MW00812753

UNIVERSITY CASEBOOK SERIES

EDITORIAL BOARD

ROBERT C. CLARK
DIRECTING EDITOR
Dean & Royall Professor of Law
Harvard University

DANIEL A. FARBER
Sho Sato Professor of Law
University of California at Berkeley

OWEN M. FISS
Sterling Professor of Law
Yale University

THOMAS H. JACKSON
President
University of Rochester

HERMA HILL KAY
Dean & Barbara Nachtrieb Armstrong Professor of Law
University of California, Berkeley

HAROLD HONGJU KOH
Gerard C. & Bernice Latrobe Smith Professor of International Law
Yale Law School

DAVID W. LEEBRON
Dean & Lucy G. Moses Professor of Law
Columbia University

SAUL LEVMORE
Dean & William B. Graham Professor of Law
University of Chicago

ROBERT L. RABIN
A. Calder Mackay Professor of Law
Stanford University

CAROL M. ROSE
Gordon Bradford Tweedy Professor of Law & Organization
Yale University

DAVID L. SHAPIRO
William Nelson Cromwell Professor of Law
Harvard University

KATHLEEN M. SULLIVAN
Dean and Richard E. Lang Professor and
Stanley Morrison Professor of Law
Stanford University

CASES AND MATERIALS

INTELLECTUAL PROPERTY AND THE INTERNET

by

MARGARET JANE RADIN
William Benjamin Scott and Luna M. Scott Professor of Law
Director, Program in Law, Science and Technology
Stanford University

JOHN A. ROTHCHILD
Associate Professor of Law
Wayne State University

GREGORY M. SILVERMAN
Associate Professor of Law
Seattle University

FOUNDATION PRESS
NEW YORK, NEW YORK
2004

Foundation Press, a Thomson business, has created this publication to provide you with accurate and authoritative information concerning the subject matter covered. However, this publication was not necessarily prepared by persons licensed to practice law in a particular jurisdiction. Foundation Press is not engaged in rendering legal or other professional advice, and this publication is not a substitute for the advice of an attorney. If you require legal or other expert advice, you should seek the services of a competent attorney or other professional.

© 2004 By FOUNDATION PRESS

       395 Hudson Street
       New York, NY 10014
       Phone Toll Free 1–877–888–1330
       Fax (212) 367–6799
       fdpress.com

Printed in the United States of America

ISBN 1–58778–654–0

TEXT IS PRINTED ON 10% POST CONSUMER RECYCLED PAPER

This book is dedicated to

JOHN W. RADIN

æ

JOAN, JULIA, AND DANIEL

æ

MARYLYN PATRICIA MULLEN.

*

PREFACE

The growing use of the Internet by both commercial interests and individuals has created a broad range of new issues relating to the legal regimes protecting intellectual property. In today's networked world, a competent lawyer needs more than a passing familiarity with these aspects of the law. Many lawyers are aware, for example, of the copyright issues raised by peer-to-peer sharing of music files, but it is equally important for them to be familiar with Internet-related copyright issues that do not make the headlines of the mainstream press, including liability based on unauthorized links to online materials, liability for use of and trafficking in technologies enabling circumvention of copyright protections, and availability of a safe harbor for online intermediaries. Many lawyers have some awareness of the upheaval in trademark law caused by the advent of commercially valuable domain names, but they need also to have some depth of familiarity both with how traditional trademark law has adapted to the Internet, and how in particular the regime for resolving trademark-based disputes over domain names functions. And many lawyers have heard of the race to the U.S. Patent and Trademark Office, and the concomitant legal uncertainties, caused by the judicial validation of business method patents, but it is important for lawyers, even those who do not specialize in patent law, to understand how this circumstance may affect a client who has an Internet presence. It is also important for lawyers to be aware of the legal status of types of information assets that are not afforded protection by the three traditional regimes—in particular, the problem of protecting databases.

The purpose of this book is to supply an in-depth survey of the emerging legal framework for the protection of intellectual property on the Internet. The book may be used to supplement a traditional survey course in intellectual property, or may serve as the basis for a course or seminar focusing on intellectual property in cyberspace.

This book consists of excerpts from our casebook, *Internet Commerce: The Emerging Legal Framework*. On our website, www.ecommercecasebook.com, you will find a glossary of technical terms, links to statutory source material, and updates on cases and legislation. We also recommend consulting the relevant portions of our 2003 Supplement. The casebook also contains appendices explaining the operation of the Internet in general and the domain name system in particular.

MJR
JAR
GMS

*

ACKNOWLEDGMENTS

We would like to thank Foundation Press for recognizing the need for a book like this, and bringing us together to create it. We thank the Roberts Program in Law and Business for support in completing the final stages of the project. A number of law students helped with this project, and we thank all of them for their fine work: Yvonne Campbell, Carole Church, Genevieve Cox, Dirk Heumueller, Masako Kanazawa, Alisa Mall, Araceli Martinez-Olguin, Corynne McSherry, Melissa Raycraft, T. Marie Satterfield, Andrew Shen, and David B. Silva. We also thank Professors Eric Chiappinelli, Mark Chinen, Margaret Chon, Sidney DeLong, Paula Lustbader, R. Anthony Reese, David M. Skover, Kellye Testy, R. Polk Wagner, Jonathan Weinberg, and Kenneth Wing for helpful comments on portions of the book. We are extremely grateful to Joan E. Hartman for first-class editing and encouragement.

Excerpts from the following materials are reprinted with the permission of the copyright owners:

Blasbalg, Gregory B., Note, *Master of Their Domain: Trademark Holders Now Have New Ways to Control Their Marks in Cyberspace,* 5 Roger Williams U.L. Rev. 563 (2000).

Dreyfuss, Rochelle Cooper, *Are Business Method Patents Bad For Business?*, 16 Santa Clara Computer & High Tech. L.J. 263 (2000).

Grusd, Jared Earl, *Internet Business Methods: What Role Does and Should Patent Law Play?*, 4 Va. J.L. & Tech. 9 (1999).

Helfer, Laurence R. & Graeme B. Dinwoodie, *Designing Non-National Systems: The Case of the Uniform Domain Name Dispute Resolution Policy,* 43 Wm. & Mary L. Rev. 141 (2001). © 2001 by the William and Mary Law Review. All rights reserved.

Lemley, Mark A., *Beyond Preemption: The Law and Policy of Intellectual Property Licensing*, 87 Calif. L. Rev. 111 (1999). © 1999 by California Law Review and Mark A. Lemley. All rights reserved. Reprinted by permission of the Regents of the University of California.

Lemley, Mark A., *The Modern Lanham Act and the Death of Common Sense*, 108 Yale L.J. 1687 (1999). Reprinted by permission of The Yale Law Journal Company and William S. Hein Company.

Lessig, Lawrence, *The Problem with Patents*, The Industry Standard, Apr. 23, 1999.

McCarthy, J. Thomas, *McCarthy on Trademarks and Unfair Competition* (2002). © 2002 by West Group, all rights reserved.

Oakes, Chris, *Patently Absurd*, Wired News, Mar. 3, 2000.

Raskind, Leo J., *The State Street Bank Decision: The Bad Business of Unlimited Patent Protection for Methods of Doing Business*, 10 Fordham I. P., Media & Ent. L.J. 61 (1999).

Reese, R. Anthony, *Copyright and Internet Music Transmissions: Existing Law, Major Controversies, Possible Solutions*, 55 U. Miami L. Rev. 237 (2001).

Stefik, Mark & Alex Silverman, *The Bit and the Pendulum: Balancing the Interests of Stakeholders in Digital Publishing,* 16 No. 1 Computer Lawyer 1 (1999). © 1999 by Aspen Publishers, Inc.

SUMMARY OF CONTENTS

TABLE OF CONTENTS

*

TABLE OF CASES

Principal cases are in bold type. Non-principal cases are in roman type. References are to Pages.

xvii

CASES AND MATERIALS

INTELLECTUAL PROPERTY AND THE INTERNET

*

CHAPTER ONE

PROTECTING COMMERCIAL IDENTITY ONLINE: TRADEMARKS

In the world of bricks and mortar, it is widely held that the success of a retail establishment is highly dependent on its physical location. In the virtual world of electronic commerce, by contrast, physical location is almost irrelevant. From the standpoint of access by potential customers, it matters very little whether a company's web server is located in New York, Paris, Hong Kong or some remote region of Siberia. On the Web, every store is as close as the nearest network access device—whether it be a desktop computer, a laptop, a personal digital assistant, a television with a set-top box or a Web-enabled cell phone. Only when e-commerce must rely upon the traditional commercial infrastructure of brick-and-mortar companies does location matter. If I buy a television from an e-commerce website, the cost of that television and the time required for its delivery to my home will depend in part on the distance of that company's distribution center from my house. By contrast, for transactions involving information goods such as software, music and other digital products that can be delivered as well as purchased online, the physical location of the company does not matter to the consumer, though it may matter to taxing and regulatory authorities.

If physical location is not an essential predicate to commercial success online, what is? While there is no consensus answer to this question, many observers believe that developing and protecting one's commercial identity is critical. A strong brand seamlessly integrated into the search and navigation technologies with which consumers identify and connect to e-commerce websites is as important online as physical location is offline.

Brand identities serve an efficiency-enhancing role by reducing the costs that consumers incur locating goods and services that meet their needs. A brand identity reduces consumer search costs by conveying important information to consumers, at a very low cost. Within a product category, a strong brand signifies that the item it marks originates from a particular company, has a known level of quality, and enjoys a specific array of product features and characteristics. Such information is important for making informed and rational choices in the marketplace.

Branding is even more important in the online commercial environment than it has been in the world of bricks and mortar. In the offline world, consumers might become physically familiar with a store they frequent, might come to know the employees personally, might even live in the same neighborhood with them. In the online world, branding is the main thing consumers have to go on in deciding whether to trust a company or its product. Moreover, in the offline world, if a product is unsatisfactory, a consumer may have some confidence that it can be exchanged if there is a known physical store the consumer can return to, but trying to fix transactions that have gone wrong becomes more uncertain in the online environment, because electronic presence seems much more shadowy and ephemeral. Brand X website might fail to deliver a satisfactory product, and might be here today and gone tomorrow.

For these reasons, trademark law is one of the most important areas of law for Internet commerce, and the advent of Internet commerce has seen significant developments in trademark law. Perhaps the most significant of these developments is the creation of an entirely new form of intangible asset, the Internet domain name, and the disputes that have arisen over who owns and controls this asset. Among the most significant features of the most popular domain names, giving rise to difficult governance questions, are their uniqueness and international scope—even if many companies around the world have the same corporate name, there is only one dotcom for that name. We will take up the issues surrounding domain names in Chapter 2.

Meanwhile, in this chapter we explore how established trademark law applies to online businesses and their efforts to protect their brands, in two different ways. Traditional trademark law is based on the danger of confusing consumers about the source and quality of the product they are buying. Contemporary trademark protection has, in the case of powerful, well-established, "famous" brands, provided additional protection in the form of actions for trademark dilution. Dilution does not turn on consumer confusion, so it establishes much broader exclusion rights for those brands that can make use of it.

In this chapter we also explore the limits of trademark protection; that is, the balance between the exclusion rights afforded to the brand owner and the needs of competitors or the general public to use the words or images that constitute or are similar to the trademark. For example, generic words for a product cannot be trademarks because competitors need to use the word to describe their own products. "Computer" cannot be the trademark for a computer product. In fact, if a trademark becomes so popular that it becomes a generic word for the product—"aspirin" is one example—trademark protection ceases. In addition to economic issues of the scope that must be afforded to competitors, free speech issues also arise. For example, can a company use trademark law to quash a parody site like chasemanhattansucks.com?

Introduction—Trademark Basics

A trademark is "a word, name, symbol, device, or other designation * * * that is distinctive of a person's goods or services and that is used in a manner that identifies those goods or services and distinguishes them from the goods or services of others." RESTATEMENT (THIRD) OF UNFAIR COMPETITION

§ 9 (1995). In addition to words and names, such designations may include, *inter alia,* numbers, letters, slogans, pictures, characters, sounds, graphic designs, and product and packaging features.

Trademarks are protectible under both state and federal law. While trademarks were originally a creature of the common law, and common-law trademarks still exist, Congress and state legislatures have enacted statutes providing for their registration and protection. At common law and under these statutes, the trademark owner has, subject to certain limitations, the exclusive right to use the protected mark in commerce.

> The purpose underlying any trade-mark statute is twofold. One is to protect the public so that it may be confident that, in purchasing a product bearing a particular trade-mark which it favorably knows, it will get the product which it asks for and wants to get. Secondly, where the owner of a trade-mark has spent energy, time, and money in presenting to the public the product, he is protected in his investment from its misappropriation by pirates and cheats.

Id. § 9 (Reporter's Notes, cmt. c) (quoting S. REP. No. 79–1333, at 3 (1946)).

To qualify for protection, a word, name or other designation must (1) be distinctive, (2) be used in commerce, (3) be affixed or otherwise associated with goods and services, and (4) signify the source or origin of those goods and services with which it is associated.

As to the first criterion, distinctiveness, marks may be either inherently distinctive, or may acquire distinctiveness through their use in commerce. Courts refer to inherently distinctive marks as *arbitrary, fanciful* or *suggestive.* EXXON is a fanciful mark, while APPLE, when applied to computers, is an arbitrary mark. The use of fanciful or arbitrary marks in connection with the goods and services with which they are associated has no meaning or significance other than as a trademark. Suggestive marks, in contrast, suggest some attribute or characteristic of the goods and services with which they are associated. For example, THE MONEY STORE suggests that the company with which it is associated provides money lending services. Similarly, EVERREADY when applied to batteries suggests that the batteries will have a long life.

Other marks, while not inherently distinctive, may acquire distinctiveness through their use in commerce. Courts call these marks *descriptive.* Descriptive marks are so called because they purport to describe some attribute or characteristic of the goods and services with which they are associated. For example, TENDER VITTLES applied to cat food suggests that the product has a certain desirable consistency. A descriptive mark that acquires distinctiveness is said to have "secondary meaning," and it is only the "secondary meaning" that is protected, not the term's primary meaning in ordinary language:

> There are but a limited number of words and images suitable for use in describing a product, and sellers own neither the English language nor common depictions of goods. * * * If descriptive words and pictures could be appropriated without evidence of a

secondary meaning, sellers could snatch for themselves the riches of the language and make it more difficult for new entrants to identify their own products; consumers would be worse off.

Scandia Down Corp. v. Euroquilt, Inc., 772 F.2d 1423, 1430 (7th Cir.1985).

A word, name, symbol or other designation that is generic is not protectible as a trademark. For example, APPLE, when applied to apples, is not protectible, and neither is SHREDDED WHEAT when applied to small edible "pillows" of shredded wheat. While a generic term can never become a trademark, a protectible trademark may lose its protection if it becomes generic. This process is sometimes called "genericide." THERMOS, ASPIRIN and DRY ICE are examples of marks that lost their protection in this fashion. The potential loss of trademark protection through genericide explains why employees of 3M and Xerox always say, respectively, "clear cellophane tape" instead of "scotch tape" and "photocopies" instead of "xeroxes." Since the use of a generic term is not protected under the law of trademark, if a term is or becomes generic, anyone can use it.

Generally, the owner of a protectible mark is the person or entity that first adopts and uses that mark in commerce. For this reason, the trademark owner is sometimes called the senior user of the mark. Anyone who subsequently uses the same or a confusingly similar mark is referred to as a junior user. Senior users have priority of use, and therefore priority of right, over junior users. Since the effective date of the Trademark Revision Act of 1988, one can establish priority of use for inherently distinctive marks that one has not yet used in commerce by filing an intent-to-use application to obtain a federal trademark registration. *See* Lanham Act § 1(b), 15 U.S.C. § 1051(b). Under this application process, the registrant must actually adopt and use the mark in commerce within six months, a period which the U.S. Patent and Trademark Office ("PTO") may extend for six month periods, up to three years. *See* 15 U.S.C. § 1051(d).

The senior user of a protectible mark may significantly increase its level of protection by registering that trademark on the Principal Register of the PTO. There are two application procedures through which one can request registration of a trademark: a use-based application pursuant to 15 U.S.C. § 1051(a) (under which the applicant must specify the date it first used the mark and the date it first used the mark in commerce, and the goods in connection with which the mark is used), and an intent-to-use application pursuant to 15 U.S.C. § 1051(b) (under which the applicant must specify the goods in connection with which the applicant has a bona fide intention to use the mark). Both types of applicants must specify the class of goods and services in connection with which the mark will be used, and must provide an actual specimen of such good.

PTO Trademark Examining Attorneys review applications to determine whether they satisfy statutory requirements and whether they are subject to any of the statutory bars set forth in 15 U.S.C. § 1052(a)–(e). These provisions of the Lanham Act prohibit the registration of marks that comprise or consist of, *inter alia*, (a) immoral, deceptive or scandalous matter, (b) the flag or coat of arms or other insignia of the United States, or any state, municipality, or foreign country, (c) the name, portrait or signature of a living person without that person's consent, (d) a word, name or other designation that is confusingly similar to another mark already registered, or (e) matter that applied to the applicant's goods is merely descriptive, deceptively misdescriptive, primarily geographically descriptive (unless it is a mark indicating regional origin such as "Made in America"), primarily geographically deceptively misdescriptive, primarily a surname, or primarily functional. If the Examining Attorney determines that the application is barred under one of these provisions, he or she will then determine whether the claimed mark has acquired secondary meaning and may nevertheless be registered under exceptions to the statutory bar set forth in 15 U.S.C. § 1052(f). If the application satisfies statutory requirements for registration, it is published in the Official Gazette of the PTO.[1] Upon publication, anyone who believes that he or she would be damaged by the registration may file an opposition. If all opposition proceedings are resolved in the applicant's favor, then a certificate of registration will be issued. Adverse determinations by the Examining Attorney may be appealed to the Trademark Trial and Appeals Board and then to the Court of Appeals for the Federal Circuit.

Federal registration of a trademark on the Principal Register confers substantial benefits on the trademark owner. The trademark owner may bring actions for trademark infringement in federal court, 15 U.S.C. § 1121(a), and may recover damages, 15 U.S.C. § 1117(a)–(c). In any legal proceeding, the trademark owner's registration is "prima facie evidence of the validity of the registered mark and of the registration of the mark, of the registrant's ownership of the mark, and of the registrant's exclusive right to use the registered mark in commerce on or in connection with the goods or services specified in the registration subject to any conditions or limitations stated therein." 15 U.S.C. § 1115(a). Moreover, under the incontestability provision of the Lanham Act, after five years the registration becomes conclusive evidence of those matters. 15 U.S.C. § 1115(c). Finally, the defenses that a junior user can raise against a trademark owner with a federal registration are significantly reduced. 15 U.S.C § 1115(b).

Descriptive marks that have not yet acquired secondary meaning may not be registered on the Principal Register but may be placed on the Supplemental Register. Once they acquire secondary meaning they may then be registered on the Principal Register. While not conferring as many benefits as the Principal Register, registration on the Supplemental Register nonetheless provides some advantages. For example, it allows the trademark owner to bring an action for infringement in federal court, prevents the registration of other marks that may cause confusion, permits registration abroad based on the United States registration, gives notice of use to all those who perform trademark searches, and permits the trademark owner to use the ® symbol. *See generally* 15 U.S.C. §§ 1091–96.

---

1. Sometimes a claimed mark will comprise both registrable and unregistrable matter. In such cases, the applicant may be required to disclaim any federal trademark rights in the unregistrable matter before the Examining Attorney will approve the application for publication in the Official Gazette. 15 U.S.C. § 1056.

Trademarks that are deemed "famous" are also entitled, under federal law and the law of many states, to protection against dilution. The Federal Trademark Dilution Act of 1995 defines "dilution" as "the lessening of the capacity of a famous mark to identify and distinguish goods or services, regardless of the presence or absence of (1) competition between the owner of the famous mark and other parties, or (2) likelihood of confusion, mistake, or deception." 15 U.S.C. § 1127. Trademark dilution can occur even when there is no infringement—that is, there is no likelihood of confusion between the diluting mark and the trademark being diluted.

Registration of a trademark with the PTO or use in commerce in the United States confers protection against infringing use only in the United States. Because there is no international registration regime, a trademark owner that wants to protect its mark must register the mark in every country where it does business. Many countries allow registration of a mark before the owner has made any use of it. This has resulted in situations where trademark owners in one country had to buy rights to marks in other countries they wanted to enter from registrants who anticipated them.

From the foregoing discussion of trademark law, we may discern a tripartite framework in which to consider the possible commercial exploitation of trademarks and other symbols, words and names. If a term is generic, then one may freely use it. No one may claim an exclusive right to use a generic term, word or symbol. If, however, a term is distinctive—inherently or because it has acquired secondary meaning—and has been used as a trademark, then one may not use in commerce or otherwise commercially exploit that mark or any other possible mark that is confusingly similar to it. Finally, if a mark has become famous from its use as a trademark, then one may not use in commerce or otherwise commercially exploit any other mark that would dilute the famous mark even if there is no likelihood of confusion between the famous mark and the possible diluting mark. The laws barring the commercial use of infringing and diluting marks are not absolute and some uses are permitted as exceptions to these rules. These exceptions are characterized as affirmative defenses that may be raised in actions for trademark infringement and trademark dilution.

The organization of the present chapter conforms to the structure of this general framework. In Part I of this chapter, we consider traditional trademark infringement. In Part II, we focus on trademark dilution. Finally, in Part III we consider various defenses that have been raised in actions for trademark infringement and dilution online.

I.   TRADITIONAL TRADEMARK INFRINGEMENT: THE REQUIREMENT OF CONSUMER CONFUSION

A.   INFRINGEMENT RESULTING FROM TRADITIONAL CONFUSION

As Oliver Wendell Holmes noted in 1890, the law of trademarks was created "to prevent one man from palming off his goods as another's, from getting another's business or injuring his reputation by unfair means and, perhaps, from defrauding the public." *Chadwick v. Covell*, 23 N.E. 1068, 1069 (Mass.1890). The law of trademarks may therefore be viewed as a branch of unfair competition law. As the First Circuit has observed, the law of unfair competition comprises a "broad class of business torts of which trademark infringement is one species." *Keebler Co. v. Rovira Biscuit Corp.*, 624 F.2d 366 (1st Cir.1980).

In a typical trademark infringement lawsuit, the senior user of a mark sues a junior user of the same or similar mark, alleging that consumers are likely to confuse the senior user's goods and services with those of the junior user. *See, e.g.,* Lanham Act § 32(1), 15 U.S.C. § 1114(1). "When comparing marks to determine the likelihood of consumer confusion, 'the correct test is whether a consumer who is somewhat familiar with the plaintiff's mark would likely be confused when presented with defendant's mark alone.' " *Clinique Laboratories, Inc. v. Dep Corp.*, 945 F.Supp. 547, 552 (S.D.N.Y.1996). Usually, the alleged consumer confusion concerns the source or origin of the goods or services in question. Equally actionable, however, is consumer confusion about whether there is an affiliation, relation of sponsorship or other connection between the senior and junior users of the mark. *See, e.g.,* Lanham Act § 43(a), 15 U.S.C. § 1125(a).

The following cases highlight the fact that infringing uses of a trademark are possible online as well as off.

Playboy Enterprises, Inc. v. Universal Tel–A–Talk, Inc.

1998 WL 767440 (E.D.Pa.1998).

■ McGlynn, District Judge.

Plaintiff, Playboy Enterprises, Inc. ("PEI") filed this action on October 2, 1996, alleging trademark infringement and related causes of action under the Lanham Act, 15 U.S.C. §§ 1114–1125 and Pennsylvania's anti-dilution law, 54 Pa.C.S.A. § 1124, *et seq.* at defendant's web site "adult-sex.com/playboy." The Court entered a temporary restraining order and later a consent decree enjoining the defendants use of PEI's trademarks. Thereafter, the complaint was amended to include a counterfeiting claim under 15 U.S.C. § 1116(d). * * *

FINDINGS OF FACT

1. Plaintiff Playboy Enterprises, Inc. (PEI), is a Delaware corporation having offices at 730 Fifth Avenue, New York, New York and a principal place of business in Chicago, Illinois.

2. Defendant Universal Tel–A–Talk, Inc. is a Pennsylvania corporation having a principal place of business in Philadelphia, Pennsylvania. Defendant Stanley Huberman is the president and sole shareholder.

3. Defendant Adult Discount Toys is a business entity having a principal place of business in Philadelphia, Pennsylvania and is owned by defendant Stanley Huberman.

* * *

5. Since 1953, PEI has published *Playboy* magazine. *Playboy* magazine is read by approximately 10 million readers each month and is published worldwide in 16 international editions.

6. *Playboy* magazine is known for its display of erotic and provocative pictorials of PEI models and adult entertainment material.

7. PEI and its licensees have sold a wide variety of merchandise; such as, wearing apparel, cosmetics, sunglasses, watches and other personal accessories under the trademark PLAYBOY, in interstate commerce, including the Commonwealth of Pennsylvania.

8. PEI is the owner of a number of U.S. trademark registrations for the mark PLAYBOY * * *.

9. Over the years, PEI has sold merchandise bearing the PLAYBOY trademark. Through its licenses, products bearing the PLAYBOY trademark are sold throughout the United States and in more than 50 countries around the world. PEI and its licensees have and continue to spend considerable time and money promoting the PLAYBOY trademark. As a result of PEI's longstanding use of the PLAYBOY trademark, the PLAYBOY trademark has become well known and has developed a secondary meaning, such that the public has come to associate it with PEI.

10. In addition to the PLAYBOY trademark, PEI also utilizes a Rabbit Head Design trademark (hereafter the "RABBIT HEAD DESIGN") in connection with *Playboy* magazine and a wide variety of goods sold by PEI and/or its licensees. Since 1954, PEI has used the RABBIT HEAD DESIGN mark in connection with *Playboy* magazine. The RABBIT HEAD DESIGN mark traditionally appears in the masthead of *Playboy* magazine. PEI has also used the RABBIT HEAD DESIGN in connection with a wide variety of merchandise and services.

11. PEI also owns a number of U.S. trademark registrations for the RABBIT HEAD DESIGN mark * * *.

12. In addition to the PLAYBOY trademarks and RABBIT HEAD DESIGN, the mark "BUNNY" has been registered by PEI with the United States Patent and Trademark Office.

* * *

14. Over the years, PEI has sold merchandise bearing the RABBIT HEAD DESIGN mark. Through its licensees, products bearing the RABBIT HEAD DESIGN mark are sold throughout the United States and in more than 50 countries around the world. Products bearing the RABBIT HEAD DESIGN mark are available worldwide by mail order catalog and through PLAYBOY specialty boutiques, department stores, art galleries and museum shops. PEI and its licensees have spent considerable time and money promoting products bearing the RABBIT HEAD DESIGN mark nationwide and throughout the world. As a result of PEI's longstanding use of the RABBIT HEAD DESIGN mark, the RABBIT HEAD DESIGN mark has become famous and has developed significant goodwill and secondary meaning, such that the public has come to associate it exclusively with PEI.

15. As a result of PEI's use and promotion of the RABBIT HEAD DESIGN mark, the mark BUNNY has also become associated with PEI in connection with adult entertainment services. Indeed, the RABBIT HEAD DESIGN trademark is commonly referred to by the public as the "Playboy Bunny."

16. The Internet is an international computer "super-network" of over 15,000 computer networks which is used by 30 million or more individuals, corporations, organization and educational institutions world-wide. Users of the Internet can access each others computers, can communicate directly with each other (by means of electronic mail or "e-mail"), and can access various types of data and information. Each Internet user has an address, consisting of one or more address components, which address is otherwise commonly referred to within the Internet as a "domain" or "domain name."

17. Domain names serve as an address for sending and receiving e-mail and for posting information or providing other services. On the Internet, a domain name serves as the primary identifier of the source of information, products or services. It is common practice for companies to form Internet domain names by combining their trade name or one of their famous trademarks as a prefix and their business category as a suffix. The suffix ".com" (usually pronounced "dot com") identifies a service provider as commercial in nature.

18. The domain name is one component of the "Uniform Resource Locator" ("URL"). The URL may also include root directories and subdirectories which serve as a guide to the contents of a website.

19. In August, 1994, PEI launched www.playboy.com on the Internet on the World Wide Web. The website currently receives approximately six million "hits" a day. The trademark www.playboy.com offers access to some of PEI's copyrighted images and other contents from *Playboy* magazine and other PEI publications. www.playboy.com has also been registered with the U.S. Patent and Trademark Office.

20. PEI also operates cyber.playboy.com, a subscription and pay per visit website (the "PLAYBOY CYBER CLUB") which allows members access to individual PLAYMATE home pages, video clips from PLAYMATE home pages, video clips from PLAYBOY home video and PLAYBOY TV and contents of *Playboy* magazine.

21. Both www.playboy.com and cyber.playboy.com are used by PEI to promote subscriptions to its monthly *Playboy* magazine, to display erotic pictorials of PEI models, and to advertise and sell PEI's merchandise and other services under PEI's trademarks. PEI's websites prominently feature the PEI trademarks PLAYBOY and RABBIT HEAD DESIGN, as well as photographs, articles of interest, PEI merchandise, videos and subscription information for *Playboy* magazine. PEI's Website contains electronic versions of *Playboy* magazine in that it displays the contents of *Playboy* magazine on-line. An Internet user is able to view the contents of *Playboy* magazine by visiting www.playboy.com or the PLAYBOY CYBER CLUB.

22.   Defendant Universal Tel–A–Talk, Inc. created and is maintaining several Internet World Wide Web sites which may be accessed throughout the United States, including the Commonwealth of Pennsylvania.

23.   On or about October 2, 1996, PEI learned that Universal–Tel–A–Talk, Inc. was using PEI's registered trademarks PLAYBOY and BUNNY in conjunction with their website to advertise on-line a collection of photographs, which both plaintiff and defendant describe as "hard core." However, neither side has defined that term, at least on this record, except as a modifier of the term sexually explicit photographs.

24.   Defendant Universal Tel–A–Talk, Inc.'s website advertises and offers a subscription service called "Playboy's Private Collection" (located at www.adult-sex.com) (hereafter "Defendant's website") for a charge of $3.95 per month, which features hard core photographs. The PLAYBOY trademark is prominently featured in defendants' website. Defendants also used the term "Bunny" on the navigational bar of the introductory page of the defendants' website. The navigational bar serves as a table of contents and appears on the bottom of the introductory screens and web pages. When a user clicks onto one of six "Bunny" segments of the navigational bar on the introductory page, the user becomes connected to another level of hard core on-line services offered by Defendants.

25.   A subscriber to defendants' "Playboy's Private Collection" service is greeted by a "home page" which is the equivalent of the cover and table of contents page of a magazine in that it displays the name of the site and a menu of information that is available for review. A subscriber to defendants' Playboy subscription service, upon assessing the URL "adult-sex.com/playboy/members" is welcomed by defendants' home page which reads: "Welcome to PLAYBOYS PRIVATE COLLECTION." Defendants' website www.adult-sex.com is an on-line collection of "hard core" photographs sold under the PLAYBOY and BUNNY trademarks and portrayed as an extension of PEI's *Playboy* magazine. Defendants' unlawful use of the PLAYBOY trademark also appears at least twice on every printed web page. "Playboys Private Collection" appears on the upper left-hand corner and the URL "adult-sex.com/playboy/members/pictures" appears at the upper right-hand corner.

26.   Subscribers can "click" onto a portion of the home page which reads: "Let me see the pictures in Playboys Private Collection" and obtain a lengthy list of hard core photographs on a variety of topics which may be viewed on screen, downloaded to disk or printed.

27.   Defendants also provided an electronic mail address which utilizes the PLAYBOY trademark in the text of defendants' website. The home page of defendants' service invites subscribers to "Send E-mail to Playboy @adult-sex.com."

28.   Defendant has also "linked" their adult-sex website to PEI's website at "Playboy.com." A "link" is a connection of one website to another.

29. Defendants are not now and never have been authorized by PEI to use the PLAYBOY trademark or the BUNNY trademark in connection with any business or service.

* * *

DISCUSSION

* * *

PEI has alleged infringement of the PLAYBOY trademark under § 32 of the Lanham Act (Count I), § 43(a) of the Lanham Act (Count II) and the common law of the Commonwealth of Pennsylvania (Count IV). The test for infringement is the same for each count, namely, whether the alleged infringement creates a likelihood of confusion. *See Scott Paper Co. v. Scott's Liquid Gold,* 589 F.2d 1225 (3d Cir.1978).

In order to succeed on the merits, a plaintiff must establish that: "(1) the marks are valid and legally protectible; (2) the marks are owned by the plaintiff; and (3) the defendants' use of the marks to identify goods or services is likely to create confusion concerning the origin of the goods and services." *Opticians Ass'n v. Independent Opticians,* 920 F.2d 187, 192 (3d Cir.1990).

The trademark PLAYBOY has attained incontestable status pursuant to 15 U.S.C. § 1065. PEI's ownership of incontestable U.S. Registrations for the PLAYBOY trademark constitutes prima facie evidence of PEI's ownership of the PLAYBOY trademark and the validity of the mark. *Optician's Ass'n v. Independent Opticians,* 920 F.2d at 194.

In determining whether a likelihood of confusion exists, the court may take into account

(1) the degree of similarity between the owner's mark and the alleged infringing mark; (2) the strength of owner's mark; (3) the price of the goods and other factors indicative of the care and attention expected of consumers when making a purchase; (4) the length of time the defendant has used the mark without evidence of actual confusion arising; (5) the intent of the defendant in adopting the mark; (6) the evidence of actual confusion; (7) whether the goods, though not competing, are marketed through the same channels of trade and advertised through [sic] the same media; (8) the extent to which the targets of the parties' sales efforts are the same; (9) the relationship of the goods in the minds of the public because of the similarity of function; (10) other facts suggesting that the consuming public might expect the prior owner to manufacture a product in the defendant's market. *Scott Paper Co. v. Scott's Liquid Gold, supra* at 1229.

Defendants' use of the words "Playboy" and "Bunny" in their website and in the identifying directories of defendants' URL's are identical to PEI's duly registered trademarks PLAYBOY and BUNNY. PEI's registered trademarks have previously been adjudicated as very strong. *See, Playboy Enterprises, Inc. v. Chuckleberry Pub., Inc.,* 687 F.2d 563 (2d Cir.1982). Suggestive marks are entitled to protection without proof of secondary meaning. *See e.g., Dominion Bankshares Corp. v. Devon Holding Co., Inc.,* 690 F.Supp. 338, 345 (E.D.Pa.1988); *American Diabetes Assn. v. National Diabetes Ass'n,* 533 F.Supp. 16, 214 U.S.P.Q. 231, 233 (E.D.Pa.1981).

Even if secondary meaning were required, PEI has established that the PLAYBOY trademark and the RABBIT HEAD DESIGN trademark for adult entertainment goods and services have become famous, and have acquired significant secondary meaning, such that the public has come to associate these trademarks with PEI.

Defendants intentionally adopted PLAYBOY and BUNNY trademarks in an effort to capitalize on PEI's established reputation in the PLAYBOY and RABBIT HEAD DESIGN marks. This is evidenced by defendant's establishment of a "link" between their website and PEI's actual PLAY-BOY website at "Playboy.com" and their appropriation of the words "playboy" and "Bunny" to advertise their own on-line service.

Evidence of actual confusion is not required. It has long been recognized that because evidence of confusion is notoriously difficult to obtain, it is not necessary to find a likelihood of confusion. *See, e.g., Coach Leatherware Co. v. AnnTaylor, Inc.,* 933 F.2d 162 (2d Cir.1991); *Lois Sportswear U.S.A., Inc. v. Levi Strauss & Co.,* 631 F.Supp. 735, 743 (S.D.N.Y.), *aff'd,* 799 F.2d 867 (2d Cir.1986); *Brockum Co. v. Blaylock,* 729 F.Supp. 438, 445 (E.D.Pa.1990) (lack of evidence of actual confusion is not a bar to injunctive relief). PEI and defendant market their services through the same channel of trade: the Internet. The consuming public is likely to believe the PEI is connected with defendants' hard core. * * *

   * * *

"Trademark policies are designed to '(1) to protect consumers from being misled as to the enterprise, or enterprises, from which the goods or services emanate or with which they are associated; (2) to prevent an impairment of the value of the enterprise which owns the trademark; and (3) to achieve these ends in a manner consistent with the objectives of free competition.'" *Intel Corp. v. Terabyte International, Inc.,* 6 F.3d 614, 618 (9th Cir.1993) (quoting *Anti–Monopoly, Inc. v. General Mills Fun Group,* 611 F.2d 296, 300–01 (9th Cir.1979)).

   * * *

Accordingly, the Court arrives at the following

CONCLUSIONS OF LAW

   * * *

2. Defendants have infringed on Plaintiff's PLAYBOY trademark.

   * * *

Albert v. Spencer

1998 WL 483462 (S.D.N.Y.1998).

■ JOHN S. MARTIN, JR., DISTRICT JUDGE.

Plaintiff and defendant both use the title AISLE SAY for theater reviews. Plaintiff whose reviews currently appear regularly in "Singles

Almanac," a magazine distributed to approximately 40,000 people in the greater New York area, has used the title AISLE SAY for nineteen years. Defendant has published theater reviews on an Internet web cite using the title AISLE SAY since 1995.

The Court is faced with the situation of two good faith users of the same trade name who operate in distinct markets. Plaintiff has never registered AISLE SAY. While the Court accepts plaintiff's testimony that she introduced herself to defendant in 1992 and mentioned AISLE SAY to him, the Court also credits the testimony of defendant that he has no recollection of this event and was not aware of the plaintiff's use of the name at the time he established his website. To avoid confusion, defendant has added a disclaimer to his web page stating that it is not connected to the plaintiff's column. Plaintiff did, however, introduce the testimony of two theater professionals who had been confused by the fact that two reviewers were using the name AISLE SAY.

DISCUSSION

As in all such cases, the parties have placed emphasis on the eight factors set forth by the Second Circuit in *Polaroid Corp. v. Polarad Elecs. Corp.*, 287 F.2d 492, 495 (2d Cir.), *cert. denied*, 368 U.S. 820 (1961). The factors are: (1) the strength of the plaintiff's mark; (2) the similarity between the two marks; (3) the proximity of the products in the marketplace; (4) the likelihood that the prior user will bridge the gap between the two products; (5) evidence of actual confusion; (6) defendant's bad faith; (7) the quality of the defendant's product; and (8) the sophistication of the relevant consumer group. *Id.*

A review of the *Polaroid* factors does not provide a clear guide to the proper outcome of this dispute:

1. Strength of the mark. A mark's strength is defined as its tendency to identify goods as emanating from a particular source. This is assessed according to two factors: first, the degree to which the mark is inherently distinctive; and second, the degree to which it is distinctive in the marketplace. The inherent distinctiveness of a mark is gauged according to whether it is generic, descriptive, suggestive or fanciful.

Plaintiff argues that AISLE SAY is a strong mark because it is fanciful, and defendant argues that it is weak because plaintiff's column is known to a relatively small number of persons. While the Court would consider the mark as more suggestive than fanciful, the mark is original enough that plaintiff would have the right to register it and enforce it against a bad faith user. Defendant is correct, however, that plaintiff's use of the mark is not widely known. Still, this factor favors plaintiff.

2. Similarity of the marks. There is no question that the marks are for practical purposes identical, and this factor favors plaintiff.

3. The competitive proximity of the products. If one considers the product simply as theater reviews, plaintiff and defendant's products are in direct competition. However, it is more appropriate to ask whether plaintiff's reviews compete with defendant's reviews for readers. The answer to that question is no, because plaintiff's reviews appear in print in a specific magazine while defendant publishes his reviews only at his website. Thus, this factor favors defendant.

4. The likelihood that plaintiff will bridge the gap. Plaintiff does not contend that she has any plans to distribute her reviews on the Internet. Thus, this factor favors defendant.

5. Actual confusion. While there was evidence showing some confusion involving two theater professionals, there was no evidence that either the magazine readers of plaintiff's reviews or the Internet visitors to the defendant's website were confused. Thus, this factor appears neutral at best.

6. The defendant's good faith. The Court is persuaded that defendant acted in complete good faith in adopting the name AISLE SAY for his website, and this factor strongly favors defendant.

7. The quality of the defendant's product. While the evidence indicates that the defendant's reviews are highly regarded, this is a subjective matter and one can understand why someone like plaintiff, who takes great pride in her work, would be concerned that someone else's reviews would be attributed to her. Thus, this factor favors plaintiff.

8. The sophistication of the buyers. To the extent that this factor focuses on the likelihood that the purchaser will be so familiar with the relevant market that he or she will not be confused as to the source of the review, it favors plaintiff, since a sophisticated playgoer may still be unsophisticated concerning the difference between reviews on the Internet and reviews in a magazine.

While four of the eight factors favor plaintiff and only three favor defendant, most of the factors favoring plaintiff tilt only slightly in her favor. Moreover, the eight factor test is not exclusive, and is not to be applied mechanically by totting up the number of factors weighing in each party's favor. * * *

"The essence of . . . unfair competition claims, under both federal and New York law 'is that the use of the infringing term creates the likelihood of consumer confusion . . . The essential inquiry is whether an appreciable number of ordinary prudent prospective [customers] are likely to be confused or misled.'" *Marshak v. Green*, 505 F. Supp. 1054, 1058 (S.D.N.Y. 1981). * * *

Here, a balancing of the relevant factors suggests that defendant should not be prohibited from using a name that he adopted in good faith, because there is no danger that an appreciable number of consumers will be misled as to the source of the review they are reading.

Given the fact that there is no real competition between plaintiff's and defendant's reviews and that defendant has added a disclaimer to his website, it is unlikely that plaintiff will suffer any real economic disadvantage or damage to her reputation if defendant is permitted to continue to use AISLE SAY to identify his website. To enjoin defendant from using the name AISLE SAY would cause him far greater harm.

CONCLUSION

For the foregoing reasons, the complaint is dismissed.

Niton Corp. v. Radiation Monitoring Devices, Inc.

27 F.Supp.2d 102 (D.Mass.1998).

■ ROBERT E. KEETON, DISTRICT JUDGE.

Two innovative enterprises of modest size are coexisting almost side-by-side without friction. They are not in direct competition. Each, however, has possibilities for success and expansion. The success of both will, some months or years away, bring them to competing with each other and with larger entities whose operations may, by then, be international or global in scope.

Enter upon this tranquil scene the Internet and its inducements to each of the two modest enterprises to obtain web sites. They do so, and soon begin to worry about each other. As they learn more, one comes into a United States district court with a complaint and prayer for preliminary injunction against the other. They accept a suggestion from the judge that the request for injunctive relief be tried along with all other claims and defenses on an expedited discovery and trial schedule.

One soon learns, by chance, that the other's web sites and means of attracting Internet users to them are deceptive and immediately harmful. Forthwith, the matter is back before the district court with a renewed request for immediate intervention.

This is a classic illustration of a new kind of litigation for which nothing in past experience comes even close to preparing trial judges and the advocates appearing before them. But the case must be decided, and quickly, unless mediation within or outside court sponsorship produces an even quicker solution.

In the matter before me, I conclude that court intervention is appropriate but not in a classic form of preliminary injunction. For the reasons summarized here, my order is more provisional and tentative in nature and is entitled Preliminary Injunction Subject to Modification.

* * *

Plaintiff Niton Corporation is in the business of manufacturing and selling x-ray fluorescence ("XRF") instruments and software designed to detect the presence or absence of lead in paint. Defendant Radiation Monitoring Devices ("RMD") is in the business of manufacturing XRF instruments that detect lead in paint. One of these products is called the LPA–1. Niton's product employs the "L–Shell" and "K-shell" methods while RMD's product employs only the "K–Shell" method. By the time this civil action is commenced, Niton and RMD are aiming to sell to the same potential entities, in many instances, one or more of their respective products. Niton contends, and RMD denies, that the two companies are the only companies in the American market for XRF instruments and software.

In its complaint, Niton alleges that RMD uses false and misleading statements in RMD's advertising, marketing and promotion of its own product in Massachusetts and interstate commerce. Niton asserts that these statements "misrepresent the true nature, characteristics, capabilities, and qualities of RMD's product" and, as a result, reflect on Niton's products. Niton further contends that these misleading statements are contained on RMD's World Wide Web page on the Internet. * * *

　　 * * *

Furthermore, Niton maintains that RMD has made false, misleading, and deceptive statements to third parties about Niton's products. * * *

　　 * * *

In response, RMD has filed in this civil action a counterclaim against Niton for using false and misleading statements in its advertising, marketing and promotion of Niton products.

As stated above, the two companies were involved in this litigation when Niton learned, by chance, that RMD's web sites and the means of attracting Internet users to the sites were deceptive and misleading. In an affidavit, a Niton employee in charge of maintaining Niton's Internet web site, Robert Bowley, asserts that, on November 5, 1998, he discovered that the "META" descriptions of RMD's web sites included references to Niton's home page that were unusual. The term "META description" refers to words that identify an Internet site, and the term "META" keywords refers to keywords that are listed by the web page creator when creating the web site. An Internet user then uses a web search engine that searches the "META" keywords and identifies a match or a "hit".

Upon further inspection of the "META" descriptions, Bowley found that several of the web addresses appeared to be for Niton's home page, but were actually for pages of RMD's web sites. Although no links to Niton were visible in the surface text of the RMD web sites, Bowley was able to use Netscape's "View Source" command to look at the source code for the RMD web sites.

Using this feature, Bowley discovered that the "META" descriptions of RMD's web sites were identical to those he had used when creating the Niton web site. Bowley discovered that several keywords, such as "radon", that were relevant to products Niton sold, but not to products sold or marketed by RMD, nevertheless appeared in RMD's web site source code.

After this discovery, Bowley asserts that he performed an Internet web search using the phrase "home page of Niton Corporation" and turned up several "hits". Only three of the "hits" were for pages on Niton's web site. The other five matches referred him to pages on RMD's web sites. According to Bowley, the "META" description of the five RMD pages is "The Home Page of Niton Corporation, makers of the finest lead, radon, and multi-element detectors."

In his affidavit, Bowley states that he repeated the search for "home page of Niton Corporation" using several other web search engines and came up with the same results. Finally, Bowley asserts that he performed a search for "Niton Corporation" and "home page" and came up with hits that described themselves as being the "Home Page of Niton Corporation" but gave the web address of RMD's web site.

I find a likelihood of success of plaintiff in establishing before the finder of fact, at trial, the credibility of Bowley's findings recited here.

For the foregoing reasons, the Clerk is directed to enter forthwith on a separate document a Preliminary Injunction Subject to Modification in the form attached to this Opinion.

Preliminary Injunction Subject to Modification

* * *

On the basis of all the oral and filed submissions, the court finds: (a) that plaintiff has shown a likelihood of success on the merits of its contention that RMD's Internet web sites and means of attracting users of the Internet to examine these web sites have been used by RMD in a way likely to lead users to believe that the employees of RMD are "makers of the finest radon detectors," that RMD is also known as Niton Corporation, that RMD is affiliated with Niton Corporation, that RMD makes for Niton products marketed by Niton, and that RMD web sites are Niton web sites * * *. For the reasons expressed here and orally at the hearings of November 13 and 18, 1998, it is ORDERED:

Defendant Radiation Monitoring Devices, Inc. ("RMD"), its officers, directors, agents, servants, employees, and those persons in active concert or participation with them who receive notice in fact of this Order are hereby enjoined from using RMD's Internet web sites and means of attracting users of the Internet to examine those web sites in a way that is likely to lead users to believe:

(1) that the employees of RMD are "makers of the finest radon detectors," or

(2) that RMD is also known as Niton Corporation, or

(3) that RMD is affiliated with Niton Corporation, or

(4) that RMD makes for Niton any product marketed by Niton, or

(5) that RMD web sites are Niton web sites.

* * *

This Order is subject to modification by this court upon motion of an interested party for good cause shown. RMD may, at any time, apply to this court for a modification of this Order upon a showing of good cause for determining that an alternative form of relief is more appropriate than an injunction. Such a showing of good cause may be made by RMD's showing that it has developed or proposes to develop a modification of its web sites and means of attracting users of the Internet to examine those web sites

(a) that, if practiced, would not be a violation of this order, or

(b) that would be a violation of the terms of this Order, absent modification, but for special reasons shown, an alternative form of remedy allowing RMD to proceed on specified conditions, including compensation or security to Niton against harm, is more appropriate than an injunction.

NOTE: METATAGGING AND SEARCH ENGINES

The most direct way to view a web site in your web browser is to type that site's web address (also known as its Uniform Resource Locator, or "URL") into the text box on the address bar of a web browser. The principal reason why so many businesses desire to use their trademark as a domain name is because it provides a highly intuitive, direct link to their company website. But not all websites have such obvious addresses, and we often find ourselves at a loss as we try to guess the URL that points to the web site we are trying to locate.

After a few unsuccessful guesses, most people enlist the aid of Internet search engines and directories. A *search engine* or *directory* is a searchable index of resources available on the Internet. A large majority of these resources are web pages, but one can also locate postings to USENET newsgroups, documents on FTP servers, and even the content of some databases. The user interface for this searchable index is usually a simple text box on a web page with a button labeled "search." The user types one or more search terms into the text box and presses the button to initiate a search. These terms, called *keywords*, are then passed off to the software that searches the index for Internet resources that contain those terms. It is not unusual for hundreds and even thousands of matches to be discovered. The web addresses of these resources are then arranged in a descending order of relevance according to relevance criteria adopted by the particular search engine or directory and returned to the user as a list of hyperlinks on a series of web pages. Often these hyperlinks are accompanied by additional information about the website. Reviewing these results pages, the user can often identify the website or other resource that she is attempting to locate and with a click of the mouse proceed directly to it.

The central difference between a search engine and a directory is that a search engine is compiled by an autonomous software agent called a *spider*. A spider moves through the Internet by following links from one website to another, searching for and retrieving various Internet resources. The manner in which a particular spider conducts its search and the decision criteria by which it decides which resources to retrieve are both determined by the programming logic and algorithms composing that spider. Well-known search engines include Altavista, Excite, Google, Hot-

Bot, Lycos and Northern Light. A directory, by contrast, is an index that is compiled by human beings. Because directories are compiled by humans, they tend to have fewer, but higher quality, links. The most widely used directories as of this writing are Yahoo!, LookSmart, Open Directory Project (ODP), NBCi and Ask Jeeves. Recognizing that their strengths are complementary, search engines and directories have begun to partner with one another, forming so-called hybrid search engines. For example, Google now provides search results for Yahoo! and is powered in part by the Open Directory Project.

The relevance ranking that a web page receives from a search engine is determined by an algorithm built into that search engine's software. As a result, if a website operator understands how a search engine's relevancy algorithm works, the operator can design and optimize the website to receive a higher ranking on the results pages that search engine returns to its users. Many search engines employ relevancy algorithms that take account of the presence of search terms (1) in certain "tagged" locations within the HTML code that comprises the web page, (2) in the text of the web page, and (3) in the URL of the web page.

Web site designers can try to increase their relevancy score under the first criterion by including as many likely keywords as possible within the HTML tags—even when the keywords have little or nothing to do with the content of the web page. This strategy, often referred to as "metatagging," has become so ubiquitous that many search engines now discount the presence of keywords within these tags.

The IBM corporate website provides a good example of how metatags are used.

```
<meta name=''DESCRIPTION'' content=''The IBM corpo-
rate home page, entry point to information about IBM
products and services''/>
```

```
<meta name=''KEYWORDS'' content=''ibm, internation-
al business machines, internet, e-business, ebusi-
ness, personal computer, personal system, e-commerce,
ecommerce, pc, workstation, mainframe, unix, techni-
cal support, homepage, home page''/>
```

www.ibm.com (page source code) (viewed July 26, 2002).

To enhance the relevance ranking of a web page under the second criterion, some website operators repeat likely keywords over and over again on a web page. To prevent this repetitive text from being seen by visitors to this website, site operators set the color of this text to the color of the background. Thus, while the repeated keywords remain invisible to humans viewing the web page through a browser, they are nonetheless visible to a search engine's spider. Keywords repeated in this fashion are sometimes referred to as buried code or invisible or hidden text.

The third strategy for enhancing the relevance ranking of a website— obtaining a domain name that contains a likely keyword, or using the keyword as part of the directory structure of the website—can be seen in

Playboy v. Universal Tel–A–Talk, supra ("www.adult-sex.com/playboy"). (Domain names are considered in Chapter 2, *infra*).

Recognizing the value that website operators place on a high relevance ranking, some search engines and directories have attempted to sell higher rankings directly. For a price, some search engines will guarantee a premium relevance ranking for searches containing certain keywords. Others allow companies to bid on keywords, giving the highest relevance ranking to the highest bidder. *See, e.g.*, www.overture.com. In a related practice, some search engines and directories sell premium placements for banner ads on the results pages of searches involving certain keywords. For example, let us say a search engine user types in the keyword "washing machine." If Maytag has purchased a premium placement for its banner ad on results pages generated from a search using the keyword "washing machine," then the results pages returned to the user would prominently display Maytag's banner ad.

Metatagging raises several trademark issues, including: Is it trademark infringement or dilution to embed another's trademark in HTML tags on your web page? What about repeating another's trademark as buried code or invisible text on your web page? Is it unlawful for a search engine or directory to sell premium placements for banner ads keyed to another's trademark? How about the sale of an enhanced relevancy ranking for searches keyed to another's trademark?

B.   INFRINGEMENT RESULTING FROM INITIAL INTEREST CONFUSION

Brookfield Communications, Inc. v. West Coast Entertainment Corp.

174 F.3d 1036 (9th Cir.1999).

■ O'SCANNLAIN, CIRCUIT JUDGE:

We must venture into cyberspace to determine whether federal trademark and unfair competition laws prohibit a video rental store chain from using an entertainment-industry information provider's trademark in the domain name of its web site and in its web site's metatags.

I

Brookfield Communications, Inc. ("Brookfield") appeals the district court's denial of its motion for a preliminary injunction prohibiting West Coast Entertainment Corporation ("West Coast") from using in commerce terms confusingly similar to Brookfield's trademark, "MovieBuff." Brookfield gathers and sells information about the entertainment industry. Founded in 1987 for the purpose of creating and marketing software and services for professionals in the entertainment industry, Brookfield initially offered software applications featuring information such as recent film submissions, industry credits, professional contacts, and future projects.

These offerings targeted major Hollywood film studios, independent production companies, agents, actors, directors, and producers.

Brookfield expanded into the broader consumer market with computer software featuring a searchable database containing entertainment-industry related information marketed under the "MovieBuff" mark around December 1993. Brookfield's "MovieBuff" software now targets smaller companies and individual consumers who are not interested in purchasing Brookfield's professional level alternative, The Studio System, and includes comprehensive, searchable, entertainment-industry databases and related software applications containing information such as movie credits, box office receipts, films in development, film release schedules, entertainment news, and listings of executives, agents, actors, and directors. This "MovieBuff" software comes in three versions—(1) the MovieBuff Pro Bundle, (2) the MovieBuff Pro, and (3) MovieBuff—and is sold through various retail stores, such as Borders, Virgin Megastores, Nobody Beats the Wiz, The Writer's Computer Store, Book City, and Samuel French Bookstores.

Sometime in 1996, Brookfield attempted to register the World Wide Web ("the Web") domain name "moviebuff.com" with Network Solutions, Inc. ("Network Solutions"), but was informed that the requested domain name had already been registered by West Coast. Brookfield subsequently registered "brookfieldcomm.com" in May 1996 and "moviebuffonline.com" in September 1996. Sometime in 1996 or 1997, Brookfield began using its web sites to sell its "MovieBuff" computer software and to offer an Internet-based searchable database marketed under the "MovieBuff" mark. Brookfield sells its "MovieBuff" computer software through its "brookfieldcomm.com" and "moviebuffonline.com" web sites and offers subscribers online access to the MovieBuff database itself at its "inhollywood.com" web site.

On August 19, 1997, Brookfield applied to the Patent and Trademark Office (PTO) for federal registration of "MovieBuff" as a mark to designate both goods and services. Its trademark application describes its product as "computer software providing data and information in the field of the motion picture and television industries." Its service mark application describes its service as "providing multiple-user access to an on-line network database offering data and information in the field of the motion picture and television industries." Both federal trademark registrations issued on September 29, 1998. Brookfield had previously obtained a California state trademark registration for the mark "MovieBuff" covering "computer software" in 1994.

In October 1998, Brookfield learned that West Coast—one of the nation's largest video rental store chains with over 500 stores—intended to launch a web site at "moviebuff.com" containing, *inter alia,* a searchable entertainment database similar to "MovieBuff." West Coast had registered "moviebuff.com" with Network Solutions on February 6, 1996 and claims that it chose the domain name because the term "Movie Buff" is part of its service mark, "The Movie Buff's Movie Store," on which a federal registration issued in 1991 covering "retail store services featuring video cassettes and video game cartridges" and "rental of video cassettes and video game cartridges." West Coast notes further that, since at least 1988, it has also used various phrases including the term "Movie Buff" to promote goods and services available at its video stores in Massachusetts, including "The Movie Buff's Gift Guide"; "The Movie Buff's Gift Store"; "Calling All Movie Buffs!"; "Good News Movie Buffs!"; "Movie Buffs, Show Your Stuff!"; "the Perfect Stocking Stuffer for the Movie Buff!"; "A Movie Buff's Top Ten"; "The Movie Buff Discovery Program"; "Movie Buff Picks"; "Movie Buff Series"; "Movie Buff Selection Program"; and "Movie Buff Film Series."

On November 10, Brookfield delivered to West Coast a cease-and-desist letter alleging that West Coast's planned use of the "moviebuff.com" would violate Brookfield's trademark rights; as a "courtesy" Brookfield attached a copy of a complaint that it threatened to file if West Coast did not desist.

The next day, West Coast issued a press release announcing the imminent launch of its web site full of "movie reviews, Hollywood news and gossip, provocative commentary, and coverage of the independent film scene and films in production." The press release declared that the site would feature "an extensive database, which aids consumers in making educated decisions about the rental and purchase of" movies and would also allow customers to purchase movies, accessories, and other entertainment-related merchandise on the web site.

Brookfield fired back immediately with a visit to the United States District Court for the Central District of California, and this lawsuit was born. In its first amended complaint filed on November 18, 1998, Brookfield alleged principally that West Coast's proposed offering of online services at "moviebuff.com" would constitute trademark infringement and unfair competition in violation of §§ 32 and 43(a) of the Lanham Act, 15 U.S.C. §§ 1114, 1125(a). Soon thereafter, Brookfield applied *ex parte* for a temporary restraining order ("TRO") enjoining West Coast "[f]rom using . . . in any manner . . . the mark MOVIEBUFF, or any other term or terms likely to cause confusion therewith, including *moviebuff.com,* as West Coast's domain name, . . . as the name of West Coast's website service, in buried code or metatags on their home page or web pages, or in connection with the retrieval of data or information on other goods or services."

* * *

V

* * *

B

[The court concluded that West Coast's use of the domain name *moviebuff.com* infringes the trademark of Brookfield.] Because Brookfield requested that we also preliminarily enjoin West Coast from using marks confusingly similar to "MovieBuff" in metatags and buried code, we must also decide whether West Coast can, consistently with the trademark and unfair competition laws, use "MovieBuff" or "moviebuff.com" in its HTML code.

At first glance, our resolution of the infringement issues in the domain name context would appear to dictate a similar conclusion of likelihood of confusion with respect to West Coast's use of "moviebuff.com" in its metatags. Indeed, all eight likelihood of confusion factors outlined [above]—with the possible exception of purchaser care, which we discuss below—apply here as they did in our analysis of domain names; we are, after all, dealing with the same marks, the same products and services, the same consumers, etc. Disposing of the issue so readily, however, would ignore the fact that the likelihood of confusion in the domain name context resulted largely from the associational confusion between West Coast's domain name "moviebuff.com" and Brookfield's trademark "MovieBuff." The question in the metatags context is quite different. Here, we must determine whether West Coast can use "MovieBuff" or "moviebuff.com" in the metatags of its web site at "westcoastvideo.com" or at any other domain address *other than* "moviebuff.com" (which we have determined that West Coast may not use).

Although entering "MovieBuff" into a search engine is likely to bring up a list including "westcoastvideo.com" if West Coast has included that term in its metatags, the resulting confusion is not as great as where West Coast uses the "moviebuff.com" domain name. First, when the user inputs "MovieBuff" into an Internet search engine, the list produced by the search engine is likely to include both West Coast's and Brookfield's web sites. Thus, in scanning such list, the Web user will often be able to find the particular web site he is seeking. Moreover, even if the Web user chooses the web site belonging to West Coast, he will see that the domain name of the web site he selected is "westcoastvideo.com." Since there is no confusion resulting from the domain address, and since West Coast's initial web page prominently displays its own name, it is difficult to say that a consumer is likely to be confused about whose site he has reached or to think that Brookfield somehow sponsors West Coast's web site.

Nevertheless, West Coast's use of "moviebuff.com" in metatags will still result in what is known as initial interest confusion. Web surfers looking for Brookfield's "MovieBuff" products who are taken by a search engine to "westcoastvideo.com" will find a database similar enough to "MovieBuff" such that a sizeable number of consumers who were originally looking for Brookfield's product will simply decide to utilize West Coast's offerings instead. Although there is no source confusion in the sense that consumers know they are patronizing West Coast rather than Brookfield, there is nevertheless initial interest confusion in the sense that, by using "moviebuff.com" or "MovieBuff" to divert people looking for "MovieBuff" to its web site, West Coast improperly benefits from the goodwill that Brookfield developed in its mark. Recently in *Dr. Seuss,* we explicitly recognized that the use of another's trademark in a manner calculated "to capture initial consumer attention, even though no actual sale is finally completed as a result of the confusion, may be still an infringement." *Dr.*

Seuss, 109 F.3d at 1405 (citing *Mobil Oil Corp. v. Pegasus Petroleum Corp.,* 818 F.2d 254, 257–58 (2d Cir.1987)).

The *Dr. Seuss* court, in recognizing that the diversion of consumers' initial interest is a form of confusion against which the Lanham Act protects, relied upon *Mobil Oil.* In that case, Mobil Oil Corporation ("Mobil") asserted a federal trademark infringement claim against Pegasus Petroleum, alleging that Pegasus Petroleum's use of "Pegasus" was likely to cause confusion with Mobil's trademark, a flying horse symbol in the form of the Greek mythological Pegasus. Mobil established that "potential purchasers would be misled into an initial interest in Pegasus Petroleum" because they thought that Pegasus Petroleum was associated with Mobil. *Id.* at 260. But these potential customers would generally learn that Pegasus Petroleum was unrelated to Mobil well before any actual sale was consummated. *See id.* Nevertheless, the Second Circuit held that "[s]uch initial confusion works a sufficient trademark injury." *Id.*

Mobil Oil relied upon its earlier opinion in *Grotrian, Helfferich, Schulz, Th. Steinweg Nachf. v. Steinway & Sons,* 523 F.2d 1331, 1341–42 (2d Cir.1975). Analyzing the plaintiff's claim that the defendant, through its use of the "Grotrian–Steinweg" mark, attracted people really interested in plaintiff's "Steinway" pianos, the Second Circuit explained:

> We decline to hold, however, that actual or potential confusion at the time of purchase necessarily must be demonstrated to establish trademark infringement under the circumstances of this case.
>
> The issue here is not the possibility that a purchaser would buy a Grotrian-Steinweg thinking it was actually a Steinway or that Grotrian had some connection with Steinway and Sons. The harm to Steinway, rather, is the likelihood that a consumer, hearing the "Grotrian–Steinweg" name and thinking it had some connection with "Steinway," would consider it on that basis. The "Grotrian–Steinweg" name therefore would attract potential customers based on the reputation built up by Steinway in this country for many years.

Grotrian, 523 F.2d at 1342.

Both *Dr. Seuss* and the Second Circuit hold that initial interest confusion is actionable under the Lanham Act, which holdings are bolstered by the decisions of many other courts which have similarly recognized that the federal trademark and unfair competition laws do protect against this form of consumer confusion. *See Green Prods.,* 992 F.Supp. 1070, 1076 (N.D.Iowa 1997) ("In essence, ICBP is capitalizing on the strong similarity between Green Products' trademark and ICBP's domain name to lure customers onto its web page."). [Eight other citations omitted.] *But see Astra Pharm. Prods., Inc. v. Beckman Instruments, Inc.,* 718 F.2d 1201, 1206–08 (1st Cir.1983) (suggesting that only confusion that affects "the ultimate decision of a purchaser whether to buy a particular product" is actionable); *Teletech Customer Care Mgmt. (Cal.), Inc. v. Tele–*

Tech Co., 977 F.Supp. 1407, 1410, 1414 (C.D.Cal.1997) (finding likelihood of initial interest confusion but concluding that such "brief confusion is not cognizable under the trademark laws").

Using another's trademark in one's metatags is much like posting a sign with another's trademark in front of one's store. Suppose West Coast's competitor (let's call it "Blockbuster") puts up a billboard on a highway reading—"West Coast Video: 2 miles ahead at Exit 7"—where West Coast is really located at Exit 8 but Blockbuster is located at Exit 7. Customers looking for West Coast's store will pull off at Exit 7 and drive around looking for it. Unable to locate West Coast, but seeing the Blockbuster store right by the highway entrance, they may simply rent there. Even consumers who prefer West Coast may find it not worth the trouble to continue searching for West Coast since there is a Blockbuster right there. Customers are not confused in the narrow sense: they are fully aware that they are purchasing from Blockbuster and they have no reason to believe that Blockbuster is related to, or in any way sponsored by, West Coast. Nevertheless, the fact that there is only initial consumer confusion does not alter the fact that Blockbuster would be misappropriating West Coast's acquired goodwill. *See Blockbuster Entertainment Group, Div. of Viacom, Inc. v. Laylco, Inc.*, 869 F.Supp. 505, 513 (E.D.Mich.1994) (finding trademark infringement where the defendant, a video rental store, attracted customers' initial interest by using a sign confusingly [similar] to its competitor's even though confusion would end long before the point of sale or rental); *see also Dr. Seuss*, 109 F.3d at 1405; *Mobil Oil*, 818 F.2d at 260; *Green Prods.*, 992 F.Supp. at 1076.

The few courts to consider whether the use of another's trademark in one's metatags constitutes trademark infringement have ruled in the affirmative. For example, in a case in which Playboy Enterprises, Inc. ("Playboy") sued AsiaFocus International, Inc. ("AsiaFocus") for trademark infringement resulting from AsiaFocus's use of the federally registered trademarks "Playboy" and "Playmate" in its HTML code, a district court granted judgment in Playboy's favor, reasoning that AsiaFocus intentionally misled viewers into believing that its web site was connected with, or sponsored by, Playboy. *See Playboy Enters. v. Asiafocus Int'l, Inc.*, No. CIV.A. 97–734–A, 1998 WL 724000, at *3, *6–*7 (E.D.Va. Apr.10, 1998).

In a similar case also involving Playboy, a district court in California concluded that Playboy had established a likelihood of success on the merits of its claim that defendants' repeated use of "Playboy" within "machine readable code in Defendants' Internet Web pages, so that the PLAYBOY trademark [was] accessible to individuals or Internet search engines which attempt[ed] to access Plaintiff under Plaintiff's PLAYBOY registered trademark" constituted trademark infringement. *See Playboy Enters. v. Calvin Designer Label*, 985 F.Supp. 1220, 1221 (N.D.Cal.1997). The court accordingly enjoined the defendants from using Playboy's marks in buried code or metatags. *See id.* at 1221–22.

In a metatags case with an interesting twist, a district court in Massachusetts also enjoined the use of metatags in a manner that resulted in initial interest confusion. *See Niton,* 27 F.Supp.2d at 102–05. In that case, the defendant Radiation Monitoring Devices ("RMD") did not simply use Niton Corporation's ("Niton") trademark in its metatags. Instead, RMD's web site directly copied Niton's web site's metatags and HTML code. As a result, whenever a search performed on an Internet search engine listed Niton's web site, it also listed RMD's site. Although the opinion did not speak in terms of initial consumer confusion, the court made clear that its issuance of preliminary injunctive relief was based on the fact that RMD was purposefully diverting people looking for Niton to its web site. *See id.* at 104–05.

Consistently with *Dr. Seuss,* the Second Circuit, and the cases which have addressed trademark infringement through metatags use, we conclude that the Lanham Act bars West Coast from including in its metatags any term confusingly similar with Brookfield's mark. West Coast argues that our holding conflicts with *Holiday Inns,* in which the Sixth Circuit held that there was no trademark infringement where an alleged infringer merely took advantage of a situation in which confusion was likely to exist and did not affirmatively act to create consumer confusion. *See Holiday Inns, Inc. v. 800 Reservation, Inc.* 86 F.3d 619, 622 (6th Cir.1996) (holding that the use of "1–800–405–4329"—which is equivalent to "1–800–H[zero-]LIDAY"—did not infringe Holiday Inn's trademark, "1–800–HOLIDAY"). Unlike the defendant in *Holiday Inns,* however, West Coast was not a passive figure; instead, it acted affirmatively in placing Brookfield's trademark in the metatags of its web site, thereby *creating* the initial interest confusion. Accordingly, our conclusion comports with *Holiday Inns.* * * *

* * *

VI

[The court concludes that "[p]reliminary injunctive relief is appropriate here to prevent irreparable injury to Brookfield's interests in its trademark 'MovieBuff' and to promote the public interest in protecting trademarks generally as well."]

* * *

Bihari v. Gross

119 F.Supp.2d 309 (S.D.N.Y.2000).

■ SCHEINDLIN, DISTRICT JUDGE.

Plaintiffs Marianne Bihari and Bihari Interiors, Inc. (collectively "Bihari") move to preliminarily enjoin defendants Craig Gross and Yolanda Truglio (collectively "Gross") from using the names "Bihari" or "Bihari Interiors" in the domain names or metatags of any of their websites ("the Gross websites"), claiming that such use violates the Anticybersquatting Consumer Protection Act ("ACPA"), 15 U.S.C. § 1125(d)(1), and infringes on Bihari's common-law service mark in violation of § 43(a) of the Lanham Act, 15 U.S.C. § 1125(a)(1)(A). * * * Neither party has requested an evidentiary hearing. For the reasons set forth below, Bihari's motion for preliminary injunctive relief is denied.

I. Introduction

[The court presents a brief description of the Internet, domain names and metatags.]

II. Background

A. *The Failed Contract*

Marianne Bihari is an interior designer who has been providing interior design services in New York City, New Jersey, Connecticut, California, Florida and Italy since 1984. Since 1989, she has been continuously doing business as Bihari Interiors or Marianne Bihari d/b/a Bihari Interiors. The Bihari Interiors name is well known, particularly in the New York City high-end residential interior design market. Bihari does not engage in paid advertising to promote her services; rather, she relies on referrals from clients and other design-industry professionals.

Craig Gross is a former client of Bihari Interiors. Yolanda Truglio is Gross's girlfriend. On February 12, 1998, Gross, on behalf of 530 East 76th Street, Inc., retained Bihari Interiors to provide interior and architectural design services for his condominium apartment on East 76th Street ("the Contract"). For various reasons not relevant to this action, the relationship between Bihari and Gross soured, and the Contract was never completed.

On June 14, 1999, Gross filed suit against Marianne Bihari and Bihari Interiors in New York State Supreme Court alleging fraud and breach of contract ("the State Suit"). On August 12, 1999, Gross submitted an amended verified complaint in the State Suit. On April 3, 2000, the state court dismissed two of the fraud claims, but granted Gross a right to replead one of those claims. Gross has since filed a second amended complaint which is currently pending in New York State Supreme Court * * *.

B. *The Alleged Harassment*

Approximately two months after Gross first filed the complaint in the State Suit, on August 10, 1999, Bihari, Gross and Truglio engaged in settlement negotiations, which were ultimately unsuccessful. Four days later, Gross registered the domain names "bihari.com" and "bihariinteriors.com". On August 16, 1999, Bihari received an anonymous facsimile alerting her to the website. The following day, Bihari accessed the website "www.bihariinteriors.com". Disturbed by the unauthorized use of her name and her business name in the domain name, as well as the disparaging statements on the website, Bihari contacted her attorney. On August 31, 1999, Bihari's attorney sent a letter to Gross demanding that he terminate the website. *See* Amended Complaint Rather than complying with Bihari's demand, Gross delivered to Bihari's residence pens bearing the words "www.bihariinteriors.com". In addition, Bihari alleges that subsequent to the delivery of the pens, Bihari received frequent "hang-up telephone calls" which lasted until approximately November 22, 1999. Bihari filed a criminal complaint for aggravated harassment against Gross and Truglio on October 3, 1999, but the District Attorney's office declined to prosecute.

Bihari was the subject of a criminal complaint several months later. Before the contract relationship between Gross and Bihari deteriorated, Bihari Interiors sold Gross three sofas purchased from a vendor. Bihari Interiors made the initial payments for the sofas. By the terms of the Contract, if Bihari Interiors failed to pay in full by a certain date, the vendor would be free to resell the sofas. After the payment deadline expired, Gross paid the vendor the balance due on the sofas, thereby avoiding payment of Bihari Interiors' commission. The sofas, however, were not delivered to Gross, but to Bihari, who took possession of them pending resolution of the State Suit. Bihari alleges that Gross then filed a criminal complaint against her for theft of the sofas. On December 20, 1999, Bihari was arrested, held for approximately six hours, and "charged with criminal possession of stolen property in the fifth degree, a misdemeanor offense." On January 24, 2000, Bihari was informed that the District Attorney's office had declined to prosecute her case.

C.   The Websites

On March 7, 2000, Bihari served Gross with the instant Complaint and motion for injunctive relief. Gross then offered to take down the "bihariinteriors.com" website pending a preliminary injunction hearing. He has since relinquished the domain names "bihari.com" and "bihariinteriors.com" and is taking all necessary steps to return those domain names to Network Solutions, Inc., the provider of domain name registrations.

On March 7, 2000, the day that Bihari served Gross with the Complaint, Bihari also learned of another website created by Gross, "designscam.com", by using an Internet search engine and searching for the words "Bihari Interiors". Bihari discovered that the "designscam.com" website contained the same content as the "bihariinteriors.com" website. Then, on March 11, 2000, Gross registered a fourth website, "manhattaninteriordesign.com", containing the identical material as "designscam.com".

All of the Gross websites use "Bihari Interiors" as metatags embedded within the websites' HTML code. The description metatags of the Gross websites state "This site deals with the problems experienced when hiring a new [sic] York City (Manhattan) designer. It discusses Marianne Bihari [,] fraud and deceit and interior decorating."

D.   The Website Content

Each of the Gross websites is critical of Bihari and her interior design services. An Internet user accessing any of the websites first sees a large caption reading "The Real Story Behind Marianne Bihari & Bihari Interiors." Directly beneath this title are three photographic reproductions of scenic New York. Beneath the photographs is a counter indicating how many visitors the website has had. As of June 26, 2000, the counter indicated that 9,774 people have visited the website since August 15, 1999. Also appearing on the first page of the websites are various hyperlinks including "Tips on Picking a Designer," "New York City Information," "Who's Who in Interior Design," "Kabalarians Philosophy," "A Humorous Look," "Tell A Friend," "Send E–Mail," "Sign or Read the Guest Book," and "Participate in the Bihari Poll."

A long block of text appears beneath these hyperlinks and it states:

> Welcome to the first website designed to protect people from the alleged ill intentions of Marianne Bihari & Bihari Interiors. Keep in mind that this site reflects only the view points and experiences of one Manhattan couple that allegedly fell prey to Marianne Bihari & Bihari Interiors. There possibly may be others that have experienced similar alleged fraud and deceit from Marianne Bihari & Bihari Interiors. Please feel free to e-mail us if you think you were victimized by Marianne Bihari & Bihari Interiors. Our goal is to protect you from experiencing the overwhelming grief and aggravation in dealing with someone that allegedly only has intentions to defraud. If you think you need advice before entering into a contract with Marianne Bihari & Bihari Interiors—Please Click Here.

Below this text a viewer finds additional hyperlinks to "The Initial Meeting," "The Contract," "The Scam," and "The Law Suit" [sic]. Viewers who connect with these links do not immediately receive the information, but are told that if they send an e-mail, they will receive a copy of the requested information.

In addition to these comments, the Gross websites contain a "guestbook" where visitors leave messages for other visitors to the websites. Some of the guestbook entries indicate that potential clients declined to retain Bihari's services because of the Gross websites. Other messages simply comment or inquire about the Gross websites' design. Many other entries disparage Bihari and Bihari Interiors. Bihari alleges that many of the guestbook entries were written by Gross and Truglio, and do not reflect true dissatisfaction with Bihari or Bihari Interiors.

The "designscam.com" and "manhattaninteriordesign.com" websites also contain a box which presents in blinking green letters the following incomplete statement quoted from Bihari's March 3, 2000 Affidavit: "I was arrested and charged with criminal possession of stolen property in the Fifth Degree." Gross neither includes the rest of the sentence—which reveals that the arrest was for a misdemeanor offense—nor informs the reader that the District Attorney's Office declined to prosecute the case.

In June 2000, Gross launched amended versions of the "designscam.com" and "manhattaninteriordesign.com" websites. The new websites are substantially identical to the former version, with two exceptions. Gross deleted the statement, "Our goal is to protect you from experiencing the overwhelming grief and aggravation in dealing with someone that allegedly only has intentions to defraud." *Second,* he added two hyperlinks—from the words "alleged fraud" and "lawsuit"—to a copy of the First Amended Complaint in the State Suit.

E.   Motive and Intent

The parties dispute defendants' motive and intent in creating the websites. Bihari alleges that Gross's motive was to harass Bihari and to pressure her into settling the State Suit. Gross counters that he created the websites because he was disturbed by Bihari's "deceitful practices," and was "dedicated to assisting consumers who are in the process of choosing a designer in New York City, as well as informing others of my experiences with Bihari." While there is no direct proof that Gross's motive is to pressure Bihari to settle the State Suit, there is proof that Gross intends to harm Bihari's business. Gross's specific intent, as memorialized in his own words on his websites, is to warn potential customers of Bihari's "alleged ill intentions" and to "protect" them from experiencing "the overwhelming grief and aggravation" he has experienced in dealing with Bihari. Undeniably, Gross's intent is to cause Bihari commercial harm. * * *

IV.   Discussion

* * *

A claim of trademark infringement under § 43(a) of the Lanham Act requires the plaintiff to show (1) that she has a valid mark that is entitled to protection under the Lanham Act, and (2) that use of that mark by another "is likely to cause confusion . . . as to the affiliation, connection, or association of such person with another person, or as to the origin, sponsorship, or approval of [the defendant's] goods, services, or commercial activities by another person." 15 U.S.C. § 1125(a)(1)(A); *Estee Lauder Inc. v. The Gap, Inc.*, 108 F.3d 1503, 1508–09 (2d Cir.1997). As discussed more fully below, Bihari has failed to demonstrate a likelihood of success on the merits of this claim because Gross's use of the "Bihari Interiors" mark in the metatags is not likely to cause confusion and is protected as a fair use.

* * *

d.   Initial Interest Confusion

Even if actual confusion is unlikely, Plaintiffs argue that there is a likelihood of "initial interest confusion." Accepting, arguendo, the concept of initial interest confusion in an Internet case,[14] Bihari has failed to prove a likelihood of initial interest confusion.

---

14. Although the Second Circuit has not explicitly applied this doctrine in an Internet case, the Ninth Circuit has. *See Brookfield Communications*, 174 F.3d at 1062–63 (relying on *Mobil Oil Corp. v. Pegasus Petroleum Corp.*, 818 F.2d 254, 257–58 (2d Cir. 1987)). In addition, at least two courts in the Second Circuit have analyzed a trademark case involving metatags by applying the initial interest confusion doctrine. *See New York State Society of Certified Public Accountants*, 79 F.Supp.2d at 341; *OBH, Inc. v. Spotlight Magazine, Inc.*, 86 F.Supp.2d 176, 190 (W.D.N.Y.2000); *but see BigStar Entertainment, Inc. v. Next Big Star, Inc.*, 105 F.Supp.2d 185, 207–210 (S.D.N.Y.2000) (refusing to apply initial interest confusion doctrine).

An infringement action may be based on a claim that the alleged infringement creates initial consumer interest, even if no actual sale is completed as a result of the confusion. In the cyberspace context, the concern is that potential customers of one website will be diverted and distracted to a competing website. The harm is that the potential customer believes that the competing website is associated with the website the customer was originally searching for and will not resume searching for the original website.

The Ninth Circuit recently provided a useful metaphor for explaining the harm of initial interest confusion in cyberspace:

> Using another's trademark in one's metatags is much like posting a sign with another's trademark in front of one's store. Suppose West Coast's, [the defendant], competitor (let's call it "Blockbuster") puts up a billboard on a highway reading—"West Coast Video: 2 miles ahead at Exit 7"—where West Coast is really located at Exit 8 but Blockbuster is located at Exit 7. Customers looking for West Coast's store will pull off at Exit 7 and drive around looking for it. Unable to locate West Coast, but seeing the Blockbuster store right by the highway entrance, they may simply rent there. Even consumers who prefer West Coast may find it not worth the trouble to continue searching for West Coast since there is a Blockbuster right there.

Brookfield Communications, 174 F.3d at 1064.[15]

The highway analogy pinpoints what is missing in this case. Inserting "Bihari Interiors" in the metatags is not akin to a misleading "billboard," which diverts drivers to a competing store and "misappropriat[es] [plaintiff's] acquired goodwill." *Id.* ("[T]he fact that there is only initial consumer confusion does not alter the fact that [the defendant] would be misappropriating [the plaintiff's] good will."). Far from diverting "people looking for information on Bihari Interiors," as plaintiffs allege, the Gross websites provide users with information about Bihari Interiors. Furthermore, the Gross websites cannot divert Internet users away from Bihari's website because Bihari does not have a competing website. *See BigStar Entertainment,* 105 F.Supp.2d at 209–10 (stating that initial interest confusion does not arise where parties are not in close competitive proximity).

Furthermore, users are unlikely to experience initial interest confusion when searching the Internet for information about Bihari Interiors. In support of their motion, Plaintiffs' counsel provided a typical search result when "Bihari Interiors" is entered into the search field. The search revealed twelve websites, eight of which appear to be the Gross websites. Of those eight, five bear the heading "Manhattan Interior Design Scam—

---

15. Use of the highway billboard metaphor is not the best analogy to a metatag on the Internet. The harm caused by a misleading billboard on the highway is difficult to correct. In contrast, on the information superhighway, resuming one's search for the correct website is relatively simple. With one click of the mouse and a few seconds delay, a viewer can return to the search engine's results and resume searching for the original website.

Bihari Interiors." Each website with that heading contains the following description underneath the title: "This site deals with the problems experienced when hiring a New York City (Manhattan) designer. It discusses Marianne Bihari[,] fraud and deceit and...." An Internet user who reads this text, and then sees the domain name of "designscam.com" or "manhattaninteriordesign.com", is unlikely to believe that these websites belong to Bihari Interiors or Bihari. * * *

The few decisions holding that use of another entity's trademark in metatags constitutes trademark infringement involved very different circumstances. *Niton Corp. v. Radiation Monitoring Devices, Inc.*, 27 F.Supp.2d 102 (D.Mass.1998), for example, provides a good example of the use of metatags to divert a competitor's customers. *First*, Radiation Monitoring Devices ("RMD") and Niton Corporation ("Niton") were direct competitors. *Second*, RMD did not simply use Niton's trademark in its metatag. Rather, RMD directly copied Niton's metatags and HTML code. As a result, an Internet search using the phrase "home page of Niton Corporation" revealed three matches for Niton's website and five for RMD's website. *See id.* at 104. RMD obviously was taking advantage of Niton's good will to divert customers to the RMD website.

Similarly, in *Playboy Enters., Inc. v. Asiafocus Int'l, Inc.*, No. Civ. A. 97–734–A, 1998 WL 724000, at *3, **6–7 (E.D.Va. Apr.10, 1998), the court enjoined use of the marks "Playboy" and "Playmate" in the domain name and metatags of defendant's website. The defendant provided adult nude photos on web pages located at "asian-playmates.com" and "playmates-asian.com". The "Playboy" and "Playmate" trademarks were embedded in the metatags such that a search for Playboy Enterprises Inc.'s ("Playboy") website would produce a list that included "asian-playmates.com". *See also Playboy Enters., Inc. v. Calvin Designer Label*, 985 F.Supp. 1220, 1221 (N.D.Cal.1997) (preliminarily enjoining defendant's website, "www.playboyxxx.com" and repeated use of the "Playboy" trademark in defendant's metatags). Defendants in these cases were clearly attempting to divert potential customers from Playboy's website to their own.

Even *Brookfield Communications*, where initial interest confusion was first applied to metatags, presents convincing proof of diversion. Brookfield sought to protect its trademark in its "MovieBuff" software, which provides entertainment-industry information. Brookfield had created a website offering an Internet-based searchable database under the "Moviebuff" mark. The defendant, West Coast, a video rental store chain, registered a site at "moviebuff.com" which also contained a searchable entertainment database. The court held that defendant's use of the "moviebuff.com" domain name constituted trademark infringement. The court also enjoined West Coast from using any term confusingly similar to "moviebuff" in the metatags based on the initial interest confusion caused by the use of Brookfield's mark, which would redound to West Coast's financial benefit.

In each of these cases, the defendant was using the plaintiff's mark to trick Internet users into visiting defendant's website, believing either that they were visiting plaintiff's website or that the defendant's website was sponsored by the plaintiff. [In contrast to those cases,] Gross's use of the "Bihari Interiors" mark in the metatags is not a bad-faith attempt to trick users into visiting his websites, but rather a means of cataloging those sites.

* * *

V.   Conclusion

For the foregoing reasons, Bihari's motion for a preliminary injunction is denied in its entirety. * * *

NOTES & QUESTIONS

1. *Initial interest confusion and metatags*. In *Bihari v. Gross*, the court rejects plaintiffs' argument that the defendant's websites cause initial interest confusion and are, therefore, infringing. One reason for the court's conclusion is that the plaintiff had no website. Would the result have changed if the plaintiff did have a website? Five of the eight websites operated by the defendant appear to have included a "description" metatag which contained the statement that "This site deals with the problems experienced when hiring a New York City (Manhattan) Designer. It discusses Marianne Bihari fraud and deceit * * *." Assuming that this description was presented on the results page containing links to defendant's websites, would this strengthen or weaken plaintiffs' argument for finding initial interest confusion?

2. *More initial interest confusion*. The only circuit court to have embraced the initial interest confusion doctrine in the Internet context is the Ninth Circuit. For another case that applies this doctrine, see *Green Products Co. v. Independence Corn By–Products Co.*, 992 F.Supp. 1070 (N.D.Iowa 1997), excerpted in Chapter 2, *infra*.

II.   TRADEMARK DILUTION

Trademark infringement protects a trademark owner from another using his or her mark in connection with competing goods and services. It does not, however, prohibit another from using that mark in connection with noncompeting goods and services. So long as the trademark is used in connection with goods and services that do not compete with the goods and services of the trademark owner, the trademark has not been infringed. A cause of action for *trademark dilution* may, however, be available to certain trademark owners to prevent use by others even absent infringement.

Trademark dilution was federalized by the Federal Trademark Dilution Act of 1995, 15 U.S.C. § 1125(c). (Previously, dilution had been available in some states under common law or by statute.) In its federal incarnation, dilution is defined as "the lessening of the capacity of a famous mark to identify and distinguish goods or services." 15 U.S.C. § 1127. Significantly, the use of another's trademark on noncompeting goods or services may dilute that trademark even if that use does not involve consumer confusion, mistake or deception. *Id*. Equally significant, however, is the limitation of this cause of action to *famous* trademarks. As we note below, attempts to define fame for the purposes of federal trademark dilution have occasioned a split in the circuits.

Historically, courts have recognized only two forms of trademark dilution: *blurring* and *tarnishment*. Thus, for example, Section 25 of the *Restatement (Third) of Unfair Competition* states:

> An actor is subject to liability under an antidilution statute if the actor uses [the trademark of another] in a manner that is likely to associate the other's mark with the goods, services, or business of the actor and:
>
> > (a) the other's mark is highly distinctive and the association of the mark with the actor's goods, services, or business is likely to cause a reduction in that distinctiveness; or
> >
> > (b) the association of the other's mark with the actor's goods, services, or business, or the nature of the actor's use, is likely to disparage the other's goods, services, or business or tarnish the images associated with the other's mark.

RESTATEMENT (THIRD) OF UNFAIR COMPETITION § 25(1) (1995). The *Restatement* distinguishes between blurring and tarnishment in paragraphs (a) and (b) respectively. In dilution by blurring,

> the assumption is that the relevant public sees the junior user's use, and intuitively knows, because of the context of the junior user's use, that there is no connection between the owners of the respective marks. However, even with those who perceive distinct sources and affiliation, the ability of the senior user's mark to serve as a unique identifier of the plaintiff's goods or services is weakened because the relevant public now also associates that designation with a new and different source. Hence, the unique and distinctive link between the plaintiff's mark and its goods or services is "blurred."

4 J. THOMAS MCCARTHY, MCCARTHY ON TRADEMARKS AND UNFAIR COMPETITION § 24:70 (4th ed.2002). In dilution by tarnishment, "[t]he selling power of a trademark * * * [is] undermined by a use of the mark with goods or services such as illicit drugs or pornography that 'tarnish' the mark's image through inherently negative or unsavory associations, or with goods or services that produce a negative response when linked in the minds of prospective purchasers with the goods or services of the [senior] user, such as the use on insecticide of a trademark similar to one previously used by [the senior user] on food products." RESTATEMENT (THIRD) OF UNFAIR COMPETITION § 25(1), cmt. c (1995). While both blurring and tarnishment require that the diluted trademark become associated with the goods or services of another, blurring occurs when this association is likely to reduce the distinctive quality of that mark, whereas tarnishment is found when this association is likely to tarnish that mark's image.

Some proponents of the Federal Trademark Dilution Act heralded it as, among other things, a means of combating "cybersquatting"—the practice of registering another's trademark as a domain name with the intent of selling it for a profit, usually to the trademark owner. In the remainder of this Part, we consider domain name disputes involving claims of dilution. In reading the following materials, consider when dilution can appropriately be found absent blurring or tarnishment. (Cybersquatting is considered in more detail in Chapter 2, *infra.*)

Federal Trademark Dilution Act

15 U.S.C. §§ 1125(c) & 1127 (§§ 43(c) & 45 of the Lanham Act).

§ 1125

(c) Remedies for dilution of famous marks.

    (1) The owner of a famous mark shall be entitled, subject to the principles of equity and upon such terms as the court deems reasonable, to an injunction against another person's commercial use in commerce of a mark or trade name, if such use begins after the mark has become famous and causes dilution of the distinctive quality of the mark, and to obtain such other relief as is provided in this subsection. In determining whether a mark is distinctive and famous, a court may consider factors such as, but not limited to—

        (A) the degree of inherent or acquired distinctiveness of the mark;

        (B) the duration and extent of use of the mark in connection with the goods or services with which the mark is used;

        (C) the duration and extent of advertising and publicity of the mark;

        (D) the geographical extent of the trading area in which the mark is used;

        (E) the channels of trade for the goods or services with which the mark is used;

        (F) the degree of recognition of the mark in the trading areas and channels of trade used by the mark's owner and the person against whom the injunction is sought;

        (G) the nature and extent of use of the same or similar marks by third parties; and

        (H) whether the mark was registered under the Act of March 3, 1881, or: the Act of February 20, 1905, or on the principal register.

    (2) In an action brought under this subsection, the owner of the famous mark shall be entitled only to injunctive relief as set forth in § 1116 of this title unless the person against whom

the injunction is sought willfully intended to trade on the owner's reputation or to cause dilution of the famous mark. If such willful intent is proven, the owner of the famous mark shall also be entitled to the remedies set forth in §§ 1117(a) and 1118 of this title, subject to the discretion of the court and the principles of equity.

(3) The ownership by a person of a valid registration under the Act of March 3, 1881, or the Act of February 20, 1905, or on the principal register shall be a complete bar to an action against that person, with respect to that mark, that is brought by another person under the common law or a statute of a State and that seeks to prevent dilution of the distinctiveness of a mark, label, or form of advertisement.

(4) The following shall not be actionable under this section:

    (A) Fair use of a famous mark by another person in comparative commercial advertising or promotion to identify the competing goods or services of the owner of the famous mark.

    (B) Noncommercial use of a mark.

    (C) All forms of news reporting and news commentary.

§ 1127

The term "dilution" means the lessening of the capacity of a famous mark to identify and distinguish goods or services, regardless of the presence or absence of—

(1) competition between the owner of the famous mark and other parties, or

(2) likelihood of confusion, mistake, or deception.

Toys "R" Us, Inc. v. Feinberg

26 F.Supp.2d 639 (S.D.N.Y.1998), *vacated & remanded*, 201 F.3d 432 (2d Cir.1999).

■ SCHWARTZ, DISTRICT JUDGE.

    * * *

Plaintiff Geoffrey, Inc. is a wholly owned subsidiary of Toys "R" Us, Inc. Geoffrey owns the rights to the Toys "R" Us and related trademarks, licensing their use to Toys "R" Us and its various subsidiaries. Plaintiffs have been making use of the Toys "R" Us mark for over 35 years. The range of products sold in Toys "R" Us stores has grown and now includes, in addition to toys, over 11,000 different items such as clothing, lamps, telephones, stereos, calculators, computers, audio and visual tapes, pools, and sporting goods. The Toys "R" Us mark is prominently featured in national and regional advertising, and throughout Toys "R" Us stores. Since 1983, Toys "R" Us has owned and operated a chain of retail children's clothing stores under the mark Kids "R" Us. There are 698 Toys "R" Us stores in the United States, and 443 in foreign countries, with annual sales over $11 billion. As a result of over $100 million in advertising annually, and an intensive effort to maintain high quality goods and services, Toys "R" Us has become one of the most famous and widely known marks in the world.

Toys "R" Us has also worked diligently to maintain its reputation as a family oriented store with a wholesome image. Toys "R" Us has sought to project the image of a store where children are the first concern, and was one of the first stores to refuse to carry or sell toy guns—a fact widely publicized.

Plaintiff Geoffrey, Inc., in addition to the Toys "R" Us mark which it licenses to its co-plaintiff, owns a number of federal trademark registrations containing the phrase " 'R' Us." For example, Geoffrey has registered Babies "R" Us, Bikes "R" Us, Books "R" Us, Computers "R" Us, Dolls "R" Us, Games "R" Us, Mathematics "R" Us, Movies "R" Us, Parties "R" Us, Portraits "R" Us, Shoes "R" Us, and Sports "R" Us. Plaintiffs also own common law rights over various other "R" Us marks, such as Treats "R" Us, Gifts "R" Us, and 1–800–Toys–R–Us, by virtue of the exclusive use of those marks.

Finally, Geoffrey also owns various internet domain names including tru.com, toysrus.com, kidsrus.com, boysrus.com, dollsrus.com, galsrus.com, girlsrus.com, babiesrus.com, computersrus.com, guysrus.com, mathematicsrus.com, moviesrus.com, opportunitiesrus.com, partiesrus.com, poolsrus.com, portraitsrus.com, racersrus.com, supervaluesrus.com, treatsrus.com, tykesrus.com, sportsrus.com, giftsrus.com, and toysrusregistry.com. Toys "R" Us operates an internet website located at www.toysrus.com

Plaintiffs make use of various of these marks and others through ownership or licensing, resulting in the extensive use of the "R" Us family of marks, under the control and supervision of plaintiffs.

Defendant Richard Feinberg is the sole proprietor of codefendant We Are Guns, a firearms store doing business at 15 Farm Lane, Norton, Massachusetts. Feinberg runs his business predominantly in Massachusetts, but also sells products on the internet and has, "on occasion, shipped products to New York firearms dealers." Feinberg's business had been previously known as "Guns Are Us." The business's name was changed to "Guns are We" and then to "We Are Guns" in response to objections by plaintiffs. Feinberg maintains a website located at www.gunsareus.com and has registered the domain name "gunsareus.com" with InterNIC.

Plaintiffs brought this suit seeking damages and an injunction prohibiting defendants from operating the website at gunsareus.com and from reverting back to either of the trade names "Guns are Us" or "Guns Are We." * * *

The Court finds no issue of material fact as to whether defendants' use of the internet domain name gunsareus.com can serve as the basis for a dilution claim under * * * § 43(c) of the Lanham Act, 15 U.S.C. § 1125(c), * * * There are two types of dilution claims, (1) blurring, and (2) tarnishment. As a matter of law, plaintiff has failed to present a prima facie case under either theory.

The owner of a famous mark is entitled to an injunction "against another person's commercial use in commerce of a mark or trade name, if such use begins after the mark has become famous and causes dilution of the distinctive quality of the mark." *See Toys "R" Us, Inc. v. Akkaoui,* 1996 WL 772709 (N.D.Cal., Oct.29, 1996) (barring the use by defendants of the name "Adults 'R Us"), *citing* 15 U.S.C. § 1125(c)(1). Dilution does not depend on a showing of either likelihood of confusion between the marks, or competition between the owner of the mark and other parties. *See* 15 U.S.C. § 1127.

First, plaintiffs have failed to establish the existence of a triable issue of fact as to whether maintaining a website with the domain name "gunsareus.com" will blur, or lessen the capacity of plaintiffs' marks to identify and distinguish their goods or services. While it is conceivable that the proliferation of trade names ending in " 'R' Us," unassociated with plaintiffs, might cause such blurring, this case is nowhere near such a situation. This case involves a website that merely uses the letters "gunsareus" as its internet domain name. Defendants neither make use of the single letter "R" nor do they space or color the letters and words in a manner remotely related to plaintiffs. The name "gunsareus" appears in all lower case letters with no spaces in between the letters. The Court finds that the use of such an internet domain name, without naming the website itself "Guns 'R' Us" or "Guns Are Us," will not, as a matter of law, blur the distinctiveness of plaintiffs' "R" Us family of marks.

Second, the Court also finds an absence of a triable issue of fact as to whether defendants have diluted plaintiffs' mark by tarnishment. Dilution by tarnishment occurs when "a famous mark is improperly associated with an inferior or offensive product or service." *See Ringling Bros.,* 937 F.Supp. at 209 (*citing Hormel Foods Corp. v. Jim Henson Prods., Inc.,* 73 F.3d 497, 506 (2d Cir.1996)). Courts have found such negative connotations in situations where a mark was used in the context of drugs, nudity, and sex. *See e.g., Dallas Cowboys Cheerleaders, Inc. v. Pussycat Cinema, Ltd.,* 467 F.Supp. 366 (S.D.N.Y.1979) (pornography); *Coca–Cola Co. v. Gemini Rising, Inc.,* 346 F.Supp. 1183 (E.D.N.Y.1972) (cocaine); *Eastman Kodak Co. v. Rakow,* 739 F.Supp. 116, 118 (W.D.N.Y.1989) (crude comedy routine).

The Court, however, finds it unlikely that defendants' website will be associated with plaintiffs' stores and products at all. As stated earlier, the differing product areas, absence of the single letter "R" in the name, and peculiarities of an internet domain name make any association with plaintiffs' products extremely unlikely. In addition, defendant does not sell to the general public outside of Massachusetts. Its internet site is used almost exclusively to sell to firearms dealers.

In sum, the parties have demonstrated an absence of any material issues of fact, requiring judgment to be issued as a matter of law. Defendants' decision to cease using the trade names "Guns Are Us" and "Guns Are We" eliminates the need or basis for the Court to decide whether those trade names infringe on or dilute plaintiffs marks. Defendants' website, entitled Guns Are We, but with the domain name gunsareus.com, does not violate any of plaintiffs' rights under federal or state trademark and unfair competition law.

CONCLUSION

For the reasons set forth above, plaintiffs' motion for summary judgment is denied in its entirety, and summary judgment is granted in favor of defendants.

Avery Dennison Corp. v. Sumpton

189 F.3d 868 (9th Cir.1999).

■ TROTT, CIRCUIT JUDGE:

Jerry Sumpton and Freeview Listings Ltd. (together, "Appellants") appeal an injunction in favor of Avery Dennison Corp., entered after summary judgment for Avery Dennison on its claims of trademark dilution under the Federal Trademark Dilution Act of 1995, 15 U.S.C. § 1125(c) (Supp. II 1996) (amending the Lanham Trademark Act of 1946, 15 U.S.C. §§ 1051–1127 (1994)), and the California dilution statute, Cal. Bus. & Prof. Code § 14330 (West 1987). The district court published an opinion, 999 F.Supp. 1337 (C.D.Cal.1998), holding that Appellants' maintenance of domain name registrations for <avery.net> and <dennison.net> diluted two of Avery Dennison's separate trademarks, "Avery" and "Dennison." (Note that when referencing Internet addresses, domain-name combinations, e-mail addresses, and other Internet-related character strings, we use the caret symbols ("< >"), in order to avoid possible confusion.) The district court then entered an injunction ordering Appellants to transfer the domain-name registrations to Avery Dennison in exchange for $300 each.

We have jurisdiction under 28 U.S.C. § 1291 (1994). Because Avery Dennison failed to create a genuine issue of fact on required elements of the dilution cause of action, we reverse and remand with instructions to enter summary judgment for Appellants and to consider Appellants' request for attorneys' fees in light of this decision.

I.   Background

We are the third panel of this court in just over a year faced with the challenging task of applying centuries-old trademark law to the newest medium of communication—the Internet. (*See Brookfield Communications, Inc. v. West Coast Enter. Corp.*, 174 F.3d 1036 (9th Cir.1999), and *Panavision Int'l, L.P. v. Toeppen*, 141 F.3d 1316 (9th Cir.1998).) Although we attempt to set out the background facts as clearly as possible, the interested reader may wish to review some of the following sources for a more complete understanding of the Internet: *Brookfield*, 174 F.3d at 1044–45;

Intermatic, Inc. v. Toeppen, 947 F.Supp. 1227, 1230–32 (N.D.Ill.1996); and Marshall Leaffer, *Domain Names, Globalization and Internet Commerce,* 6 Ind. J. Global Legal Stud. 139, 139–46 (1998).

Two communicative functions of the Internet are relevant to this appeal: the capacity to support web sites and the corollary capacity to support electronic mail ("e-mail"). A web site, which is simply an interactive presentation of data which a user accesses by dialing into the host computer, can be created by any user who reserves an Internet location—called an Internet protocol address—and does the necessary programming. Because an Internet protocol address is a string of integer numbers separated by periods, for example, <129.137.84.101>, for ease of recall and use a user relies on a "domain-name combination" to reach a given web site. The registrar of Internet domain names, Network Solutions, Inc. ("NSI"),[1] maintains a database of registrations and translates entered domain-name combinations into Internet protocol addresses. When accessing a web site, a user enters the character string <http://www.>, followed by the reserved domain-name combination. The domain-name combination must include a top-level domain ("TLD"), which can be <.com>, <.net>, <.org>, <.gov> or <.edu>, among others, although some, like <.gov> and <.edu>, are reserved for specific purposes. The combination also includes a second-level domain ("SLD"), which can be any word not already reserved in combination with the TLD. Once a domain-name combination is reserved, it cannot be used by anybody else, unless the first registrant voluntarily or otherwise relinquishes its registration.

A web site can be programmed for multiple purposes. Some merchants maintain a form of "electronic catalog" on the Internet, permitting Internet users to review products and services for sale. A web site can also be programmed for e-mail, where the provider licenses e-mail addresses in the format <alias@SLD.TLD>, with <alias> selected by the e-mail user. A person or company maintaining a web site makes money in a few different ways. A site that aids in marketing goods and services is an asset to a merchant. E-mail providers make money from licensing fees paid by e-mail users. Money is also made from advertising and links to other web sites.

II. Facts

Sumpton is the president of Freeview, an Internet e-mail provider doing business as "Mailbank." Mailbank offers "vanity" e-mail addresses to users for an initial fee of $19.95 and $4.95 per year thereafter, and has registered thousands of domain-name combinations for this purpose. Most SLDs that Mailbank has registered are common surnames, although some represent hobbies, careers, pets, sports interests, favorite music, and the like. One category of SLDs is titled "Rude" and includes lewd SLDs, and another category, titled "Business," includes some common trademark SLDs. Mailbank's TLDs consist mainly of <.net> and <.org>, but some

---

1. At the time of publication of this opinion, NSI is no longer the exclusive registrar of domain names. A new competitive scheme is being implemented by the Commerce Department, and one competitor, "register.com," is currently in operation. * * *

registered domain name combinations, including most in the "Business" and "Rude" categories, use the TLD <.com>. Mailbank's surname archives include the domain-name combinations <avery.net> and <dennison.net>.

Avery Dennison sells office products and industrial fasteners under the registered trademarks "Avery" and "Dennison," respectively. "Avery" has been in continuous use since the 1930s and registered since 1963, and "Dennison" has been in continuous use since the late 1800s and registered since 1908. Avery Dennison spends more than $5 million per year advertising its products, including those marketed under the separate "Avery" and "Dennison" trademarks, and the company boasts in the neighborhood of $3 billion in sales of all of its trademarks annually. No evidence indicates what percentage of these dollar figures apply to the "Avery" or "Dennison" trademarks. Avery Dennison maintains a commercial presence on the Internet, marketing its products at <avery.com> and <averydennison.com>, and maintaining registrations for several other domain-name combinations, all using the TLD <.com>.

Avery Dennison sued Appellants, alleging trademark dilution under the Federal Trademark Dilution Act and California Business and Professional Code § 14330. Avery Dennison also sued NSI, alleging contributory dilution and contributory infringement. The district court granted summary judgment to NSI on Avery Dennison's claims. The district court then concluded as a matter of law that the disputed trademarks were famous and denied summary judgment to Appellants and granted summary judgment to Avery Dennison on its dilution claims, entering an injunction requiring Appellants to transfer the registrations to Avery Dennison. 999 F.Supp. at 1342.

III. Trademark Law

Trademark protection is "the law's recognition of the psychological function of symbols." *Mishawaka Rubber & Woolen Mfg. Co. v. S.S. Kresge Co.,* 316 U.S. 203 (1942). Two goals of trademark law are reflected in the federal scheme. On the one hand, the law seeks to protect consumers who have formed particular associations with a mark. On the other hand, trademark law seeks to protect the investment in a mark made by the owner.

Until recently, federal law provided protection only against infringement of a registered trademark, or the unregistered trademark analog, unfair competition. *See* §§ 32 and 43(a) of the Lanham Trademark Act of 1946, as amended, 15 U.S.C. §§ 1114, 1125(a) (1994). These causes of action require a plaintiff to prove that the defendant is using a mark confusingly similar to a valid, protectable trademark of the plaintiff's. *Brookfield,* 174 F.3d at 1046.

Many states, however, have long recognized another cause of action designed to protect trademarks: trademark dilution. Lori Krafte–Jacobs, Comment, Judicial Interpretation of the Federal Trademark Dilution Act of 1995, 66 U. Cin. L.Rev. 659, 660–62 (1998) (discussing the evolution of the dilution doctrine). With the 1995 enactment of the Federal Trademark

Dilution Act, dilution became a federal-law concern. Unlike infringement and unfair competition laws, in a dilution case competition between the parties and a likelihood of confusion are not required to present a claim for relief. *See* 15 U.S.C. § 1127 (Supp. II 1996) (definition of "dilution"); Leslie F. Brown, *Note, Avery Dennison Corp. v. Sumpton*, 14 Berkeley Tech. L.J. 247, 249 (1999). Rather, injunctive relief is available under the Federal Trademark Dilution Act if a plaintiff can establish that (1) its mark is famous; (2) the defendant is making commercial use of the mark in commerce; (3) the defendant's use began after the plaintiff's mark became famous; and (4) the defendant's use presents a likelihood of dilution of the distinctive value of the mark. *Panavision Int'l, L.P. v. Toeppen*, 141 F.3d 1316, 1324 (9th Cir.1998) (interpreting 15 U.S.C. § 1125(c)(1)).

California's dilution cause of action is substantially similar, providing relief if the plaintiff can demonstrate a "[l]ikelihood of injury to business reputation or of dilution of the distinctive quality of a mark ..., notwithstanding the absence of competition between the parties or the absence of confusion as to the source of goods or services." Cal. Bus. & Prof. Code § 14330. We have interpreted § 14330, like the Federal Trademark Dilution Act, to protect only famous marks. *Fruit of the Loom, Inc. v. Girouard*, 994 F.2d 1359, 1362–63 (9th Cir.1993); *see* 3 J. Thomas McCarthy, *Trademarks and Unfair Competition* § 24:108 (Supp.1998).

   * * *

V.   Dilution Protection

We now turn to the dilution causes of action at issue in this case, brought under the Federal Trademark Dilution Act and California Business and Professional Code § 14330.

In *Panavision*, we held that both the Federal Trademark Dilution Act and § 14330 were implicated when the defendant registered domain-name combinations using famous trademarks and sought to sell the registrations to the trademark owners. 141 F.3d at 1318, 1327. Three differences made *Panavision* easier than the instant case. First, the defendant did not mount a challenge on the famousness prong of the dilution tests. *Panavision*, 141 F.3d at 1324. Second, the *Panavision* defendant did not challenge the factual assertion that he sought to profit by arbitrage with famous trademarks. *Id.* at 1324–25. Third, the diluting registrations in *Panavision* both involved the TLD <.com>. In the instant case, by contrast, Appellants contest Avery Dennison's claim of famousness, Appellants contend that the nature of their business makes the trademark status of "Avery" and "Dennison" irrelevant, and the complained-of registrations involve the TLD <. net>.

A. *Famousness*

The district court considered evidence submitted by Avery Dennison regarding marketing efforts and consumer association with its marks and concluded as a matter of law that "Avery" and "Dennison" were famous marks entitled to dilution protection. 999 F.Supp. at 1339. We hold that

Avery Dennison failed to create a genuine issue of fact on the famousness element of both dilution statutes.[4]

Dilution is a cause of action invented and reserved for a select class of marks—those marks with such powerful consumer associations that even non-competing uses can impinge on their value. *See generally* Frank L. Schechter, *The Rational Basis for Trademark Protection,* 40 Harv. L.Rev. 813 (1927) (proposing a cause of action for dilution); Krafte–Jacobs, *supra,* at 689–91. Dilution causes of action, much more so than infringement and unfair competition laws, tread very close to granting "rights in gross" in a trademark. *See* 3 McCarthy, *supra,* § 24:108. In the infringement and unfair competition scenario, where the less famous a trademark, the less the chance that consumers will be confused as to origin, *see AMF Inc. v. Sleekcraft Boats,* 599 F.2d 341, 349 (9th Cir.1979), a carefully-crafted balance exists between protecting a trademark and permitting non-infringing uses. In the dilution context, likelihood of confusion is irrelevant. *See* 15 U.S.C. § 1127; Cal. Bus. and Prof.Code § 14330; *Panavision,* 141 F.3d at 1326. If dilution protection were accorded to trademarks based only on a showing of inherent or acquired distinctiveness, we would upset the balance in favor of over-protecting trademarks, at the expense of potential non-infringing uses. *See Fruit of the Loom,* 994 F.2d at 1363 ("[The plaintiff] would sweep clean the many business uses of this quotidian word.").

We view the famousness prong of both dilution analyses as reinstating the balance—by carefully limiting the class of trademarks eligible for dilution protection, Congress and state legislatures granted the most potent form of trademark protection in a manner designed to minimize undue impact on other uses. *See San Francisco Arts & Athletics, Inc. v. United States Olympic Comm.,* 483 U.S. 522, 564 n. 25 (1987) (Brennan, J., dissenting) (citing 2 J. McCarthy, *Trademarks & Unfair Competition* § 24:16, at 229 (2d ed.1984)) (discussing limits on the dilution doctrine that help prevent overprotection of trademarks).

Therefore, to meet the "famousness" element of protection under the dilution statutes, " 'a mark [must] be truly prominent and renowned.' " *I.P. Lund Trading ApS v. Kohler Co.,* 163 F.3d 27, 46 (1st Cir.1998) (quoting 3 McCarthy, *supra,* § 24.91). In a 1987 report, which recommended an amendment to the Lanham Act to provide a federal dilution cause of action, the Trademark Review Commission of the United States Trademark Association emphasized the narrow reach of a dilution cause of action: "We believe that a limited category of trademarks, those which are truly famous and registered,[5] are deserving of national protection from

---

4. Although the famousness of "Avery" and "Dennison" is disputed, no dispute exists on the third element of dilution under *Panavision:* Appellants' use must begin after the marks became famous. Any fame that Avery Dennison's marks have acquired existed be-

fore November, 1996, when Appellants' use began.

5. The Trademark Review Commission's recommended amendment is very similar to the language of the eventually-enacted Federal Trademark Dilution Act. The main difference relevant to the famousness inquiry

dilution." Trademark Review Commission, *Report & Recommendations*, 77 Trademark Rep. 375, 455 (Sept.-Oct.1987).

The Federal Trademark Dilution Act lists eight non-exclusive considerations for the famousness inquiry, 15 U.S.C. § 1125(c)(1)(A)–(H), which are equally relevant to a famousness determination under Business and Professional Code § 14330, *see Panavision*, 141 F.3d at 1324 ("Panavision's state law dilution claim is subject to the same analysis as its federal claim.").

* * *

We note the overlap between the statutory famousness considerations and the factors relevant to establishing acquired distinctiveness, which is attained "when the purchasing public associates the [mark] with a single producer or source rather than just the product itself." *First Brands Corp. v. Fred Meyer, Inc.*, 809 F.2d 1378, 1383 (9th Cir.1987). Proof of acquired distinctiveness is a difficult empirical inquiry which a factfinder must undertake, *Taco Cabana Int'l, Inc. v. Two Pesos, Inc.*, 932 F.2d 1113, 1119–20 & n. 7 (5th Cir.1991), *aff'd*, 505 U.S. 763 (1992), considering factors including:

[1]   whether actual purchasers ... associate the [mark] with [the plaintiff];

[2]   the degree and manner of [the plaintiff's] advertising;

[3]   the length and manner of [the plaintiff's] use of the [mark]; and

[4]   whether [the plaintiff's] use of the [mark] has been exclusive.

Clamp Mfg. Co. v. Enco Mfg. Co., 870 F.2d 512, 517 (9th Cir.1989). Furthermore, registration on the principal register creates a presumption of distinctiveness—in the case of a surname trademark, acquired distinctiveness. 15 U.S.C. § 1057(b) (1994); *Americana Trading Inc. v. Russ Berrie & Co.*, 966 F.2d 1284, 1287 (9th Cir.1992) ("[R]egistration carries a presumption of secondary meaning.").

However, the Federal Trademark Dilution Act and Business and Professional Code § 14330 apply "only to those marks which are both truly distinctive *and* famous, and therefore most likely to be adversely affected by dilution." S. Rep. No. 100–515, at 42 (emphasis added). The Trademark Review Commission stated that "a higher standard must be employed to gauge the fame of a trademark eligible for this extraordinary remedy." 77 Trademark Rep. at 461. Thus, "[t]o be capable of being diluted, a mark must have a degree of distinctiveness and 'strength' beyond that needed to serve as a trademark." 3 McCarthy, *supra*, § 24:109; *see also* Krafte-Jacobs, *supra*, at 690 ("If all marks are distinctive, and a showing of distinctiveness meets the element of fame, what marks would be outside the protection of the FTDA? [T]he FTDA does not indicate that any particular degree of distinctiveness should end the inquiry." (interpreting the Federal Trademark Dilution Act)). We have previously held likewise

is that the Commission's recommendation only permitted a cause of action to the owner of a registered mark, while the owner of any protectable mark or trade name can bring a cause of action under the enacted version of the Federal Trademark Dilution Act.

under California Business and Professional Code § 14330. *Accuride Int'l, Inc. v. Accuride Corp.,* 871 F.2d 1531, 1539 (9th Cir.1989) (requiring more than mere distinctiveness).

Applying the famousness factors from the Federal Trademark Dilution Act to the facts of the case at bench, we conclude that Avery Dennison likely establishes acquired distinctiveness in the "Avery" and "Dennison" trademarks, but goes no further. Because the Federal Trademark Dilution Act requires a showing greater than distinctiveness to meet the threshold element of fame, as a matter of law Avery Dennison has failed to fulfill this burden.

1. Distinctiveness

We begin with the first factor in the statutory list: "inherent or acquired distinctiveness." § 1125(c)(1)(A). No dispute exists that "Avery" and "Dennison" are common surnames—according to evidence presented by Appellants, respectively the 775th and 1768th most common in the United States. A long-standing principle of trademark law is the right of a person to use his or her own name in connection with a business. *See Howe Scale Co. v. Wyckoff, Seamans & Benedict,* 198 U.S. 118, 140 (1905). This principle was incorporated into the Lanham Act, which states that a mark that is "primarily merely a surname" is not protectable unless it acquires secondary meaning. 15 U.S.C. § 1052(e)(4), (f) (1994); *Abraham Zion Corp. v. Lebow,* 761 F.2d 93, 104 (2d Cir.1985); *see L.E. Waterman Co. v. Modern Pen Co.,* 235 U.S. 88, 94 (1914) (pre-Lanham Act case stating that protection from confusion is available to the holder of a surname trademark that has acquired public recognition); *Horlick's Malted Milk Corp. v. Horluck's, Inc.,* 59 F.2d 13, 15 (9th Cir.1932) (pre-Lanham Act case limiting the defendant's right to use his surname as a trademark where the name had acquired public recognition from the efforts of a competitor). Avery Dennison cannot claim that "Avery" and "Dennison" are inherently distinctive, but must demonstrate acquired distinctiveness through secondary meaning.

The drafters of the Federal Trademark Dilution Act continued the concern for surnames when adding protection against trademark dilution to the federal scheme. On early consideration of the Act, the report from the Senate Judiciary Committee emphasized: "[T]he committee intended to give special protection to an individual's ability to use his or her own name in good faith." S. Rep. No. 100–515, at 43 (1988). The Federal Trademark Dilution Act imports, at a minimum, the threshold secondary-meaning requirement for registration of a surname trademark.

Avery Dennison maintains registrations of both "Avery" and "Dennison" on the principal register, prima facie evidence that these marks have achieved the secondary meaning required for protection from infringement and unfair competition. *See Americana Trading,* 966 F.2d at 1287. We reject Appellants' argument that the distinctiveness required for famousness under the Federal Trademark Dilution Act is inherent, not merely acquired distinctiveness. *See* 15 U.S.C. § 1125(c)(1)(A) (referring to "inherent or acquired distinctiveness"). However, because famousness requires a showing greater than mere distinctiveness, the presumptive secondary meaning associated with "Avery" and "Dennison" fails to persuade us that the famousness prong is met in this case.

2. Overlapping Channels of Trade

We next consider the fifth and sixth factors of the statutory inquiry: the channels of trade for the plaintiff's goods and the degree of recognition of the mark in the trading areas and channels of trade used by plaintiff and defendant. § 1125(c)(1)(E), (F). The drafters of the Federal Trademark Dilution Act broke from the Trademark Review Commission's recommendation that only marks "which have become famous throughout a substantial part of the United States" could qualify for protection. *Report & Recommendation,* 77 Trademark Rep. at 456. Instead, fame in a localized trading area may meet the threshold element under the Act if plaintiff's trading area includes the trading area of the defendant. S.Rep. No. 100–515, at 43; *Washington Speakers Bureau, Inc. v. Leading Auths., Inc.,* 33 F.Supp.2d 488, 503–04 (E.D.Va.1999) (*citing I.P. Lund,* 163 F.3d at 46; *Teletech Customer Care Mgt., Inc. v. Tele–Tech Co.,* 977 F.Supp. 1407, 1413 (C.D.Cal.1997)). The rule is likewise for specialized market segments: specialized fame can be adequate only if the "diluting uses are directed narrowly at the same market segment." *Washington Speakers,* 33 F.Supp.2d at 503. No evidence on the record supports Avery Dennison's position on these two prongs of the famousness inquiry.

In *Teletech,* fame in a narrow market segment was present when the plaintiff showed "that the Teletech Companies may be the largest provider of primarily inbound integrated telephone and Internet customer care nationwide." 977 F.Supp. at 1409. The defendant was "a contractor providing engineering and installation services to the telecommunications industry," and maintained the domain-name combination, <teletech.com>. *Id.* at 1409–10. The court held that the showing on the threshold element under the Federal Trademark Dilution Act was adequate to qualify for a preliminary injunction. *Id.* at 1413. In *Washington Speakers,* both the plaintiff and defendant were in the business of scheduling speaking engagements for well-known lecturers. 33 F.Supp.2d at 490, 503 and n. 31 (citing cases). In the instant case, by contrast, Appellants' sought-after customer base is Internet users who desire vanity e-mail addresses, and Avery Dennison's customer base includes purchasers of office products and industrial fasteners. No evidence demonstrates that Avery Dennison possesses any degree of recognition among Internet users or that Appellants direct their e-mail services at Avery Dennison's customer base.

3. Use of the Marks by Third Parties

The seventh factor, "the nature and extent of use of the same . . . marks by third parties," § 1125(c)(1)(G), undercuts the district court's conclusion as well. All relevant evidence on the record tends to establish that both "Avery" and "Dennison" are commonly used as trademarks, both on and off of the Internet, by parties other than Avery Dennison. This evidence is relevant because, when "a mark is in widespread use, it may not be famous for the goods or services of one business." *Report & Recommendation,* 77 Trademark Rep. at 461; *see Accuride,* 871 F.2d at 1539 (affirming the district court's holding that widespread use of elements of a trademark helped to defeat a dilution claim).

The record includes copies of five trademark registrations for "Avery" and "Averys," a computer printout of a list of several businesses with "Avery" in their names who market products on the Internet, and a list of business names including "Avery," which, according to a declaration submitted by NSI, is a representative sample of over 800 such businesses. The record also contains a computer printout of a list of several businesses with "Dennison" in their names which market products on the Internet and a list of business names including "Dennison," a representative sample of over 200 such businesses. Such widespread use of "Avery" and "Dennison" makes it unlikely that either can be considered a famous mark eligible for the dilution cause of action.

4. Other Famousness Factors

Avery Dennison argues that evidence of extensive advertising and sales, international operations, and consumer awareness suffices to establish fame. We agree that the remaining four statutory factors in the famousness inquiry likely support Avery Dennison's position. Both "Avery" and "Dennison" have been used as trademarks for large fractions of a century and registered for decades. Avery Dennison expends substantial sums annually advertising each mark, with some presumable degree of success due to Avery Dennison's significant annual volume of sales. In addition, Avery Dennison markets its goods internationally. *See* 15 U.S.C. § 1125(c)(1)(B)–(D), (G). However, we disagree that Avery Dennison's showing establishes fame.

Avery Dennison submitted three market research studies regarding perceptions of the "Avery" and "Avery Dennison" brands. Discussion groups through which one study was conducted were formed "using Avery client lists," and produced the conclusion that the "Avery" name has "positive associations ... among current customers." Surveyed persons in the other two studies were mostly "users and purchasers of office products" and "[o]ffice supply consumers." The one consumer group that did not necessarily include office supply purchasers for businesses was still required to be "somewhat" or "very" familiar with Avery products in order to be counted.

Avery Dennison's marketing reports are comparable to a survey we discussed in *Anti–Monopoly, Inc. v. General Mills Fun Group, Inc.,* 684 F.2d 1316 (9th Cir.1982), proving only the near tautology that consumers already acquainted with Avery and Avery Dennison products are familiar with Avery Dennison. *See id.* at 1323–24. The marketing reports add nothing to the discussion of whether consumers in general have any brand association with "Avery" and "Avery Dennison," and no evidence of product awareness relates specifically to the "Dennison" trademark. Although proper consumer surveys might be highly relevant to a showing of fame, we reject any reliance on the flawed reports submitted by Avery Dennison.

Finally, Avery Dennison—like any company marketing on the Internet—markets its products worldwide. *See* 15 U.S.C. § 1125(c)(1)(D). By itself, this factor carries no weight; worldwide use of a non-famous mark does not establish fame. Because famousness requires more than mere distinctiveness, and Avery Dennison's showing goes no further than establishing secondary meaning, we hold that Avery Dennison has not met its burden to create a genuine issue of fact that its marks are famous. Avery Dennison's failure to fulfill its burden on this required element of both dilution causes of action mandates summary judgment for Appellants.

5.   *Likelihood of Confusion Remains Irrelevant*

We recognize that our discussion of the breadth of fame and overlapping market segments begins to sound like a likelihood of confusion analysis, and we agree with Avery Dennison that likelihood of confusion should not be considered under either the Federal Trademark Dilution Act or Business and Professional Code § 14330. However, as we discuss above, the famousness element of the dilution causes of action serves the same general purpose as the likelihood of confusion element of an infringement or unfair competition analysis—preventing the trademark scheme from granting excessively broad protection at the expense of legitimate uses. *See Fruit of the Loom*, 994 F.2d at 1363 ("Whittling away will not occur unless there is at least some subliminal connection in a buyer's mind between the two parties' uses of their marks."). The close parallels between the two analyses are therefore not surprising; nor do they cause us concern.

B.   *Commercial Use*

Addressing the second element of a cause of action under the Federal Trademark Dilution Act, the district court held that Appellants' registration of <avery.net> and <dennison.net> constituted commercial use. 999 F.Supp. at 1339–40. We disagree.

Commercial use under the Federal Trademark Dilution Act requires the defendant to be using the trademark as a trademark, capitalizing on its trademark status. *See Panavision*, 141 F.3d at 1325. Courts have phrased this requirement in various ways. In a classic "cybersquatter" case, one court referenced the defendants "intention to arbitrage" the registration which included the plaintiff's trademark. *Intermatic*, 947 F.Supp. at 1239. Another court, whose decision we affirmed, noted that the defendant "traded on the value of marks as marks." *Panavision Int'l, L.P. v. Toeppen*, 945 F.Supp. 1296, 1303 (C.D.Cal.1996), *aff'd*, 141 F.3d 1316 (9th Cir.1998). In our *Panavision* decision, we considered the defendant's "attempt to sell the trademarks themselves." 141 F.3d at 1325.

All evidence in the record indicates that Appellants register common surnames in domain-name combinations and license e-mail addresses using those surnames, with the consequent intent to capitalize on the surname status of "Avery" and "Dennison." Appellants do not use trademarks qua trademarks as required by the caselaw to establish commercial use. Rather, Appellants use words that happen to be trademarks for their non-trademark value. The district court erred in holding that Appellants' use of <avery.net> and <dennison.net> constituted commercial use under the Federal Trademark Dilution Act, and this essential element of the dilution causes of action likewise mandates summary judgment for Appellants.

C. Dilution

The district court then considered the dilution requirement under both statutes, holding that Appellants' use of <avery.net> and <dennison.net> caused dilution, or a likelihood of dilution, of "Avery" and "Dennison." 999 F.Supp. at 1340–41. We hold that genuine issues of fact on this element of the causes of action should have precluded summary judgment for Avery Dennison.

Two theories of dilution are implicated in this case. First, Avery Dennison argues that Appellants' conduct is the cybersquatting dilution that we recognized in *Panavision. See* 141 F.3d at 1326–27. Second, Avery Dennison argues that Appellants' conduct in housing the <avery.net> and <dennison.net> domain names in the same database as various lewd SLDs causes tarnishment of the "Avery" and "Dennison" marks.

1. Cybersquatting

Cybersquatting dilution is the diminishment of " 'the capacity of the [plaintiff's] marks to identify and distinguish the [plaintiff's] goods and services on the Internet.' " *Panavision,* 141 F.3d at 1326 (quoting the *Panavision* district court, 945 F.Supp. at 1304). We recognized that this can occur if potential customers cannot find a web page at <trademark.com.> *Id.* at 1327; *see also Brookfield,* 174 F.3d at 1045 ("The Web surfer who assumes that 'X.com' will always correspond to the web site of company X or trademark X will, however, sometimes be misled."). Dilution occurs because " '[p]rospective users of plaintiff's services . . . may fail to continue to search for plaintiff's own home page, due to anger, frustration or the belief that plaintiff's home page does not exist.' " *Panavision,* 141 F.3d at 1327 (quoting *Jews for Jesus v. Brodsky,* 993 F.Supp. 282, 306–07 (D.N.J. 1998)).

In the instant case, Appellants registered the TLD <.net>, rather than <.com>, with the SLDs <avery> and <dennison>. As we recognized in *Panavision,* <.net> applies to networks and <.com> applies to commercial entities. 141 F.3d at 1318. Evidence on the record supports this distinction, and courts applying the dilution cause of action to domain-name registrations have universally considered <trademark.com> registrations. *See* Brown, *Note, supra,* at 251–54 (discussing cases); *id.* at 262–63 (addressing the <.com> versus <.net> distinction). Although evidence on the record also demonstrates that the <.com> and <.net> distinction is illusory, a factfinder could infer that dilution does not occur with a <trademark.net> registration. This genuine issue of fact on the question of cybersquatting dilution should have prevented summary judgment for Avery Dennison.

2. Tarnishment

Tarnishment occurs when a defendant's use of a mark similar to a plaintiff's presents a danger that consumers will form unfavorable associations with the mark. *See Hasbro, Inc. v. Internet Ent. Group, Ltd.,* 40 U.S.P.Q.2d 1479, 1480, 1996 WL 84853 (W.D.Wash.1996) (<candyland.com> as a domain-name combination for a sexually explicit web site diluted plaintiff's trademark, "Candyland," for a children's game); 3 McCarthy, *supra,* § 24:104. The district court did not reach Avery Dennison's claims regarding tarnishment.

Avery Dennison offers, as an alternative ground for affirming the district court, the fact that Appellants house <avery.net> and <dennison.net> at the same web site as lewd domain-name registrations. However, the evidence likewise indicates that to move from <avery.net> or <dennison.net> to a lewd SLD requires "linking" through the Mailbank home page, which might remove any association with the "Avery" and "Dennison" trademarks that the Internet user might have had. *See Fruit of the Loom,* 994 F.2d at 1363 (requiring some connection between the two parties' uses of their marks). Whether Appellants' use of the registrations presents a danger of tarnishment is an issue of fact that could not be decided on summary judgment. * * *

VII.   Conclusion

We reverse the district court's summary judgment in favor of Avery Dennison and remand with instructions to enter summary judgment for Sumpton and Freeview.

REVERSED and REMANDED.

NOTES & QUESTIONS

1. *Cybersquatters or entrepreneurs?* In *Avery Dennison v. Sumpton,* the district court held that "Avery" and "Dennison" were famous marks, and that defendants had made commercial use of them. These holdings were reversed on appeal. The district court went on to address the equities of the parties' claims to the two domain names. The court expressed great skepticism concerning defendants' explanation of their business model:

> Defendants allege that they have invested approximately $1,200,000 in their business. They allege that they are providing internet services to their licensees that the licensees could not offer for themselves, i.e., the ability to allow multiple uses of the same surnames as domain names, and the ability to spread the cost of maintaining the domain name registrations among all of the users.
>
> Defendants also point out that their use of the ".net" designation does not deny plaintiff access to the internet through use of its trademarks as domain names. Plaintiff has registered names corresponding to its trademarks under the ".com" designation,

which is the designation specified for commercial use. According to the defendants, the internet registration system contemplates that the ".net" designation will be reserved for use by Internet service providers, and that it will not be used for marketing of commercial products. Defendants argue that their own use of the ".net" designation is within the contemplation of the internet registration system.

Plaintiffs contend that none of defendants' arguments is apt. They contend that the internet registration system simply does not authorize "cybersquatting." They contend that it does not authorize the registration of *any* domain names that are commonly used by others to identify themselves, not for the purpose of use by the registrant as domain names, but rather for sale or license to others.

The court agrees. This is not a case involving a dispute over a domain name between persons or entities that have previously used the name to identify themselves or their products. Defendants' claimed "service" depends on their first having preempted 12,000 domain names, so that others who customarily use a name to identify themselves can use a domain name for that purpose only with the permission of the defendants. Moreover, anyone who desires to use any of those 12,000 names for any purpose, other than as an e-mail address, is entirely precluded from doing so. In light of the fact that many of the most popular on-line services provide e-mail addresses without charge, limiting domain name registrations to this purpose is almost certainly not the highest and best use. Finally, the ".net" designation has not been preserved according to the original intent, and many registrants, including trademark holders, have registered domain names with ".net" designations that are not internet providers.

The court is extremely dubious that licensing domain names for use as e-mail addresses is defendants' true business. As previously noted, this limitation is voluntary. It would be extremely difficult to enforce if defendants' right to the exclusive use of these domain names was ever held to exist. Thereafter, it would appear that the laws of economics would require the defendants to sell or license each of their 12,000 names to the highest bidder for whatever use the buyer or licensee wished to make of them.

Avery Dennison v. Sumpton, 999 F.Supp. 1337, 1341–42 (C.D.Cal.1998), *rev'd*, 189 F.3d 868 (9th Cir.1999).

Do you agree that defendants' purported business model is a sham? Was the district court too facile in condemning defendants as cybersquatters? Consider the district court's explanation: "Defendants are 'cybersquatters,' as that term has come to be commonly understood. They have registered over 12,000 internet domain names not for their own use, but rather to prevent others from using those names without defendants' consent." Is cybersquatting, as thus understood, more worthy of condemnation than the action of any other entrepreneur who gains control of a resource that is in limited supply (real estate, stock in a corporation, chromium) and makes it available to others for a price?

2. *Trademark combinatorics and domain permutations.* The court in *Toys "R" Us v. Feinberg* notes that "Geoffrey also owns various internet domain names including tru.com, toysrus.com, kidsrus.com, boysrus.com, dollsrus.com, galsrus.com, girlsrus.com, babiesrus.com, computersrus.com, guysrus.com, mathematicsrus.com, moviesrus.com, opportunitiesrus.com, partiesrus.com, poolsrus.com, portraitsrus.com, racersrus.com, supervalues-rus.com, treatsrus.com, tykesrus.com, sportsrus.com, giftsrus.com, and toysrusregistry.com." Would the registration or use of these domain names by somebody other than Geoffrey constitute trademark infringement?

3. *Fame.* While it is unsurprising that "Toys 'R' Us" is viewed as a "famous" trademark, you might find it odd that the court in *Teletech Customer Care Management v. Tele–Tech*, 977 F.Supp. 1407 (C.D.Cal.1997), excerpted in Chapter 2, *infra*, found "TeleTech" to be a famous mark. If "TeleTech" is a famous mark, one might conclude that the legal threshold for fame under 15 U.S.C. § 1125(c) is very low, but the Ninth Circuit in *Avery Dennison v. Sumpton, supra*, applied a rather more rigorous standard. The Seventh Circuit wrestled with this question in *Syndicate Sales, Inc. v. Hampshire Paper Corp.*, 192 F.3d 633 (7th Cir.1999):

> At an initial glance, there appears to be a wide variation of authority on this issue. Some cases apparently hold that fame in a niche market is insufficient for a federal dilution claim, while some hold that such fame is sufficient. However, a closer look indicates that the different lines of authority are addressing two different contexts. Cases holding that niche-market fame is insufficient generally address the context in which the plaintiff and defendant are using the mark in separate markets. On the other hand, cases stating that niche-market renown is a factor indicating fame address a context like the one here, in which the plaintiff and defendant are using the mark in the same or related markets. *See Teletech Customer Care Management, Inc. v. Tele–Tech Co.*, 977 F.Supp. 1407, 1413 (C.D.Cal.1997). The validity of this distinction is supported by the Restatement and a commentator:
>
> > A mark that is highly distinctive only to a select class or group of purchasers may be protected from diluting uses directed at that particular class or group. For example, a mark may be highly distinctive among purchasers of a specific type of product. In such circumstances, protection against a dilution of the mark's distinctiveness is ordinarily appropriate only against uses specifically directed at that particular class of purchasers; uses of the mark in broader markets, although they may produce an incidental diluting effect in the protected market, are not normally actionable.

Restatement (Third) of Unfair Competition § 25 cmt. e (1995); *see also* 4 J. Thomas McCarthy, *McCarthy on Trademarks and Unfair Competition* § 24:112, at 24–204 to 24–205 (1999).

Moreover, one of the factors in § 1125(c) for determining the existence of fame indicates that fame may be constricted to a particular market. That factor is "the degree of recognition of the mark in the trading areas and channels of trade used by the marks' owner and the person against whom the injunction is sought." 15 U.S.C. § 1125(c)(1)(F). We acknowledge, of course, that the narrowness of the market in which a plaintiff's mark has fame is a factor that must be considered in the balance. * * * However, when the defendant allegedly uses a mark in the same market as the plaintiff, the narrowness of that market is less important. We therefore hold that the district court erred in concluding that the trade dress was not famous based solely on the niche-market status of the baskets.

Syndicate Sales, Inc. v. Hampshire Paper Corp., 192 F.3d at 640–41. Do you find the Seventh Circuit's explanation of the *TeleTech* holding convincing? Apparently the Second Circuit did not. In *TCPIP Holding Company, Inc. v. Haar Communications, Inc.,* 244 F.3d 88 (2d Cir.2001), the Second Circuit notes that

the benefits of the [Federal Trademark] Dilution Act are available to owners of a "famous" mark. The Act does not tell *how* famous a mark must be. Nor does it provide any direct guidance as to how courts should answer the question. The word "famous" is susceptible to many widely different understandings. If a hypothetical Grendel's Coffee Shop in Smalltown, U.S.A. has for years been the favorite hangout of Smalltown high school students, Grendel's may well be famous among the students and graduates of Smalltown High. Or another mark for a catalogue selling rare plant specimens may be famous among 100,000 collectors scattered throughout the country. Are those then "famous" marks within the meaning of the statute? The argument might be made that if the plaintiff's mark is "famous" in any sense coming within a dictionary definition, it qualifies for the statute's protection. * * *

It seems most unlikely that Congress intended to confer on marks that have enjoyed only brief fame in a small part of the country, or among a small segment of the population, the power to enjoin all other users throughout the nation in all realms of commerce. The examples of eligible "famous marks" given in the House Report—Dupont, Buick, and Kodak, *see* H.R.Rep. No. 104–374, at 3 (1995), *reprinted in* 1995 U.S.C.C.A.N. 1029, 1030—are marks that for the major part of the century have been household words throughout the United States. They are representative of the best known marks in commerce. Once again, we recognize that examples in a legislative report cannot be taken as defining the limits of a statute's coverage. Putting together the extraordinary power the Act confers on a "famous" mark and the improbability that Congress intended to grant such outright exclusivity to marks that are famous in only a small area or segment of the nation, with the hints to be gleaned from the House Report, we think Congress envisioned that marks would qualify as "famous" only if they carried a substantial degree of fame.

TCPIP Holding Company, Inc. v. Haar Communications, Inc., 244 F.3d at 98–99. Is it possible to reconcile the Second and Seventh Circuit discussions of congressional intent? If not, which do you find more convincing?

4. *Actual harm v. likelihood of harm.* A split in the circuits has developed over the issue whether a claim for trademark dilution under the Federal Trademark Dilution Act requires proof of actual harm or merely a showing that harm is likely. In *Ringling Bros.-Barnum & Bailey Combined Shows, Inc. v. Utah Div. of Travel Development*, 170 F.3d 449 (4th Cir.1999), the Fourth Circuit required a showing of actual harm.

By contrast, in *Nabisco, Inc. v. PF Brands, Inc.*, 191 F.3d 208 (2d Cir.1999), the court held that likelihood of future harm is sufficient to support an injunction. How would you resolve this split in the circuits?

5. *A split in the circuits over descriptive trademarks.* Does a trademark have to be inherently distinctive to qualify for protection under the Federal Trademark Dilution Act? In the cases discussed above, none of the marks was descriptive (i.e., none of them had acquired distinctiveness; all were inherently distinctive). Does this mean that descriptive marks that have acquired secondary meaning are not protected under 15 U.S.C. § 1125(c)? That is exactly the conclusion reached by the Second Circuit in *TCPIP Holding Company, Inc. v. Haar Communications, Inc.*, 244 F.3d 88 (2d Cir.2001):

> In order to qualify for the Act's protection, the mark must be famous. By definition, every mark that is famous, in the sense intended by the Act, has a high degree of acquired distinctiveness. Thus, no mark can qualify for the Act's protection without acquired distinctiveness. If that acquired distinctiveness satisfies not only the fame requirement, but also the distinctiveness requirement, then there will never be a case when a court needs to consider whether the mark has inherent distinctiveness. The statute's invitation to courts to consider the mark's degree of inherent distinctiveness would serve no function.
>
> We therefore understand Clause (A) of § 1125(c)(1) to invite two inquiries: (1) Has the plaintiff's mark achieved a sufficient degree of consumer recognition ("acquired distinctiveness") to satisfy the Act's requirement of fame? (2) Does the mark possess a sufficient degree of "inherent distinctiveness" to satisfy the Act's requirement of "distinctive quality." The latter requirement cannot be satisfied by the mere fact that the public has come to associate the mark with the source. Thus, weak, non-distinctive,

descriptive marks do not qualify for the Act's protection, even if famous.

TCPIP Holding Company, Inc. v. Haar Communications, Inc., 244 F.3d at 98. In *Times Mirror Magazines, Inc. v. Las Vegas Sports News, L.L.C.*, 212 F.3d 157 (3d Cir.2000), the Third Circuit reached the opposite conclusion: that a descriptive trademark that had acquired secondary meaning was indeed covered by the Federal Trademark Dilution Act. Rejecting the idea that 15 U.S.C. § 1125(c) involves a test for distinctiveness separate and apart from its test for fame, the Third Circuit noted that

> [t]o be a "mark" eligible in the first place for protection under [§ 1125(c)(1)], basic trademark principles dictate that a designation has to be "distinctive" either inherently or through acquisition of secondary meaning.

4 *McCarthy on Trademarks and Unfair Competition* § 24:91 (footnotes omitted).

McCarthy explains the legislative history behind § 1125(c)(1)'s "distinctive and famous" language:

> The 1987 Trademark Review Commission Report, the genesis of the language contained in the 1996 federal Act, said that the dual mention of both "distinctive and famous" in the introduction to the list of factors was inserted to emphasize the policy goal that to be protected, a mark had to be truly prominent and renowned. The double-barreled language "distinctive and famous" reflected the goal that protection should be confined to marks "which are both distinctive, as established by federal registration at a minimum, and famous, as established by separate evidence." The Commission inserted the term "distinctive" as hyperbole to emphasize the requirement that the mark be registered, for without inherent or acquired distinctiveness, the designation would not have been a mark that should have federally registered in the first place. The Trademark Review Commission Report reveals that the Commission saw distinctiveness and fame as two sides of the same evidentiary coin which requires widespread and extensive customer recognition of the plaintiff's mark. However, when in the 1995 House amendment, the requirement of federal registration was dropped from the Bill, Congress neglected to also drop the mention of "distinctive" introducing the list of factors. Thus, the word "distinctive" was left floating in the statute, unmoored to either any statutory requirement or underlying policy goal.

Id. (footnotes omitted).

Accordingly, we are not persuaded that a mark be subject to separate tests for fame and distinctiveness. * * * Having decided that Times Mirror has proved that its mark had gained secondary meaning and a high degree of distinctiveness in the market, there is no necessity for proving an additional test of distinctiveness.

Times Mirror Magazines, Inc. v. Las Vegas Sports News, L.L.C., 212 F.3d at 167–68. Is there a conflict here between the language of the federal statute and the statute's legislative history? Is the statutory language sufficiently unclear so that the Third Circuit's primary reliance on the legislative history is warranted? Which approach makes the most sense to you?

III. TRADEMARK DEFENSES ONLINE

A. TRADITIONAL FAIR USE

Brookfield Communications, Inc. v. West Coast Entertainment Corp.

174 F.3d 1036 (9th Cir.1999).

■ O'SCANNLAIN, CIRCUIT JUDGE:

[The statement of facts and the Lanham Act claims are excerpted in Part I(B), *supra.*]

* * *

Contrary to West Coast's contentions, we are not in any way restricting West Coast's right to use terms in a manner which would constitute fair use under the Lanham Act. *See New Kids on the Block v. News America Pub., Inc.,* 971 F.2d 302, 306–09 (9th Cir.1992); *see also August Storck K.G. v. Nabisco, Inc.,* 59 F.3d 616, 617–18 (7th Cir.1995). It is well established that the Lanham Act does not prevent one from using a competitor's mark truthfully to identify the competitor's goods, *see, e.g., Smith v. Chanel, Inc.,* 402 F.2d 562, 563 (9th Cir.1968) (stating that a copyist may use the originator's mark to identify the product that it has copied), or in comparative advertisements, *see New Kids on the Block,* 971 F.2d at 306–09. This fair use doctrine applies in cyberspace as it does in the real world. *See Radio Channel Networks, Inc. v. Broadcast.Com, Inc.,* No. 98 Civ. 4799, 1999 WL 124455, at *5–*6 (S.D.N.Y. Mar.8, 1999); *Bally Total Fitness Holding Corp. v. Faber,* 29 F.Supp.2d 1161 (C.D.Cal.1998); *Playboy Enterprises, Inc. v. Terri Welles, Inc.* 7 F.Supp.2d 1098, 1103–04 (S.D.Cal. 1998).

In *Welles,* the case most on point, Playboy sought to enjoin former Playmate of the Year Terri Welles ("Welles") from using "Playmate" or "Playboy" on her website featuring photographs of herself. *See* 7 F.Supp.2d at 1100. Welles's website advertised the fact that she was a former Playmate of the Year, but minimized the use of Playboy's marks; it also contained numerous disclaimers stating that her site was neither endorsed by nor affiliated with Playboy. The district court found that Welles was using "Playboy" and "Playmate" not as trademarks, but rather as descriptive terms fairly and accurately describing her web page, and that her use of "Playboy" and "Playmate" in her website's metatags was a permissible, good faith attempt to index the content of her website. It accordingly concluded that her use was permissible under the trademark laws. *See id.* at 1103–04.[2]

We agree that West Coast can legitimately use an appropriate descriptive term in its metatags. But "MovieBuff" is not such a descriptive term. Even though it differs from "Movie Buff" by only a single space, that difference is pivotal. The term "Movie Buff" is a descriptive term, which is routinely used in the English language to describe a movie devotee. "MovieBuff" is not. The term "MovieBuff" is not in the dictionary. *See Merriam–Webster's Collegiate Dictionary* 762 (10th ed.1998); *American Heritage College Dictionary* 893 (3d ed.1997); *Webster's New World College Dictionary* 889 (3d ed.1997); *Webster's Third New Int'l Dictionary* 1480 (unabridged 1993). Nor has that term been used in any published federal or state court opinion. In light of the fact that it is not a word in the English language, when the term "MovieBuff" *is* employed, it is used to refer to Brookfield's products and services, rather than to mean "motion picture enthusiast." The proper term for the "motion picture enthusiast" is "Movie Buff," which West Coast certainly *can* use. It cannot, however, omit the space.

Moreover, West Coast is not absolutely barred from using the term "MovieBuff." As we explained above, that term can be legitimately used to describe Brookfield's product. For example, its web page might well include an advertisement banner such as "Why pay for MovieBuff when you can get the same thing here for FREE?" which clearly employs "MovieBuff" to refer to Brookfield's products. West Coast, however, presently uses Brookfield's trademark not to reference Brookfield's products, but instead to describe its own product (in the case of the domain name) and to attract people to its website in the case of the metatags. That is not fair use.

* * *

Bihari v. Gross

119 F.Supp.2d 309 (S.D.N.Y.2000).

■ SCHEINDLIN, DISTRICT JUDGE.

[The statement of facts and the Lanham Act claims are excerpted in Part I(B), *supra.*]

* * *

---

2. [The district court subsequently entered summary judgment in favor of Welles, and the court of appeals affirmed in substantial part. *See Playboy Enterprises, Inc. v. Terri Welles, Inc.,* 78 F.Supp.2d 1066 (S.D.Cal. 1999), *aff'd in part, rev'd in part, & remanded,* 279 F.3d 796 (9th Cir.2002). The appellate decision is excerpted in Part III(B), *infra.*—Eds.]

e. The Fair Use Doctrine

Even if the Gross websites cause consumer confusion, use of the "Bihari Interiors" mark in the metatags is protected as a fair use. The Lanham Act codified a common law fair use defense in 15 U.S.C. § 1115(b)(4). The fair use doctrine applies to the Internet as readily as to the print media. *See Radio Channel Networks, Inc. v. Broadcast.Com, Inc.,* 98 Civ. 4799, 1999 WL 124455, at **5–6 (S.D.N.Y. Mar.8, 1999) (permitting defendant's fair use of the term "The Radio Channel" on its website, which transmits broadcasts over the Internet, even though plaintiff had registered the service mark "The Radio Channel").

"Fair use is established when the challenged term is a use, otherwise than as a mark, ... of a term or device which is descriptive of and used fairly and in good faith only to describe the goods or services of such party...." 15 U.S.C. § 1115(b)(4). In other words, "fair use permits others to use a protected mark to describe aspects of their own goods." *Car-Freshner Corp. v. S.C. Johnson & Son, Inc.,* 70 F.3d 267, 270 (2d Cir.1995). It is not necessary that the plaintiff's mark be classified as "descriptive" to benefit from the fair use defense. Instead, the central considerations are whether the defendant has used the mark (1) in its descriptive sense, and (2) in good faith. *See id.*

(i) Use of the Term in its Descriptive Sense

The requirement that a trademark be used in its descriptive sense is met where the mark is used in an index or catalog, or to describe the defendant's connection to the business claiming trademark protection. *See Nihon Keizai Shimbun, Inc. v. Comline Bus. Data, Inc.,* 166 F.3d 65, 73–74 (2d Cir.1999) (permitting fair use defense where defendant, a company that gathers news articles and sells "abstracts" summarizing the articles, routinely used the plaintiff's mark in the reference line of its abstracts to identify the source of the article abstracted by the defendant); Restatement (Third) of Unfair Competition § 28 cmt. a (1995) (fair use defense protects a subsequent user's use of a personal name designation "if the name is used solely to indicate truthfully the named person's connection with the goods, services, or business."). Applying this general rule to the metatag context, Professor McCarthy states: "[T]he fair use defense applies ... if another's trademark is used in a meta tag solely to describe the defendant or defendant's goods or services...." 4 J. Thomas McCarthy, *McCarthy on Trademarks and Unfair Competition* ("McCarthy"), § 25:69 at 25–137 (4th ed.1999). This position finds support in recent cases. In *Playboy Enters., Inc. v. Welles,* 7 F.Supp.2d 1098 (S.D.Cal.1998), Playboy sought to enjoin Terri Welles, a former "Playmate of the Month" and "Playmate of the Year", from utilizing the trademarked terms "Playboy" and "Playmate" in the metatags of Welles' website. The court denied the injunction, holding that use of the trademarked terms in the metatags is a fair use. * * * *See also Brookfield Communications,* 174 F.3d at 1066 (stating that West Coast can use Brookfield's trademark on its website to "legitimately ... describe Brookfield's product. For example, [West Coast can] ... include an advertisement banner such as 'Why pay for MovieBuff when you can get the same thing here for FREE?' '').

Here, Gross has included "Bihari Interiors" in the metatags of his websites because the websites provide information about Bihari Interiors and Marianne Bihari. Gross has not used the terms "Bihari Interiors" and "Bihari" in the metatags as a mark, but rather, to fairly identify the content of his websites. In short, Gross uses the "Bihari Interiors" mark in its descriptive sense only.

Moreover, use of the "Bihari Interiors" mark in the metatags of his websites is the only way Gross can get his message to the public. *See Bally Total Fitness,* 29 F.Supp.2d at 1165 ("Prohibiting [the defendant] from using Bally's name in the machine readable code would effectively isolate him from all but the most savvy of Internet users."). A broad rule prohibiting use of "Bihari Interiors" in the metatags of websites not sponsored by Bihari would effectively foreclose all discourse and comment about Bihari Interiors, including fair comment. Courts must be particularly cautious of overextending the reach of the Lanham Act and intruding on First Amendment values. *Cf. Rogers v. Grimaldi,* 875 F.2d 994, 998 (2d Cir.1989) (holding that movie titles using a celebrity's name will not be actionable under the Lanham Act unless the title has no artistic relevance to the underlying work or if the title misleads as to the source or the content of the work); 4 *McCarthy,* § 27:91 at 27–140 ("Whether through the use of statutory interpretation or concern for free speech, traditional protections for commentators and critics on business and commercial affairs must not be jettisoned. It is important to create critical breathing space for legitimate comment and criticism about products and services."). The Second Circuit's warning in a recent Internet case to proceed cautiously when dealing with the frontier of expressive speech on the Internet is particularly instructive:

> In considering whether domain names constitute expressive speech, we observe that the lightning speed development of the Internet poses challenges for the common-law adjudicative process—a process which, ideally while grounded in the past, governs the present and offers direction for the future based on understandings of current circumstances. Mindful of the often unforeseeable impact of rapid technological change, we are wary of making legal pronouncements based on highly fluid circumstances, which almost certainly will give way to tomorrow's new realities.

Name.Space, Inc. v. Network Solutions, Inc., 202 F.3d 573 (2d Cir.2000) (stating that top level domain names may, one day, constitute expressive speech).

(ii) Gross's Good Faith

To benefit from the defense of fair use, Gross must have acted in good faith. The inquiry into a defendant's good faith focuses on whether "the defendant adopted its mark with the intention of capitalizing on plaintiff's reputation and goodwill and any confusion between his and the senior user's product." *Lang v. Retirement Living Pub. Co., Inc.,* 949 F.2d 576, 583 (2d Cir.1991).

Bihari argues, in a conclusory fashion, that Gross did not adopt the "Bihari Interiors" mark in good faith. Rather, Gross intended to divert individuals searching for information about Bihari Interiors to his websites. This argument is not persuasive. Metatags serve as a cataloging system for a search engine. Gross has the right to catalog the contents of his websites. Furthermore, the fact that Gross knew of the prior use of the "Bihari Interiors" mark does not in itself prove a lack of good faith. "[P]rior knowledge of [plaintiff's] trade name does not give rise to a necessary inference of bad faith, because adoption of a trademark with actual knowledge of another's prior registration ... may be consistent with good faith." *Lang,* 949 F.2d at 583–84; Restatement (Third) of Unfair Competition § 28 cmt. d ("Knowledge of a prior trademark use of the term does not in itself prove a lack of good faith.").

In addition, the domain names of the Gross websites and the disclaimer prove that Gross is using "Bihari Interiors" in good faith. The domain names of his websites in no way confuse Internet users into believing that his site is actually that of Bihari Interiors. *See, e.g., Planned Parenthood,* 1997 WL 133313, at **8–10 (defendant's anti-abortion website violates the Lanham Act because, among other reasons, it was registered at "www.plannedparenthood.com", and the site greeted users with "Welcome to the PLANNED PARENTHOOD HOME PAGE"). Moreover, the Gross websites include a disclaimer: "Keep in mind that this site reflects only the view points and experiences of one Manhattan couple...." Although a disclaimer cannot insulate Gross from liability, it indicates good faith use of the service marks and weighs in Gross's favor. *See Consumers Union of United States, Inc. v. General Signal Corp.,* 724 F.2d 1044, 1053 (2d Cir.1983) ("Disclaimers are a favored way of alleviating consumer confusion as to source or sponsorship"). Even if the Gross websites are mean-spirited and vindictive, bad faith cannot be imputed as well to Gross's use of the "Bihari Interiors" mark in the metatags. *See Nihon Keizai Shimbun,* 166 F.3d at 74 (holding that use of plaintiff's mark is in good faith even though "other aspects of defendants' behavior may have evidenced bad faith."). * * *

NOTES & QUESTIONS

1. *Fair use and metatags.* In *Bihari v. Gross,* Gross was successful in his fair use defense, while in *Brookfield Communications v. West Coast Entertainment,* West Coast was not. Why was one successful and the other not? Do both courts understand the fair use defense in the same way? If West Coast Entertainment had had a discussion and critique of the plaintiff's MovieBuff database on its website, would the Ninth Circuit have permitted West Coast to succeed on its fair use defense? Does it matter that the word "MovieBuff" is not a descriptive term that can be found in a dictionary? For a case where a defendant that used an affiliate's trademark as a keyword in a metatag succeeded in its fair use defense, *see Trans Union LLC v. Credit Research, Inc.*, 142 F.Supp.2d 1029 (N.D.Ill.2001).

2. *Fair use and dilution.* Is the fair use defense effective against claims of trademark dilution under 15 U.S.C. § 1125(c)? *See* 15 U.S.C. § 1125(c)(4). Does this provision resolve the question? What if the mark is being used to identify the defendant's goods and services? What if the mark is being used to identify the defendant rather than the defendant's goods and services?

B. Nominative Use

Playboy Enterprises, Inc. v. Welles

279 F.3d 796 (9th Cir.2002).

■ T.G. Nelson, Circuit Judge.

Playboy Enterprises, Inc. (PEI), appeals the district court's grant of summary judgment as to its claims of trademark infringement [and trademark dilution]* * * against Terri Welles [and] Terri Welles, Inc. * * * We have jurisdiction pursuant to 28 U.S.C. § 1291, and we affirm in part and reverse in part. * * *

I. Background

Terri Welles was on the cover of Playboy in 1981 and was chosen to be the Playboy Playmate of the Year for 1981. Her use of the title "Playboy Playmate of the Year 1981," and her use of other trademarked terms on her website are at issue in this suit. During the relevant time period, Welles' website offered information about and free photos of Welles, advertised photos for sale, advertised memberships in her photo club, and promoted her services as a spokesperson. A biographical section described Welles' selection as Playmate of the Year in 1981 and her years modeling for PEI. After the lawsuit began, Welles included discussions of the suit and criticism of PEI on her website and included a note disclaiming any association with PEI.[1]

PEI complains of four different uses of its trademarked terms on Welles' website: (1) the terms "Playboy" and "Playmate" in the metatags of the website; (2) the phrase "Playmate of the Year 1981" on the masthead of the website; (3) the phrases "Playboy Playmate of the Year 1981" and "Playmate of the Year 1981" on various banner ads, which may be transferred to other websites; and (4) the repeated use of the abbreviation "PMOY '81" as the watermark on the pages of the website.[3] PEI claimed that these uses of its marks constituted trademark infringement, dilution, false designation of origin, and unfair competition. The district

1. The disclaimer reads as follows: "This site is neither endorsed, nor sponsored, nor affiliated with Playboy Enterprises, Inc. PLAYBOY® PLAYMATE OF THE YEAR® AND PLAYMATE OF THE MONTH® ARE REGISTERED trademarks of Playboy Enterprises, Inc."

3. PEI claims that "PMOY" is an unregistered trademark of PEI, standing for "Playmate of the Year."

court granted defendants' motion for summary judgment. PEI appeals the grant of summary judgment on its infringement and dilution claims. We affirm in part and reverse in part.

* * *

III.   Discussion

A.   Trademark Infringement

Except for the use of PEI's protected terms in the wallpaper of Welles' website, we conclude that Welles' uses of PEI's trademarks are permissible, nominative uses. They imply no current sponsorship or endorsement by PEI. Instead, they serve to identify Welles as a past PEI "Playmate of the Year."

We articulated the test for a permissible, nominative use in *New Kids On The Block v. New America Publishing, Inc.*[8] The band, New Kids On The Block, claimed trademark infringement arising from the use of their trademarked name by several newspapers. The newspapers had conducted polls asking which member of the band New Kids On The Block was the best and most popular. The papers' use of the trademarked term did not fall within the traditional fair use doctrine. Unlike a traditional fair use scenario, the defendant newspaper was using the trademarked term to describe not its own product, but the plaintiff's. Thus, the factors used to evaluate fair use were inapplicable. The use was nonetheless permissible, we concluded, based on its nominative nature.

We adopted the following test for nominative use:

> First, the product or service in question must be one not readily identifiable without use of the trademark; second, only so much of the mark or marks may be used as is reasonably necessary to identify the product or service; and third, the user must do nothing that would, in conjunction with the mark, suggest sponsorship or endorsement by the trademark holder.

We noted in *New Kids* that a nominative use may also be a commercial one.

In cases in which the defendant raises a nominative use defense, the above three-factor test should be applied instead of the test for likelihood of confusion set forth in [*AMF Inc. v. Sleekcraft Boats*, 599 F.2d 341 (9th Cir.1979)]. The three-factor test better evaluates the likelihood of confusion in nominative use cases. When a defendant uses a trademark nominally, the trademark will be identical to the plaintiff's mark, at least in terms of the words in question. Thus, application of the *Sleekcraft* test, which focuses on the similarity of the mark used by the plaintiff and the defendant, would lead to the incorrect conclusion that virtually all nominative uses are confusing. The three-factor test—with its requirements that the defendant use marks only when no descriptive substitute exists, use no more of the mark than necessary, and do nothing to suggest sponsorship or

---

8.   971 F.2d 302 (9th Cir.1992).

endorsement by the mark holder—better addresses concerns regarding the likelihood of confusion in nominative use cases.

We group the uses of PEI's trademarked terms into three for the purpose of applying the test for nominative use. First, we analyze Welles' use of the terms in headlines and banner advertisements. We conclude that those uses are clearly nominative. Second, we analyze the use of the terms in the metatags for Welles' website, which we conclude are nominative as well. Finally, we analyze the terms as used in the wall-paper of the website. We conclude that this use is not nominative and remand for a determination of whether it infringes on a PEI trademark.

1. Headlines and banner advertisements.

To satisfy the first part of the test for nominative use, "the product or service in question must be one not readily identifiable without use of the trademark[.]" This situation arises "when a trademark also describes a person, a place or an attribute of a product" and there is no descriptive substitute for the trademark. In such a circumstance, allowing the trademark holder exclusive rights would allow the language to "be depleted in much the same way as if generic words were protectable." In *New Kids,* we gave the example of the trademarked term, "Chicago Bulls." We explained that "one might refer to the 'two-time world champions' or 'the professional basketball team from Chicago,' but it's far simpler (and more likely to be understood) to refer to the Chicago Bulls." Moreover, such a use of the trademark would "not imply sponsorship or endorsement of the product because the mark is used only to describe the thing, rather than to identify its source." Thus, we concluded, such uses must be excepted from trademark infringement law.

The district court properly identified Welles' situation as one which must also be excepted. No descriptive substitute exists for PEI's trademarks in this context. The court explained:

> [T]here is no other way that Ms. Welles can identify or describe herself and her services without venturing into absurd descriptive phrases. To describe herself as the "nude model selected by Mr. Hefner's magazine as its number-one prototypical woman for the year 1981" would be impractical as well as ineffectual in identifying Terri Welles to the public.

We agree. Just as the newspapers in *New Kids* could only identify the band clearly by using its trademarked name, so can Welles only identify herself clearly by using PEI's trademarked title.

The second part of the nominative use test requires that "only so much of the mark or marks may be used as is reasonably necessary to identify the product or service[.]" *New Kids* provided the following examples to explain this element: "[A] soft drink competitor would be entitled to compare its product to Coca–Cola or Coke, but would not be entitled to use Coca–Cola's distinctive lettering." Similarly, in a past case, an auto shop was allowed to use the trademarked term "Volkswagen" on a sign describing the cars it repaired, in part because the shop "did not use Volkswagen's distinctive lettering style or color scheme, nor did he display the encircled 'VW' emblem." Welles' banner advertisements and headlines satisfy this element because they use only the trademarked words, not the font or symbols associated with the trademarks.

The third element requires that the user do "nothing that would, in conjunction with the mark, suggest sponsorship or endorsement by the trademark holder." As to this element, we conclude that aside from the wallpaper, which we address separately, Welles does nothing in conjunction with her use of the marks to suggest sponsorship or endorsement by PEI. The marks are clearly used to describe the title she received from PEI in 1981, a title that helps describe who she is. It would be unreasonable to assume that the Chicago Bulls sponsored a website of Michael Jordan's simply because his name appeared with the appellation "former Chicago Bull." Similarly, in this case, it would be unreasonable to assume that PEI currently sponsors or endorses someone who describes herself as a "Playboy Playmate of the Year in 1981." The designation of the year, in our case, serves the same function as the "former" in our example. It shows that any sponsorship or endorsement occurred in the past.[25]

In addition to doing nothing in conjunction with her use of the marks to suggest sponsorship or endorsement by PEI, Welles affirmatively disavows any sponsorship or endorsement. Her site contains a clear statement disclaiming any connection to PEI. Moreover, the text of the site describes her ongoing legal battles with the company.[26]

For the foregoing reasons, we conclude that Welles' use of PEI's marks in her headlines and banner advertisements is a nominative use excepted from the law of trademark infringement.

2. Metatags.

Welles includes the terms "playboy" and "playmate" in her metatags. Metatags describe the contents of a website using keywords. Some search engines search metatags to identify websites relevant to a search. Thus, when an internet searcher enters "playboy" or "playmate" into a search engine that uses metatags, the results will include Welles' site.[28] Because Welles' metatags do not repeat the terms extensively, her site will not be at the top of the list of search results. Applying the three-factor test for nominative use, we conclude that the use of the trademarked terms in Welles' metatags is nominative.

---

25. We express no opinion regarding whether an individual's use of a current title would suggest sponsorship or endorsement.

26. By noting Welles' affirmative actions, we do not mean to imply that affirmative actions of this type are necessary to establish nominative use. *New Kids* sets forth no such requirement, and we do not impose one here.

28. We note that search engines that use their own summaries of websites, or that search the entire text of sites, are also likely to identify Welles' site as relevant to a search for "playboy" or "playmate," given the content of the site.

As we discussed above with regard to the headlines and banner advertisements, Welles has no practical way of describing herself without using trademarked terms. In the context of metatags, we conclude that she has no practical way of identifying the content of her website without referring to PEI's trademarks.

A large portion of Welles' website discusses her association with Playboy over the years. Thus, the trademarked terms accurately describe the contents of Welles' website, in addition to describing Welles. Forcing Welles and others to use absurd turns of phrase in their metatags, such as those necessary to identify Welles, would be particularly damaging in the internet search context. Searchers would have a much more difficult time locating relevant websites if they could do so only by correctly guessing the long phrases necessary to substitute for trademarks. We can hardly expect someone searching for Welles' site to imagine the same phrase proposed by the district court to describe Welles without referring to Playboy—"the nude model selected by Mr. Hefner's organization...." Yet if someone could not remember her name, that is what they would have to do. Similarly, someone searching for critiques of Playboy on the internet would have a difficult time if internet sites could not list the object of their critique in their metatags.

There is simply no descriptive substitute for the trademarks used in Welles' metatags. Precluding their use would have the unwanted effect of hindering the free flow of information on the internet, something which is certainly not a goal of trademark law. Accordingly, the use of trademarked terms in the metatags meets the first part of the test for nominative use.

We conclude that the metatags satisfy the second and third elements of the test as well. The metatags use only so much of the marks as reasonably necessary[30] and nothing is done in conjunction with them to suggest sponsorship or endorsement by the trademark holder. We note that our decision might differ if the metatags listed the trademarked term so repeatedly that Welles' site would regularly appear above PEI's in searches for one of the trademarked terms.

3. *Wallpaper/watermark.*

The background, or wallpaper, of Welles' site consists of the repeated abbreviation "PMOY '81," which stands for "Playmate of the Year 1981." Welles' name or likeness does not appear before or after "PMOY '81." The pattern created by the repeated abbreviation appears as the background of the various pages of the website. Accepting, for the purposes of this appeal, that the abbreviation "PMOY" is indeed entitled to protection, we conclude that the repeated, stylized use of this abbreviation fails the nominative use test.

---

30. It is hard to imagine how a metatag could use more of a mark than the words contained in it, but we recently learned that some search engines are now using pictures. Searching for symbols, such as the Playboy bunny, cannot be far behind. That problem does not arise in this case, however, and we need not address it.

The repeated depiction of "PMOY '81" is not necessary to describe Welles. "Playboy Playmate of the Year 1981" is quite adequate. Moreover, the term does not even appear to describe Welles—her name or likeness do not appear before or after each "PMOY '81." Because the use of the abbreviation fails the first prong of the nominative use test, we need not apply the next two prongs of the test.

Because the defense of nominative use fails here, and we have already determined that the doctrine of fair use does not apply, we remand to the district court. The court must determine whether trademark law protects the abbreviation "PMOY," as used in the wallpaper.

B.   Trademark Dilution

The district court granted summary judgment to Welles as to PEI's claim of trademark dilution. We affirm on the ground that all of Welles' uses of PEI's marks, with the exception of the use in the wallpaper which we address separately, are proper, nominative uses. We hold that nominative uses, by definition, do not dilute the trademarks.

Federal law provides protection against trademark dilution:

> The owner of a famous mark shall be entitled, subject to the principles of equity and upon such terms as the court deems reasonable, to an injunction against another person's commercial use in commerce of a mark or trade name, if such use begins after the mark has become famous and causes dilution of the distinctive quality of the mark. . . .

Dilution, which was not defined by the statute, has been described by the courts as "the gradual 'whittling away' of a trademark's value." * * *

Dilution works its harm not by causing confusion in consumers' minds regarding the source of a good or service, but by creating an association in consumers' minds between a mark and a different good or service. * * *

Uses that do not create an improper association between a mark and a new product but merely identify the trademark holder's products should be excepted from the reach of the anti-dilution statute. Such uses cause no harm. The anti-dilution statute recognizes this principle and specifically excepts users of a trademark who compare their product in "commercial advertising or promotion to identify the competing goods or services of the owner of the famous mark."[40]

For the same reason uses in comparative advertising are excepted from anti-dilution law, we conclude that nominative uses are also excepted. A nominative use, by definition, refers to the trademark holder's product. It does not create an improper association in consumers' minds between a new product and the trademark holder's mark.

When Welles refers to her title, she is in effect referring to a product of PEI's. She does not dilute the title by truthfully identifying herself as its one-time recipient any more than Michael Jordan would dilute the name

---

40.   15 U.S.C. § 1125(c)(4)(A).

"Chicago Bulls" by referring to himself as a former member of that team, or the two-time winner of an Academy Award would dilute the award by referring to him or herself as a "two-time Academy Award winner." Awards are not diminished or diluted by the fact that they have been awarded in the past. Similarly, they are not diminished or diluted when past recipients truthfully identify themselves as such. It is in the nature of honors and awards to be identified with the people who receive them. Of course, the conferrer of such honors and awards is free to limit the honoree's use of the title or references to the award by contract. So long as a use is nominative, however, trademark law is unavailing.

The one exception to the above analysis in this case is Welles' use of the abbreviation "PMOY" on her wallpaper. Because we determined that this use is not nominative, it is not excepted from the anti-dilution provisions. Thus, we reverse as to this issue and remand for further proceedings. We note that if the district court determines that "PMOY" is not entitled to trademark protection, PEI's claim for dilution must fail. The trademarked term, "Playmate of the Year" is not identical or nearly identical to the term "PMOY." Therefore, use of the term "PMOY" cannot, as a matter of law, dilute the trademark "Playmate of the Year."

                          * * *

NOTES & QUESTIONS

1. *Traditional fair use vs. nominative use.* Is Welles's use of the trademarks belonging to Playboy Enterprises protected under the traditional fair use defense as well as the nominative use defense? In *Brookfield Communications*, the court appears to suggest that the traditional fair use test privileges Welles's use of these marks when it writes:

> The district court found that Welles was using "Playboy" and "Playmate" not as trademarks, but rather as descriptive terms fairly and accurately describing her web page, and that her use of "Playboy" and "Playmate" in her website's metatags was a permissible, good faith attempt to index the content of her website. It accordingly concluded that her use was permissible under the trademark laws.

Is the court in *Brookfield Communications* correct that the marks were being used to describe Welles's website? How else might one view their use?

2. *Reference, necessity and repetition.* The first prong of the nominative use test is that "the product or service in question must be one not readily identifiable without use of the trademark." The Ninth Circuit points out that "[t]he background, or wallpaper, of Welles' site consists of the repeated abbreviation 'PMOY '81,' which stands for 'Playmate of the Year 1981.'" It then concludes that the use of "PMOY '81" as wallpaper fails the first prong of the nominative use test because "[t]he repeated depiction of 'PMOY '81' is not necessary to describe Welles. 'Playboy Playmate of the Year 1981' is quite adequate." Does the court mean that the abbreviation is not necessary because one can use the unabbreviated phrase? Is the court perhaps actually objecting to the repeated use of the abbreviation rather than to the abbreviation itself?

C. GENERICITY

Playboy Enterprises, Inc. v. Netscape Communications Corp.

55 F.Supp.2d 1070 (C.D.Cal.1999), *aff'd*, 202 F.3d 278 (9th Cir.1999).

■ STOTLER, DISTRICT JUDGE.

I. PROCEDURAL BACKGROUND

On April 15, 1999, plaintiff Playboy Enterprises, Inc. ("PEI") filed a Motion for Preliminary Injunction against defendant Netscape Communications Corp. and against defendant Excite, Inc. On May 10, 1999, defendants filed a joint opposition. PEI filed its reply on May 17, 1999. The Court heard oral argument on the motion on May 24, 1999. At the end of the hearing, the Court took the matter under advisement, and ordered the parties to lodge proposed Findings of Fact and Conclusions of Law. Plaintiff lodged its proposed Findings on June 1, 1999; defendants lodged theirs on June 8, 1999. The Court has considered all of the parties' submissions, as well as arguments presented at the hearing.

II. FACTUAL BACKGROUND

Defendants operate search engines on the Internet.[1] When a person searches for a particular topic in either search engine, the search engine compiles a list of sites matching or related to the user's search terms, and then posts the list of sites, known as "search results."

Defendants sell advertising space on the search result pages. Known as "banner ads," the advertisements are commonly found at the top of the screen. The ads themselves are often animated and whimsical, and designed to entice the Internet user to "click here." If the user does click on the ad, she is transported to the website of the advertiser.

As with other media, advertisers seek to maximize the efficacy of their ads by targeting consumers matching a certain demographic profile. Savvy website operators accommodate the advertisers by "keying" ads to search terms entered by users. That is, instead of posting ads in a random rotation, defendants program their servers to link a pre-selected set of banner ads to certain "key" search terms. Defendants market this context-sensitive advertising ability as a value-added service and charge a premium.

Defendants key various adult entertainment ads to a group of over 450 terms related to adult entertainment, including the terms "playboy" and

---

1. The Court notes that Netscape's search engine is co-branded with Excite, and programmed by Excite, but for purposes of this Motion, the Court treats them both as search engine operators.

"playmate." Plaintiff contends that inclusion of those terms violates plaintiff's trademarks rights in those words.

III.   PARTIES' CONTENTIONS

Plaintiff has a trademark on "Playboy®" and "Playmate®." Plaintiff contends that defendants are infringing and diluting its trademarks (1) by marketing and selling the group of over 450 words, including "playboy" and "playmate," to advertisers, (2) by programming the banner ads to run in response to the search terms "playboy" and "playmate" (i.e., "keying"), and (3) by actually displaying the banner ad on the search results page. As a result, plaintiff contends, Internet users are diverted from plaintiff's official website and websites sponsored or approved by plaintiff, which generally will be listed as search results, to other adult entertainment websites. Plaintiff further argues that defendants intend to divert the users to the non-PEI sites. Plaintiff does not contend, however, that defendants infringe or dilute the marks when defendants' search engines generate a list of websites related to "playboy" or "playmate."

Defendants respond that while plaintiff may have a trademark on "Playboy®" and "Playmate®," defendants do not actually "use" the trademarks qua trademarks. Moreover, even if defendants do use the trademarks, defendants argue that a trademark does not confer an absolute property right on all uses of the protected terms, and that defendants' use of the terms is permitted. Finally, defendants dispute that they have any intent to divert users from clicking on search results (such as PEI's sites) to clicking on banner ads.

IV.   DISCUSSION

A.   Legal Standard for Preliminary Injunction

In order for plaintiff to obtain a preliminary injunction, it "must show either (1) a combination of probable success on the merits and a possibility of irreparable harm, or (2) the existence of serious questions on the merits and the balance of hardships weighing heavily in its favor." *PEI v. Welles,* 7 F.Supp.2d 1098, 1099 (S.D.Cal.1998), *aff'd without opinion,* 162 F.3d 1169, 1998 WL 750954 (9th Cir.1998).

B.   Law and The Internet

"The Internet is 'a unique and wholly new medium of worldwide human communication.'" *Reno v. ACLU,* 521 U.S. 844 (1997) (citation omitted). The parties and the Court are conversant with the workings of the Internet, as well as with the constantly expanding body of law that seeks to craft a legal contour for it. The Court is mindful of the difficulty of applying well-established doctrines to what can only be described as an amorphous situs of information, anonymous messenger of communication, and seemingly endless stream of commerce. Indeed, the very vastness, and manipulability, of the Internet forms the mainspring of plaintiff's lawsuit.

C. Trademark Use

Integral to plaintiff's success on the merits of its case, on either the infringement or dilution theory, is a showing that defendants use plaintiff's trademarks in commerce. Plaintiff does not so show. Rather, plaintiff can only contend that the use of the words "playboy" and "playmate," as keywords or search terms, is equivalent to the use of the trademarks "Playboy®" and "Playmate®." However, it is undisputed that an Internet user cannot conduct a search using the trademark form of the words, i.e., Playboy® and Playmate®. Rather, the user enters the generic word "playboy" or "playmate." It is also undisputed that the words "playboy" and "playmate" are English words in their own right, and that there exist other trademarks on the words wholly unrelated to PEI. Thus, whether the user is looking for goods and services covered by PEI's trademarks or something altogether unrelated to PEI is anybody's guess. Plaintiff guesses that most users searching the Web for "playboy" and "playmate" are indeed looking for PEI sites, goods and services. Based on that theory, plaintiff argues that since defendants also speculate that users searching for "playboy" and "playmate" are looking for things related to Playboy® and Playmate®, defendants use the trademarks when they key competing adult entertainment goods and services to the generic "playboy" and "playmate."

Plaintiff has not shown that defendants use the terms in their trademark form, i.e., Playboy® and Playmate®, when marketing to advertisers or in the algorithm that effectuates the keying of the ads to the keywords. Thus, plaintiff's argument that defendants "use" plaintiff's trademarks falls short.

D. Trademark Infringement * * *

Even if use of the generic "playboy" and "playmate" were construed to use the trademark terms Playboy® and Playmate®, plaintiff still must show that the use violates trademark law. Plaintiff has asserted * * * trademark infringement * * *

1. Infringement

"The core element of trademark infringement is the likelihood of confusion, i.e., whether the similarity of the marks is likely to confuse customers about the source of the products." *Official Airline Guides, Inc. v. Goss,* 6 F.3d 1385, 1391 (9th Cir.1993). Assuming arguendo that defendants' use of "playboy" and "playmate" is use of plaintiff's marks, plaintiff must still show that confusion is likely to result from that use. Plaintiff has not so shown.

Rather, plaintiff relies on the recent case from the Court of Appeals for the Ninth Circuit, *Brookfield Communications, Inc. v. West Coast Entertainment Corp.,* 174 F.3d 1036, 1062–64 (9th Cir.1999), for the proposition that defendants cause "initial interest confusion" by the use of the words "playboy" and "playmate." Initial interest confusion, as coined by the Ninth Circuit, is a brand of confusion particularly applicable to the Internet. Generally speaking, initial interest confusion may result when a user conducts a search using a trademark term and the results of the search include websites not sponsored by the holder of the trademark search term, but rather of competitors. *Id.* The Ninth Circuit reasoned that the user may be diverted to an unsponsored site, and only realize that she has been diverted upon arriving at the competitor's site. Once there, however, even though the user knows she is not in the site initially sought, she may stay. In that way, the competitor has captured the trademark holder's potential visitors or customers. *Id.*

Brookfield is distinguishable from this case, and where applicable, supportive of defendants' position.

First, the trademark at issue in *Brookfield* was not an English word in its own right. In *Brookfield,* the Court compared Brookfield's trademark "MovieBuff" with competitor West Coast's use of the domain name "moviebuff.com," and found them to be "essentially identical" despite the differences in capitalization, which the Court considered "inconsequential in light of the fact that Web addresses are not caps-sensitive ..." *Id.* at 1054. However, the Court held that West Coast could use the term "Movie Buff" (or, presumably, "movie buff") with the space, as such is the "proper term for the 'motion picture enthusiast'.... It cannot, however, omit the space." *Id.* at 1065. On the other hand, "[i]n light of the fact that it is not a word in the English language, when the term 'MovieBuff' is employed, it is used to refer to Brookfield's products and services, rather than to mean 'motion picture enthusiast.' " *Id.* at 1065.

As English words, "playboy" and "playmate" cannot be said to suggest sponsorship or endorsement of either the websites that appear as search results (as in *Brookfield*) or the banner ads that adorn the search results page. Although the trademark terms and the English language words are undisputedly identical, which, presumably, leads plaintiff to believe that the use of the English words is akin to use of the trademarks, the holder of a trademark may not remove a word from the English language merely by acquiring trademark rights in it. *Id.*

Second, the use by defendant of plaintiff's trademark in *Brookfield* was more suspect because the parties compete in the same market—as online providers of film industry information. *See Id.,* at 1056–57 ("[n]ot only are they not non-competitors, the competitive proximity of their products is actually quite high"). The Ninth Circuit analogized the capture of unsuspecting Internet users by a competitor to highways and billboards:

> Suppose West Coast's competitor ... puts up a billboard on a highway reading—"West Coast Video: 2 miles ahead at Exit 7"— where West Coast is really located at Exit 8 but Blockbuster is located at Exit 7. Customers looking for West Coast's store will pull off at Exit 7 and drive around looking for it. Unable to locate West Coast, but seeing the Blockbuster store right by the highway entrance, they may simply rent there.

Brookfield, at 1064. Although the customer is not confused as to where she ultimately rents a video, Blockbuster has misappropriated West Coast's goodwill through causing initial consumer confusion. *Id*. The customer has been captured by the competitor in much the same way that defendant in *Brookfield* captures Internet users looking for plaintiff's website.

Here, the analogy is quite unlike that of a devious placement of a road sign bearing false information. This case presents a scenario more akin to a driver pulling off the freeway in response to a sign that reads "Fast Food Burgers" to find a well-known fast food burger restaurant, next to which stands a billboard that reads: "Better Burgers: 1 Block Further." The driver, previously enticed by the prospect of a burger from the well-known restaurant, now decides she wants to explore other burger options. Assuming that the same entity owns the land on which both the burger restaurant and the competitor's billboard stand, should that entity be liable to the burger restaurant for diverting the driver? That is the rule PEI contends the Court should adopt. * * *

CONCLUSION

Accordingly, and for the foregoing reasons, the plaintiff's motion is denied. * * *

NOTES & QUESTIONS

1. *Keywords and domain names.* Central to the court's decision in *Playboy v. Netscape Communications Corp.* is its conclusion that the Plaintiff has not shown that "defendants use plaintiff's trademarks in commerce." The court argues that the words "playboy" and "playmate" are different from the registered trademarks Playboy® and Playmate® and that plaintiffs have only shown that defendants have keyed banner ads to the former. The court notes that technical limitations on the search technologies prevent the use of registered trademarks as keywords—one cannot include the registered trademark symbol ® in a search. Do you find this argument convincing? If I had registered the domain name playboy.com, would I be liable for trademark infringement? After all, the domain name playboy.com is different from the domain name Playboy®.com. Is there any reason why domain names and keywords should be treated differently?

2. *Searching for Playboy.* The court in *Playboy v. Netscape Communications Corp.* states that "whether the user [of a search engine] is looking for goods and services covered by [Playboy Enterprises'] trademarks or something altogether unrelated is anybody's guess." Reacting to this and similar statements in the opinion, one commentator has stated:

> In the author's opinion, it is highly unlikely that a teenage boy typing the word "playboy" in a search engine does not intend to look for information about the magazine, Playmate of the Month and all of the other products of Playboy Enterprises. I think that it is highly probable that most teenage boys have never even heard of the generic dictionary meaning of "playboy" as "a wealthy, carefree man who devotes most of his time to leisure, self-amusement and hedonistic pleasures, conventionally frequenting parties and

night clubs, romancing a rapid succession of attractive young women and racing speedboats or sports cars."[3] Thus, the Playboy decision did not really grapple with the substantive issues raised by the sale of banner advertising.

4 J. THOMAS MCCARTHY, MCCARTHY ON TRADEMARKS AND UNFAIR COMPETITION § 25:70.1 (4th ed.2002). Do you agree with this analysis? Do you think the result would have been different if the court had found as a fact that most people using the search term "playboy" were searching for the goods and services of Playboy Enterprises, Inc.?

3. *Banner ads keyed to trademark.* Ought we to recognize a redressable harm to a trademark owner when a search engine keys a banner ad to the owner's trademark? How would you characterize this harm? Given that the average search engine user does not know that banner ads may be keyed to likely search terms, is there any likelihood of confusion regarding origin, sponsorship, or affiliation sufficient to support a claim of trademark infringement? If the trademark is famous, given that the average user does not associate the appearance of a particular banner ad with the entry of a particular search term, is keying this banner ad to a trademark dilutive of that mark in any way? Is either the search engine or the producer of the banner ad trading on the goodwill associated with the trademark to which the banner ad is keyed?

4. *Keyed relevancy rankings.* Is any harm suffered by a trademark owner when a search engine awards a higher relevancy ranking to a website when that owner's trademark is used in a search? Does it matter whether the search engine charges a fee for this higher ranking?

D.   FIRST AMENDMENT

Planned Parenthood Federation of America, Inc. v. Bucci

42 U.S.P.Q.2d (BNA) 1430 (S.D.N.Y.1997).

■ KIMBA M. WOOD, DISTRICT JUDGE.

Plaintiff Planned Parenthood Federation of America, Inc. ("Planned Parenthood") has moved to preliminarily enjoin defendant Richard Bucci ("Bucci"), doing business as Catholic Radio, from using the domain name "plannedparenthood.com," and from identifying his web site on the Internet under the name "www.plannedparenthood.com." The Court held a hearing on February 20, 1997 and February 21, 1997, and now issues the preliminary injunction sought by Planned Parenthood.

I.   Undisputed Facts

The parties do not dispute the following facts. Plaintiff Planned Parenthood, founded in 1922, is a non-profit, reproductive health care

---

3. Random House Unabridged Dictionary of the English Language 1104 (1983 rev.).

organization that has used its present name since 1942. Plaintiff registered the stylized service mark "Planned Parenthood" on the Principal Register of the United States Patent and Trademark Office on June 28, 1955, and registered the block service mark "Planned Parenthood" on the Principal Register of the United States Patent and Trademark Office on September 9, 1975. Plaintiff's 146 separately incorporated affiliates, in 48 states and the District of Columbia, are licensed to use the mark "Planned Parenthood." Plaintiff expends a considerable sum of money in promoting and advertising its services. The mark "Planned Parenthood" is strong and incontestable.

Plaintiff operates a web site at "www.ppfa.org," using the domain name "ppfa.org." Plaintiff's home page offers Internet users resources regarding sexual and reproductive health, contraception and family planning, pregnancy, sexually transmitted diseases, and abortion, as well as providing links to other relevant web sites. In addition, plaintiff's home page offers Internet users suggestions on how to get involved with plaintiff's mission and solicits contributions.

Defendant Bucci is the host of "Catholic Radio," a daily radio program broadcast on the WVOA radio station in Syracuse, New York. Bucci is an active participant in the anti-abortion movement. Bucci operates web sites at "www.catholicradio.com" and at "lambsofchrist.com." On August 28, 1996, Bucci registered the domain name "plannedparenthood.com" with Network Solutions, Inc. ("NSI"), a corporation that administers the assignment of domain names on the Internet. After registering the domain name, Bucci set up a web site and home page on the Internet at the address "www.plannedparenthood.com."

Internet users who type in the address "www.plannedparenthood.com," or who use a search engine such as Yahoo! or Lycos to find web sites containing the term "planned parenthood," can reach Bucci's web site and home page. Once a user accesses Bucci's home page, she sees on the computer screen the words "Welcome to the PLANNED PARENTHOOD HOME PAGE!" These words appear on the screen first, because the text of a home page downloads from top to bottom. Tr. 2/20/97 at 47. Once the whole home page has loaded, the user sees a scanned image of the cover of a book entitled *The Cost of Abortion,* by Lawrence Roberge ("Roberge"), under which appear several links: "Foreword," "Afterword," "About the Author," "Book Review," and "Biography."

After clicking on a link, the user accesses text related to that link. By clicking on "Foreword" or "Afterword," the Internet user simply accesses the foreword or afterword of the book *The Cost of Abortion.* That text eventually reveals that *The Cost of Abortion* is an anti-abortion book. The text entitled "About the Author" contains the curriculum vitae of author Roberge. It also notes that "Mr. Roberge is available for interview and speaking engagements," and provides his telephone number. The "Book Review" link brings the Internet user to a selection of quotations by various people endorsing *The Cost of Abortion.* Those quotations include exhortations to read the book and obtain the book. "Biography" offers more information about Roberge's background.

II. *Disputed Facts*

The parties dispute defendant's motive in choosing plaintiff's mark as his domain name. Plaintiff alleges that defendant used plaintiff's mark with the "specific intent to damage Planned Parenthood's reputation and to confuse unwitting users of the Internet." Pl. Rep. Mem. at 2. Discussing the difference between the domain name at issue here and defendant's other web sites, defendant's counsel states that "[t]he WWWPLANNNED-PARENTHOOD.COM [sic] website ... enables Defendant's message to reach a broader audience." Def. Mem. in Opp. at 3. Defendant's counsel made the following statement to the Court regarding defendant's use of plaintiff's mark to designate his web site:

> My belief is that it was intended to reach people who would be sympathetic to the proabortion position.... [I]t is an effort to get the ... political and social message to people we might not have been otherwise able to reach. I think it's analogous to putting an advertisement in the New York Times rather than The National Review. You are more likely to get people who are sympathetic to the proabortion position, and that's who you want to reach. I believe that is exactly what Mr. Bucci did when he selected Planned Parenthood. Tr. 2/5/97 at 23.

Defendant did not dispute that his counsel was correct in that statement. Tr. 2/21/97 at 35. Defendant's counsel also admitted that Bucci was trying to reach Internet users who thought, in accessing his web site, that they would be getting information from plaintiff. *Id.* at 23–24.

* * *

2. *The First Amendment Exception*

Defendant also argues that his use of the "planned parenthood" mark is protected by the First Amendment. As defendant argues, trademark infringement law does not curtail or prohibit the exercise of the First Amendment right to free speech. I note that plaintiff has not sought, in any way, to restrain defendant from speech that criticizes Planned Parenthood or its mission, or that discusses defendant's beliefs regarding reproduction, family, and religion. The sole purpose of the Court's inquiry has been to determine whether the use of the "planned parenthood" mark as defendant's domain name and home page address constitutes an infringement of plaintiff's trademark. Defendant's use of another entity's mark is entitled to First Amendment protection when his use of that mark is part of a communicative message, not when it is used to identify the source of a product. *Yankee Publishing Inc. v. News America Publishing, Inc.,* 809 F.Supp. 267, 275 (S.D.N.Y.1992). By using the mark as a domain name and home page address and by welcoming Internet users to the home page with the message "Welcome to the Planned Parenthood Home Page!" defendant identifies the web site and home page as being the product, or forum, of plaintiff. I therefore determine that, because defendant's use of the term "planned parenthood" is not part of a communicative message, his infringement on plaintiff's mark is not protected by the First Amendment.

Defendant argues that his use of the "Planned Parenthood" name for his web site is entitled to First Amendment protection, relying primarily on the holding of *Yankee Publishing*, 809 F.Supp. at 275. In that case, Judge Leval noted that the First Amendment can protect unauthorized use of a trademark when such use is part of an expression of a communicative message: "the Second Circuit has construed the Lanham Act narrowly when the unauthorized use of the trademark is for the purpose of a communicative message, rather than identification of product origin." *Id.* Defendant argues that his use of the "Planned Parenthood" name for his web site is a communicative message.

However, *Yankee Publishing* carefully draws a distinction between communicative messages and product labels or identifications:

> When another's trademark ... is used without permission for the purpose of source identification, the trademark law generally prevails over the First Amendment. Free speech rights do not extend to labelling or advertising products in a manner that conflicts with the trademark rights of others.

Id. at 276. Defendant offers no argument in his papers as to why the Court should determine that defendant's use of "plannedparenthood.com" is a communicative message rather than a source identifier. His use of "plannedparenthood.com" as a domain name to identify his web site is on its face more analogous to source identification than to a communicative message; in essence, the name identifies the web site, which contains defendant's home page. The statement that greets Internet users who access defendant's web site, "Welcome to the Planned Parenthood Home Page," is also more analogous to an identifier than to a communication. For those reasons, defendant's use of the trademarked term "planned parenthood" is not part of a communicative message, but rather, serves to identify a product or item, defendant's web site and home page, as originating from Planned Parenthood.

Defendant's use of plaintiff's mark is not protected as a title under *Rogers v. Grimaldi*, 875 F.2d 994, 998 (2d Cir.1989). There, the Court of Appeals determined that the title of the film "Ginger and Fred" was not a misleading infringement, despite the fact that the film was not about Ginger Rogers and Fred Astaire, because of the artistic implications of a title. The Court of Appeals noted that "[f]ilmmakers and authors frequently rely on word-play, ambiguity, irony, and allusion in titling their works." *Id.* The Court of Appeals found that the use of a title such as the one at issue in *Rogers* was acceptable "unless the title has no artistic relevance to the underlying work"; even when the title has artistic relevance, it may not be used to "explicitly mislead[ ] [the consumer] as to the source or content of the work." *Id.* Here, even treating defendant's domain name and home page address as titles, rather than as source identifiers, I find that the title "plannedparenthood.com" has no artistic implications, and that the title is being used to attract some consumers by misleading them as to the web site's source or content. Given defendant's testimony indicating that he knew, and intended, that his use of the domain name "plannedparent-hood.com" would cause some "pro-abortion" Internet users to access his web site, Tr. 2/21/97 at 36, he cannot demonstrate that his use of "planned parenthood" is entitled to First Amendment protection.

* * *

Bally Total Fitness Holding Corp. v. Faber

29 F.Supp.2d 1161 (C.D.Cal.1998).

■ PREGERSON, DISTRICT JUDGE.

Andrew S. Faber's motion for summary judgment came before the Court for oral argument on November 23, 1998. After reviewing and considering the materials submitted by the parties and hearing oral argument, the Court GRANTS Faber's motion for summary judgment.

BACKGROUND

Bally Total Fitness Holding Corp. ("Bally") brings this action for trademark infringement, unfair competition, and dilution against Andrew S. Faber ("Faber") in connection with Bally's federally registered trademarks and service marks in the terms "Bally," "Bally's Total Fitness," and "Bally Total Fitness," including the name and distinctive styles of these marks. Bally is suing Faber based on his use of Bally's marks in a website he designed.

Faber calls his site "Bally sucks." The website is dedicated to complaints about Bally's health club business. When the website is accessed, the viewer is presented with Bally's mark with the word "sucks" printed across it. Immediately under this, the website states "Bally Total Fitness Complaints! Un–Authorized."

Faber has several websites in addition to the "Bally sucks" site. The domain in which Faber has placed his websites is "www.compupix.com." Faber's other websites within "www.compupix.com" include the "Bally sucks" site (URL address "www.compupix.com/ballysucks"); "Images of Men," a website displaying and selling photographs of nude males (URL address "www.compupix.com/index.html"); a website containing information regarding the gay community (URL address "www.compupix.com/gay"); a website containing photographs of flowers and landscapes (URL address "www.compupix.com/fl/index.html"); and a website advertising "Drew Faber Web Site Services" (URL address "www.compupix.com/biz.htm").

On April 22, 1998, Bally applied for a temporary restraining order directing Faber to withdraw his website from the Internet. Bally represents that when its application for a TRO was initially filed, the "Bally sucks" site contained a direct link to Faber's "Images of Men" site. In his opposition to the application for a TRO, Faber indicated that this link had been removed. The Court denied Bally's application on April 30, 1998.

Bally brought a motion for summary judgment on its claims of trademark infringement, trademark dilution, and unfair competition which the Court denied on October 20, 1998. In that order, the Court ordered Faber to bring a motion for summary judgment. This motion is now before the Court.

DISCUSSION

* * *

g. *Defendant's intent in selecting the mark*

Here, Faber purposely chose to use Bally's mark to build a "web site that is 'dedicated to complaint, issues, problems, beefs, grievances, grumblings, accusations, and gripes with Bally Total Fitness health clubs.' " Faber, however, is exercising his right to publish critical commentary about Bally. He cannot do this without making reference to Bally.[4] In this regard, Professor McCarthy states:

> The main remedy of the trademark owner is not an injunction to suppress the message, but a rebuttal to the message. As Justice Brandeis long ago stated, "If there be time to expose through discussion the falsehood and fallacies, to avert the evil by the process of education, the remedy to be applied is more speech, not enforced silence."

5 McCarthy, § 31:148 at 31–216.

Applying Bally's argument would extend trademark protection to eclipse First Amendment rights. The courts, however, have rejected this approach by holding that trademark rights may be limited by First Amendment concerns. *See L.L. Bean, Inc. v. Drake Publishers, Inc.,* 811 F.2d 26 (1st Cir.), *cert. denied,* 483 U.S. 1013 (1987).

* * *

C. *Trademark Dilution*

* * *

[T]he courts have held that trademark owners may not quash unauthorized use of the mark by a person expressing a point of view. *See L.L. Bean,*

---

4. Bally concedes that Faber has some right to use Bally's name as part of his consumer commentary. However, Bally argues that Faber uses more than is necessary when making his commentary and that he has alternative means of communication. Specifically, Bally argues that Faber could use the name "Bally" or "Bally Total Fitness" in block lettering without using Bally's stylized "B" mark or distinctive script. This argument, however, would create an artificial distinction that does not exist under trademark law. Trademarks are defined broadly to include both names and stylized renditions of those names or other symbols. 15 U.S.C. §§ 1051, 1127 (1997). Furthermore, the purpose of a trademark is to identify the source of goods. *Id.* § 1127. An individual who wishes to engage in consumer commentary must have the full range of marks that the trademark owner has to identify the trademark owner as the object of the criticism. (*See infra* Part I–C.)

811 F.2d at 29, *citing Lucasfilm Ltd. v. High Frontier,* 622 F.Supp. 931, 933–35 (D.D.C.1985). This is so even if the opinion may come in the form of a commercial setting. *See Id.* at 33 (discussing Maine's anti-dilution statute). In *L.L. Bean,* the First Circuit held that a sexually-oriented parody of L.L. Bean's catalog in a commercial adult-oriented magazine was non-commercial use of the trademark. *See Id.* The court stated:

> If the anti-dilution statute were construed as permitting a trademark owner to enjoin the use of his mark in a noncommercial context found to be negative or offensive, then a corporation could shield itself from criticism by forbidding the use of its name in commentaries critical of its conduct. The legitimate aim of the anti-dilution statute is to prohibit the unauthorized use of another's trademark in order to market incompatible products or services. The Constitution does not, however, permit the range of the anti-dilution statute to encompass the unauthorized use of a trademark in a noncommercial setting such as an editorial or artistic context.

Id.

Here, Bally wants to protect its valuable marks and ensure that they are not tarnished or otherwise diluted. This is an understandable goal. However, for the reasons set forth above, Faber's "Bally sucks" site is not a commercial use.

Even if Faber's use of Bally's mark is a commercial use, Bally also cannot show tarnishment. Bally cites several cases such as the "Enjoy Cocaine" and "Mutant of Omaha" cases for the proposition that this site and its relationship to other sites tarnishes their mark. *See Mutual of Omaha Ins. Co. v. Novak,* 648 F.Supp. 905 (D.Neb.1986) (discussing both infringement and disparagement), *aff'd* 836 F.2d 397 (8th Cir.1987) (addressing infringement, but not disparagement); *Coca–Cola v. Gemini Rising, Inc.,* 346 F.Supp. 1183 (E.D.N.Y.1972).

There are, however, two flaws with Bally's argument. First, none of the cases that Bally cites involve consumer commentary. In *Coca–Cola,* the court enjoined the defendant's publication of a poster stating "Enjoy Cocaine" in the same script as Coca–Cola's trademark. *See Coca–Cola,* 346 F.Supp. at 1192. Likewise, in *Mutual of Omaha,* the court prohibited the use of the words "Mutual of Omaha," with a picture of an emaciated human head resembling the Mutual of Omaha's logo on a variety of products as a means of protesting the arms race. *See Mutual of Omaha,* 836 F.2d at 398. Here, however, Faber is using Bally's mark in the context of a consumer commentary to say that Bally engages in business practices which Faber finds distasteful or unsatisfactory. This is speech protected by the First Amendment. *See L.L. Bean,* 811 F.2d at 29; McCarthy, § 24:105 at 24–191. As such, Faber can use Bally's mark to identify the source of the goods or services of which he is complaining. This use is necessary to maintain broad opportunities for expression. *See Restatement (Third) of Unfair Competition* § 25(2), cmt. i (1995) (stating "extension of the antidilution statutes to protect against damaging nontrademark uses raises substantial free speech issues and duplicates other potential remedies better suited to balance the relevant interests'').

* * *

Name.Space, Inc. v. Network Solutions, Inc.

202 F.3d 573 (2d Cir.2000).

■ KATZMANN, CIRCUIT JUDGE:

[Plaintiff Name.Space, Inc. set up an alternative system of domain names, including 530 new global top-level domains (''gTLDs'') that were not included within the official domain name system. Some of the new domain names, such as ''.forpresident,'' ''.formayor,'' and ''.micro-soft.free.zone,'' had arguably expressive content, contrasting in that respect with the existing three-letter gTLDs, such as .com, .net, and .org. Name. Space asked Network Solutions, Inc. (''NSI''), then the sole domain-name registrar, to include references to the new gTLDs in the zone files of the root servers that it maintained, which would make the new gTLDs available to virtually all Internet users, but NSI refused. Name.Space filed an action against NSI, charging it with antitrust violations. NSI then sought authorization from the National Science Foundation, the federal agency that then supervised the domain name system, to comply with Name. Space's request, but NSF declined, whereupon Name.Space added NSF as a defendant. In one count of the complaint, Name.Space alleged that by refusing to incorporate the new gTLDs into the domain name system, NSF had infringed its rights under the First Amendment. In the following excerpt the court discusses the First Amendment claim.]

* * *

II.   First Amendment

Name.Space challenges the district court's holding that it ''has not met the burden of demonstrating that the three letter top level domain portion of an Internet domain name is expressive speech.'' *PGMedia*, 51 F.Supp.2d at 407 (*citing Clark v. Community for Creative Non–Violence*, 468 U.S. 288, 293 n. 5 (1984)). Although we affirm the district court's dismissal of Name.Space's First Amendment claims, we do so for different reasons. ''We may, of course, affirm on any basis for which there is a record sufficient to permit conclusions of law, including grounds upon which the district court did not rely.'' *Cromwell Assocs. v. Oliver Cromwell Owners, Inc.*, 941 F.2d 107, 111 (2d Cir.1991) (citations omitted).

In considering whether domain names constitute expressive speech, we observe that the lightning speed development of the Internet poses challenges for the common-law adjudicative process—a process which, ideally while grounded in the past, governs the present and offers direction for the future based on understandings of current circumstances. Mindful of the often unforeseeable impact of rapid technological change, we are wary of making legal pronouncements based on highly fluid circumstances, which almost certainly will give way to tomorrow's new realities. *Cf. Columbia Broad. Sys., Inc. v. Democratic Nat'l Comm.,* 412 U.S. 94, 102 (1973) ("The problems of regulation are rendered more difficult because the broadcast industry is dynamic in terms of technological change; solutions adequate a decade ago are not necessarily so now, and those acceptable today may well be outmoded 10 years hence."). "A law that changes every day is worse than no law at all." LON L. FULLER, THE MORALITY OF LAW 37, 79–81 (rev. ed.1969).

The district court adopted an analogy between Internet alphanumeric addresses and telephone numbers, and held that domain names are akin to source identifiers rather than to communicative messages. *See PGMedia,* 51 F.Supp.2d at 407–08. We disagree. It is certainly true that while "[i]t is possible to find some kernel of expression in almost every activity a person undertakes[,] . . . such a kernel is not sufficient to bring the activity within the protection of the First Amendment." *City of Dallas v. Stanglin,* 490 U.S. 19, 25 (1989). Further, the district court is not alone in suggesting that an analogy between Internet domain names and telephone number mnemonics (for example, 1–800–FLOWERS) may be appropriate. *See, e.g., Panavision Int'l, L.P. v. Toeppen,* 141 F.3d 1316, 1325 (9th Cir.1998) (comparing domain name to 1–800–HOLIDAY); *PGMedia,* 51 F.Supp.2d at 407–08 (citing cases). However, the nature of domain names is not suscepti-ble to such a uniform, monolithic characterization. As the Supreme Court has stated in an analogous and related context, "aware as we are of the changes taking place in the law, the technology, and the industrial struc-ture related to telecommunications, . . . we believe it unwise and unneces-sary definitively to pick one analogy or one specific set of words now."[12] *Denver Area Educ. Telecomms. Consortium, Inc. v. Federal Communica-tions Comm'n,* 518 U.S. 727, 742 (1996) (Breyer, J., plurality) (citations omitted). The existing gTLDs are not protected speech, but only because the current DNS and Amendment No. 11 limit them to three-letter after-thoughts such as .com and .net, which are lacking in expressive content. The district court did not address the possibility that longer and more contentful gTLDs like ".jones_for_president" and ".smith_for_senate" may constitute protected speech, such as political speech or parody. *See, e.g., Cliffs Notes, Inc. v. Bantam Doubleday Dell Publ'g Group, Inc.,* 886 F.2d 490, 493 (2d Cir.1989) (noting that title of book "Spy Notes" is parody constituting protected speech); *Rogers v. Grimaldi,* 875 F.2d 994, 998 (2d Cir.1989) (holding that title of movie "Ginger and Fred" contained "ex-pressive element" implicating First Amendment).

The Internet in general, and the DNS in particular, is marked by extraordinary plasticity. The DNS has already undergone considerable change in the Internet's brief history to date, and may undergo even more radical changes in the near future under the auspices of ICANN and DNSO. There is nothing inherent in the architecture of the Internet that prevents new gTLDs from constituting expressive speech. How broad the

---

12. Therefore, different analogies, in-cluding analogies to book and movie titles, street addresses, and telephone numbers may be appropriate in different circumstances.

permissible bandwidth of expression is in this context depends on the future direction of the DNS. Therefore, "we should be shy about saying the final word today about what will be accepted as reasonable tomorrow," particularly "when we know too little to risk the finality of precision." *Denver Area,* 518 U.S. at 777–78 (Souter, J., concurring).

Further, the functionality of domain names does not automatically place them beyond the reach of the First Amendment. Although domain names do have a functional purpose, whether the mix of functionality and expression is "sufficiently imbued with the elements of communication" depends on the domain name in question, the intentions of the registrant, the contents of the website, and the technical protocols that govern the DNS. *Spence v. Washington,* 418 U.S. 405, 409–10 (1974) ("[T]he context in which a symbol is used for purposes of expression is important, for the context may give meaning to the symbol." (citation omitted)). Functionality and expression are therefore not mutually exclusive: for example, automobile license plates have a functional purpose, but that function can be served as well by vanity plates, which in a small way can also be expressive. Similarly, domain names may be employed for a variety of communicative purposes with both functional and expressive elements, ranging from the truly mundane street address or telephone number-like identification of the specific business that is operating the website, to commercial speech and even core political speech squarely implicating First Amendment concerns.

In short, while we hold that the existing gTLDs do not constitute protected speech under the First Amendment, we do not preclude the possibility that certain domain names and new gTLDs, could indeed amount to protected speech. The time may come when new gTLDs could be used for "an expressive purpose such as commentary, parody, news reporting or criticism," comprising communicative messages by the author and/or operator of the website in order to influence the public's decision to visit that website, or even to disseminate a particular point of view. *United We Stand Am., Inc. v. United We Stand, Am. N. Y., Inc.,* 128 F.3d 86, 93 (2d Cir.1997) (citation omitted).

We do not view *Planned Parenthood Federation of America v. Bucci* as holding to the contrary. *See* No. 97 Civ. 0629, 1997 WL 133313, at *10–11 (S.D.N.Y. Mar. 24, 1997), *aff'd,* 152 F.3d 920 (2d Cir.1998) (unpublished table decision). In *Bucci,* a trademark infringement case, the court held that the defendant's particular use of the domain name "plannedparenthood.com" was as a "source identifier" rather than a "communicative message," while leaving open the possibility that a domain name could constitute such a message under other circumstances. *See id.* In reaching this conclusion, the *Bucci* court conducted precisely the kind of particularistic, context-sensitive analysis that is appropriate here, including analyses of the domain name itself, the way the domain name is being used, the motivations of the author of the website in question, the contents of the website, and so on. *See id.* Domain names and gTLDs *per se* are neither automatically entitled to nor excluded from the protections of the First

Amendment, and the appropriate inquiry is one that fully addresses particular circumstances presented with respect to each domain name.

NOTES & QUESTIONS

1. *Communication vs. source identification. Planned Parenthood v. Bucci* sets out the rule that a defendant's "use of another entity's mark is entitled to First Amendment protection when his use of that mark is part of a communicative message, not when it is used to identify the source of a product." It held that the defendant's use of "plannedparenthood.com" was not expressive. If the defendant had instead registered "plannedparenthoodsucks.com," would the case have come out the other way?

2. *Trademark as part of a URL.* In *Bally v. Faber*, the defendant used plaintiff's trademark not as part of the domain name, which is compupix.com, but rather as a subdirectory under that domain, www.compupix.com/ballysucks. Does the trademark serve as a source identifier when used in this role? Does the court recognize any distinction between use of the trademark in the URL, and use of it in the text of the website? Recognizing that the plaintiff was entitled to identify Bally as the target of its criticism, was it entitled to do so by including its trademark in the URL?

3. *Trademarks as purchasable search terms.* In *Playboy Enterprises, Inc. v. Netscape Communications Corp.*, 55 F.Supp.2d 1070 (C.D.Cal.1999), excerpted in Part III(C), *supra.*, Playboy challenged the defendant's use of its trademarks "Playboy" and "Playmate" as purchasable keywords in connection with its search engine. The court held that this use of the trademarked terms did not infringe or dilute them. It had this to say about the First Amendment implications of upholding the claims that Playboy advanced:

> Here, PEI is seeking to leverage its trademarks "Playboy®" and "Playmate®" (which cannot be searched on the Internet) into a monopoly on the *words* "playboy" and "playmate." Indeed, by seeking a prohibition on all advertisements that appear in response to the search words "playboy" and "playmate," PEI would effectively monopolize the use of these words on the Internet. This violates the First Amendment rights of (a) Excite and Netscape; (b) *other* trademark holders of "playboy" and "playmate"; as well as (c) members of the public who conduct Internet searches. *See generally Bally Total Fitness Holding Corp. v. Faber,* 29 F.Supp.2d 1161, 1165 (C.D.Cal.1998) ("prohibiting [defendant] from using [plaintiff's] name in the machine readable code would effectively isolate him from all but the most savvy of Internet users").

CHAPTER TWO

Protecting Commercial Identity Online: Domain Names

In the offline world, as long as I know the physical location of a store, I can find my way to it even if I have forgotten its name. On the web, however, a company's name or online brand often *is* the way to its website. For example, I reach the website of Amazon.com by typing "www.amazon.com" into the address bar of my web browser. The text string "www.amazon.com" is called a *uniform resource locator*, or "URL". Typically a company's URL includes the company name or a reference to a product or brand for which the company is known. A company's domain name becomes, in effect, its brand identity on the Web.[1]

If I want to locate the website of a particular company or a brand, but do not know the site's URL, I can try several expedients. I might start by guessing that the URL will be the company's name, followed by a .com, and preceded by a www. This will frequently work. If that fails, I can enter the company or brand name into a search engine such as Google, HotBot, Yahoo! or MSN Search. After completing my search, the search engine returns a list of hyperlinks. If the search engine is well designed, the URL I am seeking should be among the first group of hyperlinks that is returned.

When this system works as expected, my search costs are very low: typing in a URL is quick and easy, and using a search engine is only slightly more involved. But suppose a well-known company or brand name is registered as a domain name by a person who has no affiliation with the company or brand. In that case, my search costs may be significantly increased. Typing in "www.company_name.com" will not yield the desired website, but may instead lead to the site of a competitor; to a website offering to sell the domain name; or to a site with content completely unrelated to the company, such as one offering sexually explicit images. I may fare better typing the company name into a search engine, but depending on the search algorithm employed the link I am looking for may lie somewhere beyond the first page of returned links, and my patience may

---

1. A domain name consists of two parts separated by a period: a second-level domain ("SLD") and a top-level domain name ("TLD"). The SLD occurs to the left of the TLD. Thus, in the domain name "amazon.com," "amazon" is the SLD and "com" is the TLD. The name associated with the company or its products is typically used as the SLD. TLDs are not unique to a particular company but are used to organize SLDs into groups for the purpose of administering the Internet address system—called the domain name system—much as house numbers are grouped by street, city and state for the purpose of the postal address system.

run out before reaching it. The situation is complicated by the fact that in the world of bricks and mortar many different companies may share the same or similar trademarks under certain circumstances, whereas there is only one dot-com domain name for each word that might be a trademark. If I type www.apple.com into my browser, I could be looking for Apple Bank or Apple Records, but the site belongs to Apple Computer.

When somebody other than a trademark owner obtains a domain name consisting of or incorporating a trademark, several types of costs may arise: (1) increased search costs for consumers; (2) consumer confusion, as may occur if a consumer reaches the website of a competitor rather than that of the company he is seeking; (3) efficiency losses due to the diminished capacity of trademarks to identify companies and products; and (4) harm to companies identified by trademarks, who may lose potential customers.

The practice of obtaining domain names containing words identical or similar to trademarks owned by somebody else commenced soon after the Internet became a commercialized venue. Some people, recognizing the value of a domain name containing a certain word before the owner of a corresponding trademark did, obtained domain names by the dozen, the hundred, and in some cases even by the thousand. This entailed a modest investment—usually $35–50 a year per domain name—which these people hoped to recoup many-fold by selling the domain names to the owners of the corresponding trademarks. In some quarters (particularly among owners of well-established trademarks), it was assumed that domain names corresponding to a trademark ought "naturally" to belong to the trademark owner (or one of the owners, in case the word corresponded to more than one trademark, as in Apple Computer, Apple Bank, and Apple Records). Those who obtained such domain names hoping to sell them to trademark owners were branded as "cybersquatters" or "cyberpirates," and harshly criticized as unethically and illegally seeking to capitalize on goodwill in a trademark that was built up by somebody else. In fact, Congress responded to this practice by enacting a statute designed specifically to end it—the Anticybersquatting Consumer Protection Act ("ACPA"), Pub. L. No. 106–113 (1999), which is addressed in detail in Part II, *infra*. In other quarters (particularly among academics seeking to preserve a robust public domain), the practice has been viewed more benignly: simply a case of one group of entrepreneurs reacting more quickly to a market opportunity than others.

As mentioned earlier, difficulties arise when different companies have the same or similar words in their trademarks and thus feel that they have legitimate claims to the same web address. Just as every house has a unique street address, every website must be built on a unique domain name. Given the obvious advantages of having a Web address built around a company's name, it often happens that two companies with similar names desire the same domain name. The oldest feminist bookstore in the United States is the Amazon Bookstore in Minneapolis, Minnesota. Once it recognized the growing importance of the Web as a distribution channel, it wanted a website with the address "www.amazon.com." The Amazon Bookstore believed its claim to this Web address was superior to that of the Internet company of similar name. After all, the Amazon Bookstore is the older and more established business—a fact of some significance under the law of trademark. While this dispute was ultimately settled out of court, other disputes over web addresses have not ended so amicably. In fact, another judgmental term, "reverse domain name hijacking," has been applied to some second-comers who try to wrest a domain name from a company with a similar trademark that got there first.

Difficulties also arise when individuals have an interest in making noncommercial uses of names and symbols that are either identical or confusingly similar to somebody's trademark. For example, consider a person whose nickname is very similar to some company's trade name. One might expect that such an individual should be able to use his or her nickname as a domain name, provided it is not already claimed by another. As a noncommercial use, it should fall outside the strictures of trademark law. Yet many trademark owners have argued that the use of any domain name on the Internet is necessarily a commercial use and some courts have been receptive to these arguments.

In response to perceived abuses by both trademark owners and cyber-squatters, a new body of law has developed to provide needed regulation and dispute resolution. In this chapter, we focus on these legal issues and developments.

I.   TRADITIONAL TRADEMARK LAW AND DOMAIN NAMES

As Internet-based e-commerce began to gather steam, it wasn't long before enterprising individuals and companies recognized the value of a well-chosen domain name. Soon the domain name gold rush was on, as individuals and corporations staked their claim to control various domain names. As a group, corporate trademark owners were relatively late to the party, and often found that their trademark or brand name had already been claimed as a domain name by another. While some companies simply purchased the right to use their trademark as a domain name from the person who previously obtained it, other companies refused to negotiate, arguing that the use of their trademarks as domain names was a form of trademark infringement or dilution. Trademark owners filed lawsuits, and the courts had to come to grips with the relationship between the domain name system and the law of trademarks, balancing the interest of the public to make noncommercial use of these new and evolving digital technologies with the interests of trademark owners in preserving the commercial value of their brands. In this section, we explore how the courts have grappled with this issue and evaluate the balance that they have struck.

A.   TRADEMARK INFRINGEMENT

Lockheed Martin Corp. v. Network Solutions, Inc.

985 F.Supp. 949 (C.D.Cal.1997), *aff'd*, 194 F.3d 980 (9th Cir.1999).

■ PREGERSON, DISTRICT JUDGE.

The motion by defendant Network Solutions, Inc. ("NSI") for summary judgment came before the Court on October 6, 1997. After reviewing and considering the materials submitted by the parties and hearing oral argument, the Court grants the motion in its entirety.

I. Background

The issue presented by this litigation is whether NSI violated federal trademark law by accepting registrations of Internet domain names that are identical or similar to Lockheed Martin Corporation's ("Lockheed") SKUNK WORKS service mark. Lockheed asserts that NSI directly infringed and diluted its mark by accepting the registrations. Lockheed also asserts that NSI is liable as a contributory infringer because NSI did not comply with Lockheed's demands to cancel the registrations.

As to direct infringement, the Court concludes that NSI has not used Lockheed's service mark in connection with the sale, offering for sale, distribution or advertising of goods or services, and therefore cannot be liable for infringement under 15 U.S.C. § 1114(1)(a) or for unfair competition under 15 U.S.C. § 1125(a).

As to dilution, the Court finds that NSI has not made a commercial use of domain names as trademarks, and therefore cannot satisfy the commercial use element of dilution under 15 U.S.C. § 1125(c).

As to contributory infringement, there are two potential bases for liability. First, a defendant is liable if it intentionally induced others to infringe a mark. Second, a defendant is liable if it continued to supply a product to others when the defendant knew or had reason to know that the party receiving the product used it to infringe a mark.

Lockheed has not presented evidence that NSI induced others to infringe Lockheed's service mark. Therefore, NSI is not liable under the first basis.

As to the knowledge basis, the Court concludes that NSI's limited role as a registrar of domain names coupled with the inherent uncertainty in defining the scope of intellectual property rights in a trademark militates against finding that NSI knew or had reason to know of potentially infringing uses by others. Furthermore, contributory infringement doctrine does not impose upon NSI an affirmative duty to seek out potentially infringing uses of domain names by registrants.

A. The Parties

For over 50 years, plaintiff Lockheed and its predecessors have operated "Skunk Works," an aerospace development and production facility. Lockheed owns the federally registered "SKUNK WORKS" service mark.

Defendant NSI is a publicly traded corporation with its principal place of business in Herndon, Virginia. Under a contract with the National Science Foundation, NSI is the exclusive registrar of most Internet domain names.

B. *The Internet*

* * *

1. The Domain Name System

Web sites, like other information resources on the Internet, are currently addressed using the Internet "domain name system." A numbering system called the "Internet Protocol" gives each individual computer or network a unique numerical address on the Internet. The "Internet Protocol number," also known as an "IP number," consists of four groups of digits separated by periods, such as "192.215.247.50." For the convenience of users, individual resources on the Internet are also given names. Specialized computers known as "domain name servers" maintain tables linking domain names to IP numbers.

Domain names are arranged so that reading from right to left, each part of the name points to a more localized area of the Internet. For example, in the domain name "cacd.uscourts.gov," "gov" is the top-level domain, reserved for all networks associated with the federal government. The "uscourts" part specifies a second-level domain, a set of the networks used by the federal courts. The "cacd" part specifies a sub-network or computer used by the United States District Court for the Central District of California.

If a user knows or can deduce the domain name associated with a web site, the user can directly access the web site by typing the domain name into a Web browser, without having to conduct a time-consuming search. Because most businesses with a presence on the Internet use the ".com" top-level domain, Internet users intuitively try to find businesses by typing in the corporate or trade name as the second-level domain name, as in "acme.com." Second-level domain names, the name just to the left of ".com," must be exclusive. Therefore, although two companies can have non-exclusive trademark rights in a name, only one company can have a second-level domain name that corresponds to its trademark. For example, Juno Lighting, a maker of lamps, sought to establish a web site with the address "juno.com," a domain name already in use by Juno Online Services, which uses the domain name as part of e-mail addresses for hundreds of thousands of e-mail customers. *See Juno Online Servs., L.P. v. Juno Lighting, Inc.*, 979 F. Supp. 684 (N.D.Ill.1997). In short, the exclusive quality of second-level domain names has set trademark owners against each other in the struggle to establish a commercial presence on the Internet, and has set businesses against domain name holders who seek to continue the traditional use of the Internet as a non-commercial medium of communication.

2. NSI's Role in the Domain Naming System

Under a contract with the National Science Foundation, NSI manages domain name registrations for the ".com," ".net," ".org," ".edu," and ".gov" top-level domains. The contract authorizes NSI to charge $100 for an initial two-year registration and $50 annually starting the third year. NSI registers approximately 100,000 Internet domain names per month.

(Graves Decl. ¶ 5.) Registration applications are made via e-mail and in more than 90% of registrations no human intervention takes place. (Graves Depo. at 54.) On average, a new registration occurs approximately once every 20 seconds. (Id. at 47–48.)

NSI performs two functions in the domain name system. First, it screens domain name applications against its registry to prevent repeated registrations of the same name. Second, it maintains a directory linking domain names with the IP numbers of domain name servers. The domain name servers, which are outside of NSI's control, connect domain names with Internet resources such as web sites and e-mail systems.

NSI does not make an independent determination of an applicant's right to use a domain name. Nor does NSI assign domain names; users may choose any available second-level domain name. In 1995, NSI responded to the problem of conflicting claims to domain names by instituting a domain name dispute policy. Under the current policy, in effect since September 9, 1996,[2] NSI requires applicants to represent and warrant that their use of a particular domain name does not interfere with the intellectual property rights of third parties. (Graves Decl. Ex. 1.) Under the policy, if a trademark holder presents NSI with a United States Patent and Trademark Office registration of a trademark identical to a currently registered domain name, NSI will require the domain name holder to prove that it has a pre-existing right to use the name. If the domain name holder fails to do so, NSI will cancel the registration. (Id.) NSI's policy has been criticized as favoring trademark owners over domain name holders, and favoring owners of federally registered marks over owners of non-registered marks, because owners of federally registered marks can invoke NSI's policy to effectively enjoin the use of identical domain name's without having to make any showing of infringement or dilution. 2 Jerome Gilson & Jeffrey M. Samuels, Trademark Protection and Practice, §§ 5.11[4][B], at 5–239, 5.11[5], at 5–243 (1997) (noting that NSI's policy is tilted in favor of trademark owners, who can deprive registrants of domain names without meeting the likelihood of confusion test for infringement or showing that the domain name dilutes the mark); Gayle Weiswasser, Domain Names, the Internet, and Trademarks: Infringement in Cyberspace, 13 Santa Clara Computer & High Tech. L. J. 137, 172–73 (1997).

If a trademark holder and domain name registrant take their dispute to court, NSI will deposit the domain name in the registry of the court. This process maintains the status quo; the domain name remains active while in the registry of the court.

C. Factual Background

Most of the underlying facts of this case are not in dispute. The dispute at summary judgment is over the interpretation of the law and the

---

2. [NSI's domain name dispute policy was superseded in 1999 by the Uniform Domain Name Dispute Resolution Policy, instituted by the Internet Corporation for Assigned Names and Numbers. *See* Part III, *infra*.—Eds.]

application of the law to the facts. The Court finds that there is no genuine issue as to the following facts:

1. Lockheed owns the federally registered SKUNK WORKS service mark for "engineering, technical consulting, and advisory services with respect to designing, building, equipping, and testing commercial and military aircraft and related equipment."

* * *

6. On May 7, 1996, Lockheed sent NSI a letter advising NSI that Lockheed owned the SKUNK WORKS mark and requesting that NSI cease registering domain names that referred to or included the names "skunk works" or "skunkworks" or otherwise infringed Lockheed's mark. Lockheed also requested that NSI provide Lockheed with a list of registered domain names that contain the words "skunk works" or any variation thereof. Lockheed's letter did not include a certified copy of its trademark registration.

7. On June 18, 1996, Lockheed sent NSI a second letter, informing NSI that the registrant of "skunkworks.com" had agreed to stop using the domain name, and that the registrant of "skunkworks.net" was being sued in federal district court. (Quinto Decl. Ex. C.) The letter did not refer to the lawsuit by docket number or caption, nor did it include a copy of the complaint or other pleading.

* * *

9. On September 18, 1996, NSI's Internet business manager, David Graves, wrote to Lockheed's counsel in response to the May 7 and June 18 letters. NSI informed Lockheed that NSI could not provide a list of all domain names that included "skunk works" or any variation thereof, but that Lockheed could use the public "Whois" database of domain name registrations to find this information. NSI further informed Lockheed that upon receipt of a file-stamped copy of the complaint in the "skunk-works.net" case, NSI would immediately deposit the domain name in the registry of the court, maintaining the status quo until the court ordered otherwise.

[Paragraphs 2–5, 8, 10 and 11 describe specific individuals and the domain names that they registered with NSI. The domain names included skunkworks.com, skunkwrks.com, skunkwerks.com, skunkworx.com, and the-skunkworks.com.]

D. Procedural Background

Lockheed filed this action on October 22, 1996, alleging infringement, unfair competition, dilution and contributory infringement under the Lanham Act, and seeking injunctive and declaratory relief. NSI answered the complaint and counterclaimed for declaratory relief.

On March 19, 1997, this Court denied NSI's motion to dismiss for failure to join the domain name registrants as indispensable parties under

Federal Rule of Civil Procedure 19(b). *Lockheed Martin Corp. v. Network Solutions, Inc.*, 43 U.S.P.Q.2d 1056 (C.D.Cal.1997).

On September 29, 1997, this Court denied Lockheed's motion to file a first amended complaint adding a cause of action for "contributory dilution." The Court denied the motion on the bases of futility, undue delay and prejudice.

NSI's present motion seeks summary judgment on all of Lockheed's claims.

II. Discussion

This Court has subject matter jurisdiction over Lanham Act claims pursuant to 28 U.S.C. §§ 1331 and 1338(a). NSI has consented to personal jurisdiction by appearing in this action. Fed.R.Civ.P. 12(h)(1).

* * *

B. *Trademark Infringement Under Lanham Act § 32, 15 U.S.C. § 1114(1)*

Section 32 of the Lanham Act prohibits any person from using another's mark without permission "in connection with the sale, offering for sale, distribution or advertising of any goods or services on or in connection with which such use is likely to cause confusion, or to cause mistake, or to deceive.…" 15 U.S.C. § 1114(1). To be liable under § 32, a person must use the mark on competing or related goods in a way that creates a likelihood of confusion. *AMF Inc. v. Sleekcraft Boats*, 599 F.2d 341, 348 (9th Cir.1979). Before considering the likelihood of confusion, however, the Court must determine whether NSI, by accepting registrations, has used the SKUNK WORKS mark in connection with the sale, distribution or advertising of goods or services. *See Planned Parenthood Fed'n of America, Inc. v. Bucci*, 42 U.S.P.Q.2d 1430, 1434 (S.D.N.Y.1997).

Domain names present a special problem under the Lanham Act because they are used for both a non-trademark technical purpose, to designate a set of computers on the Internet, and for trademark purposes, to identify an Internet user who offers goods or services on the Internet. *See* 2 Gilson, *supra*, §§ 5.11[3], at 5–235, 5.11[5], at 5–243–44 (distinguishing the technical use of domain names from the trademark use to identify goods or services). When a domain name is used only to indicate an address on the Internet, the domain name is not functioning as a trademark. *See Walt–West Enters., Inc. v. Gannett Co., Inc.*, 695 F.2d 1050, 1059–60 (7th Cir.1982) (radio station frequency used in "utilitarian sense of calling the listener's attention to a location on the FM dial" is not protectable under trademark law). Like trade names, domain names can function as trademarks, and therefore can be used to infringe trademark rights. Domain names, like trade names, do not act as trademarks when they are used merely to identify a business entity; in order to infringe they must be used to identify the source of goods or services. *Cf. In re Unclaimed Salvage & Freight Co.*, 192 U.S.P.Q. 165, 168 (T.T.A.B.1976) (affirming refusal of registration of trade name as trademark where specimen demonstrated use only to identify applicant as a business); U.S. Dept. of Commerce, Patent and Trademark Office, Trademark Manual of Examining Procedure § 1202.02, at 1202–4 (2d ed. May 1993) (directing examiners to refuse registration of material that functions only to identify a business).

NSI's acceptance of domain name registrations is connected only with the names' technical function on the Internet to designate a set of computers. By accepting registrations of domain names containing the words "skunk works," NSI is not using the SKUNK WORKS mark in connection with the sale, distribution or advertising of goods and services. NSI merely uses domain names to designate host computers on the Internet. This is the type of purely "nominative" function that is not prohibited by trademark law. *See New Kids on the Block v. News America Pub., Inc.,* 971 F.2d 302, 307 (9th Cir.1992) (noting that laws against infringement do not apply to "non-trademark use of a mark"); *Lucasfilm Ltd. v. High Frontier,* 622 F.Supp. 931, 933 (D.D.C.1985) (holding that property rights in a trademark do not extend to the use of the trademark to express ideas unconnected with the sale or offer for sale of goods or services).

This is not to say that a domain name can never be used to infringe a trademark. However, something more than the registration of the name is required before the use of a domain name is infringing. In *Planned Parenthood Fed'n of America. Inc. v. Bucci,* for example, the defendant registered the domain name "plannedparenthood.com" and used it as the address of a web site promoting his book on abortion. 42 U.S.P.Q.2d 1430, 1432 (S.D.N.Y.1997). The defendant admitted that he used the domain name hoping that people looking for the Planned Parenthood's site would find his site. *Id.* at 1433. The defendant argued that registration without more is not a commercial use of a mark. *Id.* at 1436–37. The court, however, found that the defendant did "more than merely register a domain name; he has created a home page that uses plaintiff's mark as its address, conveying the impression to Internet users that plaintiff is the sponsor of defendant's web site." *Id.* at 1437. The infringing use in *Planned Parenthood* was not registration of the plaintiff's mark with NSI, but rather the use of the plaintiff's trademark "as a domain name to identify his web site" in a manner that confused Internet users as to the source or sponsorship of the products offered there. *Id.* at 1440; *cf. Teletech Customer Care Management (California), Inc. v. Tele–Tech Co.,* 977 F.Supp. 1407 (C.D.Cal.1997) (finding that the plaintiff was not likely to prevail on the merits of an infringement claim because the plaintiff demonstrated only that customers were likely to be confused as to location of web site, not as to source of goods or services).

The cases dealing with vanity telephone numbers are consistent with the conclusion that registration of a domain name, without more, does not constitute use of the name as a trademark. A toll-free telephone number with an easy-to-remember letter equivalent is a valuable business asset. As with domain names, courts have held that the promotion of a confusingly similar telephone number may be enjoined as trademark infringement and unfair competition. *Dial–A–Mattress Franchise Corp. v. Page,* 880 F.2d 675,

678 (2d Cir.1989); *American Airlines, Inc. v. A 1–800–A–M–E–R–I–C–A–N Corp.*, 622 F.Supp. 673 (N.D.Ill.1985). The infringing act, however, is not the mere possession and use of the telephone number. If it were, trademark holders would be able to eliminate every toll-free number whose letter equivalent happens to correspond to a trademark. In *Holiday Inns, Inc., v. 800 Reservation, Inc.*, 86 F.3d 619 (6th Cir.1996), the district court held that the defendant's use of 1–800 H[zero]LIDAY infringed the plaintiff's trademark in the telephone number 1–800–HOLIDAY. *Id.* at 620. The court of appeals reversed, holding that Holiday Inns's trademark rights in its vanity telephone number did not allow it to control use by others of confusingly similar telephone numbers. Although the defendant's toll-free number was often misdialed by customers seeking 1–800–HOLIDAY, the defendant never promoted the number in connection with the HOLIDAY trademark; but only promoted it as 1–800–405–4329. *Id.* at 623. Because the defendant had used the number only as a telephone number, and not as a trademark, the court of appeals held that the defendant had not infringed the plaintiff's trademark. *Id.* at 625–26.

Domain names and vanity telephone numbers both have dual functions. Domain names, like telephone numbers, allow one machine to connect to another machine. Domain names, like telephone numbers, are also valuable to trademark holders when they make it easier for customers to find the trademark holder. Where the holder of a vanity telephone number promotes it in a way that causes a likelihood of confusion, the holder has engaged in an infringing use. *American Airlines*, 622 F.Supp. at 682 (mere use of telephone number is not infringing, but misleading use of trademarked term in yellow pages advertisement is infringing). But, where, as with NSI, the pure machine-linking function is the only use at issue, there is no trademark use and there can be no infringement.

In the ordinary trademark infringement case, where there is no question that the defendant used the mark, the analysis proceeds directly to the issue of whether there is a likelihood of confusion. Here, however, because NSI has not used Lockheed's service mark in connection with goods or services, the Court need not apply the test for likelihood of confusion. NSI, therefore, is entitled to judgment as a matter of law on the § 32 claim.

1. Printer and Publisher Liability Under 15 U.S.C. § 1114(2)(A), (B)

Lockheed asserts that NSI has infringed its service mark as a "printer" of the mark under 15 U.S.C. § 1114(2)(A). This assertion misapprehends NSI's function as a domain name registrar. To the extent that registrants of SKUNK WORKS-type domain names infringed the mark, they did so by using it on web sites or other Internet resources in a way that created a likelihood of confusion as to source or sponsorship. NSI is not an Internet service provider. It does not provide host computers for web sites or other Internet resources. NSI's role is restricted to publishing a list of domain names, their holders, and the IP numbers of the domain name servers that perform the directory functions associated with the domain names. (Graves Decl. ¶ 10.)

NSI's role is fundamentally dissimilar from that of telephone directory publishers whose conduct has been found enjoinable under § 1114(2)(A). *See Century 21 Real Estate Corp. of Northern Illinois v. R.M. Post, Inc.*, 8 U.S.P.Q.2d 1614, 1617 (N.D.Ill.1988) (denying motion to dismiss where yellow pages' publishers were alleged to have printed infringing trademark in listing of former licensee who no longer had right to use trademark). There, the telephone directory printers supplied the material that directly caused the likelihood of confusion. In the domain name context, the domain name registration itself does not infringe the trademark. Infringement occurs when the domain name is used in certain ways. For example, a domain name may infringe trademark rights when it is used in connection with a web site that advertises services in competition with those of the trademark owner. *See, e.g., Cardservice International, Inc. v. McGee*, 950 F.Supp. 737, 738 (E.D.Va.1997); *Comp Examiner Agency, Inc. v. Juris, Inc.*, 1996 WL 376600 (C.D.Cal.1996). Where domain names are used to infringe, the infringement does not result from NSI's publication of the domain name list, but from the registrant's use of the name on a web site or other Internet form of communication in connection with goods or services. NSI is not a "printer or publisher" of web sites, or any other form of Internet "publication." As discussed below in the section on contributory infringement, NSI's involvement with the use of domain names does not extend beyond registration. NSI's liability cannot be premised on an argument that it prints or publishes the list of domain names, because the list is not the instrument or forum for infringement. NSI's liability, if it exists at all, would stem from registrants' use of domain names in connection with other services not provided by NSI. This type of liability is properly analyzed under contributory liability doctrine, not as printer and publisher liability under § 1114(2)(A).

C. *Unfair Competition Under Lanham Act § 43(a), 15 U.S.C. § 1125(a)*

Lockheed has followed the common practice of alleging unfair competition under § 43(a) of the Lanham Act along with trademark infringement under § 32. Both causes of action depend on a demonstration of a likelihood of confusion. 1 J. Thomas McCarthy, *McCarthy on Trademarks and Unfair Competition* § 2:8 (1997). Federal unfair competition requires use of the mark in connection with goods or services. 15 U.S.C. § 1125(a)(1). As discussed above, NSI's acceptance of registrations for domain names resembling SKUNK WORKS is not a use of the mark in connection with goods or services.

A recent district court decision illustrates the application of federal unfair competition law to the domain name context. *Juno Online Servs., L.P. v. Juno Lighting, Inc.*, 979 F.Supp. 684 (N.D.Ill. Sept.29, 1997). During a dispute over the domain name "juno.com," Juno Lighting registered the domain name "juno-online.com" in the hopes of persuading Juno Online Services to switch its e-mail service to that domain name. Juno Online sued Juno Lighting for federal unfair competition. The district court dismissed the unfair competition claim because Juno Online alleged only that Juno Lighting registered the name with NSI, and did not allege further use of the name to create a web site or to advertise its services. *Id.* at 690–92. The court held that registration of a trademark as a domain name does not constitute use of the trademark on the Internet in connection with goods or services, and therefore was not prohibited by § 43(a). *Id.* This reasoning applies more strongly to NSI, which has not registered domain names resembling SKUNK WORKS for its own use, but has merely accepted domain name registrations from others.

[The court next considered Lockheed's trademark dilution claim and concluded that "NSI's acceptance of domain name registrations is not a 'commercial use' within the meaning of the Federal Trademark Dilution Act."]

[The court also dismissed Lockheed's contributory infringement claim, finding that Lockheed lacked the requisite knowledge of the infringing activity. The Court of Appeals affirmed the ruling on contributory infringement, holding that a registrar's registration of a domain name does not constitute the supply of an infringing "product," as would be necessary for the registrar to be found a contributory infringer.]

III. Conclusion

* * *

Because summary judgment on the above claims is based on Lockheed's lack of a legal right to control the domain name registration process, there is no case or controversy between these parties. Therefore, the Court grants NSI's motion for summary judgment as to Lockheed's declaratory judgment cause of action.

If the Internet were a technically ideal system for commercial exploitation, then every trademark owner would be able to have a domain name identical to its trademark. But the parts of the Internet that perform the critical addressing functions still operate on the 1960s and 1970s technologies that were adequate when the Internet's function was to facilitate academic and military research. Commerce has entered the Internet only recently. In response, the Internet's existing addressing systems will have to evolve to accommodate conflicts among holders of intellectual property rights, and conflicts between commercial and non-commercial users of the Internet. "In the long run, the most appropriate technology to access web sites and e-mail will be directories that point to the desired Internet address. Directory technology of the necessary scale and complexity is not yet available, but when it is developed it will relieve much of the pressure on domain names." *Domain Name System, Hearings Before the Subcommittee on Basic Research of the House Science Committee,* 105th Cong., 1997 WL 14151463 (September 30, 1997) (testimony of Barbara A. Dooley, Executive Director, Commercial Internet Exchange Association). No doubt trademark owners would like to make the Internet safe for their intellectual property rights by reordering the allocation of existing domain names so that each trademark owner automatically owned the domain name corresponding to the owner's mark. Creating an exact match between Internet addresses and trademarks will require overcoming the problem of concurrent uses of the same trademark in different classes of goods and geographical areas. Various solutions to this problem are being discussed, such as a graphically-based Internet directory that would allow the presentation of trademarks in conjunction with distinguishing logos, new top-level domains for each class of goods, or a new top-level domain for trademarks only. The solution to the current difficulties faced by trademark owners on the Internet lies in this sort of technical innovation, not in attempts to assert trademark rights over legitimate non-trademark uses of this important new means of communication.

Green Products Co. v. Independence Corn By–Products Co.

992 F.Supp. 1070 (N.D.Iowa 1997).

■ MELLOY, CHIEF JUDGE.

The sole issue before the Court is whether to compel Independence Corn By–Products Co. (ICBP) to convey the domain name "greenproducts.com" to the plaintiff, Green Products Co. (Green Products), for its use during the pendency of this litigation.

Green Products claims that ICBP violated § 43(a) of the Lanham Trademark Act, 15 U.S.C. § 1125(a), as well as state laws, when ICBP registered the domain name "greenproducts.com" as one of its own domain names on the internet. Green Products moved for a preliminary injunction: (1) to enjoin ICBP from using the domain name "greenproducts.com", (2) to enjoin ICBP from using the expressions "green products" and "green pet products" as the whole or part of a trademark, trade name, or domain name, and (3) to compel ICBP to convey the ownership of the domain name "greenproducts.com" to Green Products.

In response, ICBP agreed to the first and second parts of Green Products' request, but it resisted the third part. During the pendency of the litigation, ICBP has consented (1) not to use the domain name "greenproducts.com", and (2) not to use the expressions "green products" and "green pet products" as the whole or part of any trademark, trade name, or domain name, but ICBP will continue to use those names "in ways that do not constitute trademark infringement, such as comparative advertising." In order to analyze the merits of Green Products' motion to compel ICBP to transfer ownership of the domain name "greenproducts.com" during the pendency of the litigation, the Court will begin with a brief background of relevant language and information.

Background

[The court begins with a description of the Internet and domain names.]

In the case before this Court, Green Products and ICBP are direct competitors in the corncob by-products industry. On May 30, 1997, ICBP registered two domain names, "icbp.com" and "bestcob.com", with the goal of eventually designing a website that users could find through either domain name. On June 9, 1997, ICBP registered seven other domain names—five of which are formed by using the trade names of ICBP's competitors: e.g., "greenproducts.com." On July 16, 1997, Green Products tried to register "greenproducts.com" and "freshnest.com" (a sister company's name), but was told that ICBP had already registered those two domain names. Green Products then filed a complaint and a motion for a preliminary injunction against ICBP.

Discussion

A. Preliminary Injunction Standards

To decide whether to grant the motion for a preliminary injunction, the Court must consider: (1) the probability that Green Products will succeed on the merits; (2) the threat of irreparable harm to Green Products; (3) the state of the balance between this harm and the injury that granting the injunction will inflict on other parties; and (4) the public interest. *See Dataphase Sys., Inc. v. CL Sys., Inc.,* 640 F.2d 109, 113 (8th Cir.1981) (en banc). When weighing these factors, "no single factor is itself dispositive; in each case all factors must be considered to determine on balance whether they weigh towards granting the injunction." *Calvin Klein Cosmetics Corp. v. Lenox Labs., Inc.,* 815 F.2d 500, 503 (8th Cir.1987).

* * *

B. Analysis of Dataphase Factors

1. Probability that Green Products will succeed on the merits

* * *

An essential element to a trademark infringement action is that the plaintiff must prove that a defendant's use of a particular name " 'creates a likelihood of confusion, deception, or mistake among an appreciable number of ordinary buyers as to the source or association' between the two names." *Maritz, Inc. v. Cybergold, Inc.,* 947 F.Supp. 1338, 1339 (E.D.Mo. 1996) (quoting *Duluth News–Tribune v. Mesabi Publ'g Co.,* 84 F.3d 1093, 1096 (8th Cir.1996)). Factors relevant to determine the likelihood of confusion or deception are:

(1) the strength of the trademark;

(2) the similarity between the plaintiff's and defendant's marks;

(3) the competitive proximity of the parties' products;

(4) the alleged infringer's intent to confuse the public;

(5) evidence of any actual confusion; and

(6) the degree of care reasonably expected of the plaintiff's potential customers.

Maritz, 947 F.Supp. at 1340, *citing Anheuser–Busch, Inc. v. Balducci Publications,* 28 F.3d 769, 774 (8th Cir.1994), *cert. denied,* 513 U.S. 1112

(1995). The Court will next examine each of these factors in turn, although not all of the factors are applicable in this case.

In order to determine whether the trademark is entitled to protection, the Court examines the first factor—strength of the trademark—and classifies the plaintiffs mark as either (1) arbitrary or fanciful, (2) suggestive, (3) descriptive, or (4) generic. An arbitrary or fanciful mark is the strongest type of mark and is afforded the highest level of protection. At the other end, a generic term is used by the general public to identify a category of goods, so it does not receive trademark protection. Suggestive and descriptive marks fall somewhere in between. A suggestive mark is one that requires some measure of imagination to reach a conclusion about the nature of the product. In contrast, a descriptive mark "immediately conveys the nature or function of the product and is entitled to protection only if it has become distinctive by acquiring a secondary meaning." Here, the Court finds that Green Products' trademark—the name "Green Products' "—is at least suggestive. The name "Green Products' " requires at least some imagination to connect it with corncob by-products.

The next factor requires the Court to consider the similarity between the plaintiffs and defendant's marks. ICBP concedes that its domain name "greenproducts.com" is "undisputedly similar to the mark Green Products Co." However, ICBP also argues that its use of the mark must be viewed in the context of the marketplace, and that the "domain name only has meaning as an Internet address linking to ICBP's future web site and the web site will take every precaution to ensure there is no consumer confusion."

In essence, ICBP's argument is that the Court should only compare the similarity of domain names and websites linked to those domain names— not the similarity of ICBP's domain name and Green Products' trademark—because ICBP is not "selling a product on store shelves using the mark 'greenproducts.com'."

The Court finds ICBP's argument clever, but ultimately unpersuasive. ICBP's argument is analogous to saying that ICBP has the right to hang a sign in front of its store that reads, "Green Products." When customers enter the store expecting to be able to see (and possibly, to buy) products made by Green Products, ICBP then announces, "Actually, this store isn't owned by Green Products; it's owned by ICBP. We don't sell anything made by Green Products, but as long as you're here, we'll tell you how our products are better than Green Products." In essence, ICBP is capitalizing on the strong similarity between Green Products' trademark and ICBP's domain name to lure customers onto its web page.

Turning to the third factor, the competitive proximity of the parties' products, ICBP concedes that ICBP and Green Products are both competitors in the corncob byproducts industry. Despite being direct competitors, ICBP argues that this Court should not focus on their similar corn byproducts, but on domain names and their respective websites: "the relevant 'products' for the likelihood of confusion analysis are not corncob products because ICBP does not sell any corncob products with the mark 'greenproducts.com' on a label or package design." Instead, ICBP suggests, the Court should analyze whether a website located at "greenproducts.com" is proximate to a website located at "green-products.com" or "greenproductsco.com." ICBP believes that these domain names are not proximate, because anyone who knows Green Products' domain name can use that name to go directly to Green Products' website and "will likely never even see ICBP's web site." ICBP does, however, concede that the websites are "proximate in the sense that a person guessing at Green Product Co.'s domain name might access ICBP's website if it first tries 'greenproducts.com'. . . ."

ICBP's argument basically boils down to the idea that the Court should view the domain names as mere addresses which—along with the websites attached to each name—are products in and of themselves. The Court disagrees. There is a close competitive proximity between the products that the two companies sell, and there is also a close competitive proximity between the domain name "greenproducts.com" and the trademark "Green Products". The domain name "greenproducts.com" identifies the internet site to those who reach it, "much like a person's name identifies a particular person, or, more relevant to trademark disputes, a company's name identifies a specific company." *Cardservice,* 950 F.Supp. 737. Because customers who do not know what a company's domain name is will often guess that the domain name is the same as the company's name, a "domain name mirroring a corporate name may be a valuable corporate asset, as it facilitates communication with a customer base." *MTV Networks,* 867 F.Supp. at 203–204 n. 2.

Alternatively, even if this Court were persuaded that it should only compare the alphanumeric domain names (and not the products that each company sells, nor the similarity between ICBP's domain name and Green Products' trademark), this Court would still find a close proximity between the domain name "greenproducts.com" and any of the alternative domain names that ICBP suggests, such as "green-products.com", "greenproductsco.com", or "greenproducts-co.com." Under either analysis, there is a close competitive proximity, and that close competitive proximity further increases the opportunity of consumer confusion.

Fourth, this Court examines whether ICBP intended to cause consumer confusion by creating an ICBP website accessed through the domain name "greenproducts.com." ICBP maintains that it had no intent to "pass off" its products as those of Green Products, and that its only intent was to distinguish ICBP's products from those of Green Products through comparative advertising. ICBP believes that there will be no consumer confusion because internet users will immediately know that the website belongs to ICBP once the actual web page appears on the screen (after users have typed the domain name "greenproducts.com"). To support this argument, ICBP distinguishes its planned website from that in *Planned Parenthood Fed. of Am., Inc. v. Bucci,* 42 U.S.P.Q.2d 1430 (S.D.N.Y.1997), where an anti-abortion activist who registered the domain name "plannedparenthood.com" to lure pro-abortion internet users onto his website designed a web page that deceptively announced that it was "Planned Parenthood's" site—instead of clearly announcing that the Planned Parenthood Federation of America had nothing to do with it.

While it is true that the *Planned Parenthood* court discussed how the graphics and design of the web page misled users into believing that the Planned Parenthood Federation was operating an anti-abortion web page, *see* 42 U.S.P.Q.2d at 1432, ICBP overlooks the fact that the *Planned Parenthood* court also found that a disclaimer would not have cured the confusion caused by the domain name:

> Due to the nature of Internet use, defendant's appropriation of plaintiffs mark as a domain name and home page address cannot adequately be remedied by a disclaimer. Defendant's domain name and home page address are external labels that, on their face, cause confusion among Internet users and may cause Internet users who seek plaintiffs website to expend time and energy accessing defendant's website. Therefore, I determine that a disclaimer on defendant's home page would not be sufficient to dispel the confusion induced by his home page address and domain name.

Planned Parenthood, 42 U.S.P.Q.2d at 1441.

Because ICBP's website has not been designed yet, this Court will make no finding as to whether ICBP's web page is likely to cause consumer confusion between the products of ICBP and those of Green Products. However, based on the briefs, affidavits, and evidence presented at the hearing, this Court finds that the use of plaintiff's trademark as defendant's own domain name is likely to cause consumer confusion as to who owns the site. Just as customers entering a store that advertises "Green Products" as its store name would be initially confused to find, upon entering the store, that ICBP actually owned it, so will customers typing the domain name "greenproducts.com" be initially confused to find that ICBP owns the website.

The Court acknowledges that such an interpretation of "consumer confusion" is somewhat different than that typically used to find consumer confusion in trademark infringement cases. Typically, the courts examine whether a company intended to confuse consumers into thinking that its own products were made by a competitor company. *See, e.g., SquirtCo. v. Seven-Up Co.,* 628 F.2d 1086, 1091 (8th Cir.1980) ("Intent on the part of the alleged infringer to pass off its goods as the product of another raises an inference of likelihood of confusion, but intent is not an element of a claim for trademark infringement.").

Here, ICBP did not intend to sell its corn by-products by passing them off as having been made by Green Products. However, ICBP did intend to pass off its domain name as though it belonged to Green Products. As a result of the confusion in thinking that Green Products' website could be found through the "greenproducts.com" domain name, ICBP could deceptively lure potential customers onto its own turf, where customers would be told how ICBP is better than Green Products. This Court finds that such a deceptive use of a competitor's trademark as a way to lure customers away from the competitor is a kind of consumer confusion.

Moreover, even if such an interpretation of "consumer confusion" is not the relevant mode of inquiry, this Court also finds that ICBP's ownership of the domain name "greenproducts.com"—even without an adjoining website—could cause consumer confusion about the corporate status of Green Products. Currently, if internet users browsing the web type the domain name "greenproducts.com", they are told that "[n]o documents match the query." After reading this message, users might randomly input other domain names, guessing that Green Products is registered under some variation of its trademark. Other users might try to find out who owns the domain name "greenproducts.com" by using various functions on the web where people can type specific domain names and find out who owns them.[3] Users who do this will learn that ICBP owns the "greenproducts.com" website, and they will also learn the address and phone number of ICBP. Potential customers who see this information may be confused into thinking that ICBP has taken over Green Products, or that Green Products has merged into ICBP. As a result, customers may decide to buy from ICBP, believing that Green Products no longer exists or that ICBP now owns it. The consumer confusion thereby caused by ICBP's ownership of the domain name "greenproducts.com" during the pendency of litigation would cause Green Products to lose customers.

The fifth factor is incidents of actual confusion. Green Products concedes that because the website is not yet operational, there have been no incidents of actual confusion, so the Court need not examine this factor further.

The last factor is the degree of care reasonably expected of Green Products' potential customers. To determine this, the Court looks at the "ordinary purchaser, buying under the normally prevalent conditions of the market and giving the attention such purchasers usually give in buying that class of goods." *General Mills, Inc. v. Kellogg Co.*, 824 F.2d 622, 627 (8th Cir.1987). * * * Based on all the evidence before it at this point in the proceedings * * * this Court finds that ordinary internet users do not undergo a highly sophisticated analysis when searching for domain names [and that] * * * an ordinary internet user trying to find Green Products' website would likely guess that Green Products' domain name was the same as its trademark, and thus type "greenproducts.com". * * *

Based on this overall balancing, this Court finds a substantial probability that Green Products will prevail on the merits.

2. *Irreparable harm to Green Products*

The Court next analyzes the degree of harm, if any, that Green Products would suffer if not granted a preliminary injunction. The Eighth Circuit has held that a district court can presume irreparable injury from a finding of probable success on the merits of a § 43(a) Lanham Trademark

---

3. [Here the court is referring to a "whois" search.—Eds.]

Act case. *Sports Design*, 871 F.Supp. at 1165, *citing Sanborn Mfg.*, 997 F.2d at 489. While this Court could thus presume irreparable injury based on its finding of probable success on the merits, it will also examine the specific circumstances of this case in order to decide whether allowing ICBP to retain ownership of the domain name "greenproducts.com" during the pendency of litigation would cause irreparable harm to Green Products.

Although ICBP has consented to putting the domain name "greenproducts.com" on hold until the final merits are determined, Green Products is concerned that even though ICBP would not have an actual website that could be viewed by typing the domain name "greenproducts.com", customers could use other functions on the web to discover that ICBP owns that domain name. (Hearing, Sept. 11, 1997.) As a result, potential or actual customers might mistakenly conclude that ICBP has purchased the Green Products corporation, or that Green Products has merged with ICBP. This confusion could result in Green Products losing both customers and revenue during the pendency of the litigation, and it would be impossible to calculate how much money or how many customers were lost.

For these reasons, in addition to the fact that the Court believes that Green Products is likely to succeed on the merits, the Court finds that it would cause Green Products irreparable harm if ICBP were allowed to retain ownership of the domain name "greenproducts.com" during the pendency of the litigation.

3. Balance between this harm and the injury that granting the injunction will inflict on other parties

ICBP has not finalized what its web page will look like, has not advertised that it owns a web page that can be viewed by typing the domain name "greenproducts.com", and has not listed "greenproducts.com" as one of its domain names in the Thomas Register. If ICBP is compelled to relinquish ownership of the domain name "greenproducts.com" to Green Products during the pendency of the litigation, ICBP would still be able to launch its own website via its registered domain names "icbp.com" or "bestcob.com". Furthermore, the act of transferring ownership of "greenproducts.com" would not hinder ICBP's ability to launch a website that compares its products to those of Green Products: ICBP could still design and implement a website that compares the products of ICBP to those of Green Products, and internet users could access this website through ICBP's other registered domain names.

While these factors weigh in support of compelling ICBP to transfer ownership of the domain name, there are also certain factors that weigh against the transfer. For example, if ICBP were to prevail at trial, Green Products would have to transfer the "greenproducts.com" domain name back to ICBP. This could cause some initial confusion, and possibly hostility, from customers who might have become accustomed to accessing Green Products' website through the "greenproducts.com" domain name. In addition, because Green Products would like to advertise its domain name "greenproducts.com" in the Thomas Register, and because final changes to the printed version of the Thomas Register must be made by November 1, 1997, neither Green Products nor ICBP will be able to change the 1998 edition of the printed Thomas Register if ICBP prevails at trial. As a result, ICBP worries that it "would risk incurring the anger of these customers if that domain name was suddenly switched...."

After weighing the potential harm that ICBP would experience by not being able to use its competitor's trademark as its own domain name, against the harm Green Products would experience by not being able to use its own trademark as its domain name, this Court finds that the harm to Green Products is more extensive and severe than the harm to ICBP. Although ICBP would experience some harm by transferring ownership of the domain name during the pendency of litigation, the transfer is not irreversible; if ICBP ultimately prevails on the merits, the Court will transfer ownership of the domain name back to ICBP. Additionally, even though some customers who may have become accustomed to finding Green Products' web page through the "greenproducts.com" domain name may be initially upset when they find that the domain name "greenproducts.com" has become the domain name for ICBP's web page (if ICBP prevails at trial), any harm that ICBP may experience because of Green Products' temporary ownership of the domain name could be tempered by a carefully designed web page or by hyperlinks to Green Products' web page. Moreover, given ICBP's goal of distinguishing its products from those of Green Products, the opportunity for ICBP to establish a comparative advertising website located through the "greenproducts.com" domain name could be even more advantageous to ICBP if Green Products has already attracted customers to the "greenproducts.com" domain name.

For all of the above reasons, and especially considering the fact that the transfer of ownership is not irreversible because the Court will order the domain name transferred back to ICBP if ICBP prevails in litigation, the Court finds that the harm to Green Products is more extensive and severe than the harm to ICBP.

    * * *

Cardservice International, Inc. v. McGee

950 F.Supp. 737 (E.D.Va.1997), *aff'd mem.*, 129 F.3d 1258 (4th Cir.1997).

■ CLARKE, DISTRICT JUDGE.

This matter comes before this Court for the hearing of evidence in the bench trial of whether Plaintiff Cardservice International, Inc., is entitled to a permanent injunction pursuant to 15 U.S.C. § 1116 against Defendants Webster R. McGee and WRM & Associates banning the use by the Defendants of words similar to Plaintiff's trademark "Cardservice". * * *

I.

This action was brought by Cardservice International seeking injunctive relief and damages for alleged infringements of its trademark "Cardservice" by the Defendants. Cardservice International provides credit and debit card processing and processes "billions of dollars in transactions annually." Plaintiff's Exhibit 3 at 2. Cardservice International registered the trademark "Cardservice International" with the United States Patent and Trademark Office as Reg. No. 1,864,924 effective Nov. 29, 1994. Plaintiff's Exhibit 1. No claim was made to the exclusive right to the word "international."

McGee, through his sole proprietorship WRM & Associates has also provided credit and debit card services. Cardservice International claims that in 1994, McGee applied to become a representative of Cardservice International. McGee claims that he was only associated with an agent of Cardservice International, but never sought to become associated with Cardservice International itself. In March of 1995 and without the permission of Cardservice International, McGee registered the internet domain name "cardservice.com" with Network Solutions, Inc., the company responsible for regulating use of domain names on the internet. In advertisements located at the internet site "cardservice.com", McGee advertised merchant card services through a company held out to be "EMS—Card Service on the Caprock".

In May and August 1995, Cardservice International contacted McGee by letter demanding that McGee "cease and desist all Cardservice related activity." Subsequent discussions between Cardservice International and McGee focused on McGee's use of "cardservice.com". When McGee refused to surrender the domain name, Cardservice International retained counsel, who called McGee's attention to Cardservice International's trademark and again demanded that McGee cease and desist use of the term "Cardservice" and any variation of it on the internet.

McGee refused to relinquish "cardservice.com" or to cease use of "Card Service" on the internet. McGee claimed that the name of his business inserts a space between "card" and "service" and that he is therefore not in violation of the trademark laws. He further claimed that "cardservice.com" was one word because the internet does not allow spaces in domain names. When Cardservice International expanded its services onto the internet, it was forced to use the domain name "cardsvc.com".

Cardservice International then filed this action in September 1996. Cardservice International filed counts alleging violations of § 32 of the Lanham Act, 15 U.S.C. § 1114, for trademark infringement; § 43(a) of the Lanham Act, 42 U.S.C. § 1125(a), for unfair competition; and common law unfair competition, misappropriation, and unjust enrichment. McGee answered these allegations and filed counterclaims seeking declaratory relief that he was the proper owner of the domain name "cardservice.com.", that Cardservice International had interfered with Defendants' business relationships by attempting to have the domain name "cardservice.com" transferred from McGee to Cardservice International, and that Cardservice International had engaged in trademark misuse and wire fraud. * * *

On January 13, 1997, the Court also proceeded with the bench trial on the merits of Cardservice International's claim in which Cardservice International sought attorneys fees and a permanent injunction. McGee indicated his desire to end the litigation and stated that he would not contest Cardservice International's evidence.

II.

The Court ruled from the Bench that Cardservice International is entitled to a permanent injunction against McGee and WRM & Associates requiring the Defendants to cease use of any variation of the registered mark "Cardservice" and to relinquish any interest in the domain name "cardservice.com". Federal Rule of Civil Procedure 65(d) requires this Court to state the reasons for the grant of the permanent injunction.

First, the Court addresses a preliminary issue. McGee has argued that because he registered the domain name "cardservice.com" with Network Solutions, he is entitled to the domain name. McGee cites Network Solutions' policy of granting domain names on a first-come-first-served basis. Such a policy cannot trump federal law. Holders of valid trademarks under federal law are not subject to company policy, nor can the rights of those trademark holders be changed without congressional actions. If trademark laws apply to domain names, anyone who obtains a domain name under Network Solutions' "first-come-first-served" policy must do so subject to whatever liability is provided for by federal law.

* * *

* * * The Fourth Circuit has stated that in order to prevail in actions under [Sections 32 and 43 of the Lanham Act, 15 U.S.C. §§ 1114(1) and 1125(a)], "a complainant must demonstrate that it has a valid, protectable trademark and that the defendant's use of a colorable imitation of the trademark is likely to cause confusion among consumers." *Lone Star Steakhouse & Saloon v. Alpha of Virginia,* 43 F.3d 922 (4th Cir.1995).

It is undisputed that Cardservice International owns a valid, protectable trademark. Until McGee informed the Court that he would not contest Cardservice International's evidence, he primarily argued that his use of "cardservice.com" and "Card Service on the Caprock" would not cause confusion on the internet. The Court disagrees and finds that there is a likelihood of confusion between Cardservice International's registered mark and McGee's use of "cardservice.com" and "Card Service" on the internet.

The factors relevant to a determination of whether there is a likelihood of confusion are as follows:

a) the strength or distinctiveness of the mark;

b) the similarity of the two marks;

c) the similarity of the goods/services the marks identify;

d) the similarity of the facilities the two parties use in their businesses;

e) the similarity of the advertising used by the two parties;

f) the defendant's intent;

g) actual confusion.

Pizzeria Uno Corp. v. Temple, 747 F.2d 1522, 1527 (4th Cir.1984). Not all of these factors are relevant to any given set of facts, nor must all factors be in the registrant's favor for a finding of confusion. *Id.*

In this case, several of the *Pizzeria Uno* factors favor a finding that McGee's use of "cardservice.com" and "Card Service" is likely to cause confusion. It is clear that McGee's use of "cardservice.com" and "Card Service on the Caprock" are strikingly similar to Cardservice International's registered mark. Although McGee's use of the term "Card Service" does not exactly duplicate "Cardservice", minor differences between the registered mark and the unauthorized use of the mark do not preclude liability under the Lanham Act when the unauthorized use is likely to cause confusion. *See Lone Star Steakhouse, supra* (finding use of "Lone Star Grill" to be an infringement of registered mark "Lone Star Steakhouse and Saloon"). The use of the term "cardservice" in Defendants' domain name exactly duplicates the registered mark "Cardservice".

Further, both parties are using the internet as the facility to provide their services. Because of the nature of the internet and domain names in particular, this factor becomes even more important in cases of trademark infringement over the internet. Domain names present a unique circumstance when determining the likelihood of confusion caused by possible trademark violations. Traditionally, trademark disputes involved two or more parties using the same or similar mark. *Intermatic Inc. v. Toeppen,* 947 F.Supp. 1227, 1233–34 (N.D.Ill.1996) (Williams, Mag.). With regard to domain names, however, only one party can hold any particular domain name. *Id.* Who has access to that domain name is made even more important by the fact that there is nothing on the internet equivalent to a phone book or directory assistance. A customer who is unsure about a company's domain name will often guess that the domain name is also the company's name. For this reason, "a domain name mirroring a corporate name may be a valuable corporate asset, as it facilitates communication with a customer base." *MTV Networks, Inc. v. Curry,* 867 F.Supp. 202, 203–04 n. 2 (S.D.N.Y.1994). Thus, a domain name is more than a mere internet address. It also identifies the internet site to those who reach it, much like a person's name identifies a particular person, or, more relevant to trademark disputes, a company's name identifies a specific company.

Because of McGee's use of "cardservice.com", Cardservice International has no access to an internet domain name containing its registered mark, and must use a different domain name. Cardservice International's customers who wish to take advantage of its internet services but do not know its domain name are likely to assume that "cardservice.com" belongs to Cardservice International. These customers would instead reach McGee and see a home page for "Card Service". They would find that McGee's internet site offers advertisements for and provides access to the same services as Cardservice International—credit and debit card processing. Many would assume that they have reached Cardservice International or, even if they realize that is not who they have reached, take advantage of

McGee's services because they do not otherwise know how to reach Cardservice International. Such confusion is not only likely, but, according to McGee, has actually occurred at least four or five times since he began using "cardservice.com". Transcript of Preliminary Injunction Hearing at 366.

Such a result is exactly what the trademark laws were designed to protect against. Cardservice International has obtained a trademark to ensure that the name "cardservice" will be associated by consumers only with Cardservice International. Regardless of the fact that McGee's business is small compared to Cardservice International's, confusion will result among consumers who are seeking Cardservice International by searching for its trademark as a domain name on the internet. The fact that Cardservice International has been awarded a trademark means that it should not be forced to compete with others who would also use the words "cardservice". The terms of the Lanham Act do not limit themselves in any way which would preclude application of federal trademark law to the internet. Unauthorized use of a domain name which includes a protected trademark to engage in commercial activity over the internet constitutes use "in commerce", 15 U.S.C. § 1114(1), of a registered mark. Such use is in direct conflict with federal trademark law. *See ActMedia, Inc. v. Active Media Int'l*, No. 96C3448, 1996 WL 466527 (N.D.Ill. July 17, 1996) (finding defendant's use of domain name "actmedia.com" precluded plaintiff from reserving the domain name incorporating its registered mark and therefore violated 15 U.S.C. § 1125); *see also Panavision Int'l v. Toeppen*, 945 F.Supp. 1296 (C.D.Cal.1996) (finding defendant's reservation of domain name "panavision.com" which incorporated registered mark of plaintiff to be in violation of the Federal Trademark Dilution Act of 1995, 15 U.S.C. § 1125(c)).

Accordingly, the Court finds that McGee's use of "cardservice.com" and "Card Service on the Caprock" constitutes trademark infringement in violation of the Lanham Act and that Cardservice International is entitled to a permanent injunction against such use pursuant to 15 U.S.C. § 1116. The Court emphasizes that its finding against McGee is based on evidence which McGee ultimately chose not to contest at trial.

* * *

NOTES & QUESTIONS

1. *Is registration "commercial use"?* In *Lockheed Martin Corp. v. Network Solutions, Inc.,* the court holds that mere registration of a domain name is not use "in connection with any goods or services" or "commercial use," and therefore cannot constitute trademark infringement or dilution. In *Green Products Co. v. Independence Corn By–Products Co.,* in contrast, the court finds commercial use even though the defendant has done no more than register a domain name that is similar to a trademark owned by Green Products. The *Green Products* court reasons that the act of registering a domain name creates a public record showing that the registrant owns that domain name. By conducting a "whois" search, members of the public will see this record and erroneously infer that the registrant has acquired that company and that the goods and services of this company now originate from and are affiliated with this registrant—thereby establishing a connection to goods and services as well as consumer confusion over their origin and affiliation. Which view do you find more convincing?

2. *Similar approach in U.K.* The courts in the United Kingdom have embraced the reasoning of the *Green Products* case and held that mere registration of a domain name can constitute trademark infringement. *See British Telecommunications plc v. One in a Million Ltd.*, [1998] 4 All E.R. 476 (C.A.):

> It is accepted that the name Marks & Spencer denotes Marks & Spencer plc and nobody else. Thus anybody seeing or hearing the name realises that what is being referred to is the business of Marks & Spencer plc. It follows that registration by the appellants of a domain name including the name Marks & Spencer makes a false representation that they are associated or connected with Marks & Spencer plc. This can be demonstrated by considering the reaction of a person who taps into his computer the domain name marksandspencer.co.uk and presses a button to execute a "whois" search. He will be told that the registrant is One In A Million Limited. A substantial number of persons will conclude that One In A Million Limited must be connected or associated with Marks & Spencer plc. That amounts to a false representation which constitutes passing off.

3. *Initial interest confusion and disclaimers.* Offline, initial interest confusion is sometimes condemned as a form of "bait and switch." In holding that a bar named "The Velvet Elvis" infringed trademarks held by the Elvis Presley estate, a court noted: "[O]nce in the door, the confusion has succeeded because some patrons may stay, despite realizing that the bar has no relationship with" the Elvis Presley estate. *Elvis Presley Enters. v. Capece*, 141 F.3d 188, 204 (5th Cir.1998). Does initial interest confusion have the same consequence and significance online as it does in the world of bricks and mortar? Would the presence of disclaimers on the website affect your answer? The court in *Green Products* quotes the court in *Planned Parenthood Fed. Of Am., Inc. v. Bucci*, 42 U.S.P.Q.2d (BNA) 1430 (S.D.N.Y.1997), for the proposition that disclaimers on a website will not cure confusion caused by that website's domain name. Therein the court argued that "Defendant's domain name and home page address * * * may cause Internet users who seek plaintiff's web site to expend time and energy accessing defendant's web site. Therefore, I determine that a disclaimer on defendant's home page would not be sufficient to dispel the confusion induced by his home page address and domain name." *Id.* at 1441. Do you agree with this analysis?

4. *Registration to block another's use.* Under the reasoning of the *Lockheed* court, could a company register a competitor's trademark as a domain name in order to prevent that competitor from using it as a domain name so long as the registrant did not actually use it on the Internet? *See Juno*

Online Services, L.P. v. Juno Lighting, Inc., 979 F.Supp. 684 (N.D.Ill.1997), discussed in Part II(C) of the *Lockheed Martin* opinion.

5. *E-mail addresses vs. websites.* When courts discuss the use of a domain name on the Internet, their examples involve a "fully qualified" domain name that points to a website. Is it possible to infringe another's trademark with a domain name if one only uses that domain name as part of an e-mail address? *See America Online, Inc. v. IMS*, 24 F.Supp.2d 548 (E.D.Va.1998).

6. *Directories.* Directories are the electronic file folders found on most personal computers. One can point to a directory on a host computer connected to the Internet by appending to the fully qualified domain name of that host a forward slash "/" followed by the name of the particular directory. Thus, when I type

www.whitehouse.gov/press releases/

into the address bar of my web browser, I am served the default web page contained in the "press release" directory that resides on the host computer designated by the URL www.whitehouse.gov. With respect to trademark infringement, this raises the question whether the use of another's trademark as a directory name can constitute infringement. If so, how would you defend such a lawsuit? What is the difference between using another's trademark as a domain name and as a directory name? Is the use of another's trademark as a directory name fair use? *See, e.g., Patmont Motor Werks, Inc. v. Gateway Marine, Inc.*, 1997 WL 811770 n. 6 (N.D.Cal.1997). (For material on trademark fair use, *see* Chapter 1, Part III(A), *supra*.)

B.   TRADEMARK DILUTION

Teletech Customer Care Management, Inc. v. Tele–Tech Co.

977 F.Supp. 1407 (C.D.Cal.1997).

■ PFAELZER, DISTRICT JUDGE.

On April 21, 1997, Plaintiff's Motion for Preliminary Injunction came before the Court for hearing. * * * After considering the papers filed by the parties and the arguments presented at the hearing, the Court grants Plaintiff's Motion for Preliminary Injunction and makes the following findings of fact and conclusions of law:

Findings of Fact

I.   Facts Relating to the Plaintiff's Business

1.   Plaintiff TeleTech Customer Care Management (California), Inc. ("TeleTech" or "Plaintiff") is the owner of the federally registered service mark TELETECH®, United States Service Mark Registration No. 1,996,-498. The Service Mark Registration is valid and current. Plaintiff has used the mark TELETECH® in commerce since 1982.

2. TeleTech Holdings, Inc. is the parent company of the Plaintiff, as well as several other entities whose names begin with "TeleTech": * * * All of these corporations shall be referred to collectively as the TeleTech Companies. TeleTech Holdings, Inc. is a publicly traded company, whose stock is listed on the NASDAQ stock exchange.

3. Plaintiff has shown that the TeleTech Companies may be the largest provider of primarily inbound integrated telephone and Internet customer care worldwide. The main business of the TeleTech Companies is providing "customer care" for the customers of TeleTech's clients, including receiving and responding to telephone and Internet inquiries from customers of TeleTech's clients. "Customer care" provided by the TeleTech Companies includes answering questions asked by the clients' customers before a sale, providing information on new products offered by TeleTech's clients, enrolling customers in clients' programs, arranging product shipments to customers of TeleTech's clients, providing 24–hour technical and help desk support for customers of TeleTech's clients, resolving customer complaints, and conducting satisfaction surveys. The TeleTech Companies handle service calls from customers of many types of businesses, including airlines, the United States Postal Service, telephone companies, banks, computer companies, utility companies, a package delivery service, and other types of businesses. Airline reservations, tracking of packages, bank transactions, and many other customer service calls are handled by TeleTech employees.

4. It appears that the TeleTech Companies have spent hundreds of thousands of dollars promoting their services and advertising under the TELETECH® Service Mark. In 1996 alone, the TeleTech Companies appear to have spent in excess of nine hundred thousand dollars promoting their services and advertising under the TELETECH® Service Mark. The TeleTech Companies have sold millions of dollars worth of services under the TELETECH® Service Mark. As a result of these efforts, it appears that TeleTech has built up and now owns valuable goodwill symbolized by the TELETECH® Service Mark.

II.   Facts Relating to the Defendant's Business

5. Defendant Tele–Tech Company, Inc. ("Tele–Tech" or "Defendant") is a contractor providing engineering and installation services to the telecommunications industry. Defendant began using the name Tele–Tech (with a hyphen) in 1978.

6. Defendant has not registered the service mark TELE–TECH. Defendant has not been authorized or licensed by TeleTech to use the TELETECH® Service Mark (without a hyphen). Defendant is not affiliated with or sponsored by TeleTech.

III.   Facts Relating to the Defendant's Use of the Domain Name "Teletech.Com"

7. Defendant Tele–Tech is using Plaintiff's federally registered service mark (TELETECH, without a hyphen) as an Internet domain name, "teletech.com".

8.   Plaintiff has used the TELETECH® service mark for approximately fifteen years, and began using the TELETECH® service mark long before Defendant's first use of "teletech.com" (without the hyphenation which distinguishes Defendant's name from Plaintiff's TELETECH® service mark).

9.   Only one entity may use the domain name "teletech.com." As a result, Defendant's use of the "teletech.com" domain name prevents Plaintiff TeleTech from using its registered service mark and company name as its domain name.

10.   Plaintiff's inability to use the TELETECH® company name and registered service mark as its domain name is causing hardship to Plaintiff. Customers and potential customers of Plaintiff are unable to locate Plaintiff's website by typing in "teletech.com" as part of the Uniform Resource Locator (URL).

11.   An Internet domain name may include a hyphen.

12.   Use of a hyphen would distinguish the domain name "teletech.com" from the domain name "teletech.com." Domain names such as "teletech.com" are used to identify the location of servers on the Internet. Because the hyphen is an additional character in the domain name, its inclusion or omission changes the location of the server to which an inquiry is made.

13.   Tele–Tech is not precluded from using its own name, "Tele–Tech," with its distinctive hyphenation, as its domain name. In fact, Tele–Tech appears to have established a second website that uses the domain name "tele-tech.com."

IV.   *Facts Relating to the Balance of Hardship*

14.   Injunctive relief will probably not have great negative impact on Defendant. Defendant is free to use, and in fact already appears to be using, the domain name "tele-tech.com" (which includes the hyphenation), in a second website that Defendant maintains. In fact, it may be easier for Defendant's customers to locate Defendant's website under the domain name "tele-tech.com," since that is the way the Defendant spells its name.

15.   Defendant is "attempting to inform its customers to use 'tele-tech.com' for e-mail."

16.   Defendant suggests that Plaintiff's presence on the Internet is not hindered by Defendant's use of Plaintiff's name and registered service mark as its domain name, because Internet users can locate Plaintiff's website using Internet "search engines," rather than typing in Plaintiff's name as part of the URL. That method of searching the Internet appears to generate as many as 800 to 1000 matches, however. That number of locations is likely to deter web browsers from searching for Plaintiff's particular website.

17.   TeleTech appears to have incurred a great deal of expense over a long period of time developing recognition of its TELETECH® mark, and

users of the Internet who have become familiar with that mark will probably assume that TeleTech's website will be found at "teletech.com."

18.   The balance of hardships tips sharply in Plaintiff's favor.

* * *

VI.   *Facts Relating to Dilution*

23.   The TELETECH® mark is most likely very well recognized within the teleservicing industry, because TeleTech appears to be a large provider of integrated telephone and Internet customer care worldwide and because of the extensive promotion and advertising that TeleTech has apparently undertaken.

24.   The TELETECH® mark has been continuously used in commerce by TeleTech since 1982. The mark is registered on the Principal Register.

25.   The TELETECH® mark appears to be famous.

* * *

Conclusions of Law

* * *

IV.   *Plaintiff is Likely to Succeed on the Merits.*

* * *

B.   *TeleTech Has Demonstrated a Likelihood of Success on the Merits of Its Dilution Claims.*

* * *

12.   TeleTech has demonstrated that its mark is probably famous under this statute. The evidence submitted by the Plaintiff strongly suggests that the TeleTech Companies are the largest provider of integrated telephone and Internet customer care worldwide. The TeleTech Companies appear to have spent hundreds of thousands of dollars promoting their services and advertising under the TELETECH® Service Mark. The Tele-Tech Companies seem to have sold hundreds of millions of dollars worth of services under the TELETECH® Service Mark. TeleTech Holdings, Inc. is a publicly traded company which is listed on the NASDAQ stock exchange. The TELETECH® mark is probably very well recognized and famous within the teleservicing industry, because TeleTech is probably the largest provider of integrated telephone and Internet customer care Worldwide and because of the extensive promotion and advertising that TeleTech appears to have undertaken. The TELETECH® mark has been continuously used in commerce by TeleTech since 1982. The mark is registered on the Principal Register.

13.   TeleTech is entitled to an injunction, under § 43(c) of the Lanham Act, even without a showing of a likelihood of confusion. See Intermatic, 947 F.Supp. at 1234–41, and *Panavision* in which the court found that Toeppen had diluted the plaintiffs' marks by using the plaintiffs' registered

trademarks as his domain names. In those cases, Toeppen obtained the domain names in order to force the plaintiffs to pay him money to assign those names to them. This case is somewhat different, in that Defendant claims that it obtained the "teletech.com" domain name, because it was unaware that a hyphen could be used as part of a domain name. However, Defendant in this case also demanded that Plaintiff pay money to the Defendant in order for Defendant to stop using the "teletech.com" domain name. In any event, for purposes of this motion, the reason why Defendant adopted the diluting domain name is not relevant. Plaintiff is the owner of the registered mark TELETECH®, that mark is probably famous, and Defendant's use of the "teletech.com" domain name most likely dilutes Plaintiff's mark.

* * *

15. Plaintiff is therefore entitled to an injunction under § 43(c) of the Lanham Act.

16. California Business and Professions Code § 14330 provides as follows:

> Likelihood of injury to business reputation or of dilution of the distinctive quality of a mark registered under this chapter, or a mark valid at common law, or a trade name valid at common law, shall be a ground for injunctive relief notwithstanding the absence of competition between the parties or the absence of confusion as to the source of goods or services.

17. Plaintiff is entitled to an injunction under this statute as well.

* * *

Panavision International, L.P. v. Toeppen

141 F.3d 1316 (9th Cir.1998).

■ DAVID R. THOMPSON, CIRCUIT JUDGE:

This case presents two novel issues. We are asked to apply existing rules of personal jurisdiction to conduct that occurred, in part, in "cyberspace." In addition, we are asked to interpret the Federal Trademark Dilution Act as it applies to the Internet.

Panavision accuses Dennis Toeppen of being a "cyber pirate" who steals valuable trademarks and establishes domain names on the Internet using these trademarks to sell the domain names to the rightful trademark owners.

The district court found that under the "effects doctrine," Toeppen was subject to personal jurisdiction in California. *Panavision International, L.P. v. Toeppen,* 938 F.Supp. 616, 620 (C.D.Cal.1996). The district court then granted summary judgment in favor of Panavision, concluding that Toeppen's conduct violated the Federal Trademark Dilution Act of 1995, 15 U.S.C. § 1125(c), and the California Anti-dilution statute, California Business & Professions Code § 14330. *Panavision International, L.P. v. Toeppen,* 945 F.Supp. 1296, 1306 (C.D.Cal.1996).

Toeppen appeals. He argues that the district court erred in exercising personal jurisdiction over him because any contact he had with California was insignificant, emanating solely from his registration of domain names on the Internet, which he did in Illinois. Toeppen further argues that the district court erred in granting summary judgment because his use of Panavision's trademarks on the Internet was not a commercial use and did not dilute those marks.

We have jurisdiction under 28 U.S.C. § 1291 and we affirm.

I.

BACKGROUND

[The court begins with a description of the Internet and domain names.]

Panavision holds registered trademarks to the names "Panavision" and "Panaflex" in connection with motion picture camera equipment. Panavision promotes its trademarks through motion picture and television credits and other media advertising.

In December 1995, Panavision attempted to register a website on the Internet with the domain name Panavision.com. It could not do that, however, because Toeppen had already established a website using Panavision's trademark as his domain name. Toeppen's web page for this site displayed photographs of the City of Pana, Illinois.

On December 20, 1995, Panavision's counsel sent a letter from California to Toeppen in Illinois informing him that Panavision held a trademark in the name Panavision and telling him to stop using that trademark and the domain name Panavision.com. Toeppen responded by mail to Panavision in California, stating he had the right to use the name Panavision.com on the Internet as his domain name. Toeppen stated:

> If your attorney has advised you otherwise, he is trying to screw you. He wants to blaze new trails in the legal frontier at your expense. Why do you want to fund your attorney's purchase of a new boat (or whatever) when you can facilitate the acquisition of "PanaVision.com" cheaply and simply instead?

Toeppen then offered to "settle the matter" if Panavision would pay him $13,000 in exchange for the domain name. Additionally, Toeppen stated that if Panavision agreed to his offer, he would not "acquire any other Internet addresses which are alleged by Panavision Corporation to be its property."

After Panavision refused Toeppen's demand, he registered Panavision's other trademark with NSI as the domain name Panaflex.com. Toeppen's web page for Panaflex.com simply displays the word "Hello."

Toeppen has registered domain names for various other companies including Delta Airlines, Neiman Marcus, Eddie Bauer, Lufthansa, and over 100 other marks. Toeppen has attempted to "sell" domain names for other trademarks such as intermatic.com to Intermatic, Inc. for $10,000 and americanstandard.com to American Standard, Inc. for $15,000.

* * *

II.

DISCUSSION

A. *Personal Jurisdiction*

[The court considers the issue of personal jurisdiction and concludes that the lower court properly exercised personal jurisdiction over Toeppen.]

B. *Trademark Dilution Claims*

The Federal Trademark Dilution Act provides:

The owner of a famous mark shall be entitled ... to an injunction against another person's commercial use in commerce of a mark or trade name, if such use begins after the mark has become famous and causes dilution of the distinctive quality of the mark....

15 U.S.C. § 1125(c).

The California Anti-dilution statute is similar. *See* Cal. Bus. & Prof. Code § 14330. It prohibits dilution of "the distinctive quality" of a mark regardless of competition or the likelihood of confusion. The protection extends only to strong and well recognized marks. Panavision's state law dilution claim is subject to the same analysis as its federal claim.

In order to prove a violation of the Federal Trademark Dilution Act, a plaintiff must show that (1) the mark is famous; (2) the defendant is making a commercial use of the mark in commerce; (3) the defendant's use began after the mark became famous; and (4) the defendant's use of the mark dilutes the quality of the mark by diminishing the capacity of the mark to identify and distinguish goods and services. 15 U.S.C. § 1125(c).

Toeppen does not challenge the district court's determination that Panavision's trademark is famous, that his alleged use began after the mark became famous, or that the use was in commerce. Toeppen challenges the district court's determination that he made "commercial use" of the mark and that this use caused "dilution" in the quality of the mark.

1. *Commercial Use*

Toeppen argues that his use of Panavision's trademarks simply as his domain names cannot constitute a commercial use under the Act. Case law supports this argument. *See Panavision International, L.P. v. Toeppen,* 945 F.Supp. 1296, 1303 (C.D.Cal.1996) ("Registration of a trade[mark] as a domain name, without more, is not a commercial use of the trademark and therefore is not within the prohibitions of the Act."); *Academy of Motion Picture Arts & Sciences v. Network Solutions Inc.,* 989 F.Supp. 1276, 1997 WL 810472 (C.D.Cal. Dec.22, 1997) (the mere registration of a domain name does not constitute a commercial use); *Lockheed Martin Corp. v.*

Network Solutions, Inc., 985 F.Supp. 949 (C.D.Cal.1997) (NSI's acceptance of a domain name for registration is not a commercial use within the meaning of the Trademark Dilution Act).

Developing this argument, Toeppen contends that a domain name is simply an address used to locate a web page. He asserts that entering a domain name on a computer allows a user to access a web page, but a domain name is not associated with information on a web page. If a user were to type Panavision.com as a domain name, the computer screen would display Toeppen's web page with aerial views of Pana, Illinois. The screen would not provide any information about "Panavision," other than a "location window" which displays the domain name. Toeppen argues that a user who types in Panavision.com, but who sees no reference to the plaintiff Panavision on Toeppen's web page, is not likely to conclude the web page is related in any way to the plaintiff, Panavision.

Toeppen's argument misstates his use of the Panavision mark. His use is not as benign as he suggests. Toeppen's "business" is to register trademarks as domain names and then sell them to the rightful trademark owners. He "act[s] as a 'spoiler,' preventing Panavision and others from doing business on the Internet under their trademarked names unless they pay his fee." *Panavision*, 938 F.Supp. at 621. This is a commercial use. *See Intermatic Inc. v. Toeppen*, 947 F.Supp. 1227, 1230 (N.D.Ill.1996) (stating that "[o]ne of Toeppen's business objectives is to profit by the resale or licensing of these domain names, presumably to the entities who conduct business under these names.").

As the district court found, Toeppen traded on the value of Panavision's marks. So long as he held the Internet registrations, he curtailed Panavision's exploitation of the value of its trademarks on the Internet, a value which Toeppen then used when he attempted to sell the Panavision.com domain name to Panavision.

In a nearly identical case involving Toeppen and Intermatic Inc., a federal district court in Illinois held that Toeppen's conduct violated the Federal Trademark Dilution Act. *Intermatic*, 947 F.Supp. at 1241. There, Intermatic sued Toeppen for registering its trademark on the Internet as Toeppen's domain name, intermatic.com. It was "conceded that one of Toeppen's intended uses for registering the Intermatic mark was to eventually sell it back to Intermatic or to some other party." *Id.* at 1239. The court found that "Toeppen's intention to arbitrage the 'intermatic.com' domain name constitute[d] a commercial use." *Id. See also Teletech Customer Care Management, Inc. v. Tele–Tech Co.*, 977 F.Supp. 1407 (C.D.Cal. 1997) (granting a preliminary injunction under the Trademark Dilution Act for use of a trademark as a domain name).

Toeppen's reliance on *Holiday Inns, Inc. v. 800 Reservation, Inc.*, 86 F.3d 619 (6th Cir.1996), 519 U.S. 1093 (1997) is misplaced. In *Holiday Inns*, the Sixth Circuit held that a company's use of the most commonly *misdialed* number for Holiday Inns' 1–800 reservation number was not trademark infringement.

Holiday Inns is distinguishable. There, the defendant did not use Holiday Inns' trademark. Rather, the defendant selected the most commonly misdialed telephone number for Holiday Inns and attempted to capitalize on consumer confusion.

A telephone number, moreover, is distinguishable from a domain name because a domain name is associated with a word or phrase. A domain name is similar to a "vanity number" that identifies its source. Using Holiday Inns as an example, when a customer dials the vanity number "1–800–Holiday," she expects to contact Holiday Inns because the number is associated with that company's trademark. A user would have the same expectation typing the domain name HolidayInns.com. The user would expect to retrieve Holiday Inns' web page.

Toeppen made a commercial use of Panavision's trademarks. It does not matter that he did not attach the marks to a product. Toeppen's commercial use was his attempt to sell the trademarks themselves.[5] Under the Federal Trademark Dilution Act and the California Anti-dilution statute, this was sufficient commercial use.

2. *Dilution*

"Dilution" is defined as "the lessening of the capacity of a famous mark to identify and distinguish goods or services, regardless of the presence or absence of (1) competition between the owner of the famous mark and other parties, or (2) likelihood of confusion, mistake or deception." 15 U.S.C. § 1127.

Trademark dilution on the Internet was a matter of Congressional concern. Senator Patrick Leahy (D–Vt.) stated:

> [I]t is my hope that this anti-dilution statute can help stem the use of deceptive Internet addresses taken by those who are choosing marks that are associated with the products and reputations of others.

141 Cong. Rec. § 19312–01 (daily ed. Dec. 29, 1995) (statement of Sen. Leahy). *See also Teletech Customer Care Management, Inc. v. Tele–Tech Co., Inc.,* 977 F.Supp. 1407, 1413 (C.D.Cal.1997).

To find dilution, a court need not rely on the traditional definitions such as "blurring" and "tarnishment." Indeed, in concluding that Toeppen's use of Panavision's trademarks diluted the marks, the district court

---

5. *See Boston Pro. Hockey Assoc., Inc. v. Dallas Cap & Emblem Mfg., Inc.,* 510 F.2d 1004 (1975), which involved the sale of National Hockey League logos. The defendant was selling the logos themselves, unattached to a product (such as a hat or sweatshirt). The court stated: "The difficulty with this case stems from the fact that a reproduction of the trademark itself is being sold, unattached to any other goods or services." *Id.* at 1010. The court concluded that trademark law should protect the trademark itself. "Although our decision here may slightly tilt the trademark laws from the purpose of protecting the public to the protection of the business interests of plaintiffs, we think that the two become ... intermeshed...." *Id.* at 1011. "Whereas traditional trademark law sought primarily to protect consumers, dilution laws place more emphasis on protecting the investment of the trademark owners." *Panavision,* 945 F.Supp. at 1301.

noted that Toeppen's conduct varied from the two standard dilution theories of blurring and tarnishment. *Panavision,* 945 F.Supp. at 1304. The court found that Toeppen's conduct diminished "the capacity of the Panavision marks to identify and distinguish Panavision's goods and services on the Internet." *Id. See also Intermatic,* 947 F.Supp. at 1240 (Toeppen's registration of the domain name, "lessens the capacity of Intermatic to identify and distinguish its goods and services by means of the Internet.").

This view is also supported by *Teletech.* There, TeleTech Customer Care Management Inc., ("TCCM"), sought a preliminary injunction against Tele–Tech Company for use of TCCM's registered service mark, "Tele-Tech," as an Internet domain name. *Teletech,* 977 F.Supp. at 1410. The district court issued an injunction, finding that TCCM had demonstrated a likelihood of success on the merits on its trademark dilution claim. *Id.* at 1412. The court found that TCCM had invested great resources in promoting its servicemark and Teletech's registration of the domain name teletech.com on the Internet would most likely dilute TCCM's mark. *Id.* at 1413.

Toeppen argues he is not diluting the capacity of the Panavision marks to identify goods or services. He contends that even though Panavision cannot use Panavision.com and Panaflex.com as its domain name addresses, it can still promote its goods and services on the Internet simply by using some other "address" and then creating its own web page using its trademarks.

We reject Toeppen's premise that a domain name is nothing more than an address. A significant purpose of a domain name is to identify the entity that owns the website. "A customer who is unsure about a company's domain name will often guess that the domain name is also the company's name." *Cardservice Int'l v. McGee,* 950 F.Supp. 737, 741 (E.D.Va.1997). "[A] domain name mirroring a corporate name may be a valuable corporate asset, as it facilitates communication with a customer base." *MTV Networks, Inc. v. Curry,* 867 F.Supp. 202, 203–204 n. 2 (S.D.N.Y.1994).

Using a company's name or trademark as a domain name is also the easiest way to locate that company's website. Use of a "search engine" can turn up hundreds of websites, and there is nothing equivalent to a phone book or directory assistance for the Internet. *See Cardservice,* 950 F.Supp. at 741.

Moreover, potential customers of Panavision will be discouraged if they cannot find its web page by typing in "Panavision.com," but instead are forced to wade through hundreds of websites. This dilutes the value of Panavision's trademark. We echo the words of Judge Lechner, quoting Judge Wood: "Prospective users of plaintiff's services who mistakenly access defendant's website may fail to continue to search for plaintiff's own home page, due to anger, frustration or the belief that plaintiff's home page does not exist." *Jews for Jesus v. Brodsky,* 993 F.Supp. 282, 306–07 (D.N.J.1998) (Lechner, J., quoting Wood, J. in *Planned Parenthood v. Bucci,* 1997 WL 133313 at *4); *see also Teletech,* 977 F.Supp. at 1410 (finding that use of a search engine can generate as many as 800 to 1000 matches and it is "likely to deter web browsers from searching for Plaintiff's particular web site").

Toeppen's use of Panavision.com also puts Panavision's name and reputation at his mercy. *See Intermatic*, 947 F.Supp. at 1240 ("If Toeppen were allowed to use 'intermatic.com,' Intermatic's name and reputation would be at Toeppen's mercy and could be associated with an unimaginable amount of messages on Toeppen's web page.").

We conclude that Toeppen's registration of Panavision's trademarks as his domain names on the Internet diluted those marks within the meaning of the Federal Trademark Dilution Act, 15 U.S.C. § 1125(c), and the California Anti-dilution statute, Cal.Bus. & Prof.Code § 14330.

   * * *

Mark A. Lemley, *The Modern Lanham Act and the Death of Common Sense*

108 Yale L.J. 1687 (1999).

   * * *

II.   The Expanding Boundaries of Trademark Rights

Courts seem to be replacing the traditional rationale for trademark law with a conception of trademarks as property rights, in which trademark "owners" are given strong rights over the marks without much regard for the social costs of such rights. There appear to be three basic parts to this trend. First, we sometimes seem to be making trademark law for the extreme case, but we then apply that law to a large number of run-of-the-mill trademarks. Second, courts increasingly treat brands as things owned in their own right, rather than as advertising connected with a particular product. Finally, courts have not been sufficiently sensitive to legitimate free speech concerns in cases where trademark owners seek to restrict noncompetitive uses of the trademark.

A. *Making Law for the Extreme Case*

In a number of recent instances, trademark law has been expanded quite significantly by means of new legal rules that make sense in a limited number of cases, but that then enter widespread use where they make less sense. The tendency is perhaps a natural one. If Congress creates a new statute that protects some but not all trademark owners, every trademark owner will want his or her mark to be included in the new group and will seek to receive the added protections of the new rule. If courts are not careful to restrain the new doctrine, it will soon take on a life of its own. I call this the problem of "doctrinal creep."

1. *Dilution*

The most obvious example of doctrinal creep in trademark law is dilution. Dilution laws are directed against the possibility that the unique nature of a mark will be destroyed by companies who trade on the renown of the mark by selling unrelated goods, such as Kodak pianos or Buick aspirin. But because consumers need not be confused for dilution to occur, dilution laws represent a fundamental shift in the nature of trademark protection.

Dilution laws are largely a product of the last fifty years. Approximately half of the states now have dilution statutes. But most recent attention has been focused on the federal dilution statute, which was added in 1995. The federal statute, like most state dilution statutes, protects only "famous" marks. The statute offers a nonexclusive list of eight factors for courts to consider in determining whether a mark is "distinctive and famous." The clear intention seems to have been to restrict dilution doctrine to a relatively small class of nationally known trademarks whose fame is sufficiently great that the risk of blurring by multiple noncompeting uses is significant. But courts applying the state and federal dilution statutes have been quite willing to conclude that a local favorite, or a rather obscure company, is "famous" within the meaning of the Act. Thus, marks such as Intermatic, Gazette, Dennison, Nailtiques, TeleTech, Wedgewood (for new homes, not china), Papal Visit 1999, and Wawa have been declared famous. Worse, many courts seem willing to find dilution without even inquiring into the fame of the mark. Dilution doctrine has also been expanded to encompass not only noncompeting but also nonidentical marks, to protect famous trade dress and product configurations, to attack longstanding uses of descriptive marks to describe products, to aid trademark owners in ordinary cases against competitive marks by dispensing with the need to demonstrate consumer confusion, and even to create a cause of action against consumers (or the press) who do not use marks properly. While the federal law is still relatively new, and so prediction is difficult, we may be moving toward a world in which "famous" marks protected even in the absence of consumer confusion are the rule rather than the exception. The result, as one commentator has noted, is to grant a "trademark in gross"—one unconnected to a particular product—to a wide variety of owners. * * *

3.   Cybersquatters and Domain Names

Courts have also stretched trademark doctrine to accommodate the extreme case involving Internet domain names and "cybersquatters." Cybersquatters like Dennis Toeppen acted early to lock up a number of Internet domain names that reflect trademarks or corporate names, for a variety of possible purposes. Courts that have considered suits by trademark owners against cybersquatters have uniformly held that obtaining someone else's trademark as a domain name is either trademark infringement or dilution. In many cases, this is clearly the right result. If I register my competitor's name on the Internet, so that potential customers who enter that name will arrive at my site instead, I am clearly creating confusion in an attempt to profit commercially. In other cases, though, courts have had to stretch the "commercial use in commerce" requirement to the vanishing point in order to "catch" cybersquatters. Thus, courts have held that owning a domain name that you do not use is "use in commerce" if you hope to sell the domain name to the trademark owner. And several courts have even held that noncommercial use of a domain name is "commercial use in commerce," reasoning that *any* use on the Internet is automatically a use in commerce. This is in striking contrast to the meaning of the term in ordinary trademark cases.

Toeppen and Bucci are not particularly sympathetic defendants, and trademark or some other law *should* provide a cause of action against those who capture a domain name that clearly ought to belong to someone else in order to extort money from trademark owners. Still, there is something troubling about the erosion of the commercial use and use in commerce requirements. We may find that extending trademark protection to cover noncommercial uses of a mark, however compelling the instant case, sets a dangerous precedent for the law. Indeed, we need not look too far. The cybersquatter precedents are already being used by trademark owners to take domain names away from arguably legitimate users, such as people who want to register their last names as Internet domains and those who build a "gripe site" to complain about a specific product or company.

4. *What's Going on Here?*

* * *

* * * I think the modern dilution * * * cases take a good idea and stretch it too far. * * * [M]ost trademarks are not sufficiently well-known that their use on unrelated products would create even an association in the minds of consumers. Rather, these legal doctrines are being used to serve other purposes, ones that trademark theory does not support.[91] The explosion in product configuration cases in the last twenty years has a lot more to do with acquiring or extending de facto patent and copyright protection through a back door than with protecting consumers from confusion. And the insistence by seemingly every trademark owner that its marks must be thought famous is motivated less by genuine concerns about blurring than by a desire to "keep up with the Cokes" and get the benefit of the same property protection that truly famous marks now receive. One can understand why trademark owners want these things, of course, but we must look to the public interest, not private interests, to decide whether trademark owners should get them.[93]

* * *

---

91. Kratzke argues that dilution doctrine is misguided because it ignores consumer injury. William P. Kratzke, Normative Economic Analysis of Trademark Law, 21 Memphis St. U. L. Rev. 199, 285 (1991). He has a point: Dilution statutes do not commonly require proof of consumer confusion or an appropriate substitute. Properly conceived, however, I think dilution law is protecting consumers against a real harm: the loss of the informational value of a famous trademark through crowding.

93. * * * For a delightful exposition of this critical fact, which seems to have gotten lost in the debate over trademark law, see Jessica Litman, *Breakfast with Batman: The Public Interest in the Advertising Age*, 108 Yale L.J. 1717, 1725, who notes: "There has been inexorable pressure to recognize as an axiom the principle that if something appears

III.   Restoring Common Sense to Trademark Law

If I am right that trademark owners are obtaining property rights that trademark theory cannot justify, what should be done? For the most part, I believe the courts can handle this problem, if they are vigilant in relating the protection plaintiffs seek to the principles of trademark theory and rejecting claims that are not well-founded on trademark principles. We do not need new legal rules here; what we need is the principled and vigorous application of the old rules. Courts should ask, as [Professor Ralph] Brown does, exactly what new incentives do we need trademark law to create? How are consumers hurt by the conduct at issue? And what are the interests of society at large? Brown's answer to these questions still rings true today: "[T]he only interests in trade symbols worth protecting are those against loss of sales or loss of reputation."[142]

Courts should of course protect trademarks against uses that are likely to cause confusion, and against true cases of dilution. And they should be willing to recognize that trademarks can come in many forms, including product configuration, sounds, and colors. But they should resist the inevitable attempts by trademark owners to expand these categories without limit. In particular, they should recognize that the Lanham Act is not a general anti-copying statute—and indeed that not all copying of a competitor's product is bad.

Eradicating the property rationale for trademarks, and restoring common sense to the Lanham Act, will be hard work. The forces arrayed in favor of propertization are powerful indeed. And it is true, as Brown points out, that "the restraining influence of the courts is largely passive."[144] But the courts do have some tools available for this project. The federal dilution statute vests great discretion in the courts in deciding whether a mark is famous. To date, courts have not imposed significant limitations on parties seeking to designate their marks as famous, but they certainly could (and should) do so. * * * Taking the likelihood of confusion requirement, the fair use doctrine, and the doctrine of non-trademark use seriously will also help prevent unwarranted expansion of trademark rights in ways unforeseen by the drafters of the Lanham Act. Finally, the First Amendment stands (or should stand) as a bulwark against the increasingly common effort to use trademark law to suppress speech.

* * *

NOTES & QUESTIONS

1. *Toeppen as a reseller.* The Internet Corporation for Assigned Names and Numbers ("ICANN") controls the market for registrars through the process of accreditation. Accredited registrars, however, are permitted to provide their services through unaccredited resellers so long as the accred-

---

to have substantial value to someone, the law must and should protect it as property."

142. Ralph S. Brown, Jr., *Advertising and the Public Interest: Legal Protection of Trade Symbols*, 57 Yale L.J. 1165, 1201 (1948), *reprinted in* 108 Yale L.J. 1619, 1621 (1999). * * *

144. *Id.* at 1206.

ited registrar is listed in the TLD registry as the registrar of record. Why shouldn't we construe Toeppen as such a reseller, albeit one with a limited stock of premium domain names? Looked at in this way, isn't Toeppen's business—like NSI's—"connected only with the names' technical function on the Internet"?

2. *Intent and demands for payment.* The court in *Teletech Customer Care Management v. Tele–Tech* concludes that "Defendant's use of the 'tele-tech.com' domain name most likely dilutes Plaintiff's mark." In what way does it dilute plaintiff's mark: by tarnishment, blurring, or otherwise?

3. *Commercial use.* In *Lockheed Martin v. Network Solutions,* Lockheed Martin brought a trademark dilution claim against NSI as well as a trademark infringement claim. In a part of the opinion not reproduced in the text, the court absolves NSI of liability for trademark dilution because NSI "does not make a commercial use of domain names by trading on their value as trademarks." *Lockheed Martin v. Network Solutions,* 985 F.Supp. at 960. Can we reconcile the holdings of the *Lockheed* and *Panavision* courts? If Toeppen's use is commercial, why isn't NSI's?

4. *Surnames.* Is the registration of surnames as second-level domain names and the subsequent licensing of those domain names as e-mail addresses to people with the same surname a commercial use within the meaning of the Federal Trademark Dilution Act? *See Avery Dennison Corporation v. Sumpton,* 189 F.3d 868 (9th Cir.1999), excerpted in Chapter 1, Part II, *supra.*

5. *Confusing trademarks with property?* The law of trademarks was developed to protect a company's good will, thereby creating an incentive for companies to invest in promoting and improving their products for the benefit of the public. It was a tort-like doctrine springing from the tort of unfair competition. Do you agree with Professor Lemley that trademark law as it is being applied to domain names has lost touch with its original purpose? Does the current development of trademark dilution doctrine online serve the public interest or is it a windfall to large corporate interests? How could laws designed to protect against unfair competitive practices be construed as conferring property rights?

6. *Sale of domain names.* Take a look at www.greatdomains.com, "a Verisign Company," where exchange of domain names is flourishing. Examples: On June 24, 2002, Passover.com was listed for $90,000, and DowQuotes.com was listed for $60,000. Similar exchange sites include www.domainnames-forsale.net (advising that wine.com sold for $3.3 million and asseenontv.com sold for $5 million), www.a-1domainsales.com, and many others. Are these proprietors doing anything illegal? If not, should the law be changed to make what they are doing illegal?

7. *Domain name entrepreneurs in a market economy.* We live in a society that generally employs free markets to allocate efficiently the goods and services that our country produces. Entrepreneurial initiative and vision are generally rewarded with wealth and prestige. Is it then a bit odd that the domain name entrepreneurs have been vilified as "cybersquatters"?

These entrepreneurs took some risks: they paid registration fees when the future development of Internet commerce was not yet assured. Why didn't our society permit a free market to develop in which each domain name would end up in the hands of the person or company who could put it to its highest and best use, trademark owner or not?

II. THE ANTICYBERSQUATTING CONSUMER PROTECTION ACT

Trademark infringement and dilution remain important as legal theories under which trademark owners assert rights to a domain name registered to someone else. For the trademark owner to prevail on an infringement theory, use in commerce and consumer confusion must be shown, and in some cases, these are hurdles the trademark owner might not be able to clear. For example, one who registers a domain name desired by a trademark owner but does not offer it for sale to the owner or otherwise use it in any way will likely escape liability, even if the domain name is identical or similar to the trademark. While a dilution claim does not require a showing of consumer confusion, such claims are only available to those trademark owners who can convince a court that their marks are "famous." As one scholar has commented:

> In the author's opinion, there is a very poor fit between the actions of a cybersquatter and the federal Anti-dilution Act. The prototypical cybersquatter does not use the reserved domain name as its mark before the public, so there is no traditional dilution by blurring or tarnishment. Thus, the courts have had to create a wholly new category of "dilution" in order to find a legal weapon to combat this new and different form of reprehensible commercial activity. But this legal tool only protects "famous" marks, requiring that the courts expand and devalue the category of "famous" marks in order to combat cybersquatting.

4 J. THOMAS MCCARTHY, MCCARTHY ON TRADEMARKS AND UNFAIR COMPETITION § 25:77 (4th ed.2002).

To address these problems the Congress enacted the Anticybersquatting Consumer Protection Act ("ACPA"), Pub. L. No. 106–113 (1999). While the Act codifies much of the pre–2000 caselaw, it also introduces a number of significant innovations. For example, it makes actionable the bad faith registration of a domain name that is identical or confusingly similar to another's trademark. It limits such liability, however, to domain name registrants, codifying a domain name registrar's freedom from liability established in the *Lockheed Martin* case. *See* 15 U.S.C. §§ 1125(d)(1) and 1114(D)(iii). The Act also creates an *in rem* action against offending domain names—an important new option for trademark owners when federal courts do not have *in personam* jurisdiction over the domain name registrant. *See* 15 U.S.C. § 1125(d)(2). Yet another innovation is a provision allowing the trademark owner to elect statutory damages in lieu of actual damages. *See* 15 U.S.C. §§ 1117(d). These damages can be as large as $100,000 per registered domain name. The Act also creates a cause of action against registrants who register the non-trademarked names of others without their consent with intent to profit by resale. *See* 15 U.S.C. § 1129.

In the remainder of this Part, we first consider the overview of the Act provided in the report of the United States Senate that accompanied the legislation. We then look at three cases involving, respectively, an *in personam* action against a domain name registrant, an *in rem* action against a domain name, and an action against a cybersquatter in which statutory damages are elected. While the Act clearly grants immunity to domain name registrars for acts of selling another's trademark as a domain name, it is significantly less clear whether the Act creates a statutory framework that adequately addresses the public's right to make noncommercial uses of words and names that are identical or confusingly similar to another's trademark. It also remains to be seen how the threshold requirement that registration be with "bad faith intent to profit" will be interpreted and applied.

Senate Report 106–140

The Anticybersquatting Consumer Protection Act.
(Aug. 5, 1999).

The practice of cybersquatting harms consumers, electronic commerce, and the goodwill equity of valuable U.S. brand names, upon which consumers increasingly rely to locate the true source of genuine goods and services on the Internet. Online consumers have a difficult time distinguishing a genuine site from a pirate site, given that often the only indications of source and authenticity of the site, or the goods and services made available thereon, are the graphical interface on the site itself and the Internet address at which it resides. As a result, consumers have come to rely heavily on familiar brand names when engaging in online commerce. But if someone is operating a website under another brand owner's trademark, such as a site called "cocacola.com" or "levis.com," consumers bear a significant risk of being deceived and defrauded, or at a minimum, confused. The costs associated with these risks are increasingly burdensome as more people begin selling pharmaceuticals, financial services, and even groceries over the Internet. Regardless of what is being sold, the result of online brand name abuse, as with other forms of trademark violations, is the erosion of consumer confidence in brand name identifiers and in electronic commerce generally.

Cybersquatters target distinctive marks for a variety of reasons. Some register well-known brand names as Internet domain names in order to extract payment from the rightful owners of the marks, who find their trademarks "locked up" and are forced to pay for the right to engage in electronic commerce under their own brand name. For example, * * * the Committee * * * heard testimony that Warner Bros. was reportedly asked to pay $350,000 for the rights to the names "warner-records. com", "warner-bros-records.com", "warner-pictures.com", "warner-bros-picures", and "warnerpictures.com".

Others register well-known marks as domain names and warehouse those marks with the hope of selling them to the highest bidder, whether it be the trademark owner or someone else. For example, * * * the Committee * * * heard testimony regarding a similarly enterprising cybersquatter whose partial inventory of domain names—the listing of which was limited by the fact that Network Solutions will only display the first 50 records of a given registrant—includes names such as Coca–Cola, Pepsi, Burger King, KFC, McDonalds, Subway, Taco Bell, Wendy's, BMW, Chrysler, Dodge, General Motors, Honda, Hyundai, Jaguar, Mazda, Mercedes, Nissan, Porsche, Rolls–Royce, Saab, Saturn, Toyota, and Volvo, all of which are available to the highest bidder through an online offer sheet.

In addition, cybersquatters often register well-known marks to prey on consumer confusion by misusing the domain name to divert customers from the mark owner's site to the cybersquatter's own site, many of which are pornography sites that derive advertising revenue based on the number of visits, or "hits," the site receives. For example, the Committee was informed of a parent whose child mistakenly typed in the domain name for "dosney.com," expecting to access the family-oriented content of the Walt Disney home page, only to end up staring at a screen of hardcore pornography because a cybersquatter had registered that domain name in anticipation that consumers would make that exact mistake. Other instances of diverting unsuspecting consumers to pornographic websites involve malicious attempts to tarnish a trademark owner's mark or to extort money from the trademark owner, such as the case where a cybersquatter placed pornographic images of celebrities on a site under the name "pentium3.com" and announced that it would sell the domain name to the highest bidder. Others attempt to divert unsuspecting consumers to their sites in order to engage in unfair competition. For example, the business operating under the domain name "disneytransportation.com" greets online consumers at its site with a picture of Mickey Mouse and offers shuttle services in the Orlando area and reservations at Disney hotels, although the company is in no way affiliated with the Walt Disney Company and such fact is not clearly indicated on the site. Similarly, the domain name address "wwwcarpoint.com," without a period following "www", was used by a cybersquatter to offer a competing service to Microsoft's popular Carpoint car buying service.

Finally, and most importantly, cybersquatters target distinctive marks to defraud consumers, including to engage in counterfeiting activities. For example, the Committee heard testimony regarding a cybersquatter who registered the domain names "attphonecard.com" and "attcallingcard.com" and used those names to establish sites purporting to sell calling cards and soliciting personally identifying information, including credit card numbers. * * * Of even greater concern was the example of an online drug store selling pharmaceuticals under the name "propeciasales.com" without any way for online consumers to tell whether what they are buying is a legitimate product, a placebo, or a dangerous counterfeit.

The need for legislation banning cybersquatting

Current law does not expressly prohibit the act of cybersquatting. The World Intellectual Property Organization (WIPO) has identified cybersquatting as a global problem and recognized in its report on the domain name process that, "[f]amous and well-known marks have been the special target of a variety of predatory and parasitical practices on the Internet."[10]
* * *

Instances of cybersquatting continue to grow each year because there is no clear deterrent and little incentive for cybersquatters to discontinue their abusive practices. While the Federal Trademark Dilution Act has been useful in pursuing cybersquatters, cybersquatters have become increasingly sophisticated as the case law has developed and now take the necessary precautions to insulate themselves from liability. For example, many cybersquatters are now careful to no longer offer the domain name for sale in any manner that could implicate liability under existing trademark dilution case law. And, in cases of warehousing and trafficking in domain names, courts have sometimes declined to provide assistance to trademark holders, leaving them without adequate and effective judicial remedies. This uncertainty as to the trademark law's application to the Internet has produced inconsistent judicial decisions and created extensive monitoring obligations, unnecessary legal costs, and uncertainty for consumers and trademark owners alike.

In cases where a trademark owner can sue, the sheer number of domain name infringements, the costs associated with hundreds of litigation matters, and the difficulty of obtaining damages in standard trademark infringement and dilution actions are significant obstacles for legitimate trademark holders. Frequently, these obstacles lead trademark owners to simply "pay off" cybersquatters, in exchange for the domain name registration, rather than seek to enforce their rights in court.
* * *

Under the bill, as amended, the abusive conduct that is made actionable is appropriately limited just to bad-faith registrations and uses of others' marks by persons who seek to profit unfairly from the goodwill associated therewith. * * *

The Committee intends the prohibited "use" of a domain name to describe the use of a domain name by the domain name registrant, with the bad-faith intent to profit from the goodwill of the mark of another. The concept of "use" does not extend to uses of the domain name made by those other than the domain name registrant, such as the person who includes the domain name as a hypertext link on a web page or as part of a directory of Internet addresses.

---

10.   World Intellectual Property Organization, Management of Internet Names and Addresses: Intellectual Property Issues 8 (1999).

In addition, the bill, as amended, balances the property interests of trademark owners with the interests of Internet users who would make fair use of others' marks or otherwise engage in protected speech online. First, the bill sets forth a number of balancing factors that a court may wish to consider in deciding whether the requisite bad-faith intent is present in any given case. * * * [Codified at 15 U.S.C. § 1125(d)(1)(B)(i)(I)–(IX)], [e]ach of these factors reflect indicators that, in practice, commonly suggest bad-faith intent or a lack thereof in cybersquatting cases. * * *

Second, the amended bill underscores the bad-faith requirement by requiring a court to remit statutory damages in any case where a defendant believed, and the court finds that the defendant had reasonable grounds to believe, that the registration or use of the domain name was a fair or otherwise lawful use. In addition, the bill makes clear that the newly created statutory damages shall apply only with respect to bad-faith conduct occurring on or after the date of enactment of the bill.

Definition of "domain name"

The bill, as amended, provides a narrow definition of the term "domain name" in order to tailor the bill's reach narrowly to the problem sought to be addressed. Thus, the term "domain name" describes any alphanumeric designation which is registered with or assigned by any domain name registrar, domain name registry, or other domain name registration authority as part of an electronic address on the Internet. This definition essentially covers the second-level domain names assigned by domain name registration authorities (i.e., the name located immediately to the left of the ".com," ".net", ".edu," and ".org" generic top level domains), but is technology neutral enough to accommodate names other than second-level domains that are actually registered with domain name registration authorities, as may be the case should Internet domain name registrars begin to issue third or fourth level domains. The limited nature of the definition is important in that it excludes such things as screen names, file names, and other identifiers not assigned by a domain name registrar or registry, which have little to do with cybersquatting in practice.

In rem jurisdiction

As amended, the bill provides for in rem jurisdiction, which allows a mark owner to seek the forfeiture, cancellation, or transfer of an infringing domain name by filing an in rem action against the name itself, provided the domain name itself violates substantive Federal trademark law, where the mark owner has satisfied the court that it has exercised due diligence in trying to locate the owner of the domain name but is unable to do so. A significant problem faced by trademark owners in the fight against cybersquatting is the fact that many cybersquatters register domain names under aliases or otherwise provide false information in their registration applications in order to avoid identification and service of process by the mark owner. The bill, as amended, will alleviate this difficulty, while protecting the notions of fair play and substantial justice, by enabling a mark owner to seek an injunction against the infringing property in those cases where, after due diligence, a mark owner is unable to proceed against the domain name registrant because the registrant has provided false contact information and is otherwise not to be found.

Additionally, some have suggested that dissidents and others who are online incognito for legitimate reasons might give false information to protect themselves and have suggested the need to preserve a degree of anonymity on the Internet particularly for this reason. Allowing a trademark owner to proceed against the domain names themselves, provided they are, in fact, infringing or diluting under the Trademark Act, decreases the need for trademark owners to join the hunt to chase down and root out these dissidents or others seeking anonymity on the Net. The approach in the amended bill is a good compromise, which provides meaningful protection to trademark owners while balancing the interests of privacy and anonymity on the Internet.

Encouraging cooperation and fairness in the effort to combat cybersquatting

Like the underlying bill, the substitute amendment encourages domain name registrars and registries to work with trademark owners to prevent cybersquatting by providing a limited exemption from monetary damages for domain name registrars and registries that suspend, cancel, or transfer domain names pursuant to a court order or in the implementation of a reasonable policy prohibiting the registration of infringing domain names. The amended bill goes further, however, in order to protect the rights of domain name registrants against overreaching trademark owners. Under the amended bill, a trademark owner who knowingly and materially misrepresents to the domain name registrar or registry that a domain name is infringing is liable to the domain name registrant for damages, including costs and attorneys' fees, resulting from the suspension, cancellation, or transfer of the domain name. In addition, the court may award injunctive relief to the domain name registrant by ordering the reactivation of the domain name or the transfer of the domain name back to the domain name registrant. The bill, as amended, also promotes the continued ease and efficiency users of the current registration system enjoy by codifying current case law limiting the secondary liability of domain name registrars and registries for the act of registration of a domain name.[11]

Preservation of first amendment rights and trademark defenses

Finally, the substitute amendment includes an explicit savings clause making clear that the bill does not affect traditional trademark defenses,

---

11. *See Panavision Int'l v. Toeppen,* 141 F.3d 1316, 1319 (9th Cir.1998) (holding that NSI is not responsible for making "a determination about registrant's right to use a domain name."); *Lockheed Martin Corporation v. Network Solutions, Inc.,* 985 F.Supp. 949 (C.D.Cal.1997) (holding registrar not liable); *Academy of Motion Picture Arts and Sciences v. Network Solutions Inc.,* 989 F.Supp. 1276 (C.D.Cal.1997) (holding that holder of registered trademarks could not obtain a preliminary injunction against domain name registrar).

such as fair use, or a person's first amendment rights, and it ensures that any new remedies created by the bill will apply prospectively only.

In summary, the legislation is a balanced approach to protecting the legitimate interests of businesses, Internet users, e-commerce, and consumers.

* * *

Sporty's Farm L.L.C. v. Sportsman's Market, Inc.

202 F.3d 489 (2d Cir.2000).

■ CALABRESI, CIRCUIT JUDGE:

This case originally involved the application of the Federal Trademark Dilution Act ("FTDA") to the Internet. *See* Federal Trademark Dilution Act of 1995, Pub.L. No. 104–98, 109 Stat. 985 (codified at 15 U.S.C. §§ 1125, 1127 (Supp.1996)). While the case was pending on appeal, however, the Anticybersquatting Consumer Protection Act ("ACPA"), Pub.L. No. 106–113 (1999), *see* H.R.Rep. No. 106–479 (Nov. 18, 1999), was passed and signed into law. That new law applies to this case.

BACKGROUND

I

* * *

Over the last few years, the commercial side of the Internet has grown rapidly. Web pages are now used by companies to provide information about their products in a much more detailed fashion than can be done through a standard advertisement. Moreover, many consumers and businesses now order goods and services directly from company web pages. Given that Internet sales are paperless and have lower transaction costs than other types of retail sales, the commercial potential of this technology is vast.

For consumers to buy things or gather information on the Internet, they need an easy way to find particular companies or brand names. The most common method of locating an unknown domain name is simply to type in the company name or logo with the suffix .com. If this proves unsuccessful, then Internet users turn to a device called a search engine. A search engine will find all web pages on the Internet with a particular word or phrase. Given the current state of search engine technology, that search will often produce a list of hundreds of websites through which the user must sort in order to find what he or she is looking for. As a result, companies strongly prefer that their domain name be comprised of the company or brand trademark and the suffix .com. *See* H.R.Rep. No. 106–412, at 5 (1999).

Until recently, domain names with the .com top level domain could only be obtained from Network Solutions, Inc. ("NSI"). Now other registrars may also assign them. But all these registrars grant such names primarily on a first-come, first-served basis upon payment of a small registration fee. They do not generally inquire into whether a given domain name request matches a trademark held by someone other than the person requesting the name. *See id.*

Due to the lack of any regulatory control over domain name registration, an Internet phenomenon known as "cybersquatting" has become increasingly common in recent years. *See, e.g.,* Panavision Int'l, L.P. v. Toeppen, 141 F.3d 1316 (9th Cir.1998). Cybersquatting involves the registration as domain names of well-known trademarks by non-trademark holders who then try to sell the names back to the trademark owners. Since domain name registrars do not check to see whether a domain name request is related to existing trademarks, it has been simple and inexpensive for any person to register as domain names the marks of established companies. This prevents use of the domain name by the mark owners, who not infrequently have been willing to pay "ransom" in order to get "their names" back. *See* H.R.Rep. No. 106–412, at 5–7; S.Rep. No. 106–140, at 4–7 (1999).

II

Sportsman's is a mail order catalog company that is quite well-known among pilots and aviation enthusiasts for selling products tailored to their needs. In recent years, Sportsman's has expanded its catalog business well beyond the aviation market into that for tools and home accessories. The company annually distributes approximately 18 million catalogs nationwide, and has yearly revenues of about $50 million. Aviation sales account for about 60% of Sportsman's revenue, while non-aviation sales comprise the remaining 40%.

In the 1960s, Sportsman's began using the logo *"sporty"* to identify its catalogs and products. In 1985, Sportsman's registered the trademark *sporty's* with the United States Patent and Trademark Office. Since then, Sportsman's has complied with all statutory requirements to preserve its interest in the *sporty's* mark. *Sporty's* appears on the cover of all Sportsman's catalogs; Sportsman's international toll free number is 1–800–4*sportys;* and one of Sportsman's domestic toll free phone numbers is 1–800–*Sportys*. Sportsman's spends about $10 million per year advertising its *sporty's* logo.

Omega is a mail order catalog company that sells mainly scientific process measurement and control instruments. In late 1994 or early 1995, the owners of Omega, Arthur and Betty Hollander, decided to enter the aviation catalog business and, for that purpose, formed a wholly-owned subsidiary called Pilot's Depot, LLC ("Pilot's Depot"). Shortly thereafter, Omega registered the domain name sportys.com with NSI. Arthur Hollander was a pilot who received Sportsman's catalogs and thus was aware of the *sporty's* trademark.

In January 1996, nine months after registering sportys.com, Omega formed another wholly-owned subsidiary called Sporty's Farm and sold it the rights to sportys.com for $16,200. Sporty's Farm grows and sells

Christmas trees, and soon began advertising its Christmas trees on a sportys.com web page. When asked how the name Sporty's Farm was selected for Omega's Christmas tree subsidiary, Ralph S. Michael, the CEO of Omega and manager of Sporty's Farm, explained, as summarized by the district court, that

> in his own mind and among his family, he always thought of and referred to the Pennsylvania land where Sporty's Farm now operates as *Spotty's farm*. The origin of the name ... derived from a childhood memory he had of his uncle's farm in upstate New York. As a youngster, Michael owned a dog named Spotty. Because the dog strayed, his uncle took him to his upstate farm. Michael thereafter referred to the farm as Spotty's farm. The name Sporty's Farm was ... a subsequent derivation.

Joint Appendix ("JA") at 277 (emphasis added). There is, however, no evidence in the record that Hollander was considering starting a Christmas tree business when he registered sportys.com or that Hollander was ever acquainted with Michael's dog Spotty.

In March 1996, Sportsman's discovered that Omega had registered sportys.com as a domain name. Thereafter, and before Sportsman's could take any action, Sporty's Farm brought this declaratory action seeking the right to continue its use of sportys.com. Sportsman's counterclaimed and also sued Omega as a third-party defendant for, *inter alia,* (1) trademark infringement, (2) trademark dilution pursuant to the FTDA, and (3) unfair competition under state law. Both sides sought injunctive relief to force the other to relinquish its claims to sportys.com. While this litigation was ongoing, Sportsman's used "sportys-catalogs.com" as its primary domain name.

After a bench trial, the court rejected Sportsman's trademark infringement claim and all related claims that are based on a "likelihood of [consumer] confusion" since "the parties operate wholly unrelated businesses [and t]herefore, confusion in the marketplace is not likely to develop." *Id.* at 282–83. But on Sportsman's trademark dilution action, where a likelihood of confusion was not necessary, the district court found for Sportsman's. * * * The court also held, however, that Sportsman's could only get injunctive relief and was not entitled to "punitive damages ... profits, and attorney's fees and costs" pursuant to the FTDA since Sporty Farm and Omega's conduct did not constitute willful dilution under the FTDA. *Id.* at 292–93.

Finally, the district court ruled that, although Sporty's Farm had violated the FTDA, its conduct did not constitute a violation of CUTPA [the Connecticut Unfair Trade Practices Act]. * * *

The district court then issued an injunction forcing Sporty's Farm to relinquish all rights to sportys.com. And Sportsman's subsequently acquired the domain name. Both Sporty's Farm and Sportsman's appeal. Specifically, Sporty's Farm appeals the judgment insofar as the district court granted an injunction in favor of Sportsman's for the use of the domain name. Sportsman's, on the other hand, in addition to urging this court to affirm the district court's injunction, cross-appeals, quite correctly as a procedural matter, the district court's denial of damages under both the FTDA and CUPTA. * * *

III

As we noted above, while this appeal was pending, Congress passed the ACPA. That law was passed "to protect consumers and American businesses, to promote the growth of online commerce, and to provide clarity in the law for trademark owners by prohibiting the bad-faith and abusive registration of distinctive marks as Internet domain names with the intent to profit from the goodwill associated with such marks—a practice commonly referred to as 'cybersquatting'." S.Rep. No. 106–140, at 4. In particular, Congress viewed the legal remedies available for victims of cybersquatting before the passage of the ACPA as "expensive and uncertain." H.R.Rep. No. 106–412, at 6. * * * In short, the ACPA was passed to remedy the perceived shortcomings of applying the FTDA in cybersquatting cases such as this one.

The new act accordingly amends the Trademark Act of 1946, creating a specific federal remedy for cybersquatting. New 15 U.S.C. § 1125(d)(1)(A) reads:

A person shall be liable in a civil action by the owner of a mark, including a personal name which is protected as a mark under this section, if, without regard to the goods or services of the parties, that person—

(i) has a bad faith intent to profit from that mark, including a personal name which is protected as a mark under this section; and

(ii) registers, traffics in, or uses a domain name that—

(I) in the case of a mark that is distinctive at the time of registration of the domain name, is identical or confusingly similar to that mark;

(II) in the case of a famous mark that is famous at the time of registration of the domain name, is identical or confusingly similar to or dilutive of that mark; . . .

The Act further provides that "a court may order the forfeiture or cancellation of the domain name or the transfer of the domain name to the owner of the mark," 15 U.S.C. § 1125(d)(1)(C), if the domain name was "registered before, on, or after the date of the enactment of this Act," Pub.L. No. 106–113, § 3010. It also provides that damages can be awarded for violations of the Act, but that they are not "available with respect to the registration, trafficking, or use of a domain name that occurs before the date of the enactment of this Act." *Id.*

DISCUSSION

This case has three distinct features that are worth noting before we proceed further. First, our opinion appears to be the first interpretation of the ACPA at the appellate level. Second, we are asked to undertake the interpretation of this new statute even though the district court made its ruling based on the FTDA. Third, the case before us presents a factual situation that, as far as we can tell, is rare if not unique: A Competitor X of Company Y has registered Y's trademark as a domain name and then transferred that name to Subsidiary Z, which operates a business wholly unrelated to Y. These unusual features counsel that we decide no more than is absolutely necessary to resolve the case before us.

A. Application of the ACPA to this Case

The first issue before us is whether the ACPA governs this case. The district court based its holding on the FTDA since the ACPA had not been passed when it made its decision. Because the ACPA became law while this case was pending before us, we must decide how its passage affects this case. As a general rule, we apply the law that exists at the time of the appeal. *See, e.g.,* Hamm v. City of Rock Hill, 379 U.S. 306, 312–13 (1964) (" '[I]f subsequent to the judgment and before the decision of the appellate court, a law intervenes and positively changes the rule which governs, the law must be obeyed, or its obligation denied.' " (quoting United States v. Schooner Peggy, 5 U.S. (1 Cranch) 103, 110, 2 L.Ed. 49 (1801))).

But even if a new law controls, the question remains whether in such circumstances it is more appropriate for the appellate court to apply it directly or, instead, to remand to the district court to enable that court to consider the effect of the new law. We therefore asked for additional briefing from the parties regarding the applicability of the ACPA to the case before us. After receiving those briefs and fully considering the arguments there made, we think it is clear that the new law was adopted specifically to provide courts with a preferable alternative to stretching federal dilution law when dealing with cybersquatting cases. Indeed, the new law constitutes a particularly good fit with this case. Moreover, the findings of the district court, together with the rest of the record, enable us to apply the new law to the case before us without difficulty. Accordingly, we will do so and forego a remand.

B. "Distinctive" or "Famous"

Under the new Act, we must first determine whether *sporty's* is a distinctive or famous mark and thus entitled to the ACPA's protection. *See* 15 U.S.C. § 1125(d)(1)(A)(ii)(I), (II). The district court concluded that *sporty's* is both distinctive and famous. We agree that *sporty's* is a "distinctive" mark. As a result, and without casting any doubt on the district court's holding in this respect, we need not, and hence do not, decide whether *sporty's* is also a "famous" mark.

Distinctiveness refers to inherent qualities of a mark and is a completely different concept from fame. A mark may be distinctive before it has been used—when its fame is nonexistent. By the same token, even a famous mark may be so ordinary, or descriptive as to be notable for its lack of distinctiveness. See Nabisco, Inc. v. PF Brands, Inc., 191 F.3d 208, 215–26 (2d Cir.1999). We have no doubt that *sporty's,* as used in connection with Sportsman's catalogue of merchandise and advertising, is inherently distinctive. Furthermore, Sportsman's filed an affidavit under 15 U.S.C. § 1065 that rendered its registration of the *sporty's* mark incontestable, which entitles Sportsman's "to a presumption that its registered trademark is inherently distinctive." Equine Technologies, Inc. v. Equitechnology, Inc., 68 F.3d 542, 545 (1st Cir.1995). We therefore conclude that, for the purposes of § 1125(d)(1)(A)(ii)(I), the *sporty's* mark is distinctive.

C. *"Identical and Confusingly Similar"*

The next question is whether domain name sportys.com is "identical or confusingly similar to" the *sporty's* mark.[11] 15 U.S.C. § 1125(d)(1)(A)(ii)(I). * * * [A]postrophes cannot be used in domain names. * * * As a result, the secondary domain name in this case (sportys) is indistinguishable from the Sportsman's trademark (*sporty's*). *Cf.* Brookfield Communications, Inc. v. West Coast Entertainment Corp., 174 F.3d 1036, 1055 (9th Cir.1999) (observing that the differences between the mark "MovieBuff" and the domain name "moviebuff.com" are "inconsequential in light of the fact that Web addresses are not caps-sensitive and that the '.com' top-level domain signifies the site's commercial nature"). We therefore conclude that, although the domain name sportys.com is not precisely identical to the *sporty's* mark, it is certainly "confusingly similar" to the protected mark under § 1125(d)(1)(A)(ii)(I). *Cf. Wella Corp. v. Wella Graphics, Inc.,* 874 F.Supp. 54, 56 (E.D.N.Y.1994) (finding the new mark "Wello" confusingly similar to the trademark "Wella").

D. *"Bad Faith Intent to Profit"*

We next turn to the issue of whether Sporty's Farm acted with a "bad faith intent to profit" from the mark *sporty's* when it registered the domain name sportys.com. 15 U.S.C. § 1125(d)(1)(A)(i). The statute lists nine factors to assist courts in determining when a defendant has acted with a bad faith intent to profit from the use of a mark. But we are not limited to considering just the listed factors when making our determination of whether the statutory criterion has been met. The factors are, instead, expressly described as indicia that "may" be considered along with other facts. *Id.* § 1125(d)(1)(B)(i).

We hold that there is more than enough evidence in the record below of "bad faith intent to profit" on the part of Sporty's Farm (as that term is defined in the statute), so that "no reasonable factfinder could return a verdict against" Sportsman's. Norville v. Staten Island Univ. Hosp., 196 F.3d 89, 95 (2d Cir.1999). First, it is clear that neither Sporty's Farm nor Omega had any intellectual property rights in sportys.com at the time Omega registered the domain name. *See id.* § 1125(d)(1)(B)(i)(I). Sporty's Farm was not formed until nine months after the domain name was

---

11. We note that "confusingly similar" is a different standard from the "likelihood of confusion" standard for trademark infringement adopted by this court in Polaroid Corp. v. Polarad Electronics Corp., 287 F.2d 492 (2d Cir.1961). See Wella Corp. v. Wella Graphics, Inc., 37 F.3d 46, 48 (2d Cir.1994).

registered, and it did not begin operations or obtain the domain name from Omega until after this lawsuit was filed. Second, the domain name does not consist of the legal name of the party that registered it, Omega. *See id.* § 1125(d)(1)(B)(i)(II). Moreover, although the domain name does include part of the name of Sporty's Farm, that entity did not exist at the time the domain name was registered.

The third factor, the prior use of the domain name in connection with the bona fide offering of any goods or services, also cuts against Sporty's Farm since it did not use the site until after this litigation began, undermining its claim that the offering of Christmas trees on the site was in good faith. *See id.* § 1125(d)(1)(B)(i)(III). Further weighing in favor of a conclusion that Sporty's Farm had the requisite statutory bad faith intent, as a matter of law, are the following: (1) Sporty's Farm does not claim that its use of the domain name was "noncommercial" or a "fair use of the mark," *see id.* § 1125(d)(1)(B)(i)(IV), (2) Omega sold the mark to Sporty's Farm under suspicious circumstances, *see* Sporty's Farm v. Sportsman's Market, No. 96CV0756 (D.Conn. Mar. 13, 1998), *reprinted in* Joint Appendix at A277 (describing the circumstances of the transfer of sportys.com); 15 U.S.C. § 1125(d)(1)(B)(i)(VI), and, (3) as we discussed above, the *sporty's* mark is undoubtedly distinctive, *see id.* § 1125(d)(1)(B)(i)(IX).

The most important grounds for our holding that Sporty's Farm acted with a bad faith intent, however, are the unique circumstances of this case, which do not fit neatly into the specific factors enumerated by Congress but may nevertheless be considered under the statute. We know from the record and from the district court's findings that Omega planned to enter into direct competition with Sportsman's in the pilot and aviation consumer market. As recipients of Sportsman's catalogs, Omega's owners, the Hollanders, were fully aware that *sporty's* was a very strong mark for consumers of those products. It cannot be doubted, as the court found below, that Omega registered sportys.com for the primary purpose of keeping Sportsman's from using that domain name. Several months later, and after this lawsuit was filed, Omega created another company in an unrelated business that received the name Sporty's Farm so that it could (1) use the sportys.com domain name in some commercial fashion, (2) keep the name away from Sportsman's, and (3) protect itself in the event that Sportsman's brought an infringement claim alleging that a "likelihood of confusion" had been created by Omega's version of cybersquatting. Finally, the explanation given for Sporty's Farm's desire to use the domain name, based on the existence of the dog Spotty, is more amusing than credible. Given these facts and the district court's grant of an equitable injunction under the FTDA, there is ample and overwhelming evidence that, as a matter of law, Sporty's Farm's acted with a "bad faith intent to profit" from the domain name sportys.com as those terms are used in the ACPA.[13] *See* Luciano v. Olsten Corp., 110 F.3d 210, 214 (2d Cir.1997) (stating that, as a matter of law, judgment may be granted where "the evidence in favor

---

13. We expressly note that "bad faith intent to profit" are terms of art in the ACPA and hence should not necessarily be equated with "bad faith" in other contexts.

of the movant is so overwhelming that 'reasonable and fair minded [persons] could not arrive at a verdict against [it].' " (quoting Cruz v. Local Union No. 3, 34 F.3d 1148, 1154 (2d Cir.1994) (alteration in original))).

E. Remedy

Based on the foregoing, we hold that under § 1125(d)(1)(A), Sporty's Farm violated Sportsman's statutory rights by its use of the sportys.com domain name.[14] The question that remains is what remedy is Sportsman's entitled to. The Act permits a court to "order the forfeiture or cancellation of the domain name or the transfer of the domain name to the owner of the mark," § 1125(d)(1)(C) for any "domain name [ ] registered before, on, or after the date of the enactment of [the] Act," Pub.L. No. 106–113, § 3010. That is precisely what the district court did here, albeit under the pre-existing law, when it directed a) Omega and Sporty's Farm to release their interest in sportys.com and to transfer the name to Sportsman's, and b) permanently enjoined those entities from taking any action to prevent and/or hinder Sportsman's from obtaining the domain name. That relief remains appropriate under the ACPA. We therefore affirm the district court's grant of injunctive relief.

We must also determine, however, if Sportsman's is entitled to damages either under the ACPA or pre-existing law. Under the ACPA, damages are unavailable to Sportsman's since sportys.com was registered and used by Sporty's Farm prior to the passage of the new law. *See id.* (stating that damages can be awarded for violations of the Act but that they are not "available with respect to the registration, trafficking, or use of a domain name that occurs before the date of the enactment of this Act.").

But Sportsman's might, nonetheless, be eligible for damages under the FTDA since there is nothing in the ACPA that precludes, in cybersquatting cases, the award of damages under any pre-existing law. *See* 15 U.S.C. § 1125(d)(3) (providing that any remedies created by the new act are "in addition to any other civil action or remedy otherwise applicable"). Under the FTDA, "[t]he owner of the famous mark shall be entitled only to injunctive relief unless the person against whom the injunction is sought *willfully* intended to trade on the owner's reputation or to cause dilution of the famous mark." *Id.* § 1125(c)(2) (emphasis added). Accordingly, where willful intent to dilute is demonstrated, the owner of the famous mark is— subject to the principles of equity—entitled to recover (1) damages (2) the dilutor's profits, and (3) costs. *See id.; see also id.* § 1117(a) (specifying remedies).

---

14. The statute provides that a party "shall be *liable* in a civil action by the owner of a mark" if it meets the statutory requirements. 15 U.S.C. § 1125(d)(1)(A) (emphasis added). Although the statute uses the term "liable," it does not follow that damages will be assessed. As we discuss below, damages can be awarded for violations of the Act but they are not "available with respect to the registration, trafficking, or use of a domain name that occurs [,as in this case,] before the date of the enactment of this Act." Pub.L. No. 106–113, § 3010.

We conclude, however, that damages are not available to Sportsman's under the FTDA. The district court found that Sporty's Farm did not act willfully. We review such findings of "willfulness" by a district court for clear error. *See* Bambu Sales, Inc. v. Ozak Trading Inc., 58 F.3d 849, 854 (2d Cir.1995). Thus, even assuming the *sporty's* mark to be famous, we cannot say that the district court clearly erred when it found that Sporty's Farm's actions were not willful. To be sure, that question is a very close one, for the facts make clear that, as a Sportsman's customer, Arthur Hollander (Omega's owner) was aware of the significance of the *sporty's* logo. And the idea of creating a Christmas tree business named Sporty's Farm, allegedly in honor of Spotty the dog, and of giving that business the sportys.com domain name seems to have occurred to Omega only several months after it had registered the name. Nevertheless, given the uncertain state of the law at the time that Sporty's Farm and Omega acted, we cannot say that the district court clearly erred in finding that their behavior did not amount to willful dilution. It follows that Sportsman's is not entitled to damages under the FTDA.

Sportsman's also argues that it is entitled to damages under state law. Because neither the FTDA nor the ACPA preempts state remedies such as CUTPA, damages under Connecticut law are not barred, and hence may be available to Sportsman's. *See* H.R.Rep. No. 104–374, at 4 (1995), *reprinted in* 1996 U.S.C.C.A.N. 1029, 1031; 15 U.S.C. § 1125(d)(3). [The court concludes that damages are not available.]

In sum, then, we hold that the injunction issued by the district court was proper under the new anticybersquatting law, but that damages are not available to Sportsman's under the ACPA, the FTDA, or CUTPA.

F. Retroactivity

Sporty Farm's also contends that even if its actions would today violate the FTDA or the ACPA, any injunction requiring it to relinquish use of sportys.com is impermissibly retroactive. We find Sporty's Farm's position to be meritless. * * *

CONCLUSION

The judgment of the district court is AFFIRMED in all particulars.

Alitalia–Linee Aeree Italiane S.p.A. v. Casinoalitalia.Com

128 F.Supp.2d 340 (E.D.Va.2001).

■ ELLIS, DISTRICT JUDGE.

In this trademark dispute, the plaintiff, an Italian airline, has sued both the foreign registrant of an allegedly infringing domain name *in personam* and the domain name itself *in rem*. At issue on plaintiff's summary judgment motion is whether, consistent with the Anticybersquatting Consumer Protection Act ("ACPA" or the "Act"), a mark owner may maintain *in personam* claims against a domain name registrant concurrently with an *in rem* claim against the domain name. Also presented is the related question whether the Virginia long-arm statute constitutionally reaches the foreign registrant.

I.

Plaintiff Alitalia–Linee Aeree Italiane S.p.A. ("Alitalia") is Italy's national airline and is in the business of providing air cargo service and passenger transportation between Italy and the United States, among other foreign countries. Alitalia is the owner of a United States Trademark Registration issued on March 21, 1995, for the mark "Alitalia." Alitalia's founders coined the term "Alitalia," which has been used by the airline since 1957, by combining the words "Ali," which in Italian means "wings," and "d'Italia," which means "Italian"; the term "Alitalia," therefore, literally means "Italian wings."

Since Alitalia began operation in 1957, the airline has made continuous and widespread use of the mark "Alitalia" through extensive advertising and other means by which the carrier promotes and sells its services. In this regard, Alitalia spends approximately $60 million per year in advertising and promoting the "Alitalia" logo and mark. In addition, Alitalia maintains a website for its airline business at <www.alitalia.it> and has registered the Internet domain names <www.alitalia.com> and <www.alitalia.net>. A search of the Internet for the word "alitalia," however, returns not only Alitalia's website, but also an Internet site using the domain name <casinoalitalia.com>, which has no affiliation or connection whatever to Alitalia.

Defendant Technologia JPR, Inc., ("JPR") has registered the domain name <casinoalitalia.com> with registrar Network Solutions, Inc., ("NSI"). JPR is an entity established under the laws of the Dominican Republic, and JPR's NSI registration information lists JPR's place of business (including administrative, technical, and billing contacts) as located in Santo Domingo, Dominican Republic. JPR conducts its business entirely outside of the United States, and the company has no offices or other physical presence in the United States; it neither owns nor leases property in the United States and has no employees in the United States. Alitalia claims that JPR registered the domain name on or about October 13, 1999, although it appears from NSI's registration information that JPR registered the domain name with NSI in August 1998.

It is evident from a visit to <casinoalitalia.com> that the website exists for the purpose of conducting the business of online casino gambling. A visitor to the website can play one or more online casino games—e.g., blackjack, poker, keno, slots, craps, and roulette—by opening an account with <casinoalitalia.com> and purchasing casino "credits" that may be used to play individual games. Players can then win credits that can be redeemed for U.S. currency. In this regard, the website appears to be an attempt to simulate the experience of gambling at a conventional "brick and mortar" casino.

A visit to the website also reveals that the term "Alitalia" appears on the first page. Given this, Alitalia, which has not given JPR permission to use the mark "Alitalia" or any variation thereof for any purpose, claims that the domain name <casinoalitalia.com> and JPR's unauthorized use of the term "alitalia" create a false impression that Alitalia promotes the business of online gambling and/or any other enterprise pursued by defendants. Indeed, Alitalia claims that the word "casino" means "brothel," so that a literal translation of "casinoalitalia" is "alitalia's brothel." Thus, argues Alitalia, the site appears in the minds of consumers familiar with the Italian language to offer the services of a brothel associated or affiliated with Alitalia. In this regard, plaintiff contends, the website <casinoalitalia.com> irreparably harms, tarnishes, and dilutes the goodwill, reputation, and image of the Alitalia mark.

In March of this year, Alitalia brought a four-count complaint stating claims for (i) trademark infringement, under 15 U.S.C. § 1114 *et seq.*, against JPR (Count I); (ii) violation of the Lanham Act, 15 U.S.C. §§ 1125(a), (c), against JPR (Count II); (iii) common law unfair competition against JPR (Count III); and (iv) violation of the ACPA against JPR and <casinoalitalia.com> (Count IV). Alitalia has moved for summary judgment on all four counts. In doing so, Alitalia argues, remarkably, that the ACPA entitles it to proceed concurrently both *in rem* and *in personam*. Whether this is so presents a threshold question that must be resolved before proceeding to resolve the remaining questions of personal jurisdiction and summary judgment. JPR has entered a limited appearance for the purpose of challenging personal jurisdiction.[4]

II.

The ACPA creates two avenues by which claimants may seek a remedy for "cyberpiracy." The first, found in § 1 of the ACPA, is a remedy for owners of a mark *in personam* against a person who, with "a bad faith intent to profit from that mark[,] . . . registers, traffics in, or uses a domain name" that:

> (I) in the case of a mark that is distinctive at the time of registration of the domain name, is identical or confusingly similar to that mark;
>
> (II) in the case of a famous mark that is famous at the time of registration of the domain name, is identical or confusingly similar to or dilutive of that mark; or
>
> (III) is a trademark, work, or name protected by reason of § 706 of Title 18 or § 220506 of Title 36.

---

4. See Caesars World, Inc. v. Caesars–Palace.Com, 112 F.Supp.2d 505, 509 (E.D.Va. 2000) (noting that "*in personam* jurisdiction cannot be based merely on an appearance in an *in rem* action"); Harrods Ltd. v. Sixty Internet Domain Names, 110 F.Supp.2d 420, 421–23 (E.D.Va.2000) (holding that "no personal jurisdiction over the owner of the res is acquired by bringing . . . [an *in rem*] action" under the ACPA, and a plaintiff "cannot pursue any cause of action with the potential to impose personal liability" simply by virtue of filing an ACPA *in rem* action).

15 U.S.C. § 1125(d)(1)(A). A plaintiff proceeding under § 1 has available a full panoply of legal and equitable remedies. Specifically, such a plaintiff may seek compensatory damages, including disgorgement of defendant's profits, or elect to recover, "instead of actual damages and profits, an award of statutory damages in the amount of not less than $1,000 and not more than $100,000 per domain name, as the court considers just." 15 U.S.C. § 1117(a) and (d).[5] In addition, a § 1 plaintiff may seek injunctive relief, including "the forfeiture or cancellation of the domain name or the transfer of the domain name to the owner of the mark." 15 U.S.C. § 1125(d)(1)(C); *see Sporty's Farm LLC v. Sportsman's Market, Inc.*, 202 F.3d 489, 500 (2d Cir.2000).

A mark owner's second avenue of relief is appropriately found in § 2 of the ACPA, which provides that, where a domain name infringes a federally registered trademark or violates any right of the mark's owner under the Lanham Act, "[t]he owner ... may file an *in rem* civil action against a domain name in the judicial district in which the domain name registrar, domain name registry, or other domain name authority that registered or assigned the domain name is located." 15 U.S.C. § 1125(d)(2)(A). But importantly, a mark owner may file an *in rem* cause of action only where the court finds that the owner of the mark either (i) "is not able to obtain *in personam* jurisdiction over a person who would have been a defendant in a civil action under [Section 1]" ("Option I") or (ii) "through due diligence was not able to find a person who would have been a defendant in a civil action under [Section 1]" ("Option II").[6] *Id.* § 1125(d)(2)(A)(i)–(ii).

Thus, the ACPA limits a court's *in rem* jurisdiction over a domain name on a finding that Option I or II exists.[7] And further, as a precondition to using Option II, a mark owner is required to exercise due diligence in attempting to find a suitable defendant. *See id.* § 1125(d). This attempt must include (i) "a notice of the alleged violation and intent to proceed [*in rem*] to the registrant of the domain name at the postal and e-mail address provided by the registrant to the registrar," and (ii) "publish[ed] notice of

5. The damages awarded may be "for any sum above the amount found as actual damages, not exceeding three times such amount." 15 U.S.C. § 1117(a).

6. For purposes of brevity, the term "suitable defendant" herein refers to Section 2's requirement that suit be brought against "a person who would have been a defendant in a civil action under [§ 1]"—i.e., a person who "registers, traffics in, or uses a domain name" in a way that violates the ACPA. 15 U.S.C. § 1125(d).

7. The ACPA strangely provides that the owner of a mark may "file" an *in rem* action if the court makes a finding that the requirements of either Option I or Option II are met. 15 U.S.C. § 1125(d)(2)(A). This language suggests, nonsensically, that such a

finding must precede the filing of the suit. It is evident, however, that a court cannot make such a finding *before* the *in rem* action is "filed," which ordinarily means the formality of filing a complaint with the Office of the Clerk and paying applicable filing fees. This is so because such a finding must occur within the confines of a controversy between real parties. * * * Thus, § 1125(d)(2)(A) must be interpreted to mean that a mark owner may *maintain* an *in rem* action against a domain name only if the court finds, after suit is filed, that the requirements of either Option I or Option II are met. *Cf.* Caesars World, 112 F.Supp.2d at 505 ("[T]o force plaintiff to prove its case before filing would stand the Act on its head.").

the [*in rem*] action as the court may direct promptly after filing." *Id.* § 1125(d)(2)(A)(ii)(II). Only if the owner complies with these requirements *and* nonetheless fails to find a suitable defendant who may be sued *in personam* may the owner maintain an *in rem* action against the domain name. And significantly, the relief afforded in an ACPA *in rem* action is limited to "a court order for the forfeiture or cancellation of the domain name or the transfer of the domain name to the owner of a mark." *Id.* § 1125(d)(2)(D)(i).

These provisions, given their plain meaning, compel the conclusion that the ACPA provides mark owners with two mutually exclusive avenues for relief against putative infringers. A mark owner may proceed either *in personam* against an infringer or, in certain circumstances where this cannot be done, the owner may proceed *in rem* against the domain name; a mark owner may not proceed against both at the same time.[9] This follows from the fact that the ACPA's plain language limits the use of *in rem* jurisdiction to two situations, labeled here as Options I and II, where there is no *in personam* jurisdiction over the domain name registrant. Option I allows a mark owner to proceed *in rem* only where the identity and location of the registrant or user of an infringing domain name are known, but *in personam* jurisdiction cannot be obtained over this entity. Option II deals with those situations where the registrant or user of the offending domain name cannot be found and thus simply adds that this jurisdiction may be resorted to only where an infringer cannot be identified or found. In other words, the ACPA provides for *in rem* jurisdiction against a domain name only in those circumstances where *in personam* jurisdiction is not available.[10]

Further confirmation for the conclusion that *in personam* and *in rem* jurisdictions under the ACPA are mutually exclusive is found in the different remedies available under each jurisdictional grant. Where there exists *in personam* jurisdiction over a putative infringer, a mark owner has available a full panoply of remedies, including damages and injunctive relief. *See* 15 U.S.C. § 1117(a), (d). Yet, the remedy available in the event a mark owner must proceed *in rem* is far more limited; it is restricted to the

---

9. Alitalia's argument to the contrary mistakenly relies on § 4 of the ACPA, which provides that "[t]he *in rem* jurisdiction established under [§ 2] shall be in addition to any other jurisdiction that otherwise exists, whether *in rem* or *in personam*." 15 U.S.C. § 1125(d)(4). * * * The better reading of § 4—one that harmonizes all of the ACPA's provisions and gives effect to the Act's animating purpose—is that the Section serves to facilitate § 2 Option II *in rem* relief by allowing a mark owner to maintain an *in rem* cause of action upon a showing that the owner through due diligence was not able to find a suitable defendant, but *in personam* jurisdiction over a suitable defendant might "oth-

erwise exist" were such a defendant identified and found. Thus, for example, § 4 would prevent a previously unidentified suitable defendant from attacking collaterally an *in rem* proceeding by making a showing that *in personam* jurisdiction in fact existed, notwithstanding the mark owner's inability to find the defendant through due diligence. * * *

10. This result is consistent with the settled principle that *in rem* jurisdiction is an alternative basis for jurisdiction where *in personam* jurisdiction is not available. *See generally* 4 Charles A. Wright and Arthur R. Miller, Federal Practice and Procedure § 1070 (2d ed. 1987) * * *.

forfeiture or cancellation of the domain name or the domain name's transfer to the mark owner. *See id.* § 1125(d)(2)(D)(i).[11] Significantly, this *in rem* remedy is included in the broader set of remedies available to a plaintiff proceeding *in personam* against a putative infringer. *See id.* § 1125(d)(1)(C). In other words, where *in personam* jurisdiction exists, there is no need to proceed *in rem*, for the broader *in personam* remedies include the limited *in rem* remedy. It follows from this difference in available remedies that the *in rem* and *in personam* jurisdictional grants are exclusive and may not be simultaneously invoked or pursued by a mark owner. Indeed, to conclude otherwise would attribute a nonsensical purpose to the ACPA—namely, to provide duplicative and superfluous jurisdictional grants and remedies.

Yet another factor pointing to the exclusivity of *in rem* and *in personam* jurisdiction under the ACPA is the statutory requirement in Option I that the mark owner, as a condition to proceeding *in rem*, must bear the burden of demonstrating the absence of *in personam* jurisdiction over a suitable defendant. Unless the ACPA's *in rem* and *in personam* jurisdictional grants are mutually exclusive, a mark owner pursuing both simultaneously would then be in the odd, if not absurd, position of proving at once the presence and absence of *in personam* jurisdiction over the putative infringer. A mark owner simply cannot simultaneously establish both (i) that *in personam* jurisdiction over a suitable defendant cannot be obtained *and* (ii) that *in personam* jurisdiction over a putative infringer can be obtained.[13]

A hypothetical scenario helps illustrate the ACPA's operation in this regard. When a mark owner becomes aware of an infringing use, the owner's first step, typically, is to ascertain the infringer's identity and location by reference to information available from the infringing website or the pertinent domain name registrant. With this information in hand, the owner must then proceed to determine whether the circumstances of Option I or II exist. In this regard, if the owner determines that the putative infringer resides, does business, or is otherwise present in any judicial district in the United States,[14] then the inquiry is ended, and the

---

11. This limitation is consistent with the extraordinary nature of *in rem* relief, which adjudicates the rights of interested parties in the res *in absentia* and therefore may raise serious due process concerns in certain circumstances. See, e.g., Shaffer v. Heitner, 433 U.S. 186, 206–09, 97 S.Ct. 2569, 53 L.Ed.2d 683 (1977) (observing that "if a direct assertion of personal jurisdiction over the defendant would violate the Constitution, it would seem that an indirect assertion of that jurisdiction should be equally impermissible" and holding that the exercise of *in rem* jurisdiction must comply with the due process requirements elucidated in International

Shoe Co. v. Washington, 326 U.S. 310, 66 S.Ct. 154, 90 L.Ed. 95 (1945)) * * *.

13. In this regard, a mark owner may not simultaneously file an *in rem* cause of action and an *in personam* claim in the hope that one claim will survive the court's jurisdictional inquiry. Rather, a mark owner must choose prior to filing whether to proceed *in rem* against the domain name or *in personam* against a putative infringer. Of course, if a mark owner's first choice falters, the alternative may then be pursued by refiling or seeking to amend the complaint.

14. The ACPA does not explicitly answer the question whether a mark owner

owner, in these circumstances, must proceed *in personam* against the infringer and is precluded by the ACPA from proceeding *in rem* against the offending domain name. But Congress recognized that in many circumstances mark owners may obtain some identifying information concerning an infringer, but nonetheless may be unable to locate that entity or obtain jurisdiction over the infringer. Often these situations occur where the putative infringer is located in a foreign country and/or provided the domain name registrar with inaccurate or false identifying information. To accommodate these possibilities, Congress included § 2 of the ACPA, so that in these circumstances, an owner could still seek a remedy—albeit a more limited one—by proceeding *in rem* against the domain name itself. But, before allowing a mark owner to proceed in this extraordinary fashion, Congress required the owner to exercise due diligence in the search for the infringer. *See* 15 U.S.C. § 1125(d)(2)(A)(ii)(II).

Because the ACPA's *in rem* and *in personam* jurisdictional grants are mutually exclusive, Alitalia may not invoke and pursue both simultaneously. Either there is *in personam* jurisdiction over JPR, in which event the *in rem* count must be dismissed and JPR then afforded an opportunity to appear and contest Alitalia's summary judgment arguments, or there is no *in personam* jurisdiction over JPR,[17] in which event Alitalia may proceed only *in rem* against the domain name <casinoalitalia.com> and Alitalia will be entitled to summary judgment if the record discloses no triable issue of fact. Thus, the next step in the analysis is to address whether JPR is subject to jurisdiction in Virginia pursuant to the Commonwealth's long-arm statute. *See* Va.Code § 8.01–328.1. [In the remainder of the opinion the court concludes that JPR is subject to *in personam* jurisdiction in Virginia, and therefore Alitalia cannot maintain its ACPA *in rem* cause of action against *casinoalitalia.com*.]

Electronics Boutique Holdings Corp. v. Zuccarini

56 U.S.P.Q.2d (BNA) 1705 (E.D.Pa.2000).

■ SCHILLER.

Presently before the court is plaintiff Electronics Boutique Holding Corporation's action for Internet cybersquatting against defendant John

---

must disprove the existence of *in personam* jurisdiction over a suitable defendant in any judicial district in the United States or only in the forum where the domain name registrar is located. Although this question need not be answered here, * * * the likely answer is that the mark owner must show the absence of *in personam* jurisdiction in any judicial district in the United States. *See, e.g., Heathmount A.E. Corp. v. Technodome.com.,* 106 F.Supp.2d 860, 867 (E.D.Va.2000) ("There are two situations in which [Option I] comes into play: first, where the registrant of the domain name is not subject to personal jurisdiction *in any U.S. court* and, second, where a domain name registrant has trans-

ferred ownership of the domain name to another individual who is not subject to personal jurisdiction.") (emphasis added). * * *

17. In this regard, Alitalia bears the burden of disproving jurisdiction by a preponderance of the evidence. See Heathmount, 106 F.Supp.2d at 862–63 (holding that "[u]nder § 1125(d)(2), a plaintiff must 'disprove' the presence of personal jurisdiction in order to proceed in rem," and "bear[s] the burden to demonstrate some indicia of due diligence in trying to establish personal jurisdiction over an individual who has been identified as a potential defendant but is not subject to jurisdiction.").

Zuccarini. A hearing on the merits consolidated with a hearing on damages was held on October 10, 2000. For the reasons set forth below, I find in favor of plaintiff Electronics Boutique Holdings Corporation.

I. Procedural background

On August 10, 2000, plaintiff Electronics Boutique Holding Corporation ("EB") filed a complaint against defendant John Zuccarini ("Mr. Zuccarini"), individually and trading as Cupcake Patrol and/or Cupcake Party, alleging violations of the Anticybersquatting Consumer Protection Act of 1999, 15 U.S.C. § 1125(d) ("ACPA"), violations of § 43(a) of the Lanham Act, 15 U.S.C. § 1125(a), dilution, common law service mark infringement and unfair competition.

Also on August 10, 2000, I granted EB's motion for a temporary restraining order, enjoining the use of domain names "www.electronicbou-tique.com," "www.eletronicsboutique.com," "www.electronicbotique.com," "www.ebwold.com," "www.ebworl.com." (collectively "domain misspell-ings") or any other domain name or mark identical to or confusingly similar to EB's registered service marks until August 20, 2000, and directing Mr. Zuccarini to deactivate the domain misspellings and present the Court with evidence of the deactivations within three days of the Court's Order. Additionally, I scheduled a hearing on EB's motion for a preliminary injunction to take place on August 15, 2000.

On August 15, 2000, upon representations by EB that its attempts to effect service upon Mr. Zuccarini at his home, which is also his workplace, were unsuccessful, I granted EB's motion for alternative service, extension of the temporary restraining order, and continuance of the hearing on EB's motion for a preliminary injunction. I authorized EB to effect service through the United States Marshals' service. The hearing on EB's motion for preliminary injunction was continued until August 29, 2000.

Mr. Zuccarini failed to appear, through counsel or otherwise, for the August 29 hearing. On that date, I granted EB's motion for preliminary injunction based on its ACPA claims, finding that Mr. Zuccarini had actual notice of this matter and that the requirements for the issuance of a preliminary injunction had been satisfied. I scheduled a hearing on the merits of EB's ACPA claims for October 10, 2000.

Mr. Zuccarini failed to obtain counsel and refused to appear himself for the October 10, 2000, hearing.

II. Findings of Fact

At the October 10, 2000, hearing I found as follows: EB, a specialty retailer in video games and personal computer software, operates more than 600 retail stores, primarily in shopping malls, and also sells its products via the Internet. EB has registered several service marks on the principal register of the United States Patent and Trademark Office for goods and services of electric and computer products, including "EB" and

"Electronics Boutique." EB has applications for several other service marks on the principal register of the United States Patent and Trademark Office for goods and services of electric and computer products, including "ebworld.com." EB has continuously used its service marks in its business since 1977. They have appeared in print, trade literature, advertising, and on the Internet.

EB's online store can be accessed via the Internet at "www.ebworld.com" and "www.electronicsboutique.com." EB registered its "EB-World" domain name on December 19, 1996 and its "Electronics Boutique" domain name on December 30, 1997. EB has invested heavily in promoting its website to online customers. EB has expended a considerable amount of resources towards making its website consumer friendly. An easy-to-use website is critical to EB's ability to generate revenue directly through Internet customers and indirectly as support for EB's "brick and mortar" stores. Over the last eight months, online purchases have yielded an average of more than 1.1 million in sales per month and EB has logged more than 2.6 million online visitors.

On May 23, 2000, Mr. Zuccarini registered the domain names "www.electronicboutique.com," and "www.electronicbotique.com." One week later, Mr. Zuccarini registered the domain names "www.ebwold.com" and "www.ebworl.com." When a potential or existing online customer, attempting to access EB's website, mistakenly types one of Mr. Zuccarini's domain misspellings, he is "mousetrapped"[8] in a barrage of advertising windows, featuring a variety of products, including credit cards, internet answering machines, games, and music. The Internet user cannot exit the Internet without clicking on the succession of advertisements that appears. Simply clicking on the "X" in the top right-hand corner of the screen, a common way to close a web browser window, will not allow a user to exit. Mr. Zuccarini is paid between 10 and 25 cents by the advertisers for every click. Sometimes, after wading through as many as 15 windows, the Internet user could gain access to EB's website.

III.   Conclusions of law

A.   EB's request for a permanent injunction

* * *

[The court concludes that EB is entitled to a permanent injunction on its ACPA claim.]

* * *

B.   EB's request for statutory damages

Pursuant to 15 U.S.C. § 1117(d), a plaintiff seeking recovery under the ACPA may elect to recover statutory damages in lieu of actual damages and

---

8. The term "mousetrapped" was used by Judge Dalzell, United States District Judge for the Eastern District of Pennsylvania, to describe the situation an Internet user encounters upon accessing one of Mr. Zuccarini's domain names in a matter in which Mr. Zuccarini was sued by a different plaintiff for similar conduct. *See Shields v. Zuccarini*, 89 F.Supp.2d 634, 635 (E.D.Pa.2000).

profits. A court may award statutory damages in an amount between $1,000 and $100,000 per infringing domain name based on the court's determination of what is just. *See* 15 U.S.C. § 1117(d). EB has elected to recover statutory damages in this matter. The recovery of "statutory damages in cybersquatting cases, both [ ] deter[s] wrongful conduct and [ ] provide[s] adequate remedies for trademark owners who seek to enforce their rights in court." S.REP. No. 106–140 (1999).

I emphasize that the actual damages suffered by EB as a result of lost customers and goodwill is incalculable. In proceedings before this Court, Mr. Zuccarini admitted that he yields between $800,000 and $1,000,000 annually from the thousands of domain names that he has registered. *See Shields v. Zuccarini, No.00–494*, 2000 WL 1053884, at *1 (E.D.Pa. July 18, 2000). Advertisers pay Mr. Zuccarini between 10 and 25 cents each time an Internet user clicks on one of their ads posted on Mr. Zuccarini's websites. Many of the domain names registered by Mr. Zuccarini are misspellings of famous names and infringe on the marks of others. * * *

In addition, Mr. Zuccarini has victimized a wide variety of people and entities. This Court has permanently enjoined Mr. Zuccarini from using domain names that are "substantially similar" to the marks of another plaintiff, finding Mr. Zuccarini's "conduct utterly parasitic and in complete bad faith." *Shields v. Zuccarini*, No.00–494, 2000 WL 1056400, at *1 (E.D.Pa. June 5, 2000). Other cases alleging similar conduct have been brought against Mr. Zuccarini by Radio Shack, Office Depot, Nintendo, Hewlett–Packard, the Dave Matthews Band, *The Wall Street Journal*, *Encyclopedia Britannica*, the distributor of Guinness beers and Spiegel's catalog in various federal courts and arbitration fora. Demands regarding similar conduct have been made on Mr. Zuccarini by the Sports Authority, Calvin Klein, and Yahoo!. Mr. Zuccarini's conduct even interferes with the ability of the public to access health information by preying on hospitals and prescription drugs. *Shields v. Zuccarini*, No. 00–494, (E.D.Pa.) (admitting the registration of domain names containing misspellings of the Mayo Clinic and the weight loss drug Xenical).

I also note that Mr. Zuccarini's conduct is not easily deterred. *See Shields*, No. 00–494, 2000 WL 1053884, at *1 (E.D.Pa. July 18, 2000) (observing that Mr. Zuccarini failed to get the "crystalline message" of the Court in its March 22 Opinion and June 5 Order). Strikingly, Mr. Zuccarini registered the domain misspellings at issue in this matter after this Court preliminarily enjoined him from using misspellings of another individual's mark. *See Shields*, 89 F.Supp.2d at 642–43.

Furthermore, since this Court permanently enjoined Mr. Zuccarini from using other domain misspellings, assessed statutory damages in the amount of $10,000 per infringing domain name against him, and required him to bear the plaintiff's costs and attorneys' fees, Mr. Zuccarini has unexplainedly registered hundreds of domain names which are misspellings of famous people's names, famous brands, company names, television shows, and movies, victimizing, among others, the Survivor television show, Play Station and Carmageddon video game products, singers Kylie Minogue, Gwen Stefani and J.C. Chasez, *The National Enquirer,* and cartoon characters the Power Puff Girls. Mr. Zuccarini boldly thumbs his nose at the rulings of this court and the laws of our country. Therefore, I find that justice in this case requires that damages be assessed against Mr. Zuccarini in the amount of $100,000 per infringing domain name, for a total of $500,000.

C. Attorneys' fees and costs

EB has requested that it be awarded attorneys' fees and the costs of this litigation. The ACPA authorizes this Court to award "reasonable attorney fees to the prevailing party" in "exceptional cases." 15 U.S.C. § 1117(a). In determining whether a case is "exceptional" under § 1117(a), the Third Circuit has required "a finding of culpable conduct on the part of the losing party, such as bad faith fraud, or knowing infringement." *Ferrero U.S.A., Inc. v. Ozak Trading, Inc.*, 952 F.2d 44, 47 (3d Cir.1991). As described above, Mr. Zuccarini acted in complete bad faith by knowingly and intentionally trading on the goodwill and reputation of EB in an attempt to mislead the public. Therefore, I find that EB is entitled to attorney's fees.

* * *

I will award EB the full amount of its $30,653.34 request.

* * *

NOTES & QUESTIONS

1. *Typosquatting.* In *Electronics Boutique Holdings Corp. v. Zuccarini*, the defendant engaged in what has become known as typosquatting. A typosquatter identifies common spelling, typing and keyboarding errors that people make when entering a well-known URL into the address bar of a web browser. The typosquatter then registers these variations on the domain name in order to increase traffic to his or her own website or sell the variations to the owner of the domain name from which the variations were derived.

Typosquatting has an analogy in the brick-and-mortar world. In *Holiday Inns, Inc. v. 800 Reservation, Inc.*, 86 F.3d 619 (6th Cir.1996), the court had to determine whether it was a violation of Sections 32 or 43(a) of the Lanham Act, 15 U.S.C. §§ 1114 and 1125(a), for the defendant to use a telephone number that it had derived as a common dialing error from a competitor's vanity number:

> Holiday Inns, Inc., filed this Lanham Act suit against the defendants, alleging unfair competition and infringement of its trademark telephone number, 1–800–HOLIDAY, known as a "vanity number." The defendants, Call Management Systems, Inc. (a consulting firm that obtains and services 1–800 telephone numbers for businesses), 800 Reservations, Inc. (an agency that makes reservations for a number of hotel chains, including Holiday Inns), and Earthwinds Travel, Inc. (a travel agency) had secured the use

and were engaged in using a telephone number that potential Holiday Inns customers frequently dial by mistake when they unintentionally substitute the number zero for the letter "O." That number, 1–800–405–4329, corresponds to the alphanumeric 1–800–H[zero]LIDAY, known in the trade as a "complementary number." It is referred to in this opinion as "the 405 number" to distinguish it from the Holiday Inns numeric, 1–800–465–4329. The district court, although noting that the defendants were violating only the "spirit" and not the "letter" of the Lanham Act, nevertheless granted Holiday Inns partial summary judgment and permanently enjoined 800 Reservations and Call Management from using the 405 number. * * * For the reasons stated below, we conclude that the defendants' use of the 405 number did not violate the Lanham Act * * *

> * * *

The plain language of § 32 of the Lanham Act forbids only the "*use* in commerce [of] any reproduction, counterfeit, copy, or colorable imitation of a registered mark . . . which . . . is likely *to cause* confusion." 15 U.S.C. § 1114 (emphasis added). Additionally, § 43(a) of the Act provides a cause of action only against "[a] person who . . . *uses* in commerce any word, term, name, symbol, or device . . . or any false designation of origin, false or misleading description of fact, or false or misleading representation of fact. . . ." 15 U.S.C. § 1125(a) (emphasis added). The defendants in this case never *used* Holiday Inns's trademark nor any facsimile of Holiday Inns's marks.

Moreover, the defendants did not *create* any confusion; the confusion already existed among the misdialing public. * * *

Should the Sixth Circuit's reasoning apply to typosquatting, and if so did the court in *Electronics Boutique* reach the wrong outcome? Does it matter that in *Electronics Boutique* the court was applying the ACPA, rather than the trademark infringement provisions of the Lanham Act? Is the court's comment in *Sporty's Farm, L.L.C. v. Sportsman's Market, supra,* at n.26, "that 'confusingly similar' [under the ACPA] is a different standard from the 'likelihood of confusion' standard for trademark infringement" relevant to your answer?

2. *A pure heart and empty head defense?* The ACPA, 15 U.S.C. § 1125(d)(1)(B)(ii), states that "[b]ad faith intent described under subparagraph (A) shall not be found in any case in which the court determines that the person believed and had reasonable grounds to believe that the use of the domain name was a fair use or otherwise lawful." One commentator has remarked:

> This might be dubbed the "pure heart and empty head defense" because it might appear to reward the cybersquatter who intended no harm and mistakenly thought that his or her conduct was lawful. This defense has the potential to reward both ignorance of

the law and unawareness of the fact that cybersquatting violates widely accepted standards of fair competition. Therefore, a court should, in the author's view, make use of this "reasonable belief" defense very sparingly and only in the most unusual cases. * * * Otherwise, every cybersquatter [will] solemnly aver that it [is] entitled to this defense because it believed that its conduct was lawful.

4 J. THOMAS MCCARTHY, MCCARTHY ON TRADEMARKS AND UNFAIR COMPETITION § 25:78 (4th ed.2002). Is there any way that a court might avoid this absolute ignorance-of-the-law defense and thus avoid the perverse incentives and consequences that concern Professor McCarthy? Does a cybersquatter have any duty to inquire? Should a person who is willfully blind or who deliberately fails to inquire, knowing what the answer is likely to be, avoid liability? *See, e.g., Louis Vuitton S.A. v. Lee,* 875 F.2d 584 (7th Cir.1989) (for purposes of civil damages under 15 U.S.C. § 1117(b), it is sufficient that a retailer "failed to inquire further because he was afraid of what the inquiry would yield"). On the other hand, does the statute invite courts to infer bad faith from the mere fact that the court feels that the particular conduct was unfair competition? Is this standard too loose to protect people who might have competing claims that are arguably legitimate, even if distasteful to the trademark owner?

3. *Partial bad faith.* Much human behavior is the result of mixed motives. While one motive for a particular action may be good and legitimate, another may be less laudable. A central element for liability under the ACPA is that the person have "a bad faith intent to profit from the mark." 15 U.S.C. § 1125(d)(1)(A)(i). How should the courts decide a case in which a person acts partly in good faith? In such a case the domain name registrant may have a good-faith legitimate claim to the domain name, but still realize that it might have value to another. Just this situation was presented in *Virtual Works, Inc. v. Volkswagen of America, Inc.,* 238 F.3d 264 (4th Cir.2001). In this case, the court noted that "Virtual Works chose *vw.net* over other domain names not just because 'vw' reflected the company's own initials, but also because it foresaw the ability to profit from the natural association of *vw.net* with the VW mark." 238 F.3d at 269–70.

4. *Limitations on liability.* The ACPA limits the liability of domain name registrars and registries. *See* 15 U.S.C. §§ 1114(2)(D)(iii) & 1125(d)(2)(D)(ii). One commentator has criticized this feature of the Act:

These limitations on liability, while encouraging the resolution of domain name disputes out of court, effectively transfer the burden upon the domain name holder to prove non-infringement. This presents a real danger due to the reality that the trademark holder is likely to have resources that far exceed the owner of the domain name being challenged. In addition, these provisions encourage domain name registries to cancel registrations upon presentation of evidence of any trademark that is identical to, confusingly similar to, or dilutive of a registered domain name. Since the act leaves the determination of this complicated legal question to the registrars themselves and protects them from liability for incorrect decisions, there is little incentive for a registry to deny a request to cancel from a trademark holder. The domain name registrant may not have registered the trademark, but may be conducting a legitimate commercial non-infringing use or could raise a recognized fair use defense that is disapproved of by the mark owner. Under the new system, the domain name holder would likely find his domain registration cancelled.

Gregory B. Blasbalg, Note, *Master of Their Domains: Trademark Holders Now Have New Ways to Control Their Marks in Cyberspace*, 5 ROGER WILLIAMS U.L. REV. 563, 579–80 (2000). Do you agree with the author that the ACPA encourages domain name registrars and registries to be overly deferential to trademark holders?

5. Lockheed Martin v. NSI *reprise*. Soon after the passage of the ACPA, Lockheed Martin decided to take another bite at the apple and brought suit against Network Solutions under the ACPA. Lockheed argued that defendant violated the Act by "registering, maintaining, or trafficking in ten specific domain names that allegedly infringe its LOCKHEED MARTIN and SKUNK WORKS marks." *Lockheed Martin Corp. v. Network Solutions, Inc.*, 141 F.Supp.2d 648, 654 (N.D.Tex.2001). The court held, that the word "registers" in 15 U.S.C. § 1125(d)(1)(A) "obviously refers to a person who presents a domain name for registration, not to the registrar." *Id.* The court also noted that liability for using a domain name within the meaning of 15 U.S.C. § 1125(d)(1)(A) is limited by § 1125(d)(1)(D) to "the domain name registrant or that registrant's authorized licensee." With respect to bad-faith intent, the court wrote that "[a]lthough the list [of factors under § 1125(d)(1)(B)(i)(I)–(IX) for determining bad-faith intent] is not exclusive, none of the conditions and conduct listed would be applicable to a person functioning solely as a registrar or registry of domain names." *Id.* On the basis of this analysis, the court granted summary judgment for NSI.

6. *Dilution by linking*. Imagine that an individual registers a domain name in violation of the ACPA. If I use that domain name to create a hyperlink to that person's website, am I also liable for using a domain name that is identical or confusingly similar to or dilutive of another's trademark under 15 U.S.C. § 1125(d)(1)(A)? What if I am aware that the domain name was unlawfully registered? What about individuals who operate a search engine or other directory service on the Internet: are they liable if they index a website under such a domain name?

7. *Minimum contacts and in rem jurisdiction*. In one of the first *in rem* actions brought under the ACPA, *Caesars World, Inc. v. Caesars-Palace.Com*, 112 F.Supp.2d 502 (E.D.Va.2000), the defendant challenged the constitutionality of 15 U.S.C. § 1125(d)(2) under the Due Process Clause of the United States Constitution. In this case, the court noted:

> The question before this court, therefore, is whether *in rem* jurisdiction over defendants who are not subject to the personal jurisdiction of this court, or any other, meets the due process standards under the Constitution.

In this regard, defendant Casares.com argues that under *Shaffer v. Heitner*, 433 U.S. 186 (1977), *in rem* jurisdiction is only constitutional in those circumstances where the res provides minimum contacts sufficient for *in personam* jurisdiction. The court rejects this argument, and concludes that under *Shaffer*, there must be minimum contacts to support personal jurisdiction only in those *in rem* proceedings where the underlying cause of action is unrelated to the property which is located in the forum state. Here the property, that is, the domain name, is not only related to the cause of action but is its entire subject matter. Accordingly, it is unnecessary for minimum contacts to meet personal jurisdiction standards.

To the extent that minimum contacts are required for *in rem* jurisdiction under *Shaffer*, moreover, the fact of domain name registration with Network Solutions, Inc., in Virginia supplies that. Given the limited relief afforded by the Act, namely "the forfeiture or cancellation of the domain name or the transfer of the domain name to the owner of the mark," no due process violation occurs here as to defendants personally. 15 U.S.C. § 1125(d)(2)(D). The court considers the enactment of the Anticybersquatting Consumer Protection Act a classic case of the distinction between *in rem* jurisdiction and *in personam* jurisdiction and a proper and constitutional use of *in rem* jurisdiction.

Caesars World, Inc. v. Caesars-Palace.Com, 112 F.Supp.2d at 504.

8. *General appearance.* If the owner of an offending domain name makes a general appearance to defend that domain name in an *in rem* action brought under 15 U.S.C. § 1125(d)(2), does that owner become subject to the *in personam* jurisdiction of the court? *See Caesars World, Inc. v. Caesars-Palace.Com*, 112 F.Supp.2d 505 (E.D.Va.2000) ("We have recently addressed that issue and determined that *in personam* jurisdiction cannot be based merely on an appearance in an *in rem* action.").

9. *Notice.* Often in an *in rem* action where the owner of the *res* is not known or cannot be found, notice of the action is effected by publication in newspapers for a certain period of time. Under 15 U.S.C. § 1125(d)(2)(B), notice and service of process is accomplished by

> (aa) sending a notice of the alleged violation and intent to proceed under this paragraph to the registrant of the domain name at the postal and e-mail address provided by the registrant to the registrar; and

> (bb) publishing notice of the action as the court may direct promptly after filing the action.

15 U.S.C. § 1125(d)(2)(A)(ii)(II)(aa) and (bb). If a plaintiff can confirm that the registrant received actual notice once the plaintiff sent a letter to the registrant's postal and e-mail address, may the court waive the requirement of publication under 15 U.S.C. § 1125(d)(2)(B) and (A)(ii)(II)(bb)? *See*

Banco Inverlat, S.A. v. www.inverlat.com, 112 F.Supp.2d 521 (E.D.Va. 2000).

10. *Waiting period under the ACPA.* Before filing an *in rem* action under the ACPA, the trademark owner must proceed in a manner that will permit the court to find that the owner

> (I) is not able to obtain in personam jurisdiction over a person who would have been a defendant in a civil action under paragraph (1); or

> (II) through due diligence was not able to find a person who would have been a defendant in a civil action under paragraph (1).

15 U.S.C. § 1125(d)(2)(A)(ii). Section 1125(d)(2)(A)(ii)(II)(aa) requires that due diligence include "sending a notice of the alleged violation and intent to proceed under this paragraph to the registrant of the domain name at the postal and e-mail address provided by the registrant to the registrar." These provisions raise the question of how long a trademark owner must wait after sending the required notice before filing an *in rem* action in federal court. The ACPA is silent on this question. In *Lucent Technologies, Inc. v. Lucentsucks.com*, 95 F.Supp.2d 528 (E.D.Va.2000), the plaintiff waited only 8 days. The owner of the domain name moved to dismiss on the ground that the plaintiff had failed to exercise due diligence. In resolving this issue the court wrote:

> Where Congress has specified a waiting period by statute in situations analogous to the ACPA *in rem* provision, ten days is the shortest amount of time specified. Perhaps the statutory provision most analogous to the provision at issue is Rule C of the Federal Rules of Civil Procedure, which allows an *in rem* action "to enforce any maritime lien" or whenever a federal statute provides for "a maritime action in rem or a proceeding analogous thereto." Fed. R.Civ.P. C(1). The rule permits the claimant of property that is subject to an *in rem* action 10 days after the rem has been seized to file a claim and 20 days after that to serve an answer. Fed. R.Civ.P. C(6). In the standard *in personam* action, Rule 12 of the Federal Rules of Civil Procedure allows 20 days after service of process to file an answer. Fed.R.Civ.P. 12(a)(1)(A).

> Neither Rule C nor Rule 12 are directly on point. In our case, we are considering what notice is required before an *in rem* action is instituted, and how long a plaintiff must wait to file an *in rem* action after sending notice by mail and e-mail, which may or may not reach the addressee. In contrast, Rule C specifies the waiting period *after* an *in rem* action is instituted, and Rule 12 specifies a waiting period after service of process is complete, that is, after actual notice has occurred. Nevertheless, taken together, these rules strongly suggest that Congress would not consider eight days to be a sufficient waiting period after mailing notice of a potential *in rem* action to a person who may be affected by that action.

Lucent Technologies, Inc. v. Lucentsucks.com, 95 F.Supp.2d at 533–34. Based on the discussion in *Lucent Technologies*, what is a reasonable waiting period?

11. *Bad-faith intent and in rem actions under the ACPA.* The ACPA envisions two situations in which an *in rem* action would be appropriate. The first, described in 15 U.S.C. § 1125(d)(2)(A)(ii)(I), is a situation in which the trademark owner knows the identity of the offending domain name registrant but the federal courts cannot obtain *in personam* jurisdiction over her. The second, described in 15 U.S.C. § 1125(d)(2)(A)(ii)(II), is a situation in which the identity of the offending domain name registrant is unknown. In *BroadBridge Media, L.L.C. v. Hypercd.com,* 106 F.Supp.2d 505 (S.D.N.Y.2000), a case of the first kind in which the offending domain name registrant was known, but the court could not exercise *in personam* jurisdiction over that registrant, the trademark owner questioned whether proof of the registrant's bad faith intent was necessary in an *in rem* action under the ACPA. The court said that it understood plaintiff's argument that it need not show bad faith, but concluded that

> bad faith intent to profit is a necessary element. * * * Congress clearly intended to use the bad faith element of the statute as a way to narrow the breadth of the statute. "The bill is carefully and narrowly tailored, however, to extend only to cases where the plaintiff can demonstrate the defendant ... *used* the offending domain name with bad-faith intent to profit from the goodwill of a mark belonging to someone else. Thus, the bill does not extend to innocent domain name registrations by ... someone who is aware of the trademark status of the name but registers a domain name containing the mark for any reason other than with bad faith intent to profit from the goodwill associated with that mark." H.R. Conf. Rep. 106–412 (emphasis added); *see also Northern Light Technology, Inc. v. Northern Lights Club,* 97 F.Supp.2d 96 (D.Mass.2000). Reflecting this intent, Congress limited the in rem action against a domain name to those situations where the court finds the owner is unable "to obtain in personam jurisdiction over a the person *who would have been a defendant under paragraph (1)."* 15 U.S.C. § 1125(d)(2)(A)(i)(I) (emphasis added). To be brought in as a defendant under paragraph (1) requires, in addition to other elements, a bad faith intent to profit.

Query how one would demonstrate bad faith where the registrant is unknown. Commenting on this problem, one commentator has noted that sometimes

> an in rem procedure is needed precisely because the domain name holder cannot be located. The holder usually cannot be located precisely because little or nothing is known about that person. In that event, it may be very difficult for the plaintiff to have any evidence of bad faith. Even negative evidence may be unavailable, such as the lack of the domain name registrant's IP rights in the name. It is improbable that the trademark owner can find evidence

of bad faith of a domain name owner who cannot be personally served because he or she gave a fictitious name, a non-existent address and inaccurate contact information. In such a case, the courts should interpret the "bad faith" requirement with considerable leniency and flexibility, or else the usefulness of the in rem procedure will be curtailed.

4 J. THOMAS MCCARTHY, MCCARTHY ON TRADEMARKS AND UNFAIR COMPETITION § 25:79 (4th ed.2002).

The statute provides for notice to the registrant by publication rather than by actual notice; does this lenient standard establishing who may be a defendant in an *in rem* action conflict with a narrow legal rule concluding that such defendants may not be liable absent specific proof of their bad faith?

12. *Personal names.* Section 2(b) of the ACPA, codified as 15 U.S.C. § 1129, provides protection against the registration of non-trademarked personal names by cybersquatters. It reads:

(1) In general

    (A) Civil liability. Any person who registers a domain name that consists of the name of another living person, or a name substantially and confusingly similar thereto, without that person's consent, with the specific intent to profit from such name by selling the domain name for financial gain to that person or any third party, shall be liable in a civil action by such person.

    (B) Exception. A person who in good faith registers a domain name consisting of the name of another living person, or a name substantially and confusingly similar thereto, shall not be liable under this paragraph if such name is used in, affiliated with, or related to a work of authorship protected under title 17 [the Copyright Act] including a work made for hire as defined in § 101 of title 17, and if the person registering the domain name is the copyright owner or licensee of the work, the person intends to sell the domain name in conjunction with the lawful exploitation of the work, and such registration is not prohibited by a contract between the registrant and the named person. The exception under this subparagraph shall apply only to a civil action brought under paragraph (1) and shall in no manner limit the protections afforded under the Trademark Act of 1946 (15 U.S.C. §§ 1051 et seq.) or other provision of Federal or State law.

(2) Remedies. In any civil action brought under paragraph (1), a court may award injunctive relief, including the forfeiture or cancellation of the domain name or the transfer of the domain

name to the plaintiff. The court may also, in its discretion, award costs and attorneys fees to the prevailing party.

* * *

Is the protection afforded non-trademarked personal names as broad as the protection granted trademarks under 15 U.S.C. § 1125(d)? Is the intent requirement under 15 U.S.C. § 1129(1)(A) the same as the intent requirement under 15 U.S.C. § 1125(d)(1)(A)(i)? Are all names covered? In particular, would nicknames, stage names, and pen names be covered under 15 U.S.C. § 1129(1)(A)? Are the remedies available under 15 U.S.C. § 1129(C) the same as those available for violations under 15 U.S.C. § 1125(d)(1)? Can you describe a scenario that would fall within the exception described in 15 U.S.C. § 1129(1)(B)?

13. *The ACPA and metatags.* In *Bihari v. Gross,* 119 F.Supp.2d 309 (S.D.N.Y.2000), the court held that the ACPA does not apply to the use of another's trademark as a keyword in metatags. This result is consistent with Senate Rep. 106–140, which states that the ACPA is inapplicable to "such things as screen names, file names, and other identifiers not assigned by a domain name registrar or registry, which have little to do with cybersquatting in practice."

III. NONJUDICIAL DISPUTE RESOLUTION AND ICANN'S UNIFORM DOMAIN NAME DISPUTE RESOLUTION POLICY

To avoid becoming embroiled in disputes between trademark owners and domain name registrants—which often take the form of costly court proceedings—domain name registrars have adopted dispute resolution policies and procedures. The first domain name registrar to adopt a dispute resolution policy was Network Solutions, Inc. ("NSI"), until recently the sole registrar for the .com, .net and .org top-level domains.[4] Under this policy, NSI would suspend the use of any disputed domain name if the complaining party could prove that it had a trademark registration in any country in the world for a mark identical to the disputed domain name. Thus, a complaining party could register a mark in Tunisia, a country in which marks are granted by registration only, and render someone else's domain name inoperative. Once a domain name was put "on hold," it was no longer available for use by anyone and its status could only be altered by order of a court of competent jurisdiction stating which party was entitled to use the disputed domain name. The NSI policy satisfied no one. Domain name registrants complained that NSI improperly suspended use of a domain name before a court had an opportunity to determine whether use of that domain name infringed a trademark of the complaining party. Owners of registered trademarks complained that the NSI policy did not prevent the use of domain names that were confusingly similar, but not

4. NSI adopted its first dispute resolution policy in 1995. This policy was followed by a series of revisions of which the last was NSI Policy Revision 03, effective February 25, 1998. Beginning in 1999, the successor regime under ICANN was put in place.

identical, to their trademarks. Finally, owners of unregistered, common law or state trademarks complained that the NSI policy did not recognize their trademark rights at all. General dissatisfaction with the NSI policy in large measure fueled the process that led to the creation of ICANN and the requirement that all ICANN-accredited domain name registrars adopt its Uniform Domain Name Dispute Resolution Policy ("UDRP").[5]

Like the predecessor NSI policy, the UDRP is intended to prevent ICANN as well as its approved registrars from becoming embroiled in disputes surrounding domain names. As Section 6 of the UDRP states unequivocally, a domain name registrar "will not participate in any way in any dispute between you and any party * * * regarding the registration and use of your domain name." That same section also provides that the domain name registrant "shall not name [the domain name registrar] as a party or otherwise include [it] in any such proceeding." To reduce the need for resort to the courts, the UDRP sets up a streamlined alternative dispute resolution process. Through this process, a trademark owner can challenge a domain name registrant's right to use a disputed domain name before an ICANN-approved administrative panel.

Under the rules of procedure governing UDRP proceedings,[6] the administrative panel must render a written decision concerning this challenge within approximately forty-five days of the commencement of the proceeding. Consistent with the streamlined character of the process, a panel's decision is usually based upon a single submission by each of the parties and neither party is given the opportunity for discovery. If the complaining party is successful and no other litigation is pending, then ten business days after receiving the decision, the domain name registrar will either cancel or transfer the disputed domain name registration in accordance with the panel's decision. If, however, the domain name registrant brings an action in a court of competent jurisdiction before the end of this ten-day period, then the domain name registrar will continue the status quo until a final judgment is obtained. *See* UDRP §§ 3, 4(i) and (k), and 8.

While the UDRP has been the target of considerable criticism, it is nonetheless considered a significant advance over the NSI policy for at least four reasons. First, under the UDRP the use of disputed domain names is no longer suspended. A domain name registrant may continue to use his or her domain name while the complaining party's rights in the domain name are being determined before an ICANN-approved arbitration panel or a court of competent jurisdiction. *See* UDRP § 7. Second, the UDRP permits trademark owners to challenge the use of domain names that are confusingly similar to their trademarks. It is worth noting that while the UDRP expands the grounds upon which a trademark owner may challenge the use of a domain name, unlike the Anticybersquatting Consumer Protection Act, the UDRP does not permit a trademark owner to challenge the use of a

---

5. *See* Uniform Domain Name Dispute Resolution Policy (adopted Oct. 24, 1999), www.icann.org/dndr/udrp/policy.htm.

6. *See* Rules for Uniform Domain Name Dispute Resolution Policy (adopted Oct. 24, 1999), www.icann.org/udrp/udrp-rulesoct99.htm.

domain name because it is dilutive of his or her famous trademark. *Compare* UDRP § 4(a)(i) *with* 15 U.S.C. § 1125(d)(1)(A)(ii)(II). Third, the UDRP applies not only to nationally registered trademarks but also to state and common law trademarks. Fourth, and most significantly, proceedings under the UDRP are limited to domain name disputes in which the disputed domain name "has been registered and is being used in bad faith." UDRP § 4(a)(iii). The UDRP is specifically targeted at cybersquatting. It does not apply if the domain name registrant has registered the disputed domain name in good faith. Examples of good faith registration would include those made in connection with a bona fide offering of goods or services, registration of a name by which the domain name registrant has been commonly known, as well as the registration of another's trademark so long as the domain name registrant is making a legitimate noncommercial or fair use of that mark. *See* UDRP § 4(c).

In the remainder of this Part, we focus on the general structure of the dispute resolution process created by the UDRP and how the UDRP has been interpreted by both administrative panelists and the federal courts. In particular, the first excerpt looks at whether the UDRP implements a dispute resolution framework that is conducive to the impartial resolution of disputes between trademark owners and domain name registrants and to the development of a consistent domain name jurisprudence. Next is a decision by an administrative panel that considers, among other things, the status of foreign trademarks rights under the UDRP. Finally, we consider one federal district court's view of the significance of an administrative panel's decision under the UDRP for related federal litigation involving the disputed domain name.

Laurence R. Helfer & Graeme B. Dinwoodie, *Designing Non–National Systems: The Case of the Uniform Domain Name Dispute Resolution Policy*

43 WM. & MARY L. REV. 141 (2001).

* * *

In practice as well as in construction, the UDRP has proven to be a remarkable development in the history of international dispute settlement. Even had trademark owners filed only a handful of complaints with panels and even had those complaints concerned only core domain-name abuses, the system would be worthy of serious scrutiny. But precisely the opposite trend has occurred.

In the first twenty-one months of the UDRP's existence, panels operating under the auspices of ICANN-approved dispute settlement providers have been inundated with cases. As of September 2001, filed complaints numbered over 4300. UDRP panels have issued over 3500 published decisions, with more than three-quarters of these decisions ordering domain names transferred to the complaining trademark owners. Although domain name registrants have achieved a few sporadic (but important) victories during the last few months, beginning in the earliest days of the UDRP panels interpreted the Policy and Rules expansively in ways that generally favored intellectual property owners over domain name registrants. These rulings occurred notwithstanding the clear intent of the UDRP drafters to limit the panels' authority to core cases of domain-name abuse, and at a time when both ICANN and WIPO were considering their own expansion of the UDRP to new gTLDs and existing country code domain names (ccTLDs) as well as to names and identifiers not covered by the present Policy. * * *

[T]he UDRP is composed of elements found in judicial, arbitral, and ministerial decision-making systems. * * * Within any single judicial, arbitral, or ministerial decision-making system, a variety of checking mechanisms constrain the power of decision makers. As a working typology, we divide these mechanisms into three distinct categories, which we refer to as creational, external, and internal checking functions. These checking mechanisms serve several important objectives. They bolster the legitimacy of decision-making outcomes and the accountability of decision makers, they confine decision making within the bounds of a system's institutional capacity, they correct errors, and they ensure consistent outcomes in factually and legally comparable cases.

When elements from different decision-making systems are combined, however, the checking mechanisms that operate in any one system cannot automatically be imported into the new hybrid system. In the case of the UDRP, checking devices found in one or another of the adjudicatory, arbitral, and ministerial models are insufficient in themselves to constrain UDRP panel decision making; oftentimes, they are simply inappropriate. Moreover, ambiguities and contradictions as to the source and content of the UDRP's checking functions send conflicting messages to panels and create incentives for them to act in ways the UDRP's drafters did not intend. * * *

The success of arbitration—its speed, its decision making tailored more closely to parties' intent than to default principles of law, and its finality ensured by less intrusive external review by courts—is premised upon two important characteristics not present here. First, the parties in arbitration have consented to these reduced forms of external checks, and second, the decision of the arbitrator affects only the parties and has limited if any value in articulating broader norms or rules. Neither the parties (by virtue of their consent) nor society (because the arbitration affects only the disputants) can therefore object to the truncated external checking mechanisms that are found in the arbitral model.

By contrast, parties to non-national UDRP proceedings are strangers and have not, other than formally, consented to the arbitral procedures thereunder, and the process by which the UDRP was created cannot serve as a genuine proxy for their consent. And if UDRP decision making is to effect the creation of norms, as we (and the proponents of the UDRP) intend and as the publication of decisions makes inevitable, then some of the control features found in a traditional adjudicatory model must be incorporated.

This does not mean that we should simply adopt an adjudicatory template, however. Courts remain predominantly national in nature, and court proceedings remain slow and expensive. So the wholesale adoption of the adjudicatory model is not attractive as a solution to a non-national problem. Instead, only selective incorporation of some of the checking features of that model is advisable.

Adoption of adjudicatory features, of course, will slow down the decision-making process, and thus, one might wish to reinject speed. Here, the ministerial model has a role to play. Ministerial decision making has the advantage of speed but it is restricted to cases where the application of the relevant rules is routinized. Much of the non-national decision making that occurs in the UDRP is not so routine. Consequently, although we might wish to incorporate aspects of the ministerial model, we cannot rely wholly on it as an antecedent because the functions it delegates to decision makers assume a far less discretionary form of decision making than we contemplate here. It would appear then that the non-national model could benefit from some—but not all—aspects of this pre-existing model. * * *

[M]uch of the UDRP was built in part upon an arbitral model of decision making. The resolution of disputes between private parties pursuant to what are nominally contractual obligations; the use of lawyers, academics, and retired judges as decision makers; the creation of multiple, independent dispute settlement centers; and the role of the parties in choosing the panel all reflect arbitral antecedents. * * *

When viewed in the aggregate, the most important constraints on arbitral decision makers are ex ante creational checks rather than ex post external or internal checks. The parties' ultimate control over an arbitrator's power flows from their virtually unfettered right to choose the substantive and procedural rules according to which the arbitral panel will decide their dispute. For this reason, negotiating the terms of the agreement to arbitrate is perhaps the most effective means of preserving accountability, preventing errors and controlling excesses of arbitral power. * * *

Consider the implications of this balance of arbitral checking functions for the UDRP. By imposing uniform, mandatory dispute settlement rules upon all domain-name registrants, ICANN eliminated the ability of registrants to opt out of UDRP dispute settlement proceedings or to tailor the system to their needs. When an individual registers a domain name with any registrar of names in the three unrestricted generic top level domains anywhere in the world, she confronts a non-negotiable contract of adhesion. She cannot specify the subject matter of the disputes upon which the panel is empowered to rule or the procedures that it will follow, and she has (consistent with the inapt analogy to arbitral models) only limited control (via her selection of registrar, and hence the courts of mutual jurisdiction from which to seek redress) over the mechanisms by which panel excesses or errors may be challenged or reviewed.

In effect, all of the key substantive and procedural terms of the UDRP "arbitration" agreement are prenegotiated by ICANN, which merely heightens the importance of the content of the UDRP's two foundational documents and the legitimacy of the process by which they were drafted. If these foundational documents fairly balance the substantive interests of trademark owners and domain-name registrants and if they contain equivalent procedural rights for both parties, then using ICANN as a proxy for individualized negotiation of a dispute settlement agreement may well be an acceptable and efficient alternative. If, by contrast, these foundational documents are substantively or procedurally skewed, or if the process by which they were created is open to challenge on legitimacy and accountability grounds, then the arbitral "bargain" struck by ICANN is itself called into question and a decisive check on the authority of UDRP panels has been cast into doubt. * * *

These concerns over the UDRP's creational checking functions are further exacerbated by the fact that external checks are even more attenuated in the UDRP context than they are for international arbitration, both with respect to institutional controls and controls by national courts. Consider first the external checks imposed by the four dispute settlement providers and ICANN itself. Under many systems of institutional arbitration * * * arbitral centers retain the authority to enforce each panelist's obligation to be both independent and impartial, first by requiring panelists to disclose any circumstances giving rise to doubts over those two attributes, and second by entertaining challenges from the parties to a particular panelist.

The system of neutrality enforcement contemplated under the UDRP is substantially more attenuated. Although the UDRP Rules do impose a duty on all panelists to be impartial and independent, the means by which that duty is enforced differ according to dispute settlement provider and thus vary from case to case. One provider gives no specific provision for party challenges; another allows challenges only within a fixed period of time after the initial appointment of a panelist; whereas a third (and perhaps a fourth) permits challenges at any time during the proceedings if doubts about a particular panelist arise. In addition, the grounds upon which challenges will be recognized vary widely. The fact that ICANN permits dispute settlement providers to adopt different standards of review of a panelist's independence and impartiality suggests that providers may compete with one another over the substantive and procedural bases for panelist challenges. Whether such competition is likely to lead to more or less stringent panelist review is uncertain, however, and turns in part on the decision-making incentives created by the UDRP's panel selection rules, an issue we address [below].

The absence of meaningful external controls by national courts over UDRP proceedings is even more striking. As an initial matter, however, the claim that external checking functions are more limited for the UDRP than for international arbitration seems contrary to the plain terms of the Policy. After all, the drafters expressly designed the UDRP as a soft-law system that supplements but does not supplant national court adjudication of domain name disputes. If de novo review by a national court is possible, then it would seem that the UDRP's external checking functions are far stronger than the extremely limited national court checking mechanisms at work in arbitration. Several features of the UDRP significantly undermine this argument, however, particularly with respect to external checking functions affecting domain name registrants. These features suggest that the UDRP may be soft law in theory, but much harder law in practice.

Consider first the filing of a complaint by a respondent in a court of so-called "mutual jurisdiction" to challenge a UDRP panel decision ordering her domain name to be canceled or transferred (described somewhat loosely as an "appeal" in the preparatory documents). The extremely short ten-day window within which respondents must file such a proceeding is likely to exert a significant deterrent effect on national court review. Initiating litigation is often a time-consuming and complex process, particularly for individuals and businesses with limited financial resources who may be forced to find an attorney to litigate in a foreign jurisdiction. Of course, nothing precludes a respondent from filing national court proceedings after the ten-day window has expired. The registrant's incentives to do so once a domain name has been canceled or transferred will be substantially diminished, however, particularly when the removal of the domain name disrupts her established or planned business operations. From a cost-benefit perspective, it may be preferable to transfer operations to a different domain name or even to abandon a start-up enterprise altogether. Empirical evidence on this point is anecdotal, but the most comprehensive database of national court challenges to UDRP rulings lists only twenty-five cases in federal district court and one foreign case out of the more than 3500 UDRP panel decisions to date.

Second, it is unclear whether respondents who do muster the resources to appeal panel decisions in fact possess a cause of action against a trademark owner under national laws seeking retention of the domain name. * * * [T]he Anti-Cybersquatting Consumer Protection Act * * * permits domain-name registrants whose domain name has been canceled or transferred pursuant to the UDRP (or a similar policy) to file a civil action in U.S. federal court against the prevailing party in order to establish that the registration and use of the domain name was lawful under the Lanham Act. If the domain-name registrant is successful, the court may "grant injunctive relief to the domain name registrant, including the reactivation of the domain name or transfer of the domain name to the domain name registrant." To our knowledge, no other national law provides such a cause of action.

Third, respondents who frame their claims not as an appeal of the merits of a UDRP ruling but rather as a challenge to excesses of panel power are equally unlikely to prevail. In traditional international arbitral proceedings, nation-states have enacted detailed statutory regimes to allow losing parties to challenge awards, albeit on very limited grounds. But it is doubtful that hybrid UDRP decisions qualify as arbitral awards under these statutes, particularly given the de novo national court review contemplated by the Policy. Courts in the United States, at least, have indicated that they would not be bound by panel findings, which suggests a clear intent not to treat panel decisions as arbitral awards. For this reason, it is doubtful that national courts possess any grant of power to review UDRP panel abuses as such.

* * *

Uncertainty over the location of national court review and the substantive law to be applied raises a fourth doubt regarding national courts' ability to provide adequate external checks on UDRP panel abuses. Initially, one would expect that, as a result of the mutual jurisdiction provision in the UDRP, courts in jurisdictions where registrars are based might develop an expertise and interest in reviewing UDRP panel decisions. * * * But the mutual jurisdiction provision is unlikely over time to centralize such expertise. Even assuming that trademark owners will select the domicile of the registrar as the court of mutual jurisdiction rather than the domicile of the domain-name registrant, the geographic location of registrars is slowly diversifying under ICANN's competitive registration policy. * * *

Finally, the attenuation of national courts' external checking function is manifested by the automatic nature of UDRP enforcement. Unlike international arbitrations subject to the New York Convention, there is no requirement that prevailing UDRP complainants institute separate national court proceedings to enforce their awards—a crucial check on arbitral power. Instead, enforcement of UDRP awards in favor of trademark owners are automatic unless the respondent takes steps to appeal. This shift of the burden of enforcement removes any opportunity for a "second look" at the arbitral award, thereby destabilizing one of the features that makes the strong presumption favoring enforcement of arbitral awards acceptable in the first place.

For the foregoing reasons, national courts are unlikely to exercise significant de facto external checks on abuses of authority by UDRP panels, notwithstanding the de jure power that they are given under the terms of the Policy. This leaves internal checking functions as the principal method by which arbitral-type excesses are to be checked. Yet UDRP panels have only weak incentives to limit their own authority.

[P]anelists and institutions operating in international arbitration cases compete for business of both complaining and responding parties. They thus have an incentive to stay within the boundaries of the arbitral agreement and to issue awards that encourage repeat business from both parties. In the UDRP, by contrast, competition incentives are skewed in favor of complainant intellectual property owners. It is complainants, not respondents, who choose the dispute settlement provider and who pay panel fees in all single-panelist cases. In principle, respondents may convert a single-member panel to a three-person panel after receiving the complaint. In practice, the large number of cases in which respondents fail to appear and the added cost of choosing a three-person panel for those who do significantly diminish the impact of respondents' choice on the incentives of providers and decision makers.

Confirming fears expressed by some participants during the ICANN review-and-comment process, evidence suggests that dispute settlement providers are acting on the "irresistible incentive to ... develop a reputation for deciding cases in favor of complainants." Providers now publish statistics on their win/loss records and other information about their decisions, information which serves as indirect advertising to trademark owners intent on choosing the most complainant-friendly provider. There is also anecdotal evidence that providers have adopted more overt methods to attract complainants by boasting of the tough stance their panelists have taken in UDRP disputes. These features have already created a public perception that some dispute settlement providers are more complainant friendly than others, a fact that the case statistics support (although the cause-and-effect dynamic is still unclear).

In addition, consider the identity of the individuals who serve as UDRP panelists. Most are practicing intellectual property attorneys, while a somewhat lower number are retired judges and legal academics. It is at least an open question whether decision makers from the private sector can sufficiently distance themselves from the milieu in which they practice to self-limit their own powers and develop balanced norms for the trademark-domain name interface. This is particularly true if panelists are permitted to trade on their UDRP expertise by representing trademark owners in future domain-name disputes.

Taken together, these skewed internal checking functions are likely to place significant pressure on UDRP decision makers to rule in favor of complaining trademark owners. If, however, the disputes subject to the UDRP were both unambiguous and narrow, then the Policy itself might exert an adequate constraining force to prevent panelists from acting on these pressures. As we explain below, however, the UDRP provides panelists with discretionary decision-making authority, making it unlikely that the text of the Policy will exert such a constraining effect. * * *

[T]he first three subsections of paragraph 4 of the Policy * * * set forth the elements that a complainant must prove to justify a transfer or cancellation of a domain name. Paragraphs 4(b) and 4(c) list the circumstances demonstrating, on the one hand, a respondent's "registration and use" of a domain name in bad faith, and on the other, her "rights or legitimate interests" in the domain name sufficient to defeat a complaint. If the UDRP were designed as a system of constrained judicial decision making, these enumerated circumstances would be dispositive of all claims and all defenses. Under such a system panels would admittedly still have interpretative discretion to decide in each dispute whether the facts presented fell within the parameters of the enumerated rules and to resolve ambiguities contained within the rules themselves. However, the exclusive nature of the categories would exert considerable constraining force, preventing panels from expanding the Policy very far beyond the heartland of cases circumscribed by the text.

The UDRP's drafters, however, did not limit panelists' discretion to these enumerated grounds. Instead, they labeled these exemplars as "circumstances" which existed only "in particular but without limitation" to other situations of bad faith, on the one hand, or rights and legitimate expectations, on the other. Such an obvious and open-ended invitation to lawmaking sends a clear message to panels that they can exercise independent authority in determining which sorts of unenumerated circumstances justify a ruling in favor of complainants or respondents. Without constraints on these open-ended clauses, panels are left with little to guide the exercise of their discretionary lawmaking powers. Not surprisingly, this omission has produced a schism between panels that strictly construe the UDRP and those that interpret the Policy more expansively to curb a broader range of conduct by domain-name registrants.[7] * * *

ICANN's conflicting signals to UDRP panels concerning their adjudicatory powers also affects their adoption of internal checking mechanisms. On a basic level, the requirement that all decisions be published and reasoned exerts a constraining effect on gross errors and excesses of authority. Panelists know that the decisions they author will be available to all potentially affected parties, including not only the litigants, but future litigants, other panelists, and ICANN. They thus have a significant interest in ensuring that their rulings meet at least minimal levels of competence and persuasiveness, particularly if they hope to receive future UDRP assignments.

Beyond this bare minimum level of competence, however, there are few structural incentives for panels to produce carefully reasoned decisions. Well-reasoned decisions require at least a modicum of deliberation, a quality that the time and cost-sensitive UDRP does not favor. Consider the following: Panels normally must issue a decision within less than forty-five days after a complaint is filed. Panelists are private adjudicators with other responsibilities outside of the UDRP competing for their time. Also, the modest compensation panelists receive for their services pales in comparison to the fees they can receive as practicing attorneys or deciding other arbitral matters. Each of these pressures are likely to limit the attention that panelists can devote to drafting reasoned opinions. * * *

The UDRP's hybrid decision-making structure poses a more fundamental challenge to developing a consistent domain name jurisprudence. The

---

7. [Later in a portion of their article not reproduced here, the authors document their claim that some panels have interpreted the UDRP more expansively to curb a broader range of conduct by domain-name registrants, noting the following: "Several panels have extended the UDRP to cases involving legitimate disputes over domain name ownership or to bad faith registration without corresponding bad faith use, categories of cases that the drafters expressly excluded from the Policy. More striking still is a line of cases permitting surname and geographic name owners to bring successful complaints against domain name registrants (either by ignoring the elements required to prove a claim or by very expansive interpretation of the notion of common law trademark rights). Not only did these rulings ignore the drafters' desire to limit the UDRP to trademark controversies, they also were issued at a time when WIPO was studying whether to recommend an expansion of the Policy to encompass these precise intellectual property rights."—Eds.]

arbitral model upon which much of the UDRP was founded places limited weight on past awards as sources of authority. It also focuses more on resolving disputes between the parties than on articulating governing legal norms or creating a jurisprudence to guide future conduct by nonparties. * * * [The authors conclude that] it is questionable whether the UDRP as presently constituted can achieve jurisprudential coherence.

Madonna Ciccone, p/k/a Madonna v. Dan Parisi and "Madonna.com"

Case No. D2000–0847 (WIPO Oct. 12, 2000).

1. The Parties

The Complainant is Madonna Ciccone, an individual professionally known as Madonna.

The Respondent is "Madonna.com," the registrant for the disputed domain name, located in New York, New York, U.S.A. or Dan Parisi, the listed contact for the domain name.

2. The Domain Name(s) and Registrar(s)

The disputed domain name is *madonna.com*.

The registrar is Network Solutions, Inc., 505 Huntmar Park Drive, Herndon, Virginia 20170, U.S.A.

3. Procedural History

This action was brought in accordance with the ICANN Uniform Domain Name Dispute Resolution Policy, dated October 24, 1999 ("the Policy") and the ICANN Rules for Uniform Domain Name Dispute Resolution Policy, dated October 24, 1999 ("the Rules").

The Complaint was received by the WIPO Arbitration and Mediation Center on July 21, 2000 (e-mail) and on July 24, 2000 (hardcopy). The Response was received on August 23, 2000 (e-mail) and on August 28, 2000 (hardcopy). Both parties are represented by Counsel. There have been no further submissions on the merits.

Respondent elected to have the case decided by a three-member panel. David E. Sorkin was appointed as the Respondent's nominee. James W. Dabney was selected as the Complainant's nominee. Mark V.B. Partridge was appointed as presiding panelist.

It appears that all requirements of the Policy and the Rules have been satisfied by the parties, WIPO and the Panelists.

4. Factual Background

Complainant is the well-known entertainer Madonna. She is the owner of U.S. Trademark Registrations for the mark MADONNA for entertainment services and related goods (Reg. No. 1,473,554 and 1,463,601). She has used her name and mark MADONNA professionally for entertainment services since 1979. Complainant's music and other entertainment endeavors have often been controversial for featuring explicit sexual content. In addition, nude photographs of Madonna have appeared in Penthouse magazine, and Complainant has published a coffee-table book entitled "Sex" featuring sexually explicit photographs and text.

Respondent is in the business of developing web sites. On or about May 29, 1998, Respondent, through its business Whitehouse.com, Inc., purchased the registration for the disputed domain name from Pro Domains for $20,000. On June 4, 1998, Respondent registered MADONNA as a trademark in Tunisia. On or about June 8, 1998, Respondent began operating an "adult entertainment portal web site." The web site featured sexually explicit photographs and text, and contained a notice stating "Madonna.com is not affiliated or endorsed by the Catholic Church, Madonna College, Madonna Hospital or Madonna the singer." By March 4, 1999, it appears that Respondent removed the explicit sexual content from the web site. By May 31, 1999, it appears that the site merely contained the above notice, the disputed domain name and the statement "Coming soon Madonna Gaming and Sportsbook."

On June 9, 1999, Complainant, through her attorneys, objected to Respondent's use of the Madonna.com domain name. On June 14, 1999, Respondent through its counsel stated: "As I assume you also know, Mr. Parisi's website [sic] was effectively shut down before you sent your letter, and is now shut down altogether. He is in the process of donating his registration for the domain name."

The word "Madonna," which has the current dictionary definition as the Virgin Mary or an artistic depiction of the Virgin Mary, is used by others as a trademark, trade name and personal name. After Respondent's receipt of Complainant's objection, it appears that Respondent had communication with Madonna Rehabilitation Hospital regarding the transfer of the domain name to the Hospital. It further appears that Respondent has not identified all of its communications on this matter. Nevertheless, the transfer had not taken place at the time this proceeding was commenced.

By his own admission, Respondent has registered a large number of other domain names, including names that matched the trademarks of others. Other domain names registered by Respondent include <wallstreetjournal.com> and <edgaronline.com>. See Response, Exhibit A, ¶ 30, 35.

5.   Parties' Contentions

A.   *Complainant*

Complaint contends that the disputed domain name is identical to the registered and common law trademark MADONNA in which she owns rights. She further contends that Respondent has no legitimate interest or rights in the domain name. Finally, Complainant contends that Respondent obtained and used the disputed domain name with the intent to attract

Internet users to a pornographic web site for commercial gain based on confusion with Complainant's name and mark.

B.   Respondent

Respondent does not dispute that the disputed domain name is identical or confusingly similar to Complainant's trademark. Respondent, however, claims that Complainant cannot show a lack of legitimate interest in the domain name because Respondent (a) made demonstrable preparation to use the domain name for a bona fide business purpose; (b) holds a bona fide trademark in the word MADONNA; and (c) has attempted to make bona fide noncommercial use of the name by donating it to the Madonna Rehabilitation Hospital.

Respondent also contends that it has not registered and used the domain name in bad faith because (a) there is no evidence that its primary motivation was to sell the disputed domain name; (b) the domain name was not registered with an intent to prevent Complainant from using her mark as a domain name; (c) respondent is not engaged in a pattern of registering domain names to prevent others from doing so; (d) the use of a disclaimer on the web site precludes a finding that Respondent intentional[ly] seeks to attract users for commercial gain based on confusion with Complainant's mark; and (e) the use of a generic term to attract business is not bad faith as a matter of law. Finally, Respondent claims that Complainant cannot legitimately claim tarnishment because she has already associated herself with sexually explicit creative work.

6.   Discussion and Findings

A.   The Evidentiary Standard For Decision

Paragraph 4(a) of the Policy directs that the complainant must prove each of the following:

(i) that the domain name registered by the respondent is identical or confusingly similar to a trademark or service mark in which the complainant has rights; and,

(ii) that the respondent has no legitimate interests in respect of the domain name; and,

(iii) that the domain name has been registered and used in bad faith.

A threshold question in proceedings under the Policy is to identify the proper standard for reaching a decision on each of these issues. The limited submissions allowed under the Policy makes these proceedings somewhat akin to a summary judgment motion under the United States Federal Rules of Civil Procedure. On a summary judgment motion, the movant has the burden of showing that there are no disputes of material facts. All doubts are to be resolved in favor of the non-moving party. If there are material disputes of fact, the motion must be denied and the case will advance to a hearing before a trier of fact, either judge or jury.

Although the nature of the record is similar to that found on a summary judgment motion, our role is different than that of the Court on a summary judgment motion. Paragraph 15 of the Rules states that the "Panel shall decide a complaint on the basis of the statements and documents submitted and in accordance with the Policy ..." Paragraph 10 of the Rules provides that the "Panel shall determine the admissibility, relevance, materiality and weight of the evidence." Paragraph 4 of the Policy makes repeated reference to the Panel's role in making findings of fact based on the evidence.

Based on the Policy and the Rules, we disagree with the view that disputes over material facts should not be decided in these proceedings. Rather, it is clear to us that our role is to make findings of fact as best we can based on the evidence presented provided the matters at issue are within the scope of the Policy. There may be circumstances due to the inherent limitations of the dispute resolution process or for other reasons where it would be appropriate for a panel to decline to decide a factual dispute. However, the mere existence of a genuine dispute of material fact should not preclude a panel from weighing the evidence before it and reaching a decision.

Since these proceedings are civil, rather than criminal, in nature, we believe the appropriate standard for fact finding is the civil standard of a preponderance of the evidence (and not the higher standard of "clear and convincing evidence" or "evidence beyond a reasonable doubt"). Under the "preponderance of the evidence" standard a fact is proved for the purpose of reaching a decision when it appears more likely than not to be true based on the evidence. We recognize that other standards may be employed in other jurisdictions. However, the standard of proof employed in the United States seems appropriate for these proceedings generally, and in particular for this proceeding which involves citizens of the United States, actions occurring in the United States and a domain name registered in the United States.

In this case, there are factual disputes over Respondent's intent in obtaining and using the disputed domain name. For the reasons just stated, these disputes do not preclude a decision. Instead, we reach a decision based on the preponderance of the evidence submitted by the parties on the basic issues under the Policy.

B. Similarity of the Disputed Domain Name and Complainant's Mark

As noted above, Respondent does not dispute that its domain name is identical or confusingly similar to a trademark in which the Complainant has rights. Accordingly, we find that Complainant has satisfied the requirements of Paragraph [4(a)(i)] of the Policy.

C. Lack of Rights or Legitimate Interests In Domain Name

Complainant has presented evidence tending to show that Respondent lacks any rights or legitimate interest in the domain name. Respondent's claim of rights or legitimate interests is not persuasive.

First, Respondent contends that its use of the domain name for an adult entertainment web site involved prior use of the domain name in connection with a bona fide offering of goods or services. The record supports Respondent's claim that it used the domain name in connection with commercial services prior to notice of the dispute. However, Respondent has failed to provide a reasonable explanation for the selection of Madonna as a domain name. Although the word "Madonna" has an ordinary dictionary meaning not associated with Complainant, nothing in the record supports a conclusion that Respondent adopted and used the term "Madonna" in good faith based on its ordinary dictionary meaning. We find instead that name was selected and used by Respondent with the intent to attract for commercial gain Internet users to Respondent's web site by trading on the fame of Complainant's mark. We see no other plausible explanation for Respondent's conduct and conclude that use which intentionally trades on the fame of another can not constitute a "bona fide" offering of goods or services. To conclude otherwise would mean that a Respondent could rely on intentional infringement to demonstrate a legitimate interest, an interpretation that is obviously contrary to the intent of the Policy.

Second, Respondent contends that it has rights in the domain name because it registered MADONNA as a trademark in Tunisia prior to notice of this dispute. Certainly, it is possible for a Respondent to rely on a valid trademark registration to show prior rights under the Policy. However, it would be a mistake to conclude that mere registration of a trademark creates a legitimate interest under the Policy. If an American-based Respondent could establish "rights" vis a vis an American Complainant through the expedient of securing a trademark registration in Tunisia, then the ICANN procedure would be rendered virtually useless. To establish cognizable rights, the overall circumstances should demonstrate that the registration was obtained in good faith for the purpose of making bona fide use of the mark in the jurisdiction where the mark is registered, and not obtained merely to circumvent the application of the Policy.

Here, Respondent admits that the Tunisia registration was obtained merely to protect his interests in the domain name. Respondent is not located in Tunisia and the registration was not obtained for the purpose of making bona fide use of the mark in commerce in Tunisia. A Tunisian trademark registration is issued upon application without any substantive examination. Although recognized by certain treaties, registration in Tunisia does not prevent a finding of infringement in jurisdictions outside Tunisia. Under the circumstances, some might view Respondent's Tunisian registration itself as evidence of bad faith because it appears to be a pretense to justify an abusive domain name registration. We find at a minimum that it does not evidence a legitimate interest in the disputed name under the circumstances of this case.

Third, Respondent claims that its offer to transfer the domain name to the Madonna Hospital in Lincoln, Nebraska, is a legitimate noncommercial use under Paragraph 4(c)(iii) of the Policy. We disagree. The record is incomplete on these negotiations. Respondent has failed to disclose the specifics of its proposed arrangement with Madonna Hospital. Complainant asserts that the terms of the transfer include a condition that Madonna Hospital not transfer the domain name registration to Complainant. It also appears that the negotiations started after Complainant objected to Respondent's registration and use of the domain name. These circumstances do not demonstrate a legitimate interest or right in the domain name, and instead suggest that Respondent lacks any real interest in the domain name apart from its association with Complainant. Further, we do not believe these circumstances satisfy the provisions of Paragraph 4(c)(iii), which applies to situations where the Respondent is actually making noncommercial or fair use of the domain name. That certainly was not the situation at the time this dispute arose and is not the situation now.

Respondent cites examples of other parties besides Complainant who also have rights in the mark MADONNA, but that does not aid its cause. The fact that others could demonstrate a legitimate right or interest in the domain name does nothing to demonstrate that Respondent has such right or interest.

Based on the record before us, we find that Complainant has satisfied the requirements of Paragraph 4(a)(ii) of the Policy.

D. Bad Faith Registration and Use

Under Paragraph 4(b)(iv) of the Policy, evidence of bad faith registration and use of a domain name includes the following circumstances:

(iv) by using the domain name, you have intentionally attempted to attract, for commercial gain, Internet users to your web site or other on-line location, by creating a likelihood of confusion with the complainant's mark as to the source, sponsorship, affiliation, or endorsement of your web site or location or of a product or service on your web site or location.

The pleadings in this case are consistent with Respondent's having adopted <madonna.com> for the specific purpose of trading off the name and reputation of the Complainant, and Respondent has offered no alternative explanation for his adoption of the name despite his otherwise detailed and complete submissions. Respondent has not explained why <madonna.com> was worth $20,000 to him or why that name was thought to be valuable as an attraction for a sexually explicit web site. Respondent notes that the complainant, identifying herself as Madonna, has appeared in Penthouse and has published a "Sex" book. The statement that "madonna" is a word in the English language, by itself, is no more of a defense than would be the similar statement made in reference to the word "coke". Respondent has not even attempted to tie in his web site to any dictionary definition of madonna. The only plausible explanation for Respondent's actions appears to be an intentional effort to trade upon the fame of Complainant's name and mark for commercial gain. That purpose is a violation of the Policy, as well as U.S. Trademark Law.

Respondent's use of a disclaimer on its web site is insufficient to avoid a finding of bad faith. First, the disclaimer may be ignored or misunderstood by Internet users. Second, a disclaimer does nothing to dispel initial interest confusion that is inevitable from Respondent's actions. Such confusion is a basis for finding a violation of Complainant's rights. *See Brookfield Communications, Inc. v. West Coast Entertainment Corp.*, 174 F.3d 1036 (9th Cir.1999).

The Policy requires a showing of bad faith registration and use. Here, although Respondent was not the original registrant, the record shows he acquired the registration in bad faith. The result is the equivalent of registration and is sufficient to fall within the Policy. Indeed, Paragraph 4(b)(i) of the Policy treats acquisition as the same as registration for the purposes of supporting a finding of bad faith registration. We therefore conclude that bad faith acquisition satisfies the requirement of bad faith registration under the Policy.

Respondent's reliance on a previous ICANN decision involving the domain name <sting.com> is misplaced. *See Gordon Sumner p/k/a/ Sting v. Michael Urvan*, Case No. 2000–0596 (WIPO July 24, 2000). In the Sting decision there was evidence that the Respondent had made bona fide use of the name Sting prior to obtaining the domain name registration and there was no indication that he was seeking to trade on the good will of the well-known singer. Here, there is no similar evidence of prior use by Respondent and the evidence demonstrates a deliberate intent to trade on the good will of complainant. Where no plausible explanation has been provided for adopting a domain name that corresponds to the name of a famous entertainer, other Panels have found a violation of the Policy. *See Julia Fiona Roberts v. Russell Boyd*, Case No. D2000–0210 (WIPO May 29, 2000); *Helen Folsade Adu p/k/a Sade v. Quantum Computer Services Inc.*, Case No. D2000–0794 (WIPO September 26, 2000).

There is also evidence in the record which tends to support Complainant's claim that Respondent's registration of the domain name prevents Complainant from reflecting her mark in the corresponding .com domain name and that Respondent has engaged in a pattern of such conduct. It is admitted that Respondent registers a large number of domain names and that some happen to correspond to the names or marks of others. We find, however, that the record is inconclusive on this basis for finding bad faith and do not rely on this evidence for our conclusion.

Respondent asserts that we should reject Complainant's claims because she has been disingenuous in claiming that her reputation could be tarnished by Respondent's actions. Respondent suggests that her reputation cannot be tarnished because she has already associated herself with sexually explicit creative work. That argument misses the point. Even though Complainant has produced sexually explicit content of her own, Respondent's actions may nevertheless tarnish her reputation because they resulted in association with sexually explicit content which Complainant did not control and which may be contrary to her creative intent and standards of quality. In any event, we do not rely on tarnishment as a basis for our decision.

Because the evidence shows a deliberate attempt by Respondent to trade on Complainant's fame for commercial purposes, we find that Complainant has satisfied the requirements of Paragraph 4(a)(iii) of the Policy.

7. Decision

Under Paragraph 4(i) of the Policy, we find in favor of the Complainant. The disputed domain name is identical or confusingly similar to a trademark in which Complainant has rights; Respondent lacks rights or legitimate interests in the domain name; and the domain name has been registered and used in bad faith. Therefore, we decide that the disputed domain name <madonna.com> should be transferred to the Complainant.

Weber–Stephen Products Co. v. Armitage Hardware and Building Supply, Inc.

54 U.S.P.Q.2d (BNA) 1766 (N.D.Ill.2000).

■ Aspen, Chief J.

Defendant Armitage Hardware (Armitage) owns a number of internet domain names that plaintiff Weber–Stephen Products Company (Weber) alleges intentionally and in bad faith use Weber's registered trademarks and service marks in a deceptive, confusing, and misleading manner. Weber initiated an administrative proceeding before the World Intellectual Property Organization (WIPO), pursuant to the Uniform Domain Name Dispute Resolution Policy of the Internet Corporation for Assigned Names and Numbers (ICANN Policy), requesting that the administrative panel issue a decision transferring Armitage's domain names to Weber or canceling Armitage's domain names. The following day, Weber also filed suit in this Court, alleging ''cyberpiracy'' as well as other claims, such as trademark infringement. Weber told this Court that it had commenced an ICANN proceeding to resolve the issue of whether Armitage was using its domain names in bad faith, which is the only issue that the ICANN administrative panel has power to decide under the Policy. Weber also said that because it expected a decision from the panel within 45 to 50 days from the filing of its ICANN complaint (the Policy provides for expedited review), it would not be seeking injunctive relief in this Court with respect to Armitage's registration of the Weber domain names unless the panel declines to cancel and/or to transfer the domain names to Weber.

We understand that the panel is scheduled to issue a decision as soon as May 5, 2000. Before us now is Armitage's motion to declare the administrative proceeding non-binding and to stay this case in favor of the administrative action, or alternatively—should we find the other proceeding to be binding—to stay it while we consider whether Armitage's participation in that proceeding can be compelled. Armitage's concern is that if the panel's arbitration decision is binding on this Court, Armitage will suffer irreparable harm because our review of the panel's decision will necessarily be circumscribed pursuant to the deference accorded arbitrators' decisions under the Federal Arbitration Act.

The ICANN is a new, quasi-governmental internet-regulating body, and its Policy (approved on October 24, 1999) provides for a "mandatory administrative proceeding" in disputes between domain name owners and trademark owners and purportedly applies to every domain name registrant who registers its domain names through an ICANN-accredited registrar. Armitage contends that it did not agree to the administrative proceeding and thus cannot be compelled to participate in it. However, Armitage will participate if we declare that the proceeding is non-binding, that we owe no deference to the proceeding, and that WIPO, ICANN, and Network Solutions, Inc. (Armitage's ICANN-accredited registrar) cannot take any action adverse to Armitage until this matter is resolved in this Court.

No federal court has yet considered the legal effect of a WIPO proceeding. However, the ICANN Policy and its accompanying rules do contemplate the possibility of parallel proceedings in federal court. First, the Policy provides that ICANN will cancel or transfer domain name registrations upon "our receipt of an order from a court ... of competent jurisdiction, requiring such action; *and/or* ... our receipt of a decision of an Administrative Panel requiring such action in any administrative proceeding ... conducted under this Policy." ICANN Policy at ¶ 3. Also, the procedural rules governing the Policy provide that if legal proceedings are initiated prior to or during an administrative proceeding with regard to a domain name dispute that is the subject of the administrative complaint, the panel has the discretion to decide whether to suspend or terminate the administrative proceeding or whether to proceed and make a decision. Uniform Domain Name Dispute Resolution Rules, at ¶ 18. And the language of the Policy suggests that the administrative panels' decisions are not intended to be binding on federal courts. For example, under the heading "Availability of Court Proceedings," the ICANN Policy provides:

> The mandatory administrative proceeding requirements set forth in Paragraph 4 shall not prevent either you or the complainant from submitting the dispute to a court of competent jurisdiction for independent resolution before such mandatory administrative proceeding is commenced or after such proceeding is concluded. If an Administrative Panel decides that your domain name registration should be canceled or transferred, we will wait ten (10) business days ... before implementing that decision. We will then implement the decision unless we have received from you during that ten (10) business day period official documentation (such as a copy of a complaint, file-stamped by the clerk of the court) that you have commenced a lawsuit against the complainant in a jurisdiction to which the complainant has submitted ... If we receive such documentation within the ten (10) business day period, we will not implement the Administrative Panel's decision, and we will take no further action, until we receive (i) evidence satisfactory to us of a resolution between the parties; (ii) evidence satisfactory to us that your lawsuit has been dismissed or withdrawn; or (iii) a copy of an order from such court dismissing your

lawsuit or ordering that you do not have the right to continue to use your domain name.

ICANN Policy at ¶ 4(k).[3] Furthermore, Armitage's counsel sent an e-mail inquiry to <domain.disputes@wipo.int>, and the response from the WIPO Arbitration and Mediation Center said that the administrative panel's determination would be binding on the registrar of the domain name, but that "[t]his decision is not binding upon a court, and a court may give appropriate weight to the Administrative Panel's decision." Albeit a vague and rather unhelpful interpretation, Weber does not take issue with this WIPO statement.

We conclude that this Court is not bound by the outcome of the ICANN administrative proceedings. But at this time we decline to determine the precise standard by which we would review the panel's decision, and what degree of deference (if any) we would give that decision. Neither the ICANN Policy nor its governing rules dictate to courts what weight should be given to a panel's decision, and the WIPO e-mail message stating that "a court may give appropriate weight to the Administrative Panel's decision" confirms the breadth of our discretion.

Because both parties to this case have adequate avenues of recourse should they be unhappy with the administrative panel's imminent decision, we find no need to stay the pending ICANN administrative action. Instead, we hereby stay this case pending the outcome of those proceedings. It is so ordered.

NOTES & QUESTIONS

1. *Foreign trademark rights.* In *Madonna v. Parisi* the domain name registrant had registered the disputed domain name in Tunisia. Under Tunisian law, the registrant had legitimate trademark rights in the name. Section 4(a)(ii) of the UDRP states that the complainant must show that the domain name registrant has "no rights or legitimate interests in respect of the domain name." The Panel dismissed the domain name registrant's trademark rights under Tunisian law as a source of such rights, stating:

> If an American-based Respondent could establish "rights" vis a vis an American Complainant through the expedient of securing a trademark registration in Tunisia, then the ICANN procedure would be rendered virtually useless. To establish cognizable rights, the overall circumstances should demonstrate that the registration was obtained in good faith for the purpose of making bona fide use of the mark in the jurisdiction where the mark is registered, and not obtained merely to circumvent the application of the Policy.

3. The Policy continues: "All other disputes between you and any party other than us regarding your domain name registration that are not brought pursuant to the mandatory administrative proceeding provisions . . . shall be resolved between you and such other party through any court, arbitration or other proceeding that may be available." ICANN Policy at ¶ 5.

The Panel thus seems to concede that the UDRP, read literally, might compel a result in favor of the registrant. To avoid this result, the Panel concludes that any "rights" in the mark must be "cognizable," and to be "cognizable," they must have been acquired in good faith and used in the jurisdiction conferring those rights. How far does a UDRP panel's authority to interpret its own grant of authority extend? A UDRP panel is not a court and its power to arbitrate a dispute rests ultimately on the domain name registrant's consent to the arbitration clause contained in the domain name registration agreement. Once the domain name registrant had demonstrated trademark rights under Tunisian law, should the Panel have suggested the parties proceed to a court of law to adjudicate their respective rights in the disputed domain name?

2. *Licensing rights.* Section 4(a)(i) of the UDRP requires that the complainant prove that the disputed "domain name is identical or confusingly similar to a trademark or service mark in which the complainant has rights." What kind of rights must a complainant have under the UDRP? In *NBA Properties, Inc. v. Adirondack Software Corp.*, Case No. D2000–1211 (WIPO Dec. 8, 2000), the complainant was the exclusive licensee of the trademark owner. The disputed domain name was knicks.com. The trademark "Knicks" is owned by Madison Square Garden, L.P., the owner and operator of the New York Knicks basketball team. This trademark had been exclusively licensed to the complainant, the exclusive licensing and merchandising agent for the National Basketball Association and its member teams, including the New York Knicks. The domain name registrant had registered the disputed domain name without the consent of the trademark owner or the complainant. Notwithstanding the complainant's status as the exclusive licensee of the trademark, the Panel held that the "Complainant has not shown that it has rights in the KNICKS trademark relied upon." More specifically, the Panel stated:

> The record fails to make clear what *rights in the trademark* Complainant claims to have. The rights of a licensee are contract rights with respect to, not *in*, the licensed marks. So it is also in the case of a licensing and merchandising agent.

> There may well be circumstances in which the contract rights possessed by an exclusive licensee vest in him substantially all the powers of an owner of the licensed property. However, such circumstances have not been shown to exist here.

> The Policy [i.e., the UDRP] is believed by the Panel to envision a transfer of a disputed domain name to a complainant/trademark owner as a route to unification of control over the uses of the domain name and the trademark. However, Complainant's request for an order transferring the disputed name to Complainant in this case would place ownership of the domain name in an entity other than the trademark owner without consent from the trademark owner.

Should rights in a trademark under an exclusive licensing agreement be considered "rights in a trademark" for the purposes of the UDRP? If you were negotiating or drafting a trademark licensing agreement on behalf of the licensee, how would you attempt to ensure that your client could initiate a proceeding under the UDRP?

3. *Use in bad faith*. Earlier, we saw that the Anticybersquatting Consumer Protection Act imposed liability on a domain name registrant who "registers, traffics in, *or* uses a domain name" with bad-faith intent to profit from it. 15 U.S.C. § 1125(d)(1)(A)(ii) (emphasis added). By contrast, the ICANN UDRP permits a registrar to "cancel, transfer or otherwise make changes to domain name registrations" if the disputed "domain name has been registered *and* is being used in bad faith." UDRP § 4(a)(iii) (emphasis added). Consider a domain name registrant who registers another's trademark as a domain name in bad faith but who never uses it as part of an e-mail address or fully qualified domain name. Clearly, the trademark owner could bring an action under the ACPA. Could the owner also initiate proceedings under the UDRP? In *Telstra Corp. Ltd. v. Nuclear Marshmallows*, Case No. D2000-0003 (WIPO Feb. 18, 2000), the Panel had to decide just such a case. Turning to consider Section 4(a)(iii), the Panel observed:

> It is less clear cut whether the Complainant has proved the third element in paragraph 4(a) of the Uniform Policy, namely that the domain name "has been registered and is being used in bad faith" by Respondent. The Administrative Panel notes two things about this provision. First, the provision contains the conjunction "and" rather than "or". Secondly, the provision refers to both the past tense ("has been registered") and the present tense ("is being used").

> The significance of the use of the conjunction "and" is that paragraph 4(a)(iii) requires the Complainant to prove use in bad faith as well as registration in bad faith. That is to say, bad faith registration alone is an insufficient ground for obtaining a remedy under the Uniform Policy. * * * [T]he Second Staff Report on Implementation Documents for the Uniform Dispute Resolution Policy submitted to the ICANN Board at its meeting on October 24, 1999 * * * at paragraph 4.5, contains the following relevant statement and recommendation:

>> Several comments (submitted by INTA and various trademark owners) advocated various expansions to the scope of the definition of abusive registration. For example:

>> a. These comments suggested that the definition should be expanded to include cases of either registration or use in bad faith, rather than both registration and use in bad faith. These comments point out that cybersquatters often register names in bulk, but do not use them, yet without use the streamlined dispute-resolution procedure is not available. While that argument appears to have merit on initial impression, it would involve a change in the policy adopted by the Board. The WIPO report, the DNSO recommendation, and the registrars-group recommenda-

tion all required both registration and use in bad faith before the streamlined procedure would be invoked. Staff recommends that this requirement not be changed without study and recommendation by the DNSO.

From the fact that the ICANN Board accepted the approach recommended in the Second Staff Report, and thus adopted the Uniform Policy in the form originally proposed, it is clear that ICANN intended that bad faith registration alone not give rise to a remedy under the Uniform Policy. For a remedy to be available, the Complainant must prove both that the domain was registered in bad faith and that it is being used in bad faith.

This interpretation is confirmed, and clarified, by the use of both the past and present tenses in paragraph 4(a)(iii). * * * [T]he requirement in paragraph 4(a)(iii) that the domain name "has been registered and is being used in bad faith" will be satisfied only if the Complainant proves that the registration was undertaken in bad faith *and* that the circumstances of the case are such that Respondent is continuing to act in bad faith.

Has the Complainant proved that the domain name "has been registered in bad faith" by the Respondent? [The Panel finds that it has.].

Has the Complainant proved the additional requirement that the domain name "is being used in bad faith" by the Respondent? The [disputed] domain name * * * does not resolve to a website or other on-line presence. There is no evidence that a website or other on-line presence is in the process of being established which will use the domain name. There is no evidence of advertising, promotion or display to the public of the domain name. Finally, there is no evidence that the Respondent has offered to sell, rent or otherwise transfer the domain name to the Complainant, a competitor of the Complainant, or any other person. In short, there is no positive action being undertaken by the Respondent in relation to the domain name.

This fact does not, however, resolve the question. * * * [T]he relevant issue is not whether the Respondent is undertaking a positive action in bad faith in relation to the domain name, but instead whether, in all the circumstances of the case, it can be said that the Respondent is acting in bad faith. The distinction between undertaking a positive action in bad faith and acting in bad faith may seem a rather fine distinction, but it is an important one. The significance of the distinction is that the concept of a domain name "being used in bad faith" is not limited to positive action; inaction is within the concept. That is to say, it is possible, in certain circumstances, for inactivity by the Respondent to amount to the domain name being used in bad faith.

This understanding of paragraph 4(a)(iii) is supported by the actual provisions of the Uniform Policy. Paragraph 4(b) of the Uniform Policy identifies, without limitation, circumstances that "shall be evidence of the registration and use of a domain name in bad faith", for the purposes of paragraph 4(a)(iii). Only one of these circumstances (paragraph 4(b)(iv)), by necessity, involves a positive action post-registration undertaken in relation to the domain name (using the name to attract custom to a website or other on-line location). The other three circumstances contemplate either a positive action or inaction in relation to the domain name. That is to say, the circumstances identified in paragraphs 4(b)(i), (ii) and (iii) can be found in a situation involving a passive holding of the domain name registration. Of course, these three paragraphs require additional facts (an intention to sell, rent or transfer the registration, for paragraph 4(b)(i); a pattern of conduct preventing a trade mark owner's use of the registration, for paragraph 4(b)(ii); the primary purpose of disrupting the business of a competitor, for paragraph 4(b)(iii)). Nevertheless, the point is that paragraph 4(b) recognises that inaction (eg. passive holding) in relation to a domain name registration can, in certain circumstances, constitute a domain name being used in bad faith. Furthermore, it must be recalled that the circumstances identified in paragraph 4(b) are "without limitation"—that is, paragraph 4(b) expressly recognises that *other* circumstances can be evidence that a domain name was registered and is being used in bad faith.

The question that then arises is what circumstances of inaction (passive holding) other than those identified in paragraphs 4(b)(i), (ii) and (iii) can constitute a domain name being used in bad faith? This question cannot be answered in the abstract; the question can only be answered in respect of the particular facts of a specific case. That is to say, in considering whether the passive holding of a domain name, following a bad faith registration of it, satisfies the requirements of paragraph 4(a)(iii), the Administrative Panel must give close attention to all the circumstances of the Respondent's behaviour. A remedy can be obtained under the Uniform Policy only if those circumstances show that the Respondent's passive holding amounts to acting in bad faith

Based on the rationale of this decision, under what circumstances might passive holding not constitute bad-faith use?

4. *Country-code TLDs.* In addition to the .com, .net and .org gTLD domains, as well as the more recently activated .aero, .biz, .coop, .info, .museum, and .name domains, a number of ccTLD registries have adopted the UDRP. As a result the UDRP also applies to the .ag, .as, .bs, .cy, .gt, .na, .nu, .tt, .tv, .ve and .ws TLDs.

5. *Challenging an adverse UDRP decision in federal court.* The Anticybersquatting Consumer Protection Act expressly grants a domain name registrant the right to file a civil action if a registrar pursuant to a reasonable policy—such as the UDRP—suspends, disables or transfers his or her domain name. Section 32(2)(D)(v) of the Lanham Act, 15 U.S.C. § 1114(2)(D)(v), states:

> A domain name registrant whose domain name has been suspended, disabled, or transferred under a policy described under clause (ii)(II) may, upon notice to the mark owner, file a civil action to establish that the registration or use of the domain name by such registrant is not unlawful under this chapter. The court may grant injunctive relief to the domain name registrant, including the reactivation of the domain name or transfer of the domain name to the domain name registrant.

Does this provision create a right to appeal an adverse UDRP decision in federal court? What law does a federal court apply in such an action? Why do you think this provision was included in the Anticybersquatting Consumer Protection Act? Does it merely codify a contract remedy that was already available to a domain name registrant? Is it required by 15 U.S.C. § 1114(2)(D)(i)? Does it create a quasi-intellectual property right in domain names under federal law? One commentator has stated that this provision "creates a distinct federal claim for ownership of a domain name." 4 J. Thomas McCarthy, McCarthy on Trademarks and Unfair Competition § 25:74.2 (4th ed. 2002). Do you agree?

6. *Reverse domain name hijacking and abuse of process.* Reverse domain name hijacking is defined in the UDRP Rules as "using the Policy in bad faith to attempt to deprive a registered domain-name holder of a domain name." *See* Rules for Uniform Domain Name Dispute Resolution Policy § 1 (Definitions) (Oct. 24, 1999). Pursuant to § 15(e) of the Rules:

> If after considering the submissions the Panel finds that the complaint was brought in bad faith, for example in an attempt at Reverse Domain Name Hijacking or was brought primarily to harass the domain-name holder, the Panel *shall* declare in its decision that the complaint was brought in bad faith and constitutes an abuse of the administrative proceeding.

(emphasis added). Although the panel is required to make this declaration, neither the UDRP nor the Rules provides any penalty for initiating a UDRP proceeding in bad faith. In ICANN's Second Staff Report on Implementation Documents for the Uniform Dispute Resolution Policy, penalties were rejected as "outside ICANN's scope." Regarding reverse domain name hijacking the Report observed in § 4.10:

> The final point of substantive guidance in the Board's Santiago resolutions is that the policy should define and minimize reverse domain-name hijacking. The definition of "reverse domain name hijacking" is included in paragraph 1 of the rules. The implementation documents contain several measures to minimize that practice. First, paragraph 15(e) of the rules provides that an administrative panel finding that a complaint was brought in bad faith shall note that fact in its decision. A second measure to minimize

reverse domain-name hijacking is the enhanced notice requirement for the initial complaint in paragraph 2(a) of the rules. The
clarification that the complainant bears the burden of proof (paragraph 4(a) of the policy statement) and the lengthening of the time
for a domain-name holder to seek court review of an adverse
decision (paragraph 4(k) of the policy statement) should also
minimize reverse domain-name hijacking. Some commentators
representing non-commercial interests stated that more punitive
measures should be provided to discourage reverse domain-name
hijacking. Staff believes such punishment is outside ICANN's
scope.

What does the ICANN staff mean by "outside ICANN's scope"? What is
ICANN's role in a UDRP proceeding?

For domain name registrants in the United States, ICANN's failure to
provide any remedy to the victims of those who use the UDRP process to
reverse hijack domain names was rectified by the Anticybersquatting
Consumer Protection Act. Section 32(2)(D)(iv) of the Lanham Act, 15
U.S.C. § 1114(2)(D)(iv), states:

> If a registrar, registry, or other registration authority takes an
> action described under clause (ii) based on a knowing and material
> misrepresentation by any other person that a domain name is
> identical to, confusingly similar to, or dilutive of a mark, the
> person making the knowing and material misrepresentation *shall
> be liable for any damages, including costs and attorney's fees,*
> incurred by the domain name registrant as a result of such action.
> The court may also grant injunctive relief to the domain name
> registrant, including the reactivation of the domain name or the
> transfer of the domain name to the domain name registrant.

(emphasis added). Does this provision create an action for malicious prosecution or abuse of process with respect to a UDRP proceeding? Would this
remedy be available to domain name registrants who are not United States
citizens and who live in foreign countries? Would it matter whether such a
registrant registered the domain name with a U.S.-based domain name
registrar?

7. *Charting the UDRP and ACPA.* A chart created by the International
Trademark Association and providing an excellent comparison and brief
overview of key provisions of ICANN's UDRP and the ACPA may be found
at www.inta.org/news/compchart.shtml.

CONTROLLING DIGITAL GOODS: COPYRIGHT

Businesses involved in e-commerce may confront copyright issues in several different contexts. First, almost all businesses, whether online or offline, and whether selling hard goods or information goods, will market their products using literature, catalog copy, images, and other materials that they wish to prevent others from copying. Second, some businesses, both online and offline, have information goods (software, movies, music, books, or other "content") as their stock in trade; these businesses want to prevent competitors and "pirates" from appropriating their products. Third, some businesses, native to the online environment, depend upon transmitting, aggregating, or repackaging digitized content, some of which is subject to copyrights owned by others. New copyright issues arise in all three of these contexts, due to the digitized format in which information goods and other materials are maintained on the network.

One of the great strengths of the Internet as a platform for commerce is the ease and efficiency with which information can be distributed in the global marketplace. If a company wishes to announce a new product to the world, it need only post the announcement on the company's website, or on electronic mailing lists or bulletin boards whose membership might have an interest in the product. In addition, the company can e-mail an announcement to those who have expressed an interest in learning of such a product, or discuss it in chat rooms and live online fora dedicated to a topic to which the product is relevant. The Internet may also be used to distribute customer service information quickly and inexpensively.

But the very ease and efficiency with which the Internet permits information to be copied and distributed is regarded by some as a great danger. To content producers—movie studios, book publishers, software producers, artists, composers, music publishers, and record companies—the Internet poses a threat that some perceive as of the greatest magnitude. Once an information product is reduced to a digital file, such as a movie on a DVD or a song on a CD, perfect copies of it can be distributed world-wide in unlimited numbers at virtually no cost—perfect because one of the characteristics of digital information products is that every copy perfectly duplicates the original. Accordingly, if a company loses control of its information assets on the Internet, the market value of those assets may drop to near zero—the marginal cost of copying and distributing them.

In part for this reason, traditional content companies have been slow to embrace the Internet as anything other than a marketing channel. While the Internet could also provide these companies with a low-cost, 24/7 distribution channel for delivering their digital goods and services, many content companies consider the risk to their principal assets simply too great.

In an analog world, the risk to a company's information assets was not nearly so great. It has been possible for decades, for example, to make copies of printed materials through xerography, and copies of recorded music on audio cassettes. But those technologies posed only a limited threat to content industries due to economic and technological constraints. It is usually cheaper to purchase an authorized copy of a book than to buy a pirated version reproduced through xerography, and the quality of the original is higher.[1] Copying via audiocassette usually costs less than buying an authorized version, but the quality degrades quickly with successive generations of copying further removed from the original. With the emergence of digital technologies, the economics and quality factors began to incline more favorably toward unauthorized copying and distribution. Floppy disks containing software or data, and CDs containing music, can be copied cheaply and easily, and with no loss in quality, even after multiple generations of copies. The need physically to distribute the media bearing the content, however, acts as a constraint on unauthorized distribution: special efforts must be made to conceal the factories needed to engage in large-scale piracy, and large shipments of physical media are susceptible to discovery and confiscation. Large-scale copying and distribution via the Internet largely eliminates these constraints.

Content companies have been reluctant to make their material available online for another reason as well: the law governing rights in information goods, the law of copyright, is less well settled online than offline. In many ways, the law of copyright applies online just as one would expect. Images and text posted on a web page are governed by copyright in the same way that images and text in a mail-order catalog are. Similarly, digital music files online generally receive the same protection as music recorded on an audio CD. What causes uncertainty online is not these established applications of copyright law, but rather the novel uses of digital goods in a purely digital environment.

For example, the use of any kind of digital information on a computer, and any transmission of information from one computer to another, involves temporary storage of that information. Is the unauthorized storage of such information a violation of the copyright owner's exclusive right to make copies? Is transmitting a digital file a violation of the copyright owner's exclusive distribution right? Does the appearance of an image in a web browser implicate the copyright owner's public display right? If the transmission of a file over the Internet requires its conversion from one file format to another, is that a violation of the copyright owner's exclusive

---

1. For certain types of printed works, however, such as sheet music, a photocopy may be significantly cheaper than an authorized version.

right to prepare derivative works? Also unresolved are issues concerning how the copyright laws apply to the many new and emerging business models that use, manipulate, repurpose, and repackage digital goods in ways unanticipated by the drafters of the copyright laws.

In the last few years, Congress has enacted significant amendments to federal copyright law aimed at addressing some of the unique issues raised by the Internet. Courts have also done their part, extending traditional copyright doctrine into the digital domain. Nonetheless, much uncertainty remains.

In light of these legal uncertainties and the greater threat of unauthorized copying online, some companies have embraced self-help technologies in an effort to reduce the business risks involved in making digitized content available on the Internet. Chief among these self-help measures has been the use of encryption-based software programs—sometimes called digital rights management systems or simply "trusted systems"—that control access to and copying of information goods. In recognition of the importance of these systems to the development of Internet commerce, two recent international treaties require signatory states to enact legislation making it unlawful to circumvent such systems. We address trusted systems and the laws supporting their use in Chapter 5.

In this chapter, we look at the evolving role of copyright law online. In Part I, we present an overview of the law of copyright that highlights some of the uncertainties that arise when applying it online. In Part II, we consider how the doctrines of direct, contributory, and vicarious copyright infringement apply to such online actors as website visitors, bulletin board operators, website owners, and Internet service providers. Part III reviews the defenses of fair use, the first-sale doctrine, and copyright misuse, and the right to make copies of musical sound recordings for noncommercial purposes. Part IV considers the complex statutory framework governing the streaming and downloading of music online. Finally, in Part V we consider the safe harbors that Title II of the Digital Millennium Copyright Act created for the benefit of online service providers.

I.   A BRIEF OVERVIEW OF THE LAW OF COPYRIGHT

Copyright is a set of statutory rights that writers, artists, composers, musicians, and other authors acquire in connection with their original creations. These rights constitute a legal monopoly, allowing authors (or the transferees of their rights) to prevent others for a limited time from making certain uses of the protected works, and to condition the use of those works on whatever terms they see fit.

Federal copyright law derives from Article 1, Section 8, Clause 8 of the United States Constitution, which confers on the federal government the power "[t]o promote the Progress of Science and useful Arts, by securing for limited Times to Authors * * * the exclusive Right to their * * *

Writings * * *." Exercising this power, Congress enacted the first copyright law in 1790, and has amended it many times since.

The goal of copyright is to encourage the creation and distribution of original works of authorship, by enabling authors to exploit the economic value of their creations. Works of authorship have the special property that, once disclosed to the public, they may be reproduced by others in such a way that little of their value translates into income to the author. For example, if it were cost-free to make a perfect copy of a book, and if the law did not proscribe such copying, then it is likely the publisher would be able to sell only one copy of each book at cover price, making it economically infeasible to publish. If authors are unable to convert the fruits of their labor into income, they will cease to create, or at least create less. Because society as a whole benefits from the creation of literary, artistic, musical, and other works of authorship, the law grants authors the right to prevent others from making use of their works without paying for that privilege.

The Copyright Act of 1976 accomplishes this by granting authors a set of "exclusive rights" with respect to the works they create. These are the rights (1) to reproduce the work, (2) to prepare derivative works based on the work, (3) to distribute copies of the work to the public, (4) to perform the work publicly, (5) to display the work publicly, and (6) in the case of sound recordings, to perform the copyrighted work publicly by means of a digital audio transmission. 17 U.S.C. § 106. A person who exercises any of these rights without the permission of the copyright holder is said to "infringe" the copyright, and is liable for damages and subject to injunctive relief. The *reproduction right* may be infringed by, for example, making an unauthorized copy of a text, a musical composition, a recording of a musical performance, or a software program. The copyright holder's *right to prepare derivative works* is infringed by one who creates a new work based on the original, such as by producing a motion picture that is based on a book. The *distribution right* reserves to the copyright holder the exclusive right to transfer copies of the work to the public, by sale, rental, lease, or lending. The *public performance right* may be infringed by showing a movie, playing a sound recording, or performing a dance at a location that is open to the public, or where members of the public are gathered. Similarly, the *public display right* is infringed by showing a picture or other protected work publicly.

The works of authorship that copyright protects span the range of human imagination, including literary works, computer programs, musical compositions, dramatic works, pantomimes and choreographic works, drawings, paintings, photographs, motion pictures and other audiovisual works (including computer games), sound recordings, and architectural works. 17 U.S.C. § 102(a). Works are entitled to protection only if they are original: the author must have created the work independently rather than copying it from another, and the work must involve some minimal quantum of creativity. Only the author's *expression* is protectible; the ideas, concepts, principles, and facts communicated by that expression are not within the protection of copyright. 17 U.S.C. § 102(b).

Copyright protection exists from the moment a work of authorship is fixed in some tangible medium of expression, such as by writing a text or musical composition on paper, recording a performance on audiotape or videotape, or making a drawing or painting. The observance of formalities, such as placing a © symbol on each copy of the work or timely registering it with the Copyright Office, is not a prerequisite to copyright protection, but may yield significant advantages to the copyright holder in an infringement action. Under current law, protection generally lasts until 70 years after the death of the author. In the case of "works made for hire," which are works produced by an employee within the scope of his employment as well as certain works produced by independent contractors, copyright lasts for 95 years from publication, but no more than 120 years from creation.

Copyright seeks to maintain an appropriate balance between the interests of authors in benefiting from the economic value of their works, and the interests of the public, and of subsequent authors, in having access to the works that copyright is designed to encourage. To this end, the Copyright Act imposes certain limitations on copyright holders' exercise of their exclusive rights. The most important of these limitations is known as "fair use," which allows free use of copyrighted works in circumstances where the user derives significant benefit and the copyright owner suffers only minor harm. 17 U.S.C. § 107. The copyright laws also contain a variety of narrow exemptions for libraries, nonprofit and educational users, limited uses on business premises, non-commercial copying of musical recordings, and other circumstances. *See, e.g.*, 17 U.S.C. §§ 108, 110, & 1008. In addition, the Copyright Act grants compulsory licenses for certain uses, giving anyone the right to make use of a copyrighted work upon payment of a royalty rate determined by law. *See, e.g.*, 17 U.S.C. §§ 114 & 115.

Because the socially optimal balance between authorial rights and public access changes over time as new forms of expression emerge and new uses for copyrighted works develop, the law of copyright has been regularly amended to accommodate new and emerging technologies and forms of commerce. Historically, for example, the development and commercialization of photography, telegraphy, radio, motion pictures, broadcast and cable television, xerography, audio and video recording equipment, and the computer have all led to amendments of federal copyright law.

NOTES & QUESTIONS

1. *Fixation on the Web.* Today, many web pages are created "on the fly" using technologies such as Active Server Pages ("ASP"). These technologies are used when the information that must be displayed on a web page changes frequently, such as an e-commerce site's available inventory, sports scores, stock quotations, or the identity of the viewer. Typically, once the page is requested, an ASP application will assemble that web page by first acquiring the needed information from a database or cookie and then inserting it into appropriate HTML code. The web server will then send the newly created page to the web browser that requested it. The web page created by the ASP application may only exist momentarily in the random access memory of the server before it is sent to the requesting browser. In such a case, is the web page copyrightable subject matter? Does it meet the fixation requirement? Upon what additional facts might your answer depend?

2. *RAM copies.* Utilization of a computer inevitably involves loading software code into the machine's random access memory ("RAM"). A very significant issue in copyright law is whether this temporary storage of (generally copyrighted) code constitutes "fixation" of the code in RAM. A work (such as computer code) is "fixed" for this purpose if its embodiment in a material object (such as RAM) "is sufficiently permanent or stable to permit it to be perceived, reproduced, or otherwise communicated for a period of more than transitory duration." 17 U.S.C. § 101. If code temporarily stored in RAM is considered to be "fixed," the RAM would constitute a "copy" of the work, and making the RAM copy without authorization of the copyright owner would constitute prima facie infringement. This would mean that a wide variety of ordinary uses of computers, including particularly engaging in online communications, could involve infringement of copyrights.

This issue was addressed in *MAI Systems Corp. v. Peak Computer*, 991 F.2d 511 (9th Cir.1993), in which the copyright owner of operating system software sued a computer repair company for infringement, based on the repair company's turning on a computer running the operating system for the purpose of servicing the machine. The Ninth Circuit upheld the district court's conclusion that "the loading of copyrighted computer software * * * into the memory of a central processing unit ('CPU') causes a copy to be made," which in the absence of permission from the copyright owner constitutes infringement. *Id.* at 518.

Congress responded to the decision in *MAI v. Peak* by enacting Title III of the Digital Millennium Copyright Act, known as the Computer Maintenance Competition Assurance Act, which amends 17 U.S.C. § 117 to provide that "an independent service provider may turn on a client's computer machine in order to service its hardware components" without infringing the copyright of software that is loaded during this process. H.R. Conf. Rep. No. 105-796, at 86 (1998). This amendment, however, did not settle the more general issue of whether the temporary storage of computer code in RAM is the making of a "copy" for purposes of the Copyright Act.

The view that under current law temporary storage of a work in RAM is a "copy" for purposes of the Copyright Act has been criticized by many scholars. *See, e.g.,* Jessica Litman, *The Exclusive Right to Read*, 13 Cardozo Arts & Ent. L.J. 29, 41–43 (1994); Mark A. Lemley, *Dealing with Overlapping Copyrights on the Internet*, 22 U. Dayton L. Rev. 547, 550–52 (1997). Other scholars, however, argue that temporary storage in RAM does amount to the making of a "copy." *See, e.g.,* Jane C. Ginsburg, *Putting Cars on the "Information Superhighway": Authors, Exploiters, and Copyright in Cyberspace*, 95 Colum. L. Rev. 1466, 1476 (1995). The Register of

Copyrights has expressed the same view. *See* U.S. COPYRIGHT OFFICE, DMCA SECTION 104 REPORT (2001), www.copyright.gov/reports/studies/dmca/dmca_study.html.

Professor Joseph Liu explains the significance of this issue for the balance of power between copyright owners and users in the online environment:

> Driving the sharp criticism of the result in *MAI* is a broader concern that the result drastically and unthinkingly shifts the existing balance of rights in copyrighted works from users to copyright owners in the digital environment. Because computer software is copied into RAM as a necessary incident to the use of that software, the decision in *MAI* effectively gives copyright owners the right to control any and all uses of the software, unless such uses are subject to some statutory privilege. In addition, nothing in the reasoning of the opinion prevents it from being extended from computer software to any and all works stored in digital form, such as images, text documents, sound recordings, and motion pictures. Indeed, several federal courts have extended the rule in MAI to just such digital works. * * * Taken to its logical conclusion, MAI would give copyright owners broad control, at least in theory, over nearly all computer-aided uses of copyrighted works encoded in digital form.

Joseph P. Liu, *Owning Digital Copies: Copyright Law and the Incidents of Copy Ownership*, 42 WM. & MARY L. REV. 1245, 1262-1263 (2001).

3. *Framing and derivative works.* A frame is a region within the window of a web browser that can display a single web page. By employing multiple frames within a single browser window, one can display multiple web pages simultaneously. Moreover, one can design these web pages so that they appear to be a single page. Multiple frames are sometimes used to create a persistent user interface for a website. For example, it is common to see a website with navigational elements such as buttons and dropdown menus on the left side of the browser window, a narrow unchanging header for the website running across the top, and the changing content of the site displayed in the remaining part of the browser window. The navigational bar, the header, and the content displayed in the remainder of the browser window are actually separate web pages, each one displayed in a separate frame.

From the perspective of copyright law, it is unclear how one should characterize the display of multiple web pages in a single browser window. Under 17 U.S.C. § 101, a "derivative work" is "a work based upon one or more preexisting works." If one incorporates web pages created by another, is the result a derivative work? If so, then unauthorized framing of web pages created by another may infringe the copyright owner's exclusive right "to prepare derivative works based upon the copyrighted work." 17 U.S.C. § 106(2). This was the legal theory of the plaintiff in *Futuredontics Inc. v. Applied Anagramics Inc.*, 45 U.S.P.Q.2d (BNA) 2005 (C.D.Cal.1998), *aff'd*, 152 F.3d 925 (9th Cir.1998). The defendant, Applied Anagramics, Inc.

("AAI"), had framed a web page from the plaintiff's website. The defendant caused plaintiff's web page to appear in the window of a web browser with web pages that contained the defendant's logo, information about the defendant's business, and hypertext links to other web pages created by the defendant. In denying defendant's motion to dismiss, the court said:

> The parties sharply dispute what function AAI's framed link serves. Defendant contends that AAI's window or frame provides a "lens" which enables Internet users to view the information that Plaintiff itself placed on the Internet. Plaintiff's complaint, however, alleges that defendant reproduces its copyrighted web page by combining AAI material and Plaintiff's web site. * * *
>
>   * * *
>
> The parties discuss the applicability of *Mirage Editions, Inc. v. Albuquerque A.R.T. Co.*, 856 F.2d 1341, 1343 (9th Cir.1988). In *Mirage*, the Ninth Circuit held that transferring and affixing art images with glue to ceramic tiles constituted "the creation of a derivative work in violation of the copyright laws." Id. at 1343–44. As this Court noted in its Order denying Plaintiff's request for a preliminary injunction, *Mirage* is distinguishable from the present case. In this case, AAI has not affixed an image to a ceramic tile, rather AAI appears to have placed an electronic frame or border around Plaintiff's web page.
>
> Defendants primarily rely on *Lewis Galoob Toys, Inc. v. Nintendo of America, Inc.*, 964 F.2d 965, 968 (9th Cir.1992). In that case, the Ninth Circuit held that a Game Genie which merely enhances audiovisual displays which originate in Nintendo game cartridges does not constitute a derivative work because, in part, it does "not incorporate a portion of a copyrighted work in some concrete or permanent form." * * * *Galoob* does not foreclose Plaintiff from establishing that AAI's web page incorporates Futuredontic's web page in some "concrete or permanent form" or that AAI's framed link duplicates or recasts Plaintiff's web page. Id.
>
> For these reasons, the Court finds that the cases cited by the parties do not conclusively determine whether Defendants' frame page constitutes a derivative work.

Futuredontics Inc. v. Applied Anagramics Inc., 45 U.S.P.Q.2d at 2010. How would you decide this case? As the plaintiff, how might you argue that AAI's web page incorporates Futuredontic's web page in some "concrete or permanent form"? As the defendant, how might you argue that AAI's framed link does not duplicate or recast plaintiff's web page?

4. *Filtering and derivative works.* Before allowing a web page to be displayed in a browser, filtering software may be used to screen the page and determine whether it contains a particular type of content. Web filtering technologies may employ a variety of approaches to ascertain the content of a web page. Such filtering software might screen a web page for particular keywords, attempt to interpret the images contained on the page, or identify the HTML tags used to format the page. Once targeted content is identified, the filtering software can either prevent the browser from displaying the web page, block the entire site, or excise the targeted content and permit the remainder of the page to be displayed. If the offending content is excised, how would you characterize the resulting web page for the purpose of copyright? Who, if anyone, owns the copyright in the cleansed web page? Does creation of the cleansed web page infringe any of the exclusive rights held by the copyright owner of the original web page?

5. *Criminal copyright infringement and the Internet.* An example of how the Internet brought about amendment of the copyright laws involves criminal copyright infringement under 17 U.S.C. § 506(a). In *United States v. LaMacchia*, 871 F.Supp. 535 (D.Mass.1994), David LaMacchia, a twenty-one-year-old student at the Massachusetts Institute of Technology,

> used MIT's computer network to gain entree to the Internet. Using pseudonyms and an encrypted address, LaMacchia set up an electronic bulletin board which he named Cynosure. He encouraged his correspondents to upload popular software applications (Excel 5.0 and WordPerfect 6.0) and computer games (Sim City 2000). These he transferred to a second encrypted address (Cynosure II) where they could be downloaded by other users with access to the Cynosure password. Although LaMacchia was at pains to impress the need for circumspection on the part of his subscribers, the worldwide traffic generated by the offer of free software attracted the notice of university and federal authorities.
>
> On April 7, 1994, a federal grand jury returned a one count indictment charging LaMacchia with conspiring with "persons unknown" to violate 18 U.S.C. § 1343, the wire fraud statute. According to the indictment, LaMacchia devised a scheme to defraud that had as its object the facilitation "on an international scale" of the "illegal copying and distribution of copyrighted software" without payment of licensing fees and royalties to software manufacturers and vendors. The indictment alleges that LaMacchia's scheme caused losses of more than one million dollars to software copyright holders. The indictment does not allege that LaMacchia sought or derived any personal benefit from the scheme to defraud.

Id. at 536–37. The government argued that LaMacchia's conduct fell within the purview of the wire fraud statute because he had used the Internet to copy and distribute software in violation of 17 U.S.C. § 506(a). Section 506(a) "requir[ed] prosecutors to prove that the defendant infringed a copyright 'willfully and for purpose of commercial advantage or private financial gain.'" *Id.* at 540. Since LaMacchia acted neither for commercial advantage nor financial gain, the elements of the crime were not present, and the court granted LaMacchia's motion to dismiss.

Congress reacted to the *LaMacchia* decision by enacting the No Electronic Theft ("NET") Act, Pub. L. No. 105–147, 111 Stat. 2678 (1997). The

NET Act amended the definition of "financial gain" under 17 U.S.C. § 101 to include "receipt, or expectation of receipt, of anything of value, including the receipt of other copyrighted works." It also amended the elements for criminal copyright infringement under § 506(a). As amended, § 506(a) now reads as follows:

> **(a) Criminal Infringement**.—Any person who infringes a copyright willfully either—
>
>> (1) for purposes of commercial advantage or private financial gain, or
>>
>> (2) by the reproduction or distribution, including by electronic means, during any 180–day period, of 1 or more copies or phonorecords of 1 or more copyrighted works, which have a total retail value of more than $1,000,
>
> shall be punished as provided under section 2319 of title 18, United States Code. For purposes of this subsection, evidence of reproduction or distribution of a copyrighted work, by itself, shall not be sufficient to establish willful infringement.

17 U.S.C. § 506(a).

6. *The display right on the Web.* When a person views a page of a website using her browser, it seems clear that a "display" has occurred. From the standpoint of copyright law, who should be deemed responsible for the display: the viewer, for pointing her browser at a particular web address? the website operator, for making material available for display? both? *See Playboy Enterprises, Inc. v. Frena*, 839 F.Supp. 1552 (M.D.Fla.1993), excerpted in Part II(A), *infra*; *Kelly v. Arriba Soft Corp.*, 280 F.3d 934 (9th Cir.2002), excerpted in Part II(A), *infra*; and *Intellectual Reserve, Inc. v. Utah Lighthouse Ministry, Inc.*, 75 F.Supp.2d 1290 (D.Utah 1999), excerpted in Part II(B), *infra*. *See also* R. Anthony Reese, *The Public Display Right: the Copyright Act's Neglected Solution to the Controversy over RAM "Copies,"* 2001 U. ILL. L. REV. 83.

NOTE: DIGITALLY REPURPOSED WORKS

Digital works have the significant advantage that they can be easily manipulated and reused for a variety of purposes at very low cost. For example, a traditional print publication can easily reformat the content of its print edition for display on the Web. The variety of online versions of traditional print publications is indeed a testimony to the ease and low expense with which such repurposing can be accomplished. Moreover, as broadband connections to the Internet become more pervasive, we can expect to see traditional over-the-air broadcasters also repurposing their audio and video content online. The pervasive reuse and repurposing of content on the Web raises the question whether licensees of the right to use articles and other kinds of content in traditional print publications and over-the-air broadcasts also enjoy the right to use the same content on the Web if the licensing agreement between the publisher and the author is silent on this issue. *See Random House, Inc. v. Rosetta Books LLC*, 150 F.Supp.2d 613 (S.D.N.Y.2001), *denial of prelim. inj. aff'd*, 283 F.3d 490 (2d Cir.2002).

In *New York Times Co. v. Tasini*, 533 U.S. 483 (2001), the Supreme Court addressed a closely related question, namely whether a newspaper could reuse articles from its print edition in an electronic database. The litigation was commenced by six freelance authors, and concerned articles that they had contributed to three print periodicals (two newspapers and one magazine). "Under agreements with the periodicals' publishers, but without the freelancers' consent, two computer database companies placed copies of the freelancers' articles—along with all other articles from the periodicals in which the freelancers' work appeared—into three databases." *Id*. at 487. (For a discussion of the law applicable to databases and compilations online, see Chapter 4, *infra*.)

The two database companies were LEXIS/NEXIS and University Microfilms International ("UMI"). LEXIS/NEXIS placed the articles in its online text-based database known as NEXIS. "Each article appear[ed] as a separate, isolated 'story'—without any visible link to the other stories originally published in the same newspaper or magazine edition." The NEXIS version did "not contain pictures or advertisements," nor did it "reproduce the original print publication's formatting features such as headline size, page placement (*e.g.*, above or below the fold for newspapers), or location of continuation pages." UMI placed the articles in its own text-only database, called the New York Times OnDisc ("NYTO"). UMI also placed the articles in an image-based database called General Periodicals OnDisc ("GPO"). This database shows "each article exactly as it appeared on printed pages, complete with photographs, captions, advertisements, and other surrounding materials." *Id*. at 490–91.

The plaintiffs alleged that inclusion of their articles in the databases infringed their copyrights. The publishers defended by invoking Section 201(c) of the Copyright Act, which provides:

> Copyright in each separate contribution to a collective work is distinct from copyright in the collective work as a whole, and vests initially in the author of the contribution. In the absence of an express transfer of the copyright or of any rights under it, the owner of copyright in the collective work is presumed to have acquired only the privilege of reproducing and distributing the contribution as part of that particular collective work, any revision of that collective work, and any later collective work in the same series.

17 U.S.C. § 201(c). "Specifically, the publishers maintained that, as copyright owners of collective works, *i.e.*, the original print publications, they had merely exercised 'the privilege' § 201(c) accords them to 'reproduc[e] and distribut[e]' the author's discretely copyrighted contribution." 533 U.S. at 508–09.

Applying this provision, the Court noted that

> the three Databases present articles to users clear of the context provided either by the original periodical editions or by any revision of those editions. The Databases first prompt users to search the universe of their contents: thousands or millions of files containing individual articles from thousands of collective works (*i.e.*, editions), either in one series (the Times, in NYTO) or in scores of series (the sundry titles in NEXIS and GPO). When the user conducts a search, each article appears as a separate item within the search result. In NEXIS and NYTO, an article appears to a user without the graphics, formatting, or other articles with which the article was initially published. In GPO, the article appears with the other materials published on the same page or pages, but without any material published on other pages of the original periodical. In either circumstance, we cannot see how the Database perceptibly reproduces and distributes the article "as part of" either the original edition or a "revision" of that edition.

Id. at 499–500. The Court further elaborated its position by likening the databases to an imaginary library:

> For the purpose at hand—determining whether the Authors' copyrights have been infringed—an analogy to an imaginary library may be instructive. Rather than maintaining intact editions of periodicals, the library would contain separate copies of each article. Perhaps these copies would exactly reproduce the periodical pages from which the articles derive (if the model is GPO); perhaps the copies would contain only typescript characters, but still indicate the original periodical's name and date, as well as the article's headline and page number (if the model is NEXIS or NYTO). The library would store the folders containing the articles in a file room, indexed based on diverse criteria, and containing articles from vast numbers of editions. In response to patron requests, an inhumanly speedy librarian would search the room and provide copies of the articles matching patron-specified criteria.

> Viewing this strange library, one could not, consistent with ordinary English usage, characterize the articles "as part of" a "revision" of the editions in which the articles first appeared. In substance, however, the Databases differ from the file room only to the extent they aggregate articles in electronic packages (the LEXIS/NEXIS central discs or UMI CD–ROMs), while the file room stores articles in spatially separate files. The crucial fact is that the Databases, like the hypothetical library, store and retrieve articles separately within a vast domain of diverse texts. Such a storage and retrieval system effectively overrides the Authors' exclusive right to control the individual reproduction and distribution of each Article, 17 U.S.C. §§ 106(1), (3).

> The Publishers claim the protection of § 201(c) because users can manipulate the Databases to generate search results consisting

entirely of articles from a particular periodical edition. By this logic, § 201(c) would cover the hypothetical library if, in response to a request, that library's expert staff assembled all of the articles from a particular periodical edition. However, the fact that a third party can manipulate a database to produce a noninfringing document does not mean the database is not infringing. Under § 201(c), the question is not whether a user can generate a revision of a collective work from a database, but whether the database itself perceptibly presents the author's contribution as part of a revision of the collective work. That result is not accomplished by these Databases.

Id. at 502–04. This analogy, however, was not persuasive to all members of the Court. In his dissenting opinion, Justice Stevens, joined by Justice Breyer, adopted a different analogy:

A proper analysis of this case benefits from an incremental approach. Accordingly, I begin by discussing an issue the majority largely ignores: whether a collection of articles from a single edition of the New York Times (*i.e.,* the batch of files the Print Publishers periodically send to the Electronic Databases) constitutes a "revision" of an individual edition of the paper. In other words, does a single article within such a collection exist as "part of" a "revision"? Like the majority, I believe that the crucial inquiry is whether the article appears within the "context" of the original collective work. But this question simply raises the further issue of precisely how much "context" is enough.

The record indicates that what is sent from the New York Times to the Electronic Databases (with the exception of General Periodicals on Disc (GPO)) is simply a collection of ASCII text files representing the editorial content of the New York Times for a particular day.[7] * * *

I see no compelling reason why a collection of files corresponding to a single edition of the New York Times, standing alone, cannot constitute a "revision" of that day's New York Times. * * * Once one accepts the premise that a disk containing all the files from the October 31, 2000, New York Times can constitute a "revision," there is no reason to treat any differently the same set of files, stored in a folder on the hard disk of a computer at the New York Times. * * * If my hypothetical October 31, 2000, floppy disk can be a revision, I do not see why the inclusion of other editions and other periodicals is any more significant than the placement of a single edition of the New York Times in a large public library or in a book store.

----

7. ASCII (American Standard Code for Information Interchange) is a standard means for storing textual data. It assigns a unique binary code for each letter of the alphabet, as well as for numbers, punctuation, and other characters. It cannot be used to convey graphical information. * * *

Id. at 511–12, 517. Justice Stevens then reminded the majority that " 'the primary purpose of copyright is not to reward the author, but is rather to secure "the general benefits derived by the public from the labors of authors." ' " *Id.* at 519 (quoting Melville B. Nimmer & David Nimmer, Nimmer on Copyright § 1.03[A]) (quoting *Fox Film Corp. v. Doyal*, 286 U.S. 123, 127 (1932)). He thought that the authors' victory "unnecessarily subverts this fundamental goal of copyright law in favor of a narrow focus on 'authorial rights.' " He said that while "the desire to protect such rights is certainly a laudable sentiment, copyright law demands that 'private motivation must ultimately serve the cause of promoting *broad public availability* of literature, music, and the other arts.' *Twentieth Century Music Corp. v. Aiken*, 422 U.S. 151, 156 (1975)." *Id.* at 520.

The *Tasini* majority and dissenting opinions suggest several questions.

1. *Authorial rights vs. public access.* To advance their arguments, both the majority and the dissent present thought experiments. The majority appeals to a hypothetical library containing a collection of individual articles, while the dissent appeals to a floppy disk containing the digitized articles from a single edition of a periodical. Which is more analogous to the case before the Court? Do you agree with the dissent that the floppy disk is a revision? If so, should storage of more than one revision on a single floppy disk or other medium cause these files to lose their status as revisions? How would you respond to the dissent's rhetorical query whether paper editions of a newspaper lose their status as editions when piled together in a library?

2. Tasini *on the Web.* How does the holding in *Tasini* apply to the *New York Times* website, which reproduces material from the *Times's* print publications? Would your answer change if the *Times* formatted each article on its website as a separate HTML page?

II. Copyright Infringement Online

Many acts of online copyright infringement are initiated by individual Internet users—a person posting a copyrighted text on an electronic bulletin board system ("BBS"), for example. Copyright owners would find it impractical to identify and sue such individual infringers in large numbers. In many cases the defendant would be judgment-proof; investigative and legal fees would be considerable; and success on the merits would be unlikely to deter others from engaging in the same kind of behavior, given the unlikelihood that any particular individual would be targeted in a subsequent enforcement action. Therefore, rather than pursue individual infringers, copyright owners have usually preferred to sue BBS operators and other online service providers who act as conduits for such infringing activities. These entities generally have deeper pockets than the individual infringers, and forcing them either to shut down or to police the infringing activities of their users can bring about a significant reduction of infringement online.

A person who without authorization exercises one of a copyright holder's exclusive rights, or authorizes another to do so, is liable as a direct infringer. A person may also be held liable for the infringing actions of others, under the doctrines of contributory and vicarious liability. In this Part, we consider how courts have applied these doctrines to Internet users, BBS operators, search engines, and Internet service providers.

A. DIRECT INFRINGEMENT

A claim for direct copyright infringement arises when a person infringes one of the exclusive rights that 17 U.S.C. § 106 grants to the copyright owner. A person directly infringes a copyright by reproducing, adapting, distributing, publicly performing, or publicly displaying the copyrighted work of another, without authorization. To succeed in an action for direct copyright infringement, the plaintiff must prove (1) that she owns a valid copyright in the work, and (2) that the defendant copied or authorized the copying of protected elements of the work. The courts frequently refer to each of these infringing actions as "copying," even though distribution, performance, and display need not involve copying.

Playboy Enterprises, Inc. v. Frena

839 F.Supp. 1552 (M.D.Fla.1993).

■ SCHLESINGER, DISTRICT JUDGE.

* * * Plaintiff requests that the Court grant partial summary judgment that Defendant Frena infringed Plaintiff's copyrights and specifically that the 170 image files in question * * * infringed Plaintiff's copyrights in 50 of Plaintiff's copyrighted magazines. * * *

Defendant George Frena operates a subscription computer bulletin board service, Techs Warehouse BBS ("BBS"), that distributed unauthorized copies of Plaintiff Playboy Enterprises, Inc.'s ("PEI") copyrighted photographs. BBS is accessible via telephone modem to customers. For a fee, or to those who purchase certain products from Defendant Frena, anyone with an appropriately equipped computer can log onto BBS. Once logged on subscribers may browse through different BBS directories to look at the pictures and customers may also download the high quality computerized copies of the photographs and then store the copied image from Frena's computer onto their home computer. Many of the images found on BBS include adult subject matter. One hundred and seventy of the images that were available on BBS were copies of photographs taken from PEI's copyrighted materials.

Defendant Frena admits that these materials were displayed on his BBS, that he never obtained authorization or consent from PEI, and that each of the accused computer graphic files on BBS is substantially similar to copyrighted PEI photographs. Defendant Frena also admits that each of the files in question has been downloaded by one of his customers.

Subscribers can upload material onto the bulletin board so that any other subscriber, by accessing their computer, can see that material. Defendant Frena states in his Affidavit filed August 4, 1993, that he never uploaded any of PEI's photographs onto BBS and that subscribers to BBS uploaded the photographs. Defendant Frena states that as soon as he was served with a summons and made aware of this matter, he removed the photographs from BBS and has since that time monitored BBS to prevent additional photographs of PEI from being uploaded.

* * *

I. COPYRIGHT INFRINGEMENT

The Copyright Act of 1976 gives copyright owners control over most, if not all, activities of conceivable commercial value. The statute provides that

> the owner of a copyright ... has the exclusive rights to do and to authorize any of the following: (1) to reproduce the copyrighted work in copies ...; (2) to prepare derivative works based upon the copyrighted work; (3) to distribute copies ... of the copyrighted work to the public ... and (5) in the case of ... pictorial ... works ... to display the copyrighted work publicly.

17 U.S.C. § 106. Engaging in or authorizing any of these categories without the copyright owner's permission violates the exclusive rights of the copyright owner and constitutes infringement of the copyright. *See* 17 U.S.C. § 501(a).

To establish copyright infringement, PEI must show ownership of the copyright and "copying" by Defendant Frena, see *Feist Publications, Inc. v. Rural Tel. Serv. Co.,* 499 U.S. 340 (1991); *Southern Bell Tel. & Tel. v. Assoc. Telephone Directory Publishers,* 756 F.2d 801, 810 (11th Cir.1985).

There is no dispute that PEI owns the copyrights on the photographs in question. PEI owns copyright registrations for each of the 50 issues of Playboy publications that contain the photographs on BBS. The copyright registration certificate constitutes prima facie evidence in favor of Plaintiff. Once the plaintiff has established his prima facie ownership, the burden then shifts to the defendant to counter this evidence. Defendant Frena, however, failed to rebut the appropriate inference of validity.

Next, PEI must demonstrate copying by Defendant Frena. Since direct evidence of copying is rarely available in a copyright infringement action, copying may be inferentially proven by showing that Defendant Frena had access to the allegedly infringed work, that the allegedly infringing work is substantially similar to the copyrighted work, and that one of the rights statutorily guaranteed to copyright owners is implicated by Frena's actions. *See Ford Motor Co. v. Summit Motor Products, Inc.,* 930 F.2d 277, 291 (3d Cir.1991), *cert. denied,* 502 U.S. 939.

Access to the copyrighted work is not at issue. Access is essentially undeniable because every month PEI sells over 3.4 million copies of Playboy magazine throughout the United States.

Substantial similarity is also a non-issue in this case. Defendant Frena has admitted that every one of the accused images is substantially similar to the PEI copyrighted photograph from which the accused image was produced. Moreover, not only are the accused works substantially similar to the copyrighted work, but the infringing photographs are essentially exact copies. In many cases, the only difference is that PEI's written text appearing on the same page of the photograph has been removed from the infringing copy.

The next step is to determine whether Defendant Frena violated one of the rights statutorily guaranteed to copyright owners under 17 U.S.C. § 106. *See* 17 U.S.C. § 501(a).

Public distribution of a copyrighted work is a right reserved to the copyright owner, and usurpation of that right constitutes infringement. *See Cable/Home Communication Corp. v. Network Productions, Inc.*, 902 F.2d 829, 843 (11th Cir.1990). PEI's right under 17 U.S.C. § 106(3) to distribute copies to the public has been implicated by Defendant Frena. Section 106(3) grants the copyright owner "the exclusive right to sell, give away, rent or lend any material embodiment of his work." 2 MELVILLE B. NIMMER, Nimmer on Copyright § 8.11[A], at 8–124.1 (1993). There is no dispute that Defendant Frena supplied a product containing unauthorized copies of a copyrighted work. It does not matter that Defendant Frena claims he did not make the copies itself.

Furthermore, the "display" rights of PEI have been infringed upon by Defendant Frena. *See* 17 U.S.C. § 106(5). The concept of display is broad. *See* 17 U.S.C. § 101. It covers "the projection of an image on a screen or other surface by any method, the transmission of an image by electronic or other means, and the showing of an image on a cathode ray tube, or similar viewing apparatus connected with any sort of information storage and retrieval system." H.R.Rep. No. 1476, 94th Cong., 2d Sess. 64 (Sept. 3, 1976), reprinted in 1976 U.S.Code Cong. & Admin.News 5659, 5677. The display right precludes unauthorized transmission of the display from one place to another, for example, by a computer system. *See* H.R.Rep. No. 1476, 94th Cong., 2d Sess. 80 (Sept. 3, 1976), reprinted in 1976 U.S.Code Cong. & Admin.News 5659, 5694.

"Display" covers any showing of a "copy" of the work, "either directly or by means of a film, slide, television image or any other device or process." 17 U.S.C. § 101. However, in order for there to be copyright infringement, the display must be public. A "public display" is a display "at a place open to the public or ... where a substantial number of persons outside of a normal circle of family and its social acquaintenances is gathered." 2 MELVILLE B. NIMMER, Nimmer on Copyright § 8.14[C], at 8–169 (1993). A place is "open to the public" in this sense even if access is limited to paying customers.

Defendant's display of PEI's copyrighted photographs to subscribers was a public display. Though limited to subscribers, the audience consisted of "a substantial number of persons outside of a normal circle of family and its social acquaintenances." 2 MELVILLE B. NIMMER, Nimmer on Copyright § 8.14[C], at 8–169 (1993). *See also Thomas v. Pansy Ellen Products,* 672 F.Supp. 237, 240 (W.D.North Carolina 1987) (display at a trade show was public even though limited to members); *Ackee Music, Inc. v. Williams,* 650 F.Supp. 653 (D.Kan.1986) (performance of copyrighted songs at defendant's private club constituted a public performance). * * *

There is irrefutable evidence of direct copyright infringement in this case. It does not matter that Defendant Frena may have been unaware of the copyright infringement. Intent to infringe is not needed to find copyright infringement. Intent or knowledge is not an element of infringement, and thus even an innocent infringer is liable for infringement; rather, innocence is significant to a trial court when it fixes statutory damages, which is a remedy equitable in nature. * * *

Accordingly, * * * Plaintiff's First Motion for Partial Summary Judgment (Copyright Infringement) as to Defendant Frena (Doc. No. S–1) is GRANTED.

Religious Technology Center v. Netcom On–Line Communication Services, Inc.

907 F.Supp. 1361 (N.D.Cal.1995).

■ WHYTE, DISTRICT JUDGE.

This case concerns an issue of first impression regarding intellectual property rights in cyberspace. Specifically, this order addresses whether the operator of a computer bulletin board service ("BBS"), and the large Internet access provider that allows that BBS to reach the Internet, should be liable for copyright infringement committed by a subscriber of the BBS.

Plaintiffs Religious Technology Center ("RTC") and Bridge Publications, Inc. ("BPI") hold copyrights in the unpublished and published works of L. Ron Hubbard, the late founder of the Church of Scientology ("the Church"). Defendant Dennis Erlich ("Erlich") is a former minister of Scientology turned vocal critic of the Church, whose pulpit is now the Usenet newsgroup alt.religion.scientology ("a.r.s."), an on-line forum for discussion and criticism of Scientology. Plaintiffs maintain that Erlich infringed their copyrights when he posted portions of their works on a.r.s. Erlich gained his access to the Internet through defendant Thomas Klemesrud's ("Klemesrud's") BBS "support.com." Klemesrud is the operator of the BBS, which is run out of his home and has approximately 500 paying users. Klemesrud's BBS is not directly linked to the Internet, but gains its connection through the facilities of defendant Netcom On–Line Communications, Inc. ("Netcom"), one of the largest providers of Internet access in the United States.

After failing to convince Erlich to stop his postings, plaintiffs contacted defendants Klemesrud and Netcom. Klemesrud responded to plaintiffs' demands that Erlich be kept off his system by asking plaintiffs to prove that they owned the copyrights to the works posted by Erlich. However, plaintiffs refused Klemesrud's request as unreasonable. Netcom similarly refused plaintiffs' request that Erlich not be allowed to gain access to the Internet through its system. Netcom contended that it would be impossible to prescreen Erlich's postings and that to kick Erlich off the Internet meant kicking off the hundreds of users of Klemesrud's BBS. Consequently, plaintiffs named Klemesrud and Netcom in their suit against Erlich, although only on the copyright infringement claims.

* * * For the reasons set forth below, the court grants in part and denies in part Netcom's motion for summary judgment * * *

I.   NETCOM'S MOTION FOR SUMMARY JUDGMENT OF NONINFRINGEMENT

* * *

B.   Copyright Infringement

* * * The court has already determined that plaintiffs have established that they own the copyrights to all of the * * * works, except item 4 of Exhibit A. The court also found plaintiffs likely to succeed on their claim that defendant Erlich copied the * * * works and was not entitled to a fair use defense. Plaintiffs argue that, although Netcom was not itself the source of any of the infringing materials on its system, it nonetheless should be liable for infringement, either directly, contributorily, or vicariously. Netcom disputes these theories of infringement and further argues that it is entitled to its own fair use defense.

1.   Direct Infringement

Infringement consists of the unauthorized exercise of one of the exclusive rights of the copyright holder delineated in section 106. 17 U.S.C. § 501. Direct infringement does not require intent or any particular state of mind,[10] although willfulness is relevant to the award of statutory damages. 17 U.S.C. § 504(c).

* * *

a.   Undisputed Facts

The parties do not dispute the basic processes that occur when Erlich posts his allegedly infringing messages to a.r.s. Erlich connects to Klemesrud's BBS using a telephone and a modem. Erlich then transmits his messages to Klemesrud's computer, where they are automatically briefly

---

10. The strict liability for copyright infringement is in contrast to another area of liability affecting online service providers: defamation. Recent decisions have held that where a BBS exercised little control over the content of the material on its service, it was more like a "distributor" than a "republisher" and was thus only liable for defamation on its system where it knew or should have known of the defamatory statements. *Cubby, Inc. v. CompuServe, Inc.,* 776 F.Supp. 135 (S.D.N.Y.1991). By contrast, a New York state court judge found that Prodigy was a publisher because it held itself out to be controlling the content of its services and because it used software to automatically prescreen messages that were offensive or in bad taste. *Stratton Oakmont, Inc. v. Prodigy Services Co.,* 1995 WL 323710, THE RECORDER, June 1, 1995, at 7 (excerpting May 24, 1995 Order Granting Partial Summary Judgment to Plaintiffs).

stored. According to a prearranged pattern established by Netcom's software, Erlich's initial act of posting a message to the Usenet results in the automatic copying of Erlich's message from Klemesrud's computer onto Netcom's computer and onto other computers on the Usenet. In order to ease transmission and for the convenience of Usenet users, Usenet servers maintain postings from newsgroups for a short period of time—eleven days for Netcom's system and three days for Klemesrud's system. Once on Netcom's computers, messages are available to Netcom's customers and Usenet neighbors, who may then download the messages to their own computers. Netcom's local server makes available its postings to a group of Usenet servers, which do the same for other servers until all Usenet sites worldwide have obtained access to the postings, which takes a matter of hours.

Unlike some other large on-line service providers, such as CompuServe, America Online, and Prodigy, Netcom does not create or control the content of the information available to its subscribers. It also does not monitor messages as they are posted. It has, however, suspended the accounts of subscribers who violated its terms and conditions, such as where they had commercial software in their posted files. Netcom admits that, although not currently configured to do this, it may be possible to reprogram its system to screen postings containing particular words or coming from particular individuals. Netcom, however, took no action after it was told by plaintiffs that Erlich had posted messages through Netcom's system that violated plaintiffs' copyrights, instead claiming that it could not shut out Erlich without shutting out all of the users of Klemesrud's BBS.

b.   Creation of Fixed Copies

The Ninth Circuit addressed the question of what constitutes infringement in the context of storage of digital information in a computer's random access memory ("RAM"). *MAI Systems Corp. v. Peak Computer, Inc.,* 991 F.2d 511, 518 (9th Cir.1993). In *MAI,* the Ninth Circuit upheld a finding of copyright infringement where a repair person, who was not authorized to use the computer owner's licensed operating system software, turned on the computer, thus loading the operating system into RAM for long enough to check an "error log." *Id.* at 518–19. Copyright protection subsists in original works of authorship *"fixed* in any tangible medium of expression, now known or later developed, from which they can be perceived, reproduced, or otherwise communicated, either directly or with the aid of a machine or device." 17 U.S.C. § 102 (emphasis added). A work is "fixed" when its "embodiment in a copy . . . is sufficiently permanent or stable to permit it to be perceived, reproduced, or otherwise communicated for a period of more than transitory duration." *Id.* § 101. *MAI* established that the loading of data from a storage device into RAM constitutes copying because that data stays in RAM long enough for it to be perceived. *MAI Systems,* 991 F.2d at 518.

In the present case, there is no question after *MAI* that "copies" were created, as Erlich's act of sending a message to a.r.s. caused reproductions of portions of plaintiffs' works on both Klemesrud's and Netcom's storage devices. Even though the messages remained on their systems for at most eleven days, they were sufficiently "fixed" to constitute recognizable copies under the Copyright Act. *See* Information Infrastructure Task Force, *Intellectual Property and the National Information Infrastructure: The Report of the Working Group on Intellectual Property Rights* 66 (1995) ("IITF Report").

c.   Is Netcom Directly Liable for Making the Copies?

Accepting that copies were made, Netcom argues that Erlich, and not Netcom, is directly liable for the copying. *MAI* did not address the question raised in this case: whether possessors of computers are liable for incidental copies automatically made on their computers using their software as part of a process initiated by a third party. Netcom correctly distinguishes *MAI* on the ground that Netcom did not take any affirmative action that directly resulted in copying plaintiffs' works other than by installing and maintaining a system whereby software automatically forwards messages received from subscribers onto the Usenet, and temporarily stores copies on its system. Netcom's actions, to the extent that they created a copy of plaintiffs' works, were necessary to having a working system for transmitting Usenet postings to and from the Internet. Unlike the defendants in *MAI*, neither Netcom nor Klemesrud initiated the copying. The defendants in *MAI* turned on their customers' computers thereby creating temporary copies of the operating system, whereas Netcom's and Klemesrud's systems can operate without any human intervention. Thus, unlike *MAI*, the mere fact that Netcom's system incidentally makes temporary copies of plaintiffs' works does not mean Netcom has caused the copying. The court believes that Netcom's act of designing or implementing a system that automatically and uniformly creates temporary copies of all data sent through it is not unlike that of the owner of a copying machine who lets the public make copies with it.[12] Although some of the people using the machine may directly infringe copyrights, courts analyze the machine owner's liability under the rubric of contributory infringement, not direct infringement. * * * Plaintiffs' theory would create many separate acts of infringement and, carried to its natural extreme, would lead to unreasonable liability. It is not difficult to conclude that Erlich infringes by copying a protected work

---

12. Netcom compares itself to a common carrier that merely acts as a passive conduit for information. In a sense, a Usenet server that forwards all messages acts like a common carrier, passively retransmitting every message that gets sent through it. Netcom would seem no more liable than the phone company for carrying an infringing facsimile transmission or storing an infringing audio recording on its voice mail. * * * In any event, common carriers are granted statutory exemptions for liability that might otherwise exist. Here, Netcom does not fall under this statutory exemption, and thus faces the usual strict liability scheme that exists for copyright. Whether a new exemption should be carved out for online service providers is to be resolved by Congress, not the courts. [Congress enacted a limited exemption for online service providers as part of the Digital Millennium Copyright Act of 1998. *See* Part V, *infra.*—Eds.]

onto his computer and by posting a message to a newsgroup. However, plaintiffs' theory further implicates a Usenet server that carries Erlich's message to other servers regardless of whether that server acts without any human intervention beyond the initial setting up of the system. It would also result in liability for every single Usenet server in the worldwide link of computers transmitting Erlich's message to every other computer. These parties, who are liable under plaintiffs' theory, do no more than operate or implement a system that is essential if Usenet messages are to be widely distributed. There is no need to construe the Act to make all of these parties infringers. Although copyright is a strict liability statute, there should still be some element of volition or causation which is lacking where a defendant's system is merely used to create a copy by a third party.

Plaintiffs point out that the infringing copies resided for eleven days on Netcom's computer and were sent out from it onto the "Information Superhighway." However, under plaintiffs' theory, any storage of a copy that occurs in the process of sending a message to the Usenet is an infringement. While it is possible that less "damage" would have been done if Netcom had heeded plaintiffs' warnings and acted to prevent Erlich's message from being forwarded,[13] this is not relevant to its *direct* liability for copying. The same argument is true of Klemesrud and any Usenet server. Whether a defendant makes a direct copy that constitutes infringement cannot depend on whether it received a warning to delete the message. *See D.C. Comics Inc. v. Mini Gift,* 912 F.2d 29, 35 (2d Cir.1990). This distinction may be relevant to contributory infringement, however, where knowledge is an element.

* * *

d. Playboy Case

Playboy Enterprises, Inc. v. Frena involved a suit against the operator of a small BBS whose system contained files of erotic pictures. 839 F.Supp. 1552, 1554 (M.D.Fla.1993). A subscriber of the defendant's BBS had uploaded files containing digitized pictures copied from the plaintiff's copyrighted magazine, which files remained on the BBS for other subscribers to download. *Id.* The court did not conclude, as plaintiffs suggest in this case, that the BBS is itself liable for the unauthorized *reproduction of plaintiffs' work*; instead, the court concluded that the BBS operator was liable for violating the plaintiff's right to publicly *distribute and display copies of its work. Id.* at 1556–57.

In support of their argument that Netcom is directly liable for copying plaintiffs' works, plaintiffs cite to the court's conclusion that "[t]here is no dispute that [the BBS operator] supplied a product containing unauthorized copies of a copyrighted work. It does not matter that [the BBS

13. The court notes, however, that stopping the distribution of information once it is on the Internet is not easy. The decentralized network was designed so that if one link in the chain be closed off, the information will be dynamically rerouted through another link. This was meant to allow the system to be used for communication after a catastrophic event that shuts down part of it.

operator] claims he did not make the copies [him]self." *Id.* at 1556. It is clear from the context of this discussion that the *Playboy* court was looking only at the exclusive right to distribute copies to the public, where liability exists regardless of whether the defendant makes copies. Here, however, plaintiffs do not argue that Netcom is liable for its public distribution of copies. Instead, they claim that Netcom is liable because its computers in fact made copies. Therefore, the above-quoted language has no bearing on the issue of direct liability for unauthorized reproductions. Notwithstanding *Playboy*'s holding that a BBS operator may be directly liable for *distributing or displaying* to the public copies of protected works, this court holds that the storage on a defendant's system of infringing copies and retransmission to other servers is not a direct infringement by the BBS operator of the exclusive right to *reproduce* the work where such copies are uploaded by an infringing user. *Playboy* does not hold otherwise.

* * *

f.   Public Distribution and Display?

Plaintiffs allege that Netcom is directly liable for making *copies* of their works. They also allege that Netcom violated their exclusive rights to publicly display copies of their works. There are no allegations that Netcom violated plaintiffs' exclusive right to publicly distribute their works. However, in their discussion of direct infringement, plaintiffs insist that Netcom is liable for "maintain[ing] copies of [Erlich's] messages on its server for eleven days for access by its subscribers and 'USENET neighbors'" and they compare this case to the *Playboy* case, which discussed the right of public distribution. Plaintiffs also argued this theory of infringement at oral argument. Because this could be an attempt to argue that Netcom has infringed plaintiffs' rights of public distribution and display, the court will address these arguments.

Playboy concluded that the defendant infringed the plaintiff's exclusive rights to publicly distribute and display copies of its works. 839 F.Supp. at 1556–57. The court is not entirely convinced that the mere possession of a digital copy on a BBS that is accessible to some members of the public constitutes direct infringement by the BBS operator. Such a holding suffers from the same problem of causation as the reproduction argument. Only the subscriber should be liable for causing the distribution of plaintiffs' work, as the contributing actions of the BBS provider are automatic and indiscriminate. Erlich could have posted his messages through countless access providers and the outcome would be the same: anyone with access to Usenet newsgroups would be able to read his messages. There is no logical reason to draw a line around Netcom and Klemesrud and say that they are uniquely responsible for distributing Erlich's messages. Netcom is not even the first link in the chain of distribution—Erlich had no direct relationship with Netcom but dealt solely with Klemesrud's BBS, which used Netcom to gain its Internet access. Every Usenet server has a role in the distribution, so plaintiffs' argument would create unreasonable liability. Where the BBS merely stores and passes along all messages sent by its subscribers and others, the BBS should not be seen as causing these works to be publicly distributed or displayed.

Even accepting the *Playboy* court's holding, the case is factually distinguishable. Unlike the BBS in that case, Netcom does not maintain an archive of files for its users. Thus, it cannot be said to be "suppl[ying] a product." In contrast to some of its larger competitors, Netcom does not create or control the content of the information available to its subscribers; it merely provides *access* to the Internet, whose content is controlled by no single entity. Although the Internet consists of many different computers networked together, some of which may contain infringing files, it does not make sense to hold the operator of each computer liable as an infringer merely because his or her computer is linked to a computer with an infringing file. It would be especially inappropriate to hold liable a service that acts more like a conduit, in other words, one that does not itself keep an archive of files for more than a short duration. Finding such a service liable would involve an unreasonably broad construction of public distribution and display rights. No purpose would be served by holding liable those who have no ability to control the information to which their subscribers have access, even though they might be in some sense helping to achieve the Internet's automatic "public distribution" and the users' "public" display of files.

g. Conclusion

The court is not persuaded by plaintiffs' argument that Netcom is directly liable for the copies that are made and stored on its computer. Where the infringing subscriber is clearly directly liable for the same act, it does not make sense to adopt a rule that could lead to the liability of countless parties whose role in the infringement is nothing more than setting up and operating a system that is necessary for the functioning of the Internet. Such a result is unnecessary as there is already a party directly liable for causing the copies to be made. Plaintiffs occasionally claim that they only seek to hold liable a party that refuses to delete infringing files after they have been warned. However, such liability cannot be based on a theory of direct infringement, where knowledge is irrelevant. The court does not find workable a theory of infringement that would hold the entire Internet liable for activities that cannot reasonably be deterred. Billions of bits of data flow through the Internet and are necessarily stored on servers throughout the network and it is thus practically impossible to screen out infringing bits from noninfringing bits. Because the court cannot see any meaningful distinction (without regard to knowledge) between what Netcom did and what every other Usenet server does, the court finds that Netcom cannot be held liable for direct infringement. *Cf.* IITF Report at 69 (noting uncertainty regarding whether BBS operator should be directly liable for reproduction or distribution of files uploaded by a subscriber).

* * *

Kelly v. Arriba Soft Corp.

280 F.3d 934 (9th Cir.2002).

■ NELSON, CIRCUIT JUDGE.

This case involves the application of copyright law to the vast world of the internet and internet search engines. The plaintiff, Leslie Kelly, is a professional photographer who has copyrighted many of his images of the American West. Some of these images are located on Kelly's web site or other web sites with which Kelly has a license agreement. The defendant, Arriba Soft Corp.,[1] operates an internet search engine that displays its results in the form of small pictures rather than the more usual form of text. Arriba obtained its database of pictures by copying images from other web sites.[2] By clicking on one of these small pictures, called "thumbnails," the user can then view a large version of that same picture within the context of the Arriba web page.

When Kelly discovered that his photographs were part of Arriba's search engine database, he brought a claim against Arriba for copyright infringement. The district court found that Kelly had established a prima facie case of copyright infringement based on Arriba's unauthorized reproduction and display of Kelly's works, but that this reproduction and display constituted a non-infringing "fair use" under Section 107 of the Copyright Act. Kelly appeals that decision, and we affirm in part and reverse in part. The creation and use of the thumbnails in the search engine is a fair use, but the display of the larger image is a violation of Kelly's exclusive right to publicly display his works. We remand with instructions to determine damages and the need for an injunction.

I.

The search engine at issue in this case is unconventional in that it displays the results of a user's query as "thumbnail" images. When a user wants to search the internet for information on a certain topic, he or she types a search term into a search engine, which then produces a list of web sites that have information relating to the search term. Normally, the list of results is in text format. The Arriba search engine, however, produces its list of results as small pictures.

To provide this functionality, Arriba developed a computer program that "crawls" the web looking for images to index. This crawler downloads full-sized copies of the images onto Arriba's server. The program then uses these copies to generate smaller, lower-resolution thumbnails of the images. Once the thumbnails are created, the program deletes the full-sized originals from the server. Although a user could copy these thumbnails to his computer or disk, he cannot increase the resolution of the thumbnail; any enlargement would result in a loss of clarity of the image.

---

1. Arriba Soft has changed its name since the start of this litigation. It is now known as "Ditto.com."

2. [For a discussion of the law applicable to databases and compilations online, see Chapter 4, *infra.*—Eds.]

The second component of the Arriba program occurs when the user double-clicks on the thumbnail. From January 1999 to June 1999, clicking on the thumbnail produced the "Images Attributes" page. This page contained the original full-sized image imported directly from the originating web site, along with text describing the size of the image, a link to the originating web site, the Arriba banner, and Arriba advertising. The process of importing an image from another web site is called inline linking. The image imported from another web site is displayed as though it is part of the current web page, surrounded by the current web page's text and advertising. As a result, although the image in Arriba's Image Attributes page was directly from the originating web site, and not copied onto Arriba's site, the user typically would not realize that the image actually resided on another web site.

From July 1999 until sometime after August 2000, the results page contained thumbnails accompanied by two links: "Source" and "Details." The "Details" link produced a screen similar to the Images Attributes page but with a thumbnail rather than the full-sized image. Alternatively, by clicking on the "Source" link or the thumbnail from the results page, the site produced two new windows on top of the Arriba page. The window in the forefront contained the full-sized image, imported directly from the originating web site. Underneath that was another window displaying the originating web page. This technique is known as framing. The image from a second web site is viewed within a frame that is pulled into the primary site's web page.

In January 1999, Arriba's crawler visited web sites that contained Kelly's photographs. The crawler copied thirty-five of Kelly's images to the Arriba database. Kelly had never given permission to Arriba to copy his images and objected when he found out that Arriba was using them. Arriba deleted the thumbnails of images that came from Kelly's own web sites and placed those sites on a list of sites that it would not crawl in the future. Several months later, Arriba received Kelly's complaint of copyright infringement, which identified other images of his that came from third-party web sites. Arriba subsequently deleted those thumbnails and placed those third-party sites on a list of sites that it would not crawl in the future.

The district court granted summary judgment in favor of Arriba. Although the court found that Kelly had established a prima facie case of infringement based on Arriba's reproduction and display of Kelly's photographs, the court ruled that such actions by Arriba constituted fair use.
* * *

II.

* * *

This case involves two distinct actions by Arriba that warrant analysis. The first action consists of the reproduction of Kelly's images to create the thumbnails and the use of those thumbnails in Arriba's search engine. [The court held that the reproductions were prima facie infringing but came within the doctrine of fair use. This portion of the opinion is excerpted in Part III(A), *infra.*]

* * *

B.

The second part of our analysis concerns Arriba's inline linking to and framing of Kelly's full-sized images. This use of Kelly's images does not entail copying them but, rather, importing them directly from Kelly's web site. Therefore, it cannot be copyright infringement based on the reproduction of copyrighted works * * *. Instead, this use of Kelly's images infringes upon Kelly's exclusive right to "display the copyrighted work publicly."[36]

1. Public display right.

In order for Kelly to prevail, Arriba must have displayed Kelly's work without his permission and made that display available to the public. The Copyright Act defines "display" as showing a copy of a work. This would seem to preclude Kelly from arguing that showing his original images was an infringement. However, the Act defines a copy as a material object in which a work is fixed, including the material object in which the work is first fixed. The legislative history of the Act makes clear that "[s]ince 'copies' are defined as including the material object 'in which the work is first fixed,' the right of public display applies to original works of art as well as to reproductions of them."[39] By inline linking and framing Kelly's images, Arriba is showing Kelly's original works without his permission.

The legislative history goes on to state that " 'display' would include the projection of an image on a screen or other surface by any method, the transmission of an image by electronic or other means, and the showing of an image on a cathode ray tube, or similar viewing apparatus connected with any sort of information storage and retrieval system."[40] This language indicates that showing Kelly's images on a computer screen would constitute a display.

The Act's definition of the term "publicly" encompasses a transmission of a display of a work to the public "by means of any device or process, whether the members of the public capable of receiving the performance or display receive it in the same place or in separate places and at the same time or at different times."[41] A display is public even if there is no proof that any of the potential recipients was operating his receiving apparatus at the time of the transmission.[42] By making Kelly's images available on its web site, Arriba is allowing public access to those images. The ability to view those images is unrestricted to anyone with a computer and internet access.

---

36. 17 U.S.C. § 106(5).

39. H.R.Rep. No. 94–1476, at 64 (1976), *reprinted in* 1976 U.S.C.C.A.N. 5659, 5677.

40. *Id.*

41. 17 U.S.C. § 101.

42. H.R.Rep. No. 94–1476, at 64–65 (1976), *reprinted in* 1976 U.S.C.C.A.N. 5659, 5678.

The legislative history emphasizes the broad nature of the display right, stating that "[e]ach and every method by which the images or sounds comprising a performance or display are picked up and conveyed is a 'transmission,' and if the transmission reaches the public in [any] form, the case comes within the scope of [the public performance and display rights] of section 106."[43] Looking strictly at the language of the Act and its legislative history, it appears that when Arriba imports Kelly's images into its own web page, Arriba is infringing upon Kelly's public display right. The limited case law in this area supports this conclusion.

No cases have addressed the issue of whether inline linking or framing violates a copyright owner's public display rights. However, in *Playboy Enterprises, Inc. v. Webbworld, Inc.*,[44] the court found that the owner of an internet site infringed a magazine publisher's copyrights by displaying copyrighted images on its web site. The defendant, Webbworld, downloaded material from certain newsgroups, discarded the text and retained the images, and made those images available to its internet subscribers.[46] Playboy owned copyrights to many of the images Webbworld retained and displayed. The court found that Webbworld violated Playboy's exclusive right to display its copyrighted works, noting that allowing subscribers to view copyrighted works on their computer monitors while online was a display. The court also discounted the fact that no image existed until the subscriber downloaded it. The image existed in digital form, which made it available for decoding as an image file by the subscriber, who could view the images merely by visiting the Webbworld site.

Although Arriba does not download Kelly's images to its own server but, rather, imports them directly from other web sites, the situation is analogous to *Webbworld*. By allowing the public to view Kelly's copyrighted works while visiting Arriba's web site, Arriba created a public display of Kelly's works. Arriba argues that Kelly offered no proof that anyone ever saw his images and, therefore, there can be no display. We dispose of this argument, as did the court in *Webbworld*, because Arriba made the images available to any viewer that merely visited Arriba's site. Allowing this capability is enough to establish an infringement; the fact that no one saw the images goes to the issue of damages, not liability.

In a similar case, *Playboy Enterprises, Inc. v. Russ Hardenburgh, Inc.*,[49] the court held that the owner of an electronic bulletin board system infringed Playboy's copyrights by displaying copyrighted images on its system. The bulletin board is a central system that stores information, giving home computer users the opportunity to submit information to the system (upload) or retrieve information from the system (download). In this

---

43. *Id.* at 64, *reprinted in* 1976 U.S.C.C.A.N. at 5678.

44. 991 F.Supp. 543 (N.D.Texas 1997).

46. Interestingly, the images were retained as both full-sized images and thumbnails. A subscriber could view several thumbnails on one page and then view a full-sized image by clicking on the thumbnail. However, both the thumbnail and full-sized image were copied onto Webbworld's server so no inline linking or framing was used.

49. 982 F.Supp. 503 (N.D.Ohio 1997).

case, the defendant encouraged its subscribers to upload adult photographs, screened all submitted images, and moved some of the images into files from which general subscribers could download them. Because these actions resulted in subscribers being able to download copyrighted images, it violated Playboy's right of public display. Again, the court noted that adopting a policy that allowed the defendants to place images in files available to subscribers entailed a display. This conclusion indicates that it was irrelevant whether anyone actually saw the images.

Both of these cases highlighted the fact that the defendants took an active role in creating the display of the copyrighted images. The reason for this emphasis is that several other cases held that operators of bulletin board systems and internet access providers were not liable for copyright infringement.[54] These cases distinguished direct infringement from contributory infringement and held that where the defendants did not take any affirmative action that resulted in copying copyrighted works, but only maintained a system that acted as a passive conduit for third parties' copies, they were not liable for direct infringement.

The courts in *Webbworld* and *Hardenburgh* specifically noted that the defendants did more than act as mere providers of access or passive conduits. In *Webbworld,* the web site sold images after actively trolling the internet for them and deciding which images to provide to subscribers. The court stated that "Webbworld exercised total dominion over the content of its site and the product it offered its clientele."[56] Likewise, in *Hardenburgh,* the court found that by encouraging subscribers to upload images and then screening those images and selecting ones to make available for downloading, the defendants were more than passive conduits.[57]

Like the defendants in *Webbworld* and *Hardenburgh,* Arriba is directly liable for infringement. Arriba actively participated in displaying Kelly's images by trolling the web, finding Kelly's images, and then having its program inline link and frame those images within its own web site. Without this program, users would not have been able to view Kelly's images within the context of Arriba's site. Arriba acted as more than a passive conduit of the images by establishing a direct link to the copyright-

---

54. *See e.g. Religious Tech. Ctr. v. Netcom On–Line Communication Servs., Inc.,* 907 F.Supp. 1361, 1372–73 (N.D.Cal.1995) (holding that operator of a computer bulletin board system that forwarded messages from subscribers to other subscribers was not liable for displaying copyrighted works because it took no role in controlling the content of the information but only acted as passive conduit of the information); *Marobie–Fl, Inc. v. Nat'l. Ass'n of Fire and Equip. Distribs.,* 983 F.Supp. 1167, 1176–79 (N.D.Ill.1997) (holding that company that provided a host computer for web page and access link to internet users was not directly liable for

copyright infringement when administrator of web page posted copyrighted works on the page, because it only provided the means to display the works but did not engage in the activity itself); *Costar Group Inc. v. Loopnet, Inc.,* 164 F.Supp.2d 688, 695–96 (D.Md.2001) (holding that operator of a web site that hosted real estate listings and photos was not directly liable for copyright infringement because it did not actively participate in copying or displaying the images).

56. *Webbworld,* 991 F.Supp. at 552.

57. *Hardenburgh,* 982 F.Supp. at 513.

ed images. Therefore, Arriba is liable for publicly displaying Kelly's copyrighted images without his permission.

* * *

NOTES & QUESTIONS

1. *Downloading vs. photocopying.* In *Playboy v. Frena*, how does Frena's act of making the material available for download differ from the act of a library in keeping original magazines on its shelves and allowing members of the public to make copies using an on-premises photocopy machine?

2. *Unreasonable and unnecessary liability?* The *Netcom* court, in holding that Netcom is not directly liable for copying, distributing, or publicly displaying materials by virtue of maintaining them on its server, reasons that the alternative "would lead to unreasonable liability." What are the relative costs and benefits of imposing liability on Netcom? Who would be the least cost avoider of the harm resulting from infringement? Was the court's imposition of liability in *Frena* unreasonable? The *Netcom* court also states that imposing liability on Netcom is "unnecessary as there is already a party directly liable for causing the copies to be made." Is this the usual rule in tort actions?

3. *Who engages in the display and distribution?* In *Playboy v. Frena*, did the court address the question of who engaged in the public display and distribution of Playboy's pictures? Is there an argument that it was not Frena, but rather the BBS subscribers, who engaged in these actions?

In *Kelly v. Arriba Soft*, is it clear that the display of Kelly's images is attributable to Arriba Soft? As the court indicates, the files constituting the full-sized images never resided on or even passed through Arriba Soft's computer servers. Arriba Soft's website contained only links pointing to the URLs of the images where they resided on Kelly's site. When a user clicked on such a link, the user's browser sent a request to Kelly's computer, which Kelly's server interpreted as: "Please send me the image file that you are storing at the address www.goldrush1849.com/images/coloma.jpg." Kelly's server was configured so that it automatically granted such requests, by transmitting the requested image to the user, whose browser then displayed it graphically. (It is easy to configure a server otherwise. For example, many servers are configured so that certain pages are served *only* to requesters who are linking from a page within the site.) Thus the user's browser and Kelly's server communicated directly with each other; Arriba Soft was not an intermediary.

This is the same sequence of events that occurs whenever a user clicks on a link, and is served a page, image, or other resource from the linked-to site. If Arriba Soft is responsible for the display that occurs when a user clicks a link on its site that points to an image file on another site, it would seem to follow that every other website owner is equally responsible for displaying material residing on other sites simply by virtue of pointing a link at that material. If the material is copyrighted, and the copyright owner does not authorize the display, then the owner of the website containing the link would seem to be engaging in an infringing display every time a user clicks on the link. Can this be a proper application of the Copyright Act? The previous paragraph contains a URL pointing to an image on Kelly's website; does this constitute an infringing display by the author or publisher of this book? Would it make any difference if this were an electronic book, so that the URL were a working hyperlink? Compare *Ticketmaster Corp. v. Tickets.Com*, 54 U.S.P.Q.2d (BNA) 1344 (C.D.Cal. 2000) ("[H]yperlinking does not itself involve a violation of the Copyright Act * * * since no copying is involved. The customer is automatically transferred to the particular genuine web page of the original author."), *superseded and withdrawn*, 2000 Copyright L. Dec. (CCH) ¶ 28,146 (C.D.Cal.2000).

4. *Liability under the* Netcom *standard.* In *Playboy Enterprises, Inc. v. Russ Hardenburgh, Inc.*, 982 F.Supp. 503 (N.D.Ohio 1997), the court adopted the *Netcom* approach to direct infringement but, contrary to *Netcom*, found the defendants liable under that standard. Plaintiff, Playboy Enterprises, Inc., sued a computer bulletin board system and its owner, alleging they engaged in copyright infringement by making PEI's copyrighted images available for download from the BBS. Subscribers uploaded files to the BBS, which offered them an incentive to do so: "Subscribers were given a 'credit' for each megabyte of electronic data that they uploaded onto the system. For each credit, the subscriber was entitled to download 1.5 extra megabytes of electronic information, in addition to the megabytes available under the normal terms of subscription." Once uploaded, the files were reviewed by a BBS employee, to make sure they were "not pornographic, and not blatantly protected by copyright." *Id.* at 506. Once approved, they were made available for download by other subscribers. The court expressed agreement with the principle, which it attributed to *Netcom*, "that a finding of direct copyright infringement requires some element of direct action or participation." It found the requisite "direct action or participation" in the factors that (1) defendants encouraged subscribers to upload material to the BBS, and (2) defendants employed a screening procedure before making uploaded files available for download. These two factors "transform Defendants from passive providers of a space in which infringing activities happened to occur to active participants in the process of copyright infringement." *Id.* at 512–13.

Do the two factors that the court relies upon warrant treating defendants differently from "passive providers" of a forum for infringement? Does the court's reliance on the second (screening) factor provide BBS operators with a perverse incentive to avoid screening uploads for possible copyright infringement?

B. CONTRIBUTORY INFRINGEMENT

Absent clear evidence of direct participation in acts of infringement, courts have been reluctant to hold BBS operators and Internet service providers directly liable based on the actions of their subscribers. Copyright owners have therefore argued that such entities should be held liable as contributory or vicarious infringers, based on their providing Internet access or some other service to the primary infringer. In this section and the next, we look at how courts have applied these two doctrines to the online environment.

A person is liable as a contributory infringer if the person, with knowledge of the infringing acts, induces or materially contributes to the infringing activity of another. For example, in *Elektra Records Co. v. Gem Elec. Distributors, Inc.*, 360 F.Supp. 821 (E.D.N.Y.1973), an electronics store selling blank audio tapes was found liable for contributory infringement. The offending conduct was promoting the sale of its blank tapes by allowing tape purchasers to use its dubbing equipment to duplicate pre-recorded audio tapes containing copyrighted music onto the blank tapes. The customers were the direct infringers, and the store was a contributory infringer.

Religious Technology Center v. Netcom On–Line Communication Services, Inc.

907 F.Supp. 1361 (N.D.Cal.1995).

■ WHYTE, DISTRICT JUDGE.

[The facts of this case are set forth in Part II(A), *supra.*]

* * *

2. *Contributory Infringement*

Netcom is not free from liability just because it did not directly infringe plaintiffs' works; it may still be liable as a contributory infringer. Although there is no statutory rule of liability for infringement committed by others,

> [t]he absence of such express language in the copyright statute does not preclude the imposition of liability for copyright infringement on certain parties who have not themselves engaged in the infringing activity. For vicarious liability is imposed in virtually all areas of the law, and the concept of contributory infringement is merely a species of the broader problem of identifying the circumstances in which it is just to hold one individual accountable for the actions of another.

Sony Corp. v. Universal City Studios, Inc., 464 U.S. 417, 435 (1984) (footnote omitted). Liability for participation in the infringement will be established where the defendant, "with knowledge of the infringing activity, induces, causes or materially contributes to the infringing conduct of another." *Gershwin Publishing Corp. v. Columbia Artists Management, Inc.*, 443 F.2d 1159, 1162 (2d Cir.1971).

a. Knowledge of Infringing Activity

Plaintiffs insist that Netcom knew that Erlich was infringing their copyrights at least after receiving notice from plaintiffs' counsel indicating that Erlich had posted copies of their works onto a.r.s.[3] through Netcom's system. Despite this knowledge, Netcom continued to allow Erlich to post messages to a.r.s. and left the allegedly infringing messages on its system so that Netcom's subscribers and other Usenet servers could access them. Netcom argues that it did not possess the necessary type of knowledge because (1) it did not know of Erlich's planned infringing activities when it agreed to lease its facilities to Klemesrud, (2) it did not know that Erlich would infringe prior to any of his postings, (3) it is unable to screen out infringing postings before they are made, and (4) its knowledge of the infringing nature of Erlich's postings was too equivocal given the difficulty in assessing whether the registrations were valid and whether Erlich's use was fair. The court will address these arguments in turn.

Netcom cites cases holding that there is no contributory infringement by the lessors of premises that are later used for infringement unless the lessor had knowledge of the intended use at the time of the signing of the lease. *See, e.g. Deutsch v. Arnold,* 98 F.2d 686, 688 (2d Cir.1938). The contribution to the infringement by the defendant in *Deutsch* was merely to lease use of the premises to the infringer. Here, Netcom not only leases space but also serves as an access provider, which includes the storage and transmission of information necessary to facilitate Erlich's postings to a.r.s. Unlike a landlord, Netcom retains some control over the use of its system. Thus, the relevant time frame for knowledge is not when Netcom entered into an agreement with Klemesrud. It should be when Netcom provided its services to allow Erlich to infringe plaintiffs' copyrights. *Cf. Screen Gems–Columbia Music, Inc. v. Mark–Fi Records, Inc.,* 256 F.Supp. 399, 403 (S.D.N.Y.1966) (analyzing knowledge at time that defendant rendered its particular service). It is undisputed that Netcom did not know that Erlich was infringing before it received notice from plaintiffs. Netcom points out that the alleged instances of infringement occurring on Netcom's system all happened prior to December 29, 1994, the date on which Netcom first received notice of plaintiffs' infringement claim against Erlich. Thus, there is no question of fact as to whether Netcom knew or should have known of Erlich's infringing activities that occurred more than 11 days before receipt of the December 28, 1994 letter.

However, the evidence reveals a question of fact as to whether Netcom knew or should have known that Erlich had infringed plaintiffs' copyrights following receipt of plaintiffs' letter. Because Netcom was arguably participating in Erlich's public distribution of plaintiffs' works, there is a genuine issue as to whether Netcom knew of any infringement by Erlich before it was too late to do anything about it. If plaintiffs can prove the knowledge element, Netcom will be liable for contributory infringement since its failure to simply cancel Erlich's infringing message and thereby stop an infringing copy from being distributed worldwide constitutes substantial participation in Erlich's public distribution of the message.

---

3. [Recall that "a.r.s" stands for the Usenet newsgroup alt.religion.scientology.— Eds.]

Netcom argues that its knowledge after receiving notice of Erlich's alleged infringing activities was too equivocal given the difficulty in assessing whether registrations are valid and whether use is fair. Although a mere unsupported allegation of infringement by a copyright owner may not automatically put a defendant on notice of infringing activity, Netcom's position that liability must be unequivocal is unsupportable. While perhaps the typical infringing activities of BBSs will involve copying software, where BBS operators are better equipped to judge infringement, the fact that this involves written works should not distinguish it. Where works contain copyright notices within them, as here, it is difficult to argue that a defendant did not know that the works were copyrighted. To require proof of valid registrations would be impractical and would perhaps take too long to verify, making it impossible for a copyright holder to protect his or her works in some cases, as works are automatically deleted less than two weeks after they are posted. The court is more persuaded by the argument that it is beyond the ability of a BBS operator to quickly and fairly determine when a use is not infringement where there is at least a colorable claim of fair use. Where a BBS operator cannot reasonably verify a claim of infringement, either because of a possible fair use defense, the lack of copyright notices on the copies, or the copyright holder's failure to provide the necessary documentation to show that there is a likely infringement, the operator's lack of knowledge will be found reasonable and there will be no liability for contributory infringement for allowing the continued distribution of the works on its system.

Since Netcom was given notice of an infringement claim before Erlich had completed his infringing activity, there may be a question of fact as to whether Netcom knew or should have known that such activities were infringing. Given the context of a dispute between a former minister and a church he is criticizing, Netcom may be able to show that its lack of knowledge that Erlich was infringing was reasonable. However, Netcom admits that it did not even look at the postings once given notice and that had it looked at the copyright notice and statements regarding authorship, it would have triggered an investigation into whether there was infringement. These facts are sufficient to raise a question as to Netcom's knowledge once it received a letter from plaintiffs on December 29, 1994.

b. Substantial Participation

Where a defendant has knowledge of the primary infringer's infringing activities, it will be liable if it "induces, causes or materially contributes to the infringing conduct of" the primary infringer. *Gershwin Publishing,* 443 F.2d at 1162. Such participation must be substantial. *Apple Computer, Inc. v. Microsoft Corp.,* 821 F.Supp. 616, 625 (N.D.Cal.1993), *aff'd,* 35 F.3d 1435 (9th Cir.1994).

Providing a service that allows for the automatic distribution of all Usenet postings, infringing and noninfringing, goes well beyond renting a premises to an infringer. * * * It is more akin to the radio stations that were found liable for rebroadcasting an infringing broadcast. *See, e.g.,*

Select Theatres Corp. v. Ronzoni Macoroni Co., 59 U.S.P.Q. 288, 291 (S.D.N.Y.1943). Netcom allows Erlich's infringing messages to remain on its system and be further distributed to other Usenet servers worldwide. It does not completely relinquish control over how its system is used, unlike a landlord. Thus, it is fair, assuming Netcom is able to take simple measures to prevent further damage to plaintiffs' copyrighted works, to hold Netcom liable for contributory infringement where Netcom has knowledge of Erlich's infringing postings yet continues to aid in the accomplishment of Erlich's purpose of publicly distributing the postings. Accordingly, plaintiffs do raise a genuine issue of material fact as to their theory of contributory infringement as to the postings made after Netcom was on notice of plaintiffs' infringement claim. * * *

[For similar reasons, the court also finds that the plaintiffs have raised a genuine issue of material fact as to their theory of contributory infringement against the BBS operator, Klemesrud.]

* * *

Intellectual Reserve, Inc. v. Utah Lighthouse Ministry, Inc.

75 F.Supp.2d 1290 (D.Utah 1999).

■ CAMPBELL, DISTRICT JUDGE.

This matter is before the court on plaintiff's motion for preliminary injunction. Plaintiff claims that unless a preliminary injunction issues, defendants will directly infringe and contribute to the infringement of its copyright in the *Church Handbook of Instructions* ("Handbook"). Defendants do not oppose a preliminary injunction, but argue that the scope of the injunction should be restricted to only prohibit direct infringement of plaintiff's copyright.[4]

Having fully considered the arguments of counsel, the submissions of the parties and applicable legal authorities, the court grants plaintiff's motion for a preliminary injunction. However, the scope of the preliminary injunction is limited.

Discussion

* * *

I.   Likelihood of Plaintiff Prevailing on the Merits

First, the court considers whether there is a substantial likelihood that plaintiff will eventually prevail on the merits. Plaintiff alleges that the defendants infringed its copyright directly by posting substantial portions of its copyrighted material on defendants' website, and also contributed to

---

4. [Plaintiff is the owner of copyrights in the Handbook and other materials used by the Church of Jesus Christ of Latter-day Saints (the Mormon Church). Defendant is an organization that is critical of the Mormon Church.—Eds.]

infringement of its copyright by inducing, causing or materially contributing to the infringing conduct of another. To determine the proper scope of the preliminary injunction, the court considers the likelihood that plaintiff will prevail on either or both of its claims.

* * *

B. Contributory Infringement

According to plaintiff, after the defendants were ordered to remove the Handbook from their website, the defendants began infringing plaintiff's copyright by inducing, causing, or materially contributing to the infringing conduct of others. It is undisputed that defendants placed a notice on their website that the Handbook was online, and gave three website addresses of websites containing the material defendants were ordered to remove from their website. Defendants also posted e-mails on their website that encouraged browsing those websites, printing copies of the Handbook and sending the Handbook to others.

* * *

Liability for contributory infringement is imposed when "one who, with knowledge of the infringing activity, induces, causes or materially contributes to the infringing conduct of another." *Gershwin Publ'g Corp. v. Columbia Artists Mgt., Inc.*, 443 F.2d 1159, 1162 (2d Cir.1971). Thus, to prevail on its claim of contributory infringement, plaintiff must first be able to establish that the conduct defendants allegedly aided or encouraged could amount to infringement. *See Subafilms, Ltd. v. MGM–Pathe Comms. Co.*, 24 F.3d 1088, 1092 (9th Cir.1994). Defendants argue that they have not contributed to copyright infringement by those who posted the Handbook on websites nor by those who browsed the websites on their computers.

1. Can the Defendants Be Liable Under a Theory of Contributory Infringement for the Actions of Those Who Posted the Handbook on the Three Websites?

a. Did those who posted the Handbook on the websites infringe plaintiff's copyright?

During a hearing on the motion to vacate the temporary restraining order, defendants accepted plaintiff's proffer that the three websites contain the material which plaintiff alleges is copyrighted. Therefore, plaintiff at trial is likely to establish that those who have posted the material on the three websites are directly infringing plaintiff's copyright.

b. Did the defendants induce, cause or materially contribute to the infringement?

The evidence now before the court indicates that there is no direct relationship between the defendants and the people who operate the three websites. The defendants did not provide the website operators with the plaintiff's copyrighted material, nor are the defendants receiving any kind of compensation from them. The only connection between the defendants and those who operate the three websites appears to be the information defendants have posted on their website concerning the infringing sites. Based on this scant evidence, the court concludes that plaintiff has not shown that defendants contributed to the infringing action of those who operate the infringing websites.

2. Can the Defendants Be Liable Under a Theory of Contributory Infringement for the Actions of Those Who Browse the Three Infringing Websites?

Defendants make two arguments in support of their position that the activities of those who browse the three websites do not make them liable under a theory of contributory infringement. First, defendants contend that those who browse the infringing websites are not themselves infringing plaintiff's copyright; and second, even if those who browse the websites are infringers, defendants have not materially contributed to the infringing conduct.

      a.   Do those who browse the websites infringe plaintiff's copyright?

The first question, then, is whether those who browse any of the three infringing websites are infringing plaintiff's copyright. Central to this inquiry is whether the persons browsing are merely viewing the Handbook (which is not a copyright infringement), or whether they are making a copy of the Handbook (which is a copyright infringement). *See* 17 U.S.C. § 106.

"Copy" is defined in the Copyright Act as: "material objects ... in which a work is fixed by any method now known or later developed, and from which the work can be perceived, reproduced, or otherwise communicated, either directly or with the aid of a machine or device." 17 U.S.C. § 101. "A work is 'fixed' ... when its ... [sic] sufficiently permanent or stable to permit it to be perceived, reproduced, or otherwise communicated for a period of more than transitory duration." *Id.*

When a person browses a website, and by so doing displays the Handbook, a copy of the Handbook is made in the computer's random access memory (RAM), to permit viewing of the material. And in making a copy, even a temporary one, the person who browsed infringes the copyright.[5] *See MAI Systems Corp. v. Peak Computer, Inc.*, 991 F.2d 511, 518 (9th Cir.1993) (holding that when material is transferred to a computer's RAM, copying has occurred; in the absence of ownership of the copyright or express permission by license, such an act constitutes copyright infringement); *Marobie–Fl, Inc. v. National Ass'n of Fire and Equip. Distrib.*, 983 F.Supp. 1167, 1179 (N.D.Ill.1997) (noting that liability for copyright infringement is with the persons who cause the display or distribution of the infringing material onto their computer); *see also* Nimmer on Copyright § 8.08(A)(1) (stating that the infringing act of copying may occur from

---

5. Although this seems harsh, the Copyright Act has provided a safeguard for innocent infringers. Where the infringer "was not aware and had no reason to believe that his or her acts constituted an infringement of copyright, the court in its discretion may reduce the award of statutory damages...." 17 U.S.C. § 504(c)(2).

"loading the copyrighted material . . . into the computer's random access memory (RAM)"). Additionally, a person making a printout or re-posting a copy of the Handbook on another website would infringe plaintiff's copyright.

b. Did the defendants induce, cause or materially contribute to the infringement?

The court now considers whether the defendants' actions contributed to the infringement of plaintiff's copyright by those who browse the three websites.

The following evidence establishes that defendants have actively encouraged the infringement of plaintiff's copyright[6] After being ordered to remove the Handbook from their website, defendants posted on their website: "Church Handbook of Instructions is back online!" and listed the three website addresses. Defendants also posted e-mail suggesting that the lawsuit against defendants would be affected by people logging onto one of the websites and downloading the complete handbook. One of the e-mails posted by the defendants mentioned sending a copy of the copyrighted material to the media. In response to an e-mail stating that the sender had unsuccessfully tried to browse a website that contained the Handbook, defendants gave further instruction on how to browse the material. At least one of the three websites encourages the copying and posting of copies of the allegedly infringing material on other websites. *See* Ex. 4 [to Plaintiff's Reply Brief] ("Please mirror these files. . . . It will be a LOT quicker for you to download the compressed version . . . Needless to say, we need a LOT of mirror sites, as absolutely soon as possible.").

Based on the above, the court finds that the first element necessary for injunctive relief is satisfied.

[In the remainder of the opinion, the court finds the other elements necessary for injunctive relief also satisfied and issues a preliminary injunction.]

* * *

A & M Records, Inc. v. Napster, Inc.

239 F.3d 1004 (9th Cir.2001).

■ BEEZER, CIRCUIT JUDGE:

Plaintiffs are engaged in the commercial recording, distribution and sale of copyrighted musical compositions and sound recordings. The com-

---

6. Plaintiff at this point has been unable to specifically identify persons who have infringed its copyright because they were induced or assisted by defendants' conduct, however, there is a substantial likelihood that plaintiff will be able to do so after conducting discovery. There is evidence that at least one of the websites has seen a great increase in "hits" recently. Also, plaintiff does not have to establish that the defendants' actions are the sole cause of another's infringement; rather plaintiff may prevail by establishing that defendants' conduct induces or materially contributes to the infringing conduct of another.

plaint alleges that Napster, Inc. ("Napster") is a contributory and vicarious copyright infringer. On July 26, 2000, the district court granted plaintiffs' motion for a preliminary injunction. The injunction was slightly modified by written opinion on August 10, 2000. *A & M Records, Inc. v. Napster, Inc.,* 114 F.Supp.2d 896 (N.D.Cal.2000). The district court preliminarily enjoined Napster "from engaging in, or facilitating others in copying, downloading, uploading, transmitting, or distributing plaintiffs' copyrighted musical compositions and sound recordings, protected by either federal or state law, without express permission of the rights owner." *Id.* at 927. Federal Rule of Civil Procedure 65(c) requires successful plaintiffs to post a bond for damages incurred by the enjoined party in the event that the injunction was wrongfully issued. The district court set bond in this case at $5 million.

We entered a temporary stay of the preliminary injunction pending resolution of this appeal. We have jurisdiction pursuant to 28 U.S.C. § 1292(a)(1). We affirm in part, reverse in part and remand.

I

We have examined the papers submitted in support of and in response to the injunction application and it appears that Napster has designed and operates a system which permits the transmission and retention of sound recordings employing digital technology.

In 1987, the Moving Picture Experts Group set a standard file format for the storage of audio recordings in a digital format called MPEG–3, abbreviated as "MP3." Digital MP3 files are created through a process colloquially called "ripping." Ripping software allows a computer owner to copy an audio compact disk ("audio CD") directly onto a computer's hard drive by compressing the audio information on the CD into the MP3 format. The MP3's compressed format allows for rapid transmission of digital audio files from one computer to another by electronic mail or any other file transfer protocol.

Napster facilitates the transmission of MP3 files between and among its users. Through a process commonly called "peer-to-peer" file sharing, Napster allows its users to: (1) make MP3 music files stored on individual computer hard drives available for copying by other Napster users; (2) search for MP3 music files stored on other users' computers; and (3) transfer exact copies of the contents of other users' MP3 files from one computer to another via the Internet. These functions are made possible by Napster's MusicShare software, available free of charge from Napster's Internet site, and Napster's network servers and server-side software. Napster provides technical support for the indexing and searching of MP3 files, as well as for its other functions, including a "chat room," where users can meet to discuss music, and a directory where participating artists can provide information about their music.

A. Accessing the System

In order to copy MP3 files through the Napster system, a user must first access Napster's Internet site and download the MusicShare software to his individual computer. *See* www.Napster.com. Once the software is installed, the user can access the Napster system. A first-time user is required to register with the Napster system by creating a "user name" and password.

B. Listing Available Files

If a registered user wants to list available files stored in his computer's hard drive on Napster for others to access, he must first create a "user library" directory on his computer's hard drive. The user then saves his MP3 files in the library directory, using self-designated file names. He next must log into the Napster system using his user name and password. His MusicShare software then searches his user library and verifies that the available files are properly formatted. If in the correct MP3 format, the names of the MP3 files will be uploaded from the user's computer to the Napster servers. The content of the MP3 files remains stored in the user's computer.

Once uploaded to the Napster servers, the user's MP3 file names are stored in a server-side "library" under the user's name and become part of a "collective directory" of files available for transfer during the time the user is logged onto the Napster system. The collective directory is fluid; it tracks users who are connected in real time, displaying only file names that are immediately accessible.

C. Searching For Available Files

Napster allows a user to locate other users' MP3 files in two ways: through Napster's search function and through its "hotlist" function.

Software located on the Napster servers maintains a "search index" of Napster's collective directory. To search the files available from Napster users currently connected to the network servers, the individual user accesses a form in the MusicShare software stored in his computer and enters either the name of a song or an artist as the object of the search. The form is then transmitted to a Napster server and automatically compared to the MP3 file names listed in the server's search index. Napster's server compiles a list of all MP3 file names pulled from the search index which include the same search terms entered on the search form and transmits the list to the searching user. The Napster server does not search the contents of any MP3 file; rather, the search is limited to "a text search of the file names indexed in a particular cluster. Those file names may contain typographical errors or otherwise inaccurate descriptions of the content of the files since they are designated by other users." *Napster,* 114 F.Supp.2d at 906.

To use the "hotlist" function, the Napster user creates a list of other users' names from whom he has obtained MP3 files in the past. When logged onto Napster's servers, the system alerts the user if any user on his list (a "hotlisted user") is also logged onto the system. If so, the user can access an index of all MP3 file names in a particular hotlisted user's library and request a file in the library by selecting the file name. The contents of the hotlisted user's MP3 file are not stored on the Napster system.

D. Transferring Copies of an MP3 file

To transfer a copy of the contents of a requested MP3 file, the Napster server software obtains the Internet address of the requesting user and the Internet address of the "host user" (the user with the available files). *See generally Brookfield Communications, Inc. v. West Coast Entm't Corp.*, 174 F.3d 1036, 1044 (9th Cir.1999) (describing, in detail, the structure of the Internet). The Napster servers then communicate the host user's Internet address to the requesting user. The requesting user's computer uses this information to establish a connection with the host user and downloads a copy of the contents of the MP3 file from one computer to the other over the Internet, "peer-to-peer." A downloaded MP3 file can be played directly from the user's hard drive using Napster's MusicShare program or other software. The file may also be transferred back onto an audio CD if the user has access to equipment designed for that purpose. In both cases, the quality of the original sound recording is slightly diminished by transfer to the MP3 format.

This architecture is described in some detail to promote an understanding of transmission mechanics as opposed to the content of the transmissions. The content is the subject of our copyright infringement analysis. * * *

III

Plaintiffs claim Napster users are engaged in the wholesale reproduction and distribution of copyrighted works, all constituting direct infringement.[2] The district court agreed. We note that the district court's conclusion that plaintiffs have presented a prima facie case of direct infringement by Napster users is not presently appealed by Napster. We only need briefly address the threshold requirements.

A. Infringement

Plaintiffs must satisfy two requirements to present a prima facie case of direct infringement: (1) they must show ownership of the allegedly infringed material and (2) they must demonstrate that the alleged infringers violate at least one exclusive right granted to copyright holders under 17 U.S.C. § 106. *See* 17 U.S.C. § 501(a) (infringement occurs when alleged infringer engages in activity listed in § 106); *see also Baxter v. MCA, Inc.*, 812 F.2d 421, 423 (9th Cir.1987); *see, e.g., S.O.S., Inc. v. Payday, Inc.*, 886 F.2d 1081, 1085 n. 3 (9th Cir.1989) ("The word 'copying' is shorthand for

---

2. Secondary liability for copyright infringement does not exist in the absence of direct infringement by a third party. *Religious Tech. Ctr. v. Netcom On–Line Communication Servs., Inc.*, 907 F.Supp. 1361, 1371 (N.D.Cal.1995) ("[T]here can be no contributory infringement by a defendant without direct infringement by another."). It follows that Napster does not facilitate infringement of the copyright laws in the absence of direct infringement by its users.

the infringing of any of the copyright owner's five exclusive rights....").
Plaintiffs have sufficiently demonstrated ownership. The record supports
the district court's determination that "as much as eighty-seven percent of
the files available on Napster may be copyrighted and more than seventy
percent may be owned or administered by plaintiffs." *Napster,* 114
F.Supp.2d at 911.

The district court further determined that plaintiffs' exclusive rights
under § 106 were violated: "here the evidence establishes that a majority
of Napster users use the service to download and upload copyrighted
music.... And by doing that, it constitutes—the uses constitute direct
infringement of plaintiffs' musical compositions, recordings." *A & M Records, Inc. v. Napster, Inc.,* 2000 WL 1009483, at *1 (N.D.Cal. July 26, 2000)
(transcript of proceedings). The district court also noted that "it is pretty
much acknowledged ... by Napster that this is infringement." *Id.* We
agree that plaintiffs have shown that Napster users infringe at least two of
the copyright holders' exclusive rights: the rights of reproduction, § 106(1);
and distribution, § 106(3). Napster users who upload file names to the
search index for others to copy violate plaintiffs' distribution rights. Napster users who download files containing copyrighted music violate plaintiffs' reproduction rights.

    * * *

IV

We first address plaintiffs' claim that Napster is liable for contributory
copyright infringement. Traditionally, "one who, with knowledge of the
infringing activity, induces, causes or materially contributes to the infringing conduct of another, may be held liable as a 'contributory' infringer."
Gershwin Publ'g Corp. v. Columbia Artists Mgmt., Inc., 443 F.2d 1159,
1162 (2d Cir.1971); *see also Fonovisa, Inc. v. Cherry Auction, Inc.,* 76 F.3d
259, 264 (9th Cir.1996). Put differently, liability exists if the defendant
engages in "personal conduct that encourages or assists the infringement."
Matthew Bender & Co. v. West Publ'g Co., 158 F.3d 693, 706 (2d Cir.1998).

The district court determined that plaintiffs in all likelihood would
establish Napster's liability as a contributory infringer. The district court
did not err; Napster, by its conduct, knowingly encourages and assists the
infringement of plaintiffs' copyrights.

A. *Knowledge*

Contributory liability requires that the secondary infringer "know or
have reason to know" of direct infringement. *Cable/Home Communication
Corp. v. Network Prods., Inc.,* 902 F.2d 829, 845 and 846 n. 29 (11th
Cir.1990); *Religious Tech. Ctr. v. Netcom On–Line Communication Servs.,
Inc.,* 907 F.Supp. 1361, 1373–74 (N.D.Cal.1995) (framing issue as "whether
Netcom knew or should have known of" the infringing activities). The
district court found that Napster had both actual and constructive knowledge that its users exchanged copyrighted music. The district court also
concluded that the law does not require knowledge of "specific acts of

infringement" and rejected Napster's contention that because the company cannot distinguish infringing from noninfringing files, it does not "know" of the direct infringement. 114 F.Supp.2d at 917.

It is apparent from the record that Napster has knowledge, both actual and constructive,[5] of direct infringement. Napster claims that it is nevertheless protected from contributory liability by the teaching of *Sony Corp. v. Universal City Studios, Inc.,* 464 U.S. 417 (1984). We disagree. We observe that Napster's actual, specific knowledge of direct infringement renders *Sony*'s holding of limited assistance to Napster. We are compelled to make a clear distinction between the architecture of the Napster system and Napster's conduct in relation to the operational capacity of the system.

The *Sony* Court refused to hold the manufacturer and retailers of video tape recorders liable for contributory infringement despite evidence that such machines could be and were used to infringe plaintiffs' copyrighted television shows. *Sony* stated that if liability "is to be imposed on petitioners in this case, it must rest on the fact that *they have sold equipment with constructive knowledge of the fact that their customers may use that equipment to make unauthorized copies* of copyrighted material." *Id.* at 439 (emphasis added). The *Sony* Court declined to impute the requisite level of knowledge where the defendants made and sold equipment capable of both infringing and "substantial noninfringing uses." *Id.* at 442 (adopting a modified "staple article of commerce" doctrine from patent law). *See also Universal City Studios, Inc. v. Sony Corp.,* 480 F.Supp. 429, 459 (C.D.Cal. 1979) ("This court agrees with defendants that their knowledge was insufficient to make them contributory infringers."), *rev'd,* 659 F.2d 963 (9th Cir.1981), *rev'd,* 464 U.S. 417 (1984); Alfred C. Yen, *Internet Service Provider Liability for Subscriber Copyright Infringement, Enterprise Liability, and the First Amendment,* 88 Geo. L.J. 1833, 1874 and 1893 n.210 (2000) (suggesting that, after *Sony,* most Internet service providers lack "the requisite level of knowledge" for the imposition of contributory liability).

We are bound to follow *Sony,* and will not impute the requisite level of knowledge to Napster merely because peer-to-peer file sharing technology may be used to infringe plaintiffs' copyrights. *See* 464 U.S. at 436 (rejecting argument that merely supplying the " 'means' to accomplish an infringing activity" leads to imposition of liability). We depart from the reasoning of the district court that Napster failed to demonstrate that its system is capable of commercially significant noninfringing uses. *See Napster,* 114 F.Supp.2d at 916, 917–18. The district court improperly confined the use

---

5. The district court found actual knowledge because: (1) a document authored by Napster co-founder Sean Parker mentioned "the need to remain ignorant of users' real names and IP addresses 'since they are exchanging pirated music' "; and (2) the Recording Industry Association of America ("RIAA") informed Napster of more than 12,000 infringing files, some of which are still available. 114 F.Supp.2d at 918. The district court found constructive knowledge because: (a) Napster executives have recording industry experience; (b) they have enforced intellectual property rights in other instances; (c) Napster executives have downloaded copyrighted songs from the system; and (d) they have promoted the site with "screen shots listing infringing files." *Id.* at 919.

analysis to current uses, ignoring the system's capabilities. *See generally Sony*, 464 U.S. at 442–43 (framing inquiry as whether the video tape recorder is "*capable* of commercially significant noninfringing uses") (emphasis added). Consequently, the district court placed undue weight on the proportion of current infringing use as compared to current and future noninfringing use. *See generally Vault Corp. v. Quaid Software Ltd.*, 847 F.2d 255, 264–67 (5th Cir.1988) (single noninfringing use implicated *Sony*). Nonetheless, whether we might arrive at a different result is not the issue here. *See Sports Form, Inc. v. United Press Int'l, Inc.*, 686 F.2d 750, 752 (9th Cir.1982). The instant appeal occurs at an early point in the proceedings and "the fully developed factual record may be materially different from that initially before the district court...." *Id.* at 753. Regardless of the number of Napster's infringing versus noninfringing uses, the evidentiary record here supported the district court's finding that plaintiffs would likely prevail in establishing that Napster knew or had reason to know of its users' infringement of plaintiffs' copyrights.

This analysis is similar to that of *Religious Technology Center v. Netcom On–Line Communication Services, Inc.*, which suggests that in an online context, evidence of actual knowledge of specific acts of infringement is required to hold a computer system operator liable for contributory copyright infringement. 907 F.Supp. at 1371. *Netcom* considered the potential contributory copyright liability of a computer bulletin board operator whose system supported the posting of infringing material. *Id.* at 1374. The court, in denying Netcom's motion for summary judgment of noninfringement and plaintiff's motion for judgment on the pleadings, found that a disputed issue of fact existed as to whether the operator had sufficient knowledge of infringing activity. *Id.* at 1374–75.

The court determined that for the operator to have sufficient knowledge, the copyright holder must "provide the necessary documentation to show there is likely infringement." 907 F.Supp. at 1374; *cf. Cubby, Inc. v. CompuServe, Inc.*, 776 F.Supp. 135, 141 (S.D.N.Y.1991) (recognizing that online service provider does not and cannot examine every hyperlink for potentially defamatory material). If such documentation was provided, the court reasoned that Netcom would be liable for contributory infringement because its failure to remove the material "and thereby stop an infringing copy from being distributed worldwide constitutes substantial participation" in distribution of copyrighted material. *Id.*

We agree that if a computer system operator learns of specific infringing material available on his system and fails to purge such material from the system, the operator knows of and contributes to direct infringement. *See Netcom*, 907 F.Supp. at 1374. Conversely, absent any specific information which identifies infringing activity, a computer system operator cannot be liable for contributory infringement merely because the structure of the system allows for the exchange of copyrighted material. *See Sony*, 464 U.S. at 436, 442–43. To enjoin simply because a computer network allows for infringing use would, in our opinion, violate *Sony* and potentially restrict activity unrelated to infringing use.

We nevertheless conclude that sufficient knowledge exists to impose contributory liability when linked to demonstrated infringing use of the Napster system. *See Napster*, 114 F.Supp.2d at 919 ("*Religious Technology Center* would not mandate a determination that Napster, Inc. lacks the knowledge requisite to contributory infringement."). The record supports the district court's finding that Napster has *actual* knowledge that *specific* infringing material is available using its system, that it could block access to the system by suppliers of the infringing material, and that it failed to remove the material. *See Napster*, 114 F.Supp.2d at 918, 920–21.[6]

B. Material Contribution

Under the facts as found by the district court, Napster materially contributes to the infringing activity. Relying on *Fonovisa*, the district court concluded that "[w]ithout the support services defendant provides, Napster users could not find and download the music they want with the ease of which defendant boasts." *Napster*, 114 F.Supp.2d at 919–20 ("Napster is an integrated service designed to enable users to locate and download MP3 music files."). We agree that Napster provides "the site and facilities" for direct infringement. *See Fonovisa*, 76 F.3d at 264; *cf. Netcom*, 907 F.Supp. at 1372 ("Netcom will be liable for contributory infringement since its failure to cancel [a user's] infringing message and thereby stop an infringing copy from being distributed worldwide constitutes substantial participation."). The district court correctly applied the reasoning in *Fonovisa*, and properly found that Napster materially contributes to direct infringement.

We affirm the district court's conclusion that plaintiffs have demonstrated a likelihood of success on the merits of the contributory copyright infringement claim. * * *

* * *

NOTES & QUESTIONS

1. *Knowledge of infringement.* In *RTC v. Netcom*, the court holds that Netcom may be contributorily liable for the infringement, based on application of traditional copyright principles, if it had knowledge of the infringing activity and substantially contributed to the infringement. What will constitute the requisite knowledge? The court offers several bits of guidance on this point. First, it says that "[w]here works contain copyright notices within them, as here, it is difficult to argue that a defendant did not know that the works were copyrighted." Does presence of a copyright notice necessarily imply that the posting is infringing? The court continues:

6. As stated by the district court:

Plaintiff[s] ... demonstrate that defendant had actual notice of direct infringement because the RIAA informed it of more than 12,000 infringing files. Although Napster, Inc. purportedly terminated the users offering these files, the songs are still available using the Napster service, as are the copyrighted works which the record company plaintiffs identified in Schedules A and B of their complaint.

114 F.Supp.2d at 918.

"Where a BBS operator cannot reasonably verify a claim of infringement, either because of a possible fair use defense [or] the lack of copyright notices on the copies, the operator's lack of knowledge will be found reasonable and there will be no liability for contributory infringement for allowing the continued distribution of the works on its system." Isn't there always "a possible fair use defense"?

2. *Infringement via linking and browsing.* Based on the reasoning in *Intellectual Reserve v. Utah Lighthouse Ministry*, does a search engine "materially contribute" to infringement, for purposes of contributory infringement analysis, when it presents a user with a link to a website containing infringing material? If so, what must the search engine's operator do to avoid liability if it receives notice of the website's infringement? Also under the reasoning of this case, does an individual engage in direct infringement when she comes across infringing material while browsing a website? If so, what must she do to avoid liability?

3. Napster *and the* Sony *criterion.* In *A & M Records v. Napster*, what is the role of *Sony's* approach to contributory liability? Under the standard set forth in *Sony*: "[T]he sale of copying equipment, like the sale of other articles of commerce, does not constitute contributory infringement if the product is widely used for legitimate, unobjectionable purposes. Indeed, it need merely be capable of substantial noninfringing uses." *Sony Corp. v. Universal City Studios, Inc.*, 464 U.S. 417, 442 (1984). Is there a distinction, for present purposes, between Napster's role with respect to its file-sharing technology, and a VCR manufacturer's role with respect to its tape-copying technology?

4. *Liability for age-verification services.* Numerous websites that offer adult-oriented materials make use of online age-verification services. When a prospective customer clicks to indicate he wishes to subscribe to such a website, he is transferred to the site of the associated age-verification service, which accepts the customer's credit card information, bills the card in its own name for a membership fee, and pays a portion of the fees to the website, keeping the rest for itself. Suppose that an adult-oriented website offers copyrighted materials without the authorization of the copyright owner. Is its age-verification service contributorily or vicariously liable for the website's infringement? *See Perfect 10, Inc. v. Cybernet Ventures, Inc.*, 213 F.Supp.2d 1146 (C.D.Cal.2002).

5. *Filtering and contributory infringement.* If a person purchases and installs Web-filtering software to excise banner ads from the web pages that are viewed, would the filtered web pages be infringing derivative works? If so, would the software manufacturer be liable for contributory copyright infringement?

C.   VICARIOUS LIABILITY FOR COPYRIGHT INFRINGEMENT

In the preceding section we saw that a person who does not directly violate one of the exclusive rights of a copyright owner may nonetheless be held liable as a contributory infringer. Another form of indirect liability, vicarious liability, may be found when a person who has the right and ability to control the activities of the primary infringer receives a direct financial benefit from the infringement.

Religious Technology Center v. Netcom On–Line Communication Services, Inc.

907 F.Supp. 1361 (N.D.Cal.1995).

■ WHYTE, DISTRICT JUDGE.

> [The facts of this case are set forth in Part II(A), *supra*.]

> * * *

3. Vicarious Liability

Even if plaintiffs cannot prove that Netcom is contributorily liable for its participation in the infringing activity, it may still seek to prove vicarious infringement based on Netcom's relationship to Erlich. A defendant is liable for vicarious liability for the actions of a primary infringer where the defendant (1) has the right and ability to control the infringer's acts and (2) receives a direct financial benefit from the infringement. *See Shapiro, Bernstein & Co. v. H.L. Green Co.,* 316 F.2d 304, 306 (2d Cir.1963). Unlike contributory infringement, knowledge is not an element of vicarious liability. 3 NIMMER ON COPYRIGHT § 12.04[A][1], at 12–70.

a. *Right and Ability To Control*

The first element of vicarious liability will be met if plaintiffs can show that Netcom has the right and ability to supervise the conduct of its subscribers. Netcom argues that it does not have the right to control its users' postings before they occur. Plaintiffs dispute this and argue that Netcom's terms and conditions, to which its subscribers[22] must agree, specify that Netcom reserves the right to take remedial action against subscribers. *See, e.g., Francis Depo.* at 124–126. Plaintiffs argue that under "netiquette," the informal rules and customs that have developed on the Internet, violation of copyrights by a user is unacceptable and the access provider has a duty [to] take measures to prevent this; where the immediate service provider fails, the next service provider up the transmission stream must act. Further evidence of Netcom's right to restrict infringing activity is its prohibition of copyright infringement and its requirement that its subscribers indemnify it for any damage to third parties. Plaintiffs have thus raised a question of fact as to Netcom's right to control Erlich's use of its services.

---

22. In this case, Netcom is even further removed from Erlich's activities. Erlich was in a contractual relationship only with Klemesrud. Netcom thus dealt directly only with Klemesrud. However, it is not crucial that Erlich does not obtain access directly through Netcom. The issue is Netcom's right and ability to control the use of its system, which it can do indirectly by controlling Klemesrud's use.

Netcom argues that it could not possibly screen messages before they are posted given the speed and volume of the data that goes through its system. Netcom further argues that it has never exercised control over the content of its users' postings. Plaintiffs' expert opines otherwise, stating that with an easy software modification Netcom could identify postings that contain particular words or come from particular individuals.[31] Plaintiffs further dispute Netcom's claim that it could not limit Erlich's access to Usenet without kicking off all 500 subscribers of Klemesrud's BBS. As evidence that Netcom has in fact exercised its ability to police its users' conduct, plaintiffs cite evidence that Netcom has acted to suspend subscribers' accounts on over one thousand occasions. *See* Ex. J (listing suspensions of subscribers by Netcom for commercial advertising, posting obscene materials, and off-topic postings). Further evidence shows that Netcom can delete specific postings. Whether such sanctions occurred before or after the abusive conduct is not material to whether Netcom can exercise control. The court thus finds that plaintiffs have raised a genuine issue of fact as to whether Netcom has the right and ability to exercise control over the activities of its subscribers, and of Erlich in particular.

b. *Direct Financial Benefit*

Plaintiffs must further prove that Netcom receives a direct financial benefit from the infringing activities of its users. For example, a landlord who has the right and ability to supervise the tenant's activities is vicariously liable for the infringements of the tenant where the rental amount is proportional to the proceeds of the tenant's sales. *Shapiro, Bernstein,* 316 F.2d at 306. However, where a defendant rents space or services on a fixed rental fee that does not depend on the nature of the activity of the lessee, courts usually find no vicarious liability because there is no direct financial benefit from the infringement. *See, e.g., Roy Export Co. v. Trustees of Columbia University,* 344 F.Supp. 1350, 1353 (S.D.N.Y.1972) (finding no vicarious liability of university because no financial benefit from allowing screening of bootlegged films); *Fonovisa,* 847 F.Supp. at 1496 (finding swap meet operators did not financially benefit from fixed fee);[5] *see also* Kelly Tickle, Comment, *The Vicarious Liability of Electronic Bulletin Board Operators for the Copyright Infringement Occurring on Their Bulletin Boards,* 80 IOWA L.REV. 391, 415 (1995) (arguing that BBS operators ''lease cyberspace'' and should thus be treated like landlords, who are not liable for infringement that occurs on their premises).

* * *

31. However, plaintiffs submit no evidence indicating Netcom, or anyone, could design software that could determine whether a posting is infringing.

5. [The district court opinion in *Fonovisa* was reversed on appeal. The Ninth Circuit held, contrary to the district court, that the operator of a swap meet *does* receive a direct financial benefit from the participation of vendors selling bootleg music recordings, by virtue of the admission fees, concession stand sales, and parking fees they receive from the additional customers attracted by the counterfeit recordings. *Fonovisa, Inc. v. Cherry Auction, Inc.,* 76 F.3d 259 (9th Cir.1996).—Eds.]

* * * Plaintiffs cannot provide any evidence of a direct financial benefit received by Netcom from Erlich's infringing postings. Unlike *Shapiro, Bernstein,* and like *Fonovisa,* Netcom receives a fixed fee. There is no evidence that infringement by Erlich, or any other user of Netcom's services, in any way enhances the value of Netcom's services to subscribers or attracts new subscribers. Plaintiffs argue, however, that Netcom somehow derives a benefit from its purported "policy of refusing to take enforcement actions against its subscribers and others who transmit infringing messages over its computer networks." Plaintiffs point to Netcom's advertisements that, compared to competitors like CompuServe and America Online, Netcom provides easy, regulation-free Internet access. Plaintiffs assert that Netcom's policy attracts copyright infringers to its system, resulting in a direct financial benefit. The court is not convinced that such an argument, if true, would constitute a direct financial benefit to Netcom from *Erlich's* infringing activities. *See Fonovisa,* 847 F.Supp. at 1496 (finding no direct financial benefit despite argument that lessees included many vendors selling counterfeit goods and that clientele sought "bargain basement prices"). Further, plaintiffs' argument is not supported by probative evidence. The only "evidence" plaintiffs cite for their supposition is the declaration of their counsel, Elliot Abelson, who states that

> [o]n April 7, 1995, in a conversation regarding Netcom's position related to this case, Randolf Rice, attorney for Netcom, informed me that Netcom's executives are happy about the publicity it is receiving in the press as a result of this case. Mr. Rice also told me that Netcom was concerned that it would lose business if it took action against Erlich or Klemesrud in connection with Erlich's infringements.

Abelson Decl. ¶ 2. Netcom objects to this declaration as hearsay and as inadmissible evidence of statements made in compromise negotiations. Fed.R.Ev. 801, 408. Whether or not this declaration is admissible, it does not support plaintiffs' argument that Netcom either has a policy of not enforcing violations of copyright laws by its subscribers or, assuming such a policy exists, that Netcom's policy directly financially benefits Netcom, such as by attracting new subscribers. Because plaintiffs have failed to raise a question of fact on this vital element, their claim of vicarious liability fails. * * *

[For similar reasons, the court also finds that the plaintiffs have failed to raise a genuine issue of material fact on their claim of vicarious infringement against the BBS operator, Klemesrud.]

　　* * *

A & M Records, Inc. v. Napster, Inc.

239 F.3d 1004 (9th Cir.2001).

■ BEEZER, CIRCUIT JUDGE:

[For the facts of the case and the court's finding of direct infringement by the users of the Napster service, see Part II(B), *supra.*]

V

We turn to the question whether Napster engages in vicarious copyright infringement. Vicarious copyright liability is an "outgrowth" of respondeat superior. *Fonovisa*, 76 F.3d at 262. In the context of copyright law, vicarious liability extends beyond an employer/employee relationship to cases in which a defendant "has the right and ability to supervise the infringing activity and also has a direct financial interest in such activities." *Id.* (quoting *Gershwin*, 443 F.2d at 1162); *see also Polygram Int'l Publ'g, Inc. v. Nevada/TIG, Inc.*, 855 F.Supp. 1314, 1325–26 (D.Mass.1994) (describing vicarious liability as a form of risk allocation).

Before moving into this discussion, we note that *Sony*'s "staple article of commerce" analysis has no application to Napster's potential liability for vicarious copyright infringement. *See Sony*, 464 U.S. at 434–435; *see generally* 3 Melville B. Nimmer & David Nimmer, *Nimmer On Copyright* §§ 12.04[A][2] and [A][2][b] (2000) (confining *Sony* to contributory infringement analysis: "Contributory infringement itself is of two types— personal conduct that forms part of or furthers the infringement and contribution of machinery or goods that provide the means to infringe"). The issues of Sony's liability under the "doctrines of 'direct infringement' and 'vicarious liability'" were not before the Supreme Court, although the Court recognized that the "lines between direct infringement, contributory infringement, and vicarious liability are not clearly drawn." *Id.* at 435 n. 17. Consequently, when the *Sony* Court used the term "vicarious liability," it did so broadly and outside of a technical analysis of the doctrine of vicarious copyright infringement. *Id.* at 435 ("[V]icarious liability is imposed in virtually all areas of the law, and the concept of contributory infringement is merely a species of the broader problem of identifying the circumstances in which it is just to hold one individual accountable for the actions of another."); *see also Black's Law Dictionary* 927 (7th ed. 1999) (defining "vicarious liability" in a manner similar to the definition used in *Sony*).

A. *Financial Benefit*

The district court determined that plaintiffs had demonstrated they would likely succeed in establishing that Napster has a direct financial interest in the infringing activity. *Napster*, 114 F.Supp.2d at 921–22. We agree. Financial benefit exists where the availability of infringing material "acts as a 'draw' for customers." *Fonovisa*, 76 F.3d at 263–64 (stating that financial benefit may be shown "where infringing performances enhance the attractiveness of a venue"). Ample evidence supports the district court's finding that Napster's future revenue is directly dependent upon "increases in userbase." More users register with the Napster system as the "quality and quantity of available music increases." 114 F.Supp.2d at 902. We conclude that the district court did not err in determining that

Napster financially benefits from the availability of protected works on its system.

B. *Supervision*

The district court determined that Napster has the right and ability to supervise its users' conduct. *Napster*, 114 F.Supp.2d at 920–21 (finding that Napster's representations to the court regarding "its improved methods of blocking users about whom rights holders complain . . . is tantamount to an admission that defendant can, and sometimes does, police its service"). We agree in part.

The ability to block infringers' access to a particular environment for any reason whatsoever is evidence of the right and ability to supervise. *See Fonovisa*, 76 F.3d at 262 ("Cherry Auction had the right to terminate vendors for any reason whatsoever and through that right had the ability to control the activities of vendors on the premises."); *cf. Netcom*, 907 F.Supp. at 1375–76 (indicating that plaintiff raised a genuine issue of fact regarding ability to supervise by presenting evidence that an electronic bulletin board service can suspend subscriber's accounts). Here, plaintiffs have demonstrated that Napster retains the right to control access to its system. Napster has an express reservation of rights policy, stating on its website that it expressly reserves the "right to refuse service and terminate accounts in [its] discretion, including, but not limited to, if Napster believes that user conduct violates applicable law . . . or for any reason in Napster's sole discretion, with or without cause."

To escape imposition of vicarious liability, the reserved right to police must be exercised to its fullest extent. Turning a blind eye to detectable acts of infringement for the sake of profit gives rise to liability. *See, e.g., Fonovisa*, 76 F.3d at 261 ("There is no dispute for the purposes of this appeal that Cherry Auction and its operators were aware that vendors in their swap meets were selling counterfeit recordings."); *see also Gershwin*, 443 F.2d at 1161–62 (citing *Shapiro, Bernstein & Co. v. H.L. Green Co.*, 316 F.2d 304 (2d Cir.1963), for the proposition that "failure to police the conduct of the primary infringer" leads to imposition of vicarious liability for copyright infringement).

The district court correctly determined that Napster had the right and ability to police its system and failed to exercise that right to prevent the exchange of copyrighted material. The district court, however, failed to recognize that the boundaries of the premises that Napster "controls and patrols" are limited. *See, e.g., Fonovisa*, 76 F.3d at 262–63 (in addition to having the right to exclude vendors, defendant "controlled and patrolled" the premises); *see also Polygram*, 855 F.Supp. at 1328–29 (in addition to having the contractual right to remove exhibitors, trade show operator reserved the right to police during the show and had its "employees walk the aisles to ensure 'rules compliance' "). Put differently, Napster's reserved "right and ability" to police is cabined by the system's current architecture. As shown by the record, the Napster system does not "read" the content of indexed files, other than to check that they are in the proper MP3 format.

Napster, however, has the ability to locate infringing material listed on its search indices, and the right to terminate users' access to the system. The file name indices, therefore, are within the "premises" that Napster has the ability to police. We recognize that the files are user-named and may not match copyrighted material exactly (for example, the artist or song could be spelled wrong). For Napster to function effectively, however, file names must reasonably or roughly correspond to the material contained in the files, otherwise no user could ever locate any desired music. As a practical matter, Napster, its users and the record company plaintiffs have equal access to infringing material by employing Napster's "search function."

Our review of the record requires us to accept the district court's conclusion that plaintiffs have demonstrated a likelihood of success on the merits of the vicarious copyright infringement claim. Napster's failure to police the system's "premises," combined with a showing that Napster financially benefits from the continuing availability of infringing files on its system, leads to the imposition of vicarious liability. * * *

* * *

NOTES & QUESTIONS

1. *Vicarious liability of corporate officers and employees.* In *Playboy Enterprises, Inc. v. Webbworld, Inc.*, 991 F.Supp. 543 (N.D.Tex.1997), *aff'd mem.*, 168 F.3d 486 (5th Cir.1999), the court held that defendant Webbworld, Inc. directly infringed the copyrights of plaintiff Playboy Enterprises, Inc. by posting Playboy's pictures on its website. The court then addressed the liability of the three individuals who acted as the corporation's principals, one of whom was the corporation's president and sole shareholder. In doing so, it applied the test for vicarious copyright liability: "To show vicarious liability, a plaintiff must prove that a defendant (1) has a direct financial interest in the infringing activity, and (2) has the right and ability to supervise the activity which causes the infringement." *Id.* at 553. The court concluded that all three of the individuals had a direct financial interest in the infringement, as they split the profits from the website's operations. It found that two of the three additionally had the requisite ability to supervise, and therefore held them, but not the third individual, liable as vicarious infringers. Did the court apply the correct test for liability of the individuals? Should it instead, or additionally, have determined whether they were liable as *direct* infringers, either because they themselves performed the actions constituting infringement, or through "piercing the corporate veil"?

2. *Vicarious liability of venture capitalists?* Venture capital firms collect money from investors and invest the money in start-up firms they think are likely to succeed. Of course, the venture capitalists (VCs) only make money if their start-ups succeed and their investors make money, rendering them willing to invest in other ventures sponsored by the VC firm. Thus, in order to keep control of a start-up's business model and operations during the crucial launch period, VCs often condition funding of a start-up on placement of a member of their firm as interim CEO of the company. For example, at the time the record companies launched their lawsuit against Napster for copyright infringement, its CEO was a member of a VC firm. If Napster is contributorily liable for its users' infringements, is the VC firm vicariously liable?

III.   DEFENSES TO COPYRIGHT INFRINGEMENT

In this Part, we consider the use of four defenses to copyright infringement online: the doctrine of fair use, the first-sale doctrine,[6] the defense of copyright misuse, and the right, established by the Audio Home Recording Act, to make copies of musical sound recordings for noncommercial purposes. These defenses play an important role in marking out the shifting line of demarcation between the uses of works that are under the control of the copyright owner, and the uses that are open to competitors and the public.

A.   FAIR USE ONLINE

As noted above, the law of copyright strives to accommodate two competing goals: offering sufficient incentives to motivate the creation of original works of authorship, while allowing the public access to and use of these works. One method the Copyright Act employs to maintain this balance is by granting the public the right to fair use of copyrighted materials.

Fair use is an affirmative defense that a defendant in a lawsuit for copyright infringement may raise. Fair use includes uses for such purposes as "criticism, comment, news reporting, teaching (including multiple copies for classroom use), scholarship, or research." 17 U.S.C. § 107. If a use is fair, then it "is not an infringement of copyright." *Id*. To determine whether a particular use is fair, courts evaluate it using four factors set forth in section 107.

UMG Recordings, Inc. v. MP3.com, Inc.

92 F.Supp.2d 349 (S.D.N.Y.2000).

■ RAKOFF, DISTRICT JUDGE.

The complex marvels of cyberspatial communication may create difficult legal issues; but not in this case. Defendant's infringement of plain-

---

6. In the European Union member states, and in some other countries, the doctrine that limits the extent of control by both copyright and patent holders after their products leave their hands goes by the name of "exhaustion." Thus the U.S. first-sale doctrine in copyright law is subsumed under the general concept of exhaustion in many other jurisdictions.

tiffs' copyrights is clear. Accordingly, on April 28, 2000, the Court granted defendant's motion for partial summary judgment holding defendant liable for copyright infringement. This opinion will state the reasons why.

The pertinent facts, either undisputed or, where disputed, taken most favorably to defendant, are as follows:

The technology known as "MP3" permits rapid and efficient conversion of compact disc recordings ("CDs") to computer files easily accessed over the Internet. *See generally Recording Industry Ass'n of America v. Diamond Multimedia Systems, Inc.,* 180 F.3d 1072, 1073–74 (9th Cir.1999). Utilizing this technology, defendant MP3.com, on or around January 12, 2000, launched its "My.MP3.com" service, which is advertised as permitting subscribers to store, customize and listen to the recordings contained on their CDs from any place where they have an Internet connection. To make good on this offer, defendant purchased tens of thousands of popular CDs in which plaintiffs held the copyrights, and, without authorization, copied their recordings onto its computer servers so as to be able to replay the recordings for its subscribers.

Specifically, in order to first access such a recording, a subscriber to MP3.com must either "prove" that he already owns the CD version of the recording by inserting his copy of the commercial CD into his computer CD–Rom drive for a few seconds (the "Beam-it Service") or must purchase the CD from one of defendant's cooperating online retailers (the "instant Listening Service"). Thereafter, however, the subscriber can access via the Internet from a computer anywhere in the world the copy of plaintiffs' recording made by defendant. Thus, although defendant seeks to portray its service as the "functional equivalent" of storing its subscribers' CDs, in actuality defendant is re-playing for the subscribers converted versions of the recordings it copied, without authorization, from plaintiffs' copyrighted CDs. On its face, this makes out a presumptive case of infringement under the Copyright Act of 1976 ("Copyright Act"), 17 U.S.C. § 101 *et seq. See, e.g., Castle Rock Entertainment, Inc. v. Carol Publishing Group, Inc.,* 150 F.3d 132, 137 (2d Cir.1998); *Hasbro Bradley, Inc. v. Sparkle Toys, Inc.,* 780 F.2d 189, 192 (2d Cir.1985).[1]

Defendant argues, however, that such copying is protected by the affirmative defense of "fair use." *See* 17 U.S.C. § 107. In analyzing such a defense, the Copyright Act specifies four factors that must be considered: "(1) the purpose and character of the use, including whether such use is of a commercial nature or is for nonprofit educational purposes; (2) the

---

1. Defendant's only challenge to plaintiffs' *prima facie* case of infringement is the suggestion, buried in a footnote in its opposition papers, that its music computer files are not in fact "reproductions" of plaintiffs' copyrighted works within the meaning of the Copyright Act. *See, e.g.,* 17 U.S.C. § 114(b). Specifically, defendant claims that the simulated sounds on MP3–based music files are not physically identical to the sounds on the original CD recordings. Defendant concedes, however, that the human ear cannot detect a difference between the two. *Id.* Moreover, defendant admits that a goal of its copying is to create a music file that is sonically as identical to the original CD as possible. In such circumstances, some slight, humanly undetectable difference between the original and the copy does not qualify for exclusion from the coverage of the Act.

nature of the copyrighted work; (3) the amount and substantiality of the portion used in relation to the copyrighted work as a whole; and (4) the effect of the use upon the potential market for or value of the copyrighted work." *Id.* Other relevant factors may also be considered, since fair use is an "equitable rule of reason" to be applied in light of the overall purposes of the Copyright Act. *Sony Corporation of America v. Universal City Studios, Inc.,* 464 U.S. 417, 448, 454 (1984); *see Harper & Row Publishers, Inc. v. Nation Enterprises,* 471 U.S. 539, 549 (1985).

Regarding the first factor—"the purpose and character of the use"—defendant does not dispute that its purpose is commercial, for while subscribers to My.MP3.com are not currently charged a fee, defendant seeks to attract a sufficiently large subscription base to draw advertising and otherwise make a profit. Consideration of the first factor, however, also involves inquiring into whether the new use essentially repeats the old or whether, instead, it "transforms" it by infusing it with new meaning, new understandings, or the like. *See, e.g., Campbell v. Acuff–Rose Music, Inc.,* 510 U.S. 569, 579 (1994); *Castle Rock,* 150 F.3d at 142; *See also* Pierre N. Leval, "Toward a Fair Use Standard," 103 *Harv.L.Rev.* 1105, 111 (1990). Here, although defendant recites that My.MP3.com provides a transformative "space shift" by which subscribers can enjoy the sound recordings contained on their CDs without lugging around the physical discs themselves, this is simply another way of saying that the unauthorized copies are being retransmitted in another medium—an insufficient basis for any legitimate claim of transformation, *See, e.g., Infinity Broadcast Corp. v. Kirkwood,* 150 F.3d 104, 108 (2d Cir.1998) (rejecting the fair use defense by operator of a service that retransmitted copyrighted radio broadcasts over telephone lines); *Los Angeles News Serv. v. Reuters Television Int'l Ltd.,* 149 F.3d 987 (9th Cir.1998) (rejecting the fair use defense where television news agencies copied copyrighted news footage and retransmitted it to news organizations), *cert. denied,* 525 U.S. 1141 (1999); *see also American Geophysical Union v. Texaco Inc.,* 60 F.3d 913, 923 (2d Cir.), *cert. dismissed,* 516 U.S. 1005 (1995).

Here, defendant adds no "new aesthetics, new insights and understandings" to the original music recordings it copies, *see Castle Rock,* 150 F.3d at 142 (internal quotation marks omitted), but simply repackages those recordings to facilitate their transmission through another medium. While such services may be innovative, they are not transformative.[2]

Regarding the second factor—"the nature of the copyrighted work"—the creative recordings here being copied are "close[ ] to the core of intended copyright protection," *Campbell,* 510 U.S. at 586, and, conversely,

---

2. Defendant's reliance on the Ninth Circuit's "reverse engineering" cases, *see Sony Computer Entertainment, Inc. v. Connectix Corp.,* 203 F.3d 596 (9th Cir.2000); *Sega Enterprises Ltd. v. Accolade, Inc.,* 977 F.2d 1510, 1527 (9th Cir.1992), is misplaced, because, among other relevant distinctions, those cases involved the copying of software in order to develop a new product, whereas here defendant copied CDs onto its servers not to create any new form of expression but rather to retransmit the same expression in a different medium.

far removed from the more factual or descriptive work more amenable to "fair use," *see Nihon Keizai Shimbun, Inc. v. Comline Business Data, Inc.,* 166 F.3d 65, 72–73 (2d Cir.1999); *see also Castle Rock,* 150 F.3d at 143–44.

Regarding the third factor—"the amount and substantiality of the portion [of the copyrighted work] used [by the copier] in relation to the copyrighted work as a whole"—it is undisputed that defendant copies, and replays, the entirety of the copyrighted works here in issue, thus again negating any claim of fair use.

Regarding the fourth factor—"the effect of the use upon the potential market for or value of the copyrighted work"—defendant's activities on their face invade plaintiffs' statutory right to license their copyrighted sound recordings to others for reproduction. *See* 17 U.S.C. § 106. Defendant, however, argues that, so far as the derivative market here involved is concerned, plaintiffs have not shown that such licensing is "traditional, reasonable, or likely to be developed." *American Geophysical,* 60 F.3d at 930 and n. 17. Moreover, defendant argues, its activities can only enhance plaintiffs' sales, since subscribers cannot gain access to particular recordings made available by MP3.com unless they have already "purchased" (actually or purportedly), or agreed to purchase, their own CD copies of those recordings.

Such arguments—though dressed in the garb of an expert's "opinion" (that, on inspection, consists almost entirely of speculative and conclusory statements)—are unpersuasive. Any allegedly positive impact of defendant's activities on plaintiffs' prior market in no way frees defendant to usurp a further market that directly derives from reproduction of the plaintiffs' copyrighted works. *See Infinity Broadcast,* 150 F.3d at 111. This would be so even if the copyrightholder had not yet entered the new market in issue, for a copyrighterholder's "exclusive" rights, derived from the Constitution and the Copyright Act, include the right, within broad limits, to curb the development of such a derivative market by refusing to license a copyrighted work or by doing so only on terms the copyright owner finds acceptable. *See Castle Rock,* 150 F.3d at 145–46; *Salinger v. Random House, Inc.,* 811 F.2d 90, 99 (2d Cir.), *cert. denied,* 484 U.S. 890 (1987). Here, moreover, plaintiffs have adduced substantial evidence that they have in fact taken steps to enter that market by entering into various licensing agreements.

Finally, regarding defendant's purported reliance on other factors, *see Campbell,* 510 U.S. at 577, this essentially reduces to the claim that My.MP3.com provides a useful service to consumers that, in its absence, will be served by "pirates." Copyright, however, is not designed to afford consumer protection or convenience but, rather, to protect the copyrightholders' property interests. Moreover, as a practical matter, plaintiffs have indicated no objection in principle to licensing their recordings to companies like MP3.com; they simply want to make sure they get the remuneration the law reserves for them as holders of copyrights on creative works. Stripped to its essence, defendant's "consumer protection" argument amounts to nothing more than a bald claim that defendant should be able to misappropriate plaintiffs' property simply because there is a consumer demand for it. This hardly appeals to the conscience of equity.

In sum, on any view, defendant's "fair use" defense is indefensible and must be denied as a matter of law. * * *

Accordingly, the Court, for the foregoing reasons, has determined that plaintiffs are entitled to partial summary judgment holding defendant to have infringed plaintiffs' copyrights.

* * *

A & M Records, Inc. v. Napster, Inc.

239 F.3d 1004 (9th Cir.2001).

■ BEEZER, CIRCUIT JUDGE:

[For the facts of the case and the court's finding of direct infringement by the users of the Napster service, see Part II(B), *supra*.]

* * *

B.   Fair Use

Napster contends that its users do not directly infringe plaintiffs' copyrights because the users are engaged in fair use of the material. *See* 17 U.S.C. § 107 ("[T]he fair use of a copyrighted work ... is not an infringement of copyright."). Napster identifies three specific alleged fair uses: sampling, where users make temporary copies of a work before purchasing; space-shifting, where users access a sound recording through the Napster system that they already own in audio CD format; and permissive distribution of recordings by both new and established artists.

The district court considered factors listed in 17 U.S.C. § 107, which guide a court's fair use determination. These factors are: (1) the purpose and character of the use; (2) the nature of the copyrighted work; (3) the "amount and substantiality of the portion used" in relation to the work as a whole; and (4) the effect of the use upon the potential market for the work or the value of the work. *See* 17 U.S.C. § 107. The district court first conducted a general analysis of Napster system uses under § 107, and then applied its reasoning to the alleged fair uses identified by Napster. The district court concluded that Napster users are not fair users. We agree. * * *

1.   Purpose and Character of the Use

This factor focuses on whether the new work merely replaces the object of the original creation or instead adds a further purpose or different character. In other words, this factor asks "whether and to what extent the new work is 'transformative.'" *See Campbell v. Acuff–Rose Music, Inc.,* 510 U.S. 569, 579 (1994).

The district court first concluded that downloading MP3 files does not transform the copyrighted work. *Napster,* 114 F.Supp.2d at 912. This conclusion is supportable. Courts have been reluctant to find fair use when an original work is merely retransmitted in a different medium. *See, e.g., Infinity Broadcast Corp. v. Kirkwood*, 150 F.3d 104, 108 (2d Cir.1998) (concluding that retransmission of radio broadcast over telephone lines is not transformative); *UMG Recordings, Inc. v. MP3.Com, Inc.*, 92 F.Supp.2d 349, 351 (S.D.N.Y.) (finding that reproduction of audio CD into MP3 format does not "transform" the work), *certification denied*, 2000 WL 710056 (S.D.N.Y. June 1, 2000) ("Defendant's copyright infringement was clear, and the mere fact that it was clothed in the exotic webbing of the Internet does not disguise its illegality.").

This "purpose and character" element also requires the district court to determine whether the allegedly infringing use is commercial or noncommercial. *See Campbell*, 510 U.S. at 584–85. A commercial use weighs against a finding of fair use but is not conclusive on the issue. *Id.* The district court determined that Napster users engage in commercial use of the copyrighted materials largely because (1) "a host user sending a file cannot be said to engage in a personal use when distributing that file to an anonymous requester" and (2) "Napster users get for free something they would ordinarily have to buy." *Napster*, 114 F.Supp.2d at 912. The district court's findings are not clearly erroneous.

Direct economic benefit is not required to demonstrate a commercial use. Rather, repeated and exploitative copying of copyrighted works, even if the copies are not offered for sale, may constitute a commercial use. *See Worldwide Church of God v. Philadelphia Church of God*, 227 F.3d 1110, 1118 (9th Cir.2000) (stating that church that copied religious text for its members "unquestionably profit[ed]" from the unauthorized "distribution and use of [the text] without having to account to the copyright holder"); *American Geophysical Union v. Texaco, Inc.*, 60 F.3d 913, 922 (2d Cir.1994) (finding that researchers at for-profit laboratory gained indirect economic advantage by photocopying copyrighted scholarly articles). In the record before us, commercial use is demonstrated by a showing that repeated and exploitative unauthorized copies of copyrighted works were made to save the expense of purchasing authorized copies. *See Worldwide Church*, 227 F.3d at 1117–18; *Sega Enters. Ltd. v. MAPHIA*, 857 F.Supp. 679, 687 (N.D.Cal.1994) (finding commercial use when individuals downloaded copies of video games "to avoid having to buy video game cartridges"); *see also American Geophysical*, 60 F.3d at 922. Plaintiffs made such a showing before the district court.[4]

We also note that the definition of a financially motivated transaction for the purposes of criminal copyright actions includes trading infringing copies of a work for other items, "including the receipt of other copyrighted works." *See* No Electronic Theft Act ("NET Act"), *Pub.L. No. 105–147*, 18 U.S.C. § 101 (defining "Financial Gain").

---

4. Napster counters that even if certain users engage in commercial use by downloading instead of purchasing the music, space-shifting and sampling are nevertheless *non-*commercial in nature. We address this contention in our discussion of these specific uses, *infra.*

2. The Nature of the Use

Works that are creative in nature are "closer to the core of intended copyright protection" than are more fact-based works. *See Campbell*, 510 U.S. at 586. The district court determined that plaintiffs' "copyrighted musical compositions and sound recordings are creative in nature . . . which cuts against a finding of fair use under the second factor." *Napster*, 114 F.Supp.2d at 913. We find no error in the district court's conclusion.

3. The Portion Used

"While 'wholesale copying does not preclude fair use per se,' copying an entire work 'militates against a finding of fair use.'" *Worldwide Church*, 227 F.3d at 1118 (quoting *Hustler Magazine Inc. v. Moral Majority Inc.*, 796 F.2d 1148, 1155 (9th Cir.1986)). The district court determined that Napster users engage in "wholesale copying" of copyrighted work because file transfer necessarily "involves copying the entirety of the copyrighted work." *Napster*, 114 F.Supp.2d at 913. We agree. We note, however, that under certain circumstances, a court will conclude that a use is fair even when the protected work is copied in its entirety. *See, e.g., Sony Corp. v. Universal City Studios, Inc.*, 464 U.S. 417, 449–50 (1984) (acknowledging that fair use of time-shifting necessarily involved making a full copy of a protected work).

4. Effect of Use on Market

"Fair use, when properly applied, is limited to copying by others which does not materially impair the marketability of the work which is copied." *Harper & Row Publishers, Inc. v. Nation Enters.*, 471 U.S. 539, 566–67 (1985). "[T]he importance of this [fourth] factor will vary, not only with the amount of harm, but also with the relative strength of the showing on the other factors." *Campbell*, 510 U.S. at 591 n. 21. The proof required to demonstrate present or future market harm varies with the purpose and character of the use:

> A challenge to a noncommercial use of a copyrighted work requires proof either that the particular use is harmful, or that if it should become widespread, it would adversely affect the potential market for the copyrighted work. . . . *If the intended use is for commercial gain, that likelihood [of market harm] may be presumed. But if it is for a noncommercial purpose, the likelihood must be demonstrated.*

Sony, 464 U.S. at 451 (emphases added).

Addressing this factor, the district court concluded that Napster harms the market in "at least" two ways: it reduces audio CD sales among college students and it "raises barriers to plaintiffs' entry into the market for the digital downloading of music." *Napster*, 114 F.Supp.2d at 913. The district court relied on evidence plaintiffs submitted to show that Napster use harms the market for their copyrighted musical compositions and sound recordings. In a separate memorandum and order regarding the parties' objections to the expert reports, the district court examined each report, finding some more appropriate and probative than others. *A & M Records,*

Inc. v. Napster, Inc., 2000 WL 1170106 (N.D.Cal. August 10, 2000). Notably, plaintiffs' expert, Dr. E. Deborah Jay, conducted a survey (the "Jay Report") using a random sample of college and university students to track their reasons for using Napster and the impact Napster had on their music purchases. *Id.* at *2. The court recognized that the Jay Report focused on just one segment of the Napster user population and found "evidence of lost sales attributable to college use to be probative of irreparable harm for purposes of the preliminary injunction motion." *Id.* at *3.

Plaintiffs also offered a study conducted by Michael Fine, Chief Executive Officer of Soundscan, (the "Fine Report") to determine the effect of online sharing of MP3 files in order to show irreparable harm. Fine found that online file sharing had resulted in a loss of "album" sales within college markets. After reviewing defendant's objections to the Fine Report and expressing some concerns regarding the methodology and findings, the district court refused to exclude the Fine Report insofar as plaintiffs offered it to show irreparable harm. *Id.* at *6.

Plaintiffs' expert Dr. David J. Teece studied several issues ("Teece Report"), including whether plaintiffs had suffered or were likely to suffer harm in their existing and planned businesses due to Napster use. *Id.* Napster objected that the report had not undergone peer review. The district court noted that such reports generally are not subject to such scrutiny and overruled defendant's objections. *Id.*

As for defendant's experts, plaintiffs objected to the report of Dr. Peter S. Fader, in which the expert concluded that Napster is *beneficial* to the music industry because MP3 music file-sharing stimulates more audio CD sales than it displaces. *Id.* at *7. The district court found problems in Dr. Fader's minimal role in overseeing the administration of the survey and the lack of objective data in his report. The court decided the generality of the report rendered it "of dubious reliability and value." The court did not exclude the report, however, but chose "not to rely on Fader's findings in determining the issues of fair use and irreparable harm." *Id.* at *8.

The district court cited both the Jay and Fine Reports in support of its finding that Napster use harms the market for plaintiffs' copyrighted musical compositions and sound recordings by reducing CD sales among college students. The district court cited the Teece Report to show the harm Napster use caused in raising barriers to plaintiffs' entry into the market for digital downloading of music. *Napster,* 114 F.Supp.2d at 910. The district court's careful consideration of defendant's objections to these reports and decision to rely on the reports for specific issues demonstrates a proper exercise of discretion in addition to a correct application of the fair use doctrine. Defendant has failed to show any basis for disturbing the district court's findings.

We, therefore, conclude that the district court made sound findings related to Napster's deleterious effect on the present and future digital download market. Moreover, lack of harm to an established market cannot deprive the copyright holder of the right to develop alternative markets for the works. *See L.A. Times v. Free Republic,* 54 U.S.P.Q.2d 1453, 1469–71

(C.D.Cal.2000) (stating that online market for plaintiff newspapers' articles was harmed because plaintiffs demonstrated that "[defendants] are attempting to exploit the market for viewing their articles online"); *see also UMG Recordings,* 92 F.Supp.2d at 352 ("Any allegedly positive impact of defendant's activities on plaintiffs' prior market in no way frees defendant to usurp a further market that directly derives from reproduction of the plaintiffs' copyrighted works."). Here, similar to *L.A. Times* and *UMG Recordings,* the record supports the district court's finding that the "record company plaintiffs have already expended considerable funds and effort to commence Internet sales and licensing for digital downloads." 114 F.Supp.2d at 915. Having digital downloads available for free on the Napster system necessarily harms the copyright holders' attempts to charge for the same downloads.

Judge Patel did not abuse her discretion in reaching the above fair use conclusions, nor were the findings of fact with respect to fair use considerations clearly erroneous. We next address Napster's identified uses of sampling and space-shifting.

5. *Identified Uses*

Napster maintains that its identified uses of sampling and space-shifting were wrongly excluded as fair uses by the district court.

a. *Sampling*

Napster contends that its users download MP3 files to "sample" the music in order to decide whether to purchase the recording. Napster argues that the district court: (1) erred in concluding that sampling is a commercial use because it conflated a noncommercial use with a personal use; (2) erred in determining that sampling adversely affects the market for plaintiffs' copyrighted music, a requirement if the use is noncommercial; and (3) erroneously concluded that sampling is not a fair use because it determined that samplers may also engage in other infringing activity.

The district court determined that sampling remains a commercial use even if some users eventually purchase the music. We find no error in the district court's determination. Plaintiffs have established that they are likely to succeed in proving that even authorized temporary downloading of individual songs for sampling purposes is commercial in nature. *See Napster,* 114 F.Supp.2d at 913. The record supports a finding that free promotional downloads are highly regulated by the record company plaintiffs and that the companies collect royalties for song samples available on retail Internet sites. *Id.* Evidence relied on by the district court demonstrates that the free downloads provided by the record companies consist of thirty-to-sixty second samples or are full songs programmed to "time out," that is, exist only for a short time on the downloader's computer. *Id.* at 913–14. In comparison, Napster users download a full, free and permanent copy of the recording. *Id.* at 914–15. The determination by the district court as to the commercial purpose and character of sampling is not clearly erroneous.

The district court further found that both the market for audio CDs and market for online distribution are adversely affected by Napster's service. As stated in our discussion of the district court's general fair use analysis: the court did not abuse its discretion when it found that, overall, Napster has an adverse impact on the audio CD and digital download markets. Contrary to Napster's assertion that the district court failed to specifically address the market impact of sampling, the district court determined that "[e]ven if the type of sampling supposedly done on Napster were a non-commercial use, plaintiffs have demonstrated a substantial likelihood that it would adversely affect the potential market for their copyrighted works if it became widespread." *Napster,* 114 F.Supp.2d at 914. The record supports the district court's preliminary determinations that: (1) the more music that sampling users download, the less likely they are to eventually purchase the recordings on audio CD; and (2) even if the audio CD market is not harmed, Napster has adverse effects on the developing digital download market.

Napster further argues that the district court erred in rejecting its evidence that the users' downloading of "samples" increases or tends to increase audio CD sales. The district court, however, correctly noted that "any potential enhancement of plaintiffs' sales ... would not tip the fair use analysis conclusively in favor of defendant." *Id.* at 914. We agree that increased sales of copyrighted material attributable to unauthorized use should not deprive the copyright holder of the right to license the material. *See Campbell,* 510 U.S. at 591 n. 21 ("Even favorable evidence, without more, is no guarantee of fairness. Judge Leval gives the example of the film producer's appropriation of a composer's previously unknown song that turns the song into a commercial success; the boon to the song does not make the film's simple copying fair."); *see also L.A. Times,* 54 U.S.P.Q.2d at 1471–72. Nor does positive impact in one market, here the audio CD market, deprive the copyright holder of the right to develop identified alternative markets, here the digital download market. *See id.* at 1469–71.

We find no error in the district court's factual findings or abuse of discretion in the court's conclusion that plaintiffs will likely prevail in establishing that sampling does not constitute a fair use.

b. *Space–Shifting*

Napster also maintains that space-shifting is a fair use. Space-shifting occurs when a Napster user downloads MP3 music files in order to listen to music he already owns on audio CD. *See id.* at 915–16. Napster asserts that we have already held that space-shifting of musical compositions and sound recordings is a fair use. *See Recording Indus. Ass'n of Am. v. Diamond Multimedia Sys., Inc.,* 180 F.3d 1072, 1079 (9th Cir.1999) ("Rio [a portable MP3 player] merely makes copies in order to render portable, or 'space-shift,' those files that already reside on a user's hard drive.... Such copying is a paradigmatic noncommercial personal use."). *See also generally Sony,* 464 U.S. at 423 (holding that "time-shifting," where a video tape recorder owner records a television show for later viewing, is a fair use).

We conclude that the district court did not err when it refused to apply the "shifting" analyses of *Sony* and *Diamond*. Both *Diamond* and *Sony* are inapposite because the methods of shifting in these cases did not also simultaneously involve distribution of the copyrighted material to the general public; the time or space-shifting of copyrighted material exposed the material only to the original user. In *Diamond,* for example, the copyrighted music was transferred from the user's computer hard drive to the user's portable MP3 player. So too *Sony,* where "the majority of VCR purchasers ... did not distribute taped television broadcasts, but merely enjoyed them at home." *Napster,* 114 F.Supp.2d at 913. Conversely, it is obvious that once a user lists a copy of music he already owns on the Napster system in order to access the music from another location, the song becomes "available to millions of other individuals," not just the original CD owner. *See UMG Recordings,* 92 F.Supp.2d at 351–52 (finding space-shifting of MP3 files not a fair use even when previous ownership is demonstrated before a download is allowed); *cf. Religious Tech. Ctr. v. Lerma,* 1996 WL 633131, at *6 (E.D.Va. Oct.4, 1996) (suggesting that storing copyrighted material on computer disk for later review is not a fair use).

c. *Other Uses*

Permissive reproduction by either independent or established artists is the final fair use claim made by Napster. The district court noted that plaintiffs did not seek to enjoin this and any other noninfringing use of the Napster system, including: chat rooms, message boards and Napster's New Artist Program. *Napster,* 114 F.Supp.2d at 917. Plaintiffs do not challenge these uses on appeal.

We find no error in the district court's determination that plaintiffs will likely succeed in establishing that Napster users do not have a fair use defense. * * *

* * *

Kelly v. Arriba Soft Corporation

280 F.3d 934 (9th Cir.2002).

■ NELSON, CIRCUIT JUDGE.

[The facts of this case are set forth in Part II(A), *supra.*]

* * *

II.

* * *

A.

An owner of a copyright has the exclusive right to reproduce, distribute, and publicly display copies of the work. To establish a claim of copyright infringement by reproduction, the plaintiff must show ownership of the copyright and copying by the defendant. As to the thumbnails, there is no dispute that Kelly owned the copyright to the images and that Arriba copied those images. Therefore, Kelly established a prima facie case of copyright infringement.

A claim of copyright infringement is subject to certain statutory exceptions, including the fair use exception. This exception "permits courts to avoid rigid application of the copyright statute when, on occasion, it would stifle the very creativity which that law is designed to foster."[9] The statute sets out four factors to consider in determining whether the use in a particular case is a fair use. We must balance these factors, in light of the objectives of copyright law, rather than view them as definitive or determinative tests. We now turn to the four fair use factors.

1.   Purpose and character of the use.

The Supreme Court has rejected the proposition that a commercial use of the copyrighted material ends the inquiry under this factor.[12] Instead,

> [t]he central purpose of this investigation is to see ... whether the new work merely supersede[s] the objects of the original creation, or instead adds something new, with a further purpose or different character, altering the first with new expression, meaning, or message; it asks, in other words, whether and to what extent the new work is transformative.[13]

The more transformative the new work, the less important the other factors, including commercialism, become.

There is no dispute that Arriba operates its web site for commercial purposes and that Kelly's images were part of Arriba's search engine database. As the district court found, while such use of Kelly's images was commercial, it was more incidental and less exploitative in nature than more traditional types of commercial use. Arriba was neither using Kelly's images to directly promote its web site nor trying to profit by selling Kelly's images. Instead, Kelly's images were among thousands of images in Arriba's search engine database. Because the use of Kelly's images was not highly exploitative, the commercial nature of the use only slightly weighs against a finding of fair use.

The second part of the inquiry as to this factor involves the transformative nature of the use. We must determine if Arriba's use of the images merely superseded the object of the originals or instead added a further purpose or different character. We find that Arriba's use of Kelly's images for its thumbnails was transformative.

Despite the fact that Arriba made exact replications of Kelly's images, the thumbnails were much smaller, lower-resolution images that served an entirely different function than Kelly's original images. Kelly's images are

---

9. *Dr. Seuss Enters., L.P. v. Penguin Books USA, Inc.,* 109 F.3d 1394, 1399 (9th Cir.1997) (internal quotation marks and citation omitted).

12. *Campbell v. Acuff–Rose Music, Inc.,* 510 U.S. 569, 579 (1994).

13. *Id.* (internal quotation marks and citation omitted) (alteration in original).

artistic works used for illustrative purposes. His images are used to portray scenes from the American West in an esthetic manner. Arriba's use of Kelly's images in the thumbnails is unrelated to any esthetic purpose. Arriba's search engine functions as a tool to help index and improve access to images on the internet and their related web sites. In fact, users are unlikely to enlarge the thumbnails and use them for artistic purposes because the thumbnails are of much lower resolution than the originals; any enlargement results in a significant loss of clarity of the image, making them inappropriate as display material.

Kelly asserts that because Arriba reproduced his exact images and added nothing to them, Arriba's use cannot be transformative. It is true that courts have been reluctant to find fair use when an original work is merely retransmitted in a different medium.[17] Those cases are inapposite, however, because the resulting use of the copyrighted work in those cases was the same as the original use. For instance, reproducing music CD's into computer MP3 format does not change the fact that both formats are used for entertainment purposes. Likewise, reproducing news footage into a different format does not change the ultimate purpose of informing the public about current affairs. * * *

This case involves more than merely a retransmission of Kelly's images in a different medium. Arriba's use of the images serves a different function than Kelly's use—improving access to information on the internet versus artistic expression. Furthermore, it would be unlikely that anyone would use Arriba's thumbnails for illustrative or esthetic purposes because enlarging them sacrifices their clarity. Because Arriba's use is not superseding Kelly's use but, rather, has created a different purpose for the images, Arriba's use is transformative.

> * * *

[I]n *Nunez v. Caribbean International News Corp.,*[22] the First Circuit found that copying a photograph that was intended to be used in a modeling portfolio and using it instead in a news article was a transformative use. By putting a copy of the photograph in the newspaper, the work was transformed into news, creating a new meaning or purpose for the work. The use of Kelly's images in Arriba's search engine is more analogous to the situation in *Nunez* because Arriba has created a new purpose for the images and is not simply superseding Kelly's purpose.

The Copyright Act was intended to promote creativity, thereby benefiting the artist and the public alike. To preserve the potential future use of artistic works for purposes of teaching, research, criticism, and news reporting, Congress made the fair use exception. Arriba's use of Kelly's images promotes the goals of the Copyright Act and the fair use exception.

---

17. *See Infinity Broad. Corp. v. Kirkwood,* 150 F.3d 104, 108 (2d Cir.1998) (concluding that retransmission of radio broadcast over telephone lines is not transformative); *UMG Recordings, Inc. v. MP3.Com, Inc.,* 92 F.Supp.2d 349, 351 (S.D.N.Y.2000) (finding that reproduction of audio CD into computer MP3 format does not transform the work) * * *.

22. 235 F.3d 18 (1st Cir.2000).

The thumbnails do not stifle artistic creativity because they are not used for illustrative or artistic purposes and therefore do not supplant the need for the originals. In addition, they benefit the public by enhancing information gathering techniques on the internet.

In *Sony Computer Entertainment America, Inc. v. Bleem*,[25] we held that when Bleem copied "screen shots" from Sony computer games and used them in its own advertising, it was a fair use.[26] In finding that the first factor weighed in favor of Bleem, we noted that "comparative advertising redounds greatly to the purchasing public's benefit with very little corresponding loss to the integrity of Sony's copyrighted material."[27] Similarly, this first factor weighs in favor of Arriba due to the public benefit of the search engine and the minimal loss of integrity to Kelly's images.

2. Nature of the copyrighted work.

"Works that are creative in nature are closer to the core of intended copyright protection than are more fact-based works."[28] Photographs used for illustrative purposes, such as Kelly's, are generally creative in nature. The fact that a work is published or unpublished also is a critical element of its nature.[29] Published works are more likely to qualify as fair use because the first appearance of the artist's expression has already occurred. Kelly's images appeared on the internet before Arriba used them in its search image. When considering both of these elements, we find that this factor only slightly weighs in favor of Kelly.

3. Amount and substantiality of portion used.

"While wholesale copying does not preclude fair use per se, copying an entire work militates against a finding of fair use."[31] However, the extent of permissible copying varies with the purpose and character of the use.[32] If the secondary user only copies as much as is necessary for his or her intended use, then this factor will not weigh against him or her.

This factor will neither weigh for nor against either party because, although Arriba did copy each of Kelly's images as a whole, it was reasonable to do so in light of Arriba's use of the images. It was necessary for Arriba to copy the entire image to allow users to recognize the image and decide whether to pursue more information about the image or the originating web site. If Arriba only copied part of the image, it would be more difficult to identify it, thereby reducing the usefulness of the visual search engine.

25. 214 F.3d 1022 (9th Cir.2000).

26. *Id.* at 1029.

27. *Id.* at 1027.

28. *A & M Records*, 239 F.3d at 1016 (citing *Campbell*, 510 U.S. at 586) (internal quotation marks omitted).

29. *Harper & Row, Publishers, Inc. v. Nation Enters.*, 471 U.S. 539, 564 (1985) (noting that the scope of fair use is narrower with respect to unpublished works because the author's right to control the first public appearance of his work weighs against the use of his work before its release).

31. *Worldwide Church of God*, 227 F.3d at 1118 (internal quotation marks and citation omitted).

32. *Campbell*, 510 U.S. at 586–87.

4. Effect of the use upon the potential market for or value of the copyrighted work.

This last factor requires courts to consider "not only the extent of market harm caused by the particular actions of the alleged infringer, but also 'whether unrestricted and widespread conduct of the sort engaged in by the defendant ... would result in a substantially adverse impact on the potential market for the original.' "[33] A transformative work is less likely to have an adverse impact on the market of the original than a work that merely supersedes the copyrighted work.

Kelly's images are related to several potential markets. One purpose of the photographs is to attract internet users to his web site, where he sells advertising space as well as books and travel packages. In addition, Kelly could sell or license his photographs to other web sites or to a stock photo database, which then could offer the images to its customers.

Arriba's use of Kelly's images in its thumbnails does not harm the market for Kelly's images or the value of his images. By showing the thumbnails on its results page when users entered terms related to Kelly's images, the search engine would guide users to Kelly's web site rather than away from it. Even if users were more interested in the image itself rather than the information on the web page, they would still have to go to Kelly's site to see the full-sized image. The thumbnails would not be a substitute for the full-sized images because when the thumbnails are enlarged, they lose their clarity. If a user wanted to view or download a quality image, he or she would have to visit Kelly's web site.[35] This would hold true whether the thumbnails are solely in Arriba's database or are more widespread and found in other search engine databases.

Arriba's use of Kelly's images also would not harm Kelly's ability to sell or license his full-sized images. Arriba does not sell or license its thumbnails to other parties. Anyone who downloaded the thumbnails would not be successful selling the full-sized images because of the low-resolution of the thumbnails. There would be no way to view, create, or sell a clear, full-sized image without going to Kelly's web sites. Therefore, Arriba's creation and use of the thumbnails does not harm the market for or value of Kelly's images. This factor weighs in favor of Arriba.

Having considered the four fair use factors and found that two weigh in favor of Arriba, one is neutral, and one weighs slightly in favor of Kelly,

---

33. *Id.* at 590 (quoting 3 M. Nimmer & D. Nimmer, *Nimmer on Copyright* § 13.05[A][4], at 13–102.61 (1993)) (ellipses in original).

35. We do not suggest that the inferior display quality of a reproduction is in any way dispositive, or will always assist an alleged infringer in demonstrating fair use. In this case, however, it is extremely unlikely that users would download thumbnails for display purposes, as the quality full-size versions are easily accessible from Kelly's web sites.

In addition, we note that in the unique context of photographic images, the quality of the reproduction may matter more than in other fields of creative endeavor. The appearance of photographic images accounts for virtually their entire esthetic value.

we conclude that Arriba's use of Kelly's images as thumbnails in its search engine is a fair use.

B.

* * *

2. Fair use of full-sized images.

The last issue we must address is whether Arriba's display of Kelly's full-sized images was a fair use. Although Arriba did not address the use of the full-sized images in its fair use argument, the district court considered such use in its analysis, and we will consider Arriba's fair use defense here.

Once again, to decide whom the first factor, the purpose and character of the use, favors, we must determine whether Arriba's use of Kelly's images was transformative. Unlike the use of the images for the thumbnails, displaying Kelly's full-sized images does not enhance Arriba's search engine. The images do not act as a means to access other information on the internet but, rather, are likely the end product themselves. Although users of the search engine could link from the full-sized image to Kelly's web site, any user who is solely searching for images would not need to do so. Because the full-sized images on Arriba's site act primarily as illustrations or artistic expression and the search engine would function the same without them, they do not have a purpose different from Kelly's use of them.

Not only is the purpose the same, but Arriba did not add new expression to the images to make them transformative. Placing the images in a "frame" or locating them near text that specifies the size and originating web site is not enough to create new expression or meaning for the images. In sum, Arriba's full-sized images superseded the object of Kelly's images. Because Arriba has not changed the purpose or character of the use of the images, the first factor favors Kelly.

The analysis of the second factor, the nature of the copyrighted work, is the same as in the previous fair use discussion because Kelly's images are still the copyrighted images at issue. Therefore, as before, this factor slightly weighs in favor of Kelly.

The third fair use factor turns on the amount of the work displayed and the reasonableness of this amount in light of the purpose for the display. Arriba displayed the full images, which cuts against a finding of fair use. And while it was necessary to provide whole images to suit Arriba's purpose of giving users access to the full-sized images without having to go to another site, such a purpose is not legitimate, as we noted above. Therefore, it was not reasonable to copy the full-sized display. The third factor favors Kelly.

The fourth factor often depends upon how transformative the new use is compared to the original use. A work that is very transformative will often be in a different market from the original work and therefore is less likely to cause harm to the original work's market. Works that are not transformative, however, have the same purpose as the original work and will often have a negative effect on the original work's market.

As discussed in the previous fair use analysis, Kelly's markets for his images include using them to attract advertisers and buyers to his web site, and selling or licensing the images to other web sites or stock photo databases. By giving users access to Kelly's full-sized images on its own web site, Arriba harms all of Kelly's markets. Users will no longer have to go to Kelly's web site to see the full-sized images, thereby deterring people from visiting his web site. In addition, users would be able to download the full-sized images from Arriba's site and then sell or license those images themselves, reducing Kelly's opportunity to sell or license his own images. If the display of Kelly's images became widespread across other web sites, it would reduce the number of visitors to Kelly's web site even further and increase the chance of others exploiting his images. These actions would result in substantial adverse effects to the potential markets for Kelly's original works. For this reason, the fourth factor weighs heavily in favor of Kelly.

In conclusion, all of the fair use factors weigh in favor of Kelly. Therefore, the doctrine of fair use does not sanction Arriba's display of Kelly's images through the inline linking or framing processes that puts Kelly's original images within the context of Arriba's web site.

* * *

NOTES & QUESTIONS

1. *Private property vs. public access.* In *UMG Recordings, Inc. v. MP3.Com*, the court states that "[c]opyright * * * is not designed to afford consumer protection or convenience but, rather, to protect the copyright-holders' property interests." Dismissing Defendant's attempt to invoke the fair use defense, the court continues that "[s]tripped to its essence, defendant's 'consumer protection' argument amounts to nothing more than a bald claim that defendant should be able to misappropriate plaintiffs' property simply because there is a consumer demand for it." Should the public's desire for access be a relevant consideration in determining the scope of the monopoly conferred on the copyright owner, that is, in determining the applicability of the fair use defense? Compare Justice Stevens's statement in *New York Times v. Tasini*, 533 U.S. 483, 519 (2001): " 'the primary purpose of copyright is not to reward the author, but is rather to secure 'the general benefits derived by the public from the labors of authors.' " ' " (quoting MELVILLE B. NIMMER & DAVID NIMMER, NIMMER ON COPYRIGHT § 1.03[A]) (quoting *Fox Film Corp. v. Doyal*, 286 U.S. 123, 127 (1932)).

2. *Fair use and digital video recorders.* ReplayTV is an updated, digital version of the familiar videocassette recorder. Like a VCR, ReplayTV connects to a television set, records broadcasts as they are received, and allows the recorded broadcast to be replayed at a later time. Rather than storing the broadcast on videotape, ReplayTV makes use of a hard drive, to which it saves a digitized version of the broadcast. Replay TV has two especially noteworthy features. First, a program that is saved on a Re-playTV can be sent by e-mail to up to 15 recipients who may play the program on their own ReplayTV, but the recipients may not retransmit the program to additional recipients. Second, when in playback mode ReplayTV can be set automatically to skip commercials. When it works properly (which it does more than 90 percent of the time), the commercials simply disappear: there is no pause or fast-forwarding through them. The broadcast, cable, and satellite television industries have expressed fears that these features threaten to undermine their business models. In *Sony Corp. of America v. Universal City Studios*, 464 U.S. 417 (1984), the Supreme Court held that recording a broadcast using a traditional VCR for home viewing (often referred to as "time-shifting") is a fair use under the Copyright Act. Should the same rationale lead the courts to hold that recording broadcasts with devices like Replay TV is also fair use? *See Paramount Pictures Corp. v. ReplayTV, Inc.*, CV 01–9358 FMC (Ex) (C.D.Cal. filed Oct. 31, 2001).

B.   The First-Sale Doctrine

Video Pipeline, Inc. v. Buena Vista Home Entertainment, Inc.

192 F.Supp.2d 321 (D.N.J.2002).

■ Simandle, District Judge.

* * *

In the multi-billion dollar home video industry, an increasing amount of sales takes place over the Internet. This case examines the copyright issues that arise when an entity uses the copyrighted motion pictures to make short trailers, which are then made available for money to the entity's clients, which are video retailers, for the viewing by retail customers on the retailers' Internet websites, for the purpose of promoting sales of the copyrighted videos. In this case, the copyright owners seek a preliminary injunction against the entity which creates and sells the unauthorized trailers for their copyrighted home videos.

This matter comes before the Court upon motion by defendant Buena Vista Home Entertainment, Inc. (formerly known as Buena Vista Home Video), and counterclaim-plaintiff Miramax Film Corp. (hereinafter collectively "BVHE" or "defendants") for a preliminary injunction upon their amended counterclaim against plaintiff/counterclaim-defendant Video Pipeline, Inc. Plaintiff Video Pipeline originally brought suit against defendant Buena Vista Home Entertainment, Inc., for a declaratory judgment that plaintiff's use of trailers provided by BVHE in creating its own video clips to be commercially used by Internet video retailers does not constitute copyright infringement under the Copyright Act.

* * *

* * *For the reasons now discussed, the Court will grant defendant BVHE's motion for a preliminary injunction, pursuant to the following findings of fact and conclusions of law entered under Rules 52(a) and 65(d), Fed.R.Civ.P.

BACKGROUND

In this preliminary injunction motion, Buena Vista Home Entertainment, Inc. ("BVHE") seeks to enjoin Video Pipeline from streaming video previews it created out of motion pictures upon which BVHE owns the copyright. BVHE is a wholly-owned, indirect subsidiary of The Walt Disney Company, in the business of manufacturing, distributing, and selling home video versions of copyrighted motion pictures and other entertainment content. Since 1987, BVHE has been the exclusive licensee of Walt Disney Pictures and Television for the distribution of its products in the home video market. In addition, BVHE is the exclusive distributor for Miramax, also a wholly-owned, indirect subsidiary of The Walt Disney Company, in the home video market. Video Pipeline is a company founded in 1985 that compiles and organizes promotional previews from entertainment companies into promotional videos which retailers display in their stores to promote retail sales and rentals. Since 1985, Video Pipeline had provided promotional videos to retailers for in-store use, at times editing the material sent by the movie studios, either because it contained sales and marketing information not intended for customer viewing or because Video Pipeline's retailer clients complained about certain inappropriate previews supplied by studios.

BVHE and Video Pipeline entered into a Master Clip Agreement dated November 7, 1988, by which BVHE granted Video Pipeline permission to use certain videotape promotional previews ("trailers") in compilations to be exhibited in video stores to promote home video sales and rentals. Beginning in 1995, home video retailers began using the Internet as a means of marketing home video products. In 1997, Video Pipeline began making the promotional previews available to home video retailers' Internet websites by means of an Internet service comprised of "VideoPipeline.net" to promote sales and rentals of the home video products. VideoPipeline.net is not a website, but is the network through which retailers' customers can access and stream the previews. These previews can be viewed but cannot be downloaded by Internet users.

In general, retail customers can view the previews while on the retailers' websites by clicking on the "preview" buttons for a particular motion picture, which links them immediately to VideoPipeline.net, which then "streams" the video to the customer. (Hearing Tr. at 102.) "Video Pipeline.com" is Video Pipeline's corporate website that provides information about Video Pipeline's online promotional services for retailers, and no previews are actually shown via that site itself. "VideoDetective.com" is another website that uses VideoPipeline.net to allow Internet users to access previews and to link to retail websites by means of a "Shop Now" button. Video Pipeline has approximately 25 agreements with certain retailers, including Yahoo!Shopping, Netflix, TLA, and IMDB/Amazon to provide these services. In providing these services to Internet-based retailers, Video Pipeline charges the retailers "per Mega Byte actually shown to consumers." Thus, Video Pipeline receives its income for this service from the retailers it serves, based upon the units of time that a retailer's customer is viewing the Video Pipeline previews.

On September 13, 2000, BVHE advised Video Pipeline that it did not have permission to use the studio-supplied trailers on the Internet, nor were they cleared for online use, and requested that the previews of BVHE's motion pictures be removed from the website immediately. On October 24, 2000, Video Pipeline filed suit in this Court against BVHE, seeking a declaratory judgment that its use of promotional materials provided by BVHE to Video Pipeline did not violate any of BVHE's rights under federal copyright law or any other law. BVHE subsequently terminated the Master Clip License Agreement and demanded return of all trailers previously provided to Video Pipeline. On December 21, 2000, Video Pipeline returned to BVHE 80 promotional previews subject to the Master Clip License Agreement.

Video Pipeline removed the previews subject to the agreement from the Internet at BVHE's request, but continued to make its own previews (hereinafter "clip previews") from copies of videos of BVHE's copyrighted motion pictures owned by its retailer clients, with the exception of one clip preview of the Belgian movie "Everybody Famous," which was made from material provided directly by BVHE. Each clip preview created by Video Pipeline is approximately 120 seconds in length and consist of an opening display of the Disney or Miramax trademark, the title of the motion picture being distributed by BVHE, then two or more scenes from the motion picture, followed by another display of the title. In addition, Video Pipeline's clip previews have no voice over, no editing, no use of additional music, and no use or narration or other types of marketing techniques often found in studio-produced trailers. At issue are 62 clip previews, including those for movies such as *Fantasia, Beauty and the Beast,* and *Pretty Woman,* for purposes of this preliminary injunction. It is estimated that Internet users have streamed Video Pipeline's clip previews over 30,000 times between November 3, 2000, and April 3, 2001.

BVHE alleges that Video Pipeline's creation, distribution, and provision of online streaming of clip previews to video retailers in this fashion violates § 106 of the Copyright Act. Video Pipeline alleges that its clip previews do not infringe the copyrights on the underlying motion pictures, and that they are in any event protected by the "first sale" doctrine under § 109(a) of the Copyright Act * * *

DISCUSSION

* * * Here, it is uncontested that Disney, BVHE's licensor, owns the copyright of the full-length motion pictures on which Video Pipeline's clip previews are based, as well as the trademarks of the logos of Disney, Buena Vista, Hollywood Pictures, and Touchstone, shown at the beginning of the

clip previews. To BVHE is thus conferred the exclusive rights reserved as copyright owner under § 106 of the Copyright Act.

1. Exclusive Rights Under § 106 of the Copyright Act

BVHE argues that Video Pipeline's reproduction of the video clips provided by BVHE infringes all five of the exclusive rights that are reserved to it as owner of the copyright at issue under § 106. * * *

Video Pipeline's creation of video clips is most likely a derivative work under § 106(2). *See, e.g., Lamb v. Starks,* 949 F.Supp. 753, 756 (N.D.Cal. 1996) (holding that defendant infringed copyright by copying trailer consisting of parts of scenes from plaintiff's movie). * * *

The Court finds that Video Pipeline's clip previews also constitute a public performance under § 106(4). * * *

In addition, the Court finds that Video Pipeline's service of providing clip previews online constitutes a "public display" that violates the copyright owner's exclusive right "to display the copyrighted work publicly." 17 U.S.C. § 106(5). * * *

The Court finds that because Video Pipeline's actions violate the exclusive rights of the copyright owner BVHE, plaintiff has infringed on BVHE's copyright. *See* 17 U.S.C. § 501. The next point of discussion concerns Video Pipeline's contention that, notwithstanding its violations of § 106, it is nevertheless protected by the First Sale Doctrine. * * *

2. First Sale Doctrine

Video Pipeline argues that its actions of creating its own clip previews from those provided by BVHE and subsequently allowing customers of its retailer clients to view them online is protected by the First Sale Doctrine. The first sale doctrine, codified at 17 U.S.C. § 109(a), prevents the copyright owner from controlling future transfers of a particular copy of a copyrighted work after he has transferred its "material ownership" to another. *Columbia Pictures v. Aveco, Inc.,* 800 F.2d 59, 63–64 (3d Cir.1986) (citing *Columbia Pictures Indus. v. Redd Horne,* 749 F.2d 154, 159 (3d Cir.1984)). Section 109(a) provides

> Notwithstanding the provisions of section 106(3), the owner of a particular copy or phonorecord lawfully made under this title, or any person authorized by such owner, is entitled, without the authority of the copyright owner, to sell or otherwise dispose of the possession of that copy or phonorecord.

17 U.S.C. § 109(a). "Section 109(a) is an extension of the principle that ownership of the material object is distinct from ownership of the copyright in this material." *Redd Horne,* 749 F.2d at 159 (citing 17 U.S.C. § 202). Under the first sale doctrine, the copyright owner cannot control the future transfer of a particular copy once its material ownership has been transferred. *See Redd Horne,* 749 F.2d at 159 (citations omitted).

Video Pipeline relies on *Quality King Distribs. v. L'anza Research Int'l,* 523 U.S. 135, 118 (1998), for the proposition that from the retailer's right to resell its lawfully purchased copyrighted products must come the retailer's right to advertise and promote sales of the products without the copyright holder's consent. The Supreme Court in *Quality King* involved a California manufacturer that sold its copyrighted hair care products to a Malta distributor, which subsequently sold them to an importer, which imported the products back into the United States to be sold at lower prices than the California manufacturer. The Supreme Court held that the importer was entitled to the first sale defense in the copyright infringement action, stating that "[t]he whole point of the first sale doctrine is that once the copyright owner places the copyrighted item in the stream of commerce by selling it, he has exhausted his exclusive statutory right to control its distribution." *Quality King,* 523 U.S. at 152.

Video Pipeline's reliance on *Quality King* is misplaced because it is not a retailer who has lawfully purchased copies of BVHE's product and therefore entitled to the protection afforded by the first sale doctrine. Rather, its clients, not Video Pipeline, are video retailers who may promote the sales or rentals of the products it has lawfully purchased from BVHE. Video Pipeline, in creating clip previews and providing an online service to its customer retailers, contends that the focus of this first sale analysis should more properly be placed on the actions of the retailers, arguing that the defenses afforded to its retailer customers should be transferred to it.

The Court agrees with BVHE that the actual nature of the relationship between Video Pipeline and its retailer customers is one of licensor and licensee, not one of agency. *See* Horovitz Aff. at Ex. 7. According to the agreement, the retailer customers are allowed access to previews provided by Video Pipeline either for "in-store use and/or internet point-of-sale promotional use." *See id.* Video Pipeline provides no support for the argument that one in a license agreement is entitled to the protection of the first sale doctrine defense that may be afforded to the other party.

* * *

Plaintiff's assertion that it should be entitled, as its retailer customers are, to the privilege of advertising video products, is addressed more appropriately within the confines of subsection (c) of § 109. Section 109(c), formerly subsection (b), provides:

> Notwithstanding the provisions of section 106(5), the owner of a particular copy lawfully made under this title, or any person authorized by such owner, is entitled, without the authority of the copyright owner, to display that copy publicly, either directly or by the projection of no more than one image at a time, to viewers present at the place where the copy is located.

17 U.S.C. § 109(c). Congress stated that this subsection "deals with the scope of the copyright owner's exclusive right to control the public display of a particular 'copy' of a work." H.R.Rep. No. 94–1476, 94th Cong., 2d Sess. 79 (1976). Congress further explained the boundaries of the right granted to owners of a particular copy under § 106(5):

[S]ection [109(c)] takes account of the potentialities of the new communications media, notably television, cable and optical transmission devices, and information storage and retrieval devices, for replacing printed copies with visual images. First of all, the public display of an image of a copyrighted work would not be exempted from copyright control if the copy from which the image was derived were outside the presence of the viewers. In other words, *the display of a visual image of a copyrighted work would be an infringement if the image were transmitted* by any method (by closed or open circuit television, for example, or *by a computer system*) from one place to members of the public located elsewhere.

Id. Although Congress was discussing the possibility of copyright infringement as it relates to a copy owner, its discussion of copyright infringement occurring as a result of computerized transmission is instructive here nonetheless. Under this provision, Congress intended for copyright infringement to occur when images of a copy of copyrighted work are displayed to members of the public located other than where the copy is located. By providing for this provision, Congress intended "to preserve the traditional privilege of the owner of a copy to display it directly, but to place reasonable restrictions on the ability to display it indirectly in such a way that the copyright owner's market for reproduction and distribution of copies would be affected." *Id.*

In this case, the transmittal of images of BVHE's copyrighted motion pictures to customers of retailer licensees of Video Pipeline, presents a markedly similar scenario envisioned by Congress, and therefore constitutes copyright infringement notwithstanding the retailer's right to display under § 106(5). Congress could have said that the transmission of copyrighted images to customers at a distant point of sale by electronic means is within the zone of use permitted by § 109(c), but it has not done so. Thus, Video Pipeline's argument that it is entitled to the same scope of protection as its customer retailers further fails here due to the probable unavailability of the first sale doctrine defense to retailers who have the right to advertise their copies of copyrighted work, but are displaying images of their copyrighted materials at a distance over the Internet. Accordingly, Video Pipeline is not entitled to the protection of the first sale doctrine as provided in § 109 of the Copyright Act. * * *

> * * *

NOTES & QUESTIONS

1. *"Copies" and the first-sale right.* 17 U.S.C. § 109(a) provides that "the owner of a particular copy * * * is entitled * * * to sell or otherwise dispose of the possession of that copy." A purchaser of a CD–ROM containing software does not thereby gain ownership of the copyright in the software, but only the right to use it in ways that do not conflict with the rights of the copyright owner. Does the purchaser gain ownership of the CD–ROM disk itself? If so, does the first-sale doctrine apply, allowing the purchaser to dispose of the CD–ROM as she chooses? *See* MELVILLE B. NIMMER & DAVID NIMMER, NIMMER ON COPYRIGHT § 8.12[B][1].

What if she purchases the software by downloading it from a website onto her computer's hard drive? Does the first-sale doctrine allow her to e-mail the software to somebody else, if she deletes it from her own computer's hard drive? Does it allow her to sell the computer without first deleting the software? Suppose she downloads the software directly to a floppy diskette. Does the first-sale doctrine allow her to give the diskette to somebody else?

Can a copyright owner use contract to extend his control over redistribution of material objects containing copyrighted works?

2. *Exceptions from the first-sale right for record and software rental.* In the early 1980s, record rental stores began to proliferate. These stores would rent you an LP record for a dollar or two, allowing you to keep it for a few days. As was clear to all, nearly everyone who patronized these establishments was making a copy of the record on audio cassette tape, and adding the tape to their collection. At the instance of music copyright holders, Congress enacted the Record Rental Amendment of 1984, Pub. L. No. 98–450, 98 Stat. 1727 (1984), which amended the Copyright Act's codification of the first-sale right, 17 U.S.C. § 109. The amendment limits the first-sale right, so that it no longer permits the rental, lease, or lending of phonorecords (that is, records, tapes, and other physical objects containing sound recordings) for commercial purposes. In 1990, Congress similarly limited the applicability of the first-sale right to computer programs, by enacting a parallel amendment of Section 109. *See* Computer Software Rental Amendments Act of 1990, Pub. L. No. 101–650, 104 Stat. 5089, 5134 (1990).

These two congressional actions exemplify a clash between an owner's right to dispose of his chattels as he sees fit, which is recognized in the common law's strong distaste for restraints on alienation, and a copyright holder's statutory right to control distribution of his works. The boundary between these two rights is fluid, and shifts with technological and societal developments. Can you think of any aspects of online technology, or the societal changes it has spawned, that call for a rethinking of where this boundary should be drawn?

3. *First-sale right and digital works.* Owners of copyrighted digital works, such as software, music files, and electronic books, increasingly seek to limit distribution of those works by incorporating access-control technology into the file constituting a work. For example, movies on DVD incorporate code that allows the DVD to be played on players designed for one region of the world, but not on players designed for other regions: a DVD that a friend in Europe gives to you may not be playable on the DVD player you have at your home in the United States. Electronic books and music files may contain code that allows them to be read or played only on the computer to which they are downloaded. You can transfer such a file to a friend, but it will not be usable on her computer. Does the use of such access-control technology effectively vitiate the first-sale right? Should

Congress vindicate the first-sale right by making such technology illegal, or by making use of it cause for forfeiting the copyright on a work to which it is applied? Consider how this would affect the willingness of copyright owners to make their works available in digital form. Should Congress at least regulate such technology by mandating that access-control technologies allow transfer of one copy to a second user if it is deleted from the first user's computer? Would an affirmation of the applicability of the first-sale right to digital works inevitably interfere with the central goals of the copyright laws, namely to encourage authors to create and disseminate original works? If consumers find access-control technology objectionable, is it likely to disappear from the marketplace?

Congress's actual response to the rise of access-control technology is discussed in Chapter 5, *infra.* Under 17 U.S.C. § 1201, added by the 1998 Digital Millennium Copyright Act, one who circumvents (or provides a product that may be used to circumvent) such technology is subject to civil liability and criminal penalties.

C.   COPYRIGHT MISUSE

In re Napster

191 F.Supp.2d 1087 (N.D.Cal.2002).

■ PATEL, DISTRICT JUDGE.

The recording industry plaintiffs move for summary judgment against defendant Napster, Inc. ("Napster") for willful contributory and vicarious copyright infringement. In response, Napster requests that pursuant to *Federal Rule of Civil Procedure 56(f)* the court stay any decision on the merits to allow for additional discovery. Napster's 56(f) motion asks the court to determine whether additional discovery is necessary to decide if some of largest players in the music recording industry actually own the rights to the musical works for which they allege copyright infringement by Napster. The court is also asked to permit discovery to determine whether plaintiffs have misused their copyrights by attempting to control the market for the digital distribution of music. Having considered the arguments presented, and for the reasons set forth below, the court rules as follows.

BACKGROUND

This action is one of several copyright infringement actions against Napster, an Internet service that facilitates the downloading of MP3 music files. *See In re Napster,* MDL 00–1369 MHP. Because this court and the Ninth Circuit have discussed the Napster service at length in prior orders, and because the parties are familiar with the Napster system, the court will limit this background section to information relevant to the current motions.

A. Procedural History

On December 6, 1999, A & M Records and seventeen other record companies filed a complaint for contributory and vicarious copyright infringement against Napster. These eighteen parties can be collectively grouped into five major recording companies: BMG, Sony, EMI, Universal, and Warner. *See A & M Records, Inc. v. Napster, Inc.,* 114 F.Supp.2d 896, 908 (N.D.Cal.2000). Plaintiffs' complaint alleges that Napster knew of and failed to prevent its users' unauthorized reproduction and distribution of plaintiffs' copyrighted sound recordings. Plaintiffs claim ownership to a diverse catalog of artists including many of the industry's top-grossing artists from the last five decades.

This court granted plaintiffs' request for a preliminary injunction in July 2000 and prohibited Napster from "engaging in or facilitating others in copying, downloading, uploading, transmitting, or distributing plaintiffs' copyrighted works." 114 F.Supp.2d at 927. Two days later, the Court of Appeals stayed the injunction. *See A & M Records, Inc. v. Napster, Inc.,* 2000 WL 1055915, *1 (9th Cir. July 28, 2000). In February 2001, the Ninth Circuit largely affirmed this court's findings of fact and grant of injunctive relief. *See A & M Records, Inc. v. Napster, Inc.,* 239 F.3d 1004 (9th Cir.2001). A modified preliminary injunction was entered on March 5, 2001. *See A & M Records, Inc. v. Napster, Inc.,* 2001 WL 227083 (N.D.Cal. March 5, 2001). The court continued, with the aid of a technical expert, to monitor Napster's compliance with the preliminary injunction through August 2001.

* * *

Plaintiffs filed their motion for summary judgment on liability and willfulness on July 27, 2001. On September 10, 2001, Napster filed its opposition to plaintiffs' motion for summary judgment and a corresponding Rule 56(f) motion asking to stay summary judgment to allow for further discovery. * * *

* * *

B. Plaintiffs' Entry into the Digital Distribution Market

* * * In mid–2001, plaintiffs announced the formation of two joint ventures, MusicNet and pressplay. The aim of these joint ventures is to provide platforms for the digital distribution of music. MusicNet is a joint venture between three of the five record company plaintiffs—EMI, BMG, and Warner. MusicNet is also owned in part by RealNetworks (and possibly another entity). Pressplay is a venture between the other two plaintiffs—Sony and Universal.

In June 2001, Napster signed a licensing agreement with MusicNet, allowing Napster access to all of the copyrighted works licensed to Music-Net. Prior to signing the MusicNet agreement, Napster was unable to obtain individual licenses from any of the recording company plaintiffs. The MusicNet agreement explicitly limits Napster's ability to obtain individual licenses from any of the five plaintiffs, including the non-MusicNet plaintiffs—Sony and Universal—until March 2002. The agreement also allows MusicNet to terminate the agreement within ninety days, even after March 2002, if Napster licenses content from any of the five recording companies other than through MusicNet. Additionally, the agreement mandates a separate pricing structure for *any* content that Napster licenses from anyone other than MusicNet. Napster has only provided the court with the MusicNet agreement and the court has no other information as to how MusicNet operates or exactly what content it will offer and to whom. Similarly, because Napster has not signed a licensing agreement with pressplay, the court has before it only information culled from the public record which reveals little about pressplay's intended operations. * * *

DISCUSSION

* * *

II. *Copyright Misuse*

Napster argues that the court should deny summary judgment or stay the matter to allow for further discovery because plaintiffs are engaged in copyright misuse. Copyright misuse as a defense to an infringement action finds its origins in the equitable defense of unclean hands and is similar to the patent law defense of the same name. *See Morton Salt Co. v. G.S. Suppiger,* 314 U.S. 488 (1942). This court and the Ninth Circuit dismissed Napster's misuse defense at the preliminary injunction stage, noting that copyright misuse is rarely a defense to injunctive relief and that there was not enough evidence at that stage to support a finding of misuse. *See A & M Records,* 239 F.3d at 1026–27; 114 F.Supp.2d at 923. Since those rulings, the factual and procedural landscape has changed significantly. The motion now before the court is for summary judgment, not preliminary injunctive relief. Additionally, the prior inapplicability of copyright misuse rested on the fact that none of the plaintiffs had granted licenses to Napster, let alone impermissibly restrictive ones. *See A & M Records,* 114 F.Supp.2d at 924. The evidence now shows that plaintiffs have licensed their catalogs of works for digital distribution in what could be an overreaching manner. The evidence also suggests that plaintiffs' entry into the digital distribution market may run afoul of antitrust laws.

A. *The Development of the Copyright Misuse Defense*

The legitimacy of copyright misuse as a valid defense to an infringement action was in question for some time. *See Lasercomb Am., Inc. v. Reynolds,* 911 F.2d 970, 976 (4th Cir.1990) (describing the history of the misuse doctrine). For years, courts shied away from applying the doctrine, either refusing to recognize the defense, or finding it inapplicable on the facts. *Id.* Recently, courts have displayed a greater willingness to find copyright misuse, employing two different, though interrelated approaches. The first approach requires a finding that plaintiff engaged in antitrust violations before the court will apply the doctrine of copyright misuse. *See, e.g., Saturday Evening Post v. Rumbleseat Press, Inc.,* 816 F.2d 1191, 1200 (7th Cir.1987). The second approach, adopted by the Ninth Circuit, focuses on public policy and has been applied to a greater range of conduct than the antitrust approach. *See Practice Mgmt. Info. Corp. v. American Med. Assoc.,* 121 F.3d 516 (9th Cir.1997). *See generally* Brett Frischmann & Dan Moylan, *The Evolving Common Law Doctrine of Copyright Misuse: A Unified Theory and Its Application to Software,* 15 Berkeley Tech.L.J. 865, 880–902 (Fall 2000) (comparing antitrust and public policy-based misuse). Under the "public policy" approach, copyright misuse exists when plaintiff expands the statutory copyright monopoly in order to gain control over areas outside the scope of the monopoly. *See Practice Mgmt.,* 121 F.3d at 520; *Lasercomb,* 911 F.2d at 977–79 (copyright misuse "forbids the use of the copyright to secure an exclusive right or limited monopoly not granted by the Copyright Office"). The test is whether plaintiff's use of his or her copyright violates the public policy embodied in the grant of a copyright, not whether the use is anti-competitive. *See Practice Mgmt.,* 121 F.3d at 521. However, as a practical matter, this test is often difficult to apply and inevitably requires courts to rely on antitrust principles or language to some degree. *See Lasercomb,* 911 F.2d at 977 (noting courts' "understandable" but misplaced reliance on antitrust principles).

The scope of the defense of copyright misuse has not been significantly tested in the Ninth Circuit. In fact, the court has been unable to find a single reported case that discusses beyond a mere citation the Ninth Circuit's adoption of the copyright misuse defense in *Practice Management. See, e.g., Sony Pictures Entm't, Inc. v. Fireworks Entm't Group, Inc.,* 156 F.Supp.2d 1148, 1156 (C.D.Cal.2001); *Pollstar v. Gigmania Ltd.,* 170 F.Supp.2d 974, 982 (E.D.Cal.2000). Nor did this court or the Ninth Circuit devote any discussion to *Practice Management* in previous rulings. *A & M Records,* 239 F.3d at 1026–7; 114 F.Supp.2d at 924. As a result, the doctrine of copyright misuse remains largely undeveloped, with little case law to aid this court in its inquiry.[11]

* * *

B. *Napster's Allegations of Misuse*

Napster alleges two bases for misuse. First, Napster contends that the licensing clauses in Napster's agreement with plaintiffs' joint venture, MusicNet, are unduly restrictive. In the alternative, Napster argues that even if that particular agreement is not unduly restrictive, plaintiffs' practices as they enter the market for the digital distribution of music are so anti-competitive as to give rise to a misuse defense.

1. *The MusicNet Agreement*

Napster contends that licensing requirements of plaintiffs' online venture, MusicNet, are unduly restrictive. MusicNet is a joint venture between

---

11. In comparison, there is a substantial body of case law on patent misuse. *See, e.g., Morton Salt Co. v. G.S. Suppiger,* 314 U.S. 488 (1942). Patent misuse bases its analysis on antitrust principles and consequently is doctrinally analogous to antitrust-based copyright misuse. It is less helpful when employing the "public policy" analysis adopted by the Ninth Circuit.

three of the five record company plaintiffs (EMI, BMG, and Warner) to distribute digital music. This joint venture anticipates obtaining licenses from the other two major labels (Sony and Universal) to distribute their catalogs of copyrighted music. While Napster was unable to secure licenses from any of the individual plaintiffs, Napster reached an agreement with MusicNet that allows Napster to distribute the music from the catalogs of the three participating MusicNet plaintiffs and any other label that licenses its catalog to MusicNet.

Section 19.1 of the MusicNet agreement prevents Napster from entering into any licensing agreement with any individual plaintiffs until March 1, 2002. The text of the agreement calls this space of time the "Initial Exclusivity Period." *Id.* The agreement also provides that even after March 2002 if Napster enters into any individual license with any of the major labels—i.e. the plaintiffs—including the MusicNet plaintiffs, MusicNet may terminate the agreement with ninety-day notice. Additionally, section 6.3(a) lays out a pricing structure under which Napster will be charged higher fees if it fails to use MusicNet as its exclusive licensor for content.[13]

It is unclear from the text of the agreement if the exclusivity provision operates to impermissibly extend plaintiffs' control beyond the scope of their copyright monopoly. In other misuse cases, the offending provision was exclusive and the "adverse effects of the licensing agreement [were] apparent." *Practice Mgmt.*, 121 F.3d at 521 (provision prevented defendant from using any competitor's coding system); *Lasercomb*, 911 F.2d at 978 (defendant prohibited from producing any die-making software); *Alcatel*, 166 F.3d at 793–4 (software licensing provision effectively gave plaintiff control over uncopyrighted microprocessor cards). In contrast, the MusicNet provision is non-exclusive. Napster may obtain licenses from any of the record label plaintiffs, but may only do it through its agreement with MusicNet. Despite this theoretical non-exclusivity, the provision effectively grants MusicNet control over which content Napster licenses. Napster's use of other music catalogs is predicated on MusicNet's securing an individual license to those catalogs. For example, under the MusicNet agreement, Napster no longer has the ability to obtain an individual license from Sony (a non-MusicNet plaintiff). Instead, Napster must rely on MusicNet to obtain a license to Sony's catalog. And, if MusicNet chooses not to obtain such a license, Napster is effectively prevented from using Sony's catalog. The result is an expansion of the powers of the three MusicNet plaintiffs' copyrights to cover the catalogs of the two non-MusicNet plaintiffs.

The MusicNet plaintiffs argue that this restriction is unimportant because they fully expect to obtain licenses from the other two major recording companies.[14] That the restriction only applies until MusicNet

---

13. There are also allegations by Napster that the pricing structure of the Music-Net agreement prevents Napster from obtaining licenses from parties other than the five major record companies.

14. Plaintiffs find themselves in a catch–22 because if MusicNet does not obtain these licenses, the licensing provision may be unduly restrictive, and if MusicNet does obtain licenses from the non-MusicNet plain-

contains licenses from Sony and Universal (non-MusicNet plaintiffs) or until March 2002 is irrelevant. *See Practice Mgmt.,* 121 F.3d 516, 521 ("The controlling fact is that HCFA is prohibited from using any other coding system by virtue of the binding commitment . . . to use the AMA's copyrighted material exclusively."). The critical issue is that the agreement binds Napster to obtain licenses from MusicNet and not its competitors. Napster was caught in a position where its only options were to sign the agreement to gain access to the catalogs of the major record companies and thereby incur these restrictions in all their murkiness or to refuse to sign the agreement and have virtually no access to most commercially available music.

Though the agreement is troubling on its face, too many questions remain unanswered for the court to effectively rule on the issue. It is unclear to what extent it is appropriate to impute the actions of MusicNet to plaintiffs as MusicNet is a joint venture and technically remains a separate entity from plaintiffs. However, plaintiffs cannot hide behind the shell of a joint venture to protect themselves from misuse claims. The court views with great suspicion plaintiffs' claims of ignorance as to MusicNet's activities. Surely the three parties to MusicNet discussed their joint venture before embarking on it. MusicNet did not suddenly appear full blown from the head of a fictitious entity. The evidence suggests that plaintiffs formed a joint venture to distribute digital music and simultaneously refused to enter into individual licenses with competitors, effectively requiring competitors to use MusicNet as their source for digital licensing. If this proves to be the case, the propriety of treating MusicNet as a separate entity is in question. *Cf. Copperweld Corp. v. Independence Tube Corp.,* 467 U.S. 752, 768–69 (1984).

A few of plaintiff's arguments can be disposed of summarily. First, plaintiffs argue that Napster, as a party to the MusicNet agreement, cannot now challenge an agreement that it negotiated and subsequently signed. *Practice Management* explicitly holds that it is irrelevant who includes an exclusivity provision in an agreement. 121 F.3d at 521 (even if the exclusivity provision was included at HCFA's urging, it still prohibited HCFA from using competing coding systems). That Napster is both the party alleging misuse and a party to the offending agreement does not affect the court's analysis. *See Lasercomb,* 121 F.3d at 979 ("[T]he defense of misuse is available even if the defendants have not been injured by the misuse"; "The fact that appellants were not parties to one of Lasercomb's standard license agreements is inapposite to their copyright misuse defense."); *Morton Salt,* 314 U.S. at 494 ("It is the adverse effect upon the public interest of a successful infringement suit in conjunction with the patentee's course of conduct which disqualifies him to maintain the suit, regardless of whether the particular defendant has suffered from the misuse of the patent.")[16]

tiffs, such cross-licensing implicates potential antitrust concerns.

16. Plaintiffs' argument would have merit if there was any evidence that Napster

Second, plaintiffs contend that because MusicNet is not yet in operation, there is no ongoing misuse. This argument fails. The issue is not whether MusicNet is yet in operation, but whether the exclusivity provision in the agreement is active. Because Napster is already bound by the agreement, the restriction on Napster's ability to negotiate for licenses with individual plaintiffs is *currently* restricted.

Third, plaintiffs contend that even if they are engaged in misuse, be it through restrictive licensing or antitrust violations, they should still be able to recover for infringement that occurred prior to the MusicNet agreement. Plaintiffs misunderstand the misuse doctrine. Misuse limits enforcement of rights, not remedies. *See Practice Mgmt.*, 121 F.3d at 520 n. 9 ("Copyright misuse does not invalidate a copyright, but precludes its enforcement during the period of misuse."). If plaintiffs are engaged in misuse, they cannot bring suit based on their rights until the misuse ends. *See Lasercomb*, 911 F.2d at 979 n. 22 ("Lasercomb is free to bring a suit for infringement once it has purged itself of the misuse."); *Morton Salt*, 314 U.S. at 492 ("Equity may rightly withhold its assistance . . . by declining to entertain a suit for infringement, and should do so at least until it is made to appear that the improper practice has been abandoned and that the consequences of the misuse . . . have been dissipated."). The doctrine does not prevent plaintiffs from ultimately recovering for acts of infringement that occur during the period of misuse. The issue focuses on when plaintiffs can bring or pursue an action for infringement, not for which acts of infringement they can recover.

2. *Antitrust Violations As Copyright Misuse*

Napster does not confine its argument to the particular provision of the MusicNet licensing agreement. Napster also argues that plaintiffs' entry into the digital distribution market is rife with actual anti-competitive effects and potential antitrust concerns.

Antitrust violations can give rise to copyright misuse if those violations offend the public policy behind the copyright grant. *See Lasercomb*, 911 F.2d at 977 ("[A]ntitrust law is the statutory embodiment of that public policy"). However, generalized antitrust violations will not suffice. Napster must establish a "nexus between . . . alleged anti-competitive actions and [plaintiffs'] power over copyrighted material." *Orth–O–Vision, Inc. v. Home Box Office*, 474 F.Supp. 672, 686 (S.D.N.Y.1979).

Napster's arguments are based primarily on the declaration of Roger Noll, a Stanford professor who specializes in antitrust economics and the recording industry. Based on Dr. Noll's review of the MusicNet agreement and facts in the public record, Napster alleges that there are a host of anti-

introduced and negotiated for the exclusivity provision. In that scenario, it would be unseemly to allow Napster to use the same provision as protection against infringement actions. Such a rule would create perverse incentives to artificially manufacture over-reaching clauses as liability shields under the misuse doctrine. However, the evidence thus far shows that the relevant provisions were inserted at MusicNet's urging and not as an end-run around copyright laws by Napster.

competitive behaviors by the plaintiffs that violate antitrust laws. Dr. Noll concludes that plaintiffs' joint ventures, MusicNet and pressplay, have anti-competitive features and facilitate collusive activity between plaintiffs. Dr. Noll further asserts that plaintiffs engage in vertical foreclosure of the digital distribution market through retail price squeezes, raising costs through licensing provisions, refusals to deal, and exclusive dealing. Dr. Noll also discusses myriad other behaviors that Napster alleges provide a sufficient nexus to the copyright monopoly to invoke the doctrine of copyright misuse.

* * *

Napster has raised serious questions with respect to possible copyright misuse, based on both the MusicNet agreement and plaintiffs' possible antitrust violations in their entry into digital music delivery. Nor does the court believe Napster's motion to be merely a fishing expedition to avoid summary judgment. The same conduct by plaintiffs that Napster alleges gives rise to copyright misuse is currently under investigation by the Department of Justice. For the time being, however, neither side has sufficiently developed the factual and legal bases for their arguments. The evidence presently before the court suggests that Napster needs further discovery in order to sufficiently oppose plaintiffs' motion for summary judgment. As such, the court grants Napster's Rule 56(f) motion with respect to its misuse defense. Once such discovery is completed, both sides will have an opportunity to rebrief the issue of misuse, incorporating any new discovery and focusing on legal issues that were not adequately briefed earlier.

* * *

NOTES & QUESTIONS

Intellectual property and competition policy. Like the first-sale doctrine, the doctrine of copyright misuse can be considered a device to mark the boundary between, on the one hand, the scope of the monopoly granted to an intellectual property owner as incentive for future creators, and, on the other hand, the scope of open competition necessary for a free market. What principles do you think courts and legislators should use in drawing these boundaries? Do the boundaries shift as technology changes?

D. The Audio Home Recording Act of 1992

A & M Records, Inc. v. Napster, Inc.

239 F.3d 1004 (9th Cir.2001).

■ Beezer, Circuit Judge:

[For the facts of the case and the court's finding of direct infringement by the users of the Napster service, see Part II(B), *supra.*]

VI

* * * Napster asserts that its users engage in actions protected by § 1008 of the Audio Home Recording Act of 1992, 17 U.S.C. § 1008. * * *

A. Audio Home Recording Act

The statute states in part:

> *No action may be brought under this title alleging infringement of copyright* based on the manufacture, importation, or distribution of a digital audio recording device, a digital audio recording medium, an analog recording device, or an analog recording medium, or *based on the noncommercial use by a consumer of such a device or medium* for making digital musical recordings or analog musical recordings.

17 U.S.C. § 1008 (emphases added). Napster contends that MP3 file exchange is the type of "noncommercial use" protected from infringement actions by the statute. Napster asserts it cannot be secondarily liable for users' nonactionable exchange of copyrighted musical recordings.

The district court rejected Napster's argument, stating that the Audio Home Recording Act is "irrelevant" to the action because: (1) plaintiffs did not bring claims under the Audio Home Recording Act; and (2) the Audio Home Recording Act does not cover the downloading of MP3 files. *Napster,* 114 F.Supp.2d at 916 n. 19.

We agree with the district court that the Audio Home Recording Act does not cover the downloading of MP3 files to computer hard drives. First, "[u]nder the plain meaning of the Act's definition of digital audio recording devices, computers (and their hard drives) are not digital audio recording devices because their 'primary purpose' is not to make digital audio copied recordings." *Recording Indus. Ass'n of Am. v. Diamond Multimedia Sys., Inc.,* 180 F.3d 1072, 1078 (9th Cir.1999). Second, notwithstanding Napster's claim that computers are "digital audio recording devices," computers do not make "digital music recordings" as defined by the Audio Home Recording Act. *Id.* at 1077 (citing S. Rep. 102–294) ("There are simply no grounds in either the plain language of the definition or in the legislative history for interpreting the term 'digital musical recording' to include songs fixed on computer hard drives."). * * *

* * *

NOTES & QUESTIONS

1. *The Audio Home Recording Act.* The Audio Home Recording Act of 1992 ("AHRA"), Pub. L. No. 102–563, 106 Stat. 4248 (1992), was enacted in response to the release into the consumer marketplace of digital audio tape ("DAT") recorders. A DAT recorder may be used by consumers to make copies of audio recordings in digital format. Like music recorded on a CD, music recorded on DAT can be copied repeatedly, through multiple generations, with no loss of fidelity to the original. Holders of copyrights in musical works and recordings feared that availability of DAT recorders would lead to widespread copying of recorded music, cutting into sales of tapes and CDs. Manufacturers of DAT recorders entered into negotiations involving record companies, music publishers, musicians, and other participants in the music industry, arriving at a settlement that Congress ratified by enacting the AHRA.

The central feature of the AHRA is a simple quid pro quo. First, the music industry receives a technological solution to the problem of unauthorized copying of music recordings. All DAT recorders and similar devices, which in the statute are called "digital audio recording devices" ("DARDs"), must be outfitted with a Serial Copy Management System. 17 U.S.C. § 1002(a). This technology allows an original recording to be copied any number of times, but prevents the copying of a copy. Second, the music industry receives a stream of royalty payments deriving from sales of DARDs and the media (e.g., digital audio tapes) upon which these devices record. Manufacturers and importers of these devices pay a royalty of two percent of the sales price, and manufacturers and importers of recording media pay three percent of the sales price, into a fund that is distributed to music copyright holders and to recording artists. 17 U.S.C. § 1003–06.

In return, the manufacturers of the recording devices are free to market them, without the threat of being sued as contributory infringers. This is accomplished by Section 1008 of the AHRA, addressed in the above excerpt from *A & M Records v. Napster*.

2. *MP3 player not a DARD*. In rejecting Napster's argument based on the AHRA, the court relies on its earlier decision in *Recording Industry Ass'n of America v. Diamond Multimedia Systems, Inc.*, 180 F.3d 1072 (9th Cir.1999). That case addressed the question whether the Diamond Rio, a portable MP3 player, is a "digital audio recording device" ("DARD") under the AHRA; if so, the Rio would have to incorporate a Serial Copyright Management System, and its manufacturer would have to pay royalties. The court held that the Rio is not a DARD. It reached this result through analysis of the AHRA's rather complex set of nested definitions. According to these definitions, a device is a DARD only if it is capable of reproducing a "digital music recording." A "digital music recording" is defined as a material object in which sounds are fixed, but (as the court held) excludes computer hard drives. Since the Rio is capable of recording MP3's only from a hard drive, it cannot reproduce a "digital music recording," and therefore is not a DARD.

As a consumer, should you be happy or unhappy with the decision in *RIAA v. Diamond Multimedia*?

3. *Insulation for burning?* If a computer user downloads an MP3 file from the Internet, and burns it directly onto a CD–R disk using her computer's CD–RW drive, is she insulated from infringement liability under the AHRA, 17 U.S.C. § 1008? Consult the definitions of "digital audio recording device" and "digital audio recording medium" in 17 U.S.C. § 1001.

IV. WEBCASTING, MUSIC DOWNLOADS AND STATUTORY LICENSES

In the preceding Part, we saw that several defenses may serve to limit the exclusive rights conferred on the owner of a copyright under 17 U.S.C. § 106. Another device that limits the scope of these exclusive rights is the statutory, or "compulsory," license. To promote a particular socially beneficial use of a copyrighted work by persons other than the owner of the copyright, Congress may grant a license to use such a work to anyone whose use satisfies the conditions set forth in the statute creating the license and who pays the prescribed royalty.

By creating a compulsory licensing scheme for particular socially beneficial uses of copyrighted works, Congress obviates the need for licensees to negotiate directly with copyright owners. Statutory licenses, like the privilege of fair use, thereby reduce transaction costs that might otherwise prevent such socially beneficial uses. As a tool for implementing public policy, a compulsory license has certain advantages over the fair use defense. First, a compulsory license allows Congress precisely to target the particular kinds of uses that it desires to promote. The statute granting the license can include detailed conditions that must be satisfied before a person may enjoy the benefit of this license. Second, by creating a compulsory license Congress can require the licensee to pay a royalty to the copyright owner, balancing the interests of the public and copyright owners.

Finally, a compulsory license provides the user of another's work with greater certainty that the use is noninfringing. While broad in scope, the doctrine of fair use is uncertain in application: the four factors a court must weigh when determining whether a particular defendant is entitled to this defense are very general and require a nuanced analysis of the alleged infringing activity. As a result, until the matter is fully litigated, a person cannot be certain whether use of another's work is noninfringing. Such uncertainty may chill socially beneficial uses of copyrighted works.

Compulsory licenses are a derogation from the sweeping "exclusive rights" that the Copyright Act grants to copyright owners, and apply only to a few specific categories of activity. Of particular relevance for present purposes are the two statutory licenses contained in Sections 114 and 115 of the Copyright Act, which apply to webcasting (the digital transmission of sound recordings over the Internet by means of streaming audio technologies) and digital music deliveries. *See* The Digital Performance Right in Sound Recording Act of 1995, Pub. L. No. 104–39, 109 Stat. 336 (1995), and Title IV of the Digital Millennium Copyright Act, Pub. L. No. 105–304, 112 Stat. 2860, 2887 (1998). These compulsory licenses are the focus of the next excerpt.

R. Anthony Reese, *Copyright and Internet Transmissions: Existing Law, Major Controversies, Possible Solutions*

55 U. Miami L. Rev. 237 (2001).

* * *

I. Copyright Law Relevant to Internet Music Transmissions

A. *Musical Works and Sound Recordings: Two Separate Copyrights*

Every musical recording involves two separate copyrightable works: a "musical work" and a "sound recording." A musical work is the sequence of notes, and often words, that a songwriter or composer creates. For example, when Cole Porter sat down at a piano and wrote the lyrics and music to the song "Ev'ry Time We Say Goodbye," he created a musical work protectible by copyright law. That work can be recorded in many ways, including in printed sheet music that a musician can use to play or sing the song. A sound recording, in contrast, is a fixation of sounds, including a fixation of a performance of someone playing and singing a musical work. For instance, when Ella Fitzgerald and her accompanists went into a studio in the 1950s and performed Cole Porter's song "Ev'ry Time We Say Goodbye," the recording of that performance resulted in a sound recording. When Annie Lennox recorded the same song in the 1990s, her recorded performance was another sound recording of Porter's musical work. Transmitting recorded musical performances over the Internet involves transmitting both the sound recording and the musical work embodied in the recording.[10] U.S. copyright law grants different rights and limitations to musical works and sound recordings, increasing the complexity of the copyright implications of such transmissions, particularly when the copyright rights in those works are owned or administered by different parties.

B. *The Copyright Owners' Relevant Rights: Reproduction and Public Performance*

1. *The Reproduction Right*

Copyright law grants copyright owners the right to control certain uses of their works, including the exclusive rights to reproduce and to publicly perform copyrighted works. These are the rights most relevant to Internet music transmissions. The right to reproduce a copyrighted work is the oldest right of the copyright owner and applies to both musical works and sound recordings. Copyright owners of musical works and sound recordings have the exclusive right to reproduce their works in "phonorecords," which are "material objects in which sounds ... are fixed ... and from which the

---

10. Transmitting live musical performances would generally involve only the copyright in the musical work, since a live, unfixed performance is not protected by copyright, which extends only to fixed works. Unauthorized transmission of a live performance, however, may violate 17 U.S.C. § 1101(a)(2) (1998).

sounds can be perceived, reproduced, or otherwise communicated, either directly or with the aid of a machine or device."[13] A phonorecord can be a vinyl LP, a cassette tape, a compact disc, or a hard drive or floppy diskette containing an MP3 file. These are all tangible objects in which sounds are fixed and from which, given the proper hardware (and, in some cases, software), those sounds can be made audible. The reproduction right generally encompasses making any phonorecord of a copyrighted work.

Any single phonorecord of music is a phonorecord of both the sound recording fixed in the phonorecord and any musical work performed in that sound recording. For example, a compact disc of Ella Fitzgerald's album The Cole Porter Songbook constitutes a phonorecord of Cole Porter's musical work "Ev'ry Time We Say Goodbye" and a phonorecord of Ella Fitzgerald's sound recording of that musical work. Someone who makes a tape of that compact disc therefore produces a new phonorecord, the tape, of both the musical work and the sound recording. The same is true of someone who "rips" an MP3 version of the song from a compact disc, or who downloads such a version from a Web site and stores the MP3 file on a hard drive or other storage medium.

2.   Limitations on the Reproduction Right in Musical Works: The Compulsory Mechanical License and Digital Phonorecord Deliveries

The "compulsory mechanical license" limits the copyright owner's exclusive right to make phonorecords of most musical works.[15] Once the owner allows someone to make and sell phonorecords of a musical work, anyone else can make his or her own phonorecords of that work. This requires compliance with certain procedural requirements and paying a fee established by the Copyright Office.[16] This license essentially allows the making of so-called "cover" recordings, where a performer records a song that another performer previously recorded. As long as the compulsory license requirements are complied with, one can go into a recording studio and record, for example, a performance of the song "Yesterday" as it was written by John Lennon and Paul McCartney and sell compact discs of the recording without the permission of the copyright owner of that musical work. In fact, most performers who make cover recordings do not actually get a compulsory license from the Copyright Office. Instead, they usually obtain a license from the Harry Fox Agency, which acts as licensing agent for the U.S. copyright owners (usually music publishing companies) of most musical works.

---

13. Id. § 101 ("phonorecords"). Musical work copyright owners also have the exclusive right to reproduce their works in copies, such as sheet music. See id. ("copies").

15. 17 U.S.C. § 115 (1998). The compulsory license extends to "nondramatic" musical works. Id.

16. The current rate is usually 7.55 cents for each phonorecord. For the full schedule of rates, see 37 C.F.R. §§ 255.2, 255.3 (1999). For an album containing several copyrighted musical works, the royalty would be payable for each phonorecord of each work.

The compulsory mechanical license grants reproduction and distribution rights only for musical works, not sound recordings. The license would not allow one to record and sell compact discs of the Beatles' original recording of "Yesterday" (instead of recording and selling compact discs of one's own performance of the song). Every compact disc made would be a phonorecord of both the Lennon and McCartney musical work "Yesterday" and of the Beatles' sound recording of "Yesterday." The compulsory license confers only a reproduction privilege in the musical work. In order to make the compact discs, one would need permission from the copyright owner of the Beatles' sound recording, who would be free to refuse permission or to charge any price for that permission.[19] The compulsory mechanical license therefore primarily assists recording artists and record companies who want to make and sell their own recordings of songs by other songwriters.

In 1995, Congress amended the compulsory mechanical license to allow reproducing and distributing musical works by means of "digital phonorecord delivery" (hereinafter "DPD"). A DPD is a digital transmission of a sound recording that results in a "specifically identifiable reproduction by or for any transmission recipient of a phonorecord."[20] For example, if one connects to a Web site such as MP3.com or Emusic.com and downloads an MP3 file of the song "Yesterday," the Web site digitally transmits a sound recording of a performance of "Yesterday." At the end of the transmission that MP3 file is stored on that individual's hard drive—a phonorecord. Thus, the Web site has made a digital phonorecord delivery. If the site has obtained a compulsory mechanical license for the composition "Yesterday" and pays the specified royalty rate, then its transmission will not infringe the composition's copyright. The royalty rate, currently identical to the rate for making and selling a physical compact disc or cassette, is set every two years by a two-step process that encourages voluntary, industry-wide negotiations to establish rates to be adopted by the Copyright Office. If negotiations fail, any interested party can petition the Copyright Office to hold an arbitration proceeding to set the fees. The compulsory license only confers the right to make DPDs of the musical work, not any particular sound recording. If a little-known band tries to drum up interest in its music by allowing people to download its cover version of "Yesterday" from its Web site, the band itself will likely own the copyright in the sound recording of its performance. Therefore, the band will have the right to digitally deliver phonorecords of the sound recording, in addition to the right to digitally deliver phonorecords of the Lennon and McCartney musical work given by the compulsory mechanical license. If a Web site allows users to download the Beatles' recording of "Yesterday," then the Web site will need the permission of the owner of the copyright in that sound recording.

---

19. Indeed, the compulsory mechanical license for the musical work is not available for making phonorecords of another party's sound recording unless the licensee has authorization for reproduction from the owner of the rights in the sound recording. 17 U.S.C. § 115(a)(1) (1998).

20. Id. § 115(d).

3.   *The Public Performance Right: Musical Works*

The second exclusive right relevant to Internet music transmissions is the right to publicly perform a copyrighted work. The Copyright Act defines "performing" a work very broadly. One performs Cole Porter's song, "Ev'ry Time We Say Goodbye," if one sings the lyrics to the song, plays the song on a piano, plays a compact disc of the song on a stereo, or plays an MP3 file of the song on a personal computer or a portable playback device. Although all of those activities "perform" the musical work, they infringe the copyright only if done "publicly." A performance can be public in two ways. First, one "publicly" performs a work by performing it in a public or semi-public place, such as by singing "Ev'ry Time We Say Goodbye" in a nightclub. Second, and more important for music on the Internet, transmitting a performance is a public performance if the transmission is "to the public, by means of any device or process, whether the members of the public capable of receiving the performance ... receive it in the same place or in separate places and at the same time or at different times."[23] A radio station that broadcasts a performance of "Ev'ry Time We Say Goodbye" publicly performs the musical work by transmitting a performance to the public. Similarly, a Web site that transmits the recording to users in streaming audio publicly performs the musical work by transmitting a performance to the public. This is true even if each listener is located alone in her own home and only one listener hears the song at any given time. Even if the Web site limits its transmissions to subscribing users who pay a monthly fee, its transmissions will be "to the public."

No general compulsory license exists for the public performance right in musical works; to publicly perform such a work requires the permission of the copyright owner. Because public performances of musical works are fleeting and occur in widely dispersed locations, enforcement of the public performance right has challenged copyright owners. In response, copyright owners created collective rights societies to administer and enforce the public performance right. The principal societies in the United States are the American Society of Composers, Authors and Publishers ("ASCAP"), Broadcast Music, Inc. ("BMI"), and SESAC, Inc. (formerly the Society of European State Authors and Composers). The societies are made up of copyright owners (usually songwriters and music publishers) who grant the society the nonexclusive right to license public performances of their musical works. The societies, in turn, grant blanket licenses to entities that engage in public performances, such as radio and television stations, nightclubs and concert halls, restaurants and retail establishments. In return for a license fee (generally calculated as a percentage of the licensee's revenue), the licensee obtains the right to perform publicly any work in the society's repertoire, and the ASCAP, BMI, and SESAC repertoires collectively include virtually all copyrighted American music.

---

23. *Id.* § 101 ("publicly"). The Copyright Act defines "transmit" quite broadly: "To 'transmit' a performance ... is to com- municate it by any device or process whereby ... sounds are received beyond the place from which they are sent." Id.

4. Sound Recordings: The Digital Transmission Performance Right

Congress granted the exclusive public performance right to copyright owners of musical works, but not to copyright owners of sound recordings.[26] As a result, a nightclub or radio station that plays a compact disc of Annie Lennox singing "Ev'ry Time We Say Goodbye" publicly performs both Cole Porter's musical work and Annie Lennox's sound recording but needs permission only from the copyright owner of Porter's music and lyrics and not from the copyright owner of Lennox's sound recording.

In 1995, Congress granted sound recording copyright owners a limited public performance right: the right to perform their sound recordings publicly "by means of a digital audio transmission."[27] A Web site that streams a recording of Annie Lennox singing "Ev'ry Time We Say Goodbye" to listeners over the Internet publicly performs the sound recording by means of a digital audio transmission. That activity would be covered by the digital transmission performance right. * * *

Congress also enacted significant limitations on the digital transmission performance right. The scope of the copyright owner's right varies with the type of digital transmission. There are four basic types. The first is a transmission made by an "interactive service" that either transmits a particular sound recording requested by the recipient or transmits a program specially created for the recipient. Several kinds of transmissions are interactive. The archetypal interactive service is the much-prophesied "celestial jukebox," an on-demand service that allows a recipient (who pays a monthly subscription fee or a per-use charge) to connect to a repository of sound recordings and select a particular recording that is immediately transmitted to the recipient's speakers. MusicBank.com has entered into agreements with all of the major record labels to provide, by subscription, on-demand streaming access to all of the recordings in the labels' catalogs. MusicBank will be offering an interactive service, because the subscriber will receive, on request, the transmission of a particular sound recording that she selected. Transmissions by an interactive service are subject to the sound recording copyright owner's digital transmission performance right, so the transmitter needs the permission of the copyright owner prior to making transmissions of the subject recording. The sound recording copyright owner is entitled to charge any price for such permission or to deny permission entirely.[30]

Noninteractive service transmissions basically fall into three categories. First, there are nonsubscription broadcast transmissions.[31] Such trans-

---

26. 17 U.S.C. § 106(4) (1995).

27. 17 U.S.C. § 106(6) (1995). Essentially, a digital audio transmission is a transmission in any non-analog format that embodies a sound recording. 17 U.S.C. § 114(j)(5) (1994 & Supp. IV 1998).

30. In fact, 17 U.S.C. §§ 114(d)(3) and 114(h) (1994 & Supp. IV 1998) impose some limits on the ability of sound recording copyright owners to grant exclusive licenses to interactive services and require, in certain circumstances, that owners who license the digital transmission right to affiliates make licenses available to similar services on no-less-favorable terms.

31. These are "transmission[s] made by a terrestrial broadcast station licensed as such" by the FCC. 17 U.S.C. § 114(j)(3).

missions are entirely exempt from a copyright owner's digital transmission performance right, so obtaining permission from the sound recording copyright owner is not necessary.[32] Permission for the public performance of any musical work would be required, though.[33] Many radio stations, in addition to broadcasting over the radio airwaves, now have Web sites where they simultaneously transmit identical programming in streaming audio format. For example, public radio station KUT in Austin, Texas, has a Web site (www.kut.org) that allows users to hear in real time the programming that KUT is broadcasting over the airwaves to central Texas. * * * In response to a petition by the Recording Industry Association of America ("RIAA"), the trade association for the major recording labels, the Copyright Office recently amended its regulations to provide that an Internet simulcast by a licensed AM or FM broadcaster is not within the "nonsubscription broadcast transmission" exemption from the digital transmission performance right.[35]

Second, certain noninteractive transmissions other than broadcast transmissions, although not exempt from the digital transmission performance right, are eligible for a compulsory license of the digital transmission performance right.[37] For example, a hypothetical Web site, WebJazz, that runs a jazz "Web radio station" and streams jazz music to those who visit the site, just as a radio station would broadcast jazz music over the airwaves, would be eligible for such a license.[38] The transmissions are not interactive because WebJazz's programmers, not the site's listeners, select which songs are played. A noninteractive transmitter like WebJazz must adhere to a long list of detailed conditions to qualify for the compulsory license.[39] Those conditions seek to limit the license to those transmissions thought least likely to substitute for the sale of records. Therefore, the conditions attempt to prevent listeners from getting advance notice of which songs are to be transmitted so that they could record them or listen to them "on demand." Some conditions concern the programming that is transmitted. For example, WebJazz cannot transmit, during any three-hour period, more than three different tracks from any one compact disc or more than four different tracks by the same recording artist.[41] Other conditions

---

32. Id. § 114(d)(1)(A). Certain other types of transmissions are also exempt. Id. §§ 114(d)(1)(B), (C).

33. Id. § 114(d)(4)(B)(i).

35. See Public Performance of Sound Recordings: Definition of a Service, 65 Fed. Reg. 77,292 (Dec. 11, 2000). The regulation makes clear that the compulsory license for Web transmissions of sound recordings, discussed in the next paragraph, is available to over-the-air broadcasters for their Internet simulcasts if they meet the statute's detailed conditions for the license.

37. 17 U.S.C. § 114(d)(2).

38. Both subscription and nonsubscription transmissions are eligible for the license, so the site might support itself either by limiting access to subscribers or by transmitting advertising to its listeners. See id. §§ 114(j)(9), (14). If the transmission is nonsubscription, it must, in order to qualify for the statutory license, be part of a service whose "primary purpose" is to provide audio or entertainment programming to the public and not to sell or promote particular products or services. Id. § 114(j)(6).

39. The conditions are set forth in id. §§ 114(d)(2)(A), (C).

41. 17 U.S.C. §§ 114(d)(2)(C)(i) and 114(j)(13). Other programming-related conditions include a ban on advance publication of program schedules or specific titles to be

govern the technology and interfaces used for the transmission.[42] If Web-Jazz meets all the conditions, then it can obtain a compulsory license to transmit any sound recording by complying with Copyright Office procedures and paying the license fee. As with the compulsory mechanical license for DPDs, the license fee is to be determined every two years by voluntary negotiations among the parties to establish an industry-wide consensus on rates that would then be adopted by the Copyright Office. Failing that, rates would be set by an arbitration proceeding in the Copyright Office.[43] Rates have not yet been set for the generally available compulsory license for eligible noninteractive transmissions.[7] The compulsory license, like the broadcast exemption, applies only to the digital transmission performance right in sound recordings and not to the public performance right in musical works. A transmitter that qualifies for the compulsory license will therefore still need to obtain musical work performance licenses, usually from ASCAP, BMI, and SESAC.

Third, noninteractive transmissions that are not broadcast transmissions and that do not meet the conditions for the compulsory license are fully subject to the digital transmission performance right. Persons making such transmissions must generally obtain the permission of the copyright owner. If WebJazz wanted to program "all Ella Fitzgerald, all the time," it would not be able to comply with the limit of four tracks by one artist in three hours. Thus, it would not qualify for the compulsory license. WebJazz would therefore need permission for its digital transmission of each sound recording from the copyright owners. * * *

II. Application of Copyright Law to Streaming and Download Transmissions

A. Streaming Transmissions

The provisions of U.S. copyright law outlined in Part I govern the two major types of music transmissions available over the Internet today:

---

played, § 114(d)(2)(C)(ii), minimum time limits for the program of which a transmission of a sound recording is a part, § 114(d)(2)(C)(iii), a requirement to transmit recordings from lawfully made phonorecords and not from bootleg recordings, § 114(d)(2)(C)(vii), and a bar on transmitting visual images along with the audio transmission in a way likely to confuse recipients as to the endorsement or affiliation of the recording artist or copyright owner, § 114(d)(2)(C)(iv).

42. For example, the transmitter must identify, in text displayed to the recipient during the performance, the title of the recording, the title of the record from which it comes, and the name of the recording artist. 17 U.S.C. § 114(d)(2)(C)(ix). Other conditions of this type include not causing the receiving equipment to change channel,

§ 114(d)(2)(A)(ii), transmitting any identifying information encoded in the sound recording by the copyright owner, § 114(d)(2)(A)(iii), accommodating and not interfering with technical measures used by copyright owners to identify or protect their works, § 114(d)(2)(C)(viii), not taking any affirmative steps to cause the making of a phonorecord by the recipient of the transmission and setting the transmission equipment to limit such recording if possible, § 114(d)(2)(C)(vi), and cooperating to prevent the scanning of transmissions in order to select a particular recording to be transmitted, § 114(d)(2)(C)(v).

43. 17 U.S.C. § 114(f)(2).

7. [The Librarian of Congress established these rates in June 2002. *See* Note 5, following this excerpt.—Eds.]

streaming and downloading musical files. A digital music file can be streamed to a user. Over the World Wide Web, for example, a user might connect to the Web site of the Red Hot Organization and find a streaming audio file of Annie Lennox's recording of "Ev'ry Time We Say Goodbye" from the album Red, Hot + Blue. The user might then request that the Web site transmit that file. As the site transmits the information in the file, the user's computer makes the recording audible through the computer's speakers. During the transmission, the user's computer temporarily stores or "buffers" segments of the recording before making them audible, in order to allow (usually) uninterrupted playback of the recording even if network congestion slows the transmission. As the recording is played, however, the part of the file that is played is removed from the buffer and replaced with subsequent portions of the recording. At the end of the transmission, the user has heard the entire recording. Generally, no copy of the recording remains stored on the computer. If the user wishes to hear the streamed recording again, she must again connect to the Red Hot Web site and request that it transmit the file again.

Such streaming transmissions may fit a wide variety of Internet music business models. A user might hear streaming transmissions from the Web site of a particular musician or record label that wishes to promote particular recordings, from a Web "radio station" that transmits a variety of music in the same way that over-the-air radio stations do, or from a "music locker" service that stores particular songs selected (and possibly purchased) by the user to provide the user access to those songs from any Internet-connected computer.

A streaming transmission over the Internet clearly constitutes a digital transmission performance of the sound recording transmitted and of any musical work embodied in that sound recording. Such a transmission will infringe the public performance rights unless the person making it has permission or is otherwise excused. For example, WebJazz may want to transmit Annie Lennox's recording of "Ev'ry Time We Say Goodbye" in streaming audio as part of its Webcast. With respect to Annie Lennox's sound recording, WebJazz will either be exempt from the digital transmission right entirely (if it makes a nonsubscription broadcast transmission), be entitled to transmit the stream under the a compulsory license (if the transmission is noninteractive and meets all the license conditions), or be required to obtain permission from the copyright owner (if the stream is available to listeners on demand). The transmitter will need to obtain permission to perform Cole Porter's musical work publicly. ASCAP, BMI, and SESAC each provide blanket licenses for such transmissions of the works in their respective repertoires.[46]

The major copyright question with respect to streaming audio transmissions is whether every such transmission constitutes not only a public performance of the works transmitted but also a reproduction of those

---

46. See www.ascap.com/weblicense/ webintro.html (last visited Feb. 10, 2001), www.bmi.com/iama/webcaster/automated/in- dex.asp (last visited Feb. 10, 2001), www.se- sac.com/licensing/internet_newmedia. htm (last visited Feb. 10, 2001).

works. The reproduction and performance rights are independent of one another. The statutory language and legislative history contemplate that a single transmission could involve the exercise of both reproduction and public performance rights. Such a transmission occurs where the recipient can both hear the song received and store a copy of it.

The more significant aspect of the question is whether every streaming audio transmission reproduces both the musical work and the sound recording transmitted, even if the recipient does not retain any copy of the music at the end of the transmission, as is the case with an ordinary streaming transmission. This possibility arises largely because of the temporary storage in random-access memory (hereinafter "RAM") that occurs in essentially every computer. As a streaming audio transmission is received, the digits that represent the sounds to be played back by the recipient's streaming audio software will temporarily be stored in the RAM of the recipient's computer, until they are processed by the software, played back, and replaced in RAM by subsequently transmitted digits.[49] In cases not involving streaming transmissions, at least two federal appellate courts have held that storing a copyrightable work in RAM constitutes reproduction of the work in violation of the copyright owner's exclusive reproduction right.[50] Many have criticized these decisions as inconsistent with the statutory language and the legislative history of the Copyright Act. Some lower courts and government officials have, however, adopted this view, suggesting that courts may rule that temporary RAM storage that occurs automatically in the course of every streaming audio transmission constitutes a reproduction of the copyrighted works transmitted.

The legislative history of the compulsory DPD license indicates that at least some RAM storage as part of a streaming transmission will constitute the reproduction of a phonorecord. For purposes of license rates, the statute distinguishes between ordinary DPDs and "incidental" DPDs.[55] The legislative history provides the following example to explain the distinction:

> [I]f a transmission system was designed to allow transmission recipients to hear sound recordings substantially at the time of transmission, but the sound recording was transmitted in a high-speed burst of data and stored in a computer memory for prompt playback (such storage being technically the making of a phonorecord), and the transmission recipient could not retain the phonorecord for playback on subsequent occasions (or for any other pur-

---

49. Reproduction may also occur because the streaming software may temporarily store (or cache) the received data on the hard drive of the recipient's computer, where it may remain until it is written over by other data. There is little doubt that such storage technically constitutes the reproduction of the stored work in a phonorecord.

50. *Stenograph L.L.C. v. Bossard Associates*, 144 F.3d 96 (D.C.Cir.1998); *MAI Systems Corp. v. Peak Computer, Inc.*, 991 F.2d 511 (9th Cir.1993).

55. 17 U.S.C. § 115(c)(3)(C), (D).

pose), delivering the phonorecord to the transmission recipient would be incidental to the transmission.[56]

Thus, at least streaming transmissions where the entire transmitted sound recording is stored at one time in the RAM of the recipient's computer for playback would appear to involve the making of a DPD. It is not clear, however, whether the temporary RAM storage of small portions of a sound recording involved in the buffering typically done by streaming software today would constitute a DPD. * * *

B. Download Transmissions

The other major type of Internet music transmission, aside from streaming audio, is the downloading of a file of recorded music. Over the World Wide Web, for example, a user might connect to the Red Hot Organization's Web site and find an MP3 file of Annie Lennox's recording of "Ev'ry Time We Say Goodbye." The user can direct the Web site to transmit the music file to her, and the user's computer will store the received file, typically on the computer's hard drive. At the end of the transmission, the user has her own copy of the file on her computer hard drive, and she can listen to the recording embodied in that file whenever she wants, without any need to be connected to the Web site that originally transmitted it. With appropriate equipment, the user can copy the file onto a compact disc or onto the storage device of a portable, Walkman-like player that will allow her to listen to the recording away from her computer.

Download transmissions may be provided by various types of Internet entities. A user might download a music file from the Web site of a recording artist or record label which provides downloads for promotional purposes. The user might also download a file from a Web site specializing in downloadable music by many artists, such as Emusic.com (which has over 100,000 tracks available for download for ninety-nine cents each), MP3.com (where music files from thousands of artists can be downloaded, many for free), or DownloadsDirect (which features both free and pay downloadable files). Or, instead of downloading from a Web site, the user might download a music file directly from the hard drive of another user's computer using file-sharing software such as Napster or Gnutella.

A user who downloads an MP3 file of Annie Lennox's recording of "Ev'ry Time We Say Goodbye" reproduces in a phonorecord—the new file on the user's hard drive—both Lennox's sound recording and Cole Porter's musical work. To make that phonorecord without infringing those copyrights will generally require permission from both copyright owners. Permission to reproduce Annie Lennox's sound recording can only be obtained from the owner of the copyright in that sound recording—usually the record label that originally issued the recording. Once the sound recording copyright owner has authorized the reproduction, permission to make a phonorecord of Cole Porter's musical work by means of a digital phonorec-

---

56. S. Rep. No. 104–128 at 39.

ord delivery can be obtained in the form of the compulsory mechanical license or a mechanical license from the Harry Fox Agency. Some question may exist as to who exactly is committing the act of reproduction.[72] Under any view, however, the party transmitting the file probably faces liability for copyright infringement, either direct or contributory, if the transmission is not authorized.[73] As a result, no matter who is seen, as a technical matter, to be making the new phonorecord on the download recipient's hard drive, the entity transmitting the file likely will need reproduction licenses.

The major copyright question regarding download transmissions is the flip side of the question about streaming transmissions as reproductions: do download transmissions constitute not only a reproduction of the transmitted music but also a public performance by digital transmission, such that the transmitter will need permission from the owners of the public performance rights as well? Again, the statutory language contemplates that a transmission resulting in a DPD—a download—might also be a public performance of the works delivered[74] and makes clear that the compulsory DPD license does not grant the licensee any public performance rights.[75] The statutory framework, however, does not answer the question of whether any particular download transmission is a public performance.

It is easy to conceive of a download transmission that clearly would be a public performance of the works transmitted. For example, a Web site could transmit a music file to a user so that the user's computer, as it receives the transmitted information, both stores that information on the user's hard drive and makes the transmitted recording audible through the computer's speakers. Such a transmission would be both a reproduction of the sound recording and the musical work embodied in the file (by means of a digital phonorecord delivery) and a public performance of those works (by means of a digital audio transmission to the public). Thus, the transmitter would need permission to reproduce and to publicly perform both works.

Currently, however, typical download transmissions do not allow the end user to hear the song as the digital musical file is being received. Instead, the recipient's computer stores the received file, and the recipient

---

72. One possibility would be to view the downloading end user as the party who is making the new phonorecord. The user, after all, has instructed her computer to connect to the computer where the digital musical file is stored, to request that the file be transmitted to her computer, and to store the transmitted file as it is received. Another possibility would be to view the party that transmits the file to the end user as making the reproduction: the transmission of the data from the transmitter's computer to the receiving computer's hard drive results in the new copy of the file. A third possibility would be to view both the transmitter and the downloading user as acting jointly to reproduce the file; therefore, they would be jointly liable for any infringement involved.

73. If the transmitter is considered to be the party making the new phonorecord, then the transmitter will be directly liable. If the end user is considered to be the party making the reproduction, then the transmitter will likely face liability for contributory infringement. * * *

74. 17 U.S.C. § 115(d) (Supp. IV 1998).

75. *Id.* § 115(c)(3)(K)(i) (Supp. IV 1998).

can then, at her leisure, choose to play back the file in order to hear the recording.[76] Although widely perceived as extremely generous to copyright owners in its interpretation of copyright law in the Internet context, the Clinton Administration's White Paper addressing intellectual property rights and computer networks nevertheless took the position that such a transmission, "without the capability of simultaneous 'rendering' of the work, 'rather clearly' did not constitute a public performance." ASCAP and BMI have asserted, however, that every transmission of a musical work to the public, whether or not the transmission allows the user to hear the work in the course of the transmission, is a public performance for which permission of the copyright owner is needed—generally in the form of an ASCAP or BMI blanket license.

Neither the language of the Copyright Act, nor its legislative history, appears to resolve this question conclusively, and policy arguments exist on both sides of the matter. But answering the question of whether a download transmission constitutes a public performance may not, at the moment, be of particular urgency because the answer may make little practical difference in the business operations of most transmitters.

For performances of musical works, the practical impact turns on whether Web sites that provide download transmissions also provide streaming transmissions. For example, many download sites offer users the chance to listen to a song—or an excerpt of a song—before deciding whether to download it. Some of these sites might not hold performance licenses in the belief that the fair use doctrine excuses their public performances. Their reliance on the fair use doctrine, though, is probably misplaced because the streaming of any large-scale selection—even of thirty-second excerpts from songs—would not likely qualify as fair use. To comply with copyright law, sites that offer such streaming transmissions are likely to need a performance license. If most download sites also engage in some streaming transmissions, those sites—regardless of any download transmissions—will be publicly performing musical works and will already need licenses from the relevant performing rights societies.

Performance licenses are readily available to operators of these sites because the repertoires of ASCAP, BMI, and SESAC cover the vast majority of copyrighted music, these societies grant blanket licenses that allow the performance of any work in their respective repertoire for the same fee, and at least ASCAP and BMI must, under the antitrust consent decrees that govern their operations, grant licenses to any user willing to pay a reasonable license fee.[80] Thus, applying the performance right to downloads

---

76. When the user plays back the recording, she will be performing the sound recording and the musical work it embodies, but unless she plays the song in a public or semi-public place, her performance will not infringe because it is a not a public performance.

80. *See United States v. Broad. Music, Inc.,* 1996–1 Trade Cas. (CCH) ¶ 71,378, at 76,891 (S.D.N.Y. Nov. 18, 1994); *United States v. The Am. Soc'y of Composers, Authors & Publishers,* 1950–51 Trade Cas. (CCH) P62,595, at 63, 754 (S.D.N.Y. Mar. 14, 1950). The amount of the reasonable license

does not raise issues regarding the availability of a performance license but rather raises issues regarding the cost of such a license.

Because ASCAP, BMI, and SESAC grant blanket performance licenses that cover both streaming and download transmissions of all compositions in their repertories, a Web site that already needs performance licenses for its streaming transmissions will not incur any significant additional transaction costs in securing performance licenses for its download transmissions. The cost of the licenses also should not depend on whether a license is needed only for streaming transmissions or for both streaming and download transmissions. Whatever total price the licensor and the licensee are willing to agree to for the performance license can be spread over either the licensee's total transmissions (streams and downloads) or over a subset of those transmissions (streams only). For example, if all transmissions were to be considered performances and if the parties agreed on a rate of one cent per transmission, then a site that makes a thousand transmissions (both streaming and download) would incur a license fee of ten dollars. If, however, only streaming transmissions are required to be licensed, and if only one half of the licensee's transmissions are streams, then a price of two cents per transmission yields the same total price of ten dollars for one thousand total transmissions.

Thus, with respect to musical works, whether considering downloads to be performances has any practical impact on transmitters depends on whether sites that provide downloads also engage in streaming transmissions and therefore already require performance licenses. If they do engage in streaming, the impact would seem to be minimal; if they do not, then the impact is potentially greater. Currently, the larger download sites, such as EMusic.com, MP3.com, DownloadsDirect.com, Launch.com, CDNow.com, and Virgin Jamcast, do engage in both streaming and download transmissions. At the other end of the spectrum, individual Web users who use software such as Napster or Gnutella to make musical files on their hard drives available to other people may be engaged only in downloading and not streaming, so that they would not need a performance license unless their download transmissions constitute public performances. But those users' download transmissions are not licensed even under the reproduction right, which clearly applies to download transmissions, so at least at the moment considering such download transmissions to be performances seems unlikely to have any practical impact on those activities. In between the major music sites and the individual Napster user are a wide range of possible music Web sites, some of which may offer only download and not streaming transmissions. Sites that do not stream any music would not need performance licenses unless downloads are considered public performances; thus, requiring a performance license for download transmissions could impose additional costs on these sites that they otherwise would not face.[85]

fee is subject to determination by the District Court, Southern District of New York. Id.

85. Requiring performance licenses would not have a significant impact on all

Of course, the public performance question affects sound recording copyrights as well. If a download transmission is a public performance of the musical work, then it is also a digital transmission performance of the sound recording. Here again, under current conditions, characterizing a download to be a performance seems unlikely to have a significant economic impact on download Web sites. Because the download results in a reproduction of the sound recording that is transmitted, the transmitter will already need a reproduction license for the transmission. The compulsory DPD license covers only musical works, so the transmitter will have to obtain permission to transmit the sound recording directly from the copyright owner of that work. Where reproduction and digital transmission performance rights in sound recordings are owned by the same entity, as is currently the case for most sound recordings, the copyright owner—with whom the download transmitter will already have to negotiate—will be able to grant the transmitter permission to make the download under both the reproduction and performance rights. No additional transaction costs will be incurred in locating the relevant copyright owner and negotiating permission to perform. Moreover, permission is likely to be equally available (or equally unavailable) whether a download is just a reproduction or is both a reproduction and a performance because no compulsory reproduction license is available for sound recordings. And in the absence of divided ownership and any compulsory license, the price the download transmitter would pay for a reproduction and performance license for a download transmission should not be any greater than the price for a reproduction license alone for the same transmission. If the parties can agree on a price for the license, it will make little difference to either party whether that entire price is designated as the cost for a reproduction license or whether a portion is designated as the cost for a reproduction license and the remainder is designated as the cost for a performance license. It appears that ownership of the reproduction and digital transmission performance rights is not currently divided. Therefore, a transmitter generally will be able to obtain both rights from a single party.

In summary, unless a significant number of download-only sites would need performance licenses which they could not afford, the question of

music Web sites, however. For example, if those who run such sites make available their own recordings of their own compositions, then no third-party licenses will be required whatsoever. The same holds true if a third-party site makes such works available at the request of a performer because the performer will herself be able to license the reproduction and performance rights in both the sound recording and the musical work. Transmitting recordings of other people's musical works, on the other hand, will require a mechanical DPD license at a typical cost of 7.55 cents per work per transmission, and if the site transmits recordings of those works by performers other than the site owner, then a reproduction license for the sound recording (at whatever price the copyright owner charges) will also be necessary. A Web site that can afford to pay for the necessary reproduction licenses may be able to pay the cost of a performance license. Requiring a performance license for download transmissions therefore may not necessarily make download transmissions by such sites so costly that they will not be made, but instead may raise the cost of the transmission to the end user, change the allocation of revenue from the transmission between the transmitter and the copyright owner, or both.

whether a download transmission is a public performance perhaps can await resolution until it becomes clear that answering the question will make a difference. * * *

* * *

NOTES & QUESTIONS

1. *Scope of the Section 114 statutory license.* Section 114 creates a compulsory license allowing "[t]he performance of a sound recording publicly" through certain types of digital transmissions. 17 U.S.C. § 114(d)(2). This provision also places limitations on the scope of this license:

Nothing in this section annuls or limits in any way—

(i) the exclusive right to publicly perform a musical work, including by means of a digital audio transmission, under section 106(4);

(ii) the exclusive rights in a sound recording or the musical work embodied therein under sections 106(1), 106(2) and 106(3); * * *

17 U.S.C. § 114(d)(4)(B)(i) and (ii).

Review the exclusive rights of a copyright owner set forth in 17 U.S.C. § 106(1)–(6), and bear in mind that a sound recording (the Annie Lennox recording, in Professor Reese's example) and a musical work (the Cole Porter composition) are two different copyrighted works, which receive different types of protection under Section 106. To which type of work does the Section 114 compulsory license apply? To which of the copyright holder's exclusive rights does it apply? To which rights does it not apply?

2. *Streaming as distribution and adaptation.* When a webcaster streams a sound recording over the Internet, it is clearly engaging in "public performance" of both the sound recording and the underlying musical work, thereby implicating the copyright owners' exclusive rights under 17 U.S.C. § 106(4) and (6). Professor Reese addresses the question whether a streaming transmission constitutes a "reproduction" of the two works, which would implicate the copyright owners' rights under Section 106(1), and concludes that the answer is in some circumstances unclear. Does a streaming transmission also constitute a "distribution" of the works, implicating the copyright owners' rights under Section 106(3)? Does the conversion of the sound recording into a format compatible with the recipient's software (for example, RealPlayer) constitute the preparation of a "derivative work" based on the underlying musical composition and sound recording, implicating the copyright owners' rights under Section 106(2)?

3. *Other licenses needed.* In view of your answers to the questions in the above two Notes, consider which exclusive rights, of which copyright owners, are implicated in the streaming of a sound recording over the Internet. Beyond the statutory license extended by Section 114(d)(2), what other licenses must the webcaster obtain for the transmission not to be infringing?

4. *Interactive services.* The use of the Internet to deliver music makes it technologically possible for webcasters to offer personalized programming for individual listeners. Each listener can create a channel that provides music and other programming customized in real-time to that listener's present mood and unique tastes. As a result, personalized webcasts and interactive Internet music delivery generally have caused traditional broadcasters and record companies much anxiety, fearing diversion of their customers. Reacting to the concerns of these industries, Congress limited the exemption under Section 114(d)(1) and the statutory license under Section 114(d)(2) to noninteractive services. Thus, interactive services are fully subject to the digital performance right in sound recordings. Section 114(j)(7) defines an interactive service as

> one that enables a member of the public to receive a transmission of a program specially created for the recipient, or on request, a transmission of a particular sound recording, whether or not as part of a program, which is selected by or on behalf of the recipient. The ability of individuals to request that particular sound recordings be performed for reception by the public at large, or in the case of a subscription service, by all subscribers of the service, does not make a service interactive, if the programming on each channel of the service does not substantially consist of sound recordings that are performed within 1 hour of the request or at a time designated by either the transmitting entity or the individual making such request. If an entity offers both interactive and noninteractive services (either concurrently or at different times), the noninteractive component shall not be treated as part of an interactive service.

17 U.S.C. § 114(j)(7). A music service that falls within the scope of this definition must negotiate licenses for the music it offers, company-by-company and recording-by-recording. To be successful and at the same time avoid these additional costs, Internet music services need to qualify for the statutory license under Section 114(d)(2) while offering value-added services and features that distinguish their music service from traditional broadcasters.

Consider one Internet music service that appears to be pushing the limits of the Section 114(d)(2) statutory license. The service allows a listener to create a "station" or "channel" with a playlist of up to twenty-five of the listener's favorite recording artists. The station then plays music by these artists and others who have a similar musical style. Listeners can use a radio timeline to select music from particular time periods, a tempo tuner to select "faster" or "slower" music depending on the listener's mood, as well as a feature to skip to the next song. In your opinion, should such a service be considered a noninteractive service that falls within the scope of the Section 114(d)(2) statutory license, or is it an interactive service?

5. *Licensing terms and royalty rates.* Under 17 U.S.C. § 114(f), the Librarian of Congress is charged with establishing the rates and terms for statutory licenses for certain nonexempt transmissions of digital audio music. In June 2002, the Librarian established royalty rates under which a webcaster must pay $0.0007 each time it streams a song to a recipient (i.e., seven cents each time it streams 100 songs). *See* Determination of Reasonable Rates and Terms for the Digital Performance of Sound Recordings and Ephemeral Recordings, 67 Fed. Reg. 45,239 (Jul. 8, 2002). Webcasters say they cannot afford to pay these rates, and will be driven out of business. The recording industry contends that the rates have been set so low they are effectively being forced to subsidize online broadcasters. *See* Jon Healey, *Net Radio, Labels At Odds Over Royalties*, L.A. Times, June 24, 2002, at Part 3, p.1. Should the royalty rate be set at a level that makes webcasting viable under current business models?

Should the terms and conditions set by the Librarian of Congress be reviewable by a court and, if so, what standard of review should the reviewing court employ? *See Bonneville International Corp. v. Peters,* 153 F.Supp.2d 763 (E.D.Pa.2001); *Recording Industry Association of America v. Librarian of Congress,* 176 F.3d 528 (D.C.Cir.1999).

V. A Safe Harbor for Online Service Providers

As we have seen, the Copyright Act confers several exclusive rights on copyright owners with the aim of encouraging authors to create original works, but limits those rights to ensure that the works created are reasonably available to the public. We have so far discussed several types of limitations: fair use, the first-sale doctrine, copyright misuse, the right to make copies of musical sound recordings for noncommercial purposes, and compulsory licenses. Another limitation on the exclusive rights of copyright owners is found in 17 U.S.C. § 512, which was added by Title II of the Digital Millennium Copyright Act, Pub. L. No. 105–304, 112 Stat. 2860, 2877 (1998).

Section 512 limits online service providers' liability for direct, contributory, and vicarious copyright infringement.

As to direct infringement, liability is ruled out for passive, automatic acts engaged in through a technological process initiated by another. Thus, the bill essentially codifies the result in the leading and most thoughtful judicial decision to date: *Religious Technology Center v. Netcom On-Line Communication Services, Inc.,* 907 F.Supp. 1361 (N.D.Cal.1995). In doing so, it overrules those aspects of *Playboy Enterprises, Inc. v. Frena,* 839 F.Supp. 1552 (M.D.Fla.1993), insofar as that case suggests that such acts by service providers could constitute direct infringement, and provides certainty that *Netcom* and its progeny, so far only a few district court cases, will be the law of the land.

As to secondary liability, the bill changes existing law in two primary respects: (1) no monetary relief can be assessed for the passive, automatic acts identified in *Religious Technology Center v.*

Netcom On-Line Communication Services, Inc.; and (2) the current criteria for finding contributory infringement or vicarious liability are made clearer and somewhat more difficult to satisfy.

H.R. REP. No. 105–551, pt. 1, at 11 (1998) (discussing an earlier version of the provision ultimately adopted). If a service provider is within the Section 512 safe harbor, it is not subject to monetary liability based on copyright infringement by users of its system, and is subject only to limited injunctive remedies.

U.S. COPYRIGHT OFFICE, SUMMARY OF THE DIGITAL MILLENNIUM COPYRIGHT ACT OF 1998

1998.
www.loc.gov/copyright/legislation/dmca.pdf.

TITLE II: ONLINE COPYRIGHT INFRINGEMENT LIABILITY LIMITATION

Title II of the DMCA adds a new section 512 to the Copyright Act to create four new limitations on liability for copyright infringement by online service providers. The limitations are based on the following four categories of conduct by a service provider:

1. Transitory communications;

2. System caching;

3. Storage of information on systems or networks at direction of users; and

4. Information location tools.

New section 512 also includes special rules concerning the application of these limitations to nonprofit educational institutions. Each limitation entails a complete bar on monetary damages, and restricts the availability of injunctive relief in various respects. (§ 512(j)). Each limitation relates to a separate and distinct function, and a determination of whether a service provider qualifies for one of the limitations does not bear upon a determination of whether the provider qualifies for any of the other three. (§ 512(n)).

The failure of a service provider to qualify for any of the limitations in § 512 does not necessarily make it liable for copyright infringement. The copyright owner must still demonstrate that the provider has infringed, and the provider may still avail itself of any of the defenses, such as fair use, that are available to copyright defendants generally. (§ 512(*l*)).

* * *

Eligibility for Limitations Generally

A party seeking the benefit of the limitations on liability in Title II must qualify as a "service provider." For purposes of the first limitation, relating to transitory communications, "service provider" is defined in § 512(k)(1)(A) as "an entity offering the transmission, routing, or providing of connections for digital online communications, between or among points specified by a user, of material of the user's choosing, without modification to the content of the material as sent or received." For purposes of the other three limitations, "service provider" is more broadly defined in § 512(k)(1)(B) as "a provider of online services or network access, or the operator of facilities therefor."

In addition, to be eligible for any of the limitations, a service provider must meet two overall conditions: (1) it must adopt and reasonably implement a policy of terminating in appropriate circumstances the accounts of subscribers who are repeat infringers; and (2) it must accommodate and not interfere with "standard technical measures." (§ 512(i)). "Standard technical measures" are defined as measures that copyright owners use to identify or protect copyrighted works, that have been developed pursuant to a broad consensus of copyright owners and service providers in an open, fair and voluntary multi-industry process, are available to anyone on reasonable nondiscriminatory terms, and do not impose substantial costs or burdens on service providers.

Limitation for Transitory Communications

In general terms, section 512(a) limits the liability of service providers in circumstances where the provider merely acts as a data conduit, transmitting digital information from one point on a network to another at someone else's request. This limitation covers acts of transmission, routing, or providing connections for the information, as well as the intermediate and transient copies that are made automatically in the operation of a network.

In order to qualify for this limitation, the service provider's activities must meet the following conditions:

- The transmission must be initiated by a person other than the provider.

- The transmission, routing, provision of connections, or copying must be carried out by an automatic technical process without selection of material by the service provider.

- The service provider must not determine the recipients of the material.

- Any intermediate copies must not ordinarily be accessible to anyone other than anticipated recipients, and must not be retained for longer than reasonably necessary.

- The material must be transmitted with no modification to its content.

Limitation for System Caching

Section 512(b) limits the liability of service providers for the practice of retaining copies, for a limited time, of material that has been made available online by a person other than the provider, and then transmitted to a subscriber at his or her direction. The service provider retains the material so that subsequent requests for the same material can be fulfilled by transmitting the retained copy, rather than retrieving the material from the original source on the network.

The benefit of this practice is that it reduces the service provider's bandwidth requirements and reduces the waiting time on subsequent requests for the same information. On the other hand, it can result in the delivery of outdated information to subscribers and can deprive website operators of accurate "hit" information—information about the number of requests for particular material on a website—from which advertising revenue is frequently calculated. For this reason, the person making the material available online may establish rules about updating it, and may utilize technological means to track the number of "hits."

The limitation applies to acts of intermediate and temporary storage, when carried out through an automatic technical process for the purpose of making the material available to subscribers who subsequently request it. It is subject to the following conditions:

- The content of the retained material must not be modified.

- The provider must comply with rules about "refreshing" material—replacing retained copies of material with material from the original location—when specified in accordance with a generally accepted industry standard data communication protocol.

- The provider must not interfere with technology that returns "hit" information to the person who posted the material, where such technology meets certain requirements.

- The provider must limit users' access to the material in accordance with conditions on access (e.g., password protection) imposed by the person who posted the material.

- Any material that was posted without the copyright owner's authorization must be removed or blocked promptly once the service provider has been notified that it has been removed, blocked, or ordered to be removed or blocked, at the originating site.

*Limitation for Information Residing on Systems
or Networks at the Direction of Users*

Section 512(c) limits the liability of service providers for infringing material on websites (or other information repositories) hosted on their systems. It applies to storage at the direction of a user. In order to be eligible for the limitation, the following conditions must be met:

- The provider must not have the requisite level of knowledge of the infringing activity, as described below.

- If the provider has the right and ability to control the infringing activity, it must not receive a financial benefit directly attributable to the infringing activity.

- Upon receiving proper notification of claimed infringement, the provider must expeditiously take down or block access to the material.

In addition, a service provider must have filed with the Copyright Office a designation of an agent to receive notifications of claimed infringement. The Office provides a suggested form for the purpose of designating an agent (www.loc.gov/copyright/onlinesp/) and maintains a list of agents on the Copyright Office website (www.loc.gov/copyright/onlinesp/list/).

Under the knowledge standard, a service provider is eligible for the limitation on liability only if it does not have actual knowledge of the infringement, is not aware of facts or circumstances from which infringing activity is apparent, or upon gaining such knowledge or awareness, responds expeditiously to take the material down or block access to it.

The statute also establishes procedures for proper notification, and rules as to its effect. (§ 512(c)(3)). Under the notice and takedown procedure, a copyright owner submits a notification under penalty of perjury, including a list of specified elements, to the service provider's designated agent. Failure to comply substantially with the statutory requirements means that the notification will not be considered in determining the requisite level of knowledge by the service provider. If, upon receiving a proper notification, the service provider promptly removes or blocks access to the material identified in the notification, the provider is exempt from monetary liability. In addition, the provider is protected from any liability to any person for claims based on its having taken down the material. (§ 512(g)(1)).

In order to protect against the possibility of erroneous or fraudulent notifications, certain safeguards are built into section 512. Subsection (g)(1) gives the subscriber the opportunity to respond to the notice and takedown by filing a counter notification. In order to qualify for the protection against liability for taking down material, the service provider must promptly notify the subscriber that it has removed or disabled access to the material. If the subscriber serves a counter notification complying with statutory requirements, including a statement under penalty of perjury that the material was removed or disabled through mistake or misidentification, then unless the copyright owner files an action seeking a court order against the subscriber, the service provider must put the material back up within 10–14 business days after receiving the counter notification.

Penalties are provided for knowing material misrepresentations in either a notice or a counter notice. Any person who knowingly materially misrepresents that material is infringing, or that it was removed or blocked through mistake or misidentification, is liable for any resulting damages (including costs and attorneys' fees) incurred by the alleged infringer, the copyright owner or its licensee, or the service provider. (§ 512(f)).

Limitation for Information Location Tools

Section 512(d) relates to hyperlinks, online directories, search engines and the like. It limits liability for the acts of referring or linking users to a site that contains infringing material by using such information location tools, if the following conditions are met:

- The provider must not have the requisite level of knowledge that the material is infringing. The knowledge standard is the same as under the limitation for information residing on systems or networks.

- If the provider has the right and ability to control the infringing activity, the provider must not receive a financial benefit directly attributable to the activity.

- Upon receiving a notification of claimed infringement, the provider must expeditiously take down or block access to the material.

These are essentially the same conditions that apply under the previous limitation, with some differences in the notification requirements. The provisions establishing safeguards against the possibility of erroneous or fraudulent notifications, as discussed above, as well as those protecting the provider against claims based on having taken down the material apply to this limitation. (§§ 512(f)–(g)).

Special Rules Regarding Liability of Nonprofit Educational Institutions

Section 512(e) determines when the actions or knowledge of a faculty member or graduate student employee who is performing a teaching or research function may affect the eligibility of a nonprofit educational institution for one of the four limitations on liability. As to the limitations for transitory communications or system caching, the faculty member or student shall be considered a "person other than the provider," so as to avoid disqualifying the institution from eligibility. As to the other limitations, the knowledge or awareness of the faculty member or student will not be attributed to the institution. The following conditions must be met:

- The faculty member or graduate student's infringing activities do not involve providing online access to course materials that were required or recommended during the past three years;

- The institution has not received more than two notifications over the past three years that the faculty member or graduate student was infringing; and

- The institution provides all of its users with informational materials describing and promoting compliance with copyright law.

* * *

A & M Records, Inc. v. Napster, Inc.

54 U.S.P.Q.2d 1746 (N.D.Cal.2000).

■ PATEL, CHIEF J.

On December 6, 1999, plaintiff record companies filed suit alleging contributory and vicarious federal copyright infringement and related state law violations by defendant Napster, Inc. ("Napster"). Now before this court is defendant's motion for summary adjudication of the applicability of a safe harbor provision of the Digital Millennium Copyright Act ("DMCA"), 17 U.S.C. § 512(a), to its business activities. Defendant argues that the entire Napster system falls within the safe harbor and, hence, that plaintiffs may not obtain monetary damages or injunctive relief, except as narrowly specified by subparagraph 512(j)(1)(B). In the alternative, Napster asks the court to find subsection 512(a) applicable to its role in downloading MP3 music files, as opposed to searching for or indexing such files. Having considered the parties' arguments and for the reasons set forth below, the court enters the following memorandum and order.

BACKGROUND

Napster—a small Internet start-up based in San Mateo, California—makes its proprietary MusicShare software freely available for Internet users to download. Users who obtain Napster's software can then share MP3 music files with others logged-on to the Napster system. MP3 files, which reproduce nearly CD-quality sound in a compressed format, are available on a variety of websites either for a fee or free-of-charge. Napster allows users to exchange MP3 files stored on their own computer hard-drives directly, without payment, and boasts that it "takes the frustration out of locating servers with MP3 files." Def. Br. at 4.

Although the parties dispute the precise nature of the service Napster provides, they agree that using Napster typically involves the following basic steps: After downloading MusicShare software from the Napster website, a user can access the Napster system from her computer. The MusicShare software interacts with Napster's server-side software when the user logs on, automatically connecting her to one of some 150 servers that Napster operates. The MusicShare software reads a list of names of MP3 files that the user has elected to make available. This list is then added to a directory and index, on the Napster server, of MP3 files that users who are logged-on wish to share. If the user wants to locate a song, she enters its name or the name of the recording artist on the search page of the MusicShare program and clicks the "Find It" button. The Napster software then searches the current directory and generates a list of files responsive to the search request. To download a desired file, the user highlights it on the list and clicks the "Get Selected Song(s)" button. The user may also view a list of files that exist on another user's hard drive and select a file from that list. When the requesting user clicks on the name of a file, the Napster server communicates with the requesting user's and host user's[2] MusicShare browser software to facilitate a connection between the two users and initiate the downloading of the file without any further action on either user's part.

According to Napster, when the requesting user clicks on the name of the desired MP3 file, the Napster server routes this request to the host

---

2. Napster uses the term "host user" to refer to the user who makes the desired MP3 file available for downloading.

user's browser. The host user's browser responds that it either can or cannot supply the file. If the host user can supply the file, the Napster server communicates the host's address and routing information to the requesting user's browser, allowing the requesting user to make a connection with the host and receive the desired MP3 file. The parties disagree about whether this process involves a hypertext link that the Napster server-side software provides. However, plaintiffs admit that the Napster server gets the necessary IP address information from the host user, enabling the requesting user to connect to the host. The MP3 file is actually transmitted over the Internet, *see, e.g.,* Def. Reply Br. at 3, but the steps necessary to make that connection could not take place without the Napster server.

The Napster system has other functions besides allowing users to search for, request, and download MP3 files. For example, a requesting user can play a downloaded song using the MusicShare software. Napster also hosts a chat room.

Napster has developed a policy that makes compliance with all copyright laws one of the "terms of use" of its service and warns users that:

> Napster will terminate the accounts of users who are repeat infringers of the copyrights, or other intellectual property rights, of others. In addition, Napster reserves the right to terminate the account of a user upon any single infringement of the rights of others in conjunction with use of the Napster service.

However, the parties disagree over when this policy was instituted and how effectively it bars infringers from using the Napster service. Napster claims that it had a copyright compliance policy as early as October 1999, but admits that it did not document or notify users of the existence of this policy until February 7, 2000.

* * *

DISCUSSION

Section 512 of the DMCA addresses the liability of online service and Internet access providers for copyright infringements occurring online. Subsection 512(a) exempts qualifying service providers from monetary liability for direct, vicarious, and contributory infringement and limits injunctive relief to the degree specified in subparagraph 512(j)(1)(B). Interpretation of subsection 512(a), or indeed any of the section 512 safe harbors, appears to be an issue of first impression.

Napster claims that its business activities fall within the safe harbor provided by subsection 512(a). This subsection limits liability "for infringement of copyright by reason of the [service] provider's transmitting, routing, or providing connections for, material through a system or network controlled or operated by or for the service provider, or by reason of the intermediate and transient storage of that material in the course of such transmitting, routing, or providing connections," if five conditions are satisfied:

(1) the transmission of the material was initiated by or at the direction of a person other than the service provider;

(2) the transmission, routing, provision of connections, or storage is carried out through an automatic technical process without selection of the material by the service provider;

(3) the service provider does not select the recipients of the material except as an automatic response to the request of another person;

(4) no copy of the material made by the service provider in the course of such intermediate or transient storage is maintained on the system or network in a manner ordinarily accessible to anyone other than the anticipated recipients, and no such copy is maintained on the system or network in a manner ordinarily accessible to such anticipated recipients for a longer period than is reasonably necessary for the transmission, routing, or provision of connections; and

(5) the material is transmitted through the system or network without modification of its content.

17 U.S.C. § 512(a).

Citing the "definitions" subsection of the statute, Napster argues that it is a "service provider" for the purposes of the 512(a) safe harbor. *See* 17 U.S.C. § 512(k)(1)(A).[4] First, it claims to offer the "transmission, routing, or providing of connections for digital online communications" by enabling the connection of users' hard-drives and the transmission of MP3 files "directly from the Host hard drive and Napster browser through the Internet to the user's Napster browser and hard drive." Def. Reply Br. at 3. Second, Napster states that users choose the online communication points and the MP3 files to be transmitted with no direction from Napster. Finally, the Napster system does not modify the content of the transferred files. Defendant contends that, because it meets the definition of "service provider,"[5] it need only satisfy the five remaining requirements of the safe harbor to prevail in its motion for summary adjudication.

4.   Subparagraph 512(k)(1)(A) provides:
As used in subsection (a), the term "service provider" means an entity offering the transmission, routing, or providing of connections for digital online communications, between or among points specified by a user, of material of the user's choosing, without modification to the content of the material sent or received.
Subparagraph 512(k)(1)(B) states:
As used in this section, other than subsection (a), the term "service provider" means a provider of online services or network access, or the operator of facilities therefor, and includes an entity described in subparagraph (A).

5.   It is not entirely clear to the court that Napster qualifies under the narrower subparagraph 512(k)(1)(A). However, plaintiffs appear to concede that Napster is a "service provider" within the meaning of subparagraph 512(k)(1)(A), arguing instead that Napster does not satisfy the additional limitations that the prefatory language of subsection 512(a) imposes. The court assumes, but does not hold, that Napster is a "service provider" under subparagraph 512(k)(1)(A).

Defendant then seeks to show compliance with these requirements by arguing: (1) a Napster user, and never Napster itself, initiates the transmission of MP3 files; (2) the transmission occurs through an automatic, technical process without any editorial input from Napster; (3) Napster does not choose the recipients of the MP3 files; (4) Napster does not make a copy of the material during transmission; and (5) the content of the material is not modified during transmission. Napster maintains that the 512(a) safe harbor thus protects its core function—"transmitting, routing and providing connections for sharing of the files its users choose." Def. Reply Br. at 2.

Plaintiffs disagree. They first argue that subsection 512(n) requires the court to analyze each of Napster's functions independently and that not all of these functions fall under the 512(a) safe harbor. In their view, Napster provides information location tools—such as a search engine, directory, index, and links—that are covered by the more stringent eligibility requirements of subsection 512(d), rather than subsection 512(a).

Plaintiffs also contend that Napster does not perform the function which the 512(a) safe harbor protects because the infringing material is not transmitted or routed *through* the Napster system, as required by subsection 512(a). They correctly note that the definition of "service provider" under subparagraph 512(k)(1)(A) is not identical to the prefatory language of subsection 512(a). The latter imposes the additional requirement that transmitting, routing, or providing connections must occur "through the system or network." Plaintiffs argue in the alternative that, if users' computers are part of the Napster system, copies of MP3 files are stored on the system longer than reasonably necessary for transmission, and thus subparagraph 512(a)(4) is not satisfied.

Finally, plaintiffs note that, under the general eligibility requirements established in subsection 512(i), a service provider must have adopted, reasonably implemented, and informed its users of a policy for terminating repeat infringers. Plaintiffs contend that Napster only adopted its copyright compliance policy after the onset of this litigation and even now does not discipline infringers in any meaningful way. Therefore, in plaintiffs' view, Napster fails to satisfy the DMCA's threshold eligibility requirements or show that the 512(a) safe harbor covers any of its functions.

I.   Independent Analysis of Functions

Subsection 512(n) of the DMCA states:

> Subsections (a), (b), (c), and (d) describe separate and distinct functions for purposes of applying this section. Whether a service provider qualifies for the limitation on liability in any one of those subsections shall be based solely on the criteria in that subsection and shall not affect a determination of whether that service provider qualifies for the limitations on liability under any other such subsections.

Citing subsection 512(n), plaintiffs argue that the 512(a) safe harbor does not offer blanket protection to Napster's entire system. Plaintiffs consider the focus of the litigation to be Napster's function as an information location tool—eligible for protection, if at all, under the more rigorous subsection 512(d). They contend that the system does not operate as a passive conduit within the meaning of subsection 512(a). In this view, Napster's only possible safe harbor is subsection 512(d), which applies to service providers "referring or linking users to an online location containing infringing material or infringing activity, by using information location tools, including a directory, index, reference, pointer, or hypertext link...." Subsection 512(d) imposes more demanding eligibility requirements because it covers active assistance to users.

Defendant responds in two ways. First, it argues that subsection 512(a), rather than 512(d), applies because the information location tools it provides are incidental to its core function of automatically transmitting, routing, or providing connections for the MP3 files users select. In the alternative, defendant maintains that, even if the court decides to analyze the information location functions under 512(d), it should hold that the 512(a) safe harbor protects other aspects of the Napster service.

Napster undisputedly performs some information location functions. The Napster server stores a transient list of the files that each user currently logged-on to that server wants to share. This data is maintained until the user logs off, but the structure of the index itself continues to exist. If a user wants to find a particular song or recording artist, she enters a search, and Napster looks for the search terms in the index. Edward Kessler, Napster's Vice President of Engineering, admitted in his deposition that, at least in this context, Napster functions as a free information location tool. *Cf.* Declaration of Daniel Farmer ("Farmer Dec.") ¶ 16 (stating that "Napster operates exactly like a search engine or information location tool to the user"). Napster software also has a "hot list" function that allows users to search for other users' log-in names and receive notification when users with whom they might want to communicate have connected to the service. In short, the parties agree on the existence of a searchable directory and index, and Napster representatives have used the phrase "information location tool," which appears in the heading for subsection 512(d), to characterize some Napster functions.

There the agreement ends. According to Napster, the information location tools upon which plaintiffs base their argument are incidental to the system's core function of transmitting MP3 music files, and for this reason, the court should apply subsection 512(a). Napster also disputes the contention that it organizes files or provides links to other Internet sites in the same manner as a search engine like Yahoo!. Consequently, it deems subsection 512(d) inapplicable to its activities. *Cf.* H.R.Rep. No. 105–551(II), 105th Cong., 2d Sess. (1998), 1998 WL 414916, at *147 (using Yahoo! as an example of an information location tool covered by 512(d)). Napster contrasts its operations, which proceed automatically after initial stimuli from users, with search engines like Yahoo! that depend upon the "human judgment and editorial discretion" of the service provider's staff. *Id.*

Napster's final and most compelling argument regarding subsection 512(d) is that the DMCA safe harbors are not mutually exclusive. According to subsection 512(n), a service provider could enjoy the 512(a) safe harbor even if its information location tools were also protected by (or failed to satisfy) subsection 512(d). *See* 17 U.S.C. § 512(n) ("Whether a service provider qualifies for the limitation on liability in any one of those subsections ... shall not affect a determination of whether that service provider qualifies for the limitations on liability under any other such subsections.") Similarly, finding *some* aspects of the system outside the scope of subsection 512(a) would not preclude a ruling that *other* aspects *do* meet 512(a) criteria.

Because the parties dispute material issues regarding the operation of Napster's index, directory, and search engine, the court declines to hold that these functions are peripheral to the alleged infringement, or that they should not be analyzed separately under subsection 512(d).[6] Indeed, despite its contention that its search engine and indexing functions are incidental to the provision of connections and transmission of MP3 files, Napster has advertised the ease with which its users can locate "millions of songs" online without "wading through page after page of unknown artists." Declaration of Russell J. Frackman ("Frackman Dec."), Exh. 5, 4. Such statements by Napster to promote its service are tantamount to an admission that its search and indexing functions are essential to its marketability. Some of these essential functions—including but not limited to the search engine and index—should be analyzed under subsection 512(d).

However, the potential applicability of subsection 512(d) does not completely foreclose use of the 512(a) safe harbor as an affirmative defense. *See* 17 U.S.C. § 512(n). The court will now turn to Napster's eligibility for protection under subsection 512(a). It notes at the outset, though, that a ruling that subsection 512(a) applies to a given function would not mean that the DMCA affords the service provider blanket protection.

II.   Subsection 512(a)

Plaintiffs' principal argument against application of the 512(a) safe harbor is that Napster does not perform the passive conduit function eligible for protection under this subsection. As defendant correctly notes, the words "conduit" or "passive conduit" appear nowhere in 512(a), but are found only in the legislative history and summaries of the DMCA. The court must look first to the plain language of the statute, "construing the provisions of the entire law, including its object and policy, to ascertain the intent of Congress." *United States v. Hockings,* 129 F.3d 1069, 1071 (9th Cir.1997) (quoting *Northwest Forest Resource Council v. Glickman,* 82 F.3d 825, 830 (9th Cir.1996)) (internal quotation marks omitted). If the statute

---

6. The court need not rule on the applicability of subsection 512(d) to the functions plaintiffs characterize as information location tools because defendant does not rely on subsection 512(d) as grounds for its motion for summary adjudication.

is unclear, however, the court may rely on the legislative history. *See Hockings,* 129 F.3d at 1071. The language of subsection 512(a) makes the safe harbor applicable, as a threshold matter, to service providers "transmitting, routing or providing connections for, material *through a system or network* controlled or operated by or for the service provider...." 17 U.S.C. § 512(a) (emphasis added). According to plaintiffs, the use of the word "conduit" in the legislative history explains the meaning of "through a system."

Napster has expressly denied that the transmission of MP3 files ever passes through its servers. Indeed, Kessler declared that "files reside on the computers of Napster users, and are transmitted directly between those computers." MP3 files are transmitted "from the Host user's hard drive and Napster browser, *through the Internet* to the recipient's Napster browser and hard drive." Def. Reply Br. at 3 (emphasis added). The Internet cannot be considered "a system or network controlled or operated by or for the service provider," however. 17 U.S.C. § 512(a). To get around this problem, Napster avers (and plaintiffs seem willing to concede) that "Napster's servers and Napster's MusicShare browsers on its users' computers are all part of Napster's overall system." Def. Reply Br. at 5. Defendant narrowly defines its system to include the browsers on users' computers. In contrast, plaintiffs argue that either (1) the system does not include the browsers, or (2) it includes not only the browsers, but also the users' computers themselves.

Even assuming that the system includes the browser on each user's computer, the MP3 files are not transmitted "through" the system within the meaning of subsection 512(a). Napster emphasizes the passivity of its role—stating that "[a]ll files transfer directly from the computer of one Napster user *through the Internet* to the computer of the requesting user." Def. Br. at 5 (emphasis added). It admits that the transmission bypasses the Napster server. This means that, even if each user's Napster browser is part of the system, the transmission goes *from* one part of the system *to* another, or *between* parts of the system, but not "through" the system. The court finds that subsection 512(a) does not protect the transmission of MP3 files.

The prefatory language of subsection 512(a) is disjunctive, however. The subsection applies to "infringement of copyright by reason of the provider's transmitting, routing, *or* providing connections through a system or network controlled or operated by or for the service provider." 17 U.S.C. § 512(a) (emphasis added). The court's finding that transmission does not occur "through" the system or network does not foreclose the possibility that subsection 512(a) applies to "routing" or "providing connections." Rather, each of these functions must be analyzed independently.

Napster contends that providing connections between users' addresses "constitutes the value of the system to the users and the public." Def. Br. at 15. This connection cannot be established without the provision of the host's address to the Napster browser software installed on the requesting user's computer. The central Napster server delivers the host's address.

While plaintiffs contend that the infringing material is not *transmitted* through the Napster system, they provide no evidence to rebut the assertion that Napster supplies the requesting user's computer with information necessary to facilitate a connection with the host.

Nevertheless, the court finds that Napster does not provide connections "through" its system. Although the Napster server conveys address information to establish a connection between the requesting and host users, the connection itself occurs through the Internet. The legislative history of section 512 demonstrates that Congress intended the 512(a) safe harbor to apply only to activities "in which a service provider plays the role of a 'conduit' for the communications of others." H.R.Rep. No. 105–551(II), 105th Cong., 2d Sess. (1998), 1998 WL 414916, at *130. Drawing inferences in the light most favorable to the non-moving party, this court cannot say that Napster serves as a conduit for the connection itself, as opposed to the address information that makes the connection possible. Napster enables or facilitates the initiation of connections, but these connections do not pass through the system within the meaning of subsection 512(a).

Neither party has adequately briefed the meaning of "routing" in subsection 512(a), nor does the legislative history shed light on this issue. Defendant tries to make "routing" and "providing connections" appear synonymous—stating, for example, that "the central Napster server *routes* the transmission by providing the Host's address to the Napster browser that is installed on and in use by User's computer." Def. Br. at 16. However, the court doubts that Congress would have used the terms "routing" and "providing connections" disjunctively if they had the same meaning. It is clear from both parties' submissions that the route of the allegedly infringing material goes through the Internet from the host to the requesting user, not through the Napster server. *See, e.g.,* Def. Br. at 13 ("Indeed, the content of the MP3 files are routed without even passing through Napster's Servers."). The court holds that routing does not occur through the Napster system.

Because Napster does not transmit, route, or provide connections through its system, it has failed to demonstrate that it qualifies for the 512(a) safe harbor. The court thus declines to grant summary adjudication in its favor.

III.   *Copyright Compliance Policy*

Even if the court had determined that Napster meets the criteria outlined in subsection 512(a), subsection 512(i) imposes additional requirements on eligibility for *any* DMCA safe harbor. This provision states:

> The limitations established by this section shall apply to a service provider only if the service provider—
>
> (A) has adopted and reasonably implemented, and informs subscribers and account holders of the service provider's system or network of, a policy that provides for the termination in appropri-

ate circumstances of subscribers and account holders of the service provider's system or network who are repeat infringers; and

(B) accommodates and does not interfere with standard technical measures.

17 U.S.C. § 512(i).

Plaintiffs challenge Napster's compliance with these threshold eligibility requirements on two grounds. First, they point to evidence from Kessler's deposition that Napster did not adopt a written policy of which its users had notice until on or around February 7, 2000—two months after the filing of this lawsuit. Kessler testified that, although Napster had a copyright compliance policy as early as October 1999, he is not aware that this policy was reflected in any document, or communicated to any user. Congress did not intend to require a service provider to "investigate possible infringements, monitor its service or make difficult judgments as to whether conduct is or is not infringing," but the notice requirement is designed to insure that flagrant or repeat infringers "know that there is a realistic threat of losing [their] access." H.R. Rep. 105–551(II), 1998 WL 414916, at *154.

Napster attempts to refute plaintiffs' argument by noting that subsection 512(i) does not specify when the copyright compliance policy must be in place. Although this characterization of subsection 512(i) is facially accurate, it defies the logic of making formal notification to users or subscribers a prerequisite to exemption from monetary liability. The fact that Napster developed and notified its users of a formal policy *after* the onset of this action should not moot plaintiffs' claim to monetary relief for past harms. Without further documentation, defendant's argument that it has satisfied subsection 512(i) is merely conclusory and does not support summary adjudication in its favor.

Summary adjudication is also inappropriate because Napster has not shown that it *reasonably* implemented a policy for terminating repeat infringers. *See* 17 U.S.C. § 512(i)(A) (requiring "reasonable" implementation of such a policy). If Napster is formally notified of infringing activity, it blocks the infringer's password so she cannot log on to the Napster service using that password. Napster does not block the IP addresses of infringing users, however, and the parties dispute whether it would be feasible or effective to do so.

Plaintiffs aver that Napster wilfully turns a blind eye to the identity of its users—that is, their real names and physical addresses—because their anonymity allows Napster to disclaim responsibility for copyright infringement. Hence, plaintiffs contend, "infringers may readily reapply to the Napster system to recommence their infringing downloading and uploading of MP3 music files." Pl. Br. at 24. Plaintiffs' expert, computer security researcher Daniel Farmer, declared that he conducted tests in which he easily deleted all traces of his former Napster identity, convincing Napster that "it had never seen me or my computer before." Farmer Dec. ¶ 29. Farmer also cast doubt on Napster's contention that blocking IP addresses is not a reasonable means of terminating infringers. He noted that Napster bans the IP addresses of users who runs "bots" on the service. *See id.* ¶ 27.

Hence, plaintiffs raise genuine issues of material fact about whether Napster has reasonably implemented a policy of terminating repeat infringers. They have produced evidence that Napster's copyright compliance policy is neither timely nor reasonable within the meaning of subparagraph 512(i)(A).

CONCLUSION

This court has determined above that Napster does not meet the requirements of subsection 512(a) because it does not transmit, route, or provide connections for allegedly infringing material through its system. The court also finds summary adjudication inappropriate due to the existence of genuine issues of material fact about Napster's compliance with subparagraph 512(i)(A), which a service provider must satisfy to enjoy the protection of *any* section 512 safe harbor. Defendant's motion for summary adjudication is DENIED.

Ellison v. Robertson

189 F.Supp.2d 1051 (C.D.Cal.2002).

■ COOPER, DISTRICT JUDGE.

Introduction

When an overenthusiastic fan uploads his favorite author's novels to a newsgroup on the internet, what is the liability of an internet service provider, such as AOL, for allowing the books to reside for two weeks on their USENET server? The impact of the Digital Millennium Copyright Act on this issue presents a question of first impression in the Ninth Circuit.

* * *

II.   Background

A.   *Factual History*

Plaintiff Harlan Ellison is the author of many works of fact and fiction, particularly science fiction. He is the owner of the valid copyrights to most if not all of those works and has registered his copyrights in accordance with all applicable laws. Some of his fictional works, however, have been copied and distributed on the internet without his permission.

Some time in late March or early April 2000, Stephen Robertson scanned a number of Ellison's fictional works in order to convert them to digital files. Thereafter, Robertson uploaded and copied the files onto the USENET newsgroup "alt.binaries.e-book." Robertson accessed the internet through his local internet services provider, Tehama County Online ("TCO"); his USENET service was provided by RemarQ Communities, Inc. ("RemarQ"). The USENET, an abbreviation of "User Network," is an international collection of organizations and individuals (known as "peers") whose computers connect to each other and exchange messages posted by USENET users. Messages are organized into "newsgroups," which are topic-based discussion forums where individuals exchange ideas and information. Users' messages may contain the users' analyses and opinions, copies of newspaper or magazine articles, and even binary files containing binary copies of musical and literary works. "Alt.binaries.e-book", the newsgroup at issue in this case, seems to have been used primarily to exchange pirated and unauthorized digital copies of text material, primarily works of fiction by famous authors, including Ellison.

Peers in USENET enter into peer agreements, whereby one peer's servers automatically transmit and receive newsgroup messages from another peer's servers. As most peers are parties to a large number of peer agreements, messages posted on one USENET peer's server are quickly transmitted around the world. The result is a huge informational exchange system whereby millions of users can exchange millions of messages every day.

AOL has been a USENET peer since 1994, and its USENET servers automatically transmit and receive newsgroup messages from at least 41 other peers. AOL estimates that its peer servers receive 4.5 terabytes of data in more than twenty-four million messages each week from AOL's peers. This data is automatically transmitted to and received by AOL's USENET servers, which are computers that are accessed by AOL's users when they reach the USENET system through AOL's newsgroup service. In late March and early April 2000, when Robertson posted the infringing copies of Ellison's works, AOL's retention policy provided for USENET messages containing binary files to remain on the company's servers for fourteen days.

After Robertson uploaded the infringing copies of Ellison's works to the alt.binaries.e-book newsgroup, they were then forwarded and copied throughout USENET onto servers all over the world, including those belonging to AOL. As a result, AOL users had access to the alt.binaries.e-book newsgroup containing the infringing copies of Ellison's works. As these infringing copies were in binary file form, they would have remained on AOL's servers for approximately fourteen days.

On or about April 13, 2000, Plaintiff learned of the infringing activity and contacted counsel. After researching the notification procedures of 17 U.S.C. § 512, the Digital Millennium Copyright Act ("DMCA"), Plaintiff's counsel sent an e-mail on April 17, 2000, to TCO's and AOL's agents for notice of copyright infringement. Plaintiff received an acknowledgment of receipt from TCO, but no response from AOL, which claims never to have received that e-mail.

On April 24, 2000, Plaintiff filed suit against AOL and other Defendants. After having been served by Plaintiff on April 26, 2000, AOL blocked its users' access to alt.binaries.e-book.

B.   Procedural History

* * *

On November 26, 2001, AOL filed a Motion for summary judgment, alleging that Plaintiff had failed to set forth prima facie cases of copyright infringement, and also claiming various defenses under the DMCA. * * *

IV.   Discussion

* * *

B.   DMCA Limitations on Liability

AOL claims to qualify for two of the DMCA's "safe-harbor" provisions, subsection (a), Transitory digital network communications, and subsection (c), Information residing on systems or networks at direction of users. *See* 17 U.S.C. § 512(a), (c). These safe harbors do not confer absolute immunity upon ISPs, but do drastically limit their potential liability based on specific functions they perform (e.g. user-directed information storage). *See generally* 17 U.S.C. § 512. A party satisfying the requirements for one of the safe harbors cannot be liable for monetary relief, or, with the exception of the rather narrow relief available under subsection (j), for injunctive or other equitable relief for copyright infringement. *See id.*

1.   Section 512(i)

In order to avail itself of any of section 512's limitation-on-liability safe harbors, AOL must also satisfy the two requirements laid out in section 512(i). Section 512(i) provides that all safe-harbor provisions established by the DMCA shall apply to a service provider only if the service provider:

(A) has adopted and reasonably implemented, and informs sub-scribers and account holders of the service provider's system or network of, a policy that provides for the termination in appropriate circumstances of subscribers and account holders of the service provider's system or network who are repeat infringers; and

(B) accommodates and does not interfere with standard technical measures.

17 U.S.C. § 512(i)(1).

Furthermore, in order for an ISP to comply with subsection (i) and avail itself of one of the DMCA's safe harbors, the ISP must have adopted, reasonably implemented, and notified its members of the repeat infringer termination policy at the time the allegedly infringing activity occurred. Doing so after the infringing activity has already occurred is insufficient if the ISP seeks a limitation of liability in connection with that infringing activity. As explained by the district court in *Napster,* to hold otherwise would be defeat the whole purpose of subsection (i):

> Napster attempts to refute plaintiffs' argument by noting that subsection (i) does not specify when the copyright compliance

policy must be in place. Although this characterization of subsection (i) is factually accurate, it defies the logic of making formal notification to users or subscribers a prerequisite to exemption from monetary liability. The fact that Napster developed and notified its users of a formal policy *after* the onset of this action should not moot plaintiffs' claim to monetary relief for past harms.

Napster, 2000 WL 573136 at * 9 (original emphasis).

On its face, subsection (i) is only concerned with repeat-infringer termination policies, and not with copyright infringement in general. Nonetheless, Plaintiff urges that any reasonable policy whose goal is to put repeat infringers on notice that they face possible termination must necessarily include some procedures for actually identifying such individuals in the first place, such as a mechanism whereby the public can notify an ISP of copyright infringement occurring on its system. A termination policy could not be considered "reasonably implemented" if the ISP remained willfully ignorant of users on its system who infringe copyrights repeatedly. Although the text of section 512(i) could conceivably support such an interpretation, the legislative history demonstrates that Congress's intent was far more limited regarding subsection (i):

> the Committee does not intend this provision to undermine the principles of new subsection (*l*)[13] or the knowledge standard of new subsection (c) by suggesting that a provider *must investigate possible infringements, monitor its service, or make difficult judgments as to whether conduct is or is not infringing.* However, those who repeatedly or flagrantly abuse their access to the Internet through disrespect for the intellectual property rights of others should know that there is a realistic threat of losing that access.

H.R. Rep. 105–551(II), at p. 61 (July 22, 1998) (emphasis added); *see also* S.Rep. 105–190, at p. 51–52 (May 11, 1998) (providing *verbatim* the same explanation of subsection (i)). In the face of such clear guidance from the legislative history of the DMCA, subsection (i) cannot be interpreted to require ISPs to take affirmative steps to investigate potential infringement and set up notification procedures in an attempt to identify the responsible individuals. Accordingly, many of Plaintiff's argument regarding subsection (i) are irrelevant to determining whether AOL had reasonably implemented a policy for termination of repeat infringers.[14]

It is undisputed that AOL satisfies prong (B) based on its accommodation and non-interference with standard technical measures. And AOL presents evidence to support the conclusion that it has also met the requirements of prong (A). AOL's Terms of Service, to which every AOL member must agree before becoming a member, includes a notice that AOL members may not make unauthorized copies of content protected by copyrights, trademarks, or any other intellectual property rights. They also

---

13. In the version of the DMCA actually enacted, subsection (*l*)'s equivalent is now found at subsection (m).

14. These arguments are, however, relevant to determining whether AOL complied with the requirements of subsection (c).

notify members that their AOL accounts could be terminated for making such unauthorized copies.

Plaintiff contends, however, that AOL cannot satisfy prong (A) of subsection 512(i)(1) because although the ISP has presented substantial evidence of compliance, most of that evidence comes from March 2001, nearly a year after the infringing conduct occurred. AOL's percipient witness, Elizabeth Compton, testified that AOL's procedures for notifying its users that their access could be terminated if they were to infringe others' copyrights has not changed substantively since April 2000. However, Plaintiff challenges the credibility and competency of Ms. Compton, whose grasp of the technical side of AOL's copyright infringement procedures was decidedly less than expert.

In addition, Plaintiff notes that although AOL claims to have complied with subsection (i) and adopted and reasonably implemented polices aimed at terminating repeat infringers, Compton testified that no individual has ever been terminated for being a repeat infringer. Given the millions of AOL users, Plaintiff argues, this lack of even a single termination for repeat infringement is evidence that AOL has failed to fulfill its obligation to reasonably implement its subsection(i) termination policy. Moreover, Compton testified at her deposition that at the time of the infringement, AOL had not precisely defined how many times a user had to be guilty of infringement before that user could be classified as a "repeat infringer." Plaintiff claims this is further evidence that AOL had failed to comply with the reasonable-implementation requirement of subsection (i).

As noted above in the discussion of the legislative history of the DMCA, however, subsection (i) does not require AOL to actually terminate repeat infringers, or even to investigate infringement in order to determine if AOL users are behind it.[15] That is the province of subsection (c), which provides detailed requirements related to notification of infringement and the ISPs' responsibility to investigate and, in some instances, delete or block access to infringing material on their systems. Subsection (i) only requires AOL to put its users on notice that they face a realistic threat of having their Internet access terminated if they repeatedly violate intellectual property rights.

* * *

Accordingly, the Court holds that AOL had satisfied the requirements of 17 U.S.C. § 512(i) at the time of the alleged infringement of Ellison's copyrights.

---

15. As such, the "realistic threat of losing [Internet] access" that Congress wishes ISPs to impress upon would-be infringers remains just that—a mere threat—unless the ISP decides to implement procedures aimed at identifying, investigating, and remedying infringement in hopes of meeting the requirements of subsection (c)'s safe harbor. Such an arrangement makes a certain amount of sense. If subsection (i) obligated ISPs to affir-matively seek out information regarding infringement and then investigate, eradicate, and punish infringement on their networks, then most if not all of the notice and take-down requirements of the subsection (c) safe harbor would be indirectly imported and applied to subsections (a) and (b) as well. This would upset the carefully balanced, "separate function—separate safe harbor—separate requirements" architecture of the DMCA.

2. Section 512's limitations on liability (a) through (d)

Section 512(n) explicitly provides that each of the four limitation-on-liability safe harbors found in subsections (a) through (d) "describe separate and distinct functions for purposes of applying this section." *Id.* As a result, "[w]hether a service provider qualifies for the limitation of liability in any one of the subsections shall be based solely on the criteria in that subsection, and shall not affect a determination of whether the service provider qualifies for the limitations on liability under any other such subsection." *Id.* The DMCA's legislative history provides the following instructional example:

> Section 512's limitations on liability are based on functions, and each limitation is intended to describe a separate and distinct function. Consider, for example, a service provider that provides a hyperlink to a site containing infringing material which it then caches on its system in order to facilitate access to it by its users. This service provider is engaging in at least three functions that may be subject to the limitation on liability: transitory digital network communications under subsection (a), system caching under subsection (b), and information locating tools under subsection (d).

H.R. Rep. 105–551(II), at p. 65 (July 22, 1998). In this example, if the service provider met the threshold requirements of subsection (i), "then for its acts of system caching it is eligible for that limitation on liability with corresponding narrow injunctive relief. But if the same company is committing an infringement by using information locating tools to link its users to infringing material, then its fulfillment of the requirements to claim the system caching liability limitation does not affect whether it qualifies for the liability limitation for information location tools." 3 NIMMER ON COPYRIGHT § 12B.06[A], at 12B–53, 54.

Although AOL performs many Internet-service-provider-related functions, Plaintiff's claims against AOL are based solely on its storage of USENET messages on its servers and provision of access to those USENET messages to AOL users and others accessing the AOL system from outside.

AOL claims that it is eligible under both subsections (a) and (c) for a limitation on liability regarding Plaintiff's claims against it.

3. Subsection (a)'s limitation on liability

AOL contends that it meets all the criteria for the limitation-on-liability safe harbor found in subsection (a), which provides:

(a) Transitory digital network communications.—A service provider shall not be liable for monetary relief, or, except as provided in subsection (j), for injunctive or other equitable relief, for the infringement of copyright by reason of the provider's transmitting, routing, or providing connections for, material through a system or network controlled or operated by or for the service provider, or by reason of the intermediate and transient storage of that material in the course of transmitting, routing, or providing connections, if—

(1) the transmission of the material was initiated by or at the direction of a person other than the service provider;

(2) the transmission, routing, provision of connections, or storage is carried out through an automatic technical process without selection of the material by the service provider;

(3) the service provider does not select the recipients of the material except' as an automatic response to the request of another person;

(4) no copy of the material made by the service provider in the course of such intermediate or transient storage is maintained on the system or network in a manner ordinarily accessible to anyone other than anticipated recipients, and no such copy is maintained on the system or network in a manner ordinarily accessible to such anticipated recipients for a longer period than is reasonably necessary for the transmission, routing, or provision of connections; and

(5) the material is transmitted through the system without modification of its content.

Subsection (a) does not require ISPs to remove or block access to infringing materials upon receiving notification of infringement, as is the case with subsections (c) and (d).

* * *

Plaintiff argues that AOL's USENET servers do not engage in "intermediate and transient storage" of USENET messages such as the one posted by Robertson. Instead, AOL stores USENET messages containing binary files on its servers for up to fourteen days. AOL, however, claims that the USENET message copies are "intermediate." AOL's role is as an intermediary between the original USENET user who posts a message, such as Robertson, and the recipient USENET users who later choose to view the message.

By itself, the term "intermediate and transient storage" is rather ambiguous. And it is unclear from reading the DMCA whether AOL's storage of USENET messages containing binary files on its servers for fourteen days in order to make those messages accessible to AOL users constitutes "intermediate and transient storage." Certain functions such as the provision of e-mail service or Internet connectivity clearly fall under the purview of subsection (a); other functions such as hosting a web site or chatroom fall under the scope of subsection (c). The question presented by this case is which subsection applies to the function performed by AOL when it stores USENET messages in order to provide USENET access to users. Faced with the ambiguous language in the statute itself, the Court looks to the DMCA's legislative history for guidance in interpretation. The only real guidance is provided in the House Judiciary Committee Report. *See* H.R. Rep. 105–551 (May 22, 1998).

* * *

[T]he section-by-section analysis found in the First House Report is relevant to interpreting whether AOL's storage of USENET messages in order to provide USENET access to AOL users constitutes (1) "intermediate and transient storage" of (2) copies that are not "maintained on the system or network . . . for a longer period than is reasonably necessary for the transmission, routing, or provision of connections." 17 U.S.C. § 512(a), (a)(4).

The First House Report answers both of those questions with a resounding yes:

> The exempted storage and transmissions are those carried out through an automatic technological process that is indiscriminate—i.e., the provider takes no part in the selection of the particular material transmitted—where the copies are retained no longer than necessary for the purpose of carrying out the transmission. This conduct would ordinarily include forwarding of customers' Usenet postings to other Internet sites in accordance with configuration settings that apply to all such postings . . .
>
> This exemption codifies the result of *Religious Technology Center v. Netcom On-Line Communication Services, Inc.*, 907 F.Supp. 1361 (N.D.Cal.1995) ("Netcom"), with respect to liability of providers for direct copyright infrigement.[20] *See id*. at 1368–70. In Netcom the court held that a provider is not liable for direct infringement where it takes no "affirmative action that [directly results] in copying . . . works other than by installing and maintaining a system whereby software automatically forwards messages received from subscribers . . . and temporarily stores copies on its system." *By referring to temporary storage of copies, Netcom recognizes implicitly that intermediate copies may be retained without liability for only a limited period of time. The requirement in 512(a)(1) that "no copy be maintained on the system or network . . . for a longer period than reasonably necessary for the transmission" is drawn from the facts of the Netcom case, and is intended to codify this implicit limitation in the Netcom holding.*

H.R. Rep. 105–551(I), at p. 24. (emphasis added).

In *Netcom*, infringing USENET postings were stored on Netcom's servers for up to *eleven days,* during which those postings were accessible to Netcom users. *See Netcom*, 907 F.Supp. at 1368. In AOL's case, messages containing binary files, such as the message posted by Robertson, were stored on AOL's servers for up to *fourteen days.* While "intermediate copies may be retained without liability for only a limited period of time," the

---

20. Any argument that this codification of *Netcom*'s facts regarding intermediate storage was only meant to apply to direct infringement, and not to vicarious or contributory infringement, is forestalled by subsection (2) of the version of the bill then under consideration by the Judiciary Committee.

For subsection (2) makes it clear that the same limitations on liability that apply under subsection (1) for direct infringement also apply to "contributory infringement or vicarious liability, based solely on conduct described in paragraph (1)." * * *

three-day difference between AOL's USENET storage and that of Netcom is insufficient to distinguish the two cases.

Accordingly, the Court finds that AOL's storage of Robertson's posts on its USENET servers constitutes "intermediate and transient storage" that was not "maintained on the system or network ... for a longer period than is reasonably necessary for the transmission, routing, or provision of connections."

    * * *

The Court hereby finds that AOL qualifies for the limitation-on-liability provided under subsection 512(a).

V. Conclusion

The Court hereby GRANTS Defendant AOL's Motion for summary judgment.

ALS Scan, Inc. v. RemarQ Communities, Inc.

239 F.3d 619 (4th Cir.2001).

■ NIEMEYER, CIRCUIT JUDGE:

We are presented with an issue of first impression—whether an Internet service provider enjoys a safe harbor from copyright infringement liability as provided by Title II of the Digital Millennium Copyright Act ("DMCA") when it is put on notice of infringement activity on its system by an imperfect notice. Because we conclude that the service provider was provided with a notice of infringing activity that *substantially* complied with the Act, it may not rely on a claim of defective notice to maintain the immunity defense provided by the safe harbor. Accordingly, we reverse the ruling of the district court that found the notice fatally defective, and affirm its remaining rulings.

I

ALS Scan, Inc., a Maryland corporation, is engaged in the business of creating and marketing "adult" photographs. It displays these pictures on the Internet to paying subscribers and also sells them through the media of CD ROMs and videotapes. ALS Scan is holder of the copyrights for all of these photographs.

RemarQ Communities, Inc., a Delaware corporation, is an online Internet service provider that provides access to its subscribing members. It has approximately 24,000 subscribers to its newsgroup base and provides access to over 30,000 newsgroups which cover thousands of subjects. These newsgroups, organized by topic, enable subscribers to participate in discussions on virtually any topic, such as fine arts, politics, religion, social issues, sports, and entertainment. For example, RemarQ provides access to a newsgroup entitled "Baltimore Orioles," in which users share observations or materials about the Orioles. It claims that users post over one million articles a day in these newsgroups, which RemarQ removes after about 8–

10 days to accommodate its limited server capacity. In providing access to newsgroups, RemarQ does not monitor, regulate, or censor the content of articles posted in the newsgroup by subscribing members. It does, however, have the ability to filter information contained in the newsgroups and to screen its members from logging onto certain newsgroups, such as those containing pornographic material.

Two of the newsgroups to which RemarQ provides its subscribers access contain ALS Scan's name in the titles. These newsgroups—"alt.als" and "alt.binaries.pictures.erotica.als"—contain hundreds of postings that infringe ALS Scan's copyrights. These postings are placed in these newsgroups by RemarQ's subscribers.

Upon discovering that RemarQ databases contained material that infringed ALS Scan's copyrights, ALS Scan sent a letter, dated August 2, 1999, to RemarQ, stating:

> Both of these newsgroups ["alt.als" and "alt.binaries.pictures.erotica.als"] were created for the sole purpose of violating our Federally filed Copyrights and Tradename. These newsgroups contain virtually all Federally Copyrighted images.... Your servers provide access to these illegally posted images and enable the illegal transmission of these images across state lines.
>
> This is a cease and desist letter. You are hereby ordered to cease carrying these newsgroups within twenty-four (24) hours upon receipt of this correspondence....
>
> America Online, Erol's, Mindspring, and others have all complied with our cease and desist order and no longer carry these newsgroups.
>
>   * * *
>
> Our ALS Scan models can be identified at www.alsscan.com/modlinf2.html[.] Our copyright information can be reviewed at www.alsscan.com/copyrite.html[.]

RemarQ responded by refusing to comply with ALS Scan's demand but advising ALS Scan that RemarQ would eliminate individual infringing items from these newsgroups if ALS Scan identified them "with sufficient specificity." ALS Scan answered that RemarQ had included over 10,000 copyrighted images belonging to ALS Scan in its newsgroups over the period of several months and that

> [t]hese newsgroups have apparently been created by individuals for the express sole purpose of illegally posting, transferring and disseminating photographs that have been copyrighted by my client through both its websites and its CD–ROMs. The newsgroups, on their face from reviewing messages posted thereon, serve no other purpose.

When correspondence between the parties progressed no further to resolution of the dispute, ALS Scan commenced this action, alleging violations of the Copyright Act and Title II of the DMCA, as well as unfair competition. In its complaint, ALS Scan alleged that RemarQ possessed actual knowledge that the newsgroups contained infringing material but had "steadfastly refused to remove or block access to the material." ALS Scan also alleged that RemarQ was put on notice by ALS Scan of the infringing material contained in its database. In addition to injunctive relief, ALS Scan demanded actual and statutory damages, as well as attorneys fees. It attached to its complaint affidavits establishing the essential elements of its claims.

In response, RemarQ filed a motion to dismiss the complaint or, in the alternative, for summary judgment, and also attached affidavits, stating that RemarQ was prepared to remove articles posted in its newsgroups if the allegedly infringing articles were specifically identified. It contended that because it is a provider of access to newsgroups, ALS Scan's failure to comply with the DMCA notice requirements provided it with a defense to ALS Scan's copyright infringement claim.

The district court ruled on RemarQ's motion, stating, "[RemarQ's] motion to dismiss or for summary judgment is treated as one to dismiss and, as such, is granted." In making this ruling, the district court held: (1) that RemarQ could not be held liable for *direct* copyright infringement merely because it provided access to a newsgroup containing infringing material; and (2) that RemarQ could not be held liable for *contributory* infringement because ALS Scan failed to comply with the notice requirements set forth in the DMCA, 17 U.S.C. § 512(c)(3)(A). This appeal followed.

* * *

III

For its principal argument, ALS Scan contends that it substantially complied with the notification requirements of the DMCA and thereby denied RemarQ the "safe harbor" from copyright infringement liability granted by that Act. *See* 17 U.S.C. § 512(c)(3)(A) (setting forth notification requirements). It asserts that because its notification was sufficient to put RemarQ on notice of its infringement activities, RemarQ lost its service-provider immunity from infringement liability. It argues that the district court's application of the DMCA was overly strict and that Congress did not intend to permit Internet providers to avoid copyright infringement liability "merely because a cease and desist notice failed to technically comply with the DMCA."

RemarQ argues in response that it did not have "knowledge of the infringing activity as a matter of law," stating that the DMCA protects it from liability because "ALS Scan failed to identify the infringing works in compliance with the Act, and RemarQ falls within the 'safe harbor' provisions of the Act." It notes that ALS Scan never provided RemarQ or the district court with the identity of the pictures forming the basis of its copyright infringement claim.

These contentions of the parties present the issue of whether ALS Scan complied with the notification requirements of the DMCA so as to deny RemarQ the safe-harbor defense to copyright infringement liability afforded by that Act.

* * * Neither party to this case suggests that RemarQ is not an Internet service provider for purposes of the Act.

The liability-limiting provision applicable here, 17 U.S.C. § 512(c), gives Internet service providers a safe harbor from liability for "infringement of copyright by reason of the storage at the direction of a user of material that resides on a system or network controlled or operated by or for the service provider" as long as the service provider can show that: (1) it has neither actual knowledge that its system contains infringing materials nor an awareness of facts or circumstances from which infringement is apparent, or it has expeditiously removed or disabled access to infringing material upon obtaining actual knowledge of infringement; (2) it receives no financial benefit directly attributable to infringing activity; *and* (3) it responded expeditiously to remove or disable access to material claimed to be infringing after receiving from the copyright holder a notification conforming with requirements of § 512(c)(3). *Id.* § 512(c)(1).[112] Thus, to qualify for this safe harbor protection, the Internet service provider must demonstrate that it has met all three of the safe harbor requirements, and a showing under the first prong—the lack of actual or constructive knowledge—is prior to and separate from the showings that must be made under the second and third prongs.

* * *

* * * [W]e conclude that ALS Scan substantially complied with the third prong, thereby denying RemarQ its safe harbor defense.

---

112. Section 512(c)(1) provides in full:

(c) Information residing on systems or networks at direction of users.—

(1) In general.—A service provider shall not be liable for monetary relief, or, except as provided in subsection (j), for injunctive or other equitable relief, for infringement of copyright by reason of the storage at the direction of a user of material that resides on a system or network controlled or operated by or for the service provider, if the service provider—

(A)(i) does not have actual knowledge that the material or an activity using the material on the system or network is infringing;

(ii) in the absence of such actual knowledge, is not aware of facts or circumstances from which infringing activity is apparent; or

(iii) upon obtaining such knowledge or awareness, acts expeditiously to remove, or disable access to, the material;

(B) does not receive a financial benefit directly attributable to the infringing activity, in a case in which the service provider has the right and ability to control such activity; and

(C) upon notification of claimed infringement as described in paragraph (3), responds expeditiously to remove, or disable access to, the material that is claimed to be infringing or to be the subject of infringing activity.

In evaluating the third prong, requiring RemarQ to remove materials following "notification," the district court concluded that ALS Scan's notice was defective in failing to comply strictly with two of the six requirements of a notification—(1) that ALS Scan's notice include "a list of [infringing] works" contained on the RemarQ site and (2) that the notice identify the infringing works in sufficient detail to enable RemarQ to locate and disable them. 17 U.S.C. § 512(c)(3)(A)(ii), (iii).[113]

In support of the district court's conclusion, RemarQ points to the fact that ALS Scan never provided it with a "representative list" of the infringing photographs, as required by § 512(c)(3)(A)(ii), nor did it identify those photographs with sufficient detail to enable RemarQ to locate and disable them, as required by § 512(c)(3)(A)(iii). RemarQ buttresses its contention with the observation that not all materials at the offending sites contained material to which ALS Scan held the copyrights. RemarQ's affidavit states in this regard:

> Some, but not all, of the pictures users have posted on these sites appear to be ALS Scan pictures. It also appears that users have posted other non-ALS Scan's erotic images on these newsgroups. The articles in these newsgroups also contain text messages, many of which discuss the adult images posted on the newsgroups.

ALS Scan responds that the two sites in question—"alt.als" and "alt.binaries.pictures.erotica.als"—were created solely for the purpose of publishing and exchanging ALS Scan's copyrighted images. It points out that the address of the newsgroup is defined by ALS Scan's name. As one of its affidavits states:

> [RemarQ's] subscribers going onto the two offending newsgroups for the purpose of violating [ALS Scan's] copyrights, are actually aware of the copyrighted status of [ALS Scan's] material because (1) each newsgroup has "als" as part of its title, and (2) each photograph belonging to [ALS Scan] has [ALS Scan's] name and/or the copyright symbol next to it.

> Each of these two newsgroups was created by unknown persons for the illegal purpose of trading the copyrighted pictures of [ALS Scan] to one another without the need for paying to either (1) become

---

113. Section 512(c)(3)(A)(ii), (iii) provides:

(3) Elements of notification.—

(A) To be effective under this subsection, a notification of claimed infringement must be a written communication provided to the designated agent of a service provider that includes substantially the following:

* * *

(ii) Identification of the copyrighted work claimed to have been infringed, or, if multiple copyright-

ed works at a single online site are covered by a single notification, a representative list of such works at that site.

(iii) Identification of the material that is claimed to be infringing or to be the subject of infringing activity and that is to be removed or access to which is to be disabled, and information reasonably sufficient to permit the service provider to locate the material.

members of [ALS Scan's] web site(s) or (2) purchasing the CD ROMs produced by[ALS Scan].

ALS Scan presses the contention that these two sites serve no other purpose than to distribute ALS Scan's copyrighted materials and therefore, by directing RemarQ to these sites, it has directed RemarQ to a representative list of infringing materials.

The DMCA was enacted both to preserve copyright enforcement on the Internet and to provide immunity to service providers from copyright infringement liability for "passive," "automatic" actions in which a service provider's system engages through a technological process initiated by another without the knowledge of the service provider. H.R. Conf. Rep. No. 105–796, at 72 (1998), *reprinted in* 1998 U.S.C.C.A.N. 649; H.R.Rep. No. 105–551(I), at 11 (1998). This immunity, however, is not presumptive, but granted only to "innocent" service providers who can prove they do not have actual or constructive knowledge of the infringement, as defined under any of the three prongs of 17 U.S.C. § 512(c)(1). The DMCA's protection of an innocent service provider disappears at the moment the service provider loses its innocence, i.e., at the moment it becomes aware that a third party is using its system to infringe. At that point, the Act shifts responsibility to the service provider to disable the infringing matter, "preserv[ing] the strong incentives for service providers and copyright owners to cooperate to detect and deal with copyright infringements that take place in the digital networked environment." H.R. Conf. Rep. No. 105–796, at 72 (1998), *reprinted in* 1998 U.S.C.C.A.N. 649. In the spirit of achieving a balance between the responsibilities of the service provider and the copyright owner, the DMCA requires that a copyright owner put the service provider on notice in a detailed manner but allows notice by means that comport with the prescribed format only "substantially," rather than perfectly. The Act states: "To be effective under this subsection, a notification of claimed infringement must be a written communication provided to the designated agent of a service provider that includes *substantially* the following...." 17 U.S.C. § 512(c)(3)(A) (emphasis added). In addition to substantial compliance, the notification requirements are relaxed to the extent that, with respect to multiple works, not all must be identified—only a "representative" list. *See id.* § 512(c)(3)(A)(ii). And with respect to location information, the copyright holder must provide information that is "*reasonably* sufficient" to permit the service provider to "locate" this material. *Id.* § 512(c)(3)(A)(iii) (emphasis added). This subsection specifying the requirements of a notification does not seek to burden copyright holders with the responsibility of identifying every infringing work—or even most of them—when multiple copyrights are involved. Instead, the requirements are written so as to reduce the burden of holders of multiple copyrights who face extensive infringement of their works. Thus, when a letter provides notice equivalent to a list of representative works that can be easily identified by the service provider, the notice substantially complies with the notification requirements.

In this case, ALS Scan provided RemarQ with information that (1) identified two sites created for the sole purpose of publishing ALS Scan's copyrighted works, (2) asserted that virtually all the images at the two sites were its copyrighted material, and (3) referred RemarQ to two web addresses where RemarQ could find pictures of ALS Scan's models and obtain ALS Scan's copyright information. In addition, it noted that material at the site could be identified as ALS Scan's material because the material included ALS Scan's "name and/or copyright symbol next to it." We believe that with this information, ALS Scan substantially complied with the notification requirement of providing a representative list of infringing material as well as information reasonably sufficient to enable RemarQ to locate the infringing material. To the extent that ALS Scan's claims about infringing materials prove to be false, RemarQ has remedies for any injury it suffers as a result of removing or disabling noninfringing material. *See* 17 U.S.C. § 512(f), (g).

Accordingly, we reverse the district court's ruling granting summary judgment in favor of RemarQ on the basis of ALS Scan's non-compliance with the notification provisions of 17 U.S.C. § 512(c)(3)(A)(ii) and (iii). Because our ruling only removes the safe harbor defense, we remand for further proceedings on ALS Scan's copyright infringement claims and any other affirmative defenses that RemarQ may have. * * *

NOTES & QUESTIONS

1. *The reach of Section 512.* Subsections (a), (b), (c), and (d) of Section 512 each applies to a particular category of online activity. Under which subsection, if any, would each of the following Internet services and activities fall?

- running a chat room
- streaming video over the Internet
- operating a search engine
- hosting a website
- operating a website containing hypertext links
- hosting a bulletin board system
- operating as an Internet service provider

2. *Anticircumvention and Section 512.* Title I of the Digital Millennium Copyright Act, 17 U.S.C. §§ 1201–05, imposes liability for circumventing a technological measure that effectively controls access to a protected work, as well as for providing any technology that is primarily designed or produced for the purpose of circumventing such measures. Suppose a website makes available for download software constituting such prohibited technology. Is the website operator protected by Section 512? *See Universal City Studios, Inc. v. Reimerdes,* 82 F.Supp.2d 211 (S.D.N.Y.2000), excerpted in Chapter 5, *infra.*

3. *Pirates, Internet directories, and red flags.* Under Section 512(d), the safe harbor for a service provider's use of information location tools is unavailable if the service provider has actual or constructive knowledge of the infringing activity. During the legislative process leading to the enactment of Section 512, concern was expressed that a human-compiled Internet directory, such as Yahoo!'s directory, would not meet this requirement since each website cataloged is visited and evaluated by an employee of the online service provider. Responding to this concern, a House report on the bill noted:

> A question has been raised as to whether a service provider would be disqualified from the safe harbor based solely on evidence that it had viewed the infringing Internet site. If so, there is concern that on-line directories prepared by human editors and reviewers, who view and classify various Internet sites, would be denied eligibility to the information location tools safe harbor, in an unintended number of cases and circumstances. This is an important concern because such on-line directories play a valuable role in assisting Internet users to identify and locate the information they seek on the decentralized and dynamic networks of the Internet.
>
> Like the information storage safe harbor in Section 512(c), a service provider would qualify for this safe harbor if, among other requirements, it "does not have actual knowledge that the material or activity is infringing" or, in the absence of such actual knowledge, it is "not aware of facts or circumstances from which infringing activity is apparent." Under this standard, a service provider would have no obligation to seek out copyright infringement, but it would not qualify for the safe harbor if it had turned a blind eye to "red flags" of obvious infringement.
>
> For instance, the copyright owner could show that the provider was aware of facts from which infringing activity was apparent if the copyright owner could prove that the location was clearly, at the time the directory provider viewed it, a "pirate" site of the type described below, where sound recordings, software, movies, or books were available for unauthorized downloading, public performance, or public display. Absent such "red flags" or actual knowledge, a directory provider would not be similarly aware merely because it saw one or more well known photographs of a celebrity at a site devoted to that person. The provider could not be expected, during the course of its brief cataloguing visit, to determine whether the photograph was still protected by copyright or was in the public domain; if the photograph was still protected by copyright, whether the use was licensed; and if the use was not licensed, whether it was permitted under the fair use doctrine.
>
> The intended objective of this standard is to exclude from the safe harbor sophisticated "pirate" directories—which refer Internet users to other selected Internet sites where pirate software,

books, movies, and music can be downloaded or transmitted. Such pirate directories refer Internet users to sites that are obviously infringing because they typically use words such as "pirate," "bootleg," or slang terms in their URL and header information to make their illegal purpose obvious, in the first place, to the pirate directories as well as other Internet users. Because the infringing nature of such sites would be apparent from even a brief and casual viewing, safe harbor status for a provider that views such a site and then establishes a link to it would not be appropriate. Pirate directories do not follow the routine business practices of legitimate service providers preparing directories, and thus evidence that they have viewed the infringing site may be all that is available for copyright owners to rebut their claim to a safe harbor.

H.R. REP. No. 105–551, pt. 2, at 57–58 (1998). How would you apply the "red flag" standard for actual or constructive knowledge to the *Napster* case?

CHAPTER FOUR

CONTROLLING INFORMATION ASSETS: DATABASES

Databases are a core technology of Internet commerce. An online retailer could not function if its customers could not search an online database of its inventory. A business-to-business exchange could not function if it did not provide its members with access to a database comprising the suppliers and manufacturers of different categories of goods and services. Without databases, no company conducting business on the Internet could keep track of such critical information as the identity of its customers, the sales and other transactions into which it enters, the settlement of accounts, and the shipment and delivery of its goods and services.

Many online businesses depend on their control of information maintained in databases. For example, Westlaw and Lexis each charge fees to access their comprehensive databases of legal materials. Many companies offer free access to online databases of information in order to sell space on their websites to advertisers. Still other companies compile timely and extensive databases of commercially valuable information such as stock quotes or sports scores and sell or license them to others for use on their websites. Advertisers depend on databases of names and addresses and other marketing information.

Most commercial databases are compilations of facts. Facts, however, are not protected under the law of copyright. While the selection and arrangement of facts in a database *may* qualify for protection under copyright law—provided the selection and arrangement are sufficiently original—the factual contents of these databases remain unprotected. Thus, in many circumstances, a person may use the factual contents of another's database without infringing the owner's copyright. Database owners seeking alternative legal protection through state courts and legislatures may be disappointed in their attempts, because of federal copyright law's preemption of state laws, such as the law of misappropriation or unfair competition, that otherwise might provide protection. This state of affairs has led some to call for federal *sui generis* protection for databases along the lines of the European Union's Directive on the Legal Protection of Databases.

Before proceeding to these legal matters, however, it is necessary to have some background on why federal copyright law generally does not protect databases.

I. DATABASES AND THE LAW OF COPYRIGHT

Until the Supreme Court's decision in *Feist Publications v. Rural Telephone Service Co.*, 499 U.S. 340 (1991), there was some confusion over whether factual databases were protected under the law of copyright. Historically, many courts and scholars believed that compilations of facts were protected under the "sweat of the brow" doctrine, which holds that one can acquire a copyright in a compilation of facts by dint of the effort one expends to compile it. The intuitive appeal of this doctrine is nicely set forth by Justice Story, who noted that, although all maps of the same region feature the same selection and arrangement, another person "has no right, without any such surveys and labors, to sit down and copy the whole of the map already produced by the skill and labors of the first party, and thus to rob him of all the fruit of his industry, skill, and expenditures." *Gray v. Russell*, 10 F. Cas. 1035, 1038 (C.C.D.Mass.1839). As Justice Story summarized his point in a later case, "[a] man has a right to the copy-right of a map of a state or country, which he has surveyed or caused to be compiled from existing materials, at his own expense, or skill, or labor, or money." *Emerson v. Davies*, 8 F. Cas. 615, 619 (C.C.D.Mass.1845). If return to one's labor ("sweat of the brow") is grounds for granting an intellectual property right, the lack of creativity and originality in the cartographer's selection and arrangement appears irrelevant.

In 1879, however, the Supreme Court held that "originality" is an absolute prerequisite for copyright protection. In the *Trade-Mark Cases*, 100 U.S. 82 (1879), the Court determined that the federal trademark law was not a valid exercise of Congress's power under the Constitution's Copyright Clause,[1] since trademarks do not necessarily embody the requisite originality. The Court explained that "while the word *writings* [in the Copyright Clause] may be liberally construed, as it has been, to include original designs for engravings, prints, & c., it is only such as are *original*, and are founded in the creative powers of the mind." *Id.* at 94. In *Bleistein v. Donaldson Lithographing Co.*, 188 U.S. 239, 250 (1903), the Court made clear that the quantum of originality required for copyright protection is very low: "a very modest grade of art" will suffice.

When the Supreme Court embraced the originality doctrine, it did not at the same time expressly reject the "sweat of the brow" doctrine. For much of the last century, the lower courts found compilations of facts, such as law reports and directories, protectible either because they embodied the requisite degree of originality, or because substantial labor was expended in compiling them. *See, e.g. Hutchinson Tel. Co. v. Fronteer Directory Co. of Minnesota*, 770 F.2d 128 (8th Cir.1985) (originality); *Schroeder v. William Morrow & Co.*, 566 F.2d 3 (7th Cir.1977) ("sweat of the brow"); *Adventures*

---

1. "The Congress shall have Power * * * [t]o promote the Progress of Science and useful Arts, by securing for limited Times to Authors and Inventors the exclusive Right to their respective Writings and Discoveries." U.S. CONST., art. I, § 8, cl. 8.

in Good Eating, Inc. v. Best Places to Eat, 131 F.2d 809 (7th Cir.1942) ("sweat of the brow"); *Jeweler's Circular Publishing Co. v. Keystone Publishing Co.*, 281 F. 83 (2d Cir.1922) ("sweat of the brow"); *West Pub. Co. v. Edward Thompson Co.*, 169 F. 833 (C.C.E.D.N.Y. 1909) ("sweat of the brow"); *Edward Thompson Co. v. American Law Book Co.*, 122 F. 922 (2d Cir.1903) (originality).

With passage of the 1976 Copyright Act, Congress expressly imposed the originality doctrine on compilations protected under the Act: it defined a compilation as "a work formed by the collection and assembling of preexisting materials or of data that are selected, coordinated, or arranged in such a way that the resulting work as a whole constitutes an *original* work of authorship." 17 U.S.C. § 101 (emphasis added).

The significance of this change in the definition of a compilation was not immediately clear. Some courts continued to apply the "sweat of the brow" doctrine, *see, e.g., Illinois Bell Tel. Co. v. Haines and Co.*, 683 F.Supp. 1204 (N.D.Ill.1988), *aff'd*, 905 F.2d 1081 (7th Cir.1990), *vacated and remanded*, 499 U.S. 944 (1991), while others viewed the doctrine as superseded by the new statutory language of originality, *see, e.g., Financial Info., Inc. v. Moody's Investors Serv., Inc.*, 808 F.2d 204 (2d Cir.1986), and *Worth v. Selchow & Righter Co.*, 827 F.2d 569 (9th Cir.1987). Some courts found factual compilations such as telephone directories sufficiently original to meet this standard. *See Hutchinson Tel. Co. v. Fronteer Directory Co. of Minnesota*, 770 F.2d 128 (8th Cir.1985) ("white pages" directory copyrightable); *Southern Bell Tel. and Tel. Co. v. Associated Tel. Directory Publishers*, 756 F.2d 801 (11th Cir.1985) ("yellow pages" directory copyrightable).

Such was the state of the caselaw when, in the following case, the Supreme Court established the standards that a factual compilation must meet to qualify for copyright protection.

Feist Publications, Inc. v. Rural Telephone Service Co.
499 U.S. 340 (1991).

■ JUSTICE O'CONNOR delivered the opinion of the Court.

This case requires us to clarify the extent of copyright protection available to telephone directory white pages.

I

Rural Telephone Service Company, Inc., is a certified public utility that provides telephone service to several communities in northwest Kansas. It is subject to a state regulation that requires all telephone companies operating in Kansas to issue annually an updated telephone directory. Accordingly, as a condition of its monopoly franchise, Rural publishes a typical telephone directory, consisting of white pages and yellow pages. The white pages list in alphabetical order the names of Rural's subscribers, together with their towns and telephone numbers. The yellow pages list

Rural's business subscribers alphabetically by category and feature classified advertisements of various sizes. Rural distributes its directory free of charge to its subscribers, but earns revenue by selling yellow pages advertisements.

Feist Publications, Inc., is a publishing company that specializes in area-wide telephone directories. Unlike a typical directory, which covers only a particular calling area, Feist's area-wide directories cover a much larger geographical range, reducing the need to call directory assistance or consult multiple directories. The Feist directory that is the subject of this litigation covers 11 different telephone service areas in 15 counties and contains 46,878 white pages listings—compared to Rural's approximately 7,700 listings. Like Rural's directory, Feist's is distributed free of charge and includes both white pages and yellow pages. Feist and Rural compete vigorously for yellow pages advertising.

As the sole provider of telephone service in its service area, Rural obtains subscriber information quite easily. Persons desiring telephone service must apply to Rural and provide their names and addresses; Rural then assigns them a telephone number. Feist is not a telephone company, let alone one with monopoly status, and therefore lacks independent access to any subscriber information. To obtain white pages listings for its area-wide directory, Feist approached each of the 11 telephone companies operating in northwest Kansas and offered to pay for the right to use its white pages listings.

Of the 11 telephone companies, only Rural refused to license its listings to Feist. Rural's refusal created a problem for Feist, as omitting these listings would have left a gaping hole in its area-wide directory, rendering it less attractive to potential yellow pages advertisers. In a decision subsequent to that which we review here, the District Court determined that this was precisely the reason Rural refused to license its listings. The refusal was motivated by an unlawful purpose "to extend its monopoly in telephone service to a monopoly in yellow pages advertising." *Rural Telephone Service Co. v. Feist Publications, Inc.,* 737 F.Supp. 610, 622 (D.Kan.1990).

Unable to license Rural's white pages listings, Feist used them without Rural's consent. Feist began by removing several thousand listings that fell outside the geographic range of its area-wide directory, then hired personnel to investigate the 4,935 that remained. These employees verified the data reported by Rural and sought to obtain additional information. As a result, a typical Feist listing includes the individual's street address; most of Rural's listings do not. Notwithstanding these additions, however, 1,309 of the 46,878 listings in Feist's 1983 directory were identical to listings in Rural's 1982–1983 white pages. App. 54 (¶ 15–16), 57. Four of these were fictitious listings that Rural had inserted into its directory to detect copying.

Rural sued for copyright infringement in the District Court for the District of Kansas taking the position that Feist, in compiling its own directory, could not use the information contained in Rural's white pages. Rural asserted that Feist's employees were obliged to travel door-to-door or conduct a telephone survey to discover the same information for themselves. Feist responded that such efforts were economically impractical and, in any event, unnecessary because the information copied was beyond the scope of copyright protection. The District Court granted summary judgment to Rural, explaining that "[c]ourts have consistently held that telephone directories are copyrightable" and citing a string of lower court decisions. 663 F.Supp. 214, 218 (1987). In an unpublished opinion, the Court of Appeals for the Tenth Circuit affirmed "for substantially the reasons given by the district court." App. to Pet. for Cert. 4a, judgt. order reported at 916 F.2d 718 (1990). We granted certiorari, 498 U.S. 808 (1990), to determine whether the copyright in Rural's directory protects the names, towns, and telephone numbers copied by Feist.

II

A

This case concerns the interaction of two well-established propositions. The first is that facts are not copyrightable; the other, that compilations of facts generally are. Each of these propositions possesses an impeccable pedigree. That there can be no valid copyright in facts is universally understood. The most fundamental axiom of copyright law is that "[n]o author may copyright his ideas or the facts he narrates." *Harper & Row Publishers, Inc. v. Nation Enterprises,* 471 U.S. 539, 556 (1985). Rural wisely concedes this point, noting in its brief that "[f]acts and discoveries, of course, are not themselves subject to copyright protection." Brief for Respondent 24. At the same time, however, it is beyond dispute that compilations of facts are within the subject matter of copyright. Compilations were expressly mentioned in the Copyright Act of 1909, and again in the Copyright Act of 1976.

There is an undeniable tension between these two propositions. Many compilations consist of nothing but raw data—*i.e.,* wholly factual information not accompanied by any original written expression. On what basis may one claim a copyright in such a work? Common sense tells us that 100 uncopyrightable facts do not magically change their status when gathered together in one place. Yet copyright law seems to contemplate that compilations that consist exclusively of facts are potentially within its scope.

The key to resolving the tension lies in understanding why facts are not copyrightable. The *sine qua non* of copyright is originality. To qualify for copyright protection, a work must be original to the author. * * * Original, as the term is used in copyright, means only that the work was independently created by the author (as opposed to copied from other works), and that it possesses at least some minimal degree of creativity. 1 M. Nimmer & D. Nimmer, Copyright §§ 2.01[A], [B] (1990) (hereinafter Nimmer). To be sure, the requisite level of creativity is extremely low; even a slight amount will suffice. The vast majority of works make the grade quite easily, as they possess some creative spark, "no matter how crude, humble or obvious" it might be. *Id.,* § 1.08[C][1]. Originality does not signify novelty; a work may be original even though it closely resembles other works so long as the similarity is fortuitous, not the result of copying. To illustrate, assume that two poets, each ignorant of the other, compose identical poems. Neither work is novel, yet both are original and, hence, copyrightable. * * *

Originality is a constitutional requirement. The source of Congress' power to enact copyright laws is Article I, § 8, cl. 8, of the Constitution, which authorizes Congress to "secur[e] for limited Times to Authors ... the exclusive Right to their respective Writings." In two decisions from the late 19th century—*The Trade–Mark Cases,* 100 U.S. 82 (1879); and *Burrow-Giles Lithographic Co. v. Sarony,* 111 U.S. 53 (1884)—this Court defined the crucial terms "authors" and "writings." In so doing, the Court made it unmistakably clear that these terms presuppose a degree of originality.

* * *

The originality requirement articulated in *The Trade–Mark Cases* and *Burrow–Giles* remains the touchstone of copyright protection today. * * *

It is this bedrock principle of copyright that mandates the law's seemingly disparate treatment of facts and factual compilations. "No one may claim originality as to facts." [Nimmer] § 2.11[A], p. 2–157. This is because facts do not owe their origin to an act of authorship. The distinction is one between creation and discovery: The first person to find and report a particular fact has not created the fact; he or she has merely discovered its existence. To borrow from *Burrow–Giles,* one who discovers a fact is not its "maker" or "originator." 111 U.S., at 58. "The discoverer merely finds and records." Nimmer § 2.03[E]. Census takers, for example, do not "create" the population figures that emerge from their efforts; in a sense, they copy these figures from the world around them. Denicola, Copyright in Collections of Facts: A Theory for the Protection of Nonfiction Literary Works, 81 Colum.L.Rev. 516, 525 (1981) (hereinafter Denicola). Census data therefore do not trigger copyright because these data are not "original" in the constitutional sense. Nimmer § 2.03[E]. The same is true of all facts—scientific, historical, biographical, and news of the day. "[T]hey may not be copyrighted and are part of the public domain available to every person." [*Miller v. Universal City Studios, Inc.,* 650 F.2d 1365, 1369 (CA5 1981).]

Factual compilations, on the other hand, may possess the requisite originality. The compilation author typically chooses which facts to include, in what order to place them, and how to arrange the collected data so that they may be used effectively by readers. These choices as to selection and arrangement, so long as they are made independently by the compiler and entail a minimal degree of creativity, are sufficiently original that Congress may protect such compilations through the copyright laws. Nimmer §§ 2.11[D], 3.03; Denicola 523, n.38. Thus, even a directory that contains absolutely no protectible written expression, only facts, meets the constitutional minimum for copyright protection if it features an original selection or arrangement. * * *

This protection is subject to an important limitation. The mere fact that a work is copyrighted does not mean that every element of the work may be protected. Originality remains the *sine qua non* of copyright; accordingly, copyright protection may extend only to those components of a work that are original to the author. [Patterson & Joyce, Monopolizing the Law: The Scope of Copyright Protection for Law Reports and Statutory Compilations, 36 UCLA L.Rev. 719, 800–02 (1989) (hereinafter Patterson & Joyce).] Ginsburg, Creation and Commercial Value: Copyright Protection of Works of Information, 90 Colum.L.Rev. 1865, 1868, and n. 12 (1990) (hereinafter Ginsburg). Thus, if the compilation author clothes facts with an original collocation of words, he or she may be able to claim a copyright in this written expression. Others may copy the underlying facts from the publication, but not the precise words used to present them. In *Harper & Row*, for example, we explained that President Ford could not prevent others from copying bare historical facts from his autobiography, see 471 U.S., at 556–557, but that he could prevent others from copying his "subjective descriptions and portraits of public figures." *Id.*, at 563. Where the compilation author adds no written expression but rather lets the facts speak for themselves, the expressive element is more elusive. The only conceivable expression is the manner in which the compiler has selected and arranged the facts. Thus, if the selection and arrangement are original, these elements of the work are eligible for copyright protection. See Patry, Copyright in Compilations of Facts (or Why the "White Pages" Are Not Copyrightable), 12 Com. & Law 37, 64 (Dec. 1990) (hereinafter Patry). No matter how original the format, however, the facts themselves do not become original through association. See Patterson & Joyce 776.

This inevitably means that the copyright in a factual compilation is thin. Notwithstanding a valid copyright, a subsequent compiler remains free to use the facts contained in another's publication to aid in preparing a competing work, so long as the competing work does not feature the same selection and arrangement. As one commentator explains it: "[N]o matter how much original authorship the work displays, the facts and ideas it exposes are free for the taking.... [T]he very same facts and ideas may be divorced from the context imposed by the author, and restated or reshuffled by second comers, even if the author was the first to discover the facts or to propose the ideas." Ginsburg 1868.

It may seem unfair that much of the fruit of the compiler's labor may be used by others without compensation. As Justice Brennan has correctly observed, however, this is not "some unforeseen byproduct of a statutory scheme." *Harper & Row*, 471 U.S., at 589 (dissenting opinion). It is, rather, "the essence of copyright," *ibid.*, and a constitutional requirement. The primary objective of copyright is not to reward the labor of authors, but "[t]o promote the Progress of Science and useful Arts." Art. I, § 8, cl. 8. * * * To this end, copyright assures authors the right to their original expression, but encourages others to build freely upon the ideas and information conveyed by a work. *Harper & Row, supra*, 471 U.S., at 556–557. This principle, known as the idea/expression or fact/expression dichotomy, applies to all works of authorship. As applied to a factual compilation, assuming the absence of original written expression, only the compiler's selection and arrangement may be protected; the raw facts may be copied at will. This result is neither unfair nor unfortunate. It is the means by which copyright advances the progress of science and art.

* * *

This, then, resolves the doctrinal tension: Copyright treats facts and factual compilations in a wholly consistent manner. Facts, whether alone or as part of a compilation, are not original and therefore may not be copyrighted. A factual compilation is eligible for copyright if it features an original selection or arrangement of facts, but the copyright is limited to the particular selection or arrangement. In no event may copyright extend to the facts themselves.

B

As we have explained, originality is a constitutionally mandated prerequisite for copyright protection. The Court's decisions announcing this rule predate the Copyright Act of 1909, but ambiguous language in the 1909 Act caused some lower courts temporarily to lose sight of this requirement.

* * *

Most courts construed the 1909 Act correctly, notwithstanding the less-than-perfect statutory language. They understood from this Court's decisions that there could be no copyright without originality. * * *

* * *

But some courts misunderstood the statute. * * *

Making matters worse, these courts developed a new theory to justify the protection of factual compilations. Known alternatively as "sweat of the brow" or "industrious collection," the underlying notion was that copyright was a reward for the hard work that went into compiling facts. The classic formulation of the doctrine appeared in *Jeweler's Circular Publishing Co.,* 281 F., at 88:

> "The right to copyright a book upon which one has expended labor in its preparation does not depend upon whether the materials which he has collected consist or not of matters which are publici juris, or whether such materials show literary skill *or originality,* either in thought or in language, or anything more than industrious collection. The man who goes through the streets of a town and puts down the names of each of the inhabitants, with their occupations and their street number, acquires material of which he is the author" (emphasis added).

The "sweat of the brow" doctrine had numerous flaws, the most glaring being that it extended copyright protection in a compilation beyond selection and arrangement—the compiler's original contributions—to the facts themselves. Under the doctrine, the only defense to infringement was independent creation. A subsequent compiler was "not entitled to take one word of information previously published," but rather had to "independently wor[k] out the matter for himself, so as to arrive at the same result from the same common sources of information." *Id.*, at 88–89 (internal quotation marks omitted). "Sweat of the brow" courts thereby eschewed the most fundamental axiom of copyright law—that no one may copyright facts or ideas. *See Miller v. Universal City Studios, Inc.*, 650 F.2d, at 1372 (criticizing "sweat of the brow" courts because "ensur[ing] that later writers obtain the facts independently ... is precisely the scope of protection given ... copyrighted matter, and the law is clear that facts are not entitled to such protection").

* * *

Without a doubt, the "sweat of the brow" doctrine flouted basic copyright principles. Throughout history, copyright law has "recognize[d] a greater need to disseminate factual works than works of fiction or fantasy." *Harper & Row*, 471 U.S., at 563. Accord, Gorman, Fact or Fancy: The Implications for Copyright, 29 J. Copyright Soc. 560, 563 (1982). But "sweat of the brow" courts took a contrary view; they handed out proprietary interests in facts and declared that authors are absolutely precluded from saving time and effort by relying upon the facts contained in prior works. In truth, "[i]t is just such wasted effort that the proscription against the copyright of ideas and facts ... [is] designed to prevent." *Rosemont Enterprises, Inc. v. Random House, Inc.*, 366 F.2d 303, 310 (C.A.2 1966). "Protection for the fruits of such research ... may in certain circumstances be available under a theory of unfair competition. But to accord copyright protection on this basis alone distorts basic copyright principles in that it creates a monopoly in public domain materials without the necessary justification of protecting and encouraging the creation of 'writings' by 'authors.' " Nimmer § 3.04, p. 3–23 (footnote omitted).

C

"Sweat of the brow" decisions did not escape the attention of the Copyright Office. When Congress decided to overhaul the copyright statute and asked the Copyright Office to study existing problems, * * * the Copyright Office promptly recommended that Congress clear up the confusion in the lower courts as to the basic standards of copyrightability. * * *

Congress took the Register's advice. In enacting the Copyright Act of 1976, Congress dropped the reference to "all the writings of an author" and replaced it with the phrase "original works of authorship." 17 U.S.C. § 102(a). In making explicit the originality requirement, Congress announced that it was merely clarifying existing law: "The two fundamental criteria of copyright protection [are] originality and fixation in tangible form.... The phrase 'original works of authorship,' which is purposely left undefined, is intended to incorporate without change *the standard of originality established by the courts under the present [1909] copyright statute.*" H.R.Rep. No. 94–1476, p. 51 (1976) (emphasis added) (hereinafter H.R.Rep.); S.Rep. No. 94–473, p. 50 (1975), U.S.Code Cong. & Admin.News 1976, pp. 5659, 5664 (emphasis added) (hereinafter S.Rep.). * * *

To ensure that the mistakes of the "sweat of the brow" courts would not be repeated, Congress took additional measures. * * *

First, to make clear that compilations were not copyrightable *per se,* Congress provided a definition of the term "compilation." Second, to make clear that the copyright in a compilation did not extend to the facts themselves, Congress enacted § 103.

The definition of "compilation" is found in § 101 of the 1976 Act. It defines a "compilation" in the copyright sense as "a work formed by the collection and assembling of preexisting materials or of data *that* are selected, coordinated, or arranged *in such a way that* the resulting work as a whole constitutes an original work of authorship" (emphasis added).

The purpose of the statutory definition is to emphasize that collections of facts are not copyrightable *per se.* It conveys this message through its tripartite structure, as emphasized above by the italics. The statute identifies three distinct elements and requires each to be met for a work to qualify as a copyrightable compilation: (1) the collection and assembly of pre-existing material, facts, or data; (2) the selection, coordination, or arrangement of those materials; and (3) the creation, by virtue of the particular selection, coordination, or arrangement, of an "original" work of authorship. * * *

* * *

The key to the statutory definition is the second requirement. It instructs courts that, in determining whether a fact-based work is an original work of authorship, they should focus on the manner in which the collected facts have been selected, coordinated, and arranged. This is a straightforward application of the originality requirement. Facts are never original, so the compilation author can claim originality, if at all, only in the way the facts are presented. To that end, the statute dictates that the principal focus should be on whether the selection, coordination, and arrangement are sufficiently original to merit protection.

Not every selection, coordination, or arrangement will pass muster. This is plain from the statute. It states that, to merit protection, the facts must be selected, coordinated, or arranged "in such a way" as to render the work as a whole original. This implies that some "ways" will trigger copyright, but that others will not. * * * Otherwise, the phrase "in such a way" is meaningless and Congress should have defined "compilation" simply as "a work formed by the collection and assembly of preexisting materials or data that are selected, coordinated, or arranged." * * *

As discussed earlier, however, the originality requirement is not particularly stringent. A compiler may settle upon a selection or arrangement that others have used; novelty is not required. Originality requires only that the author make the selection or arrangement independently (*i.e.,* without copying that selection or arrangement from another work), and that it display some minimal level of creativity. Presumably, the vast majority of compilations will pass this test, but not all will. There remains a narrow category of works in which the creative spark is utterly lacking or so trivial as to be virtually nonexistent. * * * Such works are incapable of sustaining a valid copyright. * * *

Even if a work qualifies as a copyrightable compilation, it receives only limited protection. This is the point of § 103 of the Act. Section 103 explains that "[t]he subject matter of copyright . . . includes compilations," § 103(a), but that copyright protects only the author's original contributions—not the facts or information conveyed:

"The copyright in a compilation . . . extends only to the material contributed by the author of such work, as distinguished from the preexisting material employed in the work, and does not imply any exclusive right in the preexisting material." § 103(b).

As § 103 makes clear, copyright is not a tool by which a compilation author may keep others from using the facts or data he or she has collected. "The most important point here is one that is commonly misunderstood today: copyright . . . has no effect one way or the other on the copyright or public domain status of the preexisting material." H.R.Rep., at 57; S.Rep., at 55, U.S.Code Cong. & Admin. News 1976, p. 5670. The 1909 Act did not require, as "sweat of the brow" courts mistakenly assumed, that each subsequent compiler must start from scratch and is precluded from relying on research undertaken by another. See, *e.g., Jeweler's Circular Publishing Co.,* 281 F., at 88–89. Rather, the facts contained in existing works may be freely copied because copyright protects only the elements that owe their origin to the compiler—the selection, coordination, and arrangement of facts.

In summary, the 1976 revisions to the Copyright Act leave no doubt that originality, not "sweat of the brow," is the touchstone of copyright protection in directories and other fact-based works. * * *

III

There is no doubt that Feist took from the white pages of Rural's directory a substantial amount of factual information. At a minimum, Feist copied the names, towns, and telephone numbers of 1,309 of Rural's subscribers. Not all copying, however, is copyright infringement. To establish infringement, two elements must be proven: (1) ownership of a valid copyright, and (2) copying of constituent elements of the work that are original. * * * The first element is not at issue here; Feist appears to concede that Rural's directory, considered as a whole, is subject to a valid copyright because it contains some foreword text, as well as original material in its yellow pages advertisements. * * *

The question is whether Rural has proved the second element. In other words, did Feist, by taking 1,309 names, towns, and telephone numbers from Rural's white pages, copy anything that was "original" to Rural? Certainly, the raw data does not satisfy the originality requirement. Rural may have been the first to discover and report the names, towns, and telephone numbers of its subscribers, but this data does not " 'ow[e] its origin' " to Rural. *Burrow–Giles,* 111 U.S., at 58. Rather, these bits of information are uncopyrightable facts; they existed before Rural reported them and would have continued to exist if Rural had never published a telephone directory. The originality requirement "rule[s] out protecting ... names, addresses, and telephone numbers of which the plaintiff by no stretch of the imagination could be called the author." Patterson & Joyce 776.

Rural essentially concedes the point by referring to the names, towns, and telephone numbers as "preexisting material." Brief for Respondent 17. Section 103(b) states explicitly that the copyright in a compilation does not extend to "the preexisting material employed in the work."

The question that remains is whether Rural selected, coordinated, or arranged these uncopyrightable facts in an original way. As mentioned, originality is not a stringent standard; it does not require that facts be presented in an innovative or surprising way. It is equally true, however, that the selection and arrangement of facts cannot be so mechanical or routine as to require no creativity whatsoever. The standard of originality is low, but it does exist. * * * As this Court has explained, the Constitution mandates some minimal degree of creativity, see *The Trade–Mark Cases,* 100 U.S., at 94; and an author who claims infringement must prove "the existence of ... intellectual production, of thought, and conception." *Burrow–Giles, supra,* 111 U.S., at 59–60.

The selection, coordination, and arrangement of Rural's white pages do not satisfy the minimum constitutional standards for copyright protection. As mentioned at the outset, Rural's white pages are entirely typical. Persons desiring telephone service in Rural's service area fill out an application and Rural issues them a telephone number. In preparing its white pages, Rural simply takes the data provided by its subscribers and lists it alphabetically by surname. The end product is a garden-variety white pages directory, devoid of even the slightest trace of creativity.

Rural's selection of listings could not be more obvious: It publishes the most basic information—name, town, and telephone number—about each person who applies to it for telephone service. This is "selection" of a sort, but it lacks the modicum of creativity necessary to transform mere selection into copyrightable expression. Rural expended sufficient effort to make the white pages directory useful, but insufficient creativity to make it original.

We note in passing that the selection featured in Rural's white pages may also fail the originality requirement for another reason. Feist points out that Rural did not truly "select" to publish the names and telephone numbers of its subscribers; rather, it was required to do so by the Kansas Corporation Commission as part of its monopoly franchise. * * * Accordingly, one could plausibly conclude that this selection was dictated by state law, not by Rural.

Nor can Rural claim originality in its coordination and arrangement of facts. The white pages do nothing more than list Rural's subscribers in alphabetical order. This arrangement may, technically speaking, owe its origin to Rural; no one disputes that Rural undertook the task of alphabetizing the names itself. But there is nothing remotely creative about arranging names alphabetically in a white pages directory. It is an age-old practice, firmly rooted in tradition and so commonplace that it has come to be expected as a matter of course. * * * It is not only unoriginal, it is practically inevitable. This time-honored tradition does not possess the minimal creative spark required by the Copyright Act and the Constitution.

We conclude that the names, towns, and telephone numbers copied by Feist were not original to Rural and therefore were not protected by the copyright in Rural's combined white and yellow pages directory. As a constitutional matter, copyright protects only those constituent elements of a work that possess more than a *de minimis* quantum of creativity. Rural's white pages, limited to basic subscriber information and arranged alphabetically, fall short of the mark. As a statutory matter, 17 U.S.C. § 101 does not afford protection from copying to a collection of facts that are selected, coordinated, and arranged in a way that utterly lacks originality. Given that some works must fail, we cannot imagine a more likely candidate. Indeed, were we to hold that Rural's white pages pass muster, it is hard to believe that any collection of facts could fail.

* * *

NOTES & QUESTIONS

1. *The protection of commercial databases after* Feist. In *Feist*, the Supreme Court held that a factual database or compilation satisfies the Copyright Act's originality requirement if "the author make[s] the selection or arrangement independently (*i.e.*, without copying that selection or arrangement from another work)" and if the selection and arrangement "display some minimal level of creativity." 499 U.S. at 358. The Court adds that "the vast majority of compilations will pass this test, but not all will." *Id.* at 359. In your opinion, will independently compiled electronic databases normally "pass the test," or will they fall into that "narrow category of works in which the creative spark is utterly lacking or so trivial as to be virtually nonexistent"? *Id.*

2. *Perverse incentives?* Imagine a website that provides access to a comprehensive database of all the hospitals in the United States. A user keys in her zip code, and the database returns a list of hospitals in her area, including each hospital's address and telephone number. How would the rule announced in *Feist* apply to such a national database of hospitals? *See Warren Pub., Inc. v. Microdos Data Corp.*, 115 F.3d 1509 (11th Cir.1997). Would it make a difference to your answer if the database of hospitals only listed those hospitals that had an acupuncture therapist on staff? *See Key Publications, Inc. v. Chinatown Today Publishing Enterprises, Inc.*, 945 F.2d 509 (2d Cir.1991). What if the database listed all the hospitals in the United States but indicated for each one whether it had an acupuncture therapist on staff?

3. *Impact on consumers.* Is the "originality" requirement for copyrightability of collections of facts pro-consumer, in that it fosters competition among businesses that use or offer facts by preventing businesses from exercising monopoly control over facts? Is it anti-consumer, in that it reduces the incentives of businesses to compile databases of value to consumers?

4. *Interface vs. database.* In *Feist*, the Supreme Court focused on a telephone "white pages" directory, in a hard-copy book format. In book form, information is presented to the reader in the same arrangement in which it is stored. In the case of an electronic database, however, there is no necessary correspondence between the arrangement of data on a hard drive and the arrangement of returned data on a user's computer monitor. Furthermore, the arrangement of data on a hard drive may change each time the database is saved anew. Under the rule announced in *Feist*, how does one gauge the originality in the arrangement of data in an electronic database?

5. *"Thin" copyright.* Even if an electronic database's selection and arrangement of facts is sufficiently original to qualify for copyright protection, the protection afforded is extremely limited. As the Court notes, "the copyright in a factual compilation is thin. Notwithstanding a valid copyright, a subsequent compiler remains free to use the facts contained in another's publication to aid in preparing a competing work, so long as the competing work does not feature the same selection and arrangement." *Feist*, 499 U.S. at 349. In light of the "thin" protection afforded to factual databases, what is the appropriate standard for determining copyright infringement? Compare *Kregos v. Associated Press*, 937 F.2d 700, 709–10 (2d Cir.1991) and *Harper House, Inc. v. Thomas Nelson, Inc.*, 889 F.2d 197, 205 (9th Cir.1989) with *Bellsouth Advertising & Publishing Corp. v. Donnelley Information Publishing, Inc.*, 999 F.2d 1436, 1445 (11th Cir. 1993) (en banc).

6. *Overruling* Feist. Can Congress overrule *Feist* by amending the Copyright Act to provide for protection of factual databases?

II. PROTECTION FOR DATABASES UNDER STATE LAW AND THE PROBLEM OF FEDERAL COPYRIGHT PREEMPTION

In *Feist*, the Supreme Court suggested that protection for uncopyrightable databases " 'may in certain circumstances be available under a theory of [state-law] unfair competition.' " 499 U.S. at 374–75 (quoting MELVILLE B. NIMMER & DAVID NIMMER, NIMMER ON COPYRIGHT § 3.04 (1990)). While the owner of a database or compilation of facts who seeks to exclude others from using those facts might seek relief under state law, the circumstances under which a state law cause of action might offer a remedy are significantly limited by federal copyright preemption of state law.

There are two forms of preemption associated with copyright law: first, the general preemption under the supremacy clause of the Constitution afforded in favor of federal law; second, preemption deriving from a specific provision in the Copyright Act, Section 301. Constitutional preemption invalidates a state law that "stands as an obstacle to the accomplishment and execution of the full purposes and objectives of Congress." *Hines v. Davidowitz*, 312 U.S. 52, 67 (1941).

Section 301(a) of the Copyright Act preempts

> all legal or equitable rights that are equivalent to any of the exclusive rights within the general scope of copyright as specified by section 106 in works of authorship that are fixed in a tangible medium of expression and come within the subject matter of copyright as specified by sections 102 and 103.

17 U.S.C. § 301(a). Under this provision, a state cause of action is preempted, and thereby rendered invalid, if two conditions are met. First, the material that the state law purports to protect must be "within the subject matter of copyright." That is, it must be a literary work, musical work, compilation, or one of the other types of works that are capable of receiving copyright protection, as set forth in Sections 102 and 103 of the Copyright Act. A database, as long as it is "fixed in a tangible medium of expression," will meet this subject-matter requirement, even if (like the telephone white pages at issue in *Feist v. Rural Telephone Service Co.*) it lacks the requisite originality to be copyrightable.

Second, the rights that the state law protects must be "equivalent to" any of the exclusive rights granted by Section 106 of the Copyright Act, namely the rights of reproduction, adaptation, distribution, public performance, and public display. It is often unclear whether a state law satisfies this criterion. As explained in *Computer Associates International v. Altai, Inc.*, 982 F.2d 693, 716–17 (2d Cir.1992), Section 301

> preempts only those state-law rights that "may be abridged by an act which, in and of itself, would infringe one of the exclusive rights" provided by federal copyright law. *See Harper & Row Publishers, Inc. v. Nation Enters.*, 723 F.2d 195, 200 (2d Cir.1983), *rev'd on other grounds,* 471 U.S. 539 (1985). If an "extra element" is "required instead of or in addition to the acts of reproduction, performance, distribution or display, in order to constitute a state-created cause of action, then the right does not lie 'within the general scope of copyright,' and there is no preemption." 1 Nimmer [on Copyright] § 1.01[B], at 1–14–15; *see also Harper & Row, Publishers, Inc.*, 723 F.2d at 200 (where state law right "is predicated upon an act incorporating elements beyond mere reproduction or the like, the [federal and state] rights are not equivalent" and there is no preemption).
>
> A state law claim is not preempted if the "extra element" changes the "nature of the action so that it is *qualitatively* different from a copyright infringement claim." *Mayer v. Josiah Wedgwood & Sons, Ltd.*, 601 F.Supp. 1523, 1535 (S.D.N.Y.1985). To determine whether a claim meets this standard, we must determine "what plaintiff seeks to protect, the theories in which the matter is thought to be protected and the rights sought to be

enforced." 1 Roger M. Milgrim, *Milgrim on Trade Secrets* § 2.06A[3], at 2–150 (1992) * * *. An action will not be saved from preemption by elements such as awareness or intent, which alter "the action's scope but not its nature...." *Mayer,* 601 F.Supp. at 1535.

Following this "extra element" test, we have held that unfair competition and misappropriation claims grounded solely in the copying of a plaintiff's protected expression are preempted by section 301. * * * We also have held to be preempted a tortious interference with contract claim grounded in the impairment of a plaintiff's right under the Copyright Act to publish derivative works. * * *

However, many state law rights that can arise in connection with instances of copyright infringement satisfy the extra element test, and thus are not preempted by section 301. These include unfair competition claims based upon breaches of confidential relationships, breaches of fiduciary duties and trade secrets.

Several types of state laws might offer database owners the protection against unauthorized use that the Copyright Act fails to provide. Among the likely candidates are state laws against misappropriation of intangible property, laws protecting trade secrets, and laws enforcing contractual restraints on the use of a database. Most recently, the common law action of trespass to chattels and computer fraud statutes have been applied to protect databases used in e-commerce.

Misappropriation. The state-law tort of misappropriation is a branch of unfair competition law, which seeks to promote the competitive process by imposing liability for forms of competition that undermine it. The competitive markets can be undermined in many ways. A company may engage in deceptive practices in order to deprive consumers of the information they need to make informed and rational choices in the marketplace, thereby undermining its efficient operation. A company may infringe the trademark of another business in order to create customer confusion over the origin of one's goods, thereby appropriating the other company's good will. A company may appropriate information from another company, thereby gaining an unfair competitive advantage. The tort of misappropriation is intended to combat this last type of harm.

A state law against misappropriation may survive preemption if it is drawn sufficiently narrowly. In *International News Service v. Associated Press,* 248 U.S. 215 (1918), the Supreme Court recognized a federal common law cause of action for misappropriation of "hot news." The hot news in question consisted of uncopyrighted news items, which were written and disseminated by a news-gathering organization, and were copied and disseminated by a competing news-gathering organization. No issue of preemption was presented in that case. But in *National Basketball Association v. Motorola, Inc.,* 105 F.3d 841 (2d Cir.1997), the court addressed the question whether Section 301 preempts a state-law cause of action for misappropriation of hot news. The NBA sought to prevent defendants from operating a service that delivered scores and other data about professional basketball games in progress to handheld pagers carried by subscribers. Defendants acquired the information from television and radio broadcasts of the games, transmitting it to subscribers with a time lag of two to three minutes. The court held that New York's misappropriation law, which protects property rights from "any form of commercial immorality," was preempted. It explained that a state misappropriation law that seeks to protect "hot news" survives preemption only if it satisfies the following conditions:

> (i) a plaintiff generates or gathers information at a cost; (ii) the information is time-sensitive; (iii) a defendant's use of the information constitutes free-riding on the plaintiff's efforts; (iv) the defendant is in direct competition with a product or service offered by the plaintiffs; and (v) the ability of other parties to free-ride on the efforts of the plaintiff or others would so reduce the incentive to produce the product or service that its existence or quality would be substantially threatened.

105 F.3d at 845. Misappropriation laws that meet these conditions, and therefore survive preemption, will offer a rather limited range of protection to database owners.

Trade Secrets. Trade secret laws are likely to survive preemption. These laws make unauthorized disclosure of trade secrets actionable if the information holder makes a reasonable effort to keep the information secret, and the defendant either acquires it by improper means or breaches a duty of confidentiality. These requirements constitute an "extra element" in the state cause of action, beyond those which are sufficient to constitute an infringement of a copyright owner's exclusive rights. *See Architectronics, Inc. v. Control Systems, Inc.*, 935 F.Supp. 425, 441 (S.D.N.Y.1996). Consequently, such a law does not meet Section 301's "equivalent rights" criterion, and it is not preempted. Like non-preempted misappropriation laws, trade secret laws will protect only a narrow category of databases, excluding, for example, all those to which subscribers are provided access.

Breach of Contract. Another state law cause of action that has been used to protect interests in databases and other compilations of fact is breach of contract. Most providers of compilations of information in digital form, whether through online access or on a tangible medium such as a CD–ROM, require a prospective user to agree to various terms and conditions of use before providing access. Online, the terms and conditions may be presented to the user in a scrollable window, with the user manifesting assent by clicking an on-screen button labeled "I accept"; or they may be presented on an interior page of the website, indicated only by a link labeled "Terms" at the bottom of the home page. If the information product is supplied on CD–ROM, the terms and conditions might be presented on the user's computer screen the first time the product is run, or might be on a sheet of paper enclosed within the CD–ROM's packaging.

These clickwrap or shrinkwrap agreements, provided they are enforceable, could give information providers and database owners a significant level of control over their information assets. To the extent that such sets of terms are standardized and widespread within a market, the terms form a substitute for the background intellectual property rights that would prevail without them. The question arises, therefore, whether such terms are preempted by federal copyright law.

State laws enforcing contractual restraints on the use of information contained in a database can be expected generally to survive preemption. In *ProCD, Inc. v. Zeidenberg*, 86 F.3d 1447, 1454 (7th Cir.1996), the court held that a shrinkwrap license limiting the purchaser's use of telephone directory information contained on a CD–ROM was enforceable under state contract law. The court reasoned:

> Rights "equivalent to any of the exclusive rights within the general scope of copyright" are rights established *by law*—rights that restrict the options of persons who are strangers to the author. Copyright law forbids duplication, public performance, and so on, unless the person wishing to copy or perform the work gets permission; silence means a ban on copying. A copyright is a right against the world. Contracts, by contrast, generally affect only their parties; strangers may do as they please, so contracts do not create "exclusive rights."

The reasoning and result in *ProCD v. Zeidenberg* have drawn a good deal of criticism.

A few courts and commentators have taken the position that federal preemption simply shouldn't apply to contract terms—or at least that it shouldn't apply in the same way—because contracts are different than state statutes. * * * Judge Easterbrook's decision in *ProCD v. Zeidenberg* seems to accept this view, and some courts have taken this logic so far as to conclude that contracts simply can't be preempted by copyright law.

There are a number of problems with the "contracts are different" idea. First, the reference to "equivalence" seems to direct the analysis only at copyright field preemption under section 301, and thus to ignore both copyright conflicts preemption and any form of patent preemption. Even if contract and copyright are not equivalent, it simply does not follow that federal law places no limits on the enforceability of contracts. Courts that take this position should also be troubled by the significant number of cases that do apply intellectual property rules to preempt contracts.

Second, the viability of the distinction between private contracts and public legislation is diminishing day by day. One of the main changes Article 2B[2] would make in current law would be to render enforceable contract "terms" to which the parties did not

---

2. [Article 2B, a proposed addition to the Uniform Commercial Code, was ultimately promulgated by the National Conference of Commissioners on Uniform State Laws as a freestanding model state law, called the Uniform Computer Information Transactions Act.—Eds.]

agree in the classic sense, and indeed of which one party may be entirely unaware. * * * In other words, Article 2B promises to usher in an era of "private legislation," in which parties who are in a position to write contracts can jointly impose uniform terms that no one can escape. * * *

* * *

Third, even truly "private" contracts affect third parties who haven't agreed to the contract terms.

Mark A. Lemley, *Beyond Preemption: The Law and Policy of Intellectual Property Licensing*, 87 CALIF. L. REV. 111, 147–49 (1999). See also David Nimmer, Elliot Brown & Gary N. Frischling, *The Metamorphosis of Contract into Expand*, 87 CALIF. L. REV. 17, 48 (1999) ("[W]hen a breach of contract cause of action—particularly one that does not result from the bargained-for agreement of both parties to its putative execution—is used as a subterfuge to control nothing other than the reproduction, adaptation, public distribution, etc., of works within the subject matter of copyright, then it too should be deemed preempted.").

For a discussion of the availability of state misappropriation and contract claims to protect databases, see Jane C. Ginsburg, *Copyright, Common Law, and Sui Generis Protection of Databases in the United States and Abroad*, 66 U. CIN. L. REV. 151 (1997).

Trespass to Chattels. Databases and compilations of fact, although themselves intangible, must reside on some tangible medium. In the case of online databases, the tangible medium is the computer system on which the database is stored, and which makes access to it possible. A computer system is tangible personal property. In part because of the limited protection factual databases receive under the law of copyright, database owners have attempted to combat unauthorized access to their online databases by bringing lawsuits predicated upon state law causes of action designed to protect against unwanted interferences with personal property. The theory is that if one can bar unauthorized access to the computer system on which one's database resides, one can bar access to the database.

In several cases, database owners have successfully invoked the common law action of trespass to chattels to prevent unauthorized access to their information. *See eBay, Inc. v. Bidder's Edge, Inc.*, 100 F.Supp.2d 1058 (N.D.Cal.2000) (entering preliminary injunction against operator of website that accessed online auction sites and aggregated information collected from them); *Register.com, Inc. v. Verio, Inc.*, 126 F.Supp.2d 238 (S.D.N.Y. 2000) (entering preliminary injunction against company that collected domain-registration information from database maintained by registrar). (These cases are excerpted and discussed in Part III, *infra*.)

Under the *Restatement* version of the trespass to chattels cause of action, "[a] trespass to a chattel may be committed by intentionally (a) dispossessing another of the chattel, or (b) using or intermeddling with a chattel in the possession of another." RESTATEMENT (SECOND) OF TORTS § 217 (1965). Based on the "extra element" criterion, at least one court has held that trespass to chattels survives preemption under Section 301. *See eBay v. Bidder's Edge, supra,* at 1072 ("The right to exclude others from using physical personal property is not equivalent to any rights protected by copyright and therefore constitutes an extra element that makes trespass qualitatively different from a copyright infringement claim.").

Computer Fraud. The federal Computer Fraud and Abuse Act, 18 U.S.C. § 1030, prohibits a range of conduct that is often referred to under the rubric of "hacking." Database owners, characterizing unauthorized access to their information as a form of hacking, have invoked several provisions of the Act to bar such access. The Act makes it illegal to "intentionally access[]" a computer "without authorization," if the access results in at least $5,000 of damage. 18 U.S.C. § 1030(a)(5)(A)(iii). It also provides an action against one who "knowingly and with intent to defraud, accesses a * * * computer without authorization, or exceeds authorized access, and by means of such conduct furthers the intended fraud and obtains anything of value," again if the result is damages of at least $5,000. 18 U.S.C. § 1030(a)(4). Courts have applied these provisions in cases involving unauthorized access to data. *See Register.com, Inc. v. Verio, Inc., supra; EF Cultural Travel BV v. Explorica, Inc.,* 274 F.3d 577 (1st Cir. 2001) (affirming entry of preliminary injunction against company that acquired price data from a competitor's website and used it to undercut the competitors prices). (These cases are excerpted and discussed in Part III, *infra.*)

Since this cause of action clearly requires elements beyond those required for copyright infringement, it is likely to survive preemption when applied to protect databases.

NOTES & QUESTIONS

1. *Preemption and copyright management systems.* A copyright management system is a technological means of enforcing the terms and conditions of a license automatically, making recourse to the courts unnecessary. Would the widespread use of copyright management systems make the preemption doctrine irrelevant? (Copyright management systems are discussed in Chapter 5, *infra.*)

2. *Future of state-law causes of action.* As we will see in the next Part, database owners have sought legislation that would grant them control over use by others of the information in their databases. Given the availability of the various state-law causes of action described above, is such legislation necessary? If such legislation is enacted, will the state-law causes of action become superfluous?

III. ACQUIRING DATA FROM ANOTHER'S WEBSITE

eBay, Inc. v. Bidder's Edge, Inc.

100 F.Supp.2d 1058 (N.D.Cal.2000).

■ WHYTE, DISTRICT JUDGE.

ORDER GRANTING PRELIMINARY INJUNCTION

Plaintiff eBay, Inc.'s ("eBay") motion for preliminary injunction was heard by the court on April 14, 2000. * * * For the reasons set forth below, the court preliminarily enjoins defendant Bidder's Edge, Inc. ("BE") from accessing eBay's computer systems by use of any automated querying program without eBay's written authorization.

I. BACKGROUND

eBay is an Internet-based, person-to-person trading site. (Jordan Decl. ¶ 3.) eBay offers sellers the ability to list items for sale and prospective buyers the ability to search those listings and bid on items. (Id.) The seller can set the terms and conditions of the auction. (Id.) The item is sold to the highest bidder. (Id.) The transaction is consummated directly between the buyer and seller without eBay's involvement. (Id.) A potential purchaser looking for a particular item can access the eBay site and perform a key word search for relevant auctions and bidding status. (Id.) eBay has also created category listings which identify items in over 2500 categories, such as antiques, computers, and dolls. (Id.) Users may browse these category listing pages to identify items of interest. (Id.)

Users of the eBay site must register and agree to the eBay User Agreement. (Id. ¶ 4.) Users agree to the seven page User Agreement by clicking on an "I Accept" button located at the end of the User Agreement. (Id. Ex. D.) The current version of the User Agreement prohibits the use of "any robot, spider, other automatic device, or manual process to monitor or copy our web pages or the content contained herein without our prior expressed written permission." (Id.) It is not clear that the version of the User Agreement in effect at the time BE began searching the eBay site prohibited such activity, or that BE ever agreed to comply with the User Agreement.

eBay currently has over 7 million registered users. (Jordan Decl. ¶ 4.) Over 400,000 new items are added to the site every day. (Id.) Every minute, 600 bids are placed on almost 3 million items. (Id.) Users currently perform, on average, 10 million searches per day on eBay's database. Bidding for and sales of items are continuously ongoing in millions of separate auctions. (Id.)

A software robot is a computer program which operates across the Internet to perform searching, copying and retrieving functions on the web sites of others.[2] (Maynor Decl. ¶ 3; Johnson–Laird Decl. P 15.) A software robot is capable of executing thousands of instructions per minute, far in excess of what a human can accomplish. (Maynor Decl. ¶ 3) Robots consume the processing and storage resources of a system, making that portion of the system's capacity unavailable to the system owner or other users. (Id.) Consumption of sufficient system resources will slow the processing of

---

2. Programs that recursively query other computers over the Internet in order to obtain a significant amount of information are referred to in the pleadings by various names, including software robots, robots, spiders and web crawlers.

the overall system and can overload the system such that it will malfunction or "crash." (Id.) A severe malfunction can cause a loss of data and an interruption in services. (Id.)

The eBay site employs "robot exclusion headers." (Id. ¶ 5.) A robot exclusion header is a message, sent to computers programmed to detect and respond to such headers, that eBay does not permit unauthorized robotic activity. (Id.) Programmers who wish to comply with the Robot Exclusion Standard design their robots to read a particular data file, "robots.txt," and to comply with the control directives it contains. (Johnson–Laird Decl. ¶ 20.)

To enable computers to communicate with each other over the Internet, each is assigned a unique Internet Protocol ("IP") address. (Maynor Decl. ¶ 6.) When a computer requests information from another computer over the Internet, the requesting computer must offer its IP address to the responding computer in order to allow a response to be sent. (Id.) These IP addresses allow the identification of the source of incoming requests. (Id.) eBay identifies robotic activity on its site by monitoring the number of incoming requests from each particular IP address. (Id. ¶ 7.) Once eBay identifies an IP address believed to be involved in robotic activity, an investigation into the identity, origin and owner of the IP address may be made in order to determine if the activity is legitimate or authorized. (Id. ¶ 8.) If an investigation reveals unauthorized robotic activity, eBay may attempt to ignore ("block") any further requests from that IP address. (Id.) Attempts to block requests from particular IP addresses are not always successful. (Id. ¶ 9; Johnson–Laird Decl. ¶ 27.)

Organizations often install "proxy server" software on their computers. (Johnson–Laird Decl. ¶ 12.) Proxy server software acts as a focal point for outgoing Internet requests. (Id.) Proxy servers conserve system resources by directing all outgoing and incoming data traffic through a centralized portal. (Id.) Typically, organizations limit the use of their proxy servers to local users. (Id.) However, some organizations, either as a public service or because of a failure to properly protect their proxy server through the use of a "firewall," allow their proxy servers to be accessed by remote users. (Id. ¶ 13.) Outgoing requests from remote users can be routed through such unprotected proxy servers and appear to originate from the proxy server. (Id.) Incoming responses are then received by the proxy server and routed to the remote user. (Id.) Information requests sent through such proxy servers cannot easily be traced back to the originating IP address and can be used to circumvent attempts to block queries from the originating IP address. (Id. ¶ 14.) Blocking queries from innocent third party proxy servers is both inefficient, because it creates an endless game of hide-and-seek, and potentially counterproductive, as it runs a substantial risk of blocking requests from legitimate, desirable users who use that proxy server. (Id. ¶ 22.)

BE is a company with 22 employees that was founded in 1997. (Carney Decl. ¶ 2.) The BE website debuted in November 1998. (Id. ¶ 3.) BE does not host auctions. (Id. ¶ 2.) BE is an auction aggregation site designed to offer on-line auction buyers the ability to search for items across numerous on-line auctions without having to search each host site individually. (Id.) As of March 2000, the BE website contained information on more that five million items being auctioned on more than one hundred auction sites. (Id. ¶ 3.) BE also provides its users with additional auction-related services and information. (Id. ¶ 2.) The information available on the BE site is contained in a database of information that BE compiles through access to various auction sites such as eBay. (Id. ¶ 4.) When a user enters a search for a particular item at BE, BE searches its database and generates a list of every item in the database responsive to the search, organized by auction closing date and time. (Id. ¶ 5.) Rather than going to each host auction site one at a time, a user who goes to BE may conduct a single search to obtain information about that item on every auction site tracked by BE. (Id. ¶ 6.) It is important to include information regarding eBay auctions on the BE site because eBay is by far the biggest consumer to consumer on-line auction site. (Id.)

* * *

In early 1998, eBay gave BE permission to include information regarding eBay-hosted auctions for Beanie Babies and Furbies in the BE database. (Id. ¶ 7.) In early 1999, BE added to the number of person-to-person auction sites it covered and started covering a broader range of items hosted by those sites, including eBay. (Id. ¶ 8.) On April 24, 1999, eBay verbally approved BE crawling the eBay website for a period of 90 days. (Id.) The parties contemplated that during this period they would reach a formal licensing agreement. (Id.) They were unable to do so.

It appears that the primary dispute was over the method BE uses to search the eBay database. eBay wanted BE to conduct a search of the eBay system only when the BE system was queried by a BE user. (Ploen Decl. Ex. 9.) This reduces the load on the eBay system and increases the accuracy of the BE data. (Id.) BE wanted to recursively crawl the eBay system to compile its own auction database. (Carney Decl. ¶ 18.) This increases the speed of BE searches and allows BE to track the auctions generally and automatically update its users when activity occurs in particular auctions, categories of auctions, or when new items are added. (Id.)

In late August or early September 1999, eBay requested by telephone that BE cease posting eBay auction listings on its site. (Id. ¶ 9; Rock Decl. ¶ 5.) BE agreed to do so. (Rock Decl. ¶ 5.) In October 1999, BE learned that other auction aggregations sites were including information regarding eBay auctions. (Carney Decl. ¶ 12.) On November 2, 1999, BE issued a press release indicating that it had resumed including eBay auction listings on its site. (Rock Decl. Ex. H.) On November 9, 1999, eBay sent BE a letter reasserting that BE's activities were unauthorized, insisting that BE cease accessing the eBay site, alleging that BE's activities constituted a civil trespass and offering to license BE's activities. (Id. Ex. I.) eBay and BE were again unable to agree on licensing terms. As a result, eBay attempted to block BE from accessing the eBay site; by the end of November, 1999, eBay had blocked a total of 169 IP addresses it believed BE was using to query eBay's system. (Maynor Decl. ¶ 12.) BE elected to continue crawling eBay's site by using proxy servers to evade eBay's IP blocks. (Mundy Depo. at 271:18–19 ("We eventually adopted the rotating proxy servers."))

Approximately 69% of the auction items contained in the BE database are from auctions hosted on eBay. (Carney Decl. ¶ 17.) BE estimates that it would lose one-third of its users if it ceased to cover the eBay auctions. (Id.)

The parties agree that BE accessed the eBay site approximate[ly] 100,000 times a day. (Felton Decl. ¶ 33.) eBay alleges that BE activity constituted up to 1.53% of the number of requests received by eBay, and up to 1.10% of the total data transferred by eBay during certain periods in October and November of 1999. (Johnson–Laird Decl. ¶ 64.) BE alleges that BE activity constituted no more than 1.11% of the requests received by eBay, and no more than 0.70% of the data transferred by eBay. (Felton Decl. ¶ 60.) eBay alleges that BE activity had fallen 27%, to 0.74% of requests and 0.61% of data, by February 20, 2000. (Johnson–Laird Decl. ¶¶ 70–71.) eBay alleges damages due to BE's activity totaling between $45,323 and $61,804 for a ten month period including seven months in 1999 and the first three months in 2000. (Meyer Decl. ¶ 28.) However, these calculations appear flawed in that they assume the maximal BE usage of eBay resources continued over all ten months. (Id.) Moreover, the calculations attribute a pro rata share of eBay expenditures to BE activity, rather than attempting to calculate the incremental cost to eBay due to BE activity. (Id.) eBay has not alleged any specific incremental damages due to BE activity. (See Rock Depo., 192:8–10.)

It appears that major Internet search engines, such as Yahoo!, Google, Excite and AltaVista, respect the Robot Exclusion Standard. (Johnson–Laird Decl. ¶¶ 81–85.)

eBay now moves for preliminary injunctive relief preventing BE from accessing the eBay computer system based on nine causes of action: trespass, false advertising, federal and state trademark dilution, computer fraud and abuse, unfair competition, misappropriation, interference with prospective economic advantage and unjust enrichment. However, eBay does not move, either independently or alternatively, for injunctive relief that is limited to restricting how BE can use data taken from the eBay site.

II. LEGAL STANDARD

To obtain preliminary injunctive relief, a movant must demonstrate "either a likelihood of success on the merits and the possibility of irreparable injury, or that serious questions going to the merits were raised and the balance of hardships tips sharply in its favor." * * * "The critical element in determining the test to be applied is the relative hardship to the parties. If the balance of harm tips decidedly toward the plaintiff, then the plaintiff need not show as robust a likelihood of success on the merits as when the balance tips less decidedly." * * *

III. ANALYSIS

A. Balance of Harm

* * *

According to eBay, the load on its servers resulting from BE's web crawlers represents between 1.11% and 1.53% of the total load on eBay's listing servers. eBay alleges both economic loss from BE's current activities and potential harm resulting from the total crawling of BE and others. In alleging economic harm, eBay's argument is that eBay has expended considerable time, effort and money to create its computer system, and that BE should have to pay for the portion of eBay's system BE uses. eBay attributes a pro rata portion of the costs of maintaining its entire system to the BE activity. However, eBay does not indicate that these expenses are incrementally incurred because of BE's activities, nor that any particular service disruption can be attributed to BE's activities. eBay provides no support for the proposition that the pro rata costs of obtaining an item represent the appropriate measure of damages for unauthorized use. In contrast, California law appears settled that the appropriate measure of damages is the actual harm inflicted by the conduct:

> Where the conduct complained of does not amount to a substantial interference with possession or the right thereto, but consists of intermeddling with or use of or damages to the personal property, the owner has a cause of action for trespass or case, and may recover only the actual damages suffered by reason of the impairment of the property or the loss of its use.

Zaslow v. Kroenert, 29 Cal. 2d 541, 551, 176 P.2d 1 (1946). Moreover, even if BE is inflicting incremental maintenance costs on eBay, potentially calculable monetary damages are not generally a proper foundation for a preliminary injunction. * * *

eBay's allegations of harm are based, in part, on the argument that BE's activities should be thought of as equivalent to sending in an army of 100,000 robots a day to check the prices in a competitor's store. This analogy, while graphic, appears inappropriate. Although an admittedly formalistic distinction, unauthorized robot intruders into a "brick and mortar" store would be committing a trespass to real property. There does not appear to be any doubt that the appropriate remedy for an ongoing trespass to business premises would be a preliminary injunction. *See e.g.,* *State v. Carriker*, 5 Ohio App. 2d 255, 214 N.E.2d 809, 811–12 (Ohio App. 1964) (interpreting Ohio criminal trespass law to cover a business invitee who, with no intention of making a purchase, uses the business premises of another for his own gain after his invitation has been revoked); *General Petroleum Corp. v. Beilby*, 213 Cal. 601, 605, 2 P.2d 797 (1931). More importantly, for the analogy to be accurate, the robots would have to make up less than two out of every one-hundred customers in the store, the robots would not interfere with the customers' shopping experience, nor would the robots even be seen by the customers. Under such circumstances, there is a legitimate claim that the robots would not pose any threat of irreparable harm. However, eBay's right to injunctive relief is also based upon a much stronger argument.

If BE's activity is allowed to continue unchecked, it would encourage other auction aggregators to engage in similar recursive searching of the eBay system such that eBay would suffer irreparable harm from reduced system performance, system unavailability, or data losses. (See Spafford Decl. ¶ 32; Parker Decl. ¶ 19; Johnson–Laird Decl. ¶ 85.[14]) BE does not appear to seriously contest that reduced system performance, system unavailability or data loss would inflict irreparable harm on eBay consisting of lost profits and lost customer goodwill. Harm resulting from lost profits and lost customer goodwill is irreparable because it is neither easily calculable, nor easily compensable and is therefore an appropriate basis for injunctive relief. *See, e.g., People of State of California ex rel. Van De Kamp v. Tahoe Reg'l Planning Agency,* 766 F.2d 1316, 1319 (9th Cir.1985). Where, as here, the denial of preliminary injunctive relief would encourage an increase in the complained of activity, and such an increase would present a strong likelihood of irreparable harm, the plaintiff has at least established a possibility of irreparable harm.

* * *

BE correctly observes that there is a dearth of authority supporting a preliminary injunction based on an ongoing to trespass to chattels. In contrast, it is black letter law in California that an injunction is an appropriate remedy for a continuing trespass to real property. *See Allred v. Harris,* 14 Cal. App. 4th 1386, 1390 (1993) (citing 5 B.E. Witkin, Summary of California Law, Torts § 605 (9th ed. 1988)). If eBay were a brick and mortar auction house with limited seating capacity, eBay would appear to be entitled to reserve those seats for potential bidders, to refuse entrance to individuals (or robots) with no intention of bidding on any of the items, and to seek preliminary injunctive relief against non-customer trespassers eBay was physically unable to exclude. The analytic difficulty is that a wrongdoer can commit an ongoing trespass of a computer system that is more akin to the traditional notion of a trespass to real property, than the traditional notion of a trespass to chattels, because even though it is ongoing, it will probably never amount to a conversion. The court concludes that under the circumstances present here, BE's ongoing violation of eBay's fundamental property right to exclude others from its computer system potentially causes sufficient irreparable harm to support a preliminary injunction.

BE argues that even if eBay is entitled to a presumption of irreparable harm, the presumption may be rebutted. The presumption may be rebutted by evidence that a party has engaged in a pattern of granting licenses to engage in the complained of activity such that it may be reasonable to expect that invasion of the right can be recompensed with a royalty rather than with an injunction, or by evidence that a party has unduly delayed in bringing suit, thereby negating the idea of irreparability. *See Polymer Technologies, Inc. v. Bridwell,* 103 F.3d 970, 974 (Fed.Cir.1996) (discussing presumption of irreparable harm in patent infringement context). BE

---

14. "Given that Bidder's Edge can be seen to have imposed a load of 1.53% on eBay's listing servers, simple arithmetic and economies reveal how only a few more such companies deploying rude robots [that do not respect the Robot Exclusion Standard] would be required before eBay would be brought to its knees by what would be then a debilitating load."

alleges that eBay has both engaged in a pattern of licensing aggregators to crawl its site as well as delayed in seeking relief. For the reasons set forth below, the court finds that neither eBay's limited licensing activities nor its delay in seeking injunctive relief while it attempted to resolve the matter without judicial intervention are sufficient to rebut the possibility of irreparable harm.

If eBay's irreparable harm claim were premised solely on the potential harm caused by BE's current crawling activities, evidence that eBay had licensed others to crawl the eBay site would suggest that BE's activity would not result in irreparable harm to eBay. However, the gravamen of the alleged irreparable harm is that if eBay is allowed to continue to crawl the eBay site, it may encourage frequent and unregulated crawling to the point that eBay's system will be irreparably harmed. There is no evidence that eBay has indiscriminately licensed all comers. Rather, it appears that eBay has carefully chosen to permit crawling by a limited number of aggregation sites that agree to abide by the terms of eBay's licensing agreement. "The existence of such a [limited] license, unlike a general license offered to all comers, does not demonstrate a decision to relinquish all control over the distribution of the product in exchange for a readily computable fee." *Ty, Inc. v. GMA Accessories, Inc.,* 132 F.3d 1167, 1173 (7th Cir.1997) (discussing presumption of irreparable harm in copyright infringement context). eBay's licensing activities appear directed toward limiting the amount and nature of crawling activity on the eBay site. Such licensing does not support the inference that carte blanche crawling of the eBay site would pose no threat of irreparable harm.

eBay first learned of BE in late 1997 or early 1998 when BE sought to retain the same public relations firm used by eBay. (See Ploen Decl. Ex. 1.) This motion was filed on January 18, 2000. An unexplained delay of two years would certainly raise serious doubts as the irreparability of any alleged harm. See *Playboy Enters., Inc. v. Netscape Communications Corp.,* 55 F.Supp.2d 1070, 1090 (C.D.Cal.1999) (noting that delay of as little as 60 days to three months has been held sufficient to rebut the presumption of irreparable harm). Here, the circumstances establish that any delay resulted from eBay's good faith efforts to resolve this dispute without judicial intervention and do not rebut a finding of the possibility of irreparable harm.

* * *

BE argues that even if eBay will be irreparably harmed if a preliminary injunction is not granted, BE will suffer greater irreparable harm if an injunction is granted. According to BE, lack of access to eBay's database will result in a two-thirds decrease in the items listed on BE, and a one-eighth reduction in the value of BE, from $80 million to $70 million. (Sweeny Decl. PP 42, 43.) Although the potential harm to BE does not appear insignificant, BE does not appear to have suffered any irreparable harm during the period it voluntarily ceased crawling the eBay site. Barring BE from automatically querying eBay's site does not prevent BE from maintaining an aggregation site including information from eBay's site. Any potential economic harm is appropriately addressed through the posting of an adequate bond.

* * * Accordingly, the court concludes that eBay has demonstrated at least a possibility of suffering irreparable system harm and that BE has not established a balance of hardships weighing in its favor.

B.   Likelihood of Success

As noted above, eBay moves for a preliminary injunction on all nine of its causes of action. * * * Since the court finds eBay is entitled to the relief requested based on its trespass claim, the court does not address the merits of the remaining claims or BE's arguments that many of these other state law causes of action are preempted by federal copyright law. The court first addresses the merits of the trespass claim, then BE's arguments regarding copyright preemption of the trespass claim, and finally the public interest.

1.   Trespass

* * *

In order to prevail on a claim for trespass based on accessing a computer system, the plaintiff must establish: (1) defendant intentionally and without authorization interfered with plaintiff's possessory interest in the computer system; and (2) defendant's unauthorized use proximately resulted in damage to plaintiff. * * * Here, eBay has presented evidence sufficient to establish a strong likelihood of proving both prongs and ultimately prevailing on the merits of its trespass claim.

a.   BE's Unauthorized Interference

eBay argues that BE's use was unauthorized and intentional. eBay is correct. BE does not dispute that it employed an automated computer program to connect with and search eBay's electronic database. BE admits that, because other auction aggregators were including eBay's auctions in their listing, it continued to "crawl" eBay's website even after eBay demanded BE terminate such activity.

BE argues that it cannot trespass eBay's website because the site is publicly accessible. BE's argument is unconvincing. eBay's servers are private property, conditional access to which eBay grants the public. eBay does not generally permit the type of automated access made by BE. In fact, eBay explicitly notifies automated visitors that their access is not permitted. "In general, California does recognize a trespass claim where the defendant exceeds the scope of the consent." *Baugh v. CBS, Inc.*, 828 F.Supp. 745, 756 (N.D.Cal.1993).

Even if BE's web crawlers were authorized to make individual queries of eBay's system, BE's web crawlers exceeded the scope of any such consent when they began acting like robots by making repeated queries. * * * Moreover, eBay repeatedly and explicitly notified BE that its use of eBay's computer system was unauthorized. The entire reason BE directed its queries through proxy servers was to evade eBay's attempts to stop this unauthorized access. The court concludes that BE's activity is sufficiently outside of the scope of the use permitted by eBay that it is unauthorized for the purposes of establishing a trespass. * * *

eBay argues that BE interfered with eBay's possessory interest in its computer system. Although eBay appears unlikely to be able to show a substantial interference at this time, such a showing is not required. Conduct that does not amount to a substantial interference with possession, but which consists of intermeddling with or use of another's personal property, is sufficient to establish a cause of action for trespass to chattel. *See Thrifty-Tel*, 46 Cal. App. 4th at 1567 (distinguishing the tort from conversion). Although the court admits some uncertainty as to the precise level of possessory interference required to constitute an intermeddling, there does not appear to be any dispute that eBay can show that BE's conduct amounts to use of eBay's computer systems. Accordingly, eBay has made a strong showing that it is likely to prevail on the merits of its assertion that BE's use of eBay's computer system was an unauthorized and intentional interference with eBay's possessory interest.

b. Damage to eBay's Computer System

A trespasser is liable when the trespass diminishes the condition, quality or value of personal property. *See CompuServe Inc. v. Cyber Promotions*, 962 F.Supp. 1015 (S.D.Ohio 1997). The quality or value of personal property may be "diminished even though it is not physically damaged by defendant's conduct." *Id.* at 1022. * * *

eBay is likely to be able to demonstrate that BE's activities have diminished the quality or value of eBay's computer systems. BE's activities consume at least a portion of plaintiff's bandwidth and server capacity. Although there is some dispute as to the percentage of queries on eBay's site for which BE is responsible, BE admits that it sends some 80,000 to 100,000 requests to plaintiff's computer systems per day. (Ritchey Decl. Ex. 3 at 391:11–12.) Although eBay does not claim that this consumption has led to any physical damage to eBay's computer system, nor does eBay provide any evidence to support the claim that it may have lost revenues or customers based on this use, eBay's claim is that BE's use is appropriating eBay's personal property by using valuable bandwidth and capacity, and necessarily compromising eBay's ability to use that capacity for its own purposes. See *CompuServe*, 962 F.Supp. at 1022 ("any value [plaintiff] realizes from its computer equipment is wholly derived from the extent to which that equipment can serve its subscriber base.").

BE argues that its searches represent a negligible load on plaintiff's computer systems, and do not rise to the level of impairment to the condition or value of eBay's computer system required to constitute a trespass. However, it is undisputed that eBay's server and its capacity are personal property, and that BE's searches use a portion of this property. Even if, as BE argues, its searches use only a small amount of eBay's computer system capacity, BE has nonetheless deprived eBay of the ability to use that portion of its personal property for its own purposes. The law recognizes no such right to use another's personal property. Accordingly, BE's actions appear to have caused injury to eBay and appear likely to continue to cause injury to eBay. If the court were to hold otherwise, it would likely encourage other auction aggregators to crawl the eBay site, potentially to the point of denying effective access to eBay's customers. If preliminary injunctive relief were denied, and other aggregators began to crawl the eBay site, there appears to be little doubt that the load on eBay's computer system would qualify as a substantial impairment of condition or value. California law does not require eBay to wait for such a disaster before applying to this court for relief. The court concludes that eBay has made a strong showing that it is likely to prevail on the merits of its trespass claim, and that there is at least a possibility that it will suffer irreparable harm if preliminary injunctive relief is not granted. eBay is therefore entitled to preliminary injunctive relief.

　　　* * *

IV. ORDER

Bidder's Edge, its officers, agents, servants, employees, attorneys and those in active concert or participation with them who receive actual notice of this order by personal service or otherwise, are hereby enjoined pending the trial of this matter, from using any automated query program, robot, web crawler or other similar device, without written authorization, to access eBay's computer systems or networks, for the purpose of copying any part of eBay's auction database. * * *

　　　* * *

NOTES & QUESTIONS

1. *Notice via robot exclusion headers.* eBay's site contained "robot exclusion headers," which are instructions in a file named "robots.txt" that are designed to affect the operation of robot software that accesses the site. A robot's programmer may design it to read the instructions contained in the robots.txt file; if the robots.txt file bars access by robots, and the robot is programmed to heed the instructions in robots.txt files, then the robot will not access the site. Should a website's implementation of a robots.txt file be deemed notice to all who deploy robots that their accessing of the site is unauthorized? Should it only be notice as to robots that have been designed to read and honor the instructions in robots.txt files?

2. *Anticipatory harm.* Do you agree with the court's holding that trespass to chattels may be premised on the likelihood that harm will result if *additional* parties begin accessing eBay's site without authorization?

3. *Degree of interference.* In *Ticketmaster Corp. v. Tickets.com, Inc.*, 2000 WL 1887522 (C.D.Cal.2000), the plaintiff, the largest seller of events tickets in the United States, sought to prevent defendant, a much smaller seller of tickets, from using robots to extract information about events from plaintiff's site, and presenting that information on its own site. The court declined to hold that defendant's actions constituted trespass to chattels. It distinguished *eBay v. Bidders Edge* on the basis that there was no showing that defendant's accessing of plaintiff's site was substantial enough to interfere with plaintiff's business. The court also observed that the case did not present "the spectre of dozens or more parasites joining the fray, the cumulative total of which could affect the operation of [Ticketmaster's] business." Is *eBay v. Bidders Edge* distinguishable on this basis?

4. *Database copying.* The injunction that eBay sought and obtained prevents "copying * * * eBay's auction database." Could eBay have obtained relief under the law of copyright? under state law of unfair competition or misappropriation? Is trespass to chattels an appropriate instrument for database protection? Reconsider Parts I and II, *supra.*

Register.com, Inc. v. Verio, Inc.

126 F.Supp.2d 238 (S.D.N.Y.2000).

■ Jones, District Judge.

Introduction

Plaintiff Register.com, a registrar of Internet domain names, moves for a preliminary injunction against the defendant, Verio, Inc. ("Verio"), a provider of Internet services. Register.com relies on claims under Section 43(a) of the Lanham Act, 15 U.S.C. § 1125(a); the Computer Fraud and Abuse Act of 1986, 18 U.S.C. § 1030, as amended; as well as trespass to chattels and breach of contract under the common law of the State of New York. In essence Register.com seeks an injunction barring Verio from using automated software processes to access and collect the registrant contact information contained in its WHOIS database and from using any of that information, however accessed, for mass marketing purposes.

I. Findings of Fact

The Parties

Plaintiff Register.com is one of over fifty domain name registrars for customers who wish to register a name in the .com, .net, and .org top-level domains. As a registrar it contracts with these second-level domain ("SLD") name holders and a registry, collecting registration data about the SLD holder and submitting zone file information for entry in the registry database. In addition to its domain name registration services, Register.com offers to its customers, both directly and through its more than 450 co-branded and private label partners, a variety of other related services, such as (i) website creation tools; (ii) website hosting; (iii) electronic mail; (iv) domain name hosting; (v) domain name forwarding, and (vi) real-time domain name management. * * *

In order to give its customers control over their receipt of commercial solicitations, Register.com provides them with the opportunity to "opt-in" during the domain name registration process to receiving sales and marketing communications from Register.com or its co-brand or private label partners. Customers who do not opt-in to such communications are not solicited by Register.com or its co-brands. Significantly, Register.com's co-brand and private label partners have contracted with Register.com for the right to have their services featured on the *www.register.com* website. (See Mornell Decl. ¶ 18).

Defendant Verio is one of the largest operators of web sites for businesses and a leading provider of comprehensive Internet services. Although not a registrar of domain names, Verio directly competes with Register.com and its partners to provide registration services and a variety of other Internet services including website hosting and development. Verio recently made a multimillion dollar investment in its computer system and facilities for its expanded force of telephone sales associates in its efforts to "provide recent domain name registration customers with the services they need, at the time they need them." (Eden Decl. ¶ 31).

The WHOIS database

To become an accredited domain name registrar for the .com, .net, and .org domains, all registrars, including Register.com are required to enter into a registrar Accreditation Agreement ("Agreement") with the Internet Corporation for Assigned Names and Numbers ("ICANN"). Under that Agreement, Register.com, as well as all other registrars, is required to provide an on-line, interactive WHOIS database. This database contains the names and contact information—postal address, telephone number, electronic mail address and in some cases facsimile number—for customers who register domain names through the registrar. The Agreement also requires Register.com to make the database freely accessible to the public via its web page and through an independent access port called port 43. These query-based channels of access to the WHOIS database allow the user to collect registrant contact information for one domain name at a time by entering the domain name into the provided search engine.

The primary purpose of the WHOIS database is to provide necessary information in the event of domain name disputes, such as those arising from cybersquatting or trademark infringement. (See Rony Decl. ¶ 18, Ex. B to McPherson Decl. at 13). The parties also agree that the WHOIS data may be used for market research.

Specifically, section II.F.5 of Register.com's Accreditation Agreement with ICANN requires that:

> In providing query-based public access to registration data as required by Sections II.F.1 and II.F.4, Registrar shall not impose terms and conditions on use of the data provided except as permitted by ICANN-adopted policy. Unless and until ICANN adopts a different policy, Registrar shall permit use of data it provides in response to queries *for any lawful purposes except to*: (a) *allow, enable, or otherwise support the transmission of mass unsolicited, commercial advertising or solicitations via e-mail (spam);* or (b) enable high volume, automated, electronic processes that apply to Registrar (or its systems).

(Ex. E to McPherson Decl.) (emphasis added).

Originally Register.com's terms and conditions for users of its WHOIS database were substantially the same. In April 2000, however, Register.com implemented the following more restrictive terms of use governing its WHOIS database:

> By submitting a WHOIS query, you agree that you will use this data *only for lawful purposes* and that, *under no circumstances will you use this data to: (1) allow, enable, or otherwise support the transmission of mass unsolicited, commercial advertising or solicitations via direct mail, electronic mail, or by telephone;* or (2) enable high volume, automated, electronic processes that apply to Register.com (or its systems). The compilation, repackaging, dissemination or other use of this data is expressly prohibited without the prior written consent of Register.com. Register.com reserves the right to modify these terms at any time. By submitting this query, you agree to abide by these terms.

(Ex. 27 to Pl.'s Sept. 8, 2000 Motion) (emphasis added).

Verio's Project Henhouse

In late 1999, to better target their marketing and sales efforts toward customers in need of web hosting services and to reach those customers more quickly, Verio developed an automated software program or "robot." With its search robot, Verio accessed the WHOIS database maintained by the accredited registrars, including Register.com, and collected the contact information of customers who had recently registered a domain name. Then, despite the marketing prohibitions in Register.com's terms of use, Verio utilized this data in a marketing initiative known as Project Henhouse and began to contact and solicit Register.com's customers, within the first several days after their registration, by e-mail, regular mail, and telephone.

Verio's Search Robots

In general, the process worked as follows: First, each day Verio downloaded, in compressed format, a list of all currently registered domain names, of all registrars, ending in .com, .net, and .org. That list or database is maintained by Network Solutions, Inc. ("NSI") and is published on 13 different "root zone" servers. The registry list is updated twice daily and provides the domain name, the sponsoring registrar, and the nameservers for all registered names. Using a computer program, Verio then compared the newly downloaded NSI registry with the NSI registry it downloaded a day earlier in order to isolate the domain names that had been registered in the last day and the names that had been removed. After downloading the list of new domain names, only then was a search robot used to query the NSI database to extract the name of the accredited registrar of each new name. That search robot then automatically made successive queries to the various registrars' WHOIS databases, via the port 43 access channels, to harvest the relevant contact information for each new domain name registered. (See Eden Depo. at 26–30; Eden Decl. PP36–38). Once retrieved, the WHOIS data was deposited into an information database maintained by Verio. The resulting database of sales leads was then provided to Verio's telemarketing staff.

* * *

IV.   Register.com's Claims

* * *

B.   Trespass To Chattels

Register.com argues that Verio's use of an automated software robot to search the "WHOIS" database constitutes trespass to chattels. Register.com states that it has made its computer system available on the Internet, and that "Verio has used 'software automation' to flood that computer system with traffic in order to retrieve the contact information of Register.com customers for the purpose of solicitation in knowing violation of Register.com's posted policies and terms of use." (Pl.'s Mem. of Law at 36.)

The standard for trespass to chattels in New York is based upon the standard set forth in the Restatement of Torts:

> One who uses a chattel with the consent of another is subject to liability in trespass for any harm to the chattel which is caused by or occurs in the course of any use exceeding the consent, even though such use is not a conversion.

City of Amsterdam v. Goldreyer, Ltd., 882 F.Supp. 1273 (E.D.N.Y.1995) (citing Restatement (Second) of Torts, § 256 (1965)).

* * *

* * * [I]t is clear since at least the date this lawsuit was filed that Register.com does not consent to Verio's use of a search robot, and Verio is on notice that its search robot is unwelcome. (Pl.'s V.C. P36)

Accordingly, Verio's future use of a search robot to access the database exceeds the scope of Register.com's consent, and Verio is liable for any harm to the chattel (Register.com's computer systems) caused by that unauthorized access. *See CompuServe*, 962 F.Supp. at 1024 (holding that defendants' continued use after CompuServe notified defendants that it no longer consented to the use of its proprietary computer equipment was a trespass) (citing Restatement (Second) of Torts §§ 252 and 892A(5)).

Having established that Verio's access to its WHOIS database by robot is unauthorized, Register.com must next demonstrate that Verio's unauthorized access caused harm to its chattels, namely its computer system. To that end, Robert Gardos, Register.com's Vice President for Technology, submitted a declaration estimating that Verio's searching of Register.com's WHOIS database has resulted in a diminishment of 2.3% of Register.com's system resources. (See Gardos Decl. P32.) However, during discovery, the basis for Gardos' estimations of the impact Verio's search robot had on Register.com's computer systems was thoroughly undercut. Gardos admitted in his deposition that he had taken measurements of neither the capacity of Register.com's computer systems nor the portion of that capacity which was consumed by Verio's search robots. Furthermore, when describing how he arrived at his conclusion that Verio's search robots occupied a certain percentage of Register.com's systems capacity, Mr. Gardos testified that the numbers he used were "all rough estimates." (Gardos Depo. at 76).

Although Register.com's evidence of any burden or harm to its computer system caused by the successive queries performed by search robots is imprecise, evidence of mere possessory interference is sufficient to demonstrate the quantum of harm necessary to establish a claim for trespass to chattels. "A trespasser is liable when the trespass diminishes the condition, quality, or value of personal property." *eBay, Inc. v. Bidder's Edge, Inc.,* 100 F.Supp.2d 1058, 1071 (N.D.Cal.2000) (*citing CompuServe,* 962 F.Supp. at 1022). "The quality or value of personal property may be 'diminished even though it is not physically damaged by defendant's conduct.' " Id. Though it does correctly dispute the trustworthiness and accuracy of Mr. Gardos' calculations, Verio does not dispute that its search robot occupies some of Register.com's systems capacity.

Although Register.com was unable to directly measure the amount by which its systems capacity was reduced, the record evidence is sufficient to establish the possessory interference necessary to establish a trespass to chattels claim. As the *eBay* Court wrote:

> BE argues that its searches present a negligible load on plaintiff's computer systems, and do not rise to the level of impairment to the condition or value of eBay's computer system required to consitute a trespass. *However, it is undisputed that eBay's server and its capacity are personal property, and that BE's searches use a portion of this property. Even if, as BE argues, its searches only use a small amount of eBay's computer system capacity, BE has nonetheless deprived eBay of the ability to use that portion of its personal property for its own purposes. The law recognizes no such right to use another's personal property.* Accordingly, BE's actions appear to have caused injury to eBay and appear likely to continue to cause injury to eBay.

(100 F.Supp.2d at 1071.) (emphasis added).

Furthermore, Gardos also noted in his declaration "if the strain on Register.com's resources generated by Verio's searches becomes large enough, it could cause Register.com's computer systems to malfunction or crash" and "I believe that if Verio's searching of Register.com's WHOIS database were determined to be lawful, then every purveryor of Internet-based services would engage in similar conduct." (Gardos Decl. ¶¶ 33, 34). Gardos' concerns are supported by Verio's testimony that it sees no need to place a limit on the number of other companies that should be allowed to harvest data from Register.com's computers. (See Ayers Depo. at 71). Furthermore, Verio's own internal documents reveal that Verio was aware that its robotic queries could slow the response times of the registrars' databases and even overload them. (See Ex. 29 & to Pl.'s Sept. 8, 2000 Motion). Because of that possibility, Verio contemplated cloaking the origin of its queries by using a process called IP aliasing. (See id.; see also Ex. 64 to Pl.'s Sept. 8, 2000 Motion).

Accordingly, Register.com's evidence that Verio's search robots have presented and will continue to present an unwelcome interference with, and a risk of interruption to, its computer system and servers is sufficient to demonstrate a likelihood of success on the merits of its trespass to chattels claim.

There is no adequate remedy at law for an ongoing trespass and without an injunction the victim of such a trespass will be irreparably harmed. The *eBay* court specifically held that eBay was entitled to preliminary injunctive relief based on the claim that if such relief were denied, other companies would be encouraged to deploy search robots against eBay's servers and would further diminish eBay's server capacity to the point of denying effective access to eBay's customers. *See id.* at 1071–72.

The same reasoning applies here. Register.com, through Mr. Gardos, has expressed the fear that its servers will be flooded by search robots deployed by competitors in the absence of injunctive relief. Register.com has therefore demonstrated both a likelihood of success on the merits of its trespass to chattels claim and the existence of irreparable harm, and is entitled to a preliminary injunction against Verio based upon that claim.

C.   Computer Fraud And Abuse Act §§ 1030(a)(2)(C) and (a)(5)(C)

The issue of the scope of Verio's authorization to access the WHOIS database is also central to the Court's analysis of Register.com's claims that Verio is violating two discrete provisions of the Computer Fraud and Abuse Act ("CFAA"), 18 U.S.C. § 1030 et seq.

Register.com claims both that the use of software robots to harvest customer information from its WHOIS database in violation of its terms of use violates 18 U.S.C. §§ 1030(a)(2)(C) and (a)(5)(C) [since redesignated § 1030(a)(5)(A)(iii)—Eds.], and that using the harvested information in violation of Register.com's policy forbidding the use of WHOIS data for marketing also violates those sections. That is, that both Verio's method of accessing the WHOIS data and Verio's end uses of the data violate the CFAA.

1.   Verio's Use of Search Robots

Both §§ 1030(a)(2)(C) and (a)(5)(C) require that the plaintiff prove that the defendant's access to its computer system was unauthorized, or in the case of § 1030(a)(2)(C) that it was unauthorized or exceeded authorized access. However, although each section requires proof of some degree of unauthorized access, each addresses a different type of harm. Section 1030(a)(2)(C) requires Register.com to prove that Verio intentionally accessed its computers without authorization *and thereby obtained information*. Section 1030(a)(5)(C) requires Register.com to show that Verio intentionally accessed its computer without authorization *and thereby caused damage.*

As discussed more fully in the context of the trespass to chattels claim, because Register.com objects to Verio's use of search robots they represent an unauthorized access to the WHOIS database.

The type of harm that Register.com alleges is caused by the search robots, including diminished server capacity and potential system shutdowns, is better analyzed under § 1030(a)(5)(C), which specifically addresses damages to the computer system. Pursuant to the pertinent part of § 1030(e)(8), "the term 'damage' means any impairment to the integrity or availability of data, a program, a system, or information that (A) causes loss aggregating at least $5000 in value during any 1–year period to one or more individuals."

On this record Register.com has demonstrated that Verio's unauthorized use of search robots to harvest registrant contact information from Register.com's WHOIS database has diminished server capacity, however slightly, and could diminish response time, which could impair the availability of data to clients trying to get registrant contact information. Moreover, Register.com has raised the possibility that if Verio's robotic queries of Register.com's WHOIS database were determined to be lawful, then other vendors of Internet services would engage in similar conduct. This Court finds that it is highly probable that other Internet service vendors would also use robots to obtain this potential customer information were it to be permitted. The use of the robot allows a marketer to reach a potential client within the first several days of the domain name registration, an optimal time to solicit the customer for other services. In contrast, if instead of using a search robot the service vendor obtains registrant contact information pursuant to a bulk license, the vendor must wait to receive the information on a weekly basis. As Eric Eden, the director of operation Henhouse wrote in an e-mail to a Verio employee "consistent testing has found that the faster we approach someone after they register a domain name, the more likely we are to sell them hosting." (Ex. 40 to Pl.'s Sept. 8, 2000 Motion).

If the strain on Register.com's resources generated by robotic searches becomes large enough, it could cause Register.com's computer systems to malfunction or crash. Such a crash would satisfy § 1030(a)(5)(C)'s threshold requirement that a plaintiff demonstrate $5000 in economic damages[12]

---

12. Register.com relies upon lost revenue from Verio's exploitation of the WHOIS data for marketing purposes to constitute the damages required under § 1030(a)(5)(C). Although lost good will or business could provide the loss figure required under § 1030(a)(5)(C), it could only do so if it resulted from the impairment or unavailability of data or systems. The good will losses cited by Register.com are not the result of the harm addressed by § 1030(a)(5)(C). How Ver- io uses the WHOIS data, once extracted, has no bearing on whether Verio has impaired the availability or integrity of Register.com's data or computer systems in extracting it. Accordingly, because violating an anti-marketing restriction on the end use of data harms neither the data nor the computer and therefore does not cause the type of harm that § 1030(a)(5)(C) addresses, the specific good will damages cited by Register.com cannot satisfy its burden under § 1030(a)(5)(C).

resulting from the violation, both because of costs relating to repair and lost data and also because of lost good will based on adverse customer reactions.

* * *

Because Register.com has demonstrated that Verio's access to its WHOIS database by means of an automated search robot is unauthorized and caused or could cause $5000 in damages by impairing the availability of data or the availability of its computer systems, Register.com has established both irreparable harm and a likelihood of success on the merits of its claim that Verio's use of the search robot violated § 1030(a)(5)(C) of the Computer Fraud And Abuse Act. Register.com is therefore entitled to injunctive relief based upon this claim.

2. Verio's Use of WHOIS Data For Marketing Purposes

With respect to its use of Register.com's WHOIS data for e-mail, direct mail and telephone marketing, Verio argues that such an act can only be analyzed under § 1030(a)(2)(C)'s provision assessing liability where a party exceeds authorized access and obtains information it is not entitled to obtain. Verio argues that because it is authorized to access the WHOIS database for some purposes its access was authorized. Verio then argues that its conduct must meet the Act's specific definition of conduct that "exceeds authorized access." Pursuant to the definition contained in § 1030(e)(6) of the CFAA, "the term 'exceeds authorized access' means to access a computer with authorization and to use such access to obtain or alter information in the computer that the accessor is not entitled to obtain or alter." 18 U.S.C. § 1030(e)(6) (emphasis added). Verio then argues that this definition does not contemplate a violation of end use restrictions placed on data as "exceeding authorized access," and therefore that Verio has not violated § 1030(a)(2)(C).

Again, neither party disputes that Verio is not authorized under Register.com's terms of use to use the data for mass marketing purposes, and neither party disputes that Verio is authorized to obtain the data for some purposes. However, Verio's distinctions between authorized access and an unauthorized end use of information strike the Court as too fine. First, the means of access Verio employs, namely the automated search robot, is unauthorized. Second, even if Verio's means of access to the WHOIS database would otherwise be authorized, that access would be rendered unauthorized ab initio by virtue of the fact that prior to entry Verio knows that the data obtained will be later used for an unauthorized purpose.

Accordingly, the Court finds that Verio's access to the WHOIS database was unauthorized and that Verio violated § 1030(a)(2)(C) by using that unauthorized access to obtain data for mass marketing purposes. As discussed above, the harvesting and subsequent use of that data has caused and will cause Register.com irreparable harm. Therefore, because Register.com has demonstrated a likelihood of success on the merits of its claim that Verio's use of its WHOIS data for mass marketing purposes violates § 1030(a)(2)(C) of the Computer Fraud And Abuse Act and has demonstrated irreparable harm stemming from that violation, Register.com is entitled to injunctive relief based on that claim.

* * *

NOTES & QUESTIONS

The domain name system and the limits of private ordering. Does the holding of *Register.com v. Verio* give domain name registrars an effective monopoly in marketing additional services to domain name registrants? How does the court treat the contract between the domain name registrar and the registrant? The contract between ICANN and the registrar? Is the situation presented in this case any different from the usual situation in which a seller has privileged access to its customer list? Should registrars have a special duty of openness, deriving from their status as part of the global administration of the domain name space, which flows from ICANN's unilateral control over the domain name system?

EF Cultural Travel BV v. Explorica, Inc.

274 F.3d 577 (1st Cir.2001).

■ Coffin, Senior Circuit Judge.

Appellant Explorica, Inc. ("Explorica") and several of its employees challenge a preliminary injunction issued against them for alleged violations of the Computer Fraud and Abuse Act ("CFAA"), 18 U.S.C. § 1030. We affirm the district court's conclusion that appellees will likely succeed on the merits of their CFAA claim, but rest on a narrower basis than the court below.

I. Background

Explorica was formed in 2000 to compete in the field of global tours for high school students. Several of Explorica's employees formerly were employed by appellee EF, which has been in business for more than thirty-five years. EF and its partners and subsidiaries make up the world's largest private student travel organization.

Shortly after the individual defendants left EF in the beginning of 2000, Explorica began competing in the teenage tour market. The company's vice president (and former vice president of information strategy at EF), Philip Gormley, envisioned that Explorica could gain a substantial advantage over all other student tour companies, and especially EF, by undercutting EF's already competitive prices on student tours. Gormley considered several ways to obtain and utilize EF's prices: by manually keying in the information from EF's brochures and other printed materials; by using a scanner to record that same information; or, by manually searching for each tour offered through EF's website. Ultimately, however,

Gormley engaged Zefer, Explorica's Internet consultant, to design a computer program called a "scraper" to glean all of the necessary information from EF's website. Zefer designed the program in three days.

The scraper has been likened to a "robot," a tool that is extensively used on the Internet. Robots are used to gather information for countless purposes, ranging from compiling results for search engines such as Yahoo! to filtering for inappropriate content. The widespread deployment of robots enables global Internet users to find comprehensive information quickly and almost effortlessly.

Like a robot, the scraper sought information through the Internet. Unlike other robots, however, the scraper focused solely on EF's website, using information that other robots would not have. Specifically, Zefer utilized tour codes whose significance was not readily understandable to the public. With the tour codes, the scraper accessed EF's website repeatedly and easily obtained pricing information for those specific tours. The scraper sent more than 30,000 inquiries to EF's website and recorded the pricing information into a spreadsheet.[2]

Zefer ran the scraper program twice, first to retrieve the 2000 tour prices and then the 2001 prices. All told, the scraper downloaded 60,000 lines of data, the equivalent of eight telephone directories of information.[3] Once Zefer "scraped" all of the prices, it sent a spreadsheet containing EF's pricing information to Explorica, which then systematically undercut EF's prices. Explorica thereafter printed its own brochures and began competing in EF's tour market.

The development and use of the scraper came to light about a year and a half later during state-court litigation regarding appellant Olsson's departure from appellee EFICE. EF then filed this action, alleging violations of the CFAA; the Copyright Act of 1976, 17 U.S.C. § 101; the Racketeer Influenced and Corrupt Organizations Act, 18 U.S.C. § 1961; and various related state laws. It sought a preliminary injunction barring Explorica and

---

2. John Hawley, one of Zefer's senior technical associates, explained the technical progression of the scraper in an affidavit:

[a.] Open an Excel spreadsheet. The spreadsheet initially contains EFTours gateway and destination city codes, which are available on the EFTours web site.

[b.] Identify the first gateway and destination city codes [on the] Excel spreadsheet.

[c.] Create a [website address] request for the EFTours tour prices page based on a combination of gateway and destination city. Example: show me all the prices for a London trip leaving JFK.

[d.] View the requested web page which is retained in the random access memory of the requesting computer in the form of HTML [computer language] code. * * *

[e.] Search the HTML for the tour prices for each season, year, etc.

[f.] Store the prices into the Excel spreadsheet.

[g.] Identify the next gateway and city codes in the spreadsheet.

[h.] Repeat steps 3–7 for all gateway and destination city combinations.

3. Appellants dispute the relevance of the size of the printed data, arguing that 60,000 printed lines, while voluminous on paper, is not a large amount of data for a computer to store. This is a distinction without a difference. The fact is that appellants utilized the scraper program to download EF's pricing data. In June 2000, EF's website listed 154,293 prices for various tours.

Zefer from using the scraper program and demanded the return of all materials generated through use of the scraper.

On May 30, 2001, the district court granted a preliminary injunction against Explorica based on the CFAA, which criminally and civilly prohibits certain access to computers. *See* 18 U.S.C. § 1030(a)(4). The court found that EF would likely prove that Explorica violated the CFAA when it used EF's website in a manner outside the "reasonable expectations" of both EF and its ordinary users. The court also concluded that EF could show that it suffered a loss, as required by the statute, consisting of reduced business, harm to its goodwill, and the cost of diagnostic measures it incurred to evaluate possible harm to EF's systems, although it could not show that Explorica's actions physically damaged its computers. In a supplemental opinion the district court further articulated its "reasonable expectations" standard and explained that copyright, contractual and technical restraints sufficiently notified Explorica that its use of a scraper would be unauthorized and thus would violate the CFAA.

The district court first relied on EF's use of a copyright symbol on one of the pages of its website and a link directing users with questions to contact the company,[6] finding that "such a clear statement should have dispelled any notion a reasonable person may have had that the 'presumption of open access' applied to information on EF's website." The court next found that the manner by which Explorica accessed EF's website likely violated a confidentiality agreement between appellant Gormley and EF, because Gormley provided to Zefer technical instructions concerning the creation of the scraper. Finally, the district court noted without elaboration that the scraper bypassed technical restrictions embedded in the website to acquire the information. The court therefore let stand its earlier decision granting the preliminary injunction. Appellants contend that the district court erred in taking too narrow a view of what is authorized under the CFAA and similarly mistook the reach of the confidentiality agreement. Appellants also argue that the district court erred in finding that appellees suffered a "loss," as defined by the CFAA, and that the preliminary injunction violates the First Amendment.

* * *

III. The Computer Fraud and Abuse Act

Although appellees alleged violations of three provisions of the CFAA, the district court found that they were likely to succeed only under § 1030(a)(4). That section provides

> [Whoever] knowingly and with intent to defraud, accesses a protected computer without authorization, or exceeds authorized access, and by means of such conduct furthers the intended fraud and obtains anything of value . . . shall be punished.

---

6. The notice stated in full:

Copyright © 2000 EF Cultural Travel BV

EF Educational Tours is a member of the EF group of companies.

Questions? Please contact us.

18 U.S.C. § 1030(a)(4).[8]

Appellees allege that the appellants knowingly and with intent to defraud accessed the server hosting EF's website more than 30,000 times to obtain proprietary pricing and tour information, and confidential information about appellees' technical abilities. At the heart of the parties' dispute is whether appellants' actions either were "without authorization" or "exceeded authorized access" as defined by the CFAA.[9] We conclude that because of the broad confidentiality agreement appellants' actions "exceeded authorized access," and so we do not reach the more general arguments made about statutory meaning, including whether use of a scraper alone renders access unauthorized.

A. "Exceeds authorized access"

Congress defined "exceeds authorized access," as accessing "a computer with authorization and [using] such access to obtain or alter information in the computer that the accesser is not entitled so to obtain or alter." 18 U.S.C. § 1030(e)(6). EF is likely to prove such excessive access based on the confidentiality agreement between Gormley and EF. Pertinently, that agreement provides:

> Employee agrees to maintain in strict confidence and not to disclose to any third party, either orally or in writing, any Confidential or Proprietary Information . . . and never to at any time (i) directly or indirectly publish, disseminate or otherwise disclose, deliver or make available to anybody any Confidential or Proprietary Information or (ii) use such Confidential or Proprietary Information for Employee's own benefit or for the benefit of any other person or business entity other than EF.
>
> * * *
>
> As used in this Agreement, the term "Confidential or Proprietary Information" means (a) any trade or business secrets or confidential information of EF, whether or not reduced to writing . . . ; (b) any technical, business, or financial information, the use or disclosure of which might reasonably be construed to be contrary to the interests of EF. . . .

The record contains at least two communications from Gormley to Zefer seeming to rely on information about EF to which he was privy only because of his employment there. First, in an e-mail to Zefer employee

---

8. Although the CFAA is primarily a criminal statute, under § 1030(g), "any person who suffers damage or loss . . . may maintain a civil action . . . for compensatory damages and injunctive relief or other equitable relief."

9. At oral argument, appellants contended that they had no "intent to defraud" as defined by the CFAA. That argument was not raised in the briefs and thus has been waived. *See Garcia-Ayala v. Parenterals, Inc.*, 212 F.3d 638, 645 (1st Cir.2000) (failure to brief an argument constitutes waiver despite attempt to raise the argument at oral argument). Likewise, at oral argument Explorica attempted to adopt appellant Zefer's argument that the preliminary injunction violates the First Amendment. The lateness of Explorica's attempt renders it fruitless. *See id.*

Joseph Alt exploring the use of a scraper, Gormley wrote: "might one of the team be able to write a program to automatically extract prices . . .? I could work with him/her on the specification." Gormley also sent the following e-mail to Zefer employee John Hawley:

> Here is a link to the page where you can grab EF's prices. There are two important drop down menus on the right. . . . With the lowest one you select one of about 150 tours. * * * You then select your origin gateway from a list of about 100 domestic gateways (middle drop down menu). When you select your origin gateway a page with a couple of tables comes up. One table has 1999–2000 prices and the other has 2000–2001 prices. * * * On a high speed connection it is possible to move quickly from one price table to the next by hitting backspace and then the down arrow.

This documentary evidence points to Gormley's heavy involvement in the conception of the scraper program. Furthermore, the voluminous spreadsheet containing all of the scraped information includes the tour codes, which EF claims are proprietary information. Each page of the spreadsheet produced by Zefer includes the tour and gateway codes, the date of travel, and the price for the tour. An uninformed reader would regard the tour codes as nothing but gibberish.[11] Although the codes can be correlated to the actual tours and destination points, the codes standing alone need to be "translated" to be meaningful.

Explorica argues that none of the information Gormley provided Zefer was confidential and that the confidentiality agreement therefore is irrelevant. The case on which they rely, *Lanier Professional Services, Inc. v. Ricci*, 192 F.3d 1, 5 (1st Cir.1999), focused almost exclusively on an employee's non-compete agreement. The opinion mentioned in passing that there was no actionable misuse of confidential information because the only evidence that the employee had taken protected information was a "practically worthless" affidavit from the employee's successor. *Id.* at 5.

Here, on the other hand, there is ample evidence that Gormley provided Explorica proprietary information about the structure of the website and the tour codes. To be sure, gathering manually the various codes through repeated searching and deciphering of the URLs theoretically may be possible. Practically speaking, however, if proven, Explorica's wholesale use of EF's travel codes to facilitate gathering EF's prices from its website reeks of use—and, indeed, abuse—of proprietary information that goes beyond any authorized use of EF's website.[14]

---

11. An example of the website address including the tour information is www.eft-ours.com/tours/PriceResult.asp?Gate=GTF & TourID=LPM. In this address, the proprietary codes are "GTF" and "LPM."

14. Among the several e-mails in the record is one from Zefer employee Joseph Alt to the Explorica "team" at Zefer:

Below is the information needed to log into EF's site as a tour leader. Please use this to gather competitor information from both a business and experience design perspective. We may also be able to glean knowledge of their technical abilities. As with all of our information, this

Gormley voluntarily entered a broad confidentiality agreement prohibiting his disclosure of any information "which might reasonably be construed to be contrary to the interests of EF." Appellants would face an uphill battle trying to argue that it was not against EF's interests for appellants to use the tour codes to mine EF's pricing data. *See Anthony's Pier Four, Inc. v. HBC Assoc.*, 411 Mass. 451, 471, 583 N.E.2d 806, 820 (1991) (imposing a duty of good faith and fair dealing in all contracts under Massachusetts law). If EF's allegations are proven, it will likely prove that whatever authorization Explorica had to navigate around EF's site (even in a competitive vein), it exceeded that authorization by providing proprietary information and know-how to Zefer to create the scraper.[16] Accordingly, the district court's finding that Explorica likely violated the CFAA was not clearly erroneous.

B.   Damage or Loss under § 1030(g)

Appellants also challenge the district court's finding that the appellees would likely prove they met the CFAA's "damage or loss" requirements. Under the CFAA, EF may maintain a private cause of action if it suffered "damage or loss." 18 U.S.C. § 1030(g). "Damage" is defined as "any impairment to the integrity or availability of data, a program, a system, or information that . . . causes loss aggregating at least $5,000 in value during any 1–year period to one or more individuals. . . ." 18 U.S.C. § 1030(e)(8). "Loss" is not defined.

The district court held that although EF could not show any "damage" it would likely be able to show "loss" under the statute. It reasoned that a general understanding of the word "loss" would fairly encompass a loss of business, goodwill, and the cost of diagnostic measures that EF took after it learned of Explorica's access to its website.[17] Appellants respond that such diagnostic measures cannot be included in the $5,000 threshold because their actions neither caused any physical damage nor placed any stress on EF's website.

---

is extremely confidential. Please do not share it with anyone.

16.   EF also claims that Explorica skirted the website's technical restraints. To learn about a specific tour, a user must navigate through several different web pages by "clicking" on various drop-down menus and choosing the desired departure location, date, tour destination, tour length, and price range. The district court found that the scraper circumvented the technical restraints by operating at a warp speed that the website was not normally intended to accommodate. We need not reach the argument that this alone was a violation of the CFAA, however, because the apparent transfer of information in violation of the Confidentiality Agreement

furnishes a sufficient basis for injunctive relief.

Likewise, we express no opinion on the district court's ruling that EF's copyright notice served as a "clear statement [that] should have dispelled any notion a reasonable person may have had the 'presumption of open access' " to EF's website.

17.   It is undisputed that appellees paid $20,944.92 to assess whether their website had been compromised. Appellees also claim costs exceeding $40,000 that they will incur to "remedy and secure their website and computer." We need not consider whether these expenses constitute loss because the initial $20,944.92 greatly exceeds the threshold.

Few courts have endeavored to resolve the contours of damage and loss under the CFAA. *See, e.g., Shaw v. Toshiba Am. Info. Sys.,* 91 F.Supp.2d 926 (E.D.Tex.1999) (noting the paucity of decisions construing the Act). Two district courts that have addressed the issue have found that expenses such as those borne by EF do fall under the statute. In *Shurgard Storage Centers v. Safeguard Self Storage, Inc.,* 119 F.Supp.2d 1121 (W.D.Wa.2000), the district court found that the need to assess whether a defendant's actions compromised the plaintiff's computers was compensable under the CFAA because the computer's integrity was called into question. The court based its finding on the legislative history of the 1996 amendments to the CFAA:

> The 1994 Amendment required both "damage" and "loss," but it is not always clear what constitutes "damage." For example, intruders often alter existing log-on programs so that user passwords are copied to a file which the hackers can retrieve later. After retrieving the newly created password file, the intruder restores the altered log-on file to its original condition. Arguably, in such a situation, neither the computer nor its information is damaged. Nonetheless, this conduct allows the intruder to accumulate valid user passwords to the system, requires all system users to change their passwords, and requires the system administrator to devote resources to re-securing the system. Thus, although there is arguably no "damage," the victim does suffer "loss." If the loss to the victim meets the required monetary threshold, the conduct should be criminal, and the victim should be entitled to relief.

S. Rep. No. 104–357, at 11 (1996) (quoted in *Shurgard,* 119 F.Supp.2d at 1126). Another district court held that this legislative history makes "clear that Congress intended the term 'loss' to target remedial expenses borne by victims that could not properly be considered direct damage caused by a computer hacker." *In re DoubleClick Inc. Privacy Litig.,* 154 F.Supp.2d 497, 521 (S.D.N.Y.2001).

We agree with this construction of the CFAA. In the absence of a statutory definition for "loss," we apply the well-known rule of assigning undefined words their normal, everyday meaning. *See Inmates of Suffolk Cty. Jail v. Rouse,* 129 F.3d 649, 653–54 (1st Cir.1997). The word "loss" means "detriment, disadvantage, or deprivation from failure to keep, have or get." The Random House Dictionary of the English Language 1137 (2d ed. 1983). Appellees unquestionably suffered a detriment and a disadvantage by having to expend substantial sums to assess the extent, if any, of the physical damage to their website caused by appellants' intrusion. That the physical components were not damaged is fortunate, but it does not lessen the loss represented by consultant fees. Congress's use of the disjunctive, "damage or loss," confirms that it anticipated recovery in cases involving other than purely physical damage. *But see In re Intuit Privacy Litig.,* 138 F.Supp.2d 1272, 1281 (C.D.Cal.2001) (loss means "irreparable damage" and any other interpretation "would render the term 'damage' superfluous''); *Register.com, Inc. v. Verio, Inc.,* 126 F.Supp.2d 238, 252 n. 12 (S.D.N.Y.2000) (lost business or goodwill could not constitute loss absent the impairment or unavailability of data or systems). To parse the words in any other way would not only impair Congress's intended scope of the Act, but would also serve to reward sophisticated intruders. As we move into an increasingly electronic world, the instances of physical damage will likely be fewer while the value to the victim of what has been stolen and the victim's costs in shoring up its security features undoubtedly will loom ever-larger. If we were to restrict the statute as appellants urge, we would flout Congress's intent by effectively permitting the CFAA to languish in the twentieth century, as violators of the Act move into the twenty-first century and beyond.

We do not hold, however, that any loss is compensable. The CFAA provides recovery for "damage" only if it results in a loss of at least $5,000. We agree with the court in *In re DoubleClick Inc. Privacy Litigation,* 154 F.Supp.2d 497 (S.D.N.Y.2001), that Congress could not have intended other types of loss to support recovery unless that threshold were met. Indeed, the Senate Report explicitly states that "if the loss to the victim meets the required monetary threshold," the victim is entitled to relief under the CFAA. S. Rep. 104–357, at 11. We therefore conclude that expenses of at least $5,000 resulting from a party's intrusion are "losses" for purposes of the "damage or loss" requirement of the CFAA.

IV.   Conclusion

For the foregoing reasons, we agree with the district court that appellees will likely succeed on the merits of their CFAA claim under 18 U.S.C. § 1030(a)(4). Accordingly, the preliminary injunction was properly ordered.

Affirmed.

NOTES & QUESTIONS

1. *Burden on remand.* The Court of Appeals affirmed the District Court's grant of a preliminary injunction, finding that the plaintiff was likely to succeed on the merits of its claim under the Computer Fraud and Abuse Act. On remand, what will the plaintiff be required to prove in order to prevail? Based on the facts presented in this opinion, how likely do you think it is that plaintiff will succeed?

2. *De-authorization via Terms of Use.* The home page of EF Tours' website contains a link at the bottom of the page labeled Terms of Use. Clicking on the link calls up a page titled "Terms of Use," which contains, in the middle of a page of text, the following:

You may not without the prior written permission of EF use any computer code, data mining software, "robot," "bot," "spider," "scraper" or other automatic device, or program, algorithm or methodology having similar processes or functionality, or any manual process, to monitor or copy any of the web pages, data or content found on this site or accessed through this site. You also may not: engage in the mass downloading of files from this site; use the computer processing power of this site for purposes other than those permitted above; flood this site with electronic traffic designed to slow or stop its operation; or establish links to or from other websites to this site.

Does the presence of this statement in the Terms of Use render any use of the site that is inconsistent with its strictures an access "without authorization" under the Computer Fraud and Abuse Act? If I place an unapproved link from my website to this site, and the site operator expends $7,000 in consultant costs attempting to render my link inoperative, am I in violation of § 1030(a)(5)(A)(iii), which provides that one who "intentionally accesses a protected computer without authorization, and as a result of such conduct, causes damage; and [by such conduct] caused * * * loss * * * aggregating at least $5,000 in value" is subject to criminal and civil liability?

3.   *Competition in the balance.* Decisions like *eBay v. Bidders Edge, Register.com v. Verio,* and *EF v. Explorica* have the potential to interfere with the gathering of information that is necessary to operate price comparison sites and search engines, prevent online information-gathering by organizations like Consumer Reports, limit linking, impede efforts by sellers to price their offerings competitively, and hinder other activities aimed at improving the flow of information to consumers and promoting competition. Yet sellers have a legitimate interest in controlling information that is critical to their business operations. Do existing legal doctrines give adequate weight to each set of conflicting interests?

CHAPTER FIVE

TECHNOLOGICAL PROTECTION OF DIGITAL GOODS

Created by a college freshman at Northeastern University in 1999, Napster used an innovative file-sharing technology to enable Internet users to download music at no cost via peer-to-peer file sharing. Napster made it easy for users to trade music encoded in the MP3 format, which compresses recordings into small and portable files without any noticeable sacrifice in sound quality. As Napster's popularity increased—at one point it claimed 60 million users—the recording industry filed multiple lawsuits, accusing Napster of encouraging the illegal copying and distribution of copyrighted music, in violation of the copyright laws. At the same time, recording artists, most notably the heavy metal group Metallica, began criticizing Napster for the large-scale distribution of copyrighted music. The company eventually shut down in response to federal court orders.[1]

Yet even after the courts' declarations that users who exchanged copyrighted music via Napster were violating the copyright laws, file sharing continued, hardly abated, through a variety of other file-trading services that sprang up to fill the void created by Napster's demise. The online sharing of digital versions of copyrighted movies has also become widespread: in some cases, pirated versions of movies are available for download from the Internet before they open on the big screen. The unauthorized uploading and downloading of copyrighted software remains a major irritant to software developers, notwithstanding years of aggressive anti-piracy efforts by industry representatives.

The Napster experience, and the persistent unauthorized trade in other information products despite copyright owners' sustained efforts to banish it from the network, suggests two propositions: first, that individuals, and in some cases businesses, are unlikely voluntarily to conform their behavior to what the courts have declared is the mandate of the copyright laws (at least under current market conditions); and second, that efforts by copyright owners to vindicate their rights by taking legal action against infringers are unlikely to reduce unauthorized reproduction and distribution to a level that copyright owners consider acceptable.

What then are copyright owners to do? One approach is to try to control unauthorized access to information products through the use of trusted systems.

---

1. For the legal history of these lawsuits, see Chapter 3, *supra*.

A trusted system, also known as a digital rights management system ("DRMS"), is a technological device—usually implemented through computer code—that controls access to or use of an accompanying information product. Such systems prevent a person from making any use of an information product beyond that which the copyright owner has authorized. A trusted system acts as a self-enforcement mechanism, cutting off access to the information product if the user does something not allowed by the license, such as attempting to send a copy to someone else. Developers of trusted systems envision that these programs will be able to structure the entire package of rights the content owner wishes to allow the user, and that they will be able to "negotiate" with the user's computer to arrive at an "agreement" about the package of rights and its price. To encourage the use of trusted systems, the Digital Millennium Copyright Act of 1998 added provisions to the Copyright Act making it unlawful both to circumvent the access controls employed by trusted systems, and to manufacture, import, or offer to the public products that are designed to circumvent controls on access and use.

The use of trusted systems has generated a good deal of controversy. Some argue that trusted systems will result in more digital products being available to more people at lower costs than ever before. Others maintain that permitting the use of trusted systems upsets the delicate balance between ownership rights and public access created by the law of copyright, shifting the balance in favor of copyright owners at the expense of the public, by allowing owners to prevent uses that the copyright law permits— for example, use of material that is not copyrightable or whose copyright has expired, or use of copyrighted material that is within fair use. Still others argue that the use of such systems permits industry to make unacceptable incursions into the domain of personal privacy, by tracking, recording, and ultimately commercializing users' personal preferences as reflected in their online use of information goods, such as music, electronic books, movies, and games.

In this chapter, we explore the use of trusted systems from several perspectives. In Part I, we look at the technology itself and the ways it can be used. In Part II, we examine the protections for trusted systems added by the Digital Millennium Copyright Act.

I. Introduction to Trusted Systems

Mark Stefik & Alex Silverman, *The Bit and the Pendulum: Balancing the Interests of Stakeholders in Digital Publishing*

16 No. 1 Computer Law. 1 (1999).

Personal computers and computer networks have the potential to become an ideal basis for digital publishing. But the potential for digital publishing remains just that—a potential. The market for digital works remains nascent, because the medium has failed so far to balance the interests of important stakeholders. Computers and the digital medium are sometimes seen as the root of this problem. In this article we explore how computers designed as trusted systems could bring things more into balance.

By digital publishing, we mean the on-line sale and distribution of digital works. A digital work can be anything in digital form: an article, a book, a program, or any multimedia combination involving programming, music, text, and video. The advantages of the digital media include nearly instant distribution, low production costs, and the convenience of 24–hour automated shopping.

When personal computers and desktop publishing first appeared in the early 1980s, many publishers saw digital publishing as too risky. Although numerous factors influenced publishers' judgments in particular cases, the dominant and recurring factor was the fear of widespread unauthorized copying. Realistically concerned about loss of control over their intellectual assets, many publishers avoided the digital medium. From the publishers' perspective, the pendulum representing the balance of power between creators and consumers had swung too far towards consumers.

In the late 1990s, trusted systems began to appear from several vendors, including Folio, IBM, Intertrust, Xerox, and Wave Systems. Trusted systems vary in their hardware and software security arrangements, but in general, they automatically enforce terms and conditions under which digital works can be used. For example, rights can expire after a period of time. Different people can pay different fees for using a work, depending on digital licenses for membership in such groups as affiliated book clubs. Trusted systems differentiate between different uses such as making a digital copy, rendering a work on a screen, printing a work on a color printer, or extracting a portion of a work for inclusion in a new work. When asked to perform an operation not licensed by a work's specific terms and conditions, a trusted system refuses to carry it out. So dramatically do trusted systems alter the balance of power between publishers and consumers, some observers have suggested that the pendulum has now swung too far towards publishers.

* * *

Copyright and Trusted Systems

Beginning in the 1990s, it was realized that computers could become part of the solution to the copyright problem that they were said to cause. The key was the development of trusted systems technology.

There are two main ideas behind trusted systems: that the terms and conditions governing the authorized use of a digital work can be expressed in a computer-interpretable language, and that computers and software can be designed to enforce those terms and conditions. An example of a rights language is Xerox's DPRL (Digital Property Rights Language).

Digital rights cluster into several categories. Transport rights include rights to copy, transfer, or loan a work. Render rights include playing and printing. Derivative work rights govern extracting portions of a work, controlled editing of changes to it, and embedding of the portion in other works. Other rights govern the making and restoring of backup copies. With trusted systems, a publisher can assign rights to a digital work. Each right can specify fees that must be paid to exercise the right. Each right can specify access conditions that govern who can exercise the right.

Trusted systems enforce the terms and conditions. They also exchange copies of the work only with systems that can prove themselves trusted via challenge-response protocols. In exchanging digital works, trusted systems form a closed network of computers that exclude non-trusted systems and collectively support use of digital works under established rules of commerce. When digital works are sent between trusted systems, the works are encrypted. When digital works are rendered—by printing them on paper, displaying them on monitors, or playing them on speakers—the rendering process can embed machine-readable watermark data in the signal to make it easier to trace the source of any external copying of the works.

In general, the higher the security of a trusted system, the higher its cost. High-security trusted systems can detect any physical tampering, set off alarms, and erase secret key information inside. Intermediate security trusted systems have more modest physical, encryption, and programmatic defenses. Using challenge-response protocols, trusted systems have the capability to recognize other trusted systems and to determine their security levels. For any particular work, publishers can specify the security level required by a trusted system that can receive it. An expensive industry report might require an expensive and secure corporate trusted system with advanced security measures. A digital newspaper for wide distribution and subsidized by advertisements might require only modest security measures for home computers.

Trusted Systems and the Balance of Interests

There are many stakeholders in digital publishing. Beyond the government itself, U.S. copyright law focuses on two parties or categories of people: rights holders (that is, the authors and publishers who hold the copyrights) and the public. However, trusted systems delegate enforcement and control to computers. One of the effects of this delegation is that it introduces third parties to the arrangement, including distributors, trusted system vendors, financial clearing houses, and multiple governments. This complicates the balance of interests, in that it introduces more parties whose interests need to be considered.

The use of trusted systems to enforce terms and conditions provides a much finer grain of control than copyright law, and moves the legal basis of protection in the direction of contracts and licenses. The finer grain of control includes distinctions between different kinds of usage rights such as copying, loaning, printing, displaying, backup, and so on. It also includes provisions for identifying specific users, specific kinds of devices for rendering, and fees for uses. Further, trusted systems provide a finer grain of control in that it becomes possible for rights holders to monitor and negotiate over transactions in copyrighted works in situations where, in the past, such monitoring and negotiation would have been impractical, if not impossible.

Copyright Law

* * *

Without trusted systems, effective enforcement of copyright in the digital medium can be nearly impossible. Like a proverbial sieve with thousands of little holes, it is too hard and expensive to find all the little infringement leaks of isolated individuals making copies. Furthermore, living with the leaks has its own deep risks. By publishing without copyright enforcement in a community that routinely makes unauthorized copies, rights holders risk that, over time, such copying could become established as common practice or even sanctioned by courts as fair use.

In sum, the move toward digital media poses challenges for copyright law and creates uncertainty for rights holders, especially for would-be publishers in the new media. The uncertainty tends to hamper the adoption of the new media and to discourage publishers from publishing in it. The impracticalities of enforcing copyright on untrusted, networked systems, the gray areas of legal interpretation for digital works, the lack of fine-grained control in copyright law, and the risk of an emerging legal claim of fair use for digital copying all motivate would-be authors and publishers in the digital medium to find means other than copyright law for protecting their interests.

Contract Law and Digital Contracts

In a representative scenario of digital publication on a trusted system, an author begins by creating a digital work. When the work is ready, the author finds a publisher (possibly himself) to develop the work further and to sell it. The publisher develops a set of terms and conditions for use of the work. Using a rights management language like DPRL, the publisher specifies the time period over which the rights apply. He determines what rights to include, for example, whether printing is allowed, whether the work can be loaned out for free, whether there is a special discount for members of a particular book club. He may assign different fees for different rights. For example, he may decide either to disallow creation of derivative works or to encourage creation of such works as a source of further revenue. He may mandate that the reader of the digital work must have proof in the form of a proper digital certificate that he is over 18. In DPRL, each right specification statement includes a type of right, a time specification governing when the right is valid, an access specification governing any special licenses required to exercise the right, and a fee specification governing billing. Using a trusted system, these rights are associated with the digital work, either by bundling them together in an encrypted file or by assigning the work a unique digital identifier and by registering the work and its rights in an on-line database.

Why would a publisher or a consumer want to have a specific and detailed agreement about use? The alternative, based on copyright as used for most printed works, is to have a single fee to purchase a work and then general legal standards about how works can be used. In the previous section we considered motivations for publishers to use specialized terms and conditions for their digital works. Specialized rules also have potential economic advantages for consumers. In the established software market, a software license is typically purchased for a fixed fee. This means that a user who expects to make little use of a software product must pay the same fee as someone who would use it for many hours a day. In some markets, this situation is bad for both publishers and consumers because many low-usage consumers will decide not to purchase the software at all. Trusted systems offer the possibility of differential pricing and "metered use" in which the amount that someone pays to use software depends on how much they use it. One way to look at metered use is that it allows "renting" software, where the rental terms can be flexible enough to provide for decreasing costs or caps with increased volume of use.

Another example of mutual economic advantages concerns the first sale doctrine. When consumers buy a paper book, they receive and own the copy of the book. When they are done with the book, they are free to give it to a friend or to sell the book to someone else. The first sale doctrine from copyright law guarantees these rights. In the DPRL language, the analogous usage right is called a transfer right. When one trusted system transfers a digital work to a second trusted system, the copy on the first trusted system is deleted or deactivated so that it can no longer be used. Analogous to handing a book to a friend, a transfer operation preserves the number of usable copies of the work. Analogous to the first sale doctrine, the terms and conditions on a digital work could allow it to be transferred at no charge.

A free transfer right is exactly what a consumer might want if he or she were buying the digital work for a friend, or intended to share the work serially with others. On the other hand, from a publisher's perspective, a free transfer right is a threat to future sales. If each person who reads a copy of a digital work needs to buy their own copy, the publisher would sell more copies. A publisher could offer two different combinations of rights with a work. In one combination, the consumer pays the "standard" amount for a work, and can transfer the work without a fee just as with the first sale doctrine. In another combination, the consumer gets a discount for a non-transferable work or must pay a fee to transfer it. This discounted purchase might be preferred by a consumer who buys the work for his personal use and who does not anticipate giving it away. Arguably, the first sale doctrine is grounded in experience with paper-based works and the copies were treated as physical objects, independent of their creative content. Like tools or food, such physical objects could be resold at the owner's convenience. Enforcement of a law to prevent resale or giving of books would be difficult in any case, so the first sale doctrine makes sense for paper-based works. For digital works and trusted systems, these considerations are less relevant. The publisher and the consumer are free to enter into an agreement that each sees as economically advantageous.

In many ways, a set of terms and conditions in DPRL is much like a contract or license agreement for using a digital work. For convenience here, we will call such a set of terms and conditions a digital contract. However, it should be remembered that a digital contract differs from an ordinary contract in crucial ways. Notably, in an ordinary contract between people, compliance is not automatic and is the responsibility of the agreeing parties. There may be provisions for monitoring and checking compliance with the terms and conditions, but the responsibility for acting in accordance with the terms falls on the parties, and enforcement of the contract is ultimately the province of the courts. In contrast, with trusted systems, a substantial part of the enforcement of a digital contract is carried out by the trusted systems themselves. In the short term, at least, the consumer does not have an option to disregard a digital contract, for example, to make infringing copies of a digital work. A trusted system will refuse to exercise a right that is not sanctioned by the digital contract. Over the longer term, it may be possible for consumers or consumer advocacy groups to negotiate with publishers to obtain different terms and conditions in the digital contracts, but even then, the new digital contracts will be subject to automatic enforcement by trusted systems.

* * *

Courts provide checks and balances in contract law by deciding what contracts to enforce and how to interpret the terms and conditions of those contracts. With properly designed trusted systems, many of these checks and balances can be made available automatically. Consider a digital publishing scenario again. The author has finished the work and the publisher assigns terms and conditions. Just as there can be conventional (so-called "boilerplate") language used in putting together an agreement, there can be digital boilerplate in the form of templates and default conditions in setting up a digital contract. Suppose that the publisher has included some very unusual terms and conditions in the agreement. When the consumer's trusted system is in communication with the publisher's trusted system, it can first retrieve the terms and conditions of the digital contract. It shows these to the consumer. Before the consumer accepts receipt of the digital work, a program can check for and highlight unusual conditions in the digital contract. Because rights management languages like DPRL are simple and formal languages with limited complexity, simple grammar and predetermined meanings, this checking is straightforward for a computer. In particular, the contract checker can look for unusual or high fees on certain rights, unrealistic expiration dates, or any other requirement that is outside of the usual practice. (As a somewhat bizarre example, consider a digital work that the consumer can copy for free but, surprisingly and inconveniently, costs $10 to delete.) The consumer is given an opportunity to agree to the terms and accept delivery or to refuse the terms and not take delivery of the work. If the consumer agrees, his trusted system can digitally sign a form marking his agreement to the contract. This signing can be digitally notarized by a third party (a "digital notary") known to both parties.

The sequence of events in this example illustrates several checks and balances in the process. Both the publisher and the consumer can use computational aids to check the normalcy and appropriateness of the contract. More than being a labor-saving or time-saving procedure, this approach also helps to compensate for the somewhat less tangible nature of information inside computers. It gives increased confidence to both parties that the terms and conditions used by the trusted systems will be reasonable.

It is helpful to think of a digital contract as encompassing several distinct legal contracts. There is the contract for access to the copyrighted work itself. Further, there is a contract for the service of delivering digital data to the consumer, irrespective of whether that data is or can be copyrighted. For example, if the publisher provides an uncopyrightable database or telephone white pages directory to the consumer via a trusted system, the publisher can fairly charge for this service, even though the consumer could, in principle, get the uncopyrightable data elsewhere or put together the database himself. Similarly, the digital publisher could charge the consumer for a copy of the complete works of Shakespeare even though that is in the public domain, just as print publishers can charge for printed copies of Shakespeare's works. Put another way, like the print publisher, the digital publisher has made life more convenient for the consumer, and the consumer pays the publisher for this convenience. What the publisher of an uncopyrightable or public domain work cannot do is to prevent another publisher from offering consumers the same or a comparable work, as would be the case if the work were copyrighted. Finally, there is a third contract implicit in the digital contract, namely, the service agreement by which the consumer is entitled to access the network of trusted systems in the first place. This agreement may be arranged between the consumer and the publisher, or between the consumer and one or more network service providers who may or may not be affiliated with the publisher.

The idea that a digital contract includes multiple legal contracts provides a coherent rationale for why digital contracts ought to be enforceable, even as to uncopyrightable works. For example, suppose that a publisher provides a public domain work, such as the complete works of Shakespeare, to the consumer via a trusted system. However, the digital contract for this work prohibits the consumer from copying or further transferring the contents of the work, at least not in digital form. The consumer is unhappy about this. He knows that the work is not protected by copyright and, when the bill arrives from the publisher, he refuses to pay, or else sues to get his money back. In court, the consumer argues that for the publisher to charge for what is no longer protected by copyright is in violation of the policy of copyright to establish limited-term monopolies for authors. Therefore, says the consumer, the digital contract should be preempted by the Copyright Act and should be held unenforceable. (The consumer might also argue that, because the publisher accepts the consumer's money while providing in return only a public domain work that ought to be available for free, the agreement fails for lack of consideration). The publisher responds that what is being sold here isn't the work, but rather the service of delivering the work. The publisher says, in effect, "Consumer, by dealing with me, you save time and energy and money over other delivery mechanisms such as conventional bookstores. But if I, as vendor, want to continue successfully to provide this service to others, then I am entitled to collect revenue at every transaction, not just the first one. Therefore, I can legitimately prevent you by this digital contract from transferring the copy of the work I just sold you." We think that the publisher has the better argument here. The consumer can pay the publisher for the right to print out the contents of the book, and can then copy the contents, for example, by hand or by scanning with an untrusted optical scanner. Also, other publishers can produce similar books containing identical texts, and a not-for-profit library could make these texts available for free. In short, the publisher has not overstepped the bounds of copyright.

Another point of possible concern with a digital contract is the extent to which a user is realistically in a position to negotiate the terms of the contract. In court cases concerning the viability of shrinkwrap licenses, one of the legal arguments used to challenge the validity of the license is that a publisher has an advantaged position of power and leaves the user with only a "take it or leave it" proposition. In this situation, many consumers do not bother to read the shrinkwrap license. In the case of trusted systems, it may be important that a consumer agent could be called upon to highlight terms and conditions likely to be unacceptable. In principle, one of the options when such terms are found is for the trusted systems to open a channel for negotiation and possible change of the terms. It is worth noting, however, that one of the main advantages of digital publishing is the possibility of fully automated systems providing 24–hour shopping convenience. In that setting, one might not expect to negotiate the terms of purchase for a mass-market digital work any more than one would expect to negotiate the price of buying a best-seller paperback at a convenience store in the middle of the night. The consumer would simply have to either accept the terms as they stand, or postpone her purchase until such time as a human agent became available to negotiate the terms.

* * *

NOTES & QUESTIONS

1. *Implementation of trusted systems.* Digital rights management systems along the lines described in this article have been implemented in several contexts. The Serial Copy Management System, discussed in Chapter 3, Part III(D), *supra*, has been required for digital audio tape machines since 1992. More recently, some music CDs have been released with coding designed to prevent them from being copied using a CD–RW drive, or even being played on a computer. Motion pictures on DVD are protected by an encryption system called the Content Scramble System, which is designed to prevent unauthorized copying. As discussed in *Universal City Studios, Inc. v. Reimerdes*, excerpted in Part II, *infra*, CSS was cracked and circumvented by a 15-year-old Norwegian computer hobbyist, giving rise to several lawsuits and creating a cause célèbre for both proponents and opponents of trusted systems. Movie DVDs also contain regional coding, which prevents a DVD purchased in one region of the world from playing on a DVD player sold in a different region of the world. Electronic books are released with DRMS technology provided by several manufacturers, including Palm, Microsoft, and Adobe. What are the obstacles to the further implementation of systems such as these?

2. *Limiting users' rights.* The rights that one has with respect to a digital product (a music CD, a movie on DVD, software, data, a text) one purchases may be limited through several methods. First, the copyright laws limit the purchaser's right to copy, adapt, distribute, perform, and display works to which copyright applies. Second, one's rights may be limited by an accompanying set of terms, usually called a license agreement, that is deemed part of the contract between the parties. Third, one's rights may be limited by a digital rights management system incorporated into the product. In what ways do these three methods of limiting the purchaser's rights differ, from the standpoint of both vendor and purchaser? Consider the extent to which such terms may be negotiated; the ability of the parties to renegotiate disputed terms; the availability of legal defenses to enforcement; the costs of enforcement.

3. *A technological arms race.* Trusted systems, like any other technology, are susceptible to circumvention. A piece of computer code designed to prevent unauthorized access to an informational good may be defeated by another piece of computer code. The latter code may itself be neutralized by a counter-measure that plugs the loophole it exploited, giving rise to a circumvention that exploits some different loophole. This has led to a sort of technological arms race, in which trusted-system creators and hackers take turns outwitting one another. Who do you think is more likely to win this arms race: the lock-makers, or the lock-breakers? Do you agree with amateur cryptographer Edgar Allen Poe: "[I]t may be roundly asserted that human ingenuity cannot concoct a cipher which human ingenuity cannot resolve."?[2]

Suppose that the locks are effective enough to keep out all but a tiny proportion of the population, the hacker aristocracy, who are able to defeat any trusted system in existence. Should copyright owners feel safe? Do you agree with the following analogy, offered by Professor Lessig?: "[F]rom the fact that 'hackers could break any security system,' it no more follows that security systems are irrelevant than it follows from the fact that 'a locksmith can pick any lock' that locks are irrelevant. Locks, like security systems on computers, will be quite effective, even if there are norm-

---

2. Edgar Allan Poe, *A Few Words on Secret Writing*, Graham's Magazine, July 1841, at 33, 33.

oblivious sorts who can break them." Lawrence Lessig, *Reading the Constitution in Cyberspace*, 45 EMORY L.J. 869, 896 n.80 (1996). In the digital world, is there an argument that any system that is less than 100 percent effective is practically worthless?

II. USING AND TRAFFICKING IN CIRCUMVENTION TECHNOLOGIES: TITLE I OF THE DIGITAL MILLENNIUM COPYRIGHT ACT

Congress responded to the technological arms race described above, weighing in on the side of the trusted-system community, with Title I of the Digital Millennium Copyright Act of 1998 ("DMCA"), 17 U.S.C. §§ 1201–05. The drive for regulation of this kind developed in the mid–1990s when the World International Property Organization ("WIPO") Copyright Treaty and the WIPO Performances and Phonograms Treaty were negotiated. Article 11 of the WIPO Copyright Treaty, titled "Obligations concerning Technological Measures," requires:

> Contracting Parties shall provide adequate legal protection and effective legal remedies against the circumvention of effective technological measures that are used by authors in connection with the exercise of their rights under this Treaty or the Berne Convention and that restrict acts, in respect of their works, which are not authorized by the authors concerned or permitted by law.

WIPO Copyright Treaty, Dec. 20, 1996, art. 11, WIPO Doc. CRNR/DC/94, www.wipo.int/eng/diplconf/distrib/94dc.htm.

In addition, Article 12 of the same treaty, "Obligations concerning Rights Management Information," states:

> (1) Contracting Parties shall provide adequate and effective legal remedies against any person knowingly performing any of the following acts knowing, or with respect to civil remedies having reasonable grounds to know, that it will induce, enable, facilitate or conceal an infringement of any right covered by this Treaty or the Berne Convention:
>
> > (i) to remove or alter any electronic rights management information without authority;
> >
> > (ii) to distribute, import for distribution, broadcast or communicate to the public, without authority, works or copies of works knowing that electronic rights management information has been removed or altered without authority.
>
> (2) As used in this Article, "rights management information" means information which identifies the work, the author of the work, the owner of any right in the work, or information about the terms and conditions of use of the work, and any numbers or codes that represent such information, when any of these items of information

> is attached to a copy of a work or appears in connection with the communication of a work to the public.

Id. art. 12. Nearly identical provisions can also be found in the WIPO Performances and Phonograms Treaty. *See* WIPO Performances and Phonograms Treaty, Dec. 20, 1996, arts. 18 & 19, WIPO Doc. CRNR/DC/95, www.wipo.org/eng/diplconf/distrib/95dc.htm. Enactment of Title I of the DMCA was intended to meet the obligations of the United States under both of these treaties.

A Senate Report on the DMCA describes Title I as follows:

> Title I implements the WIPO Copyright Treaty and the WIPO Performances and Phonograms Treaty. These treaties were concluded by the Clinton administration in December 1996. The treaties are best understood as supplements to the Berne Convention for the Protection of Literary and Artistic Works. The Berne Convention is the leading multilateral treaty on copyright and related rights, with 130 countries adhering to it. The United States ratified the Berne Convention in 1989. The two new WIPO treaties were adopted at a diplomatic conference by a consensus of over 150 countries. In general, the Copyright Treaty updates the Berne Convention for digital works and the growth of the Internet and other digital communications networks, and the Performances and Phonograms Treaty supplements the Berne Convention with comprehensive copyright protection for performances and sound recordings (called "phonograms" in international parlance).
>
> The importance of the treaties to the protection of American copyrighted works abroad cannot be overestimated. The treaties, as well as the Berne Convention, are based on the principle of national treatment; that is, that adhering countries are obliged to grant the same protection to foreign works that they grant to domestic works. Even more importantly, the Berne Convention and the treaties set minimum standards of protection. Thus, the promise of the treaties is that, in an increasing[ly] global digital marketplace, U.S. copyright owners will be able to rely upon strong, non-discriminatory copyright protection in most of the countries of the world.
>
> The copyright industries are one of America's largest and fastest growing economic assets. * * * In fact, the copyright industries contribute more to the U.S. economy and employ more workers than any single manufacturing sector, including chemicals, industrial equipment, electronics, food processing, textiles and apparel, and aircraft. More significantly for the WIPO treaties, in 1996 U.S. copyright industries achieved foreign sales and exports of $60.18 billion, for the first time leading all major industry sectors, including agriculture, automobiles and auto parts, and the aircraft industry.

The WIPO treaties contain many important provisions. For example, the Copyright Treaty contains significant provisions such as: * * * (5) an obligation to provide "legal protection and effective legal remedies" against circumventing technological measures, e.g. encryption and password protection, that are used by copyright owners to protect their works from piracy; and (6) an obligation to provide "adequate and effective legal remedies" to preserve the integrity of "rights management information." * * *

The Committee believes that in order to adhere to the WIPO treaties, legislation is necessary in two primary areas—anticircumvention of technological protection measures and protection of the integrity of rights management information, or "copyright management information" (CMI), as it is referred to in the bill. This view is shared by the Clinton administration. In drafting implementing legislation for the WIPO treaties, the Committee has sought to address those two areas, as well as avoid government regulation of the Internet and encourage technological solutions. The Committee is keenly aware that other countries will use U.S. legislation as a model.

S. REP. NO. 105–190, at 9–11 (1998).

Title I of the DMCA added Chapter 12 to Title 17 of the U.S. Code. The first section of this chapter, Section 1201, deals with using and trafficking in circumvention technologies. Section 1201(a)(1)(A) makes it illegal to "circumvent a technological measure that effectively controls access to a work protected under" the Copyright Act. Section 1201(a)(2) provides:

No person shall manufacture, import, offer to the public, provide, or otherwise traffic in any technology, product, service, device, component, or part thereof, that—

(A) is primarily designed or produced for the purpose of circumventing a technological measure that effectively controls access to a work protected under this title;

(B) has only limited commercially significant purpose or use other than to circumvent a technological measure that effectively controls access to a work protected under this title; or

(C) is marketed by that person or another acting in concert with that person with that person's knowledge for use in circumventing a technological measure that effectively controls access to a work protected under this title.

Section 1201(b)(1) further provides:

No person shall manufacture, import, offer to the public, provide, or otherwise traffic in any technology, product, service, device, component, or part thereof, that—

(A) is primarily designed or produced for the purpose of circumventing protection afforded by a technological measure that effectively protects a right of a copyright owner under this title in a work or a portion thereof;

(B) has only limited commercially significant purpose or use other than to circumvent protection afforded by a technological measure that effectively protects a right of a copyright owner under this title in a work or a portion thereof; or

(C) is marketed by that person or another acting in concert with that person with that person's knowledge for use in circumventing protection afforded by a technological measure that effectively protects a right of a copyright owner under this title in a work or a portion thereof.

Section 1201 thus addresses two types of technological protections of copyrighted works, and two types of forbidden conduct in connection with those protections. The two types of technological protections are those that prevent unauthorized *access* to a work, and those that prevent *use* of a work in a manner that infringes the copyright. The two types of forbidden conduct are the *act of circumventing* a technological protection, and the manufacturing or distribution of a device or software program that disables such a protection, generally referred to as *trafficking*. As a matter of logic, the combination of two technological protections with two types of prohibited conduct could yield four (two times two) prohibitions. In fact, however, Section 1201 only addresses three of those combinations. With respect to the first type of technological protection (preventing unauthorized access), it is illegal both to circumvent it and to traffic in technologies of circumvention. With respect to the second type of technological protection (preventing unauthorized use), it is illegal to traffic in technologies of circumvention, but there is no prohibition against the act of circumvention. The prohibitions of Section 1201 may be represented graphically:

		Type of technological protection	
		Access controls	Use controls
Type of prohibition	Prohibition on circumvention	§ 1201(a)(1)(A)	None
	Prohibition on trafficking	§ 1201(a)(2)	§ 1201(b)(1)

Why does Section 1201 contain no prohibition against the act of circumventing protection of the rights of a copyright owner? The Senate Report explains:

The prohibition in 1201(a)(1) is necessary because prior to this Act, the conduct of circumvention was never before made unlawful. The device limitation in 1201(a)(2) enforces this new prohibition on conduct. The copyright law has long forbidden copyright infringements, so no new prohibition [on conduct facilitated by the devices prohibited in 1201(b)] was necessary. The device limitation in 1201(b) enforces the longstanding prohibitions on infringements.

S. REP. NO. 105–190, *supra*, at 12.

Thus, according to the Senate Report a prohibition on the act of circumventing a technological measure that prevents infringement of a copyright—which would occupy the upper right-hand box in the above chart—is unnecessary, because it would be redundant with the central provision of the Copyright Act, 17 U.S.C. § 106.

In addition to setting forth the preceding anti-circumvention and anti-trafficking prohibitions, Section 1201 also creates a series of exceptions to them. There are exemptions from the anti-circumvention provisions for nonprofit libraries and educational institutions, law enforcement and intelligence agents, reverse engineering computer programs, encryption research, filtering Web content to determine if it is appropriate for minors, protection of privacy, and testing computer and network security. *See* 17 U.S.C. § 1201(d)–(j). (Some of these exemptions also apply, to a limited extent, to the anti-trafficking provisions.) Moreover, Section 1201(a)(1)(B)–(E) empowers the Librarian of Congress, upon recommendation from the Register of Copyrights, to create additional exceptions to the prohibition against circumventing access controls. Pursuant to this subsection, the Librarian has exempted (through October 28, 2003) two additional narrow categories of use: "(1) Compilations consisting of lists of websites blocked by filtering software applications; and (2) Literary works, including computer programs and databases, protected by access control mechanisms that fail to permit access because of malfunction, damage or obsoleteness." 37 C.F.R. § 201.40. It remains to be seen whether these exceptions can satisfy the concerns of advocates of broader rights for users of protected materials.

Beyond the prohibitions and exceptions created by this section, Section 1201(c)(1) & (2) emphasize that none of the foregoing "shall affect rights, remedies, limitations, or defenses to copyright infringement, including fair use," or "shall enlarge or diminish vicarious or contributory liability for copyright infringement in connection with any technology, product, service, device, component, or part thereof." Moreover, with one exception, Section 1201(c)(3) states that manufacturers of consumer electronics, telecommunications equipment, and computer products are not required to design their products so that they accommodate access and use controls. The one exception is created by Section 1201(k), which requires manufacturers, importers, and distributors of certain devices such as VCRs and camcorders to produce, import and traffic only in devices that employ the copy control technology developed and owned by Macrovision Corporation.[3] By requiring

---

3. The reference to Macrovision Corp. occurs not in the statute, but only in the legislative history. *See* H.R. CONF. REP. NO. 105–796, at 67–69 (1998).

the use of a specific technology, this provision contrasts sharply with the rest of the DMCA, which strives to remain technology-neutral.

To set the stage for examination of the continuing controversies surrounding the DMCA, consider the following portions of its legislative history. While reading it, think about how Congress characterizes the problem the legislation is supposed to solve, and how it conceives of the fit between this statute and pre-existing copyright law. Consider, as well, what role is played by Congress's understanding of existing and foreseeable encryption technology. What interest groups do you think were most influential in crafting this legislation?

Section–By–Section Analysis of H.R. 2281

House Committee on the Judiciary, 105th Congress.
(Comm. Print 1998).

* * *

Section 1201: Circumvention of Copyright Protection Systems.

Subsection (a) of new Section 1201 applies when a person who is not authorized to have access to a work seeks to gain access by circumventing a technological measure put in place by the copyright owner that effectively controls access to the work. * * *

[§ 1201(a)(1).] The act of circumventing a technological protection measure put in place by a copyright owner to control access to a copyrighted work is the electronic equivalent of breaking into a locked room in order to obtain a copy of a book. Subparagraph (A) establishes a general prohibition against gaining unauthorized access to a work by circumventing a technological measure put in place by the copyright owner where such measure effectively controls access to a work protected under Title 17 of the U.S. Code. * * *

* * *

* * * The technological measures—such as encryption, scrambling and electronic envelopes—that this bill protects can be deployed, not only to prevent piracy and other economically harmful unauthorized uses of copyrighted materials, but also to support new ways of disseminating copyrighted materials to users, and to safeguard the availability of legitimate uses of those materials by individuals. These technological measures may make more works more widely available, and the process of obtaining permissions easier.

For example, an access control technology under section 1201(a) would not necessarily prevent access to a work altogether, but could be designed to allow access during a limited time period, such as during a period of library borrowing. Technological measures are also essential to a distribution strategy that allows a consumer to purchase a copy of a single article from an electronic database, rather than having to pay more for a subscription to a journal containing many articles the consumer does not want.

* * *

[§ *1201(a)(2)*]. In order to provide meaningful protection and enforcement of the copyright owner's right to control access to his or her copyrighted work, this paragraph supplements the prohibition against the act of circumvention in [§ 1201(a)(1)] with prohibitions on creating and making available certain technologies, products and services used, developed or advertised to defeat technological protections against unauthorized access to a work. * * *

Specifically, [§ 1201(a)(2)] prohibits manufacturing, importing, offering to the public, providing, or otherwise trafficking in certain technologies, products, services, devices, components, or parts that can be used to circumvent a technological protection measure that otherwise effectively controls access to a work protected under Title 17. It is drafted carefully to target "black boxes," and to ensure that legitimate multipurpose devices can continue to be made and sold. For a technology, product, service, device, component, or part thereof to be prohibited under this subsection, one of three conditions must be met. It must:

(1) be primarily designed or produced for the purpose of circumventing;

(2) have only a limited commercially significant purpose or use other than to circumvent; or

(3) be marketed by the person who manufactures it, imports it, offers it to the public, provides it or otherwise traffics in it, or by another person acting in concert with that person, for use in circumventing a technological protection measure that effectively controls access to a work protected under Title 17.

This provision is designed to protect copyright owners, and simultaneously allow the development of technology.

This three-part test, established for determining when the manufacture, distribution or other provision of a product or service constitutes a violation, is the core of the anti-circumvention provisions of this legislation. This test (also spelled out in 1201(b)(1)), as explicated by the Judiciary Committee report, stands on its own. While this legislation is aimed primarily at "black boxes" that have virtually no legitimate uses, trafficking in any product or service that meets one or more of the three points in this test could lead to liability. It is not required to prove that the device in question was "expressly intended to facilitate circumvention." At the same time, the manufacturers of legitimate consumer products such as personal computers, VCR's, and the like have nothing to fear from this legislation because those legitimate devices do not meet the three-part test. The *Sony* test of "capab[ility] of substantial non-infringing uses," while still operative in cases claiming contributory infringement of copyright, is not part of this legislation, however. *Sony Corporation of America v. Universal City Studios, Inc.*, 464 U.S. 417 (1984). The relevant test, spelled out in the plain and unchanged language of the bill, is whether or not a product or service "has only limited commercially significant purpose or use other than to circumvent."

* * *

The Committee on the Judiciary, which possesses primary jurisdiction over this legislation, considered the argument that the lack of a definition of "technological measure" leaves manufacturers in the dark as to the range of protective technologies to which their products must respond. The Committee concluded that any such concern is unfounded. No legitimate manufacturer of consumer electronics devices or computer equipment could reasonably claim to be left in doubt about the course of action to be avoided, simply because the phrase "technological measure" is not itself defined in the bill. The only obligation imposed on manufacturers by this legislation is a purely negative one: to refrain from affirmatively designing a product or a component *primarily* for the purpose of circumventing a protective technology that effectively controls unauthorized access to or uses of a copyrighted work.

Any effort to read into this bill what is not there—a statutory definition of "technological measure"—or to define in terms of particular technologies what constitutes an "effective" measure, could inadvertently deprive legal protection to some of the copy or access control technologies that are or will be in widespread use for the protection of both digital and analog formats. Perhaps more importantly, this approach runs a substantial risk of discouraging innovation in the development of protective technologies. For instance, today the standard form of encryption of digital materials involves scrambling its contents so that they are unintelligible unless processed with a key supplied by the copyright owner or its agent. However, in a field that changes and advances as rapidly as encryption research, it would be short-sighted to write this definition into a statute as the exclusive technological means protected by this bill.

* * *

[§ 1201(b)] applies when a person has obtained authorized access to a copy or a phonorecord of a work, but the copyright owner has put in place technological measures that effectively protect his or her rights under Title 17 to control or limit the nature of the use of the copyrighted work.

[§ 1201(b)(1)]. Paralleling subsection (a)(2), above, [§ 1201(b)(1)] seeks to provide meaningful protection and enforcement of copyright owners' use of technological measures to protect their rights under Title 17 by prohibiting the act of making or selling the technological means to overcome these protections and facilitate copyright infringement. Paragraph (1) prohibits manufacturing, importing, offering to the public, providing, or otherwise trafficking in certain technologies, products, services, devices, components, or parts thereof that can be used to circumvent a technological measure that effectively protects a right of a copyright owner under Title 17 in a work or portion thereof. Again, for a technology, product, service, device,

component, or part thereof to be prohibited under this subsection, one of three conditions must be met. It must:

(1) be primarily designed or produced for the purpose of circumventing;

(2) have only limited commercially significant purpose or use other than to circumvent; or

(3) be marketed by the person who manufactures it, imports it, offers it to the public, provides it, or otherwise traffics in it, or by another person acting in concert with that person, for use in circumventing a technological protection measure that effectively protects the right of a copyright owner under Title 17 in a work or a portion thereof.

Like subsection (a)(2), this provision is designed to protect copyright owners, and simultaneously allow the development of technology.

[§ 1201(b)(2)] defines certain terms used in subsection (b):

(1) "circumvent protection afforded by a technological measure" is defined as "avoiding, bypassing, removing, deactivating, or otherwise impairing a technological measure."

(2) "effectively protects a right of a copyright owner under Title 17"—a technological measure effectively protects a right of a copyright owner under Title 17 "if the measure, in the ordinary course of its operation, prevents, restricts, or otherwise limits the exercise of a right under Title 17 of a copyright owner."

* * *

[§ 1201(c)] provides that section 1201 shall not have any effect on rights, remedies, limitations, or defenses to copyright infringement, including fair use, under Title 17. Paragraph (2) provides that section 1201 shall not alter the existing doctrines of contributory or vicarious liability for copyright infringement in connection with any technology, product, service, device, component or part thereof. Together, these provisions are intended to ensure that none of the provisions in section 1201 affect the existing legal regime established in the Copyright Act and case law interpreting that statute.

* * *

[§ 1201(f)] is intended to allow legitimate software developers to continue engaging in certain activities for the purpose of achieving interoperability to the extent permitted by law prior to the enactment of this chapter. The objective is to ensure that the effect of current case law interpreting the Copyright Act is not changed by enactment of this legislation for certain acts of identification and analysis done in respect of computer programs. *See Sega Enterprises Ltd.* v. *Accolade, Inc.*, 977 F.2d 1510 (9th Cir.1992). The purpose of this subsection is to avoid hindering competition and innovation in the computer and software industry.

[§ 1201(f)(1)] permits the circumvention of access control technologies for the sole purpose of achieving software interoperability. For example, this subsection permits a software developer to circumvent an access control technology applied to a portion or portions of a program in order to perform the necessary steps to identify and analyze the information needed to achieve interoperability. * * * [T]he goal of this section is to ensure that current law is not changed, and not to encourage or permit infringement. Thus, each of the acts undertaken must fall within the scope of fair use or otherwise avoid infringing the copyright of the author of the underlying computer program.

[§ 1201(f)(2)] recognizes that to accomplish the acts permitted under paragraph (1) a person may, in some instances, have to make and use certain tools. In most instances these will be generally available tools that programmers use in developing computer programs, such as compilers, trace analyzers and disassemblers, which do not fall within the prohibition of this section. In certain instances, it is possible that a person may have to develop special tools to achieve the permitted purpose of interoperability. Thus, this provision creates an exception to the prohibition on making circumvention tools contained in sections 1201(a)(2) and (b). These tools can be either software or hardware. Again, this provision is limited by a general ban on acting in a way that constitutes infringing activity.

* * *

[§ 1201(f)(4)] defines "interoperability" as the ability of computer programs to exchange information, and for such programs mutually to use the information which has been exchanged. The seamless exchange of information is a key element of creating an interoperable independently created program. This provision applies to computer programs as such, regardless of their medium of fixation and not to works generally, such as music or audiovisual works, which may be fixed and distributed in digital form. Accordingly, since the goal of interoperability is the touchstone of the exceptions contained in paragraphs (1)–(3), nothing in those paragraphs can be read to authorize the circumvention of any technological protection measure that controls access to any work other than a computer program, or the trafficking in products or services for that purpose.

[§ 1201(g)] is intended to facilitate the purpose of this bill, namely, to improve the ability of copyright owners to prevent the theft of their works, including by applying technological measures. * * *

* * * This subsection provides that generally available encryption testing tools meeting certain specifications will not be made illegal by this Act. If each of these tools has a legitimate and substantial commercial purpose—testing security and effectiveness—it is therefore explicitly excluded from the prohibition in section 1201.

In addition to the exemption contained in this subsection, the testing of specific encryption algorithms would not fall within the scope of 1201, since mathematical formulas as such are not protected by copyright. * * *

* * *

[An] example would be a company, in the course of developing a new cryptographic product, sponsoring a crypto-cracking contest with cash prizes. Contestants would not violate section 1201, since the research acts are specifically authorized.

Significantly, section 1201 does not make illegal cryptographic devices that have substantial legitimate purposes other than to circumvent technological protection measures as applied to a work. For example, many popular word processing and other computer programs include a security feature allowing users to password-protect documents (employing a low-grade form of encryption.) It is not uncommon for users of such products to forget or lose their passwords for such documents, making their own protected works unrecoverable. As a result, many independent programmers have created utilities designed to assist in the recovery of passwords or password-protected works. Several of these utilities are distributed over the Internet as freeware or shareware. Because these utilities have a substantial legitimate use, and because they would be used by persons to gain access to their own works, these devices do not violate section 1201.

* * *

Today, network and website management and security tools increasingly contain components that automatically test a system's security and identify common vulnerabilities. These programs are valuable tools for systems administrators and website operators, to use in the course of their regular testing of their systems' security. Again, because these devices are good products put to a good use, they do not fall within the scope of this statute.

In sum, the prohibition on "devices" as written does not encompass many forms of useful encryption products. Subsection (g) is specifically structured to go further, and allow the development and use of certain additional encryption products used for research purposes.

* * *

Conference Report, Digital Millennium Copyright Act

H.R. Conf. Rep. No. 105–796.
(1998).

* * *

Section 1201(j)—Security Testing. * * * It is not the intent of this act to prevent persons utilizing technological measures in respect of computers, computer systems or networks from testing the security value and effectiveness of the technological measures they employ, or from contracting with companies that specialize in such security testing.

Thus, in addition to the exception for good faith encryption research contained in Section 1201(g), the conferees have adopted Section 1201(j) to resolve additional issues related to the effect of the anti-circumvention provision on legitimate information security activities. First, the conferees were concerned that Section 1201(g)'s exclusive focus on encryption-related research does not encompass the entire range of legitimate information security activities. Not every technological means that is used to provide security relies on encryption technology, or does so to the exclusion of other methods. Moreover, an individual who is legitimately testing a security technology may be doing so not to advance the state of encryption research or to develop encryption products, but rather to ascertain the effectiveness of that particular security technology.

The conferees were also concerned that the anti-circumvention provision of Section 1201(a) could be construed to inhibit legitimate forms of security testing. It is not unlawful to test the effectiveness of a security measure before it is implemented to protect the work covered under title 17. Nor is it unlawful for a person who has implemented a security measure to test its effectiveness. In this respect, the scope of permissible security testing under the Act should be the same as permissible testing of a simple door lock: a prospective buyer may test the lock at the store with the store's consent, or may purchase the lock and test it at home in any manner that he or she sees fit—for example, by installing the lock on the front door and seeing if it can be picked. What that person may not do, however, is test the lock once it has been installed on someone else's door, without the consent of the person whose property is protected by the lock.

* * *

Section 1201(j)(4) permits an individual, notwithstanding the prohibition contained in Section 1201(a)(2), to develop, produce, distribute, or employ technological means for the sole purpose of performing acts of good faith security testing under Section 1201(j)(2), provided the technological means do not otherwise violate section 1201(a)(2). It is Congress' intent for this subsection to have application only with respect to good faith security testing. The intent is to ensure that parties engaged in good faith security testing have the tools available to them to complete such acts. The conferees understand that such tools may be coupled with additional tools that serve purposes wholly unrelated to the purposes of this Act. Eligibility for this exemption should not be precluded because these tools are coupled in such a way. The exemption would not be available, however, when such tools are coupled with a product or technology that violates section 1201(a)(2).

Section 1201(k)—Certain Analog Devices and Certain Technological Measures. The conferees included a provision in the final legislation to require that analog video cassette recorders must conform to the two forms of copy control technology that are in wide use in the market today—the automatic gain control copy control technology and the colorstripe copy control technology. Neither are currently required elements of any format of video recorder, and the ability of each technology to work as intended depends on the consistency of design of video recorders or on incorporation of specific response elements in video recorders. Moreover, they do not employ encryption or scrambling of the content being protected.

As a consequence, these analog copy control technologies may be rendered ineffective either by redesign of video recorders or by intervention of "black box" devices or software "hacks". The conferees believe, and specifically intend, that the general circumvention prohibition in Section 1201(b)(2) will prohibit the manufacture and sale of "black box" devices that defeat these technologies. Moreover, the conferees believe and intend that the term "technology" should be read to include the software "hacks" of this type, and that such "hacks" are equally prohibited by the general circumvention provision. Devices have been marketed that claim to "fix" television picture disruptions allegedly caused by these technologies. However, as described in more detail below, there is no justification for the existence of any intervention device to "fix" such problems allegedly caused by these technologies, including "fixes" allegedly related to stabilization or clean up of the picture quality. Such devices should be seen for what they are—circumvention devices prohibited by this legislation.

* * *

NOTES & QUESTIONS

1. *Interoperability.* Many products, to be useful, must be designed so as to work in tandem with some other product—they must be designed to be interoperable. Electrical plugs must fit into outlets; software must interoperate with the operating system on which it runs. In designing a plug to fit into an outlet, it is a simple matter to take apart—to disassemble—an outlet and thereby deduce how the plug must be designed to fit it. Doing so may result in destroying the outlet, but runs no risk of legal liability (as long as the dissassembler owns the outlet). In designing software to work with an operating system, it is necessary to know something about that system. The act of disassembling an operating system, to see how it works, inevitably involves copying copyrighted computer code, which may infringe rights of the copyright owner. In *Sega Enterprises Ltd. v. Accolade, Inc.,* 977 F.2d 1510 (9th Cir.1992), referenced in the House Committee's Section–By–Section Analysis of H.R. 2281, *supra,* the court considered whether the copyright holder can prevent others from engaging in copying of this sort. The manufacturer of a computer game system, Sega, sued a developer of computer game cassettes, Accolade, alleging that Accolade infringed its copyright by disassembling code contained in the game console, in order to learn how to make its game cassettes interoperate with the console. The court held that the copying involved in disassembling code for this purpose is within fair use, and therefore does not infringe Sega's copyright.

Do the anti-circumvention provisions of Section 1201 threaten to interfere with the ability of competitors to create software products that interoperate as they must in order to function? To what extent do the exemptions contained in Section 1201 allay concerns of this sort?

2. *Encryption research and security testing.* What explains the emphasis on encryption research and security testing in the legislative history? What is your prediction about whether the exemptions in Section 1201 will prove to offer sufficient safe harbors for these activities?

Consider the experience of Princeton University computer science professor Edward Felten. In September 2000, the Secure Digital Music Initiative ("SDMI"), an association of technology companies, issued a public challenge, inviting one and all to attempt to crack the digital watermarking technology that SDMI had selected as a standard for protecting digital music. SDMI offered a $10,000 prize for a successful challenger. Professor Felten and his associates accepted the challenge, and cracked the protection scheme quite readily. Felten wrote a paper about his research on the SDMI watermarks, and planned to present his findings at an academic conference. The Recording Industry Association of American ("RIAA") asked Felten to omit the details of the SDMI watermark technology from his presentation, and sent him a letter stating that revealing his research results "could subject you and you research team to actions under the Digital Millennium Copyright Act."

In the face of this perceived threat, Felten withdrew from the conference. He subsequently filed an action against the RIAA, seeking a declaration that publication of his paper would be lawful. The RIAA and SDMI hastily insisted publicly that they never had any intention of suing Felten, and the court dismissed the case on procedural grounds.

Professor Felten subsequently presented his paper at another conference. The paper, titled "Reading Between the Lines: Lessons from the SDMI Challenge," is available at www.usenix.org/publications/library/proceedings/sec01/craver.pdf. Does presentation or publication of the paper violate Section 1201?

3. *Locked room analogy.* Consider the House Committee Report's declaration that circumventing a technological management system "is the electronic equivalent of breaking into a locked room in order to obtain a copy of a book." Do you agree with this analogy? Consider the differences between "locking up" information and locking up hard goods. To what extent can copyright protection be appropriately conceptualized in terms of traditional physical property? Who would you suppose are the proponents of this analogy?

4. *Section 1201's exemptions.* Copyright law is often described as mediating two conflicting societal interests: the promotion of original works of authorship and public access to those works. Consider the various exemptions to Section 1201's prohibition on circumvention, namely those contained in § 1201(d)–(j). What goals, beyond promoting access to works of authorship, are these exemptions directed at achieving? Does the inclusion of these exemptions ameliorate the extent to which the Section 1201(a)(1)(A) & (a)(2) prohibitions disallow circumvention for purposes that do not infringe copyright—such as fair use of a work, or copying of uncopyrightable facts or ideas?

RealNetworks, Inc. v. Streambox, Inc.

2000 WL 127311 (W.D.Wash.2000).

■ PECHMAN, J.

INTRODUCTION

Plaintiff RealNetworks, Inc. ("RealNetworks") filed this action on December 21, 1999. RealNetworks claims that Defendant Streambox has violated provisions of the Digital Millennium Copyright Act ("DMCA"), *17 U.S.C. § 1201 et seq.*, by distributing and marketing products known as the Streambox VCR and the Ripper. * * *

* * *

The Court * * * concludes that a preliminary injunction should be entered to enjoin the manufacture, distribution, and sale of the Streambox VCR * * *.

FINDINGS OF FACT

RealNetworks

1.   RealNetworks is a public company based in Seattle, Washington that develops and markets software products designed to enable owners of audio, video, and other multimedia content to send their content to users of personal computers over the Internet.

2.   RealNetworks offers products that enable consumers to access audio and video content over the Internet through a process known as "streaming." When an audio or video clip is "streamed" to a consumer, no trace of the clip is left on the consumer's computer, unless the content owner has permitted the consumer to download the file.

3.   Streaming is to be contrasted with "downloading," a process by which a complete copy of an audio or video clip is delivered to and stored on a consumer's computer. Once a consumer has downloaded a file, he or she can access the file at will, and can generally redistribute copies of that file to others.

4.   In the digital era, the difference between streaming and downloading is of critical importance. A downloaded copy of a digital audio or video file is essentially indistinguishable from the original, and such copies can often be created at the touch of a button. A user who obtains a digital copy may supplant the market for the original by distributing copies of his or her own. To guard against the unauthorized copying and redistribution of their content, many copyright owners do not make their content available for downloading, and instead distribute the content using streaming technology in a manner that does not permit downloading.

5.   A large majority of all Internet Web pages that deliver streaming music or video use the RealNetworks' format.

RealNetworks' Products

6.   The RealNetworks' products at issue in this action include the "RealProducer," the "RealServer" and the "RealPlayer." These products may be used together to form a system for distributing, retrieving and playing digital audio and video content via the Internet.

7. Owners of audio or video content may choose to use a RealNetworks product to encode their digital content into RealNetworks' format. Once encoded in that format, the media files are called RealAudio or RealVideo (collectively "RealMedia") files.

8. After a content owner has encoded its content into the RealMedia format, it may decide to use a "RealServer" to send that content to consumers. A RealServer is software program that resides on a content owner's computer that holds RealMedia files and "serves" them to consumers through streaming.

9. The RealServer is not the only available means for distributing RealMedia files. RealMedia files may also be made available on an ordinary web server instead of a RealServer. An end-user can download content from an ordinary web server using nothing more than a freely available Internet browser such as Netscape's Navigator or Microsoft's Internet Explorer.

10. To download streaming content distributed by a RealServer, however, a consumer must employ a "RealPlayer." The RealPlayer is a software program that resides on an end-user's computer and must be used to access and play a streaming RealMedia file that is sent from a RealServer.

RealNetworks' Security Measures

11. RealNetworks' products can be used to enable owners of audio and video content to make their content available for consumers to listen to or view, while at the same time securing the content against unauthorized access or copying.

12. The first of these measures, called the "Secret Handshake" by RealNetworks, ensures that files hosted on a RealServer will only be sent to a RealPlayer. The Secret Handshake is an authentication sequence which only RealServers and RealPlayers know. By design, unless this authentication sequence takes place, the RealServer does not stream the content it holds.

13. By ensuring that RealMedia files hosted on a RealServer are streamed only to RealPlayers, RealNetworks can ensure that a second security measure, which RealNetworks calls the "Copy Switch," is given effect. The Copy Switch is a piece of data in all RealMedia files that contains the content owner's preference regarding whether or not the stream may be copied by end-users. RealPlayers are designed to read this Copy Switch and obey the content owner's wishes. If a content owner turns on the Copy Switch in a particular RealMedia file, when that file is streamed, an end-user can use the RealPlayer to save a copy of that RealMedia file to the user's computer. If a content owner does not turn on the Copy Switch in a RealMedia file, the RealPlayer will not allow an end-user to make a copy of that file. The file will simply "evaporate" as the user listens to or watches it stream.

14. Through the use of the Secret Handshake and the Copy Switch, owners of audio and video content can prevent the unauthorized copying of their content if they so choose.

15. Content owners who choose to use the security measures described above are likely to be seeking to prevent their works from being copied without their authorization. RealNetworks has proferred declarations from copyright owners that they rely on RealNetworks security measures to protect their copyrighted works on the Internet. Many of these copyright owners further state that if users could circumvent the security measures and make unauthorized copies of the content, they likely would not put their content up on the Internet for end-users.

16. Many copyright owners make content available on their Web site as a means to attract end-users to the Web site; that is, to drive "traffic" to the Web site. The more traffic a Web site generates, the more it can charge for advertisements placed on the Web site. Without RealNetworks' security measures, a copyright owner could lose the traffic its content generates. An end-user could obtain a copy of the content after only one visit and listen to or view it repeatedly without ever returning to the Web site. That end-user could also redistribute the content to others who would then have no occasion to visit the site in the first instance.

17. Copyright owners also use Real Networks' technology so that end-users can listen to, but not record, music that is on sale, either at a Web site or in retail stores. Other copyright owners enable users to listen to content on a "pay-per-play" basis that requires a payment for each time the end-user wants to hear the content. Without the security measures afforded by RealNetworks, these methods of distribution could not succeed. End-users could make and redistribute digital copies of any content available on the Internet, undermining the market for the copyrighted original.

18. RealNetworks' success as a company is due in significant part to the fact that it has offered copyright owners a successful means of protecting against unauthorized duplication and distribution of their digital works.

* * *

Streambox VCR

23. The Streambox VCR enables end-users to access and download copies of RealMedia files that are streamed over the Internet. While the Streambox VCR also allows users to copy RealMedia files that are made freely available for downloading from ordinary web servers, the only function relevant to this case is the portions of the VCR that allow it to access and copy RealMedia files located on RealServers.

24. In order to gain access to RealMedia content located on a RealServer, the VCR mimics a RealPlayer and circumvents the authentication procedure, or Secret Handshake, that a RealServer requires before it will stream content. In other words, the Streambox VCR is able to convince the RealServer into thinking that the VCR is, in fact, a RealPlayer.

25. Having convinced a RealServer to begin streaming content, the Streambox VCR, like the RealPlayer, acts as a receiver. However, unlike the RealPlayer, the VCR ignores the Copy Switch that tells a RealPlayer whether an end-user is allowed to make a copy of (i.e., download) the RealMedia file as it is being streamed. The VCR thus allows the end-user to download RealMedia files even if the content owner has used the Copy Switch to prohibit end-users from downloading the files.

26. The only reason for the Streambox VCR to circumvent the Secret Handshake and interact with a RealServer is to allow an end-user to access and make copies of content that a copyright holder has placed on a RealServer in order to secure it against unauthorized copying. In this way, the Streambox VCR acts like a "black box" which descrambles cable or satellite broadcasts so that viewers can watch pay programming for free. Like the cable and satellite companies that scramble their video signals to control access to their programs, RealNetworks has employed technological measures to ensure that only users of the RealPlayer can access RealMedia content placed on a RealServer. RealNetworks has gone one step further than the cable and satellite companies, not only controlling access, but also allowing copyright owners to specify whether or not their works can be copied by end-users, even if access is permitted. The Streambox VCR circumvents both the access control and copy protection measures.

* * *

31. The Streambox VCR poses a threat to RealNetworks' relationships with existing and potential customers who wish to secure their content for transmission over the Internet and must decide whether to purchase and use RealNetworks' technology. If the Streambox VCR remains available, these customers may opt not to utilize RealNetworks' technology, believing that it would not protect their content against unauthorized copying.

* * *

CONCLUSIONS OF LAW

* * *

RealNetworks Has Demonstrated a Reasonable Likelihood of Success on its DMCA Claims With Respect to the Streambox VCR

* * *

Parts of the VCR Are Likely to Violate Sections 1201(a)(2) and 1201(b)

7. Under the DMCA, the Secret Handshake that must take place between a RealServer and a RealPlayer before the RealServer will begin streaming content to an end-user appears to constitute a "technological measure" that "effectively controls access" to copyrighted works. *See* 17 U.S.C. § 1201(a)(3)(B) (measure "effectively controls access" if it "requires the application of information or a process or a treatment, with the authority of the copyright holder, to gain access to the work"). To gain

access to a work protected by the Secret Handshake, a user must employ a RealPlayer, which will supply the requisite information to the RealServer in a proprietary authentication sequence.

8. In conjunction with the Secret Handshake, the Copy Switch is a "technological measure" that effectively protects the right of a copyright owner to control the unauthorized copying of its work. *See* 17 U.S.C. § 1201(b)(2)(B) (measure "effectively protects" right of copyright holder if it "prevents, restricts or otherwise limits the exercise of a right of a copyright owner"); 17 U.S.C. § 106(a) (granting copyright holder exclusive right to make copies of its work). To access a RealMedia file distributed by a RealServer, a user must use a RealPlayer. The RealPlayer reads the Copy Switch in the file. If the Copy Switch in the file is turned off, the RealPlayer will not permit the user to record a copy as the file is streamed. Thus, the Copy Switch may restrict others from exercising a copyright holder's exclusive right to copy its work.

9. Under the DMCA, a product or part thereof "circumvents" protections afforded a technological measure by "avoiding, bypassing, removing, deactivating or otherwise impairing" the operation of that technological measure. 17 U.S.C. §§ 1201(b)(2)(A), 1201(a)(2)(A). Under that definition, at least a part of the Streambox VCR circumvents the technological measures RealNetworks affords to copyright owners. Where a RealMedia file is stored on a RealServer, the VCR "bypasses" the Secret Handshake to gain access to the file. The VCR then circumvents the Copy Switch, enabling a user to make a copy of a file that the copyright owner has sought to protect.

10. Given the circumvention capabilities of the Streambox VCR, Streambox violates the DMCA if the product or a part thereof: (i) is primarily designed to serve this function; (ii) has only limited commercially significant purposes beyond the circumvention; or (iii) is marketed as a means of circumvention. 17 U.S.C. §§ 1201(a)(2)(A–C), [1201(b)(1)(A–C)]. These three tests are disjunctive. *Id.* A product that meets only one of the three independent bases for liability is still prohibited. Here, the VCR meets at least the first two.

11. The Streambox VCR meets the first test for liability under the DMCA because at least a part of the Streambox VCR is primarily, if not exclusively, designed to circumvent the access control and copy protection measures that RealNetworks affords to copyright owners. 17 U.S.C. §§ 1201(a)(2)(A), [1201(b)(1)(A)].

12. The second basis for liability is met because a portion of the VCR that circumvents the Secret Handshake so as to avoid the Copy Switch has no significant commercial purpose other than to enable users to access and record protected content. 17 U.S.C. § 1201(a)(2)(B), [1201(b)(1)(B)]. There does not appear to be any other commercial value that this capability affords.

13. Streambox's primary defense to Plaintiff's DMCA claims is that the VCR has legitimate uses. In particular, Streambox claims that the VCR

allows consumers to make "fair use" copies of RealMedia files, notwithstanding the access control and copy protection measures that a copyright owner may have placed on that file.

14. The portions of the VCR that circumvent the secret handshake and copy switch permit consumers to obtain and redistribute perfect digital copies of audio and video files that copyright owners have made clear they do not want copied. For this reason, Streambox's VCR is not entitled to the same "fair use" protections the Supreme Court afforded to video cassette recorders used for "time-shifting" in *Sony Corp. v. Universal City Studios, Inc.*, 464 U.S. 417 (1984).

15. The *Sony* decision turned in large part on a finding that substantial numbers of copyright holders who broadcast their works either had authorized or would not object to having their works time-shifted by private viewers. *See Sony*, 464 U.S. at 443, 446. Here, by contrast, copyright owners have specifically chosen to prevent the copying enabled by the Streambox VCR by putting their content on RealServers and leaving the Copy Switch off.

16. Moreover, the *Sony* decision did not involve interpretation of the DMCA. Under the DMCA, product developers do not have the right to distribute products that circumvent technological measures that prevent consumers from gaining unauthorized access to or making unauthorized copies of works protected by the Copyright Act. Instead, Congress specifically prohibited the distribution of the tools by which such circumvention could be accomplished. The portion of the Streambox VCR that circumvents the technological measures that prevent unauthorized access to and duplication of audio and video content therefore runs afoul of the DMCA.

* * *

18. Streambox also argues that the VCR does not violate the DMCA because the Copy Switch that it avoids does not "effectively protect" against the unauthorized copying of copyrighted works as required by [§ 1201(b)(2)(B)]. Streambox claims this "effective" protection is lacking because an enterprising end-user could potentially use other means to record streaming audio content as it is played by the end-user's computer speakers. This argument fails because the Copy Switch, in the ordinary course of its operation when it is on, restricts and limits the ability of people to make perfect digital copies of a copyrighted work. The Copy Switch therefore constitutes a technological measure that effectively protects a copyright owner's rights under section [1201(b)(2)(B)].

19. In addition, the argument ignores the fact that before the Copy Switch is even implicated, the Streambox VCR has already circumvented the Secret Handshake to gain access to a unauthorized RealMedia file. That alone is sufficient for liability under the DMCA. *See* 17 U.S.C. [§ 1201(a)(1)(A)].

20. Streambox's last defense to liability for the VCR rests on § 1201(c)(3) of the DMCA which it cites for the proposition that the VCR is not required to respond to the Copy Switch. Again, this argument fails to

address the VCR's circumvention of the Secret Handshake, which is enough, by itself, to create liability under § 1201(a)(2).

21.   Moreover, § 1201(c)(3) states that "[n]othing in this section shall require ... a response to any particular technological measure, so long as ... the product ... does not otherwise fall within the prohibitions of subsections (a)(2) or (b)(1)." 17 U.S.C. § 1201(c)(3). As the remainder of the statute and the leading copyright commentator make clear, § 1201(c)(3) does not provide immunity for products that circumvent technological measures in violation of §§ 1201(a)(2) or (b)(1). *See* 17 U.S.C. § 1201(c)(3) (a product need not respond to a particular measure *"so long as such ... product ... does not otherwise fall within the prohibitions of subsections (a)(2) or (b)(1))."* (emphasis added); 1 *Nimmer on Copyright* (1999 Supp.), § 12A.05[C]. If the statute meant what Streambox suggests, any manufacturer of circumvention tools could avoid DMCA liability simply by claiming it chose not to respond to the particular protection that its tool circumvents.

22.   As set forth above, the Streambox VCR falls within the prohibitions of §§ 1201(a)(2) and 1201(b)(1). Accordingly, § 1201(c)(3) affords Streambox no defense.

* * *

Universal City Studios, Inc. v. Reimerdes

111 F.Supp.2d 294 (S.D.N.Y.2000), *aff'd*, 273 F.3d 429 (2d Cir.2001).

■ LEWIS A. KAPLAN, DISTRICT JUDGE.

Plaintiffs, eight major United States motion picture studios, distribute many of their copyrighted motion pictures for home use on digital versatile disks ("DVDs"), which contain copies of the motion pictures in digital form. They protect those motion pictures from copying by using an encryption system called CSS. CSS-protected motion pictures on DVDs may be viewed only on players and computer drives equipped with licensed technology that permits the devices to decrypt and play—but not to copy—the films.

Late last year, computer hackers devised a computer program called DeCSS that circumvents the CSS protection system and allows CSS-protected motion pictures to be copied and played on devices that lack the licensed decryption technology. Defendants quickly posted DeCSS on their Internet web site, thus making it readily available to much of the world. Plaintiffs promptly brought this action under the Digital Millennium Copyright Act (the "DMCA") to enjoin defendants from posting DeCSS and to prevent them from electronically "linking" their site to others that post DeCSS. Defendants responded with what they termed "electronic civil disobedience"—increasing their efforts to link their web site to a large number of others that continue to make DeCSS available.

Defendants contend that their actions do not violate the DMCA * * *.

Defendants argue first that the DMCA should not be construed to reach their conduct, principally because the DMCA, so applied, could prevent those who wish to gain access to technologically protected copyrighted works in order to make fair—that is, non-infringing—use of them from doing so. They argue that those who would make fair use of technologically protected copyrighted works need means, such as DeCSS, of circumventing access control measures not for piracy, but to make lawful use of those works.

Technological access control measures have the capacity to prevent fair uses of copyrighted works as well as foul. Hence, there is a potential tension between the use of such access control measures and fair use. Defendants are not the first to recognize that possibility. As the DMCA made its way through the legislative process, Congress was preoccupied with precisely this issue. Proponents of strong restrictions on circumvention of access control measures argued that they were essential if copyright holders were to make their works available in digital form because digital works otherwise could be pirated too easily. Opponents contended that strong anti-circumvention measures would extend the copyright monopoly inappropriately and prevent many fair uses of copyrighted material.

Congress struck a balance. The compromise it reached, depending upon future technological and commercial developments, may or may not prove ideal. But the solution it enacted is clear. The potential tension to which defendants point does not absolve them of liability under the statute. There is no serious question that defendants' posting of DeCSS violates the DMCA. * * *

I. The Genesis of the Controversy

As this case involves computers and technology with which many are unfamiliar, it is useful to begin by defining some of the vocabulary.

A. *The Vocabulary of this Case*

   * * *

4. *Portable Storage Media*

Digital files may be stored on several different kinds of storage media, some of which are readily transportable. Perhaps the most familiar of these are so called floppy disks or "floppies," which now are 3 1/2 inch magnetic disks upon which digital files may be recorded. For present purposes, however, we are concerned principally with two more recent developments, CD–ROMs and digital versatile disks, or DVDs.

A CD–ROM is a five-inch wide optical disk capable of storing approximately 650 MB of data. To read the data on a CD–ROM, a computer must have a CD–ROM drive.

DVDs are five-inch wide disks capable of storing more than 4.7 GB of data. In the application relevant here, they are used to hold full-length motion pictures in digital form. They are the latest technology for private home viewing of recorded motion pictures and result in drastically improved audio and visual clarity and quality of motion pictures shown on televisions or computer screens.

5. *The Technology Here at Issue*

CSS, or Content Scramble System, is an access control and copy prevention system for DVDs developed by the motion picture companies, including plaintiffs. It is an encryption-based system that requires the use of appropriately configured hardware such as a DVD player or a computer DVD drive to decrypt, unscramble and play back, but not copy, motion pictures on DVDs. The technology necessary to configure DVD players and drives to play CSS-protected DVDs has been licensed to hundreds of manufacturers in the United States and around the world.

DeCSS is a software utility, or computer program, that enables users to break the CSS copy protection system and hence to view DVDs on unlicensed players and make digital copies of DVD movies. The quality of motion pictures decrypted by DeCSS is virtually identical to that of encrypted movies on DVD.

DivX is a compression program available for download over the Internet. It compresses video files in order to minimize required storage space, often to facilitate transfer over The Internet or other networks.

B. *Parties*

Plaintiffs are eight major motion picture studios. Each is in the business of producing and distributing copyrighted material including motion pictures. Each distributes, either directly or through affiliates, copyrighted motion pictures on DVDs. Plaintiffs produce and distribute a large majority of the motion pictures on DVDs on the market today.

Defendant Eric Corley is viewed as a leader of the computer hacker community and goes by the name Emmanuel Goldstein, after the leader of the underground in George Orwell's classic, *1984*. He and his company, defendant 2600 Enterprises, Inc., together publish a magazine called *2600: The Hacker Quarterly*, which Corley founded in 1984, and which is something of a bible to the hacker community. The name "2600" was derived from the fact that hackers in the 1960's found that the transmission of a 2600 hertz tone over a long distance trunk connection gained access to "operator mode" and allowed the user to explore aspects of the telephone system that were not otherwise accessible. Mr. Corley chose the name because he regarded it as a "mystical thing," commemorating something that he evidently admired. Not surprisingly, *2600: The Hacker Quarterly* has included articles on such topics as how to steal an Internet domain name, access other people's e-mail, intercept cellular phone calls, and break into the computer systems at Costco stores and Federal Express. One issue contains a guide to the federal criminal justice system for readers charged with computer hacking. In addition, defendants operate a web site located at <http://www.2600.com> ("2600.com"), which is managed primarily by Mr. Corley and has been in existence since 1995.[47]

Prior to January 2000, when this action was commenced, defendants posted the source and object code for DeCSS on the 2600.com web site, from which they could be downloaded easily. At that time, 2600.com contained also a list of links to other web sites purporting to post DeCSS.

C. The Development of DVD and CSS

The major motion picture studios typically distribute films in a sequence of so-called windows, each window referring to a separate channel of distribution and thus to a separate source of revenue. The first window generally is theatrical release, distribution, and exhibition. Subsequently, films are distributed to airlines and hotels, then to the home market, then to pay television, cable and, eventually, free television broadcast. The home market is important to plaintiffs, as it represents a significant source of revenue.

Motion pictures first were, and still are, distributed to the home market in the form of video cassette tapes. In the early 1990's, however, the major movie studios began to explore distribution to the home market in digital format, which offered substantially higher audio and visual quality and greater longevity than video cassette tapes. This technology, which in 1995 became what is known today as DVD, brought with it a new problem—increased risk of piracy by virtue of the fact that digital files, unlike the material on video cassettes, can be copied without degradation from generation to generation. In consequence, the movie studios became concerned as the product neared market with the threat of DVD piracy.

Discussions among the studios with the goal of organizing a unified response to the piracy threat began in earnest in late 1995 or early 1996. They eventually came to include representatives of the consumer electronics and computer industries, as well as interested members of the public, and focused on both legislative proposals and technological solutions. In 1996, Matsushita Electric Industrial Co. ("MEI") and Toshiba Corp., presented—and the studios adopted—CSS.

CSS involves encrypting, according to an encryption algorithm, the digital sound and graphics files on a DVD that together constitute a motion picture. A CSS-protected DVD can be decrypted by an appropriate decryption algorithm that employs a series of keys stored on the DVD and the DVD player. In consequence, only players and drives containing the appropriate keys are able to decrypt DVD files and thereby play movies stored on DVDs.

As the motion picture companies did not themselves develop CSS and, in any case, are not in the business of making DVD players and drives, the technology for making compliant devices, i.e., devices with CSS keys, had to

---

47. Interestingly, defendants' copyright both their magazine and the material on their web site to prevent others from copying their works.

be licensed to consumer electronics manufacturers.[60] In order to ensure that the decryption technology did not become generally available and that compliant devices could not be used to copy as well as merely to play CSS-protected movies, the technology is licensed subject to strict security requirements. Moreover, manufacturers may not, consistent with their licenses, make equipment that would supply digital output that could be used in copying protected DVDs. Licenses to manufacture compliant devices are granted on a royalty-free basis subject only to an administrative fee. At the time of trial, licenses had been issued to numerous hardware and software manufacturers, including two companies that plan to release DVD players for computers running the Linux operating system.

With CSS in place, the studios introduced DVDs on the consumer market in early 1997. All or most of the motion pictures released on DVD were, and continue to be, encrypted with CSS technology. Over 4,000 motion pictures now have been released in DVD format in the United States, and movies are being issued on DVD at the rate of over 40 new titles per month in addition to re-releases of classic films. Currently, more than five million households in the United States own DVD players, and players are projected to be in ten percent of United States homes by the end of 2000.

DVDs have proven not only popular, but lucrative for the studios. Revenue from their sale and rental currently accounts for a substantial percentage of the movie studios' revenue from the home video market. Revenue from the home market, in turn, makes up a large percentage of the studios' total distribution revenue.

D.   The Appearance of DeCSS

In late September 1999, Jon Johansen, a Norwegian subject then fifteen years of age, and two individuals he "met" under pseudonyms over the Internet, reverse engineered a licensed DVD player and discovered the CSS encryption algorithm and keys. They used this information to create DeCSS, a program capable of decrypting or "ripping" encrypted DVDs, thereby allowing playback on non-compliant computers as well as the copying of decrypted files to computer hard drives. Mr. Johansen then posted the executable code on his personal Internet web site and informed members of an Internet mailing list that he had done so. Neither Mr. Johansen nor his collaborators obtained a license from the DVD CCA.

Although Mr. Johansen testified at trial that he created DeCSS in order to make a DVD player that would operate on a computer running the Linux operating system, DeCSS is a Windows executable file; that is, it can be executed only on computers running the Windows operating system. Mr. Johansen explained the fact that he created a Windows rather than a Linux program by asserting that Linux, at the time he created DeCSS, did not

---

60. The licensing function initially was performed by MEI and Toshiba. Subsequently, MEI and Toshiba granted a royalty free license to the DVD Copy Control Association ("DVD CCA"), which now handles the licensing function. The motion picture companies themselves license CSS from the DVD CCA.

support the file system used on DVDs. Hence, it was necessary, he said, to decrypt the DVD on a Windows computer in order subsequently to play the decrypted files on a Linux machine. Assuming that to be true, however, the fact remains that Mr. Johansen created DeCSS in the full knowledge that it could be used on computers running Windows rather than Linux. Moreover, he was well aware that the files, once decrypted, could be copied like any other computer files.

In January 1999, Norwegian prosecutors filed charges against Mr. Johansen stemming from the development of DeCSS. The disposition of the Norwegian case does not appear of record.

E. The Distribution of DeCSS

In the months following its initial appearance on Mr. Johansen's web site, DeCSS has become widely available on the Internet, where hundreds of sites now purport to offer the software for download. A few other applications said to decrypt CSS-encrypted DVDs also have appeared on the Internet.

In November 1999, defendants' web site began to offer DeCSS for download. It established also a list of links to several web sites that purportedly "mirrored" or offered DeCSS for download. * * *

F. The Preliminary Injunction and Defendants' Response

The movie studios, through the Internet investigations division of the Motion Picture Association of America ("MPAA"), became aware of the availability of DeCSS on the Internet in October 1999. The industry responded by sending out a number of cease and desist letters to web site operators who posted the software, some of which removed it from their sites. In January 2000, the studios filed this lawsuit against defendant Eric Corley and two others.[91]

After a hearing at which defendants presented no affidavits or evidentiary material, the Court granted plaintiffs' motion for a preliminary injunction barring defendants from posting DeCSS. At the conclusion of the hearing, plaintiffs sought also to enjoin defendants from linking to other sites that posted DeCSS, but the Court declined to entertain the application at that time in view of plaintiffs' failure to raise the issue in their motion papers.

Following the issuance of the preliminary injunction, defendants removed DeCSS from the 2600.com web site. In what they termed an act of "electronic civil disobedience," however, they continued to support links to other web sites purporting to offer DeCSS for download, a list which had grown to nearly five hundred by July 2000. Indeed, they carried a banner saying "Stop the MPAA" and, in a reference to this lawsuit, proclaimed: "We have to face the possibility that we could be forced into submission. For that reason it's especially important that as many of you as possible, all

---

91. The other two defendants entered into consent decrees with plaintiffs. Plaintiffs subsequently amended the complaint to add 2600 Enterprises, Inc. as a defendant.

throughout the world, take a stand and mirror these files." Thus, defendants obviously hoped to frustrate plaintiffs' recourse to the judicial system by making effective relief difficult or impossible.

At least some of the links currently on defendants' mirror list lead the user to copies of DeCSS that, when downloaded and executed, successfully decrypt a motion picture on a CSS-encrypted DVD.

G.   Effects on Plaintiffs

The effect on plaintiffs of defendants' posting of DeCSS depends upon the ease with which DeCSS decrypts plaintiffs' copyrighted motion pictures, the quality of the resulting product, and the convenience with which decrypted copies may be transferred or transmitted.

As noted, DeCSS was available for download from defendants' web site and remains available from web sites on defendants' mirror list. Downloading is simple and quick—plaintiffs' expert did it in seconds. The program in fact decrypts at least some DVDs. Although the process is computationally intensive, plaintiffs' expert decrypted a store-bought copy of *Sleepless in Seattle* in 20 to 45 minutes. The copy is stored on the hard drive of the computer. The quality of the decrypted film is virtually identical to that of encrypted films on DVD. The decrypted file can be copied like any other.

The decryption of a CSS-protected DVD is only the beginning of the tale, as the decrypted file is very large—approximately 4.3 to 6 GB or more depending on the length of the film—and thus extremely cumbersome to transfer or to store on portable storage media. One solution to this problem, however, is DivX, a compression utility available on the Internet that is promoted as a means of compressing decrypted motion picture files to manageable size.

DivX is capable of compressing decrypted files constituting a feature length motion picture to approximately 650 MB at a compression ratio that involves little loss of quality. While the compressed sound and graphic files then must be synchronized, a tedious process that took plaintiffs' expert between 10 and 20 hours, the task is entirely feasible. Indeed, having compared a store-bought DVD with portions of a copy compressed and synchronized with DivX (which often are referred to as "DivX'd" motion pictures), the Court finds that the loss of quality, at least in some cases, is imperceptible or so nearly imperceptible as to be of no importance to ordinary consumers.

The fact that DeCSS-decrypted DVDs can be compressed satisfactorily to 650 MB is very important. A writeable CD–ROM can hold 650 MB. Hence, it is entirely feasible to decrypt a DVD with DeCSS, compress and synchronize it with DivX, and then make as many copies as one wishes by burning the resulting files onto writeable CD–ROMs, which are sold blank for about one dollar apiece. Indeed, even if one wished to use a lower compression ratio to improve quality, a film easily could be compressed to about 1.3 GB and burned onto two CD–ROMs. But the creation of pirated copies of copyrighted movies on writeable CD–ROMs, although significant, is not the principal focus of plaintiffs' concern, which is transmission of pirated copies over the Internet or other networks.

Network transmission of decrypted motion pictures raises somewhat more difficult issues because even 650 MB is a very large file that, depending upon the circumstances, may take a good deal of time to transmit. But there is tremendous variation in transmission times. Many home computers today have modems with a rated capacity of 56 kilobits per second. DSL lines, which increasingly are available to home and business users, offer transfer rates of 7 megabits per second. Cable modems also offer increased bandwidth. Student rooms in many universities are equipped with network connections rated at 10 megabits per second. Large institutions such as universities and major companies often have networks with backbones rated at 100 megabits per second. While effective transmission times generally are much lower than rated maximum capacities in consequence of traffic volume and other considerations, there are many environments in which very high transmission rates may be achieved. Hence, transmission times ranging from three to twenty minutes to six hours or more for a feature length film are readily achievable, depending upon the users' precise circumstances.

At trial, defendants repeated, as if it were a mantra, the refrain that plaintiffs, as they stipulated, have no direct evidence of a specific occasion on which any person decrypted a copyrighted motion picture with DeCSS and transmitted it over the Internet. But that is unpersuasive. Plaintiffs' expert expended very little effort to find someone in an IRC chat room who exchanged a compressed, decrypted copy of *The Matrix,* one of plaintiffs' copyrighted motion pictures, for a copy of *Sleepless in Seattle.* While the simultaneous electronic exchange of the two movies took approximately six hours, the computers required little operator attention during the interim. An MPAA investigator downloaded between five and ten DVD-sourced movies over the Internet after December 1999. At least one web site contains a list of 650 motion pictures, said to have been decrypted and compressed with DivX, that purportedly are available for sale, trade or free download. And although the Court does not accept the list, which is hearsay, as proof of the truth of the matters asserted therein, it does note that advertisements for decrypted versions of copyrighted movies first appeared on the Internet in substantial numbers in late 1999, following the posting of DeCSS.

The net of all this is reasonably plain. DeCSS is a free, effective and fast means of decrypting plaintiffs' DVDs and copying them to computer hard drives. DivX, which is available over the Internet for nothing, with the investment of some time and effort, permits compression of the decrypted files to sizes that readily fit on a writeable CD–ROM. Copies of such CD–ROMs can be produced very cheaply and distributed as easily as other pirated intellectual property. While not everyone with Internet access now will find it convenient to send or receive DivX'd copies of pirated motion pictures over the Internet, the availability of high speed network connections in many businesses and institutions, and their growing availability in homes, make Internet and other network traffic in pirated copies a growing threat.

These circumstances have two major implications for plaintiffs. First, the availability of DeCSS on the Internet effectively has compromised plaintiffs' system of copyright protection for DVDs, requiring them either to tolerate increased piracy or to expend resources to develop and implement a replacement system unless the availability of DeCSS is terminated. It is analogous to the publication of a bank vault combination in a national newspaper. Even if no one uses the combination to open the vault, its mere publication has the effect of defeating the bank's security system, forcing the bank to reprogram the lock. Development and implementation of a new DVD copy protection system, however, is far more difficult and costly than reprogramming a combination lock and may carry with it the added problem of rendering the existing installed base of compliant DVD players obsolete.

Second, the application of DeCSS to copy and distribute motion pictures on DVD, both on CD–ROMs and via the Internet, threatens to reduce the studios' revenue from the sale and rental of DVDs. It threatens also to impede new, potentially lucrative initiatives for the distribution of motion pictures in digital form, such as video-on-demand via the Internet.

In consequence, plaintiffs already have been gravely injured. As the pressure for and competition to supply more and more users with faster and faster network connections grows, the injury will multiply.

II.   The Digital Millennium Copyright Act

A.   Background and Structure of the Statute

* * *

The DMCA contains two principal anticircumvention provisions. The first, Section 1201(a)(1), governs "[t]he act of circumventing a technological protection measure put in place by a copyright owner to control access to a copyrighted work," an act described by Congress as "the electronic equivalent of breaking into a locked room in order to obtain a copy of a book."[131] The second, Section 1201(a)(2), which is the focus of this case, "supplements the prohibition against the act of circumvention in paragraph (a)(1) with prohibitions on creating and making available certain technologies ... developed or advertised to defeat technological protections against unauthorized access to a work."[132] As defendants are accused here only of posting and linking to other sites posting DeCSS, and not of using it themselves to bypass plaintiffs' access controls, it is principally the second of the anticircumvention provisions that is at issue in this case.

B.   Posting of DeCSS

1.   Violation of Anti–Trafficking Provision

Section 1201(a)(2) of the Copyright Act, part of the DMCA, provides that:

---

131. H.R.REP. NO. 105–551(I), 105th Cong., 2d Sess. ("JUDICIARY COMM. REP."), at 17 (1998).

132. *Id.* at 18.

No person shall . . . offer to the public, provide or otherwise traffic in any technology . . . that—

(A) is primarily designed or produced for the purpose of circumventing a technological measure that effectively controls access to a work protected under [the Copyright Act];

(B) has only limited commercially significant purpose or use other than to circumvent a technological measure that effectively controls access to a work protected under [the Copyright Act]; or

(C) is marketed by that person or another acting in concert with that person with that person's knowledge for use in circumventing a technological measure that effectively controls access to a work protected under [the Copyright Act].

17 U.S.C. § 1201(a)(2).

In this case, defendants concededly offered and provided and, absent a court order, would continue to offer and provide DeCSS to the public by making it available for download on the 2600.com web site. DeCSS, a computer program, unquestionably is "technology" within the meaning of the statute. "[C]ircumvent a technological measure" is defined to mean descrambling a scrambled work, decrypting an encrypted work, or "otherwise to avoid, bypass, remove, deactivate, or impair a technological measure, without the authority of the copyright owner," so DeCSS clearly is a means of circumventing a technological access control measure. In consequence, if CSS otherwise falls within paragraphs (A), (B) or (C) of Section 1201(a)(2), and if none of the statutory exceptions applies to their actions, defendants have violated and, unless enjoined, will continue to violate the DMCA by posting DeCSS.

a. Section 1201(a)(2)(A)

(1) CSS Effectively Controls Access to Copyrighted Works

During pretrial proceedings and at trial, defendants attacked plaintiffs' Section 1201(a)(2)(A) claim, arguing that CSS, which is based on a 40–bit encryption key, is a weak cipher that does not "effectively control" access to plaintiffs' copyrighted works. They reasoned from this premise that CSS is not protected under this branch of the statute at all. Their post-trial memorandum appears to have abandoned this argument. In any case, however, the contention is indefensible as a matter of law.

First, the statute expressly provides that "a technological measure 'effectively controls access to a work' if the measure, in the ordinary course of its operation, requires the application of information or a process or a treatment, with the authority of the copyright owner, to gain access to a work." One cannot gain access to a CSS-protected work on a DVD without application of the three keys that are required by the software. One cannot lawfully gain access to the keys except by entering into a license with the DVD CCA under authority granted by the copyright owners or by purchasing a DVD player or drive containing the keys pursuant to such a license. In consequence, under the express terms of the statute, CSS "effectively controls access" to copyrighted DVD movies. It does so, within the meaning of the statute, whether or not it is a strong means of protection.

This view is confirmed by the legislative history, which deals with precisely this point. The House Judiciary Committee section-by-section analysis of the House bill, which in this respect was enacted into law, makes clear that a technological measure "effectively controls access" to a copyrighted work if its *function* is to control access:

> The bill does define the *functions* of the technological measures that are covered—that is, what it means for a technological measure to "effectively control access to a work" ... and to "effectively protect a right of a copyright owner under this title".... The practical, common-sense approach taken by H.R.2281 is that if, in the ordinary course of its operation, a technology actually works in the defined ways to control access to a work ... then the "effectiveness" test is met, and the prohibitions of the statute are applicable. This test, which focuses on the function performed by the technology, provides a sufficient basis for clear interpretation.[140]

Further, the House Commerce Committee made clear that measures based on encryption or scrambling "effectively control" access to copyrighted works,[141] although it is well known that what may be encrypted or scrambled often may be decrypted or unscrambled. As CSS, in the ordinary course of its operation—that is, when DeCSS or some other decryption program is not employed—"actually works" to prevent access to the protected work, it "effectively controls access" within the contemplation of the statute.

Finally, the interpretation of the phrase "effectively controls access" offered by defendants at trial—viz., that the use of the word "effectively" means that the statute protects only successful or efficacious technological means of controlling access—would gut the statute if it were adopted. If a technological means of access control is circumvented, it is, in common parlance, ineffective. Yet defendants' construction, if adopted, would limit the application of the statute to access control measures that thwart circumvention, but withhold protection for those measures that can be circumvented. In other words, defendants would have the Court construe the statute to offer protection where none is needed but to withhold protection precisely where protection is essential. The Court declines to do so. Accordingly, the Court holds that CSS effectively controls access to plaintiffs' copyrighted works.

140. HOUSE COMM. ON JUDICIARY, SECTION–BY–SECTION ANALYSIS OF H.R.2281 AS PASSED BY THE UNITED STATES HOUSE OF REPRESENTATIVES ON AUGUST 4, 1998 ("SECTION–BY–SEC-TION ANALYSIS"), at 10 (Comm.Print 1998) (emphasis in original).

141. H.R.REP. NO. 105–551(II), 105th Cong., 2d Sess. ("COMMERCE COMM. REP."), at 39 (1998).

(2) DeCSS Was Designed Primarily to Circumvent CSS

As CSS effectively controls access to plaintiffs' copyrighted works, the only remaining question under Section 1201(a)(2)(A) is whether DeCSS was designed primarily to circumvent CSS. The answer is perfectly obvious. By the admission of both Jon Johansen, the programmer who principally wrote DeCSS, and defendant Corley, DeCSS was created solely for the purpose of decrypting CSS—that is all it does. Hence, absent satisfaction of a statutory exception, defendants clearly violated Section 1201(a)(2)(A) by posting DeCSS to their web site.

b. Section 1201(a)(2)(B)

As the only purpose or use of DeCSS is to circumvent CSS, the foregoing is sufficient to establish a *prima facie* violation of Section 1201(a)(2)(B) as well.

c. The Linux Argument

Perhaps the centerpiece of defendants' statutory position is the contention that DeCSS was not created for the purpose of pirating copyrighted motion pictures. Rather, they argue, it was written to further the development of a DVD player that would run under the Linux operating system, as there allegedly were no Linux compatible players on the market at the time. * * *

* * *

[T]he question whether the development of a Linux DVD player motivated those who wrote DeCSS is immaterial to the question whether the defendants now before the Court violated the anti-trafficking provision of the DMCA. The inescapable facts are that (1) CSS is a technological means that effectively controls access to plaintiffs' copyrighted works, (2) the one and only function of DeCSS is to circumvent CSS, and (3) defendants offered and provided DeCSS by posting it on their web site. Whether defendants did so in order to infringe, or to permit or encourage others to infringe, copyrighted works in violation of other provisions of the Copyright Act simply does not matter for purposes of Section 1201(a)(2). The offering or provision of the program is the prohibited conduct—and it is prohibited irrespective of why the program was written, except to whatever extent motive may be germane to determining whether their conduct falls within one of the statutory exceptions.

2. Statutory Exceptions

Earlier in the litigation, defendants contended that their activities came within several exceptions contained in the DMCA and the Copyright Act and constitute fair use under the Copyright Act. Their post-trial memorandum appears to confine their argument to the reverse engineering exception. In any case, all of their assertions are entirely without merit.

a. Reverse engineering

Defendants claim to fall under Section 1201(f) of the statute, which provides in substance that one may circumvent, or develop and employ technological means to circumvent, access control measures in order to achieve interoperability with another computer program provided that doing so does not infringe another's copyright and, in addition, that one may make information acquired through such efforts "available to others, if the person [in question] ... provides such information solely for the purpose of enabling interoperability of an independently created computer program with other programs, and to the extent that doing so does not constitute infringement...." They contend that DeCSS is necessary to achieve interoperability between computers running the Linux operating system and DVDs and that this exception therefore is satisfied. This contention fails.

First, Section 1201(f)(3) permits information acquired through reverse engineering to be made available to others only by the person who acquired the information. But these defendants did not do any reverse engineering. They simply took DeCSS off someone else's web site and posted it on their own.

Defendants would be in no stronger position even if they had authored DeCSS. The right to make the information available extends only to dissemination "solely for the purpose" of achieving interoperability as defined in the statute. It does not apply to public dissemination of means of circumvention, as the legislative history confirms. These defendants, however, did not post DeCSS "solely" to achieve interoperability with Linux or anything else.

Finally, it is important to recognize that even the creators of DeCSS cannot credibly maintain that the "sole" purpose of DeCSS was to create a Linux DVD player. DeCSS concededly was developed on and runs under Windows—a far more widely used operating system. The developers of DeCSS therefore knew that DeCSS could be used to decrypt and play DVD movies on Windows as well as Linux machines. They knew also that the decrypted files could be copied like any other unprotected computer file. Moreover, the Court does not credit Mr. Johansen's testimony that he created DeCSS solely for the purpose of building a Linux player. Mr. Johansen is a very talented young man and a member of a well known hacker group who viewed "cracking" CSS as an end it itself and a means of demonstrating his talent and who fully expected that the use of DeCSS would not be confined to Linux machines. Hence, the Court finds that Mr. Johansen and the others who actually did develop DeCSS did not do so solely for the purpose of making a Linux DVD player if, indeed, developing a Linux-based DVD player was among their purposes.

Accordingly, the reverse engineering exception to the DMCA has no application here.

* * *

d. Fair use

Finally, defendants rely on the doctrine of fair use. Stated in its most general terms, the doctrine, now codified in Section 107 of the Copyright Act, limits the exclusive rights of a copyright holder by permitting others to make limited use of portions of the copyrighted work, for appropriate purposes, free of liability for copyright infringement. For example, it is permissible for one other than the copyright owner to reprint or quote a suitable part of a copyrighted book or article in certain circumstances. The doctrine traditionally has facilitated literary and artistic criticism, teaching and scholarship, and other socially useful forms of expression. It has been viewed by courts as a safety valve that accommodates the exclusive rights conferred by copyright with the freedom of expression guaranteed by the First Amendment.

The use of technological means of controlling access to a copyrighted work may affect the ability to make fair uses of the work. Focusing specifically on the facts of this case, the application of CSS to encrypt a copyrighted motion picture requires the use of a compliant DVD player to view or listen to the movie. Perhaps more significantly, it prevents exact copying of either the video or the audio portion of all or any part of the film. This latter point means that certain uses that might qualify as "fair" for purposes of copyright infringement—for example, the preparation by a film studies professor of a single CD–ROM or tape containing two scenes from different movies in order to illustrate a point in a lecture on cinematography, as opposed to showing relevant parts of two different DVDs— would be difficult or impossible absent circumvention of the CSS encryption. Defendants therefore argue that the DMCA cannot properly be construed to make it difficult or impossible to make any fair use of plaintiffs' copyrighted works and that the statute therefore does not reach their activities, which are simply a means to enable users of DeCSS to make such fair uses.

Defendants have focused on a significant point. Access control measures such as CSS do involve some risk of preventing lawful as well as unlawful uses of copyrighted material. Congress, however, clearly faced up to and dealt with this question in enacting the DMCA.

The Court begins its statutory analysis, as it must, with the language of the statute. Section 107 of the Copyright Act provides in critical part that certain uses of copyrighted works that otherwise would be wrongful are "not ... infringement[s] of copyright." Defendants, however, are not here sued for copyright infringement. They are sued for offering and providing technology designed to circumvent technological measures that control access to copyrighted works and otherwise violating Section 1201(a)(2) of the Act. If Congress had meant the fair use defense to apply to such actions, it would have said so. Indeed, as the legislative history demonstrates, the decision not to make fair use a defense to a claim under Section 1201(a) was quite deliberate.

Congress was well aware during the consideration of the DMCA of the traditional role of the fair use defense in accommodating the exclusive rights of copyright owners with the legitimate interests of noninfringing users of portions of copyrighted works. It recognized the contention, voiced by a range of constituencies concerned with the legislation, that technological controls on access to copyrighted works might erode fair use by preventing access even for uses that would be deemed "fair" if only access might be gained.[162] And it struck a balance among the competing interests.

The first element of the balance was the careful limitation of Section 1201(a)(1)'s prohibition of the act of circumvention to the act itself so as not to "apply to subsequent actions of a person once he or she has obtained authorized access to a copy of a [copyrighted] work...."[163] By doing so, it left "the traditional defenses to copyright infringement, including fair use, ... fully applicable" provided "the access is authorized."[164]

Second, Congress delayed the effective date of Section 1201(a)(1)'s prohibition of the act of circumvention for two years pending further investigation about how best to reconcile Section 1201(a)(1) with fair use concerns. Following that investigation, which is being carried out in the form of a rule-making by the Register of Copyright, the prohibition will not apply to users of particular classes of copyrighted works who demonstrate that their ability to make noninfringing uses of those classes of works would be affected adversely by Section 1201(a)(1).

Third, it created a series of exceptions to aspects of Section 1201(a) for certain uses that Congress thought "fair," including reverse engineering, security testing, good faith encryption research, and certain uses by non-profit libraries, archives and educational institutions.

Defendants claim also that the possibility that DeCSS might be used for the purpose of gaining access to copyrighted works in order to make fair use of those works saves them under *Sony Corp. v. Universal City Studios, Inc.*, 464 U.S. 417 (1984). But they are mistaken. *Sony* does not apply to the activities with which defendants here are charged. Even if it did, it would not govern here. *Sony* involved a construction of the Copyright Act that has been overruled by the later enactment of the DMCA to the extent of any inconsistency between *Sony* and the new statute.

Sony was a suit for contributory infringement brought against manufacturers of video cassette recorders on the theory that the manufacturers were contributing to infringing home taping of copyrighted television broadcasts. The Supreme Court held that the manufacturers were not liable in view of the substantial numbers of copyright holders who either had authorized or did not object to such taping by viewers. But *Sony* has no application here.

When *Sony* was decided, the only question was whether the manufacturers could be held liable for infringement by those who purchased equipment from them in circumstances in which there were many noninfringing uses for their equipment. But that is not the question now before

---

162. *See, e.g.,* COMMERCE COMM. REP. 25–26.

163. JUDICIARY COMM.REP. 18.

164. *Id.*

this Court. The question here is whether the possibility of noninfringing fair use by someone who gains access to a protected copyrighted work through a circumvention technology distributed by the defendants saves the defendants from liability under Section 1201. But nothing in Section 1201 so suggests. By prohibiting the provision of circumvention technology, the DMCA fundamentally altered the landscape. A given device or piece of technology might have "a substantial noninfringing use, and hence be immune from attack under *Sony*'s construction of the Copyright Act—but nonetheless still be subject to suppression under Section 1201."[169] Indeed, Congress explicitly noted that Section 1201 does not incorporate *Sony*.[170]

The policy concerns raised by defendants were considered by Congress. Having considered them, Congress crafted a statute that, so far as the applicability of the fair use defense to Section 1201(a) claims is concerned, is crystal clear. In such circumstances, courts may not undo what Congress so plainly has done by "construing" the words of a statute to accomplish a result that Congress rejected. The fact that Congress elected to leave technologically unsophisticated persons who wish to make fair use of encrypted copyrighted works without the technical means of doing so is a matter for Congress unless Congress' decision contravenes the Constitution * * *. Defendants' statutory fair use argument therefore is entirely without merit.

C. Linking to Sites Offering DeCSS

Plaintiffs seek also to enjoin defendants from "linking" their 2600.com web site to other sites that make DeCSS available to users. Their request obviously stems in no small part from what defendants themselves have termed their act of "electronic civil disobedience"—their attempt to defeat the purpose of the preliminary injunction by (a) offering the practical equivalent of making DeCSS available on their own web site by electronically linking users to other sites still offering DeCSS, and (b) encouraging other sites that had not been enjoined to offer the program. The dispositive question is whether linking to another web site containing DeCSS constitutes "offer[ing DeCSS] to the public" or "provid[ing] or otherwise traffic[king]" in it within the meaning of the DMCA.[171] Answering this question requires careful consideration of the nature and types of linking.

Most web pages are written in computer languages, chiefly HTML, which allow the programmer to prescribe the appearance of the web page on the computer screen and, in addition, to instruct the computer to perform an operation if the cursor is placed over a particular point on the screen and the mouse then clicked. Programming a particular point on a screen to transfer the user to another web page when the point, referred to as a hyperlink, is clicked is called linking. Web pages can be designed to

---

169. *RealNetworks, Inc.,* 2000 WL 127311, at *8 * * *.

170. SECTION–BY–SECTION ANALYSIS 9 ("The *Sony* test of 'capab[ility]' of substantial non-infringing uses,' while still operative in cases claiming contributory infringement of copyright, is not part of this legislation. . . .").

171. 17 U.S.C. § 1201(a)(2).

link to other web pages on the same site or to web pages maintained by different sites.

[T]he links that defendants established on their web site are of several types. Some transfer the user to a web page on an outside site that contains a good deal of information of various types, does not itself contain a link to DeCSS, but that links, either directly or via a series of other pages, to another page on the same site that posts the software. It then is up to the user to follow the link or series of links on the linked-to web site in order to arrive at the page with the DeCSS link and commence the download of the software. Others take the user to a page on an outside web site on which there appears a direct link to the DeCSS software and which may or may not contain text or links other than the DeCSS link. The user has only to click on the DeCSS link to commence the download. Still others may directly transfer the user to a file on the linked-to web site such that the download of DeCSS to the user's computer automatically commences without further user intervention.

The statute makes it unlawful to offer, provide or otherwise traffic in described technology. To "traffic" in something is to engage in dealings in it, conduct that necessarily involves awareness of the nature of the subject of the trafficking. To "provide" something, in the sense used in the statute, is to make it available or furnish it. To "offer" is to present or hold it out for consideration. The phrase "or otherwise traffic in" modifies and gives meaning to the words "offer" and "provide." In consequence, the anti-trafficking provision of the DMCA is implicated where one presents, holds out or makes a circumvention technology or device available, knowing its nature, for the purpose of allowing others to acquire it.

To the extent that defendants have linked to sites that automatically commence the process of downloading DeCSS upon a user being transferred by defendants' hyperlinks, there can be no serious question. Defendants are engaged in the functional equivalent of transferring the DeCSS code to the user themselves.

Substantially the same is true of defendants' hyperlinks to web pages that display nothing more than the DeCSS code or present the user only with the choice of commencing a download of DeCSS and no other content. The only distinction is that the entity extending to the user the option of downloading the program is the transferee site rather than defendants, a distinction without a difference.

Potentially more troublesome might be links to pages that offer a good deal of content other than DeCSS but that offer a hyperlink for downloading, or transferring to a page for downloading, DeCSS. If one assumed, for the purposes of argument, that the *Los Angeles Times* web site somewhere contained the DeCSS code, it would be wrong to say that anyone who linked to the *Los Angeles Times* web site, regardless of purpose or the manner in which the link was described, thereby offered, provided or otherwise trafficked in DeCSS merely because DeCSS happened to be available on a site to which one linked. But that is not this case. Defendants urged others to post DeCSS in an effort to disseminate DeCSS and to inform defendants that they were doing so. Defendants then linked their site to those "mirror" sites, after first checking to ensure that the mirror sites in fact were posting DeCSS or something that looked like it, and proclaimed on their own site that DeCSS could be had by clicking on the hyperlinks on defendants' site. By doing so, they offered, provided or otherwise trafficked in DeCSS, and they continue to do so to this day.

* * *

[The court's discussion of defendants' First Amendment argument is omitted.]

VI. Conclusion

In the final analysis, the dispute between these parties is simply put if not necessarily simply resolved.

Plaintiffs have invested huge sums over the years in producing motion pictures in reliance upon a legal framework that, through the law of copyright, has ensured that they will have the exclusive right to copy and distribute those motion pictures for economic gain. They contend that the advent of new technology should not alter this long established structure.

Defendants, on the other hand, are adherents of a movement that believes that information should be available without charge to anyone clever enough to break into the computer systems or data storage media in which it is located. Less radically, they have raised a legitimate concern about the possible impact on traditional fair use of access control measures in the digital era.

Each side is entitled to its views. In our society, however, clashes of competing interests like this are resolved by Congress. For now, at least, Congress has resolved this clash in the DMCA and in plaintiffs' favor. * * * Accordingly, plaintiffs are entitled to appropriate injunctive and declaratory relief.

In the following decision, the Second Circuit affirmed the decision of the district court that is excerpted above.

Universal City Studios, Inc. v. Corley

273 F.3d 429 (2d Cir.2001).

■ Jon O. Newman, Circuit Judge.

When the Framers of the First Amendment prohibited Congress from making any law "abridging the freedom of speech," they were not thinking about computers, computer programs, or the Internet. But neither were they thinking about radio, television, or movies. Just as the inventions at the beginning and middle of the 20th century presented new First Amendment issues, so does the cyber revolution at the end of that century. This appeal raises significant First Amendment issues concerning one aspect of computer technology—encryption to protect materials in digital form from unauthorized access. The appeal challenges the constitutionality of the Digital Millennium Copyright Act ("DMCA"), 17 U.S.C. § 1201 *et seq.* (Supp. V 1999) and the validity of an injunction entered to enforce the DMCA.

Defendant–Appellant Eric C. Corley and his company, 2600 Enterprises, Inc., (collectively "Corley," "the Defendants," or "the Appellants") appeal from the amended final judgment of the United States District Court for the Southern District of New York (Lewis A. Kaplan, District Judge), entered August 23, 2000, enjoining them from various actions concerning a decryption program known as "DeCSS." *Universal City Studios, Inc. v. Reimerdes,* 111 F.Supp.2d 346 (S.D.N.Y.2000) ("*Universal II*"). The injunction primarily bars the Appellants from posting DeCSS on their web site and from knowingly linking their web site to any other web site on which DeCSS is posted. *Id.* at 346–47. We affirm.

* * *

Discussion

* * *

II.   Constitutional Challenge Based on the Copyright Clause

In a footnote to their brief, the Appellants appear to contend that the DMCA, as construed by the District Court, exceeds the constitutional authority of Congress to grant authors copyrights for a "limited time," *U.S. Const. art. I, § 8, cl. 8,* because it "empower[s] copyright owners to effectively secure perpetual protection by mixing public domain works with copyrighted materials, then locking both up with technological protection measures." Brief for Appellants at 42 n.30. This argument is elaborated in the *amici curiae* brief filed by Prof. Julie E. Cohen on behalf of herself and 45 other intellectual property law professors. *See also* David Nimmer, *A Riff on Fair Use in the Digital Millennium Copyright Act,* 148 U. Pa. L. Rev. 673, 712 (2000). For two reasons, the argument provides no basis for disturbing the judgment of the District Court.

First, we have repeatedly ruled that arguments presented to us only in a footnote are not entitled to appellate consideration. * * * Although an *amicus* brief can be helpful in elaborating issues properly presented by the parties, it is normally not a method for injecting new issues into an appeal, at least in cases where the parties are competently represented by counsel. * * * Second, to whatever extent the argument might have merit at some future time in a case with a properly developed record, the argument is entirely premature and speculative at this time on this record. There is not even a claim, much less evidence, that any Plaintiff has sought to prevent copying of public domain works, or that the injunction prevents the Defendants from copying such works. As Judge Kaplan noted, the possibility that encryption would preclude access to public domain works "does not yet appear to be a problem, although it may emerge as one in the future." *Universal I*, 111 F.Supp.2d at 338 n. 245.

III. Constitutional Challenges Based on the First Amendment

A. *Applicable Principles*

* * *

[The court finds that computer code can merit First Amendment protection.]

3. The Scope of First Amendment Protection for Computer Code

Having concluded that computer code conveying information is "speech" within the meaning of the First Amendment, we next consider, to a limited extent, the scope of the protection that code enjoys. As the District Court recognized, *Universal I*, 111 F.Supp.2d at 327, the scope of protection for speech generally depends on whether the restriction is imposed because of the content of the speech. Content-based restrictions are permissible only if they serve compelling state interests and do so by the least restrictive means available. *See Sable Communications of California, Inc. v. FCC*, 492 U.S. 115, 126 (1989). A content-neutral restriction is permissible if it serves a substantial governmental interest, the interest is unrelated to the suppression of free expression, and the regulation is narrowly tailored, which "in this context requires ... that the means chosen do not 'burden substantially more speech than is necessary to further the government's legitimate interests.'" *Turner Broadcasting System, Inc. v. FCC*, 512 U.S. 622, 662 (1994) (*quoting Ward v. Rock Against Racism*, 491 U.S. 781, 799 (1989)).

"[G]overnment regulation of expressive activity is 'content neutral' if it is justified without reference to the content of regulated speech." *Hill v. Colorado*, 530 U.S. 703, 720, (2000). "The government's purpose is the controlling consideration. A regulation that serves purposes unrelated to the content of expression is deemed neutral, even if it has an incidental effect on some speakers or messages but not others." *Ward*, 491 U.S. at 791. * * *

* * *

The Appellants vigorously reject the idea that computer code can be regulated according to any different standard than that applicable to pure speech, *i.e.*, speech that lacks a nonspeech component. Although recognizing that code is a series of instructions to a computer, they argue that code is no different, for First Amendment purposes, than blueprints that instruct an engineer or recipes that instruct a cook. *See* Supplemental Brief for Appellants at 2, 3. We disagree. Unlike a blueprint or a recipe, which cannot yield any functional result without human comprehension of its content, human decision-making, and human action, computer code can instantly cause a computer to accomplish tasks and instantly render the results of those tasks available throughout the world via the Internet. The only human action required to achieve these results can be as limited and instantaneous as a single click of a mouse. These realities of what code is and what its normal functions are require a First Amendment analysis that treats code as combining nonspeech and speech elements, *i.e.*, functional and expressive elements. *See Red Lion Broadcasting Co. v. FCC*, 395 U.S. 367, 386 (1969) ("[D]ifferences in the characteristics of new media justify differences in the First Amendment standards applied to them." (footnote omitted)).

* * *

The functionality of computer code properly affects the scope of its First Amendment protection.

4. The Scope of First Amendment Protection for Decryption Code

In considering the scope of First Amendment protection for a decryption program like DeCSS, we must recognize that the essential purpose of encryption code is to prevent unauthorized access. Owners of all property rights are entitled to prohibit access to their property by unauthorized persons. Homeowners can install locks on the doors of their houses. Custodians of valuables can place them in safes. Stores can attach to products security devices that will activate alarms if the products are taken away without purchase. These and similar security devices can be circumvented. Burglars can use skeleton keys to open door locks. Thieves can obtain the combinations to safes. Product security devices can be neutralized.

Our case concerns a security device, CSS computer code, that prevents access by unauthorized persons to DVD movies. The CSS code is embedded in the DVD movie. Access to the movie cannot be obtained unless a person has a device, a licensed DVD player, equipped with computer code capable of decrypting the CSS encryption code. In its basic function, CSS is like a lock on a homeowner's door, a combination of a safe, or a security device attached to a store's products.

DeCSS is computer code that can decrypt CSS. In its basic function, it is like a skeleton key that can open a locked door, a combination that can open a safe, or a device that can neutralize the security device attached to a store's products. DeCSS enables anyone to gain access to a DVD movie without using a DVD player.

* * *

At first glance, one might think that Congress has as much authority to regulate the distribution of computer code to decrypt DVD movies as it has to regulate distribution of skeleton keys, combinations to safes, or devices to neutralize store product security devices. However, despite the evident legitimacy of protection against unauthorized access to DVD movies, just like any other property, regulation of decryption code like DeCSS is challenged in this case because DeCSS differs from a skeleton key in one important respect: it not only is capable of performing the function of unlocking the encrypted DVD movie, it also is a form of communication, albeit written in a language not understood by the general public. As a communication, the DeCSS code has a claim to being "speech," and as "speech," it has a claim to being protected by the First Amendment. But just as the realities of what any computer code can accomplish must inform the scope of its constitutional protection, so the capacity of a decryption program like DeCSS to accomplish unauthorized—indeed, unlawful—access to materials in which the Plaintiffs have intellectual property rights must inform and limit the scope of its First Amendment protection. * * *

With all of the foregoing considerations in mind, we next consider the Appellants' First Amendment challenge to the DMCA as applied in the specific prohibitions that have been imposed by the District Court's injunction.

B. First Amendment Challenge

The District Court's injunction applies the DMCA to the Defendants by imposing two types of prohibition, both grounded on the anti-trafficking provisions of the DMCA. The first prohibits posting DeCSS or any other technology for circumventing CSS on any Internet web site. *Universal II*, 111 F.Supp.2d at 346–47, ¶ 1(a), (b). The second prohibits knowingly linking any Internet web site to any other web site containing DeCSS. *Id.* at 347, ¶ 1(c). The validity of the posting and linking prohibitions must be considered separately.

1. Posting

The initial issue is whether the posting prohibition is content-neutral, since, as we have explained, this classification determines the applicable constitutional standard. The Appellants contend that the anti-trafficking provisions of the DMCA and their application by means of the posting prohibition of the injunction are content-based. They argue that the provisions "specifically target . . . scientific expression based on the particular topic addressed by that expression—namely, techniques for circumventing CSS." Supplemental Brief for Appellants at 1. We disagree. The Appellants' argument fails to recognize that the target of the posting provisions of the injunction—DeCSS—has both a nonspeech and a speech component, and that the DMCA, as applied to the Appellants, and the posting prohibition of the injunction target only the nonspeech component. Neither the DMCA nor the posting prohibition is concerned with whatever capacity DeCSS might have for conveying information to a human being, and that capacity, as previously explained, is what arguably creates a speech component of the decryption code. The DMCA and the posting prohibition are applied to DeCSS solely because of its capacity to instruct a computer to decrypt CSS. That functional capability is not speech within the meaning of the First Amendment. The Government seeks to "justif[y]," *Hill*, 530 U.S. at 720, both the application of the DMCA and the posting prohibition to the Appellants solely on the basis of the functional capability of DeCSS to instruct a computer to decrypt CSS, *i.e.*, "without reference to the content of the regulated speech," *id*. This type of regulation is therefore content-neutral, just as would be a restriction on trafficking in skeleton keys identified because of their capacity to unlock jail cells, even though some of the keys happened to bear a slogan or other legend that qualified as a speech component.

As a content-neutral regulation with an incidental effect on a speech component, the regulation must serve a substantial governmental interest, the interest must be unrelated to the suppression of free expression, and the incidental restriction on speech must not burden substantially more speech than is necessary to further that interest. *Turner Broadcasting*, 512 U.S. at 662. The Government's interest in preventing unauthorized access to encrypted copyrighted material is unquestionably substantial, and the regulation of DeCSS by the posting prohibition plainly serves that interest. Moreover, that interest is unrelated to the suppression of free expression. The injunction regulates the posting of DeCSS, regardless of whether DeCSS code contains any information comprehensible by human beings that would qualify as speech. Whether the incidental regulation on speech burdens substantially more speech than is necessary to further the interest in preventing unauthorized access to copyrighted materials requires some elaboration.

Posting DeCSS on the Appellants' web site makes it instantly available at the click of a mouse to any person in the world with access to the Internet, and such person can then instantly transmit DeCSS to anyone else with Internet access. Although the prohibition on posting prevents the Appellants from conveying to others the speech component of DeCSS, the Appellants have not suggested, much less shown, any technique for barring them from making this instantaneous worldwide distribution of a decryption code that makes a lesser restriction on the code's speech component. It is true that the Government has alternative means of prohibiting unauthorized access to copyrighted materials. For example, it can create criminal and civil liability for those who gain unauthorized access, and thus it can be argued that the restriction on posting DeCSS is not absolutely necessary to preventing unauthorized access to copyrighted materials. But a content-neutral regulation need not employ the least restrictive means of accomplishing the governmental objective. *Id.* It need only avoid burdening "substantially more speech than is necessary to further the government's legitimate interests." *Id.* (internal quotation marks and citation omitted). The prohibition on the Defendants' posting of DeCSS satisfies that standard.[30]

2. Linking

* * *

In applying the DMCA to linking (via hyperlinks), Judge Kaplan recognized, as he had with DeCSS code, that a hyperlink has both a speech and a nonspeech component. It conveys information, the Internet address

---

30. We have considered the opinion of a California intermediate appellate court in *DVD Copy Control Ass'n v. Bunner,* 93 Cal. App.4th 648, 113 Cal.Rptr.2d 338 (2001), declining, on First Amendment grounds, to is-sue a preliminary injunction under state trade secrets law prohibiting a web site operator from posting DeCSS. To the extent that *DVD Copy Control* disagrees with our First Amendment analysis, we decline to follow it.

of the linked web page, and has the functional capacity to bring the content of the linked web page to the user's computer screen (or, as Judge Kaplan put it, to "take one almost instantaneously to the desired destination." *Id.*). As he had ruled with respect to DeCSS code, he ruled that application of the DMCA to the Defendants' linking to web sites containing DeCSS is content-neutral because it is justified without regard to the speech component of the hyperlink. *Id.* The linking prohibition applies whether or not the hyperlink contains any information, comprehensible to a human being, as to the Internet address of the web page being accessed. The linking prohibition is justified solely by the functional capability of the hyperlink.

Applying the *O'Brien/Ward/Turner Broadcasting* requirements for content-neutral regulation, Judge Kaplan then ruled that the DMCA, as applied to the Defendants' linking, served substantial governmental interests and was unrelated to the suppression of free expression. *Id.* We agree. He then carefully considered the "closer call," *id.*, as to whether a linking prohibition would satisfy the narrow tailoring requirement. In an especially carefully considered portion of his opinion, he observed that strict liability for linking to web sites containing DeCSS would risk two impairments of free expression. Web site operators would be inhibited from displaying links to various web pages for fear that a linked page might contain DeCSS, and a prohibition on linking to a web site containing DeCSS would curtail access to whatever other information was contained at the accessed site. *Id.* at 340.

To avoid applying the DMCA in a manner that would "burden substantially more speech than is necessary to further the government's legitimate interests," *Turner Broadcasting,* 512 U.S. at 662 (internal quotation marks and citation omitted), Judge Kaplan adapted the standards of *New York Times Co. v. Sullivan,* 376 U.S. 254, 283 (1964), to fashion a limited prohibition against linking to web sites containing DeCSS. He required clear and convincing evidence

> that those responsible for the link (a) know at the relevant time that the offending material is on the linked-to site, (b) know that it is circumvention technology that may not lawfully be offered, and (c) create or maintain the link for the purpose of disseminating that technology.

Universal I, 111 F.Supp.2d at 341. He then found that the evidence satisfied his three-part test by his required standard of proof. *Id.*

    * * *

At oral argument, we asked the Government whether its undoubted power to punish the distribution of obscene materials would permit an injunction prohibiting a newspaper from printing addresses of bookstore locations carrying such materials. In a properly cautious response, the Government stated that the answer would depend on the circumstances of the publication. The Appellants' supplemental papers enthusiastically embraced the arguable analogy between printing bookstore addresses and displaying on a web page links to web sites at which DeCSS may be accessed. Supplemental Brief for Appellants at 14. They confidently asserted that publication of bookstore locations carrying obscene material cannot be enjoined consistent with the First Amendment, and that a prohibition against linking to web sites containing DeCSS is similarly invalid. *Id.*

Like many analogies posited to illuminate legal issues, the bookstore analogy is helpful primarily in identifying characteristics that *distinguish* it from the context of the pending dispute. If a bookstore proprietor is knowingly selling obscene materials, the evil of distributing such materials can be prevented by injunctive relief against the unlawful distribution (and similar distribution by others can be deterred by punishment of the distributor). And if others publish the location of the bookstore, preventive relief against a distributor can be effective before any significant distribution of the prohibited materials has occurred. The digital world, however, creates a very different problem. If obscene materials are posted on one web site and other sites post hyperlinks to the first site, the materials are available for instantaneous worldwide distribution before any preventive measures can be effectively taken.

This reality obliges courts considering First Amendment claims in the context of the pending case to choose between two unattractive alternatives: either tolerate some impairment of communication in order to permit Congress to prohibit decryption that may lawfully be prevented, or tolerate some decryption in order to avoid some impairment of communication. Although the parties dispute the extent of impairment of communication if the injunction is upheld and the extent of decryption if it is vacated, and differ on the availability and effectiveness of techniques for minimizing both consequences, the fundamental choice between impairing some communication and tolerating decryption cannot be entirely avoided.

In facing this choice, we are mindful that it is not for us to resolve the issues of public policy implicated by the choice we have identified. Those issues are for Congress. Our task is to determine whether the legislative solution adopted by Congress, as applied to the Appellants by the District Court's injunction, is consistent with the limitations of the First Amendment, and we are satisfied that it is.

IV.   Constitutional Challenge Based on Claimed Restriction of Fair Use

Asserting that fair use "is rooted in and required by both the Copyright Clause and the First Amendment," Brief for Appellants at 42, the Appellants contend that the DMCA, as applied by the District Court, unconstitutionally "*eliminates* fair use" of copyrighted materials, *id.* at 41 (emphasis added). We reject this extravagant claim.

Preliminarily, we note that the Supreme Court has never held that fair use is constitutionally required, although some isolated statements in its opinions might arguably be enlisted for such a requirement. * * *

We need not explore the extent to which fair use might have constitutional protection, grounded on either the First Amendment or the Copyright Clause, because whatever validity a constitutional claim might have as to an application of the DMCA that impairs fair use of copyrighted materials, such matters are far beyond the scope of this lawsuit for several reasons. In the first place, the Appellants do not claim to be making fair use of any copyrighted materials, and nothing in the injunction prohibits them from making such fair use. They are barred from trafficking in a decryption code that enables unauthorized access to copyrighted materials.

Second, as the District Court properly noted, to whatever extent the anti-trafficking provisions of the DMCA might prevent others from copying portions of DVD movies in order to make fair use of them, "the evidence as to the impact of the anti-trafficking provision[s] of the DMCA on prospective fair users is scanty and fails adequately to address the issues." *Universal I,* 111 F.Supp.2d at 338 n. 246.

Third, the Appellants have provided no support for their premise that fair use of DVD movies is constitutionally required to be made by copying the original work in its original format. Their examples of the fair uses that they believe others will be prevented from making all involve copying in a digital format those portions of a DVD movie amenable to fair use, a copying that would enable the fair user to manipulate the digitally copied portions. One example is that of a school child who wishes to copy images from a DVD movie to insert into the student's documentary film. We know of no authority for the proposition that fair use, as protected by the Copyright Act, much less the Constitution, guarantees copying by the optimum method or in the identical format of the original. Although the Appellants insisted at oral argument that they should not be relegated to a "horse and buggy" technique in making fair use of DVD movies, the DMCA does not impose even an arguable limitation on the opportunity to make a variety of traditional fair uses of DVD movies, such as commenting on their content, quoting excerpts from their screenplays, and even recording portions of the video images and sounds on film or tape by pointing a camera, a camcorder, or a microphone at a monitor as it displays the DVD movie. The fact that the resulting copy will not be as perfect or as manipulable as a digital copy obtained by having direct access to the DVD movie in its digital form, provides no basis for a claim of unconstitutional limitation of fair use. A film critic making fair use of a movie by quoting selected lines of dialogue has no constitutionally valid claim that the review (in print or on television) would be technologically superior if the reviewer had not been prevented from using a movie camera in the theater, nor has an art student a valid constitutional claim to fair use of a painting by photographing it in a museum. Fair use has never been held to be a guarantee of access to copyrighted material in order to copy it by the fair user's preferred technique or in the format of the original.

Conclusion

We have considered all the other arguments of the Appellants and conclude that they provide no basis for disturbing the District Court's judgment. Accordingly, the judgment is affirmed.

NOTES & QUESTIONS

1. *Injunctive relief and the Internet.* From the perspective of content producers, the Internet is worrisome due to the ease and efficiency with which digital goods can be copied and distributed. A case in point is the DeCSS computer program that is the focus of the *Reimerdes* decision. In *Reimerdes*, by the time the court issued a preliminary injunction enjoining the defendants from distributing the DeCSS program, it was already available on many websites around the world. Although after the preliminary injunction one could no longer obtain a copy of the program from the defendants' websites, a visit to a search engine would have revealed numerous other sites from which the program could be downloaded. Enjoining distribution of certain digital goods over the Internet once such goods are already available online is arguably an exercise in futility—an argument that the defendants made, by observing that granting "an injunction would be comparable to locking the barn door after the horse is gone." *Reimerdes,* 111 F.Supp.2d at 344. The court admitted that it "has been troubled by that possibility," but concluded that "the countervailing arguments overcome that concern." *Id.*

> To begin with, any such conclusion effectively would create all the wrong incentives by allowing defendants to continue violating the DMCA simply because others, many doubtless at defendants' urging, are doing so as well. Were that the law, defendants confronted with the possibility of injunctive relief would be well advised to ensure that others engage in the same unlawful conduct in order to set up the argument that an injunction against the defendants would be futile because everyone else is doing the same thing.

> Second, and closely related, is the fact that this Court is sorely "troubled by the notion that any Internet user ... can destroy valuable intellectual property rights by posting them over the Internet."[273] While equity surely should not act where the controversy has become moot, it ought to look very skeptically at claims that the defendant or others already have done all the harm that might be done before the injunction issues.

> The key to reconciling these views is that the focus of injunctive relief is on the defendants before the Court. If a plaintiff seeks to enjoin a defendant from burning a pasture, it is no answer that there is a wild fire burning in its direction. If the defendant itself threatens the plaintiff with irreparable harm, then equity will enjoin the defendant from carrying out the threat even if other threats abound and even if part of the pasture already is burned.

> These defendants would harm plaintiffs every day on which they post DeCSS on their heavily trafficked web site and link to

---

273. *Religious Technology Center v. Netcom On–Line Communication Services, Inc.,* 923 F.Supp. 1231, 1256 (N.D.Cal.1995).

other sites that post it because someone who does not have DeCSS thereby might obtain it. They thus threaten plaintiffs with immediate and irreparable injury. They will not be allowed to continue to do so simply because others may do so as well. * * *

Id. Are you convinced by the court's conclusion that the controversy is not moot? Do you find the court's analogy to a wildfire apposite? Does the Internet, more than any other medium of communication, give rise to cases in which damages are inadequate and an injunction is ineffective? If so, how should the legal system respond?

2. *How much authority does a copyright owner have?* In a footnote in *Reimerdes*, the court notes that "[d]ecryption or avoidance of an access control measure is not 'circumvention' within the meaning of the statute unless it occurs 'without the authority of the copyright owner.' 17 U.S.C. § 1201(a)(3)(A)." Apparently, defendants' counsel had argued that the defendants' acts did not constitute circumvention within the meaning of § 1201(a)(3)(A). The court sets out defendants' view as follows:

> Defendants posit that purchasers of a DVD acquire the right "to perform all acts with it that are not exclusively granted to the copyright holder." Based on this premise, they argue that DeCSS does not circumvent CSS within the meaning of the statute because the Copyright Act does not grant the copyright holder the right to prohibit purchasers from decrypting. As the copyright holder has no statutory right to prohibit decryption, the argument goes, decryption cannot be understood as unlawful circumvention.

Reimerdes, 111 F.Supp.2d at 317 n.137. The court is blunt in its evaluation of this line of reasoning: "The argument is pure sophistry." Should the court have been so quick to dismiss defendants' argument? Does the applicability of the statute turn on the rights of a copyright owner qua copyright owner? If not, does the statute grant rights to a copyright owner which are over and above the rights granted by the Copyright Act? Consider also whether the result is consistent with Section 1201(c)(1), which provides: "Nothing in this section shall affect rights, remedies, limitations, or defenses to copyright infringement, including fair use, under this title."

3. *Is trafficking under Section 1201 a form of secondary liability?* Under the law of copyright, secondary liability for copyright infringement requires proof of direct infringement by another. Is this also the case for liability under Section 1201(b)? Similarly, does liability under Section 1201(a)(2) require proof of a violation of Section 1201(a)(1)? That is, in order to be liable for making or selling tools that will facilitate breaking into a technological protection system to obtain access to information, or disabling technological use restrictions on information, must unauthorized access or copyright infringement by means of those tools actually be shown?

4. *Criminal penalties under Section 1204.* Section 1204 prescribes criminal penalties for those who violate Section 1201 or 1202 "willfully and for purposes of commercial advantage or private financial gain." For a first offense, the penalties are a fine of up to $500,000, a prison term up to five years, or both. 17 U.S.C. § 1204(a)(1). In July 2001, a Russian computer programmer named Dmitri Sklyarov was arrested by the Federal Bureau of Investigation and charged with violating the anti-circumvention provisions, based on his creation of a program that defeated use controls built into electronic books distributed by Adobe Systems, Inc. The arrest occurred in Las Vegas at the annual Def Con convention, known as a gathering of hackers, where Sklyarov had presented a paper describing the research that led to his creation of the program. The program, as he explained in the paper, had grown out of research about security flaws in e-document security systems that he had done for his Ph.D. dissertation. After three weeks in jail, Sklyarov was released on bail. A grand jury returned a five-count indictment against both Sklyarov and his employer, a Russian software development company called ElcomSoft Co., Ltd., for violations of the anti-trafficking provision, Section 1201(b)(1). Under the indictment, Sklyarov was subject to up to 25 years in prison and a $2,250,000 fine. Sklyarov was not allowed to return to Russia until making a deal with prosecutors, under which he agreed to testify against his employer.

In *United States v. Elcom Ltd.*, 203 F.Supp.2d 1111 (N.D.Cal.2002), the district court rejected arguments that Section 1201 is unconstitutionally vague in violation of the Due Process Clause, that it is vague and overbroad in violation of the First Amendment, and that it is beyond Congress's legislative powers. As this book goes to press, the trial of ElcomSoft is in progress.

CHAPTER SIX

CONTROLLING ONLINE BUSINESS METHODS: PATENT

The application of patent protection to methods for transacting business, electronic and otherwise, is a relatively recent phenomenon, but one that has rapidly become widespread. Be Free, Inc. holds a patent on the ability to target Internet advertising based on user preferences. Priceline.com owns a patent on reverse auctions, a method of selling goods and services through an Internet bidding system whereby a customer commits to buying an item at a specified price if a seller can be found to supply it at that price. DoubleClick, Inc., owns a patent on Web-based banner advertising. And Amazon.com holds a patent on its "One–Click" ordering system, which allows online customers to save time by entering their credit and personal information only once.

Less than a decade ago, many legal experts would have considered patents such as these invalid, because business methods were believed to be specifically excluded from patent protection. In 1998, however, in *State Street Bank & Trust Co. v. Signature Financial Group, Inc.*, 149 F.3d 1368 (Fed.Cir.1998), the Court of Appeals for the Federal Circuit[1] declared that business methods are not categorically outside the subject matter of patent. In other words, an inventive business method, like any other invention, could receive patent protection if the United States Patent and Trademark Office ("PTO") found it to be new, non-obvious, and useful.

State Street Bank prompted a rapid increase in applications for patents on business methods, particularly those involving electronic commerce operations. *See* Julia King, *Patent Examiners Pending: Tech/Business Skills Combo Needed to Handle Onslaught*, COMPUTERWORLD, Sept. 13, 1999, www.idg.net/crd_idgsearch_84983.html. Some commentators have argued that the Patent Office was unprepared for the flood, and that, as a result, it has failed properly to evaluate patent applications and has issued patents for "inventions" that are obvious and/or non-novel. Others compare the current "flood" with the early years of biotechnology patents, when the patent standards were not yet clear and a solid prior-art database had not yet been established. The PTO and patent applicants may simply be experiencing a similar period of transition. In the meantime, entrepreneurs

1. The Federal Circuit, a division of the U.S. Court of Appeals, was created in 1982 through a merger of the U.S. Court of Customs and Patent Appeals and the U.S. Court of Claims. The Federal Circuit's jurisdiction is limited to cases involving patents, claims against the United States, and certain other specialized areas of law. Its jurisdiction over such cases is exclusive of the other Circuits.

all over the country are being urged to reexamine their business practices to determine (1) whether those practices might be patentable; and (2) whether those practices have been patented by others.

I. PATENT BASICS

What does it mean to gain patent protection for a business method? A patent is a limited right, granted by the federal government, to prevent others from making, using, selling or offering to sell an invention. In other words, it is a right to exclude competitors for the term of the patent. In the United States, the granting of patents is authorized by Article 1, Section 8, Clause 8 of the Constitution, which gives Congress the power "[t]o promote the Progress of Science and useful Arts, by securing for limited Times to * * * Inventors the exclusive Right to their * * * Discoveries." In the absence of some incentive to do otherwise, inventors will choose to keep their inventions secret so as to forestall direct competition. The primary goals of the patent system are to encourage inventors to reveal their secrets to the public, and to encourage investment in the development of new inventions, by granting the inventor a temporary monopoly over the use of her inventions.

Title 35 of the U.S. Code contains the statutory basis for the patent system. Sections 101, 102, 103 and 112 are particularly important. Section 101 defines patentable subject matter as any "new and useful process, machine, manufacture or composition of matter, or any new and useful improvement thereof." 35 U.S.C. § 101. (We will be particularly interested here in the first "new and useful" subject matter identified by Section 101—the process—which is defined as a "process, art or method [including] a new use of a known process, machine, manufacture, composition of matter, or material." 35 U.S.C. § 100(b).) In contrast to copyright law, in which the first creator is the owner of the derivative work right, so that subsequent creators must get the first owner's permission for follow-on works, in patent law, new and non-obvious improvements to existing technology are patentable by the improver. This means that the owner of the original technology must get the permission of the follow-on innovator in order to practice the state of the art, and vice versa—a situation known as "blocking patents."

Section 102 explains the meaning of "new": that which was not anticipated by printed literature or a patent anywhere in the world more than one year prior to the application and any time prior to the actual "invention" date shown by the applicant; not anticipated by public use in this country more than one year prior to the application date or any time before the invention date; and not commercialized in this country more than one year prior to the application date. 35 U.S.C. § 102(a) & (b). Section 102 requires that the patent applicant be the actual inventor or inventors; a patent applied for in the name of the wrong person or from which one or more co-inventors were excluded can be invalidated. Section 103 adds a non-obviousness requirement: an invention that would have been obvious at the time of invention to a person of ordinary skill in the art to which the patent pertains is not patentable. 35 U.S.C. § 103(a).[2]

Thus, in order to receive patent protection, any business method, including Internet commerce techniques and software processes, must satisfy the basic threshold requirements for patents generally:

1. *Patentable subject matter.* The types of inventions that may be entitled to patent protection include any process, machine, manufacture, or composition of matter, as well as any improvements on such inventions. 35 U.S.C. § 101. Laws of nature, physical phenomena, and abstract ideas (including mathematical algorithms) are not patentable, although a useful process that is otherwise within patentable subject matter does not lose that status merely because it implements one of the foregoing.

2. *Utility.* The process described must be "useful"—it must have a functional purpose and must produce a concrete and tangible result. 35 U.S.C. § 101.

3. *Novelty.* The method must be "new": it must be different from what is already known, and must add something new to the prior art. 35 U.S.C. §§ 101 & 102.

4. *Non-obviousness.* The described process must not be obvious (in light of the state of the prior art) to one of ordinary skill in the art at the time of invention. 35 U.S.C. § 103.

5. *Legally sufficient disclosure.* As quid pro quo for the privilege of monopoly, the patent must describe the invention in sufficient detail so that one who is skilled in the subject matter can construct it, must describe the best mode of making and using it, and must claim the invention in a clear and distinct manner which can give notice of what is to claimed to competitors and the public. 35 U.S.C. § 112.

A patent document consist of several parts: (1) an "abstract," which briefly summarizes the invention; (2) a list of references to the "prior art"—that is, citations to publications, other patents, and other inventions, which may be relevant to establishing whether the invention meets the requirements of novelty and non-obviousness; (3) the "specification," which describes the related art and the advantages of the invention with respect to that art, provides drawings of the invention, explains how to make and use the invention, and outlines the "best mode" of using it; and (4) a set of "claims," which is technically part of the specification, but is normally set out in a separate section of the patent document. The PTO makes a complete set of patent documents available via its website, www.uspto.gov.

The claims delineate exactly what is to be covered by the exclusion right and are the operative part of the patent. Claims usually consist of a preamble, a transitional phrase, and a body that lists the elements of the

---

2. Outside the United States, this requirement usually goes by the name of "inventive step."

invention and how they interact. If the application is successful, those claims set the bounds of the property right. Inventions must be "definitely" claimed, that is, the nature and function of the invention must be clear and clearly delimited. 35 U.S.C.A. § 112.

Claims are especially important in questions concerning infringement and validity, when a patent will be evaluated claim by claim. That is, patents may have more than one claim, and some of them have a great many. (Often the broadest claim will be the first one, and narrower claims will be further down the list.) To be liable for patent infringement, it is enough to infringe any one of the patent's claims.

Business method patents allow the owner to prevent others from making, using, selling, or offering to sell a specific operation or set of operations for transacting business. The United States is one of the few countries in which the patentability of business methods is clearly established. In other countries, some business methods have been found patentable, while others have not. Until recently the United States excluded business methods from patentable subject matter—but the exclusion was embedded in common law rather than the Patent Act, and, as we shall see in the *State Street Bank* case, *infra*, it was not robust. Put simply, judges distinguished, at least conceptually, a system for transacting business from a specific apparatus or process for implementing that system. The former was considered to be unpatentable because more akin to an abstract mathematical principle than to a machine or mechanical process. It is possible, too, that judges believed business methods were almost all already known (not novel); if so, the digital era changed that assumption.

II.   BACKGROUND: THE (FORMER) BUSINESS METHOD EXCEPTION

Prior to the Federal Circuit's holding in *State Street Bank* (discussed *infra*), most patent attorneys would have advised their clients not to apply for a patent on a pure business practice. The so-called "business methods exception" precluded patentability of business practices for most of the twentieth century.

The business methods exception made an early appearance in *Hotel Security Checking Co. v. Lorraine Co.*, 160 F. 467 (2d Cir.1908), in which the Second Circuit invalidated a patent that described an accounting system designed to prevent fraud by waiters and cashiers in restaurants and hotels. The system tracked the orders handled by different workers, allowing owners to determine whether money was missing and trace its source: "If there has been no carelessness or dishonesty, the amounts will agree and if there has been, it is easy to discover where the fault lies." *Id.* at 468.

The court held that "there is no patentable novelty either in the physical means employed or in the method described and claimed":

Section 4886 of the Revised Statutes [the predecessor of 35 U.S.C. § 101] provides, under certain conditions, that "any person who has invented or discovered any new and useful art, machine, manufacture or composition of matter" may obtain a patent therefor. It is manifest that the subject-matter of the claims is not a machine, manufacture or composition of matter. If within the language of the statute at all, it must be as a "new and useful art." One of the definitions given by Webster of the word "art" is as follows: "The employment of means to accomplish some desired end; the adaptation of things in the natural world to the uses of life; the application of knowledge or power to practical purposes." In the sense of the patent law, an art is not a mere abstraction. A system of transacting business disconnected from the means for carrying out the system is not, within the most liberal interpretation of the term, an art. Advice is not patentable. As this court said in Fowler v. City of New York, 121 Fed. 747, 58 C.C.A. 113: "No mere abstraction, no idea, however brilliant, can be the subject of a patent irrespective of the means designed to give it effect."

It cannot be maintained that the physical means described by Hicks,—the sheet and the slips,—apart from the manner of their use, present any new and useful feature. A blank sheet of paper ruled vertically and numbered at the top cannot be the subject of a patent, and, if used in carrying out a method, it can impart no more novelty thereto, than the pen and ink which are also used. In other words, if the "art" described in the specification be old, the claims cannot be upheld because of novelty in the appliances used in carrying it out,—for the reason that there is no novelty.

Id. at 469.

The *Hotel Security* court characterized business methods as abstractions rather than contributions to the progress of the useful arts. Subsequent cases built the court's observation into apparently solid doctrine. In *Berardini v. Tocci*, 200 F. 1021 (2d Cir.1912), a method of transmitting money via a set of coded telegraph messages was found unpatentable on the ground that the method was simply an advisory system for devising code messages, akin to advice on how to improve the practice of painting or baseball. *Conover v. Coe*, 99 F.2d 377 (D.C.Cir.1938), stated the theory plainly, declaring it to be "a rule of universal application that an object is not patentable where its novelty consists wholly in * * * a method or system of doing business." *Id.* at 379.

The exclusion was said to apply even where the business in question was arguably "new," though this was dictum in cases where the court also held the business method to be non-novel. In *Loew's Drive–In Theatres v. Park–In Theatres*, 174 F.2d 547 (1st Cir.1949), the Court of Appeals invalidated a patent for a system of parking cars in the lot of a drive-in movie theater so as to improve patrons' view of the screen. Noting that the arrangement of cars simply adapted an ancient system for arranging seats in a theater, and was therefore neither new nor non-obvious, the Court added that "a system for the transaction of business * * * however novel, useful, or commercially successful is not patentable apart from the means for making the system practically useful." *Id*. at 552.

The business method exception was buttressed by the development of the "mental steps" doctrine. The essence of this doctrine, which still has not been entirely rejected, is that patents embrace only physical effects, rather than the mental steps leading to the effects. *See, e.g., Gottschalk v. Benson*, 409 U.S. 63 (1972); *In re Abrams*, 188 F.2d 165 (C.C.P.A.1951); *In re Shao Wen Yuan*, 188 F.2d 377 (C.C.P.A.1951); *but see In re Musgrave*, 431 F.2d 882 (C.C.P.A.1970). Mental steps were viewed as too abstract to be acceptable subject matter for a patent. Processes that were primarily mental and/or that involved substantial human decisionmaking in their operation were seen as too difficult to describe with the reasonable definiteness required by patent law. Furthermore, human judgment, however well-trained, was seen as a general skill rather than a specific way of achieving a predictable and useful result, and therefore unpatentable. Finally, mental activity—including mental judgments involved in many business practices—was seen as more akin to writing than to machine-building, and therefore appropriately regulated by copyright law.

III.   SOFTWARE PATENTS: THE CHANGING LEGAL LANDSCAPE

The business method exception was thus apparently firmly rooted in case law. To understand how this changed, it is helpful to look first to developments in the legal treatment of software. Many business method patent applications involve computer-implemented practices, and, as we will see, it was not coincidental that the demise of the business method exception occurred as a result of litigation over a computer-related invention.

Computer technologies presented serious difficulties for courts evaluating patents, principally because in the 1960s and 70s judges viewed software "inventions" as essentially comprising mathematical formulas—abstract ideas, which are unpatentable, rather than the application of ideas toward a useful end. Thus, for example, the Supreme Court firmly rejected as inherently unpatentable a method for converting binary coded decimal ("BCD") numbers into pure binary numerals that was not limited to any particular art, technology, apparatus, or even a particular end use.

> It is conceded that one may not patent an idea. But in practical effect that would be the result if the formula for converting BCD numerals to pure binary numerals were patented in this case. The mathematical formula involved here has no substantial practical application except in connection with a digital computer, which means that if the judgment below is affirmed, the patent would wholly pre-empt the mathematical formula and in practical effect would be a patent on the algorithm itself.

Gottschalk v. Benson, 409 U.S. 63, 71–72 (1972).

The Supreme Court softened its position considerably several years later, and laid out a kind of "physical transformation" test for software patentability. The crucial case was *Diamond v. Diehr*, 450 U.S. 175 (1981), in which the Court declared patentable an industrial process that automated a rubber molding process by using a computer to calculate repetitively the mathematical equation governing how long to leave the mold closed, and to open the mold automatically when the curing was complete. The Court distinguished this process from an abstract mathematical formula or algorithm by noting that the algorithm in question was used to accomplish *physical transformation* of matter (in this case, uncured rubber).

> [W]hen a claim containing a mathematical formula implements or applies that formula in a structure or process which, when considered as a whole, is performing a function which the patent laws were designed to protect (e.g., transforming or reducing an article to a different state or thing), then the claim satisfies the requirements of § 101.

Id. at 192. In a series of subsequent decisions, the Court of Customs and Patent Appeals developed a counterpart to the physical transformation inquiry established in *Diehr*. *In re Freeman*, 573 F.2d 1237 (C.C.P.A.1978); *In re Walter*, 618 F.2d 758 (C.C.P.A.1980); *In re Abele*, 684 F.2d 902 (C.C.P.A.1982). The test has been summarized as follows: "First, the claim is analyzed to determine whether a mathematical algorithm is directly or indirectly recited. Next, if a mathematical algorithm is found, the claim as a whole is further analyzed to determine whether the algorithm is 'applied in any manner to physical elements or process steps,' and, if it is, it 'passes muster under § 101.'" *In re Pardo*, 684 F.2d 912, 915 (C.C.P.A.1982).

Some members of the Court of Appeals for the Federal Circuit were suspicious of the test, however, and those suspicions were not alleviated by the increasingly attenuated nature of the physicality requirement. In one case, a claim based primarily on an algorithm that reorganized data to produce a picture of the condition of a patient's heart on a hospital monitor was accepted as patentable on the theory that converting electrocardiograph signals into digital signals involved a physical transformation and that the conversion process began with the independent physical activity of a patient's heart function. *Arrhythmia Research Technology, Inc. v. Corazonix Corp.*, 958 F.2d 1053 (Fed.Cir.1992). Two years later, a programmed computer was found to be a machine that produced a "useful concrete and tangible result," even though the program in question clearly embodied a mathematical algorithm. *In re Alappat*, 33 F.3d 1526 (Fed.Cir.1994). After *Alappat*, it appeared that a patent applicant need only show practical application of an algorithm to pass as statutory subject matter. In other words, few inventions would be deemed too abstract, by definition, to be excluded from patentability.

Yet the limits of patentability remained unclear. In 1994, a system for calculating auction bids that used simple linear math to group and regroup bids was deemed unpatentable on the theory that bids were not "physical" and, therefore, their reorganization could not involve a physical effect or transformation. *In re Schrader*, 22 F.3d 290 (Fed.Cir.1994).

Schrader brought into sharper relief the potential impact of the computing technology cases—and the erosion of the mathematical algorithm exception—on the continuing viability of the business method exception. Though the opinion turned on the physical transformation test, *Schrader*'s majority made reference to the business method exception as well, prompting a prescient dissent from Judge Newman:

> [The business method exception is] an unwarranted encumbrance to the definition of statutory subject matter in § 101, * * * that [should] be discarded as error-prone, redundant, and obsolete. It merits retirement from the glossary of § 101. * * * All of the "doing business" cases could have been decided using the clearer concepts of Title 35. Patentability does not turn on whether the claimed method does "business" instead of something else, but on whether the method, viewed as a whole, meets the requirements of patentability as set forth in §§ 102, 103, and 112 of the Patent Act.

In re Schrader, 22 F.3d at 298 (Newman, J., dissenting).

IV.   THE DEMISE OF THE BUSINESS METHOD EXCEPTION

Many observers have argued, as Judge Newman suggested in her *In re Schrader* dissent, that the business methods exception, though appropriately removing commonplace or obvious business practices from the realm of patentability, unfairly penalizes inventors who devise new methods of conducting business that would otherwise meet the requirements of patentability.

Though the business methods exception generally acted as a bar to patentability, some courts declined to invalidate patents that met the novelty and non-obviousness requirements, just because the invention was a "method" related to business procedures. In *Paine, Webber, Jackson & Curtis v. Merrill Lynch, Pierce, Fenner & Smith*, 564 F.Supp. 1358 (D.Del. 1983), the court rejected Paine Webber's argument that Merrill Lynch's patent on a computer-implemented, data-processing system was "nothing more than familiar business systems, that is, the financial management of individual brokerage accounts." Instead, the court found that the patent met the threshold requirements for statutory subject matter under Section 101.

The court's reasoning carved out a niche allowing some computerized business methods to be patented, by re-articulating the mechanics of the business methods test:

> the "technological" or "useful" arts inquiry *must* focus on whether the claimed subject matter (a method of operating a machine to translate) is statutory [i.e., within patentable subject matter], not

on whether the product of the claimed subject matter (a translated text) is statutory, not on whether the prior art which the claimed subject matter purports to replace (translation by human mind) is statutory, and *not* on whether the claimed subject matter is presently perceived to be an improvement over the prior art, e.g., whether it "enhances" the operation of a machine.

Paine, Webber v. Merrill Lynch, 564 F.Supp. at 1369 (quoting *In re Toma,* 575 F.2d 872, 877–78 (C.C.P.A.1978)). Applying this reasoning, the court held that though Merrill Lynch's financial integration method "would be unpatentable if done by hand, * * * the focus of analysis should be on the operation of the program on the computer." 564 F.Supp. at 1369. Because the method was implemented through a machine—the computer—the court held that the patent was within statutory subject matter.

Paine, Webber v. Merrill Lynch demonstrates that long before the official demise of the business methods exception in *State Street Bank,* courts were avoiding the business methods bar by treating computer-implemented business methods like any other computer-implemented invention. *State Street Bank* eliminated the need for this indirect approach to business method patents.

State Street Bank & Trust Co. v. Signature Financial Group, Inc.

149 F.3d 1368 (Fed.Cir.1998).

■ Rich, Circuit Judge.

Signature Financial Group, Inc. (Signature) appeals from the decision of the United States District Court for the District of Massachusetts granting a motion for summary judgment in favor of State Street Bank & Trust Co. (State Street), finding U.S. Patent No. 5,193,056 (the '056 patent) invalid on the ground that the claimed subject matter is not encompassed by 35 U.S.C. § 101 (1994). See *State Street Bank & Trust Co. v. Signature Financial Group, Inc.,* 927 F.Supp. 502 (D.Mass.1996). We reverse and remand because we conclude that the patent claims are directed to statutory subject matter.

BACKGROUND

Signature is the assignee of the '056 patent which is entitled "Data Processing System for Hub and Spoke Financial Services Configuration." The '056 patent issued to Signature on 9 March 1993, naming R. Todd Boes as the inventor. The '056 patent is generally directed to a data processing system (the system) for implementing an investment structure which was developed for use in Signature's business as an administrator and accounting agent for mutual funds. In essence, the system, identified by the proprietary name Hub and Spoke ®, facilitates a structure whereby mutual funds (Spokes) pool their assets in an investment portfolio (Hub) organized as a partnership. This investment configuration provides the administrator of a mutual fund with the advantageous combination of economies of scale in administering investments coupled with the tax advantages of a partnership.

State Street and Signature are both in the business of acting as custodians and accounting agents for multi-tiered partnership fund financial services. State Street negotiated with Signature for a license to use its patented data processing system described and claimed in the '056 patent. When negotiations broke down, State Street brought a declaratory judgment action asserting invalidity, unenforceability, and noninfringement in Massachusetts district court, and then filed a motion for partial summary judgment of patent invalidity for failure to claim statutory subject matter under § 101. The motion was granted and this appeal followed.

DISCUSSION

* * *

The following facts pertinent to the statutory subject matter issue are either undisputed or represent the version alleged by the nonmovant. See *Anderson v. Liberty Lobby, Inc.*, 477 U.S. 242, 255 (1986). The patented invention relates generally to a system that allows an administrator to monitor and record the financial information flow and make all calculations necessary for maintaining a partner fund financial services configuration. As previously mentioned, a partner fund financial services configuration essentially allows several mutual funds, or "Spokes," to pool their investment funds into a single portfolio, or "Hub," allowing for consolidation of, inter alia, the costs of administering the fund combined with the tax advantages of a partnership. In particular, this system provides means for a daily allocation of assets for two or more Spokes that are invested in the same Hub. The system determines the percentage share that each Spoke maintains in the Hub, while taking into consideration daily changes both in the value of the Hub's investment securities and in the concomitant amount of each Spoke's assets.

In determining daily changes, the system also allows for the allocation among the Spokes of the Hub's daily income, expenses, and net realized and unrealized gain or loss, calculating each day's total investments based on the concept of a book capital account. This enables the determination of a true asset value of each Spoke and accurate calculation of allocation ratios between or among the Spokes. The system additionally tracks all the relevant data determined on a daily basis for the Hub and each Spoke, so that aggregate year end income, expenses, and capital gain or loss can be determined for accounting and for tax purposes for the Hub and, as a result, for each publicly traded Spoke.

It is essential that these calculations are quickly and accurately performed. In large part this is required because each Spoke sells shares to the public and the price of those shares is substantially based on the Spoke's percentage interest in the portfolio. In some instances, a mutual fund administrator is required to calculate the value of the shares to the nearest penny within as little as an hour and a half after the market closes. Given the complexity of the calculations, a computer or equivalent device is a virtual necessity to perform the task.

* * *

* * * [C]laim 1, properly construed, claims a machine, namely, a data processing system for managing a financial services configuration of a portfolio established as a partnership * * *. A "machine" is proper statutory subject matter under § 101. We note that, for the purposes of a § 101 analysis, it is of little relevance whether claim 1 is directed to a "machine" or a "process," as long as it falls within at least one of the four enumerated categories of patentable subject matter, "machine" and "process" being such categories.

This does not end our analysis, however, because the court concluded that the claimed subject matter fell into one of two alternative judicially-created exceptions to statutory subject matter. The court refers to the first exception as the "mathematical algorithm" exception and the second exception as the "business method" exception. Section 101 reads:

> Whoever invents or discovers any new and useful process, machine, manufacture, or composition of matter, or any new and useful improvement thereof, may obtain a patent therefor, subject to the conditions and requirements of this title.

The plain and unambiguous meaning of § 101 is that any invention falling within one of the four stated categories of statutory subject matter may be patented, provided it meets the other requirements for patentability set forth in Title 35, i.e., those found in §§ 102, 103, and 112, ¶ 2.

The repetitive use of the expansive term "any" in § 101 shows Congress's intent not to place any restrictions on the subject matter for which a patent may be obtained beyond those specifically recited in § 101. Indeed, the Supreme Court has acknowledged that Congress intended § 101 to extend to "anything under the sun that is made by man." *Diamond v. Chakrabarty*, 447 U.S. 303, 309 (1980); *see also Diamond v. Diehr*, 450 U.S. 175, 182 (1981). Thus, it is improper to read limitations into § 101 on the subject matter that may be patented where the legislative history indicates that Congress clearly did not intend such limitations. See *Chakrabarty*, 447 U.S. at 308 ("We have also cautioned that courts 'should not read into the patent laws limitations and conditions which the legislature has not expressed.' " (citations omitted)).

The "Mathematical Algorithm" Exception

The Supreme Court has identified three categories of subject matter that are unpatentable, namely "laws of nature, natural phenomena, and abstract ideas." *Diehr*, 450 U.S. at 185. Of particular relevance to this case, the Court has held that mathematical algorithms are not patentable subject matter to the extent that they are merely abstract ideas. See *Diehr*, 450 U.S. 175, passim; *Parker v. Flook*, 437 U.S. 584 (1978); *Gottschalk v. Benson*, 409 U.S. 63 (1972). In *Diehr*, the Court explained that certain types of mathematical subject matter, standing alone, represent nothing more than abstract ideas until reduced to some type of practical application, i.e., "a useful, concrete and tangible result." *Alappat*, 33 F.3d at 1544.[4]

Unpatentable mathematical algorithms are identifiable by showing they are merely abstract ideas constituting disembodied concepts or truths that are not "useful." From a practical standpoint, this means that to be patentable an algorithm must be applied in a "useful" way. In *Alappat*, we held that data, transformed by a machine through a series of mathematical calculations to produce a smooth waveform display on a rasterizer monitor, constituted a practical application of an abstract idea (a mathematical algorithm, formula, or calculation), because it produced "a useful, concrete and tangible result"—the smooth waveform.

Similarly, in *Arrhythmia Research Technology, Inc. v. Corazonix Corp.*, 958 F.2d 1053 (Fed.Cir.1992), we held that the transformation of electrocardiograph signals from a patient's heartbeat by a machine through a series of mathematical calculations constituted a practical application of an abstract idea (a mathematical algorithm, formula, or calculation), because it corresponded to a useful, concrete or tangible thing—the condition of a patient's heart.

Today, we hold that the transformation of data, representing discrete dollar amounts, by a machine through a series of mathematical calculations into a final share price, constitutes a practical application of a mathematical algorithm, formula, or calculation, because it produces "a useful, concrete and tangible result"—a final share price momentarily fixed for recording and reporting purposes and even accepted and relied upon by regulatory authorities and in subsequent trades.

The district court erred by applying the *Freeman–Walter–Abele* test to determine whether the claimed subject matter was an unpatentable abstract idea. The *Freeman–Walter–Abele* test was designed by the Court of Customs and Patent Appeals, and subsequently adopted by this court, to extract and identify unpatentable mathematical algorithms in the aftermath of *Benson* and *Flook*. See *In re Freeman*, 573 F.2d 1237 (CCPA 1978) as modified by *In re Walter*, 618 F.2d 758 (CCPA 1980). The test has been thus articulated:

> First, the claim is analyzed to determine whether a mathematical algorithm is directly or indirectly recited. Next, if a mathematical algorithm is found, the claim as a whole is further analyzed to determine whether the algorithm is "applied in any manner to physical elements or process steps," and, if it is, it "passes muster under § 101."

In re Pardo, 684 F.2d 912, 915 (CCPA 1982) (citing *In re Abele*, 684 F.2d 902 (CCPA 1982)).

---

4. This has come to be known as the mathematical algorithm exception. This designation has led to some confusion, especially given the *Freeman–Walter–Abele* analysis. By keeping in mind that the mathematical algorithm is unpatentable only to the extent that it represents an abstract idea, this confusion may be ameliorated.

After *Diehr* and *Chakrabarty*, the *Freeman–Walter–Abele* test has little, if any, applicability to determining the presence of statutory subject matter. As we pointed out in *Alappat*, 33 F.3d at 1543, application of the test could be misleading, because a process, machine, manufacture, or composition of matter employing a law of nature, natural phenomenon, or abstract idea is patentable subject matter even though a law of nature, natural phenomenon, or abstract idea would not, by itself, be entitled to such protection. The test determines the presence of, for example, an algorithm. Under *Benson*, this may have been a sufficient indicium of nonstatutory subject matter. However, after *Diehr* and *Alappat*, the mere fact that a claimed invention involves inputting numbers, calculating numbers, outputting numbers, and storing numbers, in and of itself, would not render it nonstatutory subject matter, unless, of course, its operation does not produce a "useful, concrete and tangible result." *Alappat*, 33 F.3d at 1544. After all, as we have repeatedly stated,

> every step-by-step process, be it electronic or chemical or mechanical, involves an algorithm in the broad sense of the term. Since § 101 expressly includes processes as a category of inventions which may be patented and § 100(b) further defines the word "process" as meaning "process, art or method, and includes a new use of a known process, machine, manufacture, composition of matter, or material," it follows that it is no ground for holding a claim is directed to nonstatutory subject matter to say it includes or is directed to an algorithm. This is why the proscription against patenting has been limited to mathematical algorithms....

In re Iwahashi, 888 F.2d 1370, 1374 (Fed.Cir.1989) (emphasis in the original).

The question of whether a claim encompasses statutory subject matter should not focus on which of the four categories of subject matter a claim is directed to—process, machine, manufacture, or composition of matter—but rather on the essential characteristics of the subject matter, in particular, its practical utility. Section 101 specifies that statutory subject matter must also satisfy the other "conditions and requirements" of Title 35, including novelty, nonobviousness, and adequacy of disclosure and notice. See *In re Warmerdam*, 33 F.3d 1354, 1359, (Fed.Cir.1994). For purpose of our analysis, as noted above, claim 1 is directed to a machine programmed with the Hub and Spoke software and admittedly produces a "useful, concrete, and tangible result." *Alappat*, 33 F.3d at 1544. This renders it statutory subject matter, even if the useful result is expressed in numbers, such as price, profit, percentage, cost, or loss.

The Business Method Exception

As an alternative ground for invalidating the '056 patent under § 101, the court relied on the judicially-created, so-called "business method" exception to statutory subject matter. We take this opportunity to lay this ill-conceived exception to rest. Since its inception, the "business method" exception has merely represented the application of some general, but no longer applicable legal principle, perhaps arising out of the "requirement for invention"—which was eliminated by § 103. Since the 1952 Patent Act, business methods have been, and should have been, subject to the same legal requirements for patentability as applied to any other process or method.

The business method exception has never been invoked by this court, or the CCPA, to deem an invention unpatentable. Application of this particular exception has always been preceded by a ruling based on some clearer concept of Title 35 or, more commonly, application of the abstract idea exception based on finding a mathematical algorithm. Illustrative is the CCPA's analysis in *In re Howard*, 394 F.2d 869 (CCPA 1968), wherein the court affirmed the Board of Appeals' rejection of the claims for lack of novelty and found it unnecessary to reach the Board's § 101 ground that a method of doing business is "inherently unpatentable." 394 F.2d at 872.

Similarly, *In re Schrader*, 22 F.3d 290 (Fed.Cir.1994), while making reference to the business method exception, turned on the fact that the claims implicitly recited an abstract idea in the form of a mathematical algorithm and there was no "transformation or conversion of subject matter representative of or constituting physical activity or objects." 22 F.3d at 294 (emphasis omitted).[13]

* * *

Even the case frequently cited as establishing the business method exception to statutory subject matter, *Hotel Security Checking Co. v. Lorraine Co.*, 160 F. 467 (2d Cir.1908), did not rely on the exception to strike the patent. In that case, the patent was found invalid for lack of novelty and "invention," not because it was improper subject matter for a patent. The court stated "the fundamental principle of the system is as old as the art of bookkeeping, i.e., charging the goods of the employer to the agent who takes them." *Id.* at 469. "If at the time of [the patent] application, there had been no system of bookkeeping of any kind in restaurants, we would be confronted with the question whether a new and useful system of cash registering and account checking is such an art as is patentable under the statute." *Id.* at 472.

This case is no exception. The district court announced the precepts of the business method exception as set forth in several treatises, but noted as its primary reason for finding the patent invalid under the business method exception as follows:

> If Signature's invention were patentable, any financial institution desirous of implementing a multi-tiered funding complex modelled (sic) on a Hub and Spoke configuration would be required to seek Signature's permission before embarking on such a project. *This is so because the '056 Patent is claimed [sic] sufficiently broadly to*

---

13. Any historical distinctions between a method of "doing" business and the means of carrying it out blur in the complexity of modern business systems. See *Paine, Webber,* *Jackson & Curtis v. Merrill Lynch*, 564 F.Supp. 1358 (D.Del.1983), (holding a computerized system of cash management was held to be statutory subject matter.)

foreclose virtually any computer-implemented accounting method necessary to manage this type of financial structure.

927 F Supp, 502, 516 (emphasis added). Whether the patent's claims are too broad to be patentable is not to be judged under § 101, but rather under §§ 102, 103 and 112. Assuming the above statement to be correct, it has nothing to do with whether what is claimed is statutory subject matter.

In view of this background, it comes as no surprise that in the most recent edition of the Manual of Patent Examining Procedures (MPEP) (1996), a paragraph of § 706.03(a) was deleted. In past editions it read:

> Though seemingly within the category of process or method, a method of doing business can be rejected as not being within the statutory classes. See *Hotel Security Checking Co. v. Lorraine Co.*, 160 F. 467 (2d Cir. 1908) and *In re Wait*, 73 F.2d 982, 22 C.C.P.A. 822 (1934).

MPEP § 706.03(a) (1994). This acknowledgment is buttressed by the U.S. Patent and Trademark 1996 Examination Guidelines for Computer Related Inventions which now read:

> Office personnel have had difficulty in properly treating claims directed to methods of doing business. Claims should not be categorized as methods of doing business. Instead such claims should be treated like any other process claims.

Examination Guidelines, 61 Fed. Reg. 7478, 7479 (1996). We agree that this is precisely the manner in which this type of claim should be treated. Whether the claims are directed to subject matter within § 101 should not turn on whether the claimed subject matter does "business" instead of something else.

CONCLUSION

The appealed decision is reversed and the case is remanded to the district court for further proceedings consistent with this opinion.

NOTES & QUESTIONS

1. *Limited to computer-related inventions?* State Street's patent application claimed a computer-related invention, and some commentators have characterized the Federal Circuit opinion as accepting only computer-related business methods as statutory (i.e., patentable) subject matter. Do you agree that the decision should be so interpreted? Or does the decision mean that any business method is potentially patentable?

2. *The mathematical algorithm exception.* The "tangibility" or "physicality" dimensions of the transformation inquiry, were largely abandoned in *State Street Bank.* The question whether a claim comprises statutory subject matter, the Federal Circuit insisted, should focus simply on the "practical utility" of the claim, or whether it produced a concrete, tangible and useful result. Numbers were concrete enough to "count" as such a result. What meaning is left for the word "tangible"?

The view that a numerical output can be concrete, tangible and useful was affirmed shortly thereafter, in *AT&T v. Excel Communications, Inc.*, 172 F.3d 1352 (Fed.Cir.1999), which concerned a patent on a process for transmitting billing information relating to long-distance telephone calls. The district court had found AT & T's patent to be invalid because, as a mathematical algorithm, it failed to satisfy the statutory subject matter requirements: "The court was of the view that the only physical step in the claims involves data-gathering for the algorithm. Though the court recognized that the claims require the use of switches and computers, it nevertheless concluded that use of such facilities to perform a non-substantive change in the data's format could not serve to convert non-patentable subject matter into patentable subject matter." *Id.* at 1355.

The Federal Circuit reversed, explaining that the statutory subject matter requirements were intended to exclude only "laws of nature, natural phenomena, and abstract ideas," and sharply narrowed the mathematical algorithm exception to "mathematical algorithms in the abstract." *Id.* at 1356. Further, the court interpreted *Diamond v. Diehr* as holding that "even though a mathematical algorithm is not patentable in isolation, a process that applies an equation to a new and useful end 'is at the very least not barred at the threshold by 101.' " *Id.* at 1357 (quoting *Diamond v. Diehr*, 450 U.S. at 188).

In sum, the court explicitly limited the previous "mathematical algorithm exception" to a simple inquiry of patentability: whether "the claimed subject matter as a whole is a disembodied mathematical concept representing nothing more than a 'law of nature' or an 'abstract idea,' or if the mathematical concept has been reduced to some practical application rendering it 'useful.' " *Id.* at 1357.

Applying this criterion, the Federal Circuit found that AT & T's invention fell within the purview of Section 101 statutory requirements, and reversed the holding of the district court:

> Excel argues that method claims containing mathematical algorithms are patentable subject matter only if there is a "physical transformation" or conversion of subject matter from one state into another. The physical transformation language appears in *Diehr*, *see* 450 U.S. at 184 ("That respondents' claims involve the transformation of an article, in this case raw, uncured synthetic rubber, into a different state or thing cannot be disputed."), and has been echoed by this court in *Schrader*, 22 F.3d at 294, ("Therefore, we do not find in the claim any kind of data transformation.").

> The notion of "physical transformation" can be misunderstood. In the first place, it is not an invariable requirement, but merely one example of how a mathematical algorithm may bring about a useful application. As the Supreme Court itself noted, "when [a claimed invention] is performing a function which the patent laws were designed to protect (e.g., transforming or reduc-

ing an article to a different state or thing), then the claim satisfies the requirements of § 101."

172 F.3d at 1358–59. Indeed, as a Federal Circuit judge remarked a few months later: "We have come a long way from the days when judges frowned on patents as pernicious monopolies deserving scant regard. Today, patents are the backbone of much of the national economy, and, as this court has recently held, virtually anything is patentable." *Hughes Aircraft v. United States*, 148 F.3d 1384, 1385 (Fed.Cir.1998) (Clevenger, J., dissenting).

A. The Prior-User Defense

In the wake of the *State Street Bank* decision, entrepreneurs in many fields expressed concern that they might have to pay license fees for the right to continue engaging in longstanding business practices, simply because they had not sought patent protection for those practices and somebody else had. The fact that a user of a practice had invented it independently would not be a defense in a patent infringement suit, unless the defendant were able to show that the patent must be invalidated. Entrepreneurs were concerned that an attempt to invalidate a competitor's patent on the basis of prior invention might not succeed if the patentee could prove that he was in fact first to reduce the method to practice; and where the prior user had been keeping the method secret, an attempt to invalidate the patent based upon prior public use might fail. Responding to these concerns, Congress enacted the First Inventor Defense Act of 1999, Pub. L. No. 106–113, 113 Stat. 1501A–555 (1999), which added Section 273 to Title 35. Section 273 provides:

> It shall be a defense to an action for infringement under section 271 of this title with respect to any subject matter that would otherwise infringe one or more claims for a method in the patent being asserted against a person, if such person had, acting in good faith, actually reduced the subject matter to practice at least 1 year before the effective filing date of such patent, and commercially used the subject matter before the effective filing date of such patent.

35 U.S.C. § 273(b)(1).

Although this provision grants prior user rights for "a method," the statute defines "method" as "a method of doing or conducting business." 35 U.S.C. § 273(a)(3).

A House Report on the bill noted that it would be "administratively and economically impossible to expect any inventor to apply for a patent on all business methods and processes now deemed patentable." H.R. Rep. No. 106–287, at 45 (1999). The person asserting the defense must prove its applicability by clear and convincing evidence. 35 U.S.C. § 273(b)(4). If the defense is asserted unsuccessfully, and the person asserting it is found not to have had a "reasonable basis" for asserting it, the defendant is liable for the plaintiff's attorney's fees. 35 U.S.C. § 273(b)(8).

To understand how the prior-user exception can be expected to work, and to appreciate its limitations, consider the following hypothetical and discussion:

Take the example of Bugs Bunny and Yosemite Sam. Bugs invented a method of systematically marketing carrots (and other roots) via the Rabbitnet (a network of computer networks), and filed for a patent on his "carrot pushing" method on January 15, 1998. Sam, a bitter competitor of Bugs, markets various roots (including carrots) using the same method. When precisely Sam started doing so is clouded in some mystery. The only thing Bugs knows for sure is that whenever he asks Sam to purchase a license on the carrot pushing technology, he is treated to all manner of verbal abuse.

Bugs receives his patent on January 18, 2000 and promptly sues Sam for patent infringement. Sam insists that he was pushing carrots via the Rabbitnet when Bugs was in diapers. How does Sam turn that tough talk into a viable defense?

First, Sam must prove that he was *actually commercially exploiting* the patented method before Bugs filed his application in the Patent Office. Second, Sam must prove that he reduced the patented method to practice * * * at least one year before Bugs' filing date at the Patent Office. The real kicker is that Sam has to prove these things by evidence that meets the high standard of "clear and convincing." This elevated standard is an explicit requirement in the new law. Although Congress created a loophole, they didn't want it to be an easy one to wiggle through.

Can Sam squeeze through this loophole? He has to put on testimony about events that happened over three years ago, and he needs to corroborate that testimony with objective evidence such as paper documents. That corroborating evidence is critical to meeting the clear and convincing standard, and it may not be available after such a long time, assuming that it ever existed in the first place.

The worst case for Bugs is that Sam convinces the judge that he truly was a prior user. This is not the end of the world for Bugs' carrot business. Successfully proving oneself to be a prior user does not invalidate the patent, so Bugs still has his patent. He can still enforce it against other people besides Sam. Although Sam gets a free license to infringe at will, Sam is boxed in and cannot improve on his method in any way that would take advantage of any improvements that Bugs patented. Essentially, Sam's business is frozen in the form it was when Bugs filed his patent application. Even worse for Sam is that he cannot practice his rights at any sites other than the ones he was using on the day Bugs filed his patent application. And, Sam cannot sell his prior user rights; they have no market value in theory.

Suddenly Sam doesn't sound like such a big winner. Sure he gets to stay in business, but the growth of his business is permanently hobbled. And slow growth is death for a Rabbitnet business.

Let's take a look at the downside for Sam if the judge rules against him on his prior user rights defense: Sam has already *admitted* he is an infringer! Bugs doesn't have to prove this element, because Sam shot off his mouth. Unless Sam can scrape up some evidence for another defense (insanity?) he is doomed.

In all seriousness, the practical effect of this new wrinkle in the law is that, in rare cases where an infringer has credible evidence that they can fit through the prior user loophole, it will promote early settlement of the lawsuit. This defense increases risks for both sides, and will motivate them to think twice before going to trial.

Kevin L. Pontius, *Prior User Rights In Business Methods*, www.vienna-pat.com/newsletter/vol4iss1/prioruserrightsinbusinessmethods.htm.

NOTES & QUESTIONS

1. *Limitation to business methods.* The prior-user defense is limited to business method patents. Is there a convincing reason not to extend the defense to other types of patents? Proponents of the defense have argued that it is particularly necessary in this field, where the PTO has had difficulty sorting out what is patentable and what is not. It is also arguably more difficult for prospective inventors and PTO examiners to search for relevant prior art, because a comprehensive body of prior art does not exist and prior uses may not even be documented. Business methods may be more frequently wholly "internal" to a business's operations than other processes it uses in manufacturing or marketing its products—or so it might be argued. Might a better solution be to go to the root of the problem—the Patent Office—and formulate more rigorous standards for determining patentability? While prior user rights might help resolve some of the unique problems presented by business method patents in the short-run, what effect might they have on the patent system in the long run?

2. *What exactly is a method of doing business?* What criteria should the courts use in determining whether a given method used in commerce is or is not a "method of doing business" for purposes of granting or withholding prior user rights?

3. *Patents vs. trade secrets.* Some prior users may have elected trade secrecy for their business methods because they did not realize, prior to *State Street Bank*, that such processes could be patented. When a developer of an innovative method chooses trade secrecy, it assumes the risk that someone else may obtain a patent on the method, just as it assumes the risk that the secret will leak out and be lost. The coexistence of patent (federal law) and trade secret (state law) rests partly on the fact that trade secrecy is fragile. By giving a defense to prior users of business methods who choose trade secrecy, even after *State Street Bank* made it clear that a patent may be available, has Congress undermined the balance between patent and trade secret law? *See* James R. Barney, *The Prior User Defense: A Reprieve for Trade Secret Owners or a Disaster for the Patent Law?*, 82 J. PAT. & TRADEMARK OFF. SOC'Y 261 (2000).

B.   THE IMPACT OF *STATE STREET BANK* ON THE PATENT AND TRADEMARK OFFICE AND ON THE PATENT SYSTEM AS A WHOLE

Many commentators have argued that the blitz of patent applications on computer-related inventions starting in the 1970s caught the PTO unprepared—without examiners trained in computer science, without the resources to research thoroughly whether the claimed invention was original. Hence, these commentators believe that there are a large number of patents on computer-related inventions whose validity is questionable. Once it became well known that repetitive calculations are better performed by a computer, should an invention that consists of inserting a computer into a process where repetitive calculations are needed count as non-obvious?

Since the early 1990s, the number of patent examiners has increased dramatically, and the PTO reports that the bulk of new examiners are assigned to computer technologies and biotechnologies. Yet the PTO's 2000 Corporate Plan anticipates "continuing recruitment difficulties" due to budget shortfalls and competition from private industry for qualified examiners. Q. Todd Dickinson, Remarks at the American Bar Association's Summer IPL Conference (June 23, 2000), www.uspto.gov/web/offices/speeches/speeches.html; USPTO Corporate Plan—FY 2001, Executive Summary at 19.

Much of the criticism of the *State Street Bank* decision and business method patents in general has centered on the problem of patent quality and prior art. Patent examiners look closely at relevant publications (including scholarly articles, issued patents, and other printed materials) to see whether an invention is either non-novel or obvious. The ability of patent examiners to conduct such a search may be hampered in the case of business method applications. Professor Rochelle Cooper Dreyfuss summarizes the problem.

> First, because business methods have not been patented in the past, there is very little patent-related prior art readily at hand to the examiner corps. More important, because knowledge about business methods resides mainly in the practices and policies of the firms that use them, even common methods may not be documented in the sorts of materials that examiners can efficiently consult. Unless these difficulties are taken care of—and it is hard to see how the latter can ever be dealt with effectively—invalid patents will inevitably issue.

Rochelle Cooper Dreyfuss, *Are Business Method Patents Bad For Business?*, 16 SANTA CLARA COMPUTER & HIGH TECH. L.J. 263, 269 (2000).

Other commentators concede the point, but note that similar complaints were advanced with respect to biotechnology patent applications in the early 1980s, until the PTO built up a good database of prior art and gained greater evaluative experience. *See, e.g.*, Robert Merges, *As Many as Six Impossible Patents Before Breakfast: Property Rights for Business Concepts and Patent System Reform*, 14 Berkeley Tech. L.J. 577, 589 (1999). If business method patents are similarly in a transition period, patent quality will soon improve. Are there qualitative differences between biotechnological research and business method development that might undermine this "transition" analogy? Consider the following analysis, also from Professor Dreyfuss.

> One could dismiss the problem of invalid patents as ephemeral—if a patent covers a business method that is really important, it will be challenged and invalidated. But while the potential for successful challenge is certainly real, it is not clear that it is an adequate solution. After all, patents have in terrorem effects: no one wants to invest in a business that cannot succeed without first winning a lawsuit. Moreover, much can happen during the transition period between allowance and invalidation. For example, many industries experience shake outs. These have the beneficial effect of culling out those firms that are the least competent. But to some extent, business method patents protect businesses from competition. Thus, they can function in a way that preserves inefficiencies in the marketplace.

> In some fields, there is another, more enduring, problem[:] * * * lock in. Consider, for example, Amazon.com's patented one-click technology, which has been enforced against BarnesandNoble.com.[3] One click is very nice for shoppers because once they have inputted various bits of shipping and billing information, they can check out quickly on subsequent visits. Accordingly, if Amazon has the exclusive right to one-click, we can expect that many customers will patronize its site. What happens if the patent is eventually invalidated—will there then be effective competition? Probably not because once a book buyer has entered information at Amazon, there is no reason to go elsewhere, particularly now that Amazon has the capacity to further analyze the information and offer its patrons useful suggestions about future purchases. Buyers who rely on such services will not care if the patent is invalidated, and rival sites are permitted to utilize one-click: once locked in to Amazon, shoppers will not likely visit a site that is less informative and requires more work.

> Another way to make customers stick is with network effects. An example of a network effect is AOL's instant messenger. A user's ability to exchange e-mail in real time is useful only when

---

3. [The district court's preliminary injunction enforcing the patent against Barnesandnoble.com was overturned on appeal, and the parties subsequently settled. The case is discussed and excerpted in Part VI, *infra*.—Eds.]

the people the user wishes to reach are also on the same system. As a result, the value of the system as a whole depends directly on its size. I do not know whether AOL has protected its system with a patent, but if it has, then instant messenger is a good example of the problem with relying on invalidation. The reason is this: if there were such a patent, it would be extremely significant because it would force everyone interested in instant messenger to sign up with AOL. But once a large (and valuable) network is created, invalidation will not matter at all. True, rivals would appear, but because they would necessarily start small, they would not be able to deliver the same value to their customers. The bottom line is thus a terrible transition problem: patents do not need to be in force for long to exert a substantial effect on competition.

Dreyfuss, *supra*, 16 SANTA CLARA COMPUTER & HIGH TECH. L.J. at 270–272.

Several commentators have argued that even valid business method patents are unnecessary to encourage innovation.

[T]he broad grant of patent protection for methods of doing business is something of a square peg in a sinkhole of uncertain dimensions. Nowhere in the substantial literature on innovation is there a statement that the United States economy suffers from a lack of innovation in methods of doing business. Compared with the business practices of comparable economies we seem to be innovators in distribution and in the service industries. By the casual empiricism of counting the number of graduate business schools, the United States is ahead of other developed economies. This datum, plus the substantial enrollment of foreign students in the graduate schools of business in the United States, permits the inference that business methods in this country as presently practiced, are considered innovative and attractive, despite the prior absence of patent protection.

There is, moreover, substantial anecdotal evidence that competition alone serves as a sufficient spur to innovation in business methods. The rapid cluster of development in the following businesses casts doubt on the need for the added incentive of patents. Consider the growth of fast food restaurants, self-service gasoline stations, quick oil change facilities, supermarkets for food and office supplies, automatic teller devices and other banking services, electronic fund transfers, supplemental insurance for physician services, and alternatives for long-distance telephone services. To the argument that the economy of the United States would function even better with such patent protection, the model casts doubt. The case for broad patent protection, plausible as a matter of theory, has been qualified by the historical/empirical studies of industries in which there had been broad patent protection.

Moreover, conceding the possibility of free-riding as well as outright piracy of business methods, the absence of patent protection would not leave a total void of legal remedies. There are a variety of federal and state alternative regimes of protection. Copyright, misappropriation, unfair competition, and deceptive practices statutes may serve as alternative means of protection. These regimes may serve to furnish the incentive of protection as well as a means of redress against "dirty tricks" by competitors.

Leo J. Raskind, *The State Street Bank Decision: The Bad Business of Unlimited Patent Protection for Methods of Doing Business*, 10 Fordham I. P., Media & Ent. L.J. 61, 92–93 (1999).

Some commentators have hinted that the problems created by trying to apply business method patents to the Internet might be impossible to resolve—and that the Internet would be best served if allowed to develop freely (at least for the time being) without the competitive impediment of patent monopolies. Will the desire to encourage technological development in cyberspace be better served by allowing or not allowing patent protection? Considering the traditional reliance on patents to encourage innovation, could limiting or even eliminating patent protection on the Internet actually lead to *more* innovation? Here is one view.

A patent is a form of regulation. It is a government-granted monopoly—an exclusive right backed by the power of the state. This monopoly is granted by a bureaucrat—a well-meaning, hard-working bureaucrat no doubt, but a bureaucrat nonetheless. This government employee decides whether an idea is novel, useful and nonobvious. If it is, the government guarantees the inventor an exclusive right to the idea for 20 years. Last year, some 150,000 such exclusive rights were granted, up one-third from the year before.

No doubt we are better off with a patent system than without one. Lots of research and invention wouldn't occur without the government's protection. But just because some protection is good, more isn't necessarily better. Especially in cyberspace.

There is growing skepticism among academics about whether such state-imposed monopolies help a rapidly evolving market such as the Internet. What is "novel," "nonobvious" or "useful" is hard enough to know in a relatively stable field. In a transforming market, it's nearly impossible for anyone—let alone an underpaid worker in the U.S. Department of Commerce who spends on average of eight hours evaluating the prior art in a patent and gets paid based on how many he processes—to identify what's "novel." Costly mistakes get made. On average it takes $1.2 million to challenge the validity of a patent, which means it is often cheaper simply to pay the royalties than to establish that the patent isn't deserved.

"Bad patents" thus become the space debris of cyberspace. Nowhere is this clearer than in the context of business-method patents. At a recent conference in Israel, I watched as a lawyer terrified the assembled crowd of Internet startups with stories of the increasing number of business-method patents that now haunt Internet space. Patent No. 5,715,314, for example, gives the holder a monopoly over "network-based sales systems"—we call that e-commerce. Patent No. 5,797,127 forms the basis for Priceline.com and effectively blocks any competitor. Patent No. 4,949,257 covers the purchase of software over a network.

To West Coast coders, it seems bizarre that East Coast coders—the Patent Office—consider these ideas nonobvious. But the real problem is the incentives such a system creates. Awarding patents of that type siphons off resources from technologists to lawyers—from people making real products to people applying for regulatory privilege and protection. An increasingly significant cost of Net startups involves both defensive and offensive lawyering—making sure you don't "steal" someone else's "idea" and quickly claiming as yours every "idea" you can describe in a patent application.

But this is absurd. When the world was given TCP/IP and the collection of protocols it induced, a billion ideas became obvious to anyone who took the time to think. These were not ideas that were discovered because some lone inventor spent years toiling away in his basement, but because TCP/IP was a language with which practically anything could be done. And with very little promise of protection by government, lots was done. The Internet revolution was born long before lawyers arrived on the scene.

Lawrence Lessig, *The Problem with Patents*, THE INDUSTRY STANDARD, Apr. 23, 1999, www.thestandard.com/article/display/0,1151,4296,00.html.

NOTES & QUESTIONS

1. *Software patents problematic*? Other than the courts' outmoded concerns with the metaphysics of patentable subject matter, which ended with *State Street Bank*, there are at least two reasons why software patents are a troubled area of patent law: (1) the fact that most software developments lose their value in a short time, so that the time it takes to get a patent may exhaust the invention's value; (2) the overlap in protection between patent law and copyright law.

Software became protectible under copyright law in the 1970s when the courts were refusing patent protection. Under copyright law, computer code—both source and object code—is protectible as a literary work. In addition, the structural elements of a computer program, if found to constitute "expression" rather than "ideas," can be copyrighted. It is arguable that patent and copyright were meant to be mutually exclusive, and that this situation is anomalous. Professor Radin argues that this anomaly is symptomatic of a broader breakdown of the distinction between text and machine:

Computer programs are both text and machine. They are text when considered as code statements, they are machines when considered as devices (for accomplishing a task. Copyright law reflects the text perspective (programs are considered literary works); patent law reflects the machine perspective (a programmed computer is a "new machine"). The fact that computer programs are both copyrightable and patentable is anomalous for intellectual property law. Copyright is supposed to exclude works that are functional; patent is supposed to focus on functionality and exclude texts. Computer programs are the only large area covered both by patent and copyright. This anomaly is obscured to some extent by the fact that copyright and patent regard programs differently: patent focuses on the protocol for accomplishing the task, however the programmer chooses to code it, whereas copyright focuses on the code statements, but also their structure, sequence and organization. The difference between structure, sequence and organization (copyrightable) and useful algorithm, protocol or method (patentable) is, however, conceptually difficult to maintain. This difficulty reflects the fact that computer programs can be understood either as text or machine. Those who write code sometimes genuinely feel that it is their speech and should be protected by the First Amendment. At the same time, it is clear that the primary *raison d'etre* for programs is their technological function, their ability to accomplish a task.

Margaret Jane Radin, *Online Standardization and the Integration of Text and Machine*, 70 FORDHAM L. REV. 1125, 1143–44 (2002).

Had software not been brought within the protection of copyright law, perhaps Congress would have enacted a new form of protection particularly suited to software, perhaps less onerous to apply for and of shorter duration than patents. Commentators argued at the time for such *sui generis* protection, but their arguments did not convince policy makers. *See, e.g.*, Pamela Samuelson, Randall Davis, Mitchell D. Kapor & J.H. Reichman, *A Manifesto Concerning the Legal Protection of Computer Programs*, 94 COLUM. L. REV. 2308 (1994).

2. *Availability of prior art.* Is Professor Dreyfuss correct to see little hope of effectively addressing the problem that prior art may reside in the heads of managers rather than the pages of any accessible publication? Would the proliferation of business method patents, perhaps ironically, help resolve the difficulty she identifies?

3. *Improving the system.* Commentators have advanced several proposals aimed at remedying the perceived flaws in the business method patent application examination process. Which of the following strategies would best answer the criticisms advanced above? Would some be harder to implement than others? What reforms would you suggest?

    a. *Reforming the PTO.* Professor Robert Merges has proposed a series of changes in PTO examination procedures to improve patent quality. These include: (1) subcontracting patent examination and search procedures to outside firms that can conduct more comprehensive, efficient searches focusing on specific technologies and/or industries; (2) raising pay and benefits to encourage senior examiners to remain with the office and train new examiners; (3) restructuring the examiner bonus system, which may now encourage examiners to issue more patents and thereby raise their case completion rate, by introducing "error" tracking systems; and (4) revamping the reexamination system to allow more participation by interested third parties and to allow third parties to appeal adverse reexamination decisions. *See* Robert Merges, *As Many as Six Impossible Patents Before Breakfast: Property Rights for Business Concepts and Patent System Reform*, 14 BERKELEY TECH. L.J. 577 (1999). For an argument that putting more resources into the patent-examining process would be inefficient, see Mark A. Lemley, *Rational Ignorance at the Patent Office*, 95 Nw. U. L. REV. 1495 (2001).

b. *An opposition procedure.* Many countries allow interested members of the public to file oppositions to a patent during a designated period of time. In 1999 Congress amended the Patent Act to implement such a procedure, called "inter partes reexamination." Optional Inter Partes Reexamination Procedure Act of 1999, Pub. L. No. 106–113, 113 Stat. 1501A–567 (1999), 35 U.S.C. §§ 311–18. Under this procedure, any person may at any time bring to the attention of the PTO prior art that may be relevant to a patent, and may request reexamination of the patent. If the PTO determines that the request raises a substantial new question concerning validity of the patent, it must open a reexamination of the patent. Both the person requesting reexamination and the patentee are entitled to participate in the reexamination. Reexamination may lead to invalidation of the patent. 35 U.S.C. §§ 311–18. Does this procedure address the concerns about patent quality? The procedure has so far been infrequently invoked. According to the PTO Director, as of October 24, 2000, no one had chosen to take advantage of the new reexamination procedures with respect to a business method patent.

c. *A bounty system.* Professor John R. Thomas argues that the patent system needs bounty hunters. One of the basic assumptions of the patent system is that the validity of patents will be checked by private parties. According to this assumption, a competitor that wishes to use a patented invention, and believes the patent to be invalid, will ignore it; if the patentee seeks to bring an infringement action, she will lose because the competitor will be able to show the invention in question is obvious or non-novel. But this basic assumption may ignore the reality that competitors may decide the costs or risks of litigation are too high. Thomas suggests, therefore, the development of a kind of private bounty system that would reward persons who can show a patent to be invalid. Because the bounty would be paid by the patent applicant, applicants would be encouraged to research potential prior art carefully prior to filing an application. *See* John R. Thomas,

Collusion and Collective Action in the Patent System: A Proposal for Patent Bounties, 2001 U. ILL. L. REV. 305.

Versions of a bounty system already exist. BountyQuest.com, launched in October 2000, promises to pay users a reward for finding prior art applicable to specific patents or technologies described on the site. Rewards generally range from $10,000 to $50,000, depending on the patent. Companies interested in finding relevant prior art (potential infringers of a patent, for example), and/or inventors who want to be sure their invention is really new and non-obvious, pay the reward, as well as a fee to the BountyQuest Corporation. Internet-commerce-related patents featured on the site have included those on Web-based banner advertising, the Amazon.com "One–Click" feature, the Priceline.com reverse auction, and the BountyQuest business concept itself.

The ground for BountyQuest.com's effort was paved by the Software Patent Institute ("SPI"), a nonprofit organization that collects information pertaining to software technologies. Funded primarily by small grants and subscription fees, SPI focuses specifically on the "prior art" problem with respect to all computer-related inventions, including computer-related business method inventions. SPI does not offer a bounty, but has similarly sought to build up a body of information that can be used by patent applicants and possible infringers to determine whether an invention has been anticipated by prior art. Drawing on contributions from thousands of knowledgeable members of the computing community, SPI has developed a Database of Software Technologies consisting of source documents that are generally not readily available online or in electronic form elsewhere. Because it seeks to fill in major gaps in the prior art used to evaluate computer-related inventions, SPI does not include patents and most current trade publications; rather it seeks to track and corral the "folklore" of the computing industry. Available source documents, some of which date to 1955, include computer manuals, older textbooks and older journal articles, conference proceedings, computer science theses, and other materials that can provide pointers to prior art relevant to a given technology. Anyone with access to the Web can submit new materials and search the database. *See* www.spi.org.

For an argument that the problems with the PTO are institutional, and will not be solved by approaches such as those discussed above, see Brian Kahin, *The Expansion of the Patent System: Politics and Political Economy*, FIRST MONDAY, vol. 6, no. 1 (Jan. 2001), firstmonday.org/issues/issue6_1/kahin/index.html.

C.   PATENTS OUTSIDE THE UNITED STATES

In contrast to the expansiveness of the current U.S. approach to patentability of business methods, other countries are taking a more cautious approach. Many nations have been engaged in a drive toward international harmonization of intellectual property law, driven in part by the globalization of commerce, and some have begun to reconsider their limits on patentability in light of U.S. developments. The patent offices of the United States, Japan, and Europe have repeatedly met to discuss software and business method patentability. In June 2000, these three offices reported a "consensus" opinion consisting of two propositions: (1) "A technical aspect is necessary for a computer-implemented business method to be eligible for patenting." and (2) "To merely automate a known human transaction process using well known automation techniques is not patentable." *See* Report on Comparative Study Carried Out Under Trilateral Project B3b (June 14–16, 2000), www.european-patent-office.org/tws/front_page.pdf. An Appendix to the report, issued by the President of the European Patent Office, specifies guidelines for evaluating computer-implemented business methods, the key test being whether the invention solves an objective technical problem. *Id.*, app. 6. According to a September 2000 study, at least eight business method patents already have been issued in Japan, with many more expected as the number of applications increases. Economic Research Institute, *Impact of Business Model (Method) Patents: Implications for Corporate Management*, www.marubeni.co.jp/research/eindex/00082.html. The patentability of business methods outside the United States remains an open question, though it seems the trend toward patentability will continue.

Likewise uncertain is the enforceability of U.S. business method patents against infringers based in other countries. Patent law is territorial. The Patent Act includes as infringements importing an infringing product into the United States, or importing into the United States an unpatented product made abroad by a process patented in the United States. U.S. patent law also makes it an infringement to ship all of the components of a patented invention abroad and manufacture it there. 35 U.S.C. § 271. But in general, those acting outside the territory of the United States are not covered by the U.S. patent law, and may engage in activities which if they occurred in the United States would infringe a patent.

The United States is working with other countries to address these questions. An important international agreement governing patents, to which the United States is a signatory, is the Agreement on Trade–Related Aspects of Intellectual Property Rights ("TRIPS"), www.wto.org/english/tratop_e/trips_e/t_agm0_e.htm. Under Article 1 of TRIPS, signatory countries must treat citizens and foreigners equally under the law; that is, foreigners are free to file applications for U.S. patents on the same terms as U.S. citizens. TRIPS also requires signatory countries to implement certain legal standards for patentability and sets forth a uniform patent term as well. Countries are not required to enforce each other's laws, however, nor are they prevented from excluding some forms of subject matter from protection—apparently including business methods if not sufficiently technological.[4]

---

4. Article 27(1) of TRIPS provides:

[P]atents shall be available for any inventions, whether products or processes, in all fields of technology, provided that they are new, involve an inventive step and are capable of industrial application. * * * [P]atents shall be available and patent rights enjoyable without discrimi-

NOTES & QUESTIONS

Extraterritorial effects. Should a French Web-based company using a business method patented in the United States be liable for patent infringement if the company targets U.S. citizens in its advertising? What if does not target U.S. citizens but its website is nevertheless accessible in the United States? Does it matter if actual goods are shipped to the United States?

V. Examples of E–Commerce Business Method Patents

The availability of business method patents following *State Street Bank* has had a profound effect on the operation and strategy of e-commerce, as inventors and businesses have flocked to the PTO seeking to patent their methods of doing business. Following are some examples of patents that have issued for Internet-commerce-related business methods. Note that the excerpts include only Claim One of each patent. Claim One is often the shortest and most general in wording—therefore, it often is the *broadest* of the claims of the patent. Because Claim One is often the broadest, it might be deemed by a court or a patent examiner to be invalid, while other narrower claims, more specifically delineating the actual embodiment of the invention developed by the patentee, might be upheld (remember, a patent is evaluated claim by claim).

A. Amazon.com's One–Click Patent

Patent Number: 5,960,411

Date of Patent: September 28, 1999

METHOD AND SYSTEM FOR PLACING A PURCHASE ORDER VIA A COMMUNICATIONS NETWORK

* * *

Abstract

A method and system for placing an order to purchase an item via the Internet. The order is placed by a purchaser at a client system and received by a server system. The server system receives purchaser information including identification of the purchaser, payment information, and shipment information from the client system. The server system then assigns a client identifier to the client system and associates the assigned client identifier with the received purchaser information. The server system sends to the client system the assigned client identifier and an HTML document identifying the item and including an order button. The client system receives and stores the assigned client identifier and receives and displays

---

nation as to the place of invention, the field of technology and whether products are imported or locally produced.

the HTML document. In response to the selection of the order button, the client system sends to the server system a request to purchase the identified item. The server system receives the request and combines the purchaser information associated with the client identifier of the client system to generate an order to purchase the item in accordance with the billing and shipment information whereby the purchaser effects the ordering of the product by selection of the order button.

* * *

BACKGROUND OF THE INVENTION

* * *

The World Wide Web is especially conducive to conducting electronic commerce. Many Web servers have been developed through which vendors can advertise and sell products. The products can include items (e.g., music) that are delivered electronically to the purchaser over the Internet and items (e.g., books) that are delivered through conventional distribution channels (e.g., a common carrier). A server computer system may provide an electronic version of a catalog that lists the items that are available. A user, who is a potential purchaser, may browse through the catalog using a browser and select various items that are to be purchased. When the user has completed selecting the items to be purchased, the server computer system then prompts the user for information to complete the ordering of the items. This purchaser-specific order information may include the purchaser's name, the purchaser's credit card number, and a shipping address for the order. The server computer system then typically confirms the order by sending a confirming Web page to the client computer system and schedules shipment of the items.

Since the purchaser-specific order information contains sensitive information (e.g., a credit card number), both vendors and purchasers want to ensure the security of such information. Security is a concern because information transmitted over the Internet may pass through various intermediate computer systems on its way to its final destination. The information could be intercepted by an unscrupulous person at an intermediate system. To help ensure the security of the sensitive information, various encryption techniques are used when transmitting such information between a client computer system and a server computer system. Even though such encrypted information can be intercepted, because the information is encrypted, it is generally useless to the interceptor. Nevertheless, there is always a possibility that such sensitive information may be successfully decrypted by the interceptor. Therefore, it would be desirable to minimize the sensitive information transmitted when placing an order.

The selection of the various items from the electronic catalogs is generally based on the "shopping cart" model. When the purchaser selects an item from the electronic catalog, the server computer system metaphorically adds that item to a shopping cart. When the purchaser is done selecting items, then all the items in the shopping cart are "checked out" (i.e., ordered) when the purchaser provides billing and shipment information. In some models, when a purchaser selects any one item, then that item is "checked out" by automatically prompting the user for the billing and shipment information. Although the shopping cart model is very flexible and intuitive, it has a downside in that it requires many interactions by the purchaser. For example, the purchaser selects the various items from the electronic catalog, and then indicates that the selection is complete. The purchaser is then presented with an order Web page that prompts the purchaser for the purchaser-specific order information to complete the order. That Web page may be prefilled with information that was provided by the purchaser when placing another order. The information is then validated by the server computer system, and the order is completed. Such an ordering model can be problematic for a couple of reasons. If a purchaser is ordering only one item, then the overhead of confirming the various steps of the ordering process and waiting for, viewing, and updating the purchaser-specific order information can be much more than the overhead of selecting the item itself. This overhead makes the purchase of a single item cumbersome. Also, with such an ordering model, each time an order is placed sensitive information is transmitted over the Internet. Each time the sensitive information is transmitted over the Internet, it is susceptible to being intercepted and decrypted.

* * *

[Claims]

We claim:

1. A method of placing an order for an item comprising:

under control of a client system,

> displaying information identifying the item; and

> in response to only a single action being performed, sending a request to order the item along with an identifier of a purchaser of the item to a server system;

under control of a single-action ordering component of the server system,

> receiving the request;

> retrieving additional information previously stored for the purchaser identified by the identifier in the received request; and

generating an order to purchase the requested item for the purchaser identified by the identifier in the received request using the retrieved additional information; and

fulfilling the generated order to complete purchase of the item whereby the item is ordered without using a shopping cart ordering model.

* * *

B.   PRICELINE.COM'S PATENT ON REVERSE AUCTIONS

Patent Number: 5,794,207

Date of Patent: August 11, 1998

METHOD AND APPARATUS FOR A CRYPTOGRAPHICALLY ASSISTED COMMERCIAL NETWORK SYSTEM DESIGNED TO FACILITATE BUYER–DRIVEN CONDITIONAL PURCHASE OFFERS

Abstract

The present invention is a method and apparatus for effectuating bilateral buyer-driven commerce. The present invention allows prospective buyers of goods and services to communicate a binding purchase offer globally to potential sellers, for sellers conveniently to search for relevant buyer purchase offers, and for sellers potentially to bind a buyer to a contract based on the buyer's purchase offer. In a preferred embodiment, the apparatus of the present invention includes a controller which receives binding purchase offers from prospective buyers. The controller makes purchase offers available globally to potential sellers. Potential sellers then have the option to accept a purchase offer and thus bind the corresponding buyer to a contract. The method and apparatus of the present invention have applications on the Internet as well as conventional communications systems such as voice telephony.

* * *

SUMMARY OF THE INVENTION

In a preferred embodiment, the present invention provides a method and apparatus for prospective buyers of goods or services to communicate a binding purchase offer globally to potential sellers, for sellers conveniently to search for relevant buyer purchase offers, and for sellers to bind a buyer to a contract based on the buyer's purchase offer. Additionally, the present invention can effectuate performance of the agreement between the buyer and seller by guaranteeing buyer payment for the purchase. The present invention is therefore a highly effective bilateral buyer-driven commerce system which improves the ability of buyers to reach sellers capable of satisfying the buyers' purchasing needs and improves sellers' ability to identify interested buyers.

In one embodiment of this invention, communications between buyers and sellers are conducted using an electronic network and central controller. A buyer who wishes to make a purchase accesses the central controller located at a remote server. The buyer will then create a conditional purchase offer ("CPO") by specifying the subject of the goods he wishes to purchase, a description of the goods he wishes to obtain, and any other conditions the buyer requires. For example, a typical CPO could specify that the buyer wants to purchase a block of four airline tickets from Chicago's O'Hare Airport to Dallas, Tex., the tickets must be from any of the six largest U.S. carriers, the buyer is willing to change planes no more than once so long as the scheduled layover is less than two hours, and the buyer is willing to pay $180 per ticket, plus any applicable taxes.

The buyer then attaches a user identification to the CPO and transmits the CPO to the central controller. Under the present invention, the CPO may be transmitted via numerous means including a world-wide-web interface, electronic mail, voice mail, facsimile, or postal mail. Standard legal provisions and language are then integrated with the CPO to "fill in the gaps" of the buyer's purchase offer. Alternatively, the CPO may be developed while the buyer is on-line with the central controller.

Before communicating the CPO to potential sellers, the central controller authenticates the buyer's identification number against a buyer database. The central controller may require that the buyer provide a credit card number and may also ensure that the buyer has sufficient credit available to cover the purchase price specified in the CPO by contacting the credit card clearinghouse. The central controller then assigns a unique tracking number to the CPO and globally displays the CPO in a manner such that it is available to be viewed by any interested potential sellers. CPOs may be displayed by subject category to make it easier for potential sellers to identify relevant CPOs. Thus, a seller could log onto a website, for example, and see a listing of CPO subject categories. The seller could then choose a particular subject and have the ability to browse CPOs which correspond to that subject category. In one embodiment, the seller may be required to provide qualifications in order to view the CPOs of a given subject category.

If, after reviewing a particular CPO, a potential seller wishes to accept the CPO, the seller communicates his intent to the central controller. The central controller then timestamps the message from the seller and authenticates the identity of the seller and his capacity to deliver the goods sought by the buyer. The system then verifies that the particular CPO is still "active" and capable of being accepted. If a CPO is capable of being accepted only by one seller, it is "completed" when the first qualified seller accepts it. Subsequent sellers will not be able to accept a "completed" CPO. If a seller accepts an active CPO, a unique tracking number is assigned to the seller's acceptance. The acceptance is then stored in a database. The buyer and seller are now parties to a legally binding contract.

* * *

The present invention can also be practiced in off-line embodiments. Instead of using electronic mail or web-based servers, buyers and sellers may communicate with the central controller via telephone, facsimile, postal mail, or another off-line communication tool. For example, buyers may use telephones to create CPOs (with or without the assistance of live agents) and potential sellers may use a telephone to browse and bind CPOs.

* * *

What the present invention accomplishes, which no previous system has done before, is literally to hang buyer money on a "clothesline" for sellers to see. Attached to the money is a note describing what the seller has to agree to do in order to take the money down off the clothesline. There is no uncertainty or waste of time on the part of the seller. He knows that if he can meet the conditions set forth by the buyer, he can immediately close the sale and get paid for it. No hassles. No negotiations.

The invention also allows buyers to reach a large number of remotely located sellers who normally would not be able to afford to find the buyer, but who may be able to provide the buyer with the exact deal the buyer desires. For instance, this might be the case for a car buyer who could precisely define the car and option packages he wanted for a specified price. The present invention allows such a buyer to issue a binding purchase offer which is globally communicated to authorized dealers in the U.S. Any one of those dealers could then decide whether or not to accept the offer. The buyer's advantage is particularly significant when the sellers of products sought by the buyer have no inventory carrying costs, as is the case with insurance sales. Insurance buyers could use the present invention to cast a wide net to reach thousands of potential insurance sellers and potentially find a seller willing to satisfy the buyer's specified purchase conditions.

It is a goal of the present invention to provide a robust system which matches buyers' requirements with sellers capable of satisfying those requirements. The invention provides a global bilateral buyer-driven system for creating binding contracts incorporating various methods of communication, commerce and security for the buyer and the seller. The power of a central controller to field binding offers from buyers, communicate those offers globally in a format which can be efficiently accessed and analyzed by potential sellers, effectuate performance of resulting contracts, resolve disputes arising from those contracts, and maintain billing, collection, authentication, and anonymity makes the present invention an improvement over conventional systems.

[Claims]

What is claimed:

1. A method for using a computer to facilitate a transaction between a buyer and at least one of sellers, comprising:

inputting into the computer a conditional purchase offer which includes an offer price;

inputting into the computer a payment identifier specifying a credit card account, the payment identifier being associated with the conditional purchase offer;

outputting the conditional purchase offer to the plurality of sellers after receiving the payment identifier;

inputting into the computer an acceptance from a seller, the acceptance being responsive to the conditional purchase offer; and

providing a payment to the seller by using the payment identifier.

* * *

NOTES & QUESTIONS

1. *Broad claims and obviousness.* After reading these sample patents, do you agree with numerous commentators who argue that Internet commerce patents have been wrongly granted with broadly sweeping claims that, if ever enforced, would severely injure e-commerce? What are the implications of allowing broad claims in Internet-related patents, as compared to broad claims in more traditional technologies?

One author has criticized the breadth of the Priceline.com patent claims as follows:

> * * * This patent could permit Priceline.com to exclude all other business methods in which buyers propose a price for a product or service, and then sellers bid to supply it. The reach of this patent could extend beyond the airfare context (as it is currently being used) to all industries. Accordingly, it would seem as though the scope of the patent would render it too broad to satisfy the various scope provisions. The issuance of the Priceline.com patent suggests that the USPTO is willing to permit potential patentees to claim extremely broad matter in the Internet context.

> The Priceline.com patent also represents a good example of the lenient treatment of the nonobviousness requirement as applied to Internet business methods. Although reverse Dutch Auctions have existed for centuries, the USPTO did not find that it was obvious for Priceline.com to apply the reverse Dutch Auction method to the Internet. The issuance of this patent implies that it would not be obvious for a firm to take any standard business practice and apply it to the Internet. Such a loose interpretation of the nonobviousness doctrine implies that the nonobviousness requirement is no longer being used as a significant bar on commonplace inventions. As such, this interpretation seems to pave the way for the issuance of many Internet business method patents on seemingly regular business methods.

Jared Earl Grusd, *Internet Business Methods: What Role Does and Should Patent Law Play?*, 4 Va. J.L. & Tech. 9, 28–29 (1999).

Do you agree that, pushed to its logical extreme, Claim One of the Priceline patent implies that "any standard business practice" would become patentable when applied to the Internet? If not, can you justify the PTO's determination that the Priceline method satisfies the requirement of non-obviousness?

In October 1999, Priceline.com filed suit against Expedia.com, claiming that Expedia's "Price–Matcher" service, which allowed customers to place bids on airline tickets and hotel rooms, violated Priceline's patent. After a little over a year, the two companies settled the lawsuit in a deal that requires Expedia to pay Priceline royalties for the right to continue to offer its "Price–Matcher" service.

Given the widespread condemnation of the Priceline.com patent, the questionable breadth of the claim, and the issue of possible obviousness, why would Expedia, in which Microsoft at the time held a majority stake, settle the lawsuit rather than seek to have the patent invalidated?

2. *Business method patent factory.* Walker Digital Corp., a creation of Jay Walker, the founder of Priceline.com, is a self-styled laboratory for new business models. The company's business is devising, obtaining, and marketing business method patents of all kinds. According to the company's website, as of mid–2002, 70 patents had been issued and hundreds more were pending. *See* www.walkerdigital.com. The patents range from an automated system for monitoring hospital patients and calling in an expert when needed, to controlling the prices charged by a vending machine. Is Walker Digital's business model the wave of the future? Is it a development that proves our patent system has gone astray in declaring business methods to be propertizable?

3. *Strategic use of Internet commerce patents.* Priceline.com patented its reverse auction business method to solidify its first-mover advantage on the Internet, creating a legal monopoly of its market and blocking out competitors. Arguably, this strategy worked well—it (initially) bolstered investor confidence and enabled Priceline to maintain a strong hold on the reverse-auction market. Most importantly, competitors did not opt to challenge the patent.

As with all patents, Internet business method patents can be used *offensively*, to stop infringing uses by a company's competitors, or *defensively*, as part of settlement or licensing negotiations with a competitor. Competitors frequently enter into agreements to "live and let live" with respect to patent infringement, in order to avoid costly litigation.

The following excerpt addresses some possible defensive and offensive uses of a business's patent portfolio, and the misguided incentive structure that often results. The excerpt suggests that for large businesses, procuring patents is less about promoting progress and innovation than it is about preventing lawsuits:

> In the high-technology age, the patent has become more than a way to protect legitimate intellectual property. It's often the legal equivalent of a Cold War nuclear stockpile: Sue me over your patents and I'll sue you over mine.
>
> "Internet-involved enterprises of all types continue building their own patent portfolios, for both offensive and defensive purposes," said intellectual property attorney Alan Fisch.
>
> * * *
>
> As a weapon against competitors, a patent can be a potent offense. "If you have a patent and approach someone else, you can get an injunction [and] cause a lot of harm up front," [Gregory] Aharonian said.

As a result, there's little incentive for companies not to patent everything they can.

"People will throw something into the patent office just to see if they can get something issued," [patent attorney Virginia] Medlen said. "Once it's issued, under law the presumption is that it's valid. And to knock it down the challenger has to produce clear and convincing evidence that the patent is not valid, and that clear and convincing evidence is very difficult to prove."

That's where the defensive counter-patent comes in.

A judge faced with two similar, but competing patents is likely to tell the opponents to settle the issue themselves, rather than try to wade through the subtle differences in court.

"[The counter-patent] is a relatively inexpensive way to present evidence of invalidity," Medlen said.

* * *

* * * One industry source said the practice is so common that some big-name companies chock full of communications technology patents have struck agreements not to sue each other. Their other competitors may not be so lucky.

Chris Oakes, *Patently Absurd*, WIRED NEWS (Mar. 3, 2000), www.wired.com/news/politics/0,1283,34695,00.html.

Would it be appropriate to discourage these sorts of settlements and cross-licensing? Though it is debatable whether the current system is truly rewarding and promoting innovation, as it is supposed to, allowing businesses to use patents as defensive bargaining chips might reduce the costs of litigation to both private parties and the courts. *See, e.g.*, Carl Shapiro, *Navigating the Patent Thicket: Cross Licenses, Patent Pools, and Standard Setting, in* INNOVATION POLICY AND THE ECONOMY, VOL. I (Adam B. Jaffe, Josh Lerner, & Scott Stern eds., 2001).

VI. PATENT LITIGATION: AMAZON.COM V. BARNESANDNOBLE.COM

Despite the prevalence of strategic behavior and cross-licensing to settle disputes, some cases do go to trial. To show infringement of an Internet business method patent, a plaintiff must demonstrate that the defendant's conduct matches up exactly to *all* of the elements of one (or more) of the plaintiff's patent claims—that is, that the claim "reads on" the conduct. In addition, a court might find infringement under the "doctrine of equivalents" even if no literal infringement has occurred. The doctrine of equivalents prevents would-be infringers from escaping liability by making trivial changes but copying the essence of the invention. Nonetheless, many business method patents seem to present a fairly easy opportunity to "design around" to avoid infringement.

Amazon.com brought an infringement action against Barnesandnoble.com, alleging that the latter's "Express Lane" checkout system infringed its "One–Click" business method patent, excerpted in Part V(A), *supra*. In the district court, Amazon sought and obtained a preliminary injunction preventing Barnes & Noble from using its "Express Lane" checkout. *See Amazon.com, Inc. v. Barnesandnoble.com, Inc.,* 73 F.Supp.2d 1228 (W.D.Wash.1999).

The district court rejected Barnesandnoble.com's argument that the Amazon.com patent was invalid as obvious and anticipated by the relevant prior art. After analyzing the prior art references, the court found that there were sufficient "differences between each of the prior art references cited by Defendants and the method and system described in the claims of the '411 patent" and that there was no evidence "regarding a teaching, suggestion, or motivation in the prior art that would lead one of ordinary skill in the art of e-commerce to combine the references," *id.* at 1235, which is the kind of evidence needed to establish invalidity on the ground of obviousness.

Further, Amazon.com presented other evidence of non-obviousness that the court found very convincing: "[D]espite their experience with prior art shopping cart models of on-line purchasing, both sides' technical experts acknowledged that they had never conceived of the invention." *Id.* at 1236–37. One expert testified that he found the Amazon.com One–Click technology to be "a huge leap from what was done in the past" and testified that "I've been working in electronic commerce for years now. And I've never thought of the idea of being able to turn a shopping cart or take the idea of clicking on an item and suddenly having the item ship—having the complete process done." *Id.* at 1237. The district court held that the One–Click patent "addressed an unsolved need that had been long-felt (at least in the relatively short period of time that e-commerce has existed), namely streamlining the on-line ordering process to reduce the high percentage of orders that are begun but never completed, i.e., abandoned shopping carts." *Id.* One final objective indicator of non-obviousness cited by the district court was the vast commercial success of the one-click ordering method, as used by both Amazon.com and Barnesandnoble.com. *Id.*

After Barnesandnoble.com lost on its claim of invalidity, there was little evidence to dispute that it had directly copied from Amazon.com. Barnesandnoble.com had consistently promoted its "Express Lane" feature as "One Click Ordering," both internally and to customers. The court found that continuing infringement by Barnesandnoble.com would irreparably harm Amazon.com. The court noted that "customers become loyal to sites with which they become familiar," and allowing Barnesandnoble.com to continue benefiting from the "easy-to-use and easy-to-learn consumer interfaces" Amazon.com had invented would be extremely detrimental to Amazon.com's commercial success. *Id.* at 1238. An important factor weighing in favor of issuing the injunction was the approaching holiday season:

As many as 10 million new users are expected to make their first on-line purchases during the 1999 holiday season. Millions of these new customers are likely to be shopping at Amazon.com and Barnesandnoble.com for the first time. Long-term success in e-commerce depends on establishing positive relationships with these new on-line buyers now, to preserve the ability to compete effectively for future sales, which by some estimates will reach $78 billion by the year 2003.

Id. The district court granted Amazon.com's request for a preliminary injunction requiring Barnesandnoble.com to remove the "Express Lane" feature in time for holiday ordering. The injunction, as we will see shortly, was overturned on appeal.

Following the issuance of the preliminary injunction in Amazon.com's favor, Barnesandnoble.com changed its checkout to a two-click scheme. The decision, however, was widely criticized.

An ad-hoc Internet-based opposition emerged to express outrage over Amazon's actions. The one-click concept, they argued, should be unpatentable—it's an utterly obvious use of cookies, which existed long before Amazon's patent application. Richard Stallman, president of the Free Software Foundation and a ringleader of the backlash, launched a boycott against the company, proclaiming that "foolish government policies gave Amazon the opportunity—but an opportunity is not an excuse. Amazon made the choice to obtain this patent, and the choice to use it in court for aggression. The ultimate moral responsibility for Amazon's actions lies with Amazon's executives."

Stallman's boycott didn't get much attention until late February, when Amazon announced yet another business-method patent, this one for its "affiliate program," a revenue-sharing scheme in which other sites refer customers to Amazon's store via Web links. Again, protesters viewed the patent as obvious and absurdly broad. Tim O'Reilly, a prominent publisher of computer books, posted an open letter on his website denouncing Amazon, gathering 10,000 protest signatures in a few days. A cowed Jeff Bezos [Amazon's founder and CEO] responded with an open letter of his own, declining to "give up our patents unilaterally," but expressing concern about the role of patents in the new economy and calling for major patent reform.

Bezos' move turned patents into front-page news. In March, the PTO bowed to the mounting pressure and announced a few quick-fix changes: among them, increased supervision for the patent examiners who oversee business-method patent applications, as well as a promise to hold an open discussion on patent reform with Internet leaders this summer.

Evan Ratliff, *Patent Upending*, WIRED, June 2000, www.wired.com/wired/archive/8.06/patents_pr.html

NOTES & QUESTIONS

1. *District court's analysis.* Do you agree with the district court's analysis of validity and irreparable harm? Do you believe that there was really a "long-felt" need in e-commerce to come up with a more efficient ordering method? If so, how would the existence of such a long-felt need give rise to an inference that Amazon.com's one-click method was non-obvious when invented? Should the commercial success of one-click ordering also be considered as evidence of non-obviousness? Courts routinely consider long-felt need and commercial success in evaluating non-obviousness. But is it possible to distinguish between the commercial success of the one-click method and Amazon.com's business method generally? Were people coming to the site because of the novel method of ordering, or because of the nature of the business?

2. *Responsibility to play nice?* Stallman seems to demand that Amazon.com pursue only patent applications that it truly believes are legitimate. But, if the patent examiner is willing to grant a patent, why would Amazon.com be ethically obligated to refuse it? Can convincing distinctions be drawn between companies that seek business method patents on any possible innovation, and *any* company that attempts to draft its application such that as much as possible is claimed, with as little possible disclosure, when applying for a patent? Where should the responsibility for assuring patent validity lie—with the applicant? the examiner? Congress? the courts?

———

The district court's ruling on validity was overturned on appeal. While the Federal Circuit agreed that Amazon.com had made a convincing case for infringement, it held that Barnesandnoble.com had raised a substantial question as to the validity of the "One–Click" patent, and remanded the case for further consideration.

Amazon.com, Inc. v. Barnesandnoble.com, Inc.

239 F.3d 1343 (Fed.Cir.2001).

■ CLEVENGER, CIRCUIT JUDGE.

This is a patent infringement suit brought by Amazon.com, Inc. ("Amazon") against barnesandnoble.com, inc., and barnesandnoble.com llc (together, "BN"). Amazon moved for a preliminary injunction to prohibit BN's use of a feature of its website called "Express Lane." BN resisted the preliminary injunction on several grounds, including that its Express Lane feature did not infringe the claims of Amazon's patent, and that substantial questions exist as to the validity of Amazon's patent. The United States District Court for the Western District of Washington rejected BN's contentions. Instead, the district court held that Amazon had presented a case showing a likelihood of infringement by BN, and that BN's challenges to the validity of the patent in suit lacked sufficient merit to avoid awarding extraordinary preliminary injunctive relief to Amazon. The district court granted Amazon's motion, and now BN brings its timely appeal from the order entering the preliminary injunction. We have jurisdiction to review the district court's order under 28 U.S.C. § 1292(c)(1) (1994).

After careful review of the district court's opinion, the record, and the arguments advanced by the parties, we conclude that BN has mounted a substantial challenge to the validity of the patent in suit. Because Amazon is not entitled to preliminary injunctive relief under these circumstances, we vacate the order of the district court that set the preliminary injunction in place and remand the case for further proceedings.

I

This case involves United States Patent No. 5,960,411 ("the '411 patent"), which issued on September 28, 1999, and is assigned to Amazon. On October 21, 1999, Amazon brought suit against BN alleging infringement of the patent and seeking a preliminary injunction.

Amazon's patent is directed to a method and system for "single action" ordering of items in a client/server environment such as the Internet. In the context of the '411 patent, a client/server environment describes the relationship between two computer systems in which a program executing on a client computer system makes a service request from another program executing on a server computer system, which fulfills the request. *See* col. 1, ll. 10–31; col. 3, ll. 31–33; col. 5, l. 56 to col. 6, l. 21; Fig. 2. Typically, the client computer system and the server computer system are located remotely from each other and communicate via a data communication network.

The '411 patent describes a method and system in which a consumer can complete a purchase order for an item via an electronic network using only a "single action," such as the click of a computer mouse button on the client computer system. Amazon developed the patent to cope with what it considered to be frustrations presented by what is known as the "shopping cart model" purchase system for electronic commerce purchasing events. In previous incarnations of the shopping cart model, a purchaser using a client computer system (such as a personal computer executing a web browser program) could select an item from an electronic catalog, typically by clicking on an "Add to Shopping Cart" icon, thereby placing the item in the "virtual" shopping cart. Other items from the catalog could be added to the shopping cart in the same manner. When the shopper completed the selecting process, the electronic commercial event would move to the checkout counter, so to speak. Then, information regarding the purchaser's identity, billing and shipping addresses, and credit payment method would be inserted into the transactional information base by the soon-to-be purchaser. Finally, the purchaser would "click" on a button displayed on the screen or somehow issue a command to execute the completed order, and the server computer system would verify and store the information concerning the transaction.

As is evident from the foregoing, an electronic commerce purchaser using the shopping cart model is required to perform several actions before achieving the ultimate goal of the placed order. The '411 patent sought to reduce the number of actions required from a consumer to effect a placed order. In the words of the written description of the '411 patent:

> The present invention provides a method and system for single-action ordering of items in a client/server environment. The single-action ordering system of the present invention reduces the number of purchaser interactions needed to place an order and reduces the amount of sensitive information that is transmitted between a client system and a server system.

Col. 3, ll. 31–37. How, one may ask, is the number of purchaser interactions reduced? The answer is that the number of purchaser interactions is reduced because the purchaser has previously visited the seller's website and has previously entered into the database of the seller all of the required billing and shipping information that is needed to effect a sales transaction. Thereafter, when the purchaser visits the seller's website and wishes to purchase a product from that site, the patent specifies that only a single action is necessary to place the order for the item. In the words of the written description, "once the description of an item is displayed, the purchaser need only take a single action to place the order to purchase that item." Col. 3, ll. 64–66.

II

* * * We set forth below the text of the claims pertinent to our deliberations (*i.e.*, claims 1, 2, 6, 9, and 11), with emphasis added to highlight the disputed claim terms:

[Claim 1 is set forth in Part V(A), *supra*. Claims 2, 6, 9, and 11 are drawn to narrower versions of the one-click method. The court emphasizes the term "single action" as used in each claim.]

The district court interpreted the key "single action" claim limitation, which appears in each of the pertinent claims, to mean:

> The term "single action" is not defined by the patent specification.... As a result, the term "single action" as used in the '411 patent appears to refer to one action (such as clicking a mouse button) that a user takes to purchase an item once the following information is displayed to the user: (1) a description of the item; and (2) a description of the single action the user must take to complete a purchase order for that item.

With this interpretation of the key claim limitation in hand, the district court turned to BN's accused ordering system. BN's short-cut ordering system, called "Express Lane," like the system contemplated by the patent, contains previously entered billing and shipping information for the customer. In one implementation, after a person is presented with BN's initial web page (referred to as the "menu page"), the person can [click] on an icon on the menu page to get to what is called the "product page." BN's product page displays an image and a description of the selected product, and also presents the person with a description of a single action that can be taken to complete a purchase order for the item. If the single action described is taken, for example by a mouse click, the person will have effected a purchase order using BN's Express Lane feature.

BN's Express Lane thus presents a product page that contains the description of the item to be purchased and a "description" of the single action to be taken to effect placement of the order. Because only a single action need be taken to complete the purchase order once the product page is displayed, the district court concluded that Amazon had made a showing of likelihood of success on its allegation of patent infringement.

In response to BN's contention that substantial questions exist as to the validity of the '411 patent, the district court reviewed the prior art references upon which BN's validity challenge rested. The district court concluded that none of the prior art references anticipated the claims of the '411 patent under 35 U.S.C. § 102 (1994) or rendered the claimed invention obvious under 35 U.S.C. § 103 (1994).

III

* * * As the moving party, Amazon is entitled to a preliminary injunction if it can succeed in showing: (1) a reasonable likelihood of success on the merits; (2) irreparable harm if an injunction is not granted; (3) a balance of hardships tipping in its favor; and (4) the injunction's favorable impact on the public interest. * * * Irreparable harm is presumed when a clear showing of patent validity and infringement has been made. * * *

Our case law and logic both require that a movant cannot be granted a preliminary injunction unless it establishes *both* of the first two factors, *i.e.*, likelihood of success on the merits and irreparable harm. * * *

In order to demonstrate a likelihood of success on the merits, Amazon must show that, in light of the presumptions and burdens that will inhere at trial on the merits, (1) Amazon will likely prove that BN infringes the '411 patent, and (2) Amazon's infringement claim will likely withstand BN's challenges to the validity and enforceability of the '411 patent. *Genentech, Inc. v. Novo Nordisk, A/S*, 108 F.3d 1361, 1364 (Fed.Cir.1997). If BN raises a substantial question concerning either infringement or validity, *i.e.*, asserts an infringement or invalidity defense that the patentee cannot prove "lacks substantial merit," the preliminary injunction should not issue. *Id.*

Of course, whether performed at the preliminary injunction stage or at some later stage in the course of a particular case, infringement and validity analyses must be performed on a claim-by-claim basis. * * *

Both infringement and validity are at issue in this appeal. It is well settled that an infringement analysis involves two steps: the claim scope is first determined, and then the properly construed claim is compared with the accused device to determine whether all of the claim limitations are present either literally or by a substantial equivalent.* * *

Only when a claim is properly understood can a determination be made whether the claim "reads on" an accused device or method, or whether the prior art anticipates and/or renders obvious the claimed invention. Because the claims of a patent measure the invention at issue, the claims must be interpreted and given the same meaning for purposes of both validity and infringement analyses. * * *

IV

BN contends on appeal that the district court committed legal errors that undermine the legitimacy of the preliminary injunction. In particular, BN asserts that the district court construed key claim limitations one way for purposes of its infringement analysis, and another way when considering BN's validity challenges. BN asserts that under a consistent claim interpretation, its Express Lane feature either does not infringe the '411 patent, or that if the patent is interpreted so as to support the charge of infringement, then the claims of the patent are subject to a severe validity challenge. When the key claim limitations are properly interpreted, BN thus asserts, it will be clear that Amazon is not likely to succeed on the merits of its infringement claim, or that BN has succeeded in calling the validity of the '411 patent into serious question. In addition, BN asserts that the district court misunderstood the teaching of the prior art references, thereby committing clear error in the factual predicates it established for comprehension of the prior art references.

Amazon understandably aligns itself with the district court, asserting that no error of claim interpretation and no clear error in fact-finding has occurred that would undermine the grant of the preliminary injunction. We thus turn to the legal gist of this appeal.

V

It is clear from the district court's opinion that the meaning it ascribed to the "single action" limitation includes a temporal consideration. The "single action" to be taken to complete the purchase order, according to the district court, only occurs after other events have transpired. These preliminary events required pursuant to the district court's claim interpretation are the presentation of a description of the item to be purchased and the presentation of the single action the user must take to complete the purchase order for the item.

* * *

Our analysis begins with the plain language of the claims themselves. The term "single action" appears in the independent claims of the '411 patent in the following forms: "in response to only a single action being performed" (claims 1 and 9), "single-action ordering component" (claims 1, 6, and 9), "in response to performance of only a single action" (claim 6), "in response to only the indicated single action being performed" (claim

11), and "displaying an indication of a single action that is to be performed to order the identified item" (claim 11).

In claims 1, 6, and 11, the context of the claim makes it clear that the single action is performed after some information about the item is displayed. Claim 1 provides for "displaying information identifying the item," and then immediately recites that "in response to only a single action being performed," a request to purchase the item is sent to a server system. Claim 6 provides for "a display component for displaying information identifying the item," and then immediately recites "the single action ordering component that in response to performance of only a single action" sends a request to purchase the item to a server system. Claim 11 provides for "displaying information identifying the item and displaying an indication of the single action," and then immediately recites that "in response to only the indicated single action being performed" a request to purchase the item is sent to a server system. The context also indicates that the single action is performed, or is capable of being performed, after information about the item is displayed, without any intervening action. Nothing suggests, however, that the single action must be performed after every display or even immediately after the first display of information. Claim 9 does not explicitly provide for displaying information. It merely recites that a request to order an item is "sent in response to only a single action being performed." However, although claim 9 does not recite "displaying," the written description defines the claim 9 language of "single action being performed" to require that information has been displayed.

The ordinary meaning of "single action" as used in the various claims is straightforward, but the phrase alone does not indicate when to start counting actions. Therefore, we must look first to the written description of the '411 patent for further guidance.

The written description supports a construction that after information is "displayed," single-action ordering is an option available to the user, and the counting falls within the scope of the claim when single-action ordering is actually selected by the user. To the extent that the claims are considered ambiguous on this point, the written description defines "single action" to require as much. In the Summary of the Invention, the written description describes an embodiment that "displays information that identifies the item and displays an indication of an action ... [and] [i]n response to the indicated action being performed" orders the item. Col. 2, ll. 54–59. Similarly, in the Detailed Description of the Invention, the written description states that "[o]nce the description of an item is displayed, the purchaser need only take a single action." Col. 3, ll. 65–66. This is consistent for all of the disclosed embodiments.

Therefore, neither the written description nor the plain meaning of the claims require that single action ordering be possible after each and every display of information (or even immediately after the first display of information). The plain language of the claims and the written description require only that single action ordering be possible after some display of information. Indeed, the written description allows for and suggests the possibility that previous displays of information will have occurred before the display immediately preceding an order.

* * *

VI

A

When the correct meaning of the single action limitation is read on the accused BN system, it becomes apparent that the limitations of claim 1 are likely met by the accused system. The evidence on the record concerning the operation of BN's "Express Lane" feature is not in dispute. At the time that the '411 patent was issued, BN offered customers two purchasing options. One was called "Shopping Cart," and the other was called "Express Lane." The Shopping Cart option involved the steps of adding items to a "virtual" shopping cart and then "checking out" to complete the purchase. In contrast, the Express Lane option allowed customers who had registered for the feature to purchase items simply by "clicking" on the "Express Lane" button provided on the "detail page" or "product page" describing and identifying the book or other item to be purchased. The text beneath the Express Lane button invited users to "Buy it now with just 1 click!"

BN's allegedly infringing website thus may be characterized as having "page 1," (the "menu" page) which displays a catalog listing several items but which does not contain an "order" icon, and "page 2," (the "product" or "detail" page) which includes information on one item and also shows an order icon. Someone shopping at this website would look at the catalog on page 1 and perform a first click to go to page 2. Once at page 2, a second click on the ordering icon would cause the order request to be sent. Under the claim construction set forth herein, BN likely infringes claim 1 because on page 2, the item is there displayed (meeting step 1 of the claim) and only a single action thereafter causes the order request to be transmitted (meeting step 2). The method implemented on page 1 of the BN website does not infringe, but the method on page 2 does. This has nothing to do with the state of mind of the purchaser, but simply reflects the ordinary meaning of the words of the claim in the context of the written description and in light of the prosecution history.

* * *

E

After full review of the record before us, we conclude that under a proper claim interpretation, Amazon has made the showing that it is likely to succeed at trial on its infringement case. Given that we conclude that Amazon has demonstrated likely literal infringement of at least the four independent claims in the '411 patent, we need not consider infringement under the doctrine of equivalents. The question remaining, however, is whether the district court correctly determined that BN failed to mount a substantial challenge to the validity of the claims in the '411 patent.

VII

The district court considered, but ultimately rejected, the potentially invalidating impact of several prior art references cited by BN. Because the district court determined that BN likely infringed all of the asserted claims, it did not focus its analysis of the validity issue on any particular claim. Instead, in its validity analysis, the district court appears to have primarily directed its attention to determining whether the references cited by BN implemented the single action limitation.

* * *

In this case, we find that the district court committed clear error by misreading the factual content of the prior art references cited by BN and by failing to recognize that BN had raised a substantial question of invalidity of the asserted claims in view of these prior art references.

Validity challenges during preliminary injunction proceedings can be successful, that is, they may raise substantial questions of invalidity, on evidence that would not suffice to support a judgment of invalidity at trial. *See, e.g., Helifix Ltd. v. Blok–Lok, Ltd.*, 208 F.3d 1339, 1352 (Fed.Cir.2000) (holding that the allegedly anticipatory prior art references sufficiently raised a question of invalidity to deny a preliminary injunction, even though summary judgment of anticipation based on the same references was not supported). The test for invalidity at trial is by evidence that is clear and convincing. *WMS Gaming, Inc. v. Int'l Game Tech.*, 184 F.3d 1339, 1355 (Fed.Cir.1999). To succeed with a summary judgment motion of invalidity, for example, the movant must demonstrate a lack of genuine dispute about material facts and show that the facts not in dispute are clear and convincing in demonstrating invalidity. *Robotic Vision Sys., Inc. v. View Eng'g, Inc.*, 112 F.3d 1163, 1165 (Fed.Cir.1997). In resisting a preliminary injunction, however, one need not make out a case of actual invalidity. Vulnerability is the issue at the preliminary injunction stage, while validity is the issue at trial. The showing of a substantial question as to invalidity thus requires less proof than the clear and convincing showing necessary to establish invalidity itself. That this is so is plain from our cases.

* * *

When the heft of the asserted prior art is assessed in light of the correct legal standards, we conclude that BN has mounted a serious challenge to the validity of Amazon's patent. We hasten to add, however, that this conclusion only undermines the prerequisite for entry of a preliminary injunction. Our decision today on the validity issue in no way resolves the ultimate question of invalidity. That is a matter for resolution at trial. It remains to be learned whether there are other references that may be cited against the patent, and it surely remains to be learned whether any shortcomings in BN's initial preliminary validity challenge will be magnified or dissipated at trial. All we hold, in the meantime, is that BN cast enough doubt on the validity of the '411 patent to avoid a preliminary injunction, and that the validity issue should be resolved finally at trial.

A

One of the references cited by BN was the "CompuServe Trend System." The undisputed evidence indicates that in the mid–1990s, CompuServe offered a service called "Trend" whereby CompuServe subscribers could obtain stock charts for a surcharge of 50 cents per chart. Before the district court, BN argued that this system anticipated claim 11 of the '411 patent. The district court failed to recognize the substantial question of invalidity raised by BN in citing the CompuServe Trend reference, in that this system appears to have used "single action ordering technology" within the scope of the claims in the '411 patent.

First, the district court dismissed the significance of this system partly on the basis that "[t]he CompuServe system was not a world wide web application." This distinction is irrelevant, since none of the claims mention either the Internet or the World Wide Web (with the possible exception of dependent claim 15, which mentions HTML, a program commonly associated with both the Internet and the World Wide Web). Moreover, the '411 patent specification explicitly notes that "[o]ne skilled in the art would appreciate that the single-action ordering techniques can be used in various environments other than the Internet." Col. 6, ll. 22–24.

More importantly, one of the screen shots in the record (reproduced below) indicates that with the CompuServe Trend system, once the "item" to be purchased (*i.e.*, a stock chart) has been displayed (by typing in a valid stock symbol), only a single action (*i.e.*, a single mouse click on the button labeled "*C*hart ($.50)") is required to obtain immediate electronic delivery (*i.e.*, "fulfillment") of the item. Once the button labeled "*C*hart ($.50)" was activated by a purchaser, an electronic version of the requested stock chart would be transmitted to the purchaser and displayed on the purchaser's computer screen, and an automatic process to charge the purchaser's account 50 cents for the transaction would be initiated. In terms of the language of claims 2 and 11 in the CompuServe Trend system, the item to be ordered is "displayed" when the screen echoes back the characters of the stock symbol typed in by the purchaser before clicking on the ordering button.

* * *

* * * Amazon's counsel claimed that the CompuServe Trend system was different from the claims of the '411 patent because it required a user to "log in" at the beginning of each session, and therefore would not send the claimed "identifier" along with a request to purchase each item. However, claim 11 does not require transmission of an identifier along with a request to order an item. This requirement is found only in claims 1, 6, and 9, and their respective dependent claims.

On its face, the CompuServe Trend reference does not mention transmission of the claimed identifier along with a request to purchase each item. Nor does the evidence in the record at this stage indicate that the CompuServe Trend system transmitted such an identifier. BN has therefore not demonstrated that the CompuServe Trend reference anticipates the asserted claims of the '411 patent requiring transmission of such an identifier with the degree of precision necessary to obtain summary judgment on this point. However, as noted above, validity challenges during preliminary injunction proceedings can be successful on evidence that would not suffice to support a judgment of invalidity at trial. *See Helifix*, 208 F.3d at 1352. The record in this case is simply not yet developed to the point where a determination can be made whether the CompuServe Trend system transmits the claimed identifier along with a request to order an item, or whether this limitation is obvious in view of the prior art. * * *

* * *

In view of the above, we conclude that the district court erred in failing to recognize that the CompuServe Trend reference raises a substantial question of invalidity. Whether the CompuServe Trend reference either anticipates and/or renders obvious the claimed invention in view of the knowledge of one of ordinary skill in the relevant art is a matter for decision at trial.

B

In addition to the CompuServe Trend system, other prior art references were cited by BN, but ultimately rejected by the district court. For example, BN's expert, Dr. Lockwood, testified that he developed an on-line ordering system called "Web–Basket" in or around August 1996. The Web–Basket system appears to be an embodiment of a "shopping cart ordering component": it requires users to accumulate items into a virtual shopping basket and to check these items out when they are finished shopping. Because it is an implementation of a shopping cart model, Web Basket requires several confirmation steps for even pre-registered users to complete their purchases.

However, despite the fact that Web–Basket is an embodiment of a shopping cart model, it is undisputed that Web–Basket implemented the Internet Engineering Task Force ("IETF") draft "cookie" specification, and stored a customer identifier in a cookie for use by a web server to retrieve information from a database. In other words, when a user first visited the Web–Basket site, a cookie (*i.e.*, a file stored by the server system on the client system for subsequent use) was used to store an identifier on the user's computer. The first time that a user purchased an item on the Web–Basket site, the information entered by the user necessary to complete the purchase (*e.g.*, name, address) would be stored in a database on the server system indexed by an identifier stored in the cookie on the client system. On subsequent visits, the cookie could be used to retrieve the user identifier, which would serve as the key to retrieve the user's information from the database on the server system.

At the preliminary injunction stage, based on Dr. Lockwood's declaration and testimony during the hearing, BN argued that the Web–Basket reference—combined with the knowledge of one of ordinary skill in the art at the relevant time—renders obvious the claimed invention.

The district court concluded that the Web–Basket system was "inconsistent with the single-action requirements of the '411 patent" because "it requires a multiple-step ordering process from the time that an item to be purchased is displayed." However, as discussed earlier, the undisputed evidence demonstrates that the accused BN Express Lane feature also requires a multiple-step ordering process (*i.e.*, at least two "clicks") *from the time that an item to be purchased is first displayed on the menu page*, yet the district court concluded that BN's Express Lane feature infringed all of the asserted claims of the '411 patent. The district court's failure to recognize the inconsistency in these two conclusions was erroneous.

Moreover, the district court did not address the "cookie" aspects of the Web–Basket reference, and failed to recognize that a reasonable jury could find that the step of storing purchaser data on the server system for subsequent retrieval indexed by an identifier transmitted from the client system was anticipated and/or rendered obvious by the Web–Basket reference.

* * * "[T]he district court apparently based its conclusion of nonobviousness on Dr. Lockwood's "admission" that he personally never thought of combining or modifying the prior art to come up with the claimed "single action" invention. This approach was erroneous as a matter of law. Whatever Dr. Lockwood did or did not *personally* realize at the time based on his actual knowledge is irrelevant. The relevant inquiry is what a hypothetical ordinarily skilled artisan would have gleaned from the cited references at the time that the patent application leading to the '411 patent was filed. *See Kimberly–Clark Corp. v. Johnson & Johnson*, 745 F.2d 1437, 1453 (Fed.Cir.1984) (discussing the origin and significance of the hypothetical ordinarily skilled artisan in detail).

C

BN also presented as a prior art reference an excerpt from a book written by Magdalena Yesil entitled *Creating the Virtual Store* that was copyrighted in 1996. Before the district court, BN argued that this reference anticipated every limitation of claim 11. Before this court, BN also alleges that many other claim limitations are disclosed in the reference, but that there was insufficient time to prepare testimony concerning these limitations, given the district court's accelerated briefing and hearing schedule at the preliminary injunction stage.

In general terms, the reference apparently discusses software to implement a shopping cart ordering model. However, BN focuses on the following passage from Appendix F of the book:

Instant Buy Option

Merchants also can provide shoppers with an Instant Buy button for some or all items, enabling them to skip check out review. This provides added appeal for customers who already know the single item they want to purchase during their shopping excursion.

The district court dismissed the significance of this passage, stating that "[r]ead in context, the few lines relied on by Defendants appear to describe only the elimination of the checkout review step, leaving at least two other required steps to complete a purchase." However, the district court failed to recognize that a reasonable jury could find that this passage provides a motivation to modify shopping cart ordering software to skip unnecessary steps. Thus, we find that this passage, viewed in light of the rest of the reference and the other prior art references cited by BN, raises a substantial question of validity with respect to the asserted claims of the '411 patent.

D

Another reference cited by BN, a print-out from a web page describing the "Oliver's Market" ordering system, generally describes a prior art multi-step shopping cart model. BN argued that this reference anticipates at least claim 9. The reference begins with an intriguing sentence:

A single click on its picture is all it takes to order an item.

Read in context, the quote emphasizes how easy it is to order things on-line. The district court failed to recognize that a reasonable jury could find that this sentence provides a motivation to modify a shopping cart model to implement "single-click" ordering as claimed in the '411 patent. In addition, the district court failed to recognize that other passages from this reference could be construed by a reasonable jury as anticipating and/or rendering obvious the allegedly novel "single action ordering technology" of the '411 patent. For example, the reference states that "[o]ur solution allows one-click ordering anywhere you see a product picture or a price." The reference also describes a system in which a user's identifying information (*e.g.*, username and password) and purchasing information (*e.g.*, name, phone number, payment method, delivery address) is captured and stored in a database "the very first time a user clicks on an item to order," and in which a corresponding cookie is stored on the client system. In this system, the stored information may be retrieved automatically during subsequent visits by reading the cookie. All of these passages further support BN's argument that a substantial question of validity is raised by this prior art reference, either alone or in combination with the other cited references.

E

* * *

The district court also cited certain "secondary considerations" to support its conclusion of nonobviousness. Specifically, the district court cited (1) "copying of the invention" by BN and other e-commerce retailers following Amazon's introduction of its "1–Click®" feature, and (2) "the need to solve the problem of abandoned shopping carts." First, we note that evidence of copying Amazon's "1–Click®" feature is legally irrelevant unless the "1–Click®" feature is shown to be an embodiment of the claims. To the extent Amazon can demonstrate that its "1–Click®" feature embodies any asserted claims of the '411 patent under the correct claim interpretation, evidence of copying by BN and others is not sufficient to demonstrate nonobviousness of the claimed invention, in view of the substantial question of validity raised by the prior art references cited by BN and discussed herein.

With respect to the abandoned shopping carts, this problem is not even mentioned in the '411 patent. Moreover, Amazon did not submit any evidence to show either that its commercial success was related to the "1–Click®" ordering feature, or that single-action ordering caused a reduction in the number of abandoned shopping carts. Therefore, we fail to see how this "consideration" supports Amazon's nonobviousness argument.

CONCLUSION

While it appears on the record before us that Amazon has carried its burden with respect to demonstrating the likelihood of success on infringement, it is also true that BN has raised substantial questions as to the validity of the '411 patent. For that reason, we must conclude that the necessary prerequisites for entry of a preliminary injunction are presently lacking. We therefore vacate the preliminary injunction and remand the case for further proceedings.

NOTES & QUESTIONS

1. *The value of questionable patents.* Litigating a patent all the way through the Federal Circuit to a final determination of validity can take several years, and cost several million dollars. A bit more than half of these litigated patents are upheld. Those who hold questionable, but colorable, patents therefore have quite a bit of room for maneuvering: they can license them cheaply enough so that prospective licensees will not have an incentive to litigate. It is therefore possible to make a good deal of money in licensing questionable patents. Is there reason to think this process will be even worse with Internet-commerce patents than with others?

2. *Computerization and patentability.* As the caselaw on "methods" patents has established, a commercial method that is unpatentable when performed in the traditional manner by hand may become patentable if performed by a computer. Nobody owns the method of writing checks to pay bills, but a method of electronic check writing and clearing might well be patentable. Nobody owns the method of payment by cash, but there are dozens of patents on e-cash implementations. This trend may be expected to continue, as nearly all commercial methods become computerized. Is the trend worrisome from the standpoint of competition policy? From the standpoint of individual liberty?

3. *Patentability of contracts.* Contracts are normally not thought of as patentable, though as texts they are generally copyrightable. Yet contracts perform a function. Can a standardized contract be patented? If it is in digital form? If it is embedded in delivery of a digital product? Is the method of achieving formation of a contract containing the desired terms, through the use of a shrinkwrap license, patentable?

†